# ACCOUNTING THEORY AND POLICY

*A Reader*

---

**SECOND EDITION**

# ACCOUNTING THEORY AND POLICY

## *A Reader*

SECOND EDITION

Edited by

### Robert Bloom, Ph.D.

*John Carroll University*

### Pieter T. Elgers, D.B.A., C.P.A.

*University of Massachusetts*

Harcourt Brace Jovanovich, Publishers

*San Diego     New York     Chicago     Austin     Washington, D.C.*

*London     Sydney     Tokyo     Toronto*

657
a172b
236350

# PREFACE

The basic structure and educational objectives of *Accounting Theory and Policy*, Second Edition, remain the same as in the first edition and are restated below. Yet there have been important structural and topical changes, reflecting the suggestions of present and former users of the book in addition to the evolving interests of the editors. The number of articles has been expanded from 37 in the former edition to 45 in this edition; 30 of these are new to the collection. The larger number of articles reflects two features of the revision: a) new sections dealing with agency theory and international accounting, and b) a commitment to representing sharply contrasting points of view on specific issues.

The primary audience for this collection of readings continues to be students in upper-level undergraduate and graduate accounting courses. The articles selected, therefore, emphasize the application of theory to practice, and have been drawn from both academic and professional journals. They follow an orderly progression from a consideration of the basic nature of accounting theory (as compared to theories in the physical or social sciences, for example) through a discussion of the criteria by which competing theories might be validated or discarded, to the resolution of specific disputes, such as those listed in the current agenda of the Financial Accounting Standards Board (FASB). The articles we have included should convince the reader that, though necessary in the policy-making process, current accounting theory is inadequate, and that new theories and pertinent findings in related fields such as economics, finance, and psychology have implications for both its subject matter and its methodology.

The structure of *Accounting Theory and Policy* allows the coverage of fundamental issues to serve as a framework for the later discussion of more specific issues:

• Part I covers the nature of accounting theory and its relationship to accounting policy, the insights available from agency theory which contribute to an understanding of accounting practices, the implications of capital market efficiency and disclosure rules, and economic consequences as a consideration in the setting of accounting policies.

• Part II deals with the nature of accounting income and the problem of allocation in income measurement.

• Part III reviews various proposed alternatives to historical cost-based asset and income measurement.

• Part IV addresses international accounting issues, including international harmonization of accounting standards, the rationale for functional currency choice, the Soviet accounting framework, and arguments for an accounting court.

• Part V presents various current controversies, including reporting for pensions, deferred income taxes, liquidity and solvency, and various other areas.

The previous edition of *Accounting Theory and Policy* served as both a primary and a supplemental text in masters-level accounting courses as well as in senior undergraduate accounting theory seminars. Graduate-level courses typically stress the first four parts of the outline. Undergraduate courses, while incorporating selected portions of Parts I through III, often emphasize the discussions of specific issues in Parts IV and V.

We have selected articles primarily according to how provocative and stimulating they are, rather than for their compatibility with our own views. Our effort has been to provide a catalyst for discussion rather than to present, or lead the reader to, our own conclusions. For the same reason, our interstitial comments on individual articles are brief and descriptive rather than evaluative.

The editors gratefully acknowledge the helpful comments furnished by the following professors on the outline for this Second Edition: Richard Asebrook, University of Massachusetts; Louis Corsini, Boston College; Ronald Mannino, University of Massachusetts; Gary Maydew, Iowa State University; Gerhard Mueller, University of Washington; Thomas Musser, Concordia University; and Keith Stanga, University of Tennessee. Our debt of gratitude extends to the authors of each of the articles contained in this volume and to the various academic and professional journals in which these articles originally appeared for permitting us to reprint the selections. We also appreciate the administrative assistance provided by a number of staff members in the School of Business at John Carroll University and the Faculty of Commerce and Administration at Concordia University.


Robert Bloom
Pieter T. Elgers

# Contents

# I  Foundations

This book focuses on accounting theory and policy in a decision-making context, exposing readers to the dilemmas confronted by accounting policy makers such as the Financial Accounting Standards Board, the Accounting Standards Committee of the Canadian Institute of Chartered Accountants, and the Accounting Standards Committee of the Institute of Chartered Accountants in England and Wales. Accounting theory is not an end *per se*. Theories reflect either descriptive or prescriptive behavior—the way individuals or firms act or should act, respectively. Accounting policy-making consists of developing accounting standards guided by a basic theoretical framework of financial reporting. It is important to understand accounting theory in order to examine accounting policy decisions, which have economic, political, and social consequences. The papers included in Part I of this book provide a frame of reference for evaluating the specific accounting theories and issues covered in the subsequent parts.

Section I-A, entitled "Accounting Theory," consists of ten papers addressing problems in defining the subject matter and methodology of accounting theory, as well as formulating a theory of accounting policy selection. The authors offer different perspectives on the reasons for disputes in accounting and attempt to explain the reasons for the alleged failure of accounting theory to significantly affect accounting policy.

The initial paper by Brief (1975) offers an historical perspective on current accounting controversies and suggests that perennial accounting disputes are rooted in uncertainty about the future. Brief argues that providing direct forecasts of cash flows and other future-oriented information in financial reports might cause the concept of profit to become obsolete as a measure of past performance or as a predictor of future performance. If the concept of profit becomes obsolete, then theoretical debates concerning accounting concepts of income and value also lose importance.

Watts and Zimmerman (1979) assert that accounting theory is an economic good and, as such, is subject to the forces of supply and demand. The authors contend that the demand for accounting theories pertains to the demand for rationales or excuses, couched in terms of the "public interest" but actually reflecting the needs of particular parties who lobby for specific accounting standards. The function of accounting theories is to supply excuses which, in turn, satisfy the demand engendered by political processes. Watts and Zimmerman hypothesize that there are three functions of accounting theories: *pedagogic* demand, *information* demand, and *justification* demand. In the government-regulated economy the most prominent demand in their view is the justification demand, since the government needs to justify its actions. The authors then provide historical evidence to corroborate their hypothesis that accounting theories are used to buttress governmental interventions, e.g., railroad legislation, income tax acts, and the Securities Acts of 1933–4. In all cases cited, relevant accounting theories appeared subsequent to governmental intervention. Watts and Zimmerman conclude that no one theory of accounting will ever be able to explain or justify accounting standards, due to the nature and diversity of the demand function.

Sorter (1969) argues that the myriad uses of accounting data, as well as the array of decision models presently in use (and from a normative point of view, the variety of "correct" decision models, many of which are still undeveloped) make it impossible to produce income and asset numbers that are optimal for a wide range of users. As an alternative, Sorter proposes an "events" theory under which accountants would provide "information about relevant economic events that allows users to generate their own input values for their own decision models." To state this differently, the conventional accounting emphasis on income and valuations as well as aggregations generated by the accountant may be less useful than disaggregated data.

Dopuch and Sunder (1980) provide a critical review of FASB *Statement of Financial Accounting Concepts No. 1* (1978). This document, as well as its antecedents, is judged to be a failure because it is unlikely to aid in the resolution of specific accounting issues. The authors suggest a set of modest objectives for the FASB, primarily directed toward achieving compromise solutions to accounting issues based on consideration of the interests of affected groups in society.

Miller (1985) examines several myths associated with the FASB's conceptual framework. Miller asserts that such a framework serves to describe existing practice, prescribe future practice, and define terminology and issues. However, there are conflicts among these goals due to a lack of consensus among concerned parties. Three of the eight myths that Miller criticizes are:

A conceptual framework will lead to consistent standards.
A conceptual framework will eliminate the problem of standards overload.
The FASB's conceptual framework captures only the status quo of accounting practices.

The conceptual framework is a "political document" rather than "a purely conceptual effort." It is flexible rather than rigid. In Miller's view, it has served to assist the FASB in its deliberations and to improve communications with its constituents.

Peasnell (1982) sets forth the rationale for a conceptual framework of financial reporting. In his view, the U.S. has a greater need than the U.K. for a conceptual framework because of differences in the nature of the standard-setting process in these two countries. Accounting standard-setting in Britain is more of a bargaining process than in the U.S., which has the Securities and Exchange Commission overseeing its work. Peasnell argues that a conceptual framework is most appropriate where both the responsibility and power for establishing accounting standards are given to one specific body, which is the case in Canada. The author asserts that a conceptual framework should at least furnish "the basic principles of, and sources of authority for, 'accountability' and 'rights to know'; the consequences which financial reports are intended to have (and to avoid); the trade-offs which have to be made." A conceptual framework cannot, however, eliminate conflicts over perceived differences about the consequences of accounting standards.

Beaver, Kennelly, and Voss (1968) argue that alternative accounting measurements are similar to competing scientific hypotheses, and thus may be evaluated based upon their ability to predict events of interest to decision-makers. The authors caution that this predictive ability criterion is not to be interpreted as an indiscriminate search for a method of accounting which maximizes some measure of statistical association. Accounting theory has an important role to play because theory provides an explanation of why a given association exists and enables the researcher to generalize from the sample data to a new set of observations.

Wells (1976) argues that accounting theories are similar to scientific theories, apart from the fact that accounting theories deal with financial rather than physical phenomena. This leads Wells to interpret the apparent disarray in accounting theory as a war of competing paradigms, which is a prerequisite and a harbinger of theoretical progress.

Benston (1980) examines different types of accounting standards and different means of establishing and enforcing such standards, laying the groundwork for an analysis of the benefits and costs of accounting standards to investors, public accountants, government, and society. The benefits and costs of different establishment and enforcement methods—such as, public sector versus private sector—are comparatively evaluated. Benston emphasizes that "... whether one system of standard-setting and enforcement is 'best' cannot be determined."

May and Sundem (1976) provide a way of examining the accounting policy-setting process. They contend that the most auspicious benefit of accounting policy research is to assist in the formulation of theories for policy choices. Viewing such theories in a social context, May and Sundem point to the role of political organizations such as the Financial Accounting Standards Board in affecting social welfare. In light of our ignorance of individual and collective decision-making processes, a social ordering of accounting policies cannot be set forth, according to the authors. Nevertheless, May and Sundem discuss various research strategies which may help to enlighten the policy decision. These strategies include security price-based research, *a priori* research, sensitivity of accounting time series, modeling individual and aggregate decision-making, and behavioral research with regard to empirical studies on the association of accounting data with security prices.

Section B deals with applications of agency theory to financial reporting. Zimmerman (1980) discusses the rationale for positive research in accounting with a view to the development of a theory, e.g., to explain why managers adopt one particular accounting method as opposed to another. Such a theory would provide a foundation for the measurement of the benefits and costs of alternative accounting methods. Zimmerman perceives several pitfalls in the formulation of a positive theory, including the lack of a theory of the political process and an incomplete knowledge of auditors' incentives. Nonetheless, the author expects significant findings to emerge from research on this subject in the near future. Kelly (1983) emphasizes that a positive theory searches for reasons to explain observed phenomena in contrast to descriptive research, which simply seeks to indicate what actually happens. Positive theory is consistent with the efficient market hypothesis, Kelly stresses. The author provides an agency model to reflect management's choices of accounting standards, emphasizing the effects of those actions on management's wealth, and in doing so, synthesizes previous research findings. Kelly asserts in the conclusion to her paper that it is possible that accounting changes are firm-specific and thus that generalizations from empirical research are invalid. Watts and Zimmerman (1978) examine factors affecting managers' views on accounting standards in an attempt to develop a positive theory of the determination of accounting standards. Such factors include taxes, regulation, management compensation agreements, accounting costs, and political costs. A model is developed incorporating these factors, suggesting that firms having contact with governments through regulation or intervention can influence their cash flows by reporting lower income and thereby discouraging governmental action. The model was tested with corporate responses to the FASB Discussion Memorandum on General Price Level Accounting (1974).

Section C develops the implications of market efficiency and modern portfolio theory for accounting policy. Beaver (1973) develops a set of objectives for the FASB based upon a large body of empirical research suggestions that capital markets are reasonably "efficient" in the sense that security prices behave as if they reflect all publicly available information. Beaver's interpretation of this evidence suggests that many current controversies in accounting are "much ado about nothing." The substantive questions concern what information should be publicly disclosed and whether accounting reports are the best medium for disclosing this information.

The papers by Wyatt (1983) and Deitrick and Harrison (1984) offer contrasting interpretations of the evidence on market efficiency and its practical impact on the accounting profession. Wyatt (1983) argues that the decisions of managers, bankers, and investor analysts appear to be affected by accounting rules. Management's perceptions of how a transaction will affect earnings influence lease arrangements, business combinations, foreign operations, inventory accounting, and various other activities. Often, managers choose economically less efficient arrangements in order to have a more favorable effect upon reported earnings. Moreover, Wyatt suggests that the emphasis on disclosure implies that financial statements should be dispensed with, and financial reporting should be limited to narrative disclosures.

Dietrick and Harrison (1984) defend the efficient market hypothesis and argue that the incidents described by Wyatt have no implications for the validity of the hypothesis. The beliefs and actions of managers, bankers, and investor analysts are irrelevant to the truth (or falsity) of the hypothesis. While capital markets may be efficient in the processing of accounting and other disclosures, this does not necessarily lead to economically efficient decisions by managers and others.

Section D considers the economic and political consequences of financial accounting. Solomons (1978) examines the role that politics should play in the accounting policy-making process. While acknowledging various ways in

which accounting numbers may have an economic impact, Solomons argues
that if accounting is "... used to achieve other than purely measurement ends,
faith in it would be destroyed," and he describes the proper function of accounting
as "financial cartography." This implies to Solomons that the role of
accountants is to present the "facts" in as neutral a fashion as possible and that
the use of such facts for achieving economic policy objectives should be left to
others. Zeff (1978) suggests that the recent prominence of arguments based on the
economic consequences of accounting standards reflects a veritable revolution
in accounting thought. The FASB must be expected to consider the possible
adverse economic consequences of its proposed actions, though accounting
principles of fair presentation should continue to be the basic foundations
for accounting policy decisions.

# I-A  Nature of Accounting Theory

## I-A 1  *The Accountant's Responsibility in Historical Perspective*

RICHARD P. BRIEF

$S$everal years ago it was reported (*The New York Times*, January 4, 1972) that many accountants, "like victims of an earthquake or the fist of Joe Frazier, ... wander dazedly asking what happened; where did the force come from; why wasn't it foreseen; how could it have been avoided...?" The article elaborated on the current state of the profession, indicating that "now, from within the profession itself, revolt is brewing.... And for more than 100,000 accountants themselves, the preservation of their professional credibility could not have higher significance. This credibility is under attack in the Congress, in the courts and within the profession itself." This revolt is not new. It has been brewing for nearly 100 years.

One way to gain insight into the vexing and unsettled questions connected with the responsibility of accountants is to approach the subject from an historical perspective. In the pages that follow we examine nineteenth and early twentieth century thought on various topics which have been, and continue to be, of concern to

The original version of this paper was written while the author was a Visiting Professor of Finance, Dartmouth College. It was presented at the annual meeting of the American Accounting Association in August, 1974, during a session sponsored by the Academy of Accounting Historians. Comments and suggestions by the discussants, Professor David Green, Jr. and Mr. Leonard Spacek, and by Mr. Walter Oliphant, Professor Louis Goldberg, and the reviewers of *The Accounting Review* changed the manuscript in important ways. Their help is appreciated. In addition, some of the ideas expressed in this paper are a joint product of several years of discussion with my colleague, Professor Joel Owen. Research support was provided by the Tuck Associates Program, Dartmouth College, and it is gratefully acknowledged. Naturally, the author is solely responsible for this paper.

Richard P. Brief, "The Accountant's Responsibility in Historical Perspective," *The Accounting Review*, April 1975, pp. 285–297. Reprinted by permission of *The Accounting Review*.

accountants. It will become evident that "history repeats itself" and that most of the basic problems considered by accountants now are also those which have perplexed the profession for nearly a century. Thus despite all the changes in the business environment, controversy within the accounting profession today has remarkable similarities to the discussion taking place decades ago. Why do certain accounting problems appear to be perennial and why has regulation and legislation apparently not solved many of the fundamental disputes in accounting?

The thesis of this study is that accounting controversy persists because profit calculations involve "uncertainty about the future." Legislation and regulation cannot reduce this controversy because they cannot eliminate the element of uncertainty from the problem of profit determination. Consequently, until the subject of uncertainty is given a central position in accounting theory, the problems recognized in earlier times will continue to be deferred to later generations for resolution.

The paper is divided into three sections. The first surveys accounting thought on the subjects of disclosure and alternative techniques and questions concerning the scope of audit and audit certificate. Although there has been an enormous amount of legislation and regulation in these areas, many of today's problems are no different from those which preoccupied the profession during the last century. In the second section, the attitude toward the accountant's responsibility for forecasts and estimates is examined. Historically, an effort was made to minimize uncertainty-related problems by arguing that the accountant's main responsibility was for "prosaic facts" and "dry realities." The third section concludes that this emphasis on the past rather than the future conflicts with the idea of profit as a return for risk bearing. However, the modern corporate concept of profit is a product of lawyers, not of accountants, and legislation governing the payment of dividends has had a significant impact on the development of accounting.

## LEGISLATION AND PROBLEMS OF THE ACCOUNTANT'S RESPONSIBILITY

This section considers two broad topics relating to the accountant's responsibility: full disclosure and alternative techniques and the scope of the audit and audit certificate. Nineteenth century accountants were concerned with the improvement of practice in these areas and many of them, like their twentieth century counterparts, advocated more effective regulation to reduce the degrees of freedom in accounting behavior. The profession was almost unanimous in its belief that accountants should take the lead in promulgating reform. However, there was a diversity of opinion on the specific changes in practice that were needed and some cautioned that certain kinds of regulation would have undesirable consequences.

### Full Disclosure and Alternative Techniques

In the last quarter of the nineteenth century debate over the interpretation of the legal requirement that "dividends must not be paid out of capital" and the determination of "profits available for dividends" were inextricably connected to the depreciation problem and other familiar subjects (Brief, 1970). During this period accountants attempted for the first time to formulate theory, to codify methodology, and to clarify their responsibility. The development of accounting was marked by angry argument, caustic rhetoric, and more important, a very sophisticated and penetrating dialogue on a wide range of subjects.

Underlying much of the debate was the belief that reported profits had an effect on investor behavior. The nature of this relationship was boldly and sarcastically described in 1837 (*Railway Magazine*, p. 2): "Let it only be seen by six months working of that line [Grand Junction] that a profit will accrue to proprietors of 8 or 10 percent per annum and there is little hazard in predicting that other lines of great intercourse will be amply supported." Thus, when a railroad charged £14,625 to capital and paid a dividend by arguing that "the efficiency and the value of the engines have been materially increased" after the severe winter of 1838, the sufficiency of disclosure and capitalization policy were criticized by the *Railway Magazine*, which stated: "a more puny and meagre document we have never witnessed" (1838, p. 189). The subject of accounting error, its economic effect, and the accountant's responsibility for this error were a source of continuing argument throughout the period (Brief, 1965).

Many accountants advocated that the profession should take the lead in writing new legislation to improve business practices. One writer put it this way (*The Accountant*, December 12, 1885):

> Is there a single word in the whole of the Acts restraining the payment of dividends out of capital? There is not; what is said seems to amount to this, that the payment of dividends out of capital can be made.... What are accountants doing towards drawing up formal suggestions on this and other equally important points on which the Companies Acts are notoriously at fault? Not going to sleep, let us hope.

In addition, a very competitive attitude towards others, notably lawyers, also is observed in the profession's formative years. This attitude is illustrated by the common complaint that "Existing law is deplorably defective, and ... the Chartered Accountants acting through their Institute should be the first to move in the matter, and not allow the work to be done, and the honour to be appropriated by other and less capable hands" (*The Accountant*, December 19, 1885).

At an early date *The Accountant* (April 30, 1881) stated that "If a balance sheet be correct although condensed he [the auditor] is bound to sign it" because the auditor should not publicly disagree with management. But *The Accountant* also advocated full disclosure of the amounts charged to depreciation, the method of valuation, etc.:

> A shareholder is entitled to know, not what is the true value of his shares, for that in most instances is a matter of opinion, but *how* the value of fixed assets has been estimated—whether at cost, at a valuation ..., or otherwise, and what sums have been placed in reserve or written off for depreciation, running out of leases or other decreases in value...

However, although the editor argues that "Much of the information ... might be given if the legislature made its publication compulsory upon all," he also believed that "it is difficult to enforce full information without committing an act of injustice towards companies, as opposed to private concerns, which need never print any balance-sheets" (June 4, 1881).

Although many accountants, in the nineteenth century as in the twentieth, argued that legislation which increases the amount of disclosure in financial statements and reduces the number of alternative methods is a desirable goal, others, like the editor of *The Accountant*, also considered some of the undesirable by-products of achieving these objectives. The extreme position was that "as I don't approve of too much grandmotherly legislation in a free country where a people should learn from their own experience how to take care of themselves, I don't approve of the State preventing undertakings being floated with an inducement of this sort" [returning interest on capital during construction] (*The Accountant*, December 4, 1886). In the same vein, when the editor of *The Accountant* discussed (October 8, 1881) the balance sheet of John Crossley and Son, Limited, which was criticized on the basis of inadequate disclosure by the *Citizen* newspaper, he reasoned, in effect, that inadequate disclosure would increase a firm's cost of capital:

> Here, indeed, the entire assets are lumped together in one line, and we infer that no outsider is expected to take shares; in fact, none but a semi-private concern would issue such a balance sheet. Any ordinary company would assuredly separate its freehold and plant, its stock-in-trade, its book-debts, and its cash, though it might include "minerals" perhaps with freeholds. The *et cetera* at the end of the liabilities means the reserves, no doubt, against discounts, bad debts and any other drawbacks. But the true answer of the public to such a balance sheet, however respectably audited, is to respectfully let the company's shares alone. *We therefore, consider that the "dissatisfied shareholder" must be deemed a goose.* (italics added)

Dicksee, doubtless the most influential nineteenth century accountant, also questioned the effect of legislating accounting practices (*The Accountant*, March 1, 1902):

> ... even with regard to such important questions as the value of assets, provision for depreciation, the assessments of profits earned, and the distribution of unrealised profits, the Courts have shown a marvelous disinclination [to provide] principles for the safe guidance of the auditor.... No doubt it has acted wisely in adopting this course, however, because any attempt to state explicitly what the duties of auditors are in all cases would afford the best possible excuse in such cases for the insufficiency of the audit that has been performed.

And seventeen years earlier Matheson, responding to a criticism of failing to specify exact methods in his book on depreciation, had the same apprehensive attitude about fixed rules (*The Accountant*, January 3, 1885):

> ... [regarding] the absence from my book of exact rates of depreciation for different classes of plant, I am more on my ground, and I venture to assert that any positive statements of rates would be more likely to mislead than inform... fixed rules are impossible, and examples, if offered for imitation, dangerous.

More recently, a strikingly similar view was expressed by the Chief Accountant of the Securities Exchange Commission, John C. Burton: "He was not happy with the old 18-man, part-time board. 'By writing precise rules,' he asserted, 'the board made it possible for people to observe the letter and avoid the spirit with the blessing—and often the assistance—of their auditors'" (*The New York Times*, June 25, 1972).

There were other arguments against regulation and they concerned the depreciation problem. For example, one writer said that legal requirements to charge depreciation before declaring dividends would be "injurious to companies and the public.... It would stop all enterprise because it would be absolutely impossible for companies to pay dividends in the early years of their existence" (*The Accountant*, December 14, 1889). Similarly, Lord Justice Lindley, in the landmark 1889 decision in *Lee v. Neuchatel* (41 LR Ch. 1, 19) went so far as to argue that the legal requirement to charge depreciation regularly and periodically would "paralyze the trade of the country."

Still another argument against legally requiring depreciation, which the business historian might usefully consider, was made by "an eminent accountant in the north of England." He argued (*The Accountant*, November 29, 1884) that the provision for depreciation ("money retained out of profits"):

> enables managers and directors to undertake continual new work without consulting their shareholders. It is only another way of providing fresh capital or avoiding a call, which might be resisted by those interested if it came in that form; and further in cases where you have several classes of shares upon which the capital is not equally paid up, or where you have debenture holders as well as ordinary shareholders, the rights of the respective parties are prejudicially affected by what can only be styled the misappropriation of funds intended for a specific object.

There were differences of opinion among accountants over basic questions and they were vigorously debated. However, judicial and statutory authority did not play a significant role in resolving these differences (Brief, 1966). Rather, the profession attempted to establish the limits of its own responsibility and the aims were, according to Dicksee (1915, p. xiv), somewhat Utopian:[1]

> If it should be thought that the standard I have throughout advocated is somewhat Utopian in character, and unattainable in practice, I can only reply that I maintain that, to me, an incomplete investigation seems worse than useless, and I am convinced that it is only by voluntarily accepting, and even increasing the responsibilities of our position that we can hope to maintain and to increase the large measure of public confidence we at present enjoy.

Throughout the period, accountants fought to establish the profession as a permanent institution, but the battle still rages to determine whether "the honour [will be] appropriated by other and less capable hands."

> It is now likely that unless accountants and their corporate clients take the initiative in reducing the number of acceptable accounting practices,

---

[1] The quote is taken from the preface to the first edition (1892) which was reprinted in subsequent editions.

financial disclosure will become much more a matter of law. There seems to be increasing pressure to limit the diversity of accounting methods by establishing an arbitrary set of rules.... If the accounting profession does not do so, "its position of eminence may be lost to those who seize the larger opportunity"[2] (Chatfield, 1974, p. 280).

Although the business setting has changed, nineteenth century debate on disclosure and alternative methods has a modern tone and many of the issues before the profession in the present day are those which concerned its original members. How can disclosure be improved? How much disclosure is desirable? How can the range of accounting alternatives be reduced? What are the effects of regulation? Then, as now, accountants were searching for satisfactory answers to these questions. Nineteenth century debate on the audit certificate is also relevant to today's problems.

### Scope of Audit and Audit Certificate

The pure laissez-faire attitude in the last century towards the scope of the audit was illustrated in the early legal case of *Turquand* v. *Marshall* which was decided in 1869 (20 LT 766):

> As to the publication of false balance sheets and including in them debts which were hopelessly bad, it was difficult to say where a debt was hopeless; and besides, if any shareholders were deceived into buying shares he might have his separate remedy, but each would have a different case, and the whole body could not sue.

The debtor in this case was the Confederacy! However, although the courts generally did not interfere in business affairs, accountants and other groups were more active in their advocacy of reform, and the audit and related problems quickly became a major issue which was actively discussed.

As early as 1883 there was an interesting controversy on the audit, sparked by a series of articles in a magazine called *Vanity Fair*. Significantly, *The Accountant* reprinted them in entirety, even though the comments were harshly critical of accounting practice.

Apparently, *Vanity Fair* thought that "auditors' certificates might be longer and better" and "legislation is needed" to achieve this objective. However, the editor of *The Accountant* argued that "In a simple matter such as an auditor's certificate we fail

---

[2] Chatfield is quoting from Mautz and Sharaf (1961, p. 200). Similar comments can be found elsewhere. For example, Hawkins (1963, p. 168) commented, "Once more, the possibility of further government intervention in industrial reporting matters is imminent, principally because of the accounting profession's inability to narrow the areas of difference in accounting principles and management's resistance to its critics' demands for improved corporate disclosure." The same idea is echoed by *Business Week* (April 22, 1972). "Before such sweeping moves are widely demanded, the Wheat proposals give the accounting profession another chance to demonstrate that workable accounting and auditing procedures can be set in the private sector, with the broad-based cooperation of accountants, financial executives, security analysts, and educators."

to see why any legal interference is called for. What the public and shareholders want is a readable assurance from the accountants, stating in plain English what they really have done" (October 27, 1883). With great sarcasm, the editor elaborated on this point (November 3, 1883):

> We would suggest that in future the auditors' certificates should, in accordance with the defense now made for them, run thus:— We having been allowed to audit not from month to month, but only once a year; having had too little time to make an exhaustive report, because the documents are required for the printer; knowing that shareholders are generally impatient to get through the business; being paid a fee out of all proportion to the work required to be done; and being aware that the voting power is in the absolute control of the Board—certify that, so far as we, under these disabilities, can ascertain and dare disclose the facts, it is all right. This would at any rate let shareholders know from the certificate, as we know from the general chorus of certifiers, what the true meaning and value of the certificate really amounts to. Our complaint was and is that at present they do not know this, but that they are led and are meant to imagine that bladders are lanterns and auditors' certificates proofs of all excellences and complete solvency and security.
>
> We are not to be drawn off the scent by any invitation to discuss the powers of auditors or the technicalities of auditing. That is not the question. The question is—What is worth, and what, therefore, the use of an auditorial certificate in its various forms as it is now commonly given? We say it is worth next to nothing. Our critics say, not that it is worth much, but that it is very hard to make it worth anything. Very well. Then we and our critics are agreed. The certificate *is* worth next to nothing, and this being so, it is a delusion and a snare.

Then, in response to a letter, the editor of *The Accountant* argued that to remedy the audit's deficiencies, a direct approach was called for: "Cease making those damnable faces which are called Auditors' Certificates." Rather than paraphrase, these remarks are quoted in entirety in order to give the flavor of the lively debate which took place during the profession's first decade of development:

> There is however one correspondent of *The Accountant* who signs himself "Anti-Twaddle," and who deserves special remark. He is very rude, but not more rude than illogical and ungrammatical. He too sets forth the difficulties of the poor auditor, and so feelingly that he has evidently suffered from them. The auditor gets no power, no time, and no money to talk of; he is not responsible except for the verification of figures put before him; he is the slave of the directors, who do not like to look at the worst side of affairs, and he has to satisfy also the shareholders, for we believe that if they have sometimes a strong objection to knowing the truth, they have at least as often as strong an objection to having lies told to them. And it is quite clear that, if this venerable Aunty were herself set to audit accounts and to frame thereon an auditorial certificate, she would unhesitatingly avoid any difference of opinion with directors, would carefully abstain from looking at the worst side of affairs, would very generously indulge the shareholders' strong objection to knowing the truth, and would, in spite of the insufficient time, power, and money, frame and publish a certificate that would make

everything pleasant for everybody, and above all for Aunty. This is exactly what we complain of.

And yet, in spite of this injurious disclosure of the way in which certificates are moulded from the dirty mud of facts by the Sculptor-Director, and invested with artistic merit by the Ghost-Auditor, Aunty wants to have herself fastened on all concerns by an Act of Parliament which shall supersede directors and everybody else, and make Aunty a first charge on the concern, just as though she were an official liquidator or trustee. And she proposes that *we* should get her Act passed for her! No; we cannot do this. On the contrary, we say—Amend your certificates and not your Statutes; tell the truth if you know it, and shame the Director. If you don't know and can't find out—why say that; but in any case, cease making those merely damnable faces which are now called Auditors' Certificates. (November 3, 1883)

Some leading accountants took a constructive view of this criticism. Thomas Welton, President of the Institute of Chartered Accountants in England and Wales in 1891–2, believed that *The Accountant's* remarks on the auditors' certificate "would do great good even if they did no more than induce shareholders to more closely scan the wording of these documents..." (October 27, 1883). But the basic complaint was that accountants lacked authority to impose exacting standards. For example, the problem of requiring firms to charge "adequate" depreciation was of great concern in those days and Pixley (1887, p. 127) complained that "It is in the earlier years of a company's existence the auditor has the greatest difficulty in inducing Directors to charge an amount sufficient to provide for the past depreciation of the period." A similar comment appears in the preface to the second edition of the first book on depreciation (Matheson, 1910, p. ix–x): "Auditors, and especially those who have to deal with joint stock or other concerns, where the remuneration of the management is made wholly or partly dependent upon declared profits, know in what varied forms resistance to an adequate charge against profits for Depreciation is presented."

This conflict between the accountant and management, and its effect on the accountant's responsibility to shareholders, was recognized in the first years of the profession's existence, and questions relating to the auditor's independence were connected to the proxy system which permitted persons in fiduciary positions to vote on matters affecting their own interest. Once again, *The Accountant* (October 27, 1883) identified a critical problem:

The audit of Public Companies' accounts was designed to control and check the action of directors in their administration of the affairs of Public Companies: and yet, as a rule, the auditors who are chosen for this purpose owe their employment to the very directors whom they are presumed so to control and check in the interests of the shareholders. This is one of the evils arising out of the proxy system, which I trust we may some day see abolished, as being utterly pernicious and vicious in root and branch. It should be laid down as an invariable rule that directors, trustees, or other persons in fiduciary positions should never be allowed the direct or indirect use of proxies in voting, or in fact to vote personally, on any subject affecting the performance of the duties imposed upon them by the trusts under which they act, or on the passing of the accounts as presented by them to their proprietary or *cestui que* trust.

This problem of the auditor's autonomy remains a topic of current interest, and recent suggestions for reform (Hawes, 1974) echo *The Accountant's* earlier argument:

> At a time when auditors are subject to a staggering number of lawsuits, intense pressures from managements to adopt accounting treatment that will put the best face on the financial statements and the difficult task of codifying accounting principles, legislation is needed to make stockholder approval of the appointment of auditors mandatory.
>
> Such legislation would underscore the fact that the auditor's client is the stockholders and thus would have an important therapeutic effect on the corporation.

This historical review of the audit certificate and scope of audit has demonstrated that many modern problems are not new. From the first, accountants recognized the limitations of the audit certificate and they raised questions concerning the auditor's independence. Many recommended more effective regulation but some took a more straightforward approach: "Amend your certificates and not your statutes." In summarizing this section, one conclusion is inescapable. After nearly a century of debate,

> ...there is still no comprehensive, integrated statement of concepts on which accountants and statement readers can agree and rely. There is still no consensus as to the exact meaning of the standard audit opinion that financial statements present the results of operations "fairly" in accordance with generally accepted accounting principles. One result is that accounting methods have changed much more slowly than the accounting environment. And the profession has not solved its basic problems of disclosure, consistency and statement comparability (Chatfield, 1974, pp. 298–99).

The thesis of this paper is that accounting controversy persists because profit calculations involve "uncertainty about the future." The next section surveys the attitude toward the accountant's responsibility for estimates and forecasts.

## ATTITUDE TOWARD ACCOUNTANT'S RESPONSIBILITY FOR ESTIMATES AND FORECASTS

In the discussion that follows it should be borne in mind that a formal framework for studying decision problems under uncertainty has become generally available only in the last decade or so. Therefore, nineteenth century accountants quite naturally made an effort to avoid uncertainty-related problems. Nevertheless, these early theorists did begin to discuss topics related to the subject, and their attitude towards them had a significant influence on the progress in accounting.

### Historical Attitude Toward Uncertainty

One of the earliest references to the problem of uncertainty in accounting can be found in a series of articles on audits which appeared in several 1881 issues of *The Accountant*. Referring to balance sheet audits, the editor asserted (April 23, 1881) "that the real object to be aimed at is such a verification that will be practically sufficient." The auditor's task is then compared to a judge and jury who are often obliged to be content with "little more than a reasonable probability." Thus, at the end of a period "some matters outstanding ... must be introduced by estimation ... to make the apparent profit a real measure of what has been accomplished in the period under review." However, the auditor should not "indulge in forecasts or in expressions of feeling, but rather adhere as coldly and impassively as he can to facts— hard, dry realities."

This logical contradiction between the necessity to make estimates and the adherence to dry realities is not resolved, but the writer does suggest a "trend analysis" for specific problems like estimating "probable losses" such as "bad and doubtful debts." Since the facts "keep changing almost hourly," the auditor should study past trends and advocate reserves in good years to be used in years when losses exceed the average. However, when a loss is certain, "no rule can be laid down," but "broad principles" which "favour moderation in the distribution of dividends, and ... ample reserves is [sic] desirable. Yet he should likewise remember the possibility of excess in the latter direction" which might induce shareholders "to part with their shares at an insufficient valuation."

The principle of conservatism and the auditor's responsibility for estimates is discussed again (June 4, 1881):

> Generally he [the shareholder] should be enabled to see in the balance sheet which of the assets are matters of opinion, and which are matters of fact. When this part of the subject is clear, little doubt can rest upon the estimate of profit or loss, which may be deemed correct or otherwise according to the spirit in which matters of opinion are apparently handled.
> Estimates are often proper things to make use of, where they relate to subsidiary matters, and enables the balance sheet to be speedily prepared, but all estimates should be slightly to the disadvantage of the company, rather than tending the other way.

In the first paper on the ethics of accountancy in 1888 (*The Accountant*, December 12, 1888), John Mather flatly opposed any idea of chance or uncertainty in accounting. However, once again, the views on this subject are not perfectly consistent:

> What is called the "glorious uncertainty of the Law"—illustrated not only in the varying interpretations of enactments, but often in the evidence of opposing experts in law suits—conveys an idea that rarely attaches to the figures, statements, or certificates of Chartered Accountants. And it is our hope and belief, that as we succeed in gradually raising the standard of the skill and the ethics of the profession, any such idea of chance or uncertainty will be still more foreign to its work in the future.

In other words, "There seems a general agreement that ... the accountant may not prophecy 'unless he knows' ... he must avoid the tempting region of fancy and stick to the prosaic facts." Stated differently, "in most cases an accountant is no better able than other people to forecast the business prospects of an undertaking which, however sound at the outset, may ultimately fail through mismanagement, change of fashion, invalidity of patents, or numberless unforeseen causes." Yet, according to

Mather, the accountant, "in the opinion of many . . . is fully justified in dealing with those facts in their bearing upon the future. . . ." But how can the accountant do this if he must stick to the prosaic facts?

Further insight into the accountant's conflicting attitudes towards uncertainty is provided by Dickinson twenty-six years later. In concluding a discussion of the accountant's responsibility for earnings projections Dickinson (1914, pp. 226–27) said that:

> It should be clear, therefore, from the above considerations that any estimate of future earnings must necessarily depend upon so many contingencies that it would hardly seem desirable that it should be put forth without calling specific attention to the assumptions involved; and an estimate with such qualification attached would hardly be of much service to the promoter and would not be incorporated in the prospectus.

However,

> *In as much as the community is being educated to consider that statements emanating from a public accountant deal only with facts*, it may be said in conclusion that in such a case as that supposed, the accountant's duty should end with the submission on request of a carefully prepared estimate, accompanied by all necessary qualifications, without, however, any certificate there to. . . . (italics added)

Even though Dickinson rejects the inclusion of estimates in the prospectus, his proposal that all estimates should be accompanied by the assumptions on which they are based reflects modern thinking on the subject. Of greater significance, however, is his remark concerning the effort *to educate* the community that financial statements deal only with facts. It suggests that a conscious attempt was made by the profession to convince the public that the accountant is responsible only for "facts," and it also helps to explain why so many generations have come to regard accounting as an essentially historical discipline.

At the same time, accountants understood the tenuous nature of their argument. Even Dickinson (p. 236) recognized that "Every balance sheet is a matter of opinion." But he failed to make any explicit connection between the problems which require the accountant to exercise his "opinion" and the conditions which give rise to these problems—namely, uncertainty about the future.

These references to the uncertainty problem are generally in terms of estimating balances in asset and liability accounts at the end of each period. This perspective is consistent with a balance sheet approach to income determination. However, there were also discussions about another class of estimation and forecasting problems in accounting and they concerned the relationship between reported profits and future profits.

The first of these provides an amusing illustration of the "interim reporting problem." In 1883 The Hotels and City Properties Share Trust, Limited issued a four-month report and estimated the year's results by doubling the figures for the interim period. *The Accountant* (October 27, 1883) published a scathing criticism of this report:

Mr. Daniels has furnished the public with the result of working the Royal during the best four months of the year. But are we to understand that he pledges his professional reputation that *any* appreciable profit can be made during the remaining eight months, when Southend is little better than a howling wilderness, and when a stray Londoner at the Royal is looked upon with as much curiosity as if he were a friendly Zulu? During those dark and dreary months is there not an entire absence of excursionists, and as a rule are not the only occupants and best customers of that spacious bar which the prospectus says is a great source of profit, the neglected piermaster and the boatman?

In another reference to this general subject, Montgomery (1909, p. 324) seems to argue that the purpose of reporting the results of operations in past periods is to predict profits of future periods:

the certificate, therefore, should be a clear and unconditional certificate of accomplished facts, and not a mere estimate of possible—or even probable—future results, misnamed a "certificate." To the limited extent already mentioned it may be permissible, and even desirable, to modify the past results so that they may more usefully serve the purpose for which they are primarily intended—namely, provide a reliable index of future profits. But at the same time a certificate should relate not to the future, but to the past....

Although Montgomery argues unequivocally that financial statements should reflect "accomplished facts," i.e., financial statements should be historical, he also points out that the primary purpose of reporting past results is to provide an index (estimate) of future profits. Clearly, the methods used to calculate past performance will influence this "index," but questions about this relationship were not raised.

### Effect on Modern Accounting Thought

The early ideas on uncertainty and its relevance to accounting have not changed very much in the twentieth century. There are few extended discussions of the subject in modern texts and theoretical treatises and most references to the uncertainty problem are vague and ambiguous.

For example, van Pelt (1972, pp. 13–4) defines profitability as the "excess of revenues ... over *known* costs ..." (italics added), but also states that "estimates ... will be required for the purpose of allocating costs." The *APB Accounting Principles* (1973, 1, p. 15) states that "Accountants have considered themselves primarily historians, not prophets.... However, *even* present accounting practices require estimates of the future" (italics added). How are estimates used in allocating costs? Which accounting practices require estimates of the future? What quantities must be estimated? What assumptions are the estimates based on? What estimating procedures are used? Questions such as these, and there are many others, have rarely been asked.

This historical review of the accountant's attitude towards uncertainty shows that the profession has always recognized that many of the numbers in financial statements are based on estimates of uncertain future events. At the same time, it also indicates that many accountants repeatedly stated that the accounts should reflect "prosaic facts" and "dry realities." This attitude toward uncertainty dominated thought; accountants, as well as the public, have been educated to believe that financial statements are essentially historical.

In the final section this attitude towards uncertainty is at least partly explained by the legal origin of the modern corporate concept of profit.

## UNCERTAINTY AND THE CORPORATE CONCEPT OF PROFIT

It is uncertainty about the future that makes profit a return for risk bearing (Edwards and Bell, 1961, p. 9). It is also uncertainty about the future that provides the *logical* motivation for calculating the "profit of a period," and the common procedure in accounting of assuming certainty about the future completely obscures the information content of period earnings reports (Brief and Owen, 1970, p. 167). Thus, by assuming that the future is known with certainty (or by deemphasizing and minimizing the importance of uncertainty), accountants have eliminated, or at least have obscured, that which they set out to measure.

However, as a practical matter, the origin of the modern corporate concept of profit is in dividend law, not accounting, and the purpose of this legislation was to protect the rights of creditors and different classes of shareholders. This legal origin of the profit concept had an important influence on accounting.

Kehl (1941, p. 14) indicates that "During the 1600's charters began including dividend regulations among their provisions. The most common limitation required that dividends be paid from profits. Such was the restriction used in 1620 in the charter of James I to the New River Company." And "By 1700, there had already been adopted in England two statutory standards, one or the other of which still controls dividend distributions under present day statutes in a great many American states" (Kehl, p. 4).

This legislation governing the payment of dividends produced the "capital impairment rule" and the "profits tests" which were the first statutory references to the modern corporate concept of profit. Dividends cannot be paid out of capital and/or dividends must be paid out of the *profit of a period*.

Historically, railroads, utilities, and other quasi-public enterprise used a cash receipts-less-disbursements method of calculating profit. This method implied that the value of assets was "permanent." And although it became evident that this assumption was not valid, the cameralistic origin of the method seems to have blocked accounting reform for this class of enterprise.

The profit calculations of other firms are more difficult to assess. At the beginning of the nineteenth century the "inventory method" was employed. This method was a balance sheet (direct valuation) approach to profit determination. Eventually, this method was replaced by the modern accounting concept of profit that assumes a going concern and computes profit by "matching" revenues and expenses. All of these approaches have been sanctioned by the courts at various times (Brief, 1966).

Leake (1912, p. 2) correctly observed that "when commerce was carried on by individuals, each on his own account, in a vast number of small undertakings, and there was no regular income tax, it was a matter of small moment ... whether the surplus of receipts ... was economic profits." On the other hand, the coming of modern corporation and the development of capital markets interacted with dividend law to make the concept of a year's profit one of the most important ideas in economics and, as May (1936, II, p. 307) put it, "the central question of modern accounting." Yet, Hatfield's comment (1927, p. 241) about the profit concept is as valid today as it was nearly fifty years ago:

> It is a peculiar fact that while all business is carried on for the purpose of securing profits, while the distribution of profits is continually the subject of controversy in the courts, while the ascertainment of profits enters largely into the discussion of every economist, the term is still vaguely and loosely used and without definition by either economist, man of affairs, jurist, or accountant.

Thus, whereas dividend law conditioned businessmen, investors, and creditors to think in terms of the concept of "profit of a period," traditional accounting models that attempt to explain operationally the meaning of this concept in the context of the modern firm have been unsatisfactory. And as long as the term, "profit," is vaguely and loosely used and without definition, all areas of accounting responsibility that touch on questions concerning profit calculations must be a continuing source of controversy and dispute. This controversy will not subside until accountants become willing to acknowledge that in theory it is uncertainty about the future, not dividend law, that gives rise to the problem of determining the profit of a period.


## CONCLUSION

Accounting thought in the nineteenth century is especially relevant to contemporary issues because the laissez-faire business environment produced a free and uninhibited exchange of views. The courts at this time were reluctant to interfere in business affairs and, unless fraud were an issue, business practices were determined by businessmen. Similarly, the statutes did not lay down specific rules governing accounting practices, and quasi-judicial administrative bodies such as the Securities Exchange Commission did not yet exist.

The last two decades of the nineteenth century were a "golden age" in accounting and most of the major issues connected with the subject of the accountant's responsibility were brought out in the period. Questions concerning full disclosure, alternative techniques, scope of audit and the meaning of the audit certificate were widely discussed in the first few years after the profession was formally established.

However, nineteenth century accountants did not "solve" most of the problems which they debated. One explanation for the perennial nature of controversy is the accountant's early attitude toward uncertainty. During the last century, the profession began to emphasize the historical nature of accounting calculations even though many theorists recognized that forecasts and estimates were inherent in most problems.

Thus one explanation for the persistence of accounting controversy is the failure to recognize that profit calculations involve uncertainty about the future. But given the legal origin of the profit concept, it is not surprising to find that accountants became more concerned with statutory and judicial references to profit than with the more abstruse questions associated with an uncertain future. What implications can be drawn from this historical study of the accountant's responsibility?

First, many modern proposals for reform can be traced directly to the nineteenth century. Indeed, the basic perspective of the accountant's responsibility has not changed very much, and recent suggestions for improving practice often repeat earlier ideas. Thus even though the economic environment was very different 100 years ago, the basic problems in accounting today closely resemble those which confronted the profession in the last century. Therefore, regulation and legislation do not seem to have produced many of the improvements in practice which were expected.

Second, there is recent evidence that the accounting profession's attitude toward uncertainty may be changing. The report of the Study Group on the Objectives of Financial Statements (1973) gives explicit attention to the problem of forecasting future cash flows. And the Forecasting Task Force of the MAS Development and Liaison Subcommittee of the AICPA (1974) considered questions concerning past profit as an "index" of future profit. This work could produce a radical change in the concept of profit.

If direct forecasts of cash flows and other information about the future are given in financial reports, the modern corporate concept of profit might become obsolete as a measure of either past performance or as an index of future performance. In the last analysis, a firm's performance depends on its cash flows, and if information about cash flows were provided by accountants, what purpose would be served by reporting profit figures that are based on conventional methods in accounting? And what purpose would be served by forecasting future profits, if direct estimates of future cash flows already were available? Questions like these will inevitably arise when more attention is devoted to the subject of uncertainty.[3]

Third, if the traditional opposition to forecasting and estimation overrides the current effort being made in some quarters to integrate forecasting and estimation problems within the mainstream of accounting theory, then the lesson of history will not have been learned. For most debate in accounting inevitably must lead to a discussion of uncertainty about the future. This is the one area of thought which nineteenth century accountants were unable to deal with, and twentieth century accountants have not yet faced the problem squarely.

## REFERENCES

American Institute of Certified Public Accountants, Study Group on the Objectives of Financial Statements, *Objectives of Financial Statements* (1973).

American Institute of Certified Public Accountants, Forecasting Task Force of the MAS Development and Liaison Subcommittee, March 28, 1974 Exposure Draft, *Standards for Systems for the Preparation of Financial Forecasts* (1974).

*APB Accounting Principles*, Current Text as of June 30, 1973 (Commerce Clearing House, 1973).

Brief, R. P., "Nineteenth Century Accounting Error," *Journal of Accounting Research* (Spring 1965), pp. 167–77.

———, "The Origin and Evolution of Nineteenth Century Asset Accounting," *Business History Review* (Spring 1966), pp. 1–23.

---

[3] See, e.g., Thomas (1974).

————, "Depreciation Theory in Historical Perspective," *The Accountant* (December 26, 1970), pp. 737–39.

———— and Owen, J., "The Estimation Problem in Financial Accounting," *Journal of Accounting Research* (Autumn 1970), pp. 167–78.

Chatfield, M., *A History of Accounting Thought* (Dryden Press, 1974).

Dickinson, A. L., *Accounting Practice and Procedure* (Ronald Press, 1914).

Dicksee, L. R., *Auditing*, 10th ed., (Gee & Co., 1915).

Edwards, E. O. and Bell, P. W., *The Theory and Measurement of Business Income* (University of California Press, 1965).

Hatfield, H. R., *Modern Accounting—Its Principles and Some of Its Problems* (D. Appleton & Co., 1927).

Hawes, D. W., "Towards a More Muscular Audit," *New York Times*, April 14, 1974.

Hawkins, D. F., "The Development of Modern Financial Reporting Practices Among American Manufacturing Corporations," *Business History Review* (Autumn 1963), pp. 135–168.

Kehl, D., *Corporate Dividends—Legal and Accounting Problems Pertaining to Corporate Distributions* (Ronald Press, 1941).

Leake, P. D., *Depreciation and Wasting Assets* (Henry Good & Son, 1912).

Matheson, E., *Depreciation of Factories*, 4th ed., (E. & F. Spon, 1910).

Mautz, R. K. and Sharaf, H. A., *The Philosophy of Auditing*, American Accounting Association Monograph Number Six (American Accounting Association, 1961).

May, G. O., *Twenty-Five Years of Accounting Responsibility 1911–1936*, B. S. Hunt, ed. (American Institute Publishing Co., 1936).

Montgomery, R. H. ed., *Dicksee's Auditing*, 2nd ed. (New York, 1909).

Pixley, F. W., *Auditors: Their Duties and Responsibilities*, 4th ed., (Henry Good & Son, 1887).

Thomas, A. L., *The Allocation Problem: Part II*, Studies in Accounting Research #9 (American Accounting Association, 1974).

van Pelt III, J .V., "The Future of Accepted Accounting Principles," A Digest of the 1971–72 Gold Medal Award Winning Article, *Management Accounting* (August 1972), pp. 11–14.

# I-A 2 *The Demand for and Supply of Accounting Theories: The Market for Excuses*

ROSS L. WATTS AND JEROLD L. ZIMMERMAN

## I. INTRODUCTION

The literature we commonly call financial accounting theory is predominantly prescriptive.[1] Most writers are concerned with what the contents of published financial statements should be; that is, how firms should account. Yet, it is generally concluded that financial accounting theory has had little substantive, direct impact on accounting practice or policy formulation despite half a century of research. Often the lack of impact is attributed to basic methodological weaknesses in the research. Or, the prescriptions offered are based on explicit or implicit objectives which frequently differ among writers.[2] Not only are the researchers unable to agree on the

This research was supported by the Center for Research in Government Policy and Business, Graduate School of Management, University of Rochester. The authors wish to acknowledge the suggestions of Ray Ball, George Benston, Richard Brief, Nicholas Dopuch, Nicholas Gonedes, David Henderson, Robert Holthausen, Michael Jensen, Melvin Krasney, Richard Leftwich, Janice Maquire, William Meckling, Philip Meyers, Katherine Schipper, William Schwert, Clifford Smith, and Jerold Warner. We also acknowledge the suggestions received on an earlier version of this paper presented at the Stanford Summer Research Colloquium, August 2, 1977, and the comments of the anonymous reviewers.

Ross L. Watts and Jerold L. Zimmerman, "The Demand for and Supply of Accounting Theories: The Market for Excuses" *The Accounting Review*, April 1979, pp. 273–304. Reprinted with the permission of *The Accounting Review*.

[1] For example, see Canning [1929], Paton [1922], Edwards and Bell [1961], Sprouse and Moonitz [1962], Gordon [1964], Chambers [1966], and American Accounting Association [1966]. We would prefer to reserve the term "theory" for principles advanced to explain a set of phenomena, in particular for sets of hypotheses which have been confirmed. However, such a definition of theory would exclude much of the prescriptive literature and generate a semantic debate. To avoid that consequence, in this paper (unless qualified) we use the word "theory" as a generic term for the existing accounting literature.

[2] For example, Chambers [1966, Chapters 9–11] apparently adopts economic efficiency as an objective while the American Institute of Certified Public Accountants (AICPA) Study Group on the Objectives of Financial Statements [1973, p. 17] decided that "financial statements should meet the needs of those with the least ability to obtain information...."

objectives of financial statements, but they also disagree over the methods of deriving the prescriptions from the objectives.[3]

One characteristic common to the prescriptions and proposed accounting methodologies, however, is their failure to satisfy all practicing accountants and to be accepted generally by accounting standard-setting bodies. A committee of the American Accounting Association recently concluded that "a single universally accepted basic accounting theory does not exist at this time."[4]

The preceding observations lead us to pose the following question: What is the role of accounting theory in determining accounting practice? Our objective in this paper is to begin building a theory of the determinants of accounting theory. This theory is intended to be a positive theory, that is, a theory capable of explaining the factors determining the extant accounting literature, predicting how research will change as the underlying factors change, and explaining the role of theories in the determination of accounting standards.[5] It is *not* normative or prescriptive.[6]

Other writers have examined the relationship between accounting theory and practice. For example, Zeff [1974, p. 177] examines the historical relationship and concludes:

> A study of the U.S. experience clearly shows that the academic literature has had remarkably little impact on the writings of practitioners and upon the accounting policies of the American Institute and the SEC. *Too often, accounting theory is invoked more as a tactic to buttress one's preconceived notions, rather than as a genuine arbiter of contending views* (emphasis added).

Horngren [1973, p. 61] goes further and suggests an explanation for accounting theory's limited impact on the setting of accounting standards:[7]

> My hypothesis is that the setting of accounting standards is as much a product of political action as of flawless logic or empirical findings.

Our tentative theory is consistent with both Zeff's and Horngren's observations. It predicts that accounting theory will be used to "buttress preconceived notions" and further, it explains why. Our contribution to Zeff's and Horngren's ideas is to give them more structure so that we can make additional predictions about accounting theory. The source of that structure is economics. We view accounting theory

---

[3] Some writers (*e.g.*, Chambers [1966]) make assumptions about the world without regard to *formal* empirical evidence and derive their prescriptions using those assumptions. Others (*e.g.*, Gonedes and Dopuch [1974]) argue that prescriptions to achieve any given objective must be based on hypotheses which have been subjected to formal statistical tests and confirmed.

[4] American Accounting Association, [1977, p. 1]. This report also reviews the major accounting theories.

[5] The Committee on Concepts and Standards for External Reports, American Accounting Association [1977] examines many of these same questions, and the interested reader should refer to this committee report for an alternative explanation of these phenomena, specifically Chapter 4.

[6] The terms "normative" and "prescriptive" are used interchangeably. See Mautz and Gray [1970] for an example of prescriptions to "improve" accounting research and hence its impact on practice.

[7] See Sterling [1974, pp. 180–181] for Horngren's response to Zeff's initial remark.

as an economic good and examine the nature of the demand for and the supply of that good.

Understanding why accounting theories are as they are requires a theory of the political process. We model that process as competition among individuals for the use of the coercive power of government to achieve wealth transfers. Because accounting procedures[8] are one means of effecting such transfers, individuals competing in the political process demand theories which prescribe the accounting procedures conducive to their desired wealth transfers. Further, because individual interests differ, a variety of accounting prescriptions, hence a variety of accounting theories, is demanded on any one issue. We argue that it is this diversity of interests which prevents general agreement on accounting theory.

While individuals want a theory which prescribes procedures conducive to their own interest, they do *not* want a normative theory which has their self-interest as its stated objective. The reason is that information is costly to obtain. Some voters will not obtain information on political issues personally. Those voters are not likely to support political actions which have as their stated objective the self-interest of others. The most useful theories for persuading uninformed voters are theories with stated objectives appealing to those voters, *e.g.*, the "public interest." As a result, individuals demand normative accounting theories which make prescriptions based on the "public interest." In other words, the demand is for rationales or excuses. Because it arises from the political process, the demand for normative, "public interest"-oriented accounting theories depends on the extent of the government's role in the economy.

Section II analyzes the demand for financial accounting and accounting theory first in an unregulated economy, in which the only role of government is to enforce contracts, and then in a regulated economy. In Section III, we examine the nature of the supply of accounting theories. Because of the diverse demands for prescriptions, we expect to observe a variety of normative theories. Further, we expect theories to change over time as government intervention changes. In Section IV we examine the effect of government intervention on extant accounting theory during the last century. Section V summarizes the issues and presents our conclusions.

## II. THE DEMAND FOR ACCOUNTING THEORIES

This section analyzes the demand for accounting theories in an unregulated economy (Part A) and the additional demands generated by government intervention (Part B).

### A. The Demand for Accounting Theories in an Unregulated Economy

*1. Accounting in an Unregulated Economy*    Audited corporate financial statements were voluntarily produced prior to government mandate.[9] Watts [1977]

---

[8] Accounting "procedures," "techniques," and "practices" are defined as any computational algorithm used or suggested in the preparation of financial accounting statements. "Accounting standards" are those "procedures" sanctioned or recommended by an "authoritative" body such as the APB, FASB, SEC, ICC, *etc.*

[9] Benston [1969a] reports that as of 1926 all firms listed on the New York Stock Exchange published a balance sheet, 55 percent disclosed sales, 45 percent disclosed cost of goods sold, 71 percent disclosed depreciation, 100 percent disclosed net income, and 82 percent were audited by a CPA.

concludes that the original promoters of corporations or, subsequently, corporate managers have incentives to contract to supply audited financial statements. Agreements to supply financial statements were included in articles of incorporation (or by-laws) and in private lending contracts between corporations and creditors.[10] These contracts increase the welfare of the promoter or manager (who is raising the new capital) because they reduce the *agency costs*[11] which he bears.

Agency costs arise because the manager's (the agent's) interests do not necessarily coincide with the interests of shareholders or bondholders (the principals). For example, the manager (if he owns shares) has incentives to convert assets of the corporation into dividends, thus leaving the bondholders with the "shell" of the corporation. Similarly, the manager has incentives to transfer wealth to himself at the expense of both the shareholders and bondholders (*e.g.*, via perquisites).

Bondholders and shareholders anticipate the manager's behavior and appropriately discount the price of the bonds or shares at the time of issue. Hence, the promoter (or manager) of a new corporation receives less for the shares and bonds he sells than he would if he could guarantee that he would continue to act as he did when he owned the firm (*i.e.*, when there were no outside shareholders or bondholders). This difference in the market value of the securities is part of the cost of an agency relationship, it is part of agency costs, and is borne by the promoter (or manager).[12] Jensen and Meckling [1976, p. 308] call it the "residual loss."

Because he bears the residual loss, the manager has incentives to make expenditures to guarantee that he will not take certain actions which harm the principal's interest or that he will compensate the principal if he does. These are "bonding" and "monitoring" expenditures and are additional elements of agency costs. Examples of such expenditures include contracting to restrict dividend payments and expenditures to monitor such dividend convenants.

The final element of agency costs is the utility of the increase in perquisites, wealth transfers, *etc.*, the manager receives because of his actions as an agent. An equilibrium occurs when the net costs of an agency relationship, the agency costs, are minimized by trading off the decreases in the promoter's (or manager's) utility due to the residual loss, the monitoring and bonding expenditures, and the increased utility due to increased perquisites. The promoter or manager will write contracts for monitoring and bonding as long as the marginal benefits of these contracts (*e.g.*, reduction of the residual loss) are greater than the marginal costs (*e.g.*, the costs of contracting and the utility of any perquisites foregone). Moreover, since he bears the agency costs, the manager or promoter will try to write the contracts and perform the bonding or monitoring at minimum cost. In fact, the Jensen and Meckling analysis

---

[10] In the period 1862–1900, many U.K. companies voluntarily adopted the optional articles included in Table A of the 1862 U.K. Companies Act. See Edey [1968], Edey and Panitpakdi [1956] and Watts [1977]. Examples of private contracts can be found today in any note or bond indenture agreement.

[11] Jensen and Meckling [1976, p. 308] define an agency relationship as "a contract under which one or more persons (the principal(s)) engage another person (the agent) to perform some service on their behalf which involves delegating some decision making authority to the agent." There are at least two agency relationships which cause corporate promoters and managers to bear agency costs. The first is the relationship between shareholders (the principals) and the manager (the agent) and the second is the relationship between the bondholders (the principals) and the manager (the agent).

[12] See Jensen and Meckling [1976] for a formal proof that he bears this cost.

suggests that the equilibrium set of contractual devices is the one which minimizes the agency costs associated with the separation of management and control and with the conflict of interests associated with the different classes of investors.

Promoters and managers voluntarily included bonding covenants in corporate articles and by-laws in the nineteenth century. Dividend covenants were voluntarily included in company charters as early as 1620.[13]

Watts's [1977] analysis of agency relationships suggests that the function of audited financial statements in an unregulated economy is to reduce agency costs. This theory predicts that accounting practices (i.e., the form, content, frequency, etc., of external reporting) would vary across corporations in an unregulated economy depending on the nature and magnitude of the agency costs. Agency costs, in turn, are, among other things, a function of the amount of corporate debt outstanding and of the relative share of equity owned by the manager.[14] These variables affect the manager's incentive to take actions which conflict with the interests of shareholders and bondholders. Agency costs also vary with the costs of monitoring managers, which, in turn depend on the physical size, dispersion, and complexity of the firm. Further, the practices underlying financial statements will vary across firms because an accounting practice which minimizes agency costs in one industry may not minimize those costs in another.

As an example of the association between agency costs and accounting procedures, consider management compensation schemes in the nineteenth century. Some management compensation schemes in the nineteenth century were included in corporate articles. Those schemes tied management compensation to the firms' "profits" [Matheson, 1893, pp. vii–viii] to reduce the divergence between the interests of the managers and shareholders.[15] At that time "profits" were effectively operating cash flows, since accrual accounting was not used. [Litherland, 1968, pp. 171–172]. However, a cash flow "profit" index is susceptible to shortrun manager manipulation. The manager can reduce repairs and maintenance expenditures and increase cash flows and "profits,"[16] which would increase the manager's compensation.[17] In addition, reduced maintenance increases the ability of the corporation to pay current dividends. Such dividends could reduce the value of the creditors' claims and increase the shareholders' wealth.[18]

To reduce these agency costs of equity and debt, several contractual devices were used to decrease the likelihood that managers and shareholders would run down the value of the capital stock.

---

[13] See Kehl [1941, p. 4].

[14] Agency costs are also a function of the tastes of managers for non-pecuniary income, the extent of managerial competition, the degree to which the capital markets and the legal system are able to reduce agency costs, etc. See Jensen and Meckling [1976, pp. 328–330].

[15] The terms "shareholders" and "stockholders" are used interchangeably.

[16] See Matheson [1893, p. 5] for a report that managers did in fact adopt this tactic in the nineteenth century.

[17] See Matheson [1893, p. vii] for a statement that managers did in fact resist depreciation charges because of the effect on their compensation.

[18] See Smith [1976, p. 42]. Also, we find labor managed firms in socialist countries faced with the same agency problem. Labor has less incentive to maintain physical capital than an owner-manager. Jensen and Meckling [1977].

    *i)*   Dividends were restricted to a fixed proportion of profits, thereby creating a buffer.[19]

    *ii)*  Reserve funds of fixed amounts had to be maintained if dividends were to be paid.[20]

    *iii)* Fixed assets were treated as merchandise accounts with changes in value (usually not called depreciation) closed to profits prior to dividend distributions.[21]

In the latter procedure, depreciation was treated as a valuation technique which had to be estimated only in profitable years, since dividends were paid only in these years. A typical company charter requiring depreciation is:

> The directors shall, before recommending any dividend, set aside out of the profits of the company, but subject to the sanction of the company in general meeting, such sum as they think proper as a reserve fund for maintenance, repairs, depreciation and renewals.[22]

The court interpreted this article and the term "proper reserve" as a mechanism to account for declines in the capital stock.[23] Thus, the existence of a depreciation covenant (and hence the presence of depreciation in the financial statement) or other restrictions on dividends was a function of the amount of fixed assets and the nature and magnitude of the agency costs of debt.

    Capital market participants contract to supply capital. Managers and owners seeking capital have incentives to enter into contracts which limit the agency costs they incur. But these contracts must then be monitored and enforced since managers have incentives to circumvent the contracts. For example, the promoter or manager of a corporation may contract to restrict dividends to, or base management compensation on, profits after a deduction for depreciation because such a covenant enables him to sell bonds and shares at a higher price. However, *after* the contract is written the manager has incentives to minimize that depreciation charge, thereby leading to increased profits (and potentially increased management compensation) and dividends which transfer wealth from bondholders to shareholders (including management). Thus, contracts will reduce agency costs only if they include provisions for monitoring. Since audited financial statements are useful devices to monitor these voluntary agreements between owners and managers, these statements

---

[19] For example, the General Bank of India had a provision in its charter limiting dividends to not more than $\frac{2}{3}$ of net (cash) profits [DuBois, 1938, p. 365].

[20] The Phoenix Insurance Company, 1781, required a reserve fund of £52,000 before any dividends could be paid. *Ibid.*

[21] See Littleton [1933, pp. 223–227].

[22] *Dent v. London Tramways Company*, 1880, in Brief [1976, p. 193].

[23] "Take the case of a warehouse: supposing a warehouse keeper, having a new warehouse, should find at the end of the year that he had no occasion to expend money in repairs, but thought that, by reason of the usual wear and tear of the warehouse, it was 1,000*l.* worse than it was at the beginning of the year, he would set aside 1,000*l.* for a repair or renewal or depreciation fund, before he estimated any profits; because, although that sum is not required to be paid in that year, it is still the sum of money which is lost, so to say, out of capital, and which must be replaced." *Ibid.*

serve a useful role in the capital markets and owner-managers will agree to provide them in advance.

2. *The Function of Accounting Theories*   The preceding analysis suggests that accounting theories will serve three overlapping functions in an unregulated economy.

*i) Pedagogic demand.* Accounting procedures are devised in order to reduce agency costs of contracts. Since these costs vary across firms, accounting procedures will vary, giving rise to diversity of techniques, formats, *etc.*[24] However, diversity in accounting procedures increases the difficulty of teaching the practice of accounting. Consequently, accounting teachers develop pedagogic devices (rules-of-thumb) to assist learning and to structure the variation found in practice. Theorists examine existing systems of accounts and summarize differences and similarities. These descriptions of practice highlight the tendencies of firms with particular attributes to follow certain accounting procedures.

Nineteenth century accounting texts and articles indicate that accounting theorists recognized the diversity of practice and attempted to distill general tendencies from the diversity. For example:

> No fixed rules, or rates of depreciation can be established for general use, because not only do trades and processes of manufacture differ, but numerous secondary circumstances have to be considered in determining the proper course. It may, however, be possible to lay down some general principles which will always apply, or which, at any rate, may with advantage be held in view in deciding particular cases. [Matheson, 1893, p. 1]

Similarly, Dicksee and Tillyard's [1906] treatise describes current accounting practice for goodwill and the relevant court cases. Based on this description, the authors "enunciate general business principles and explain their practical application" [Dicksee and Tillyard, 1906, p. vii].

*ii) Information Demand.* In an unregulated economy there is a demand for writers to do more than just describe variations in accounting practice. There is a demand for predictions of the effects of accounting procedures on both the manager's and auditor's welfare via exposure to law suits. The auditor contracts with the shareholders (and creditors) to monitor management, and he is legally liable if he fails to report breaches of covenants in the corporation's articles or by-laws.[25] Furthermore, the demand for a given auditor's services is a function of the auditor's

---

[24] Prior to the creation of the Securities and Exchange Commission (SEC) in 1934, much variation existed in accounting procedures. See Blough [1937, p. 7]. In an unregulated economy, the market itself regulates the amount of diversity of accounting procedures. There are economies associated with using existing practices and terminology. If the firm adopts previously unknown accounting practices, then the users of the statements (*i.e.*, creditors monitoring shareholders and shareholders monitoring management) will incur costs in learning the new accounting procedures. If creditors and shareholders have alternative uses of their capital (*i.e.*, capital markets are competitive) the costs of the new procedures are ultimately borne by the shareholders and managers. Hence, new procedures (and increased diversity) will be implemented only if their added benefits offset the added costs they impose.

[25] See the *Leeds Estate Building Company* case in Edwards [1968b, p. 148].

efficiency in monitoring management.[26] Hence, the auditor again has an incentive to understand how management's choice of accounting procedures affects agency costs.

Auditors would value information in the form of theories predicting how agency costs vary with accounting procedures. In particular, auditors would like to know how managers' actions and hence agency costs would be affected by alternative accounting procedures.

*iii) Justification Demand.* Early accounting textbooks warned that managers would use accounting to serve their own interests at the expense of shareholders. The second edition of Matheson [1893] contains examples of such warnings. Matheson provides illustrations of how managers can take advantage of deficiencies in the definition of depreciation, repairs, and maintenance charges to increase "profits" and their own compensation at the expense of shareholders and/or bondholders. For example, on page 5 he writes:

> The temptation to treat as Profit the Surplus of Income over Expenditure, without sufficient allowance for Deterioration, appears to be often irresistible. Thus, in the case of a Tramway undertaking in its first years of working, a dividend may be possible only by writing off little or nothing from the capital value of the cars, the harness, and the horses. This, of course, cannot last without the introduction of new capital, but in undertakings long established there yet may be epochs of fictitious profits due to various causes. For instance there may be neglect of repairs, which, when the necessity for them becomes evident, will involve a heavy outlay for renewals; or it may arise from actual fraud in postponing expenditure, so as to show large profits, which will raise the value of shares for stock-jobbing purposes. There are railways where the dividend income and the corresponding value of the shares have fluctuated considerably, not according to alterations in the real earnings, but according to alternate neglect and attention in regard to plant.

Accounting texts (and theories) which detail how managers seek to manipulate profits and the consequent effects of those manipulations on shareholders and bondholders not only improve the auditor's ability to monitor such behavior, but also provide the auditor with ready-made arguments to use against such practices in discussions with management. It is clear that Matheson's work fulfilled this role. William Jackson, a member of the Council of the Institute of Chartered Accountants in England and Wales, stated that he used Matheson's book in that fashion:

> To those who honestly and from conviction treat the subject on the only sound basis, it may seem superfluous to urge due consideration of the arguments so convincingly set out in these pages; but Auditors, and especially those who have to deal with joint-stock or other concerns where

---

[26] Share prices are unbiased estimates of the extent to which the auditor monitors management and reduces agency costs (see Fama [1970] and Gonedes and Dopuch [1974] for a review of the evidence on market efficiency). The larger the reduction in agency costs effected by an auditor (net of the auditor's fees), the higher the value of the corporation's shares and bonds and, *ceteris paribus*, the greater the demand for that auditor's services. If the market observes the auditor failing to monitor management, it will adjust downwards the share price of all firms who engage this auditor (to the extent to which the auditor does not reduce agency costs), and this will reduce the demand for his services.

the remuneration of the management is made wholly or partly dependent upon declared Profits, know in what varied forms resistance to an adequate Charge against profits for Depreciation is presented.

The fallacies underlying these objections present themselves again and again with the modifications caused by the lack of apprehension in some, or the ingenuity of others. *Mr. Matheson's work provides the Auditor with true antidotes to these fallacies, and it has been in past times used by the writer with satisfactory effect, where his own less-reasoned arguments have failed to convince.*

He therefore recommends it afresh to the notice and for the support, where necessary, of members of his own profession, and of those who, untrained in the practice of Auditing, are confronted with unfamiliar and specious pretexts for avoiding the unwelcome charge against Profits [Matheson, 1893, pp. vii-viii] (emphasis added).

### B. The Demand for Accounting Theories in a Regulated Economy

This section extends the previous analysis of the demand for theories to include the effects of government. We assume that private citizens, bureaucrats, and politicians have incentives to employ the powers of the state to make themselves better off and to coalesce for that purpose. One way by which coalitions of individuals are made better off is by legislation that redistributes (i.e., confiscates) wealth.

*1. Accounting and the Political Process*    Farm subsidies, tariffs, welfare, social security, even regulatory commissions[27] are examples of special interest legislation which transfer wealth. The business sector is both the source (via taxes, anti-trust, affirmative action, *etc.*) and the recipient of many of these wealth transfers (via tax credits, tariffs, subsidies, *etc.*).

Financial accounting statements perform a central role in these wealth transfers and are affected both directly and indirectly by the political process. The Securities and Exchange Commission (SEC) regulates the contents of financial statements directly (upward asset revaluations are not allowed, statements of changes in financial position must be prepared, *etc.*). The Federal Revenue Acts also affect the contents of financial statements directly (*e.g.*, LIFO). In addition, regulatory commissions (*e.g.*, state public utility boards, various banking and insurance commissions, the Interstate Commerce Commission, the Federal Trade Commission) often affect the contents of financial statements.

Besides these more direct effects, there are indirect effects. Government commissions often use the contents of financial statements in the regulatory process (rate setting, antitrust, *etc.*). Further, Congress often bases legislative actions on these statements.[28] This, in turn, provides management with incentives to select accounting procedures which either reduce the costs they bear or increase the benefits they receive as a result of the actions of government regulators and legislators.[29]

---

[27] See Stigler [1971], Posner [1974], and Peltzman [1976].

[28] The reported profits of U.S. oil companies during the Arab oil embargo were used to justify bills to break up these large firms.

[29] See Watts and Zimmerman [1978] for a test of this proposition. Also, see Prakash and Rappaport [1977] for further discussion of these feedback effects. See a bill introduced into the Senate by Senator Bayh (U.S. Congress, Senate, Subcommittee on Anti-trust and Monopoly [1975, pp. 5–13] and [1976, p. 1893]). Note that it is absolute size and profits which are used as a justification. On this point, see the "Curse of Bigness," *Barron's* [June 30, 1969, pp. 1 and 8]. Also see Alchian and Kessel [1962, p. 162].

Since public utilities have incentives to propose accounting procedures for rate making purposes which increase the market value of the firm, their arguments are assisted if accounting standard-setting bodies such as the Financial Accounting Standards Board (FASB) mandate the same accounting procedures for financial reporting.[30] Consequently, managers of utilities and other regulated industries (*e.g.*, insurance, bank and transportation) lobby on accounting standards not only with their regulatory commissions but also with the Accounting Principles Board (APB) and the FASB.

Moonitz [1974 a and b] and Horngren [1973 and 1977] document instances of regulated firms seeking or opposing accounting procedures which affect the value of the firm via direct and indirect wealth transfers. Examples of other firms lobbying on accounting standards exist. Most of the major U.S. oil companies made submissions regarding the FASB's Discussion Memorandum on General Price Level Adjustments [Watts and Zimmerman, 1978].

*2. The Effect of Government Intervention on the Demand for Accounting Theories*    The rules and regulations which result from government regulation of business increase the pedagogic and information demands for accounting theories. Even beginning accounting textbooks report the income tax requirements of LIFO, depreciation, *etc.* Practitioners demand detailed texts explaining SEC requirements (*e.g.*, Rappaport [1972]), tax codes, and other government regulations.

The justification demand for theories also expands with regulation. The political process in the U.S. is characterized as an advocacy proceeding. Proponents and opponents of special interest legislation (or petitioners before regulatory and administrative committees) must give arguments for the positions they advocate. If these positions include changes in accounting procedures, accounting theories which serve as justifications (*i.e.*, excuses) are useful. These advocacy positions (including theories) will tend to be based on contentions that the political action is in the public interest,[31] that everyone is made better off, that most are made better off and no one is harmed, or that the action is "fair," since those contentions are likely to generate less opposition than arguments based on self-interest. Often, those public interest arguments rely upon the notion that the unregulated market solution is inefficient. The typical argument is that there is a market failure which can only be remedied by government intervention.

Politicians and bureaucrats charged with the responsibility for promoting the general welfare demand public interest testimony not only to inform them of the trade-offs but also for use in justifying their actions to the press and their constituencies. Consequently, when politicians support (or oppose) legislation, they tend to adopt the public interest arguments advanced by the special interests who promote (oppose) the legislation.

*i) Examples of Public Interest or Market Failure Justifications.* The reported objective of the Securities Exchange Act of 1934 and of required disclosure is stated

---

[30] The Interstate Commerce Commission based its decision to allow tax deferral accounting on APB Opinion No. 11. See Interstate Commerce Commission, *Accounting for Federal Income Taxes*, 318 I.C.C. 803.

[31] Other writers have also recognized the tendency for advocates to use public interest arguments. For example, Pichler [1974, pp. 64–65] concludes that the accounting profession has increased its economic power via control over entry "through legislation justified as protecting the public interest" (p. 64). "In most cases, *public rather than professional interest was cited as the primary reason for* [the legislation]" (p. 65) (emphasis added).

by Mundheim [1964, p. 647]:

> The theory of the Securities Act is that if investors are provided with sufficient information to permit them to make a reasoned decision concerning the investment merits of securities offered to them, investor interests can be adequately protected without unduly restricting the ability of business ventures to raise capital.

This objective stresses economic efficiency. The statement suggests that required disclosure can increase investors' welfare at virtually zero cost (*i.e.*, that there is a market failure).

Examples of "public interest" justifications of accounting procedures are observed in rate-setting hearings for public utilities. For example, Public Systems, an organization that represents municipalities and rural electrification agencies, applied for a hearing on the Federal Power Commission's (FPC) Order 530 which allowed the use of income tax allocation in setting rates.[32] Order 530 increases the cash flow of electric utilities "at the expense of customers using electricity" and hence harms the interests of Public Systems. But, Public Systems did not argue that it is in its self-interest to oppose Order 530. Instead, it argued that "normalization [income tax allocation] represents an *inefficient* means of subsidizing the public utility industry" [U.S. Congress, Senate, 1976, p. 683] (emphasis added).

Bureaucrats also use public interest arguments to justify their actions.[33] For example, the former SEC Chief Accountant, John Burton, a bureaucrat, justified the disclosure regulations imposed during his term in office by arguing:

> In a broad sense we hope [that disclosure regulations] will contribute to a more efficient capital market.... The way in which we hope that will be achieved is first by giving investors more confidence that they are getting the whole story and second by encouraging the development of better tools of analysis and more responsibility on the part of the professional analyst to understand what's going on. We think that by giving them better data we can encourage them in the direction of doing a better job, thus leading, we hope, to more effective [sic] capital markets [Burton, 1975, p. 21].

Government regulation creates a demand for normative accounting theories employing public interest arguments, that is, for theories purporting to demonstrate that certain accounting procedures *should* be used because they lead to better decisions by investors, more efficient capital markets, *etc.* Further, the demand is not for *one* theory, but rather for diverse prescriptions. On any political issue such as utility rate determination, there will be at least two sides. In the FPC Order 530 example, Coopers & Lybrand, who opposed Public Systems, wanted a theory which prescribed income tax allocation, while Public Systems wanted a theory which did not. When we consider that accounting methods are relevant to taxes, antitrust cases, union negotiations, disclosure regulations, *etc.*, as well as utility rate-setting, we expect a demand for a multitude of prescriptions.

---

[32] U.S. Congress, Senate [1976, p. 59]. "Metcalf Staff Report."
[33] McGraw [1975, p. 162]. Also, see U.S. Securities and Exchange Commission [1945, pp. 1–10].

With increased government intervention in business, the demand for theories which justify particular accounting procedures (proposed in the self-interest of various parties) has come to eclipse the demand for theories which fulfill the pedagogic and information roles. We present evidence to support this proposition in Section V.

*ii) Rationality or "Theory Illusion."* Until recently, it had been popular in the economics literature to assume that politicians, elected officials, bureaucrats, *etc.*, acted in the "public interest" (the public interest assumption).[34] In order to determine which actions are in the public interest, politicians require theories which predict the consequences of alternative actions. "Rational," "public interest"-oriented politicians/bureaucrats would tend to use the theories which best predict (*i.e.*, the "best" theories)[35] and hence those theories would predominate. Leading articles in the accounting literature are implicitly based on the public interest premise (AAA [1966, p. 5], AICPA [1973, p. 17], Gonedes and Dopuch [1974, pp. 48–49 and pp. 114–118], Beaver and Demski [1974, p. 185]) that the "best" theories prevail.

In recent years, however, economists have questioned whether the public interest assumption is consistent with observed phenomena.[36] They have proposed an alternative assumption—that individuals involved in the political process act in their own interest (the self-interest assumption). This assumption yields implications which are more consistent with observed phenomena than those based on the public interest assumption.[37]

The costs and benefits to voters of becoming informed, of lobbying, of forming coalitions, and of monitoring their representatives' actions are of central importance in a self-interest model of the political process. Downs [1957] suggests that the expected effect of one individual's vote on the outcome of an election is trivial, and, hence, the individual voter has very little incentive to incur the costs of becoming informed on political issues. On the other hand, individual voters do have incentives to act as groups in the political process. Economies of scale in political action encourage group participation. When several voters have similar interests on particular issues (*e.g.*, members of a trade union), those voters can share the "fixed" costs of becoming informed and moreover can increase the likelihood of affecting the outcome of an election by voting as a bloc.[38]

The costs of political action also depend on the existing political institutions (*e.g.*, whether political decisions are made by referendum or a vote of elected representatives) [Leffler and Zimmerman, 1977]. If we call the sum of the costs of political action the "transactions costs" of political decisions, the crucial question is "what is the magnitude of these transactions costs?" If the transactions costs of political decisions are high, self-interest motivated government servants will not

---

[34] For a summary of this literature see Posner [1974] and McCraw [1975].

[35] By "best" theory, we mean the theory most consistent with observed phenomena. Such theories allow public officials to predict the outcomes of their actions, thereby helping them select actions which increase social welfare.

[36] See Posner [1974].

[37] For analyses of the political process based on this assumption see Downs [1957], Jensen [1976], Meckling [1976a and b], Mueller [1976], Niskanen [1971], Peltzman [1976], Stigler [1971], and Leffler and Zimmerman [1977].

[38] Stigler [1971] attempts to explain the regulation of an industry on the basis of variation of coalition costs, free-rider costs, *etc.*, with such variables as group size, homogeneity of interest, *etc.*

always act in the public interest; if they are zero, they will.[39] Hence, if the transactions costs of the political process are high, government officials will not use the "best" theory available; if they are zero, they will.

As an example of the importance of positive political transactions costs, consider the manager of a utility advocating deferred tax accounting because of its effects on utility rates. The manager will argue that recognizing deferred taxes as current operating costs is in the public interest. The official responsible for allowing or not allowing this practice has a greater incentive to resist the lobbying efforts of the utility manager if other individuals (e.g., consumer advocates) lobby against the procedure. Whether those individuals lobby depends on the costs of consumers being informed about the effects of the accounting procedures on their welfare (which requires human capital), the costs of forming groups to oppose the procedure, etc. The manager's public interest theory (which is an "excuse" to cover a self-interest motive and need not be valid) increases the costs of others being informed and will tend to be accepted by the public official if the transactions costs are large enough.

We assume that political transactions costs are large enough to cause the acceptance of "invalid" theories, that the competition among excuses does not always lead to acceptance of the "best" theory. The usefulness of the assumption depends on the empirical consistency of its implications. It is an empirical question. The work by Posner [1974], Stigler [1971], and Peltzman [1976] supports the assumption.

The assumption that the transactions costs of the political process are non-zero is analogous to the assumption of non-zero transactions costs in capital markets.[40] In capital market theory it is typically assumed that transactions costs are zero despite the fact they obviously are not, because that assumption yields empirically confirmed hypotheses. Why then, should political transactions costs be sufficiently more important than capital market transactions costs to warrant their inclusion in a political theory?

We suggest that there is an important difference between capital markets and the political process which make transactions costs important in the latter case. There is, in the capital markets, a direct market for control. If the manager of a corporation is not maximizing the market value of the corporation's shares, then an individual can, by buying its shares, acquire control of the corporation in the capital markets and, therefore, obtain the right to make the decisions. That individual can change the corporation's decisions and reap for himself the capital gain from the increase in the value of the corporation's stock. If the Chairman of the Securities and Exchange Commission were not making decisions in the public interest, an individual could not directly buy the right to make those decisions and capture the benefits of the changed decision. Because direct payments to elected officials are illegal and payments in kind are generally more expensive, it is costlier to bribe Congressmen, Senators, etc., than to purchase a controlling interest in a corporation. It is also costly to establish indirect ways of achieving the same result.[41]

---

[39] The social choice literature (see Mueller [1976]) discusses the conditions which guarantee Pareto-efficient decisions by regulators.

[40] See Fama [1976] for a review of capital market theory.

[41] See Zimmerman [1977] for further discussion of this issue. Essentially, the reason it is costlier to purchase "control" of the political system (via a system of bribes, payoffs, etc.) is that the legal system does not enforce these contracts to the same extent that the state enforces the property rights of residual claimants in corporations. Hence, more (costly) monitoring is required to enforce contracts between politicians/bureaucrats and other parties.

Notice that in our model of the political process everyone is rational. No one is being "fooled" by accounting theories; they are not "fooled" by "theory illusion."[42] If people do not investigate the validity of theories, it is because they do not expect such investigation to be worthwhile. If the expected benefits of investigation to an individual are small, he will make only a limited investigation.

Our assumption of high political costs is crucial to our theory. As we shall see in the next section, the assumption enables us to discriminate between the empirical implications of our theory and the implications of an alternative theory. This allows empirical testing. Ultimately, the test of the political cost assumption is whether the implications of the theory based on the assumption are confirmed or not by empirical tests. Thus, the merit of an assumption is judged by the predictions it generates. Those accounting researchers who build theories on the assumption that information is a pure public good (*e.g.*, Gonedes and Dopuch [1974] and Beaver [1976]) often assert that information is a pure public good. Yet, no tests of these theories have been provided. In Section IV we argue that implications of our theory are consistent with the evidence.

## III. THE SUPPLY OF ACCOUNTING THEORIES

Accounting theorists often view themselves as expert critics or defenders of accounting prescriptions (*e.g.*, replacement cost, historical cost, *etc.*). They argue that accounting theory should be used to determine accounting practice and standards.[43] The ideal state of affairs to them is one in which theorists logically and objectively determine the merits of alternative procedures.[44] For example, Hendriksen [1977, p. 1] writes: "...the most important goal of accounting theory should be to provide a coherent set of logical principles that form the general frame of reference for the evaluation and development of sound accounting practices." Theorists tend to bemoan the fact that this ideal state does not exist and that corporate managers, auditors, and politicians do not allow them to determine accounting standards.[45]

Most theorists probably believe that an objective of their research and the reason they supply theories to provide knowledge which will ultimately improve accounting practice. They would not regard themselves as supplying "excuses." But we suggest that the predominant contemporary demand for accounting theories (the demand for accounting in a regulated economy) is the demand for justifications—"excuses." If

---

[42] Buchanan and Wagner [1977, pp. 128–130] introduce the concept of "fiscal illusion" as a systematic bias in individuals' perceptions of the differential effects of alternative taxing procedures. They hypothesize "that complex and indirect payment structures create a fiscal illusion that will systematically produce higher levels of public outlay than those that would be observed under simple-payment structures." (p. 129) It could be argued that individuals also suffer from "theory illusion" (*i.e*, that more complex theories obscure political behavior). We do not subscribe to this phenomenon, but offer it as an alternative explanation.

[43] Mautz [1966, p. 6] and Sterling [1973, p. 49].

[44] Ijiri [1971, p. 26] states, "Accounting theorists are scientific observers of accounting practices and their surrounding environment. Their theories are required to have the highest degree of objectivity."

[45] Moonitz [1974b] does not believe that accounting research should be the sole source for setting practice, but that it should have a role, "Almost everyone agrees that research is an essential component of the process of establishing accounting standards" (p. 58). He goes on to suggest that "accountants must curb the power of the management" (p. 68).

that empirical proposition is correct, the question is: How responsive is the supply side (accounting research) to changes in the nature and quantity of the economic good being demanded?

As long as there exists a large number of individuals who are able to supply a wide diversity of theories (*i.e.*, as long as numerous close substitutes exist) at relatively low cost, then supply will be very responsive to demand. Stigler's observation succinctly summarizes this point:

> ... consumers generally determine what will be produced, and producers make profits by discovering more precisely what consumers want and producing it more cheaply. Some may entertain a tinge of doubt about this proposition, thanks to the energy and skill of Professor Galbraith, but even his large talents hardly raise a faint thought that I live in a house rather than a tent because of the comparative advertising outlays of the two industries. This Cambridge eccentricity aside, then, *it is useful to say that consumers direct production—and therefore, do they not direct the production of the words and ideas of intellectuals, rather than, as in the first view, vice-versa?* [Stigler, 1976, p. 347] (emphasis added).

The consumers ("vested interests") determine the production of accounting research through the incentives they provide for accounting theorists. The greater the prestige and articulation skills of an accounting researcher, the more likely practitioners, regulators and other academics will know his work and the greater the flow of both students and funds to his university. Researchers have non-pecuniary incentives to be well-known, and this reputation is rewarded by a higher salary and a plenitude of research funds.[46] Practitioners, regulators, and those teaching future practitioners are more likely to read or hear of the output of an accounting researcher if it bears on topics of current interest. As a result, the researcher who is motivated by pecuniary and non-pecuniary factors (*e.g.,* "free" trips to conferences) will tend to write on the current controversies in accounting. Therein lies the connection to the demands of vested interests. Controversies arise in accounting when vested interests disagree over accounting standards. For example, the LIFO controversy arose when the Supreme Court outlawed the base stock method of valuing inventory for tax purposes and the American Petroleum Institute recommended LIFO to replace it, thereby reducing the present value of its members' taxes. The Internal Revenue Service resisted because of the effect on revenues. The parties demanded pro and con LIFO theories which were eventually produced [Moonitz, 1974, pp. 33–34].

Accounting researchers often include a set of policy recommendations as part of their research project.[47] Those recommendations, made on the basis of some objective assumed by the researcher, may never have been intended to serve as an "excuse" for the corporate manager, practitioner or politician who prefers the recommended procedure for self-interest reasons. Nevertheless, the research findings will be

---

[46] Even though we have argued the existence of close substitutes, all researchers will not be earning the same compensation. Higher compensation will accrue to the most prolific, articulate, and creative advocates—to those who are able to establish early property rights in a topic and thus must be cited by later theorists.

[47] See Beaver [1973] for an example of policy prescriptions based on accounting research.

favorably quoted by those with vested interests.[48] The more readable the research, the more frequently it is quoted, the more the researcher's fame increases. Similarly, criticisms of alternative accounting practices will be quoted by vested interests and will also increase the researcher's reputation.

The link between suppliers of accounting theory and consumers goes further than mere quotation. Partners in accounting firms, bureaucrats in government agencies and corporate managers will seek out accounting researchers who have eloquently and consistently advocated a particular practice which happens to be in the practitioner's, bureaucrat's, or manager's self-interest and will appoint the researcher as a consultant, or expert witness, or commission him to conduct a study of that accounting problem. Consistency in the researcher's work allows the party commissioning the work to predict more accurately the ultimate conclusions. Thus, research and consulting funds will tend to flow to the most eloquent and consistent advocates of accounting practices where there are vested interests who benefit by the adoption or rejection of these accounting practices.

The tendency of vested interests to seek out researchers who support their position produces a survival bias.[49] The bias is introduced by the vested interests. We do not mean to impugn the motives of accounting researchers who advocate particular practices. In fact, the more consistent the positions of the researcher and the greater his integrity, the more support he lends to the vested interest's position.

Given the rewards for supply theories on controversial issues, we expect to observe competition in the supply of accounting theories related to those issues. The prescriptions for an issue are likely to be as diverse as the positions of vested interests. But despite this diversity, we do not necessarily expect accounting researchers to be inconsistent from issue to issue. Academic evaluation and criticism create incentives for each researcher to be consistent. However, the rationales given for observed accounting standards may well be inconsistent across issues and different sections of the same accounting standard.

Rationales differ (and are inconsistent) across accounting standards because a standard is the result of political action. The outcome depends on the relative costs which the various involved parties are willing to incur to achieve their goals. And these costs will vary with the expected benefits. The rationale given for a standard

[48] An interesting case in point is the work of Ijiri [1967 and 1975]. Ijiri claims to be a positivist— "...the purpose [of this book] is a better understanding of the foundations of accounting as it is and not as someone thinks it ought to be." [1967, p. x] He states that his work "is not intended to be pro-establishment or to promote the maintenance of the status quo. The purpose of such an exercise is to highlight where changes are most needed and where they are feasible." [1975, p. 28] But, then, in the same monograph (pp. 85–90), Ijiri presents a defense of historical costs, saying, "Our defense of historical cost should not, however, be interpreted to mean that historical cost is without any flaw" (p. 85). Ijiri concludes this defense with a statement, "We should in fact try to improve the accounting system based on historical cost not by abandoning it, but by modifying it (e.g., through price level adjustments) and supplementing it with data based on other valuation methods" (p. 90). Despite being a professed positivist, Ijiri is making a strong normative statement. No wonder the AAA [1977, p. 10] committee when summarizing Ijiri [1975] concludes, "[he] defends historical cost against the criticisms of current-cost and current value...." At least part of the "market" views Ijiri as a defender of the status quo.

[49] Just as in any market, those who produce what is demanded have a better chance of survival than those who do not.

will be the successful party's rationale; and if it is a compromise, such as APB Opinion 16 on business combinations, mixtures of rationales will be used.[50] The same party is not successful in every issue; indeed many are not even involved in every issue. Further, vested interests (*e.g.*, an insurance company) are less constrained to give consistent rationales across issues. Hence, we observe a party supporting historical cost valuation in some cases and market valuation in others.[51]

If political transactions costs are high so that there is a demand for excuses which are useful weapons in the political arena, if the demand for accounting theory is dominated by that demand for excuses, and if demand determines production, accounting theories will be generated by, not generate, political debates. We will observe the nature of accounting theory changing as political issues change. Accounting theory will change *contemporaneously* with or *lag* political issues. We will *not* observe accounting theory generally *leading* political action.

Contrast the preceding predictions to what we would expect under alternative theories of accounting theory. The only alternative theory which we can even partially specify is that theories in the accounting literature are used to further the "public interest" (*i.e.*, they assist politicians or bureaucrats in producing regulations to further the "public interest"). In order for politicians or bureaucrats to use that literature we would have to observe the theories appearing in the literature before or, at best, at the same time as the relevant regulation. The appearance of the theories in the literature could not *lag* the regulation. Thus, we can discriminate between our theory and the alternative public interest theory if the appearance of theories in the literature tends to lead or lag regulation. If it tends to lead, the public interest hypothesis is supported. If it lags, our theory is supported. On the other hand, if the literature and regulation are contemporaneous we cannot discriminate between the two hypotheses.

It is important to remember that we are attempting to explain accounting theory as it is represented in the accounting literature (see footnote 1). It is conceivable that an accounting theory could be produced and used in the political process to institute a regulation, but not appear until later in the accounting literature. In other words, the "public interest" could, in fact, motivate the theory and the regulation, but the publication of the theory nonetheless, could, lag legislation. In that case, neither the public interest theory nor our theory could explain the accounting literature. In essence, we would be left without a theory of the literature. However, those who would argue such a scenario must then produce another explanation for, or theory of, the accounting literature.

In Section IV we compare the timing of general movements in the accounting literature to the timing of regulation to see if *a priori* the evidence supports our theory or the public interest theory. We do not present any formal tests which discriminate between the two theories, although we believe such tests could be performed (*e.g.*, by using citation tests). However, the serious problem in doing a formal test is that the public interest theory, like other alternative theories, is poorly specified. Hopefully, this paper will cause others to specify the public interest theory better or specify alternative theories of the accounting literature so that testing is facilitated.

---

[50] See Zeff [1972, pp. 212–216] for an account of this compromise.

[51] Ernst & Ernst [1976] has proposed that replacement cost be used for depreciable assets while historical costs be continued for other assets.

One or two papers discussing a topic prior to the time the topic becomes politically active is not sufficient to reject our theory, just as one or two "heads" is not sufficient to reject the hypothesis that a given coin is "fair." It is important to remember that as in all empirical theories we are concerned with *general* trends. Our predictions are for the accounting literature in general. We are not purporting to have a theory that explains the behavior of all accounting researchers or the acceptance, or lack of acceptance, of every published paper. There are many interesting phenomena that this theory, at this stage of development, cannot yet explain. But this does not *ipso facto* destroy the value of the theory.

Our analysis suggests that the accounting literature is not the simple accumulation of knowledge and consequent development of techniques. It is not a literature in which, as Littleton suggests,[52] concepts become better understood and consequently leads to "better" accounting practices. Instead it is a literature in which the concepts are altered to permit accounting practices to adapt to changes in political issues and institutions.

In this section, the existence of close substitute suppliers of theories was shown to make the supply of accounting "excuses" very responsive to the demand. In the next section we argue that the evidence we have gathered is consistent with the proposition that the market for accounting research is the market for "excuses" and suggests that the theory will be confirmed in formal testing.

## IV. THE EMPIRICAL RELATIONSHIP BETWEEN GOVERNMENT INTERVENTION AND ACCOUNTING THEORY

If the demand for "excuses" is important in determining the output of accounting theorists, we expect to observe changes in accounting theory when a new law is passed which impinges on accounting practice. This section examines how accounting practice and theories were affected by several major types of legislation. We have selected three types of legislation which we believe have had a pronounced impact on accounting theory: the laws regulating railroads, the income tax laws, and the securities acts.

In this section we do not purport to present an exhaustive list of legislation which has created a demand for accounting "excuses" or to present a complete analysis of each type of legislation. Our objective is merely to present *prima facie* support for the hypothesis that accounting theory has changed *after* the introduction of government regulation.

When dealing with historical events such as government regulation, the "evidence" presented is always subject to interpretation and the *ex post* selection bias of the researchers. Critics can always charge that "strategic sampling" of references produced the results. In fact, much of the economic theory of regulation suffers from this *ex post* rationalization. However, at this early stage in the development of the theory, an *ex post* case study approach has yielded insights [Posner, 1974] and appears

---

[52] "There is little evidence of fresh ideas regarding depreciation until the middle of the nineteenth century. The appearance of steam railroads at that time directed attention as never before to fixed assets and their associated problems of maintenance, renewal and improvement. Out of the discussion and experience which followed, new ideas about depreciation took form and the ground was prepared for a better comprehension of the real nature of depreciation itself" [Littleton 1933, p. 227].

to be the logical and necessary precursor to a general theory of regulation. We are aware of these methodological problems. Even though the evidence we present is somewhat "casual," and not as "rigorous" as we would like, it is, nonetheless, evidence.[53] Furthermore, we have endeavored to choose the references from the standard, classical accounting literature. Undoubtedly, conflicting citations and references exist. Critics can, will, and should raise these conflicting citations, keeping in mind the statistical fallacies of drawing inferences based on sample sizes of one. We do not contend that all issues are settled, but rather encourage others to pursue, correct, and extend our analysis.

### A. Railroad Legislation

The growth of railroads is considered by many accountants to have been very important in the development of accounting theory, Hendriksen [1977, p. 40] lists it as one of the main influences on accounting theory in the period from 1800 to 1930. Littleton [1933, pp. 239–241] is more specific; he ascribes the development of depreciation accounting and the concern with depreciation in the literature in the nineteenth century to the growth of railroads.

There is no doubt that the development of railroads both in the U.S. and the U.K. affected the accounting literature on the nature of depreciation, including the question of charging depreciation as an expense [Pollins, 1956; and Boockholdt, 1977]. Holmes [1975, p. 18] writes:

> Depreciation was a knotty problem for these early railroad accountants. They argued over it, scorned it, denied it, anatomized it, and misused their own concepts. But in the end it was from the very ashes of their disagreements that our modern concepts of depreciation rose Phoenix-like fifty years later.

This literature existed at least by 1841 in the U.K. [*The Railway Times*, October 30, 1841, quoted in Pollins, 1956] and by 1850 in the U.S. [Dionysius Lardner's book quoted in Pollins, 1956]. Although the debate did not result in depreciation being treated as an expense in either the U.S. or U.K.,[54] theories of depreciation were enunciated. Consequently, given our theory, we have to answer two questions: (1) why did this depreciation debate arise with the railroads (*i.e.*, was there some government regulation or political action present in the case of the railroads that was not present for earlier corporations); and if so, (2) did that government regulation or political action precede the literature?

(1) *The reason for the debate* was investigated by Littleton [1933]. He asserts that two conditions were necessary to the development of depreciation accounting — corporations with limited liability and long-lived assets. He suggests that limited liability was a necessary condition, because it led to covenants restricting dividends

---

[53] It is tempting to suggest citation tests of the theory (*i.e.*, the frequency of articles on a subject increases with regulation). Besides the obvious cost of such a test, it suffers from the interpretation bias of the researchers. Also, how should changes in terminology be controlled? We would welcome anyone who can overcome these methodological difficulties to perform the tests.

[54] The general practice in both countries came to be the writing-off of the value of fixed assets at the time of retirement of the asset.

to profits and thereby created the demand for financial statements which report profits (see Section II). Long-lived assets were important because, if they had not existed, there would have been no necessity to calculate depreciation to determine profits.

We think that Littleton's analysis is incomplete. *First*, agency costs of debt and equity exist whether or not a corporation has legally limited liability. Limited liability merely shifts some of the risk [Jensen and Meckling, 1976, pp. 331–332]. Given that the function of dividend covenants is to reduce the agency costs of debt, it is not surprising to observe them existing as early as 1620 for U.K. companies, long before limited liability was generally recognized for companies. We can easily amend Littleton's argument for this defect; for the first condition of limited liability, we substitute the existence of dividend covenants.

*Second*, dividend covenants and long-lived assets would not necessarily lead to depreciation being treated as an *expense*. The dividend covenants put a lower bound on the equity participation of shareholders. As long as sufficient earnings have been retained in the past to cover the depreciation of fixed assets to the current time, there would be no necessity to deduct depreciation systematically each year. We do not observe depreciation being treated as an expense prior to this century. Instead it was treated as an allocation of profits.

This suggests that Littleton's analysis has not been supported empirically. Observation of his two conditions would not necessarily be accompanied by depreciation being treated as an expense. Littleton's two conditions existed in the seventeenth and eighteenth centuries (dividend covenants can be observed as early as 1620 and were included in company charters as a general practice in the eighteenth century). Limited liability for U.K. companies existed *de facto* at least by the 1730s and was explicitly recognized by 1784.[55] The U.K. trading companies of the seventeenth and eighteenth centuries certainly had long-lived assets—forts and ships. Yet, we do not observe any real concern with depreciation expense until the nineteenth century.

Littleton recognized that his analysis was inconsistent with observed phenomena and that some other variable was necessary to explain the absence of concern about depreciation expense in both accounting theory and practice. He eloquently expresses the inconsistency [Littleton, 1933, p. 240]:

> The simultaneous appearance of these two elements—active, long-lived assets and a special need for the careful calculation of net profit—seems to be essential to the recognition of the importance of depreciation. Before these two are joined depreciation is incidental to the profit calculation; afterward it becomes indispensable. First in the trading companies, later in

---

[55] See DuBois [1938, pp. 94–95] for a report on the incorporation proceedings of the Albion Flour Mill in 1784. In those proceedings, the Attorney General gave an opinion on limited liability which caused DuBois to conclude that, "for England at any rate, the fact of incorporation either by the Crown or by Parliament came to be the criterion for the extent of limited liability" (p. 96). Note, however, that it was theoretically possible for shareholders of insolvent companies to be made subject to calls. (See DuBois, pp. 98–103). DuBois (p. 95) recognized that *de facto* limited liability existed in the 1730s and 1740s: "it should be noted that through the financial tribulations of the Charitable Corporation, the York Buildings Company, and the Royal African Company, which in the thirties and forties were making life miserable for their creditors, there was no suggestion of any attempt to proceed against the personal estates of the members of the corporations."

the railroads, these two elements were united and the foundations for depreciation accounting were laid. But, so far as could be learned, the depreciation of ships and forts did not receive consideration in the trading companies' bookkeeping, while the railroads, as has been seen, did give considerable attention to the problem of wear and tear of roadway and equipment. *Apparently some third element was also needed, which was present in the case of the railroads* but not earlier (emphasis added).

Littleton [1933, p. 240] suggests that the missing variable is knowledge, that it took 200 years for the nature of the corporation to become known. We suggest that a more plausible explanation is that, in the case of railroads, fares and rates were regulated by government on the basis of "profits."

Both in the U.S. and the U.K., some transportation prices were regulated before the existence of railroads. For example, the rates of the Fort Point Ferry (U.S.), incorporated in 1807, were, according to its charter, to be fixed by the court. [Dodd, 1954, p. 258]. However, railroad rates came to be tied to profits. The early U.S. railroad charters often had provisions for the adjustment of their rates based on profits. For example, the charter of the Franklin Railroad Company, incorporated in Massachusetts in 1830, included the following provision:

if at any time after the expiration of four years from the completion of the Road, the net income shall have amounted to more than ten percent per annum, from the date of the completion aforesaid, upon the actual cost of said Road, the Legislature may take measures to alter and reduce the rates of toll and income, in such manner as to take off the overplus for the next four years, calculating the amount of transportation and income to be the same as the four preceding years; and, at the expiration of every four years thereafter the same proceeding may be had [Dodd, 1954, p. 260].

The charters of three other railroads incorporated in Massachusetts in the same year included a similar provision. [Dodd, 1954, p. 261].

The private acts of Parliament incorporating the early U.K. railroads typically fixed the maximum rates explicitly; but, in one notable exception, the Liverpool and Manchester Railway Act in 1826 limited the company's dividends to ten percent of the capital and required that its rates be reduced by five percent for each one percent of dividend above ten percent [Pollins, 1956, pp. 337–338]. Parliament soon began regulating railroad profits. In 1836, James Morrison sought to have Parliament restrict the profits of all railways. Clauses in Gladstone's 1844 Bill,

authorized the Board of Trade to consider the position and profits of any railway which had a charter for fifteen years and to decide whether to buy it up on prescribed terms or, alternatively, to revise all its charges if it had made a profit of more than ten percent on its capital for three consecutive years [Cooke, 1950, p. 135].

Though these clauses were weakened in the actual Railways Regulation Act of 1844, a principle was established. Cooke [1950, p. 136] explains,

The Act therefore fell short of the designs of Gladstone's committee and it is notable not for any reform it accomplished but rather for the principle embodied in it, that railway companies were one example of a class of company which was formed under special Parliamentary sanction to carry on an undertaking of a special public nature. Since for this purpose it had special powers, it should therefore be subject to special scrutiny and (if necessary) control by the State on behalf of the public.

The question of railroad profits and the public interest was raised in the political process in both the U.S. and the U.K. in the nineteenth century. Hence, it is not surprising that questions of calculating profits and whether depreciation should be charged as an expense were raised. The accounting methods of treating capital additions, depreciation, repairs and renewals, *etc.*, could affect reported profits and hence the rates and market values of railroads. Thus, there was a demand for rationalizations of alternative procedures.

The political issue of railroad profits led several U.S. states (Virginia (1837), New Hampshire and Rhode Island (1841), New York (1855), Massachusetts (1869) and Illinois (1869)) to pass legislation which in some way regulated railroads, usually by "controlling extortionate rates." [Boockholdt, 1977, p. 13; Johnson, 1965, p. 218; and Nash, 1947, p. 2]. According to Nash [1947, p. 3], "Several of the early state laws called for statements of provision for depreciation in annual reports but without definition as to what such provisions should be." Arguments for depreciation are expected to follow such regulations. Finally, in 1887 federal legislation established the Interstate Commerce Commission to prohibit unreasonable rates and price discrimination, control mergers, and prescribe a uniform system of accounts. The Interstate Commerce Commission adopted an accounting policy of charging "repairs or renewals of ties, rails, roadway, locomotives and cars under the classification 'operating expenses' [which typically results in higher reported expenses than depreciation] but did not mention depreciation" [Littleton, 1933, p. 236].

Although railroads were the prime target of regulation, the rates of other public utilities were also regulated in the nineteenth century. A Gas Commission was established in Massachusetts in 1885 and two years later was expanded to regulate electric companies. Later, it was given control over capitalization and rates [Nash, 1947, p. 3]. Municipalities regulated water company rates (*Spring Valley Water Works v. Schottler* (1883)) [Clay, 1932, p. 33] and such regulation led to legal disputes over whether depreciation should be considered in determining rates (*San Diego Water Co. v. San Diego*) [Riggs, 1922, pp. 155–157]. In addition, states regulated the charges for grain elevators (*Munn v. Illinois* (1877)) [Clay, 1932, p. 30].

It is our hypothesis that rate regulation (primarily of the railroads) created a demand for theories rationalizing depreciation as an expense. Furthermore, we expect that the more popular of these theories would stress that it is in the "public interest" for depreciation to be treated as an expense. Without regulation there was no necessity for depreciation to be a charge, systematically deducted each year in determining net income. However, because rate regulation was justified in terms of restricting the economic profits of monopolists (or eliminating "ruinous" competition), regulation created a demand for justifications arguing for depreciation to be treated as an annual charge to profits. Furthermore, because regulatory legislation was often based on economic arguments, theories of depreciation came to be couched in terms of economic costs.

(2) *The timing of the debate* appears to confirm our hypothesis that political action generated accounting theory, not vice-versa. As we have seen, the early U.S.

railroad charters in the 1830s included provisions for regulation of profits. Those charters *precede* the debates observed in the accounting literature. The move by Morrison to have Parliament regulate the profits of U.K. railroads also *precedes* the debates.

### B. Income Tax Acts

The influence of the income tax laws on financial reporting *practice* is well known and much lamented by academics.[56] That influence is very obvious in the practice of charging depreciation to net income, rather than treating it as an allocation of profit. Saliers [1939, pp. 17–18] describes the effect of the 1909 Excise Tax Law, the forerunner of the 1913 Income Tax Law:

> "Financial looseness" describes the accounting practices of industries in general at that time. The company bookkeepers, when closing their books, based the amount of the depreciation charge on the amount of profit earned in that year. A lean year caused the property to receive little or no charge for depreciation, while a prosperous year caused a liberal allowance to be made. The authorities had reason for either action at their fingertips, shifting one side to the other as conditions warranted. But after the year 1909 the shift was to the side of larger depreciation charges, for in that year the Corporation Excise Tax Law was enacted. This law levied a 1% tax on net income of corporations in excess of $5,000. This net income was said to be the figure resulting after deducting ordinary and necessary expenses and all losses, including an allowance for depreciation, from gross profit. Depreciation expense was made an allowable deduction and was universally deducted by those corporations affected by the act. The effect of this act on the growth of the use of the depreciation charge cannot be overemphasized. *It was the first instance in which the writing off of depreciation as expense was definitely advantageous. That fact alone insured its general application* (emphasis added).

The influence of tax laws on accounting theory appears to be as dramatic as Saliers' description of the U.S. tax laws' effect on accounting practice, particularly with respect to depreciation. Concern with depreciation as an expense existed only in the *railroad* accounting literature until the 1880s. In that decade we observe a spate of U.K. journal articles and textbooks on the question of depreciation for corporations in *general*. We do not observe the same concern in the U.S. at that time. This raises the question of why the sudden concern with depreciation in the U.K., not just for public utilities, but for all corporations. Further, why did such a concern with depreciation for all corporations not manifest itself in the U.S.?

Brief [1976, p. 737] suggests that the U.K. literature was motivated by a concern with "paying dividends out of capital" and that "accountants sought first of all to clarify theory, and second, to understand their responsibility in these matters.

---

[56] Hendriksen [1977, p. 49] states, "The effect on accounting theory of taxation of business incomes in the United States and in other countries has been considerable, but it has been primarily indirect in nature.... While the revenue acts did hasten the adoption of good accounting practices and thus brought about a more critical analysis of accepted accounting procedures and concepts, they have also been a deterrent to experimentation and the acceptance of good theory."

However, they were offered little assistance from judicial and statutory authority which failed to specify rules of accounting behavior." Although the accounting authors of the time may have suggested that was the problem, we think it is a very unsatisfactory answer to the question of what really motivated the literature for two reasons. First, we have already noted that the "profits available for dividends" question had existed for 260 years. Second, there was no uncertainty in the law as to when depreciation should or should not be deducted before determining "profits available for dividends." The legal decisions were consistent: if the corporate articles required a provision for depreciation, it had to be taken; if not it did not. As Litherland [1968, p. 171] states, "the question of depreciation was a matter of internal management with which the law had nothing to do. The Articles of the given company were to govern."

We suggest that the reason a general concern with the depreciation for all corporations (and not just railroads) appeared in the U.K. literature in the 1880s and not before is that, prior to 1878, the U.K. tax laws made no allowance for depreciation. "In 1878 the law was modified to permit the deduction of a reasonable amount for the diminished value of machinery and plant resulting from wear and tear. Depreciation was not mentioned in the law and no amount was permitted for obsolescence" [Saliers, 1939, p. 255]. Now there was an additional reason for arguing over the concept of annual depreciation and its level—taxes [Leake, 1912, p. 180].

The income tax explanation for the late nineteenth century depreciation debate also explains the absence of that debate in the U.S. Brief's hypothesis does not. The first effective U.S. corporate income tax law was the Excise Tax Act of 1909 (which went into effect before it was delared unconstitutional).[57] Thus, in 1880 there was no federal tax motivation driving a debate over depreciation. There was in the U.S. in 1880 the problem of determining "profits available for dividends."

The tax laws affected not only the timing of depreciation discussions, but also the resulting concepts of depreciation and of accounting income. In the legal cases on "dividends out of profits," depreciation was regarded as a valuation procedure (see p. 278). Whether the amount of depreciation taken was sufficient would be decided in the event of a dispute. Administering the tax laws is less costly if the periodic valuation is replaced by an arbitrary proportion of historical cost. This saving was recognized in the early literature [Matheson, 1893, p. 15] and was the likely reason that both U.S. and U.K. income tax allowances for depreciation were based on historical cost. The demand for a rationalization of this procedure and other accruals under the tax law eventually resulted in the concept of income based on matching and the realization concept. Storey [1959, p. 232] reports this effect of the tax law as follows:

> [The realization concept] probably did not exist at all before the First World War, and at least one writer states that the first official statement of the concept was made in 1932 in the correspondence between the Special Committee on Cooperation with Stock Exchanges of the American Institute

---

[57] An increase in the effective corporate tax rate from less than 1 percent in 1909 to over 7 percent in 1918 further stimulated the concern for depreciation in the U.S. (Source: *Historical Survey of the United States*, U.S. Department of Commerce [1975, p. 1109]).

of Accountants and the Stock List Committee of the New York Stock Exchange. The letter referred to rejects the method of determining income by the inventorying of assets as the beginning and end of each period in favor of the recognition of profit at the time of sale. This concept of profit was gradually taking form during the period after the First World War and had become dominant in the field of accounting determination of net income by the late 1930's. *That it was influenced by the concept of income laid down by the Supreme Court in early income tax litigation is obvious* (emphasis added).

The timing of the depreciation debates in the U.K. also appears to confirm our hypothesis that political action caused the observed change in accounting theory. The tax allowance of the depreciation deduction (1878) *precedes* the 1880s debates.

It might appear that the development of the profession could explain the difference in the timing of the concern with depreciation in the U.K. and U.S. The professional bodies did not really develop until the 1870s in the U.K. and until the 1890s in the U.S. [Edwards, 1968a, pp. 197–199]. Hence, we could not observe depreciation debates in either country until those times. However, this alternative hypothesis is unsatisfactory on several counts. *First*, while the first professional society was not formed in the U.K. until 1854, Littleton [1933, p. 265] reports evidence of individuals (primarily lawyers) practicing accounting in the U.K. in the eighteenth century and suggests it is highly likely that accounting was practiced by lawyers in earlier times also. Similarly, there were public accountants in the U.S. at least as early as 1866 [Edwards, 1968a, p. 198]. *Second*, the lack of a *formal* accounting profession did not prevent the appearance of the railroad depreciation literature in both the U.S. and U.K. in the 1840s and 1850s. *Third*, the formation of professional societies, itself, is likely to be due, at least partly, to political action. Accountants have incentives to lobby on government prescription of accounting practices. Given some economies of scale in lobbying, government intervention in accounting would be expected to produce professional bodies.

### C. Securities Acts

There appear to be at least two major effects of the U.S. Securities Acts of 1933–34 on the accounting literature: they caused the objective of accounting to shift to what we call the "information objective"; and they stimulated a search for accounting principles. Both *follow* the Securities Acts.

(1) *The Information Objective.* Prior to the Securities Acts accounting theorists tended to describe and base their prescriptions on the multiple objectives of accounting, and they listed the numerous users. Consistent with our analysis of accounting in an unregulated economy, the control, or stewardship role, was frequently stressed. For example, Leake [1912, pp. 1–2] includes as reasons for calculating profit and loss:

1.  the stewardship role of management to "uphold the value of the capital investment and to ascertain and distribute the annual profits with due regard to the differential rights" of the various classes of capital;
2.  profit sharing schemes between capital and labor;
3.  income taxes; and
4.  public utility regulation.

Daines [1929, p. 94] describes the "orthodox" or dominant objective of accounting as being "to reflect that income which is legally available for dividends." Sweeney [1936, p. 248] states that "the fundamental purpose of accounting should consist of an attempt to distinguish between capital and income."

In his book based on his doctoral dissertation, Sweeney adds other functions to the stewardship role:

> Business management guides the affairs of business. For its own guidance it depends heavily on reports submitted to it by its employees. Periodically it renders reports of its stewardship to the owners of the business. From time to time it also renders reports to bankers who have lent money to the business, to federal and state governments that tax or regulate business, and to the general financial public.
>
> The whole system of business, therefore, depends upon reports. Reports are made up largely of accounting statements [Sweeney, 1936, p. xi].

Managers were frequently cited as important users of accounting. Paton [1924, p. 1] defines accounting as a

> mechanism and body of principles by means of which the financial data of the particular concern are recorded, classified, and periodically presented and interpreted, with a view, thereby, to the *rational administration of the enterprise* (emphasis added).

*After* the Securities Acts the providing of information to investors and creditors in order to aid them in making rational investment choices became the dominant objective in the literature. We call this the information objective. One of the earliest documents which illustrates this new emphasis on the investor's decision is the AAA's 1936 "Tentative Statement on Accounting Principles." A number of "unsatisfactory" accounting procedures are discussed, including upward asset revaluations:

> Occasional uncoordinated "appraisals" produce in the average financial statement a hodgepodge of unrelated values of no explicable significance to *the ordinary investor*, if indeed they have any to the managements of the enterprises affected [American Accounting Association, 1936, p. 189] (emphasis added).

Notice the emphasis given to investors. Hendriksen [1977, p. 54] also supports our contention that the objective changed "from presenting financial information to management and creditors to that of providing financial information to investors and stockholders." In a more recent example, *A Statement of Basic Accounting Theory* [American Accounting Association, 1966, p. 4], the information objective is listed first among four objectives of accounting. The objectives are:

1.  to provide information for decisions concerning limited resources by "individuals acting in their own behalf, such as the stockholders or creditors of a firm, by agents serving in fiduciary capacities, or by individuals or groups in business firms, in government, in not-for-profit organizations and elsewhere" [p. 4].

2. to effectively direct and control an organization's human and material resources,
3. to maintain and report on the custodianship of resources,
4. "to facilitate the operations of an organized society for the welfare of all" [p. 5].

Recent writers no longer even list management as a principal user of financial statements. The dichotomy of internal and external accounting has become complete. The recent statement on accounting objectives, the FASB's Conceptual Framework Study [1976], also excludes management:

> Financial statements of business enterprises should provide information, within the limits of financial accounting, that is useful to present and potential investors and creditors in making rational investment and credit decisions [FASB, 1976, p. 10].

The dominance of the information objective arose, we suspect, as a public interest justification consistent with and in support of the *raison d'être* of the Securities Acts. The SEC was justified in terms of, and charged with, maintaining the orderly functioning of the capital markets. In particular the SEC was to protect the public from another stock market crash. That crash was alleged to have been caused in part by inadequate corporate disclosure, although very little evidence exists to support this claim.[58]

Although the SEC delegated the power to determine accounting standards for corporate disclosure to the accounting profession, there is evidence that it still exercised control over that determination. According to Horngren [1973] and Zeff [1972, pp. 150–160] the SEC managed by exception, threatening to intervene, or actually intervening in the standard-setting process whenever the Committee on Accounting Procedure (CAP) or the APB proposed a standard of which it did not approve. Consequently, proponents advocating particular accounting procedures would justify those procedures in terms of the SEC's stated objective—the public interest (which "requires" the information objective).

The hypothesis that the dominance of the information objective was caused by the Securities Acts is supported not only by the tendency of modern writers to cite the public interest as an objective along with the information objective [*e.g.*, the fourth objective of *A Statement of Basic Accounting Theory* listed above], but by the tendency to argue that fulfillment of the information objective is necessary to the "public interest." An example of that latter tendency is provided by the FASB [1976, p. 3]:

> Financial accounting and reporting is an important source of information on which investment, lending, and related decisions are based. Confidence in financial information is vital not only to ensure that individual decisions result in an equitable allocation of capital but to ensure continuing public support of the free enterprise system as a whole.

---

[58] See Benston [1969a and b]. The U.S. Securities and Exchange Commission [1945, pp. 1–3 and Part X] makes this claim, although Sanders [1946, pp. 9–10] disputes much of their argument.

The close relationship between the information objective and the "public interest" is exemplified by the argument recently raised in the literature that information provided in accounting reports is a public good and that as a consequence, there may be an underproduction of information from society's viewpoint (*i.e.*, there may be a market failure). If there is a market failure, the argument proceeds, the "public interest" may require disclosure laws requiring the provision of information to investors [Beaver, 1976, p. 66].

(2) *The Search for Accounting Principles.* Before the Securities Acts most of the accounting literature did not stray far from practice, and prescriptions were usually based on rationalizations of practice (*e.g.*, the matching concept). Even Sweeney's price-level accounting proposals of the 1920s were based on practice. According to the author [Sweeney, 1936, p. xii] the work "has its roots in methods that were developed in Germany and France during the late inflation periods in those countries." There was, with the notable exceptions of Paton [1922] and Canning [1929], little effort devoted to establishing a theory of accounting.[59] Indeed, Chambers [1955a, p. 18] claims that except for Paton [1922] the word theory was not attached to any work in the accounting literature until after World War II.

Taggart describes the general situation in 1922 as follows:

> Some of the writers on theory, notably Sprague and Hatfield, not satisfied merely to describe practice, had earnestly addressed themselves to exposition of pure theory; but the textbook writers, for the most part, had quite naturally concerned themselves primarily with practice and with not much more than an occasional nod toward theory, where it seemed to bolster practice. Paton's *Accounting Theory* is concerned only with theory; it touches on practice only for illustration or contrast; and it is quite the opposite of an apologia for practice, [Foreword in the 1962 re-issue of Paton, 1922, p. v.].

Canning [1929, p. 160] himself wrote, "accountants have no complete philosophical system of thought about income; *nor is there evidence that they have ever greatly felt the need for one*"[60] (emphasis added).

A potential explanation for the two famous departures from the orthodox accounting thought of the 1920s [Canning, 1929; and Paton, 1922] is that both were based on doctoral dissertations written in economics departments [Zeff, 1978, p. 16]. Undoubtedly, both authors were influenced heavily by economists as well as accountants. Canning himself writes, "I need not declare my obligation to Professor [Irving] Fisher for the influence of his writings upon my thought—that obligation appears throughout the whole book" [Canning, 1929, p. iv].

If Paton and Canning were harbingers of a change in accounting thought, we would expect to observe a shift in the orthodox accounting view during the 20s,

---

[59] The Federal Reserve Board published a 1917 bulletin (*Uniform Accounting*) written by Price, Waterhouse & Co. in response to the Federal Trade Commission threatening to establish a federal accountant's register, but the bulletin "consisted of mainly audit procedures" [Carey, 1969, pp. 1:129–135].

[60] Canning's principal intentions were not to reform existing practice or to construct a general theory but rather to make "the work of the professional accountant more fully intelligible to those in other branches of learning" [1929, p. iii].

following publication of their books. Alternatively, if Canning's and Paton's views were outliers or aberrations due to their economics training, we would expect to observe them modifying their views towards the orthodox position to ensure their survival as accounting academics.

Zeff [1978] presents evidence that Paton's views, at least, moved more towards the orthodox view during the 1920s and 1930s, than the orthodox view moved towards Paton's. Thus, it is difficult to argue that Paton and Canning were representative of a change in the accounting literature which influenced the passage of the Securities Acts. Instead, we suspect that much of the attention which Paton's and Canning's views received after the Securities Acts was a result of the Acts themselves.

The literature's concern with practice before the Securities Acts is not surprising (given our theory). Prescriptions based on rationalizations of practice are to be expected in an economy in which corporate reporting is not regulated. Theorists would base their prescriptions for individual firms on the current institutional arrangements determining practice (*i.e.*, in the terms of the agency or stewardship relationships, utility regulation, taxes, *etc.*). Hence, theory would be very concerned with practice. Further, because the advantages are to the individual firms, the theorist would not *require* all firms to follow his prescriptions, but expect his prescriptions to be adopted because of self-interest. The theorist would not try to specify accounting principles which all firms *should* adopt.

As we have noted, the Securities Acts were based on the argument that required disclosure is necessary to the "public interest." The idea was that without required disclosure capital markets would be less efficient. We do not observe this theory being generally advanced in the accounting literature prior to the Securities Acts.[61]

The justification for required disclosure is that the private incentives to adopt accounting prescriptions are insufficient. Hence, current accounting practice cannot serve as a basis for prescriptions. This justification sets accounting theory free from practice. It makes it possible to "build up a theory of accounting without reference to the practice of accounting" [Chambers, 1955a, p. 19]. Further, the justification caused the SEC to demand such theories. Because they were to reform existing accounting practice, the SEC commissioners could not base regulations on practice; they required a theory or a set of accounting principles to justify their rulings.

Zeff [1972, pp. 133–173] documents the AICPA's initial search for accounting principles and the SEC's passing the responsibility for the determination of principles to the profession in SEC Accounting Series Release No. 4 [U.S. SEC, ASR 4].[62] Zeff also documents the search for accounting principles (or standards) by the succession of standard-setting bodies established by the profession. As noted, the SEC exercised control over the standard-setting bodies' search for accounting principles. Thus, we expect these bodies (like the SEC) to search for or demand accounting principles which do *not* describe existing practice.

---

[61] The theory does appear in *The Journal of Accountancy* in October, 1930 (see Hoxsey [1930], but the author is not an accounting theorist; instead he is an employee of the New York Stock Exchange. The theory also appears in the writings of Ripley in the popular financial literature in the 1920s (*e.g.*, Ripley [1926]). However, Ripley is also not representative of the financial literature.

[62] ASR 4 stated that "financial statements filed with this Commission ... [which] are prepared in accordance with accounting principles for which there is *no substantial authoritative support*, ... will be presumed to be misleading or inaccurate" (emphasis added). ASR 4 created a demand for some procedure or device to provide "substantial authoritative" support.

We expect accounting theorists, who are accustomed to developing rules based on practice, to be perplexed by a demand for accounting principles not based on practice. *After* the SEC's call (in ASR 4) for accounting principles for which there is substantial authoritative support [1938], the accounting literature begins to discuss the nature of principles [Scott, 1941; Wilcox and Hassler, 1941; and Kester, 1942].[63] Further, as theorists come to observe less emphasis being placed on the practicality of their approach, we observe philosophical works becoming far removed from practice such as Chambers [1955a, 1955b, 1966], Mattessich [1957] and Edwards and Bell [1961].

It is instructive to compare the search for accounting principles in the U.S. to that in the U.K. where there has not been a government regulatory body with the statutory power to prescribe accounting procedures [Benston, 1976, pp. 14–30; Zeff, 1972, pp. 1–69].[64] Until recently there has been considerably less "progress" in the U.K. in the search for accounting principles [Zeff, 1972, p. 310 and Shackleton, 1977, pp. 17–21] and further, "the English began late" [Zeff, 1972, p. 310]. The evidence suggests that the U.K. search for principles is also a response to government pressure which arose out of various financial crises [Zeff, 1972, pp. 39–40; Benston, 1976, pp. 15–17; and Shackleton, 1977, pp. 17–21].

The difference in the timing of the search for principles in the two countries is reminiscent of the 30-year difference in the timing of the general depreciation debates in the U.K. and the U.S. That 30-year difference also coincides with a difference in the timing of government regulation (*i.e.*, corporate income tax laws allowing depreciation as a deduction). The difference in timing cannot be explained *per se* by the fact that we are comparing two different countries. In the depreciation debates, the U.K. led, while the U.S. led in the search for principles.

The discussion in this section has suggested that much of accounting theory (*e.g.*, the concepts of depreciation, accrual accounting, the application of the concept of economic income, and the idea that the objective of financial statements is generally to provide information to investors rather than to control agency costs), *follows* government intervention. Thus, the evidence is consistent with our hypothesis that much of accounting theory is the product of government intervention and that accounting theory satisfies the demand for excuses. The evidence appears to be inconsistent with what we have called the "public interest" hypothesis. Undoubtedly there are alternative theories which can also explain the timing of the accounting literature. The challenge is to those who would support those alternative theories to specify them and show that they are more consistent with the evidence than ours.

## V. CONCLUSIONS

In our view, accounting theories have had an important role in determining the content of financial statements—although it might not be the role envisioned by the theorists. Instead of providing "an underlying framework" for the promulgation of "sound" financial reporting practices by standard-setting boards, accounting theory has proven a useful "tactic to buttress one's preconceived notions" [Zeff, 1974, p. 177].

---

[63] Storey [1964, p. 3] supports our contention that the Securities Acts were "landmark events" and directly related to the search for accounting principles.

[64] See Sanders [1946] for an overview of the different prevailing attitudes in the U.S. and U.K. in the 1940s.

While accounting theories have always served a justification role in addition to information and pedagogic roles, government intervention has expanded the justification role. The predominant function of accounting theories is now to supply excuses which satisfy the demand created by the political process; consequently accounting theories have become increasingly normative.

We are not offering any judgments on the desirability of accounting theories fulfilling an excuse role. What we are arguing, however, is that *given* the existing economic and political institutions and the incentives of voters, politicians, managers, investors, *etc.* to become involved in the process by which accounting standards are determined, the only accounting theory that will provide a set of predictions that are consistent with observed phenomena is one based on self-interest. No other theory, *no normative theory currently in the accounting literature*, (e.g., *current value theories) can explain or will be used to justify all accounting standards*, because:

1. accounting standards are justified using the theory (excuse) of the vested interest group which is benefitted by the standard;
2. vested interest groups use different theories (excuses) for different issues; and
3. different vested interest groups prevail on different issues.

While a self-interest theory can explain accounting standards, such a theory will not be used to justify accounting standards because self-interest theories are politically unpalatable. As a consequence, *not only is there no generally accepted accounting theory to justify accounting standards, there will never be one.*

## REFERENCES

Accounting Principles Board, *Opinion 16: Business Combinations*, American Institute of Certified Public Accountants, 1970).

Alchian, Armen and Reuben Kessel, "Competition, Monopoly and the Pursuit of Money," in *Aspects of Labor Economics*, (Princeton University Press: N.B.E.R., 1962), pp. 157–175.

American Accounting Association, "A Tentative Statement of Accounting Principles Affecting Corporate Reports," THE ACCOUNTING REVIEW, (June 1936), pp. 187–191.

———, Committee on Basic Accounting Theory, *A Statement of Basic Accounting Theory* (American Accounting Association, 1966).

———, Committee on Concepts and Standards for External Reports, *Statement on Accounting Theory and Theory Acceptance* (American Accounting Association, 1977).

American Institute of Certified Public Accountants, *Objectives of Financial Statements*, (Trueblood) Report of the Study Group on the Objectives of Financial Statements (American Institute of Certified Public Accountants, 1973).

Beaver, William H., "What Should Be the FASB's Objectives?", *Journal of Accountancy*, (August, 1973), pp. 49–56.

———, "The Implications of Security Price Research for Disclosure Policy and the Analyst Community," in A. R. Abdel-khalik and T. F. Keller (eds.), *Financial Information Requirements for Security Analysis*, Duke Second Accounting Symposium, Duke University (December 1976), pp. 65–81.

———— and Joel S. Demski, "The Nature of Financial Accounting Objectives: A Summary and Synthesis," *Studies on Financial Accounting Objectives*, supplement to the *Journal of Accounting Research* (1974), pp. 170–187.

Benston, George J., "The Value of the SEC's Accounting Disclosure Requirements," THE ACCOUNTING REVIEW, (July 1969a), pp. 515–532.

————, "The Effectiveness and Effects of the SEC's Accounting Disclosure Requirements," in Henry G. Manne (ed.), *Economic Policy and the Regulation of Corporate Securities*, (American Enterprise Institute, 1969b), pp. 23–79.

————, *Corporate Financial Disclosure in the UK and the USA* (Saxon House, 1976).

Blough, Carman G., "Some Accounting Problems of the Securities and Exchange Commission," *The New York Certified Public Accountant*, (April 1937), pp. 3–14.

Boockholdt, James L., "Influence of Nineteenth and Early Twentieth Century Railroad Accounting on Development of Modern Accounting Theory," unpublished working paper 31, University of Alabama (July 1977).

Brief, Richard P. (ed.), *The Late Nineteenth Century Debate Over Depreciation, Capital and Income* (Arno Press, 1976).

Buchanan, James M. and Richard E. Wagner, *Democracy in Deficit: The Political Legacy of Lord Keynes*, (Academic Press, 1977).

Burton, John C., "An Interview with John C. Burton," *Management Accounting*, (May 1975), pp. 19–23.

Canning, John B., *The Economics of Accountancy* (Ronald Press, 1929).

Carey, John L., *The Rise of the Accounting Profession*, Vols. 1 & 2 (American Institute of Certified Public Accountants, 1969–70).

Chambers, Raymond J., "Blueprint for a Theory of Accounting," *Accounting Research*, (January 1955a), pp. 17–25.

————, "A Scientific Pattern for Accounting Theory," *Australian Accountant* (October 1955b), pp. 428–434.

————, *Accounting, Evaluation and Economic Behavior* (Prentice-Hall, 1966).

Clay, Cassius M., *Regulation of Public Utilities*, (Henry Holt and Company, 1932).

Cooke, C. A., *Corporation, Trust and Company* (Manchester University Press, 1950).

"Curse of Bigness," *Barron's*, (June 30, 1969), pp. 1 and 8.

Daines, H. C., "The Changing Objectives of Accounting," THE ACCOUNTING REVIEW, (June 1929), pp. 94–110.

Dicksee, Lawrence, *Depreciation, Reserves and Reserve Funds* (1903), reprinted by Arno Press, 1976.

Dodd, Edwin M., *American Business Corporations Until 1860* (Harvard University Press, 1954).

Downs, Anthony, *An Economic Theory of Democracy* (Harper and Row, 1957).

DuBois, Armand B., *The English Business Company After the Bubble Act 1720–1800* (The Commonwealth Fund, 1938).

Edey, Harold C., "Company Accounting in the Nineteenth and Twentieth Centuries," reprinted in Michael Chatfield (ed.), *Contemporary Studies in the Evolution of Accounting Thought* (Dickenson Publishing Co. Inc., 1968), pp. 135–143.

———— and Prot Panitpakdi, "British Company Accounting and the Law 1844–1900," in A. C. Littleton and B. S. Yamey (eds.), *Studies in the History of Accounting* (Richard D. Irwin, Inc., 1956), pp. 356–379.

Edwards, Edgar O. and Philip W. Bell, *The Theory and Measurement of Business Income* (University of California Press, 1961).

Edwards, James D., "Some Significant Developments of Public Accounting in the United States," *Business History Review* (June 1956), reprinted in Michael Chatfield (ed.), *Contemporary Studies in the Evolution of Accounting Thought* (Dickenson Publishing Co., 1968a), pp. 196–209.

———, "The Antecedents of American Public Accounting," *Accounting Research* (January 1956), reprinted in Michael Chatfield (ed.), *Contemporary Studies in the Evolution of Accounting Thought* (Dickenson Publishing Co., 1968b), pp. 144–166.

Ernst & Ernst, *Accounting Under Inflationary Conditions*, (Ernst & Ernst, 1976).

Fama, Eugene F., "Efficient Capital Markets: A Review of Theory and Empirical Work," *Journal of Finance* (May 1970), pp. 381–417.

———, *Foundations of Finance* (Basic Books, Inc., 1976).

Financial Accounting Standards Board, *An Analysis of Issues Related to Conceptual Framework for Financial Accounting and Reporting: Elements of Financial Statements and Their Measurement* (FASB, 1976).

Gonedes, Nicholas and Nicholas Dopuch, "Capital Market Equilibrium, Information Production and Selecting Accounting Techniques: Theoretical Framework and Review of Empirical Work," *Studies on Financial Accounting Objectives*, supplement to the *Journal of Accounting Research* (1974), pp. 48–129.

Gordon, Myron J., "Postulates, Principles and Research in Accounting," THE ACCOUNTING REVIEW (April 1964), pp. 251–263.

Hendriksen, Eldon, *Accounting Theory*, 3rd Edition (Richard D. Irwin, Inc., 1977).

Holmes, William, "Accounting and Accountants in Massachusetts," *Massachusetts CPA Review* (May—June 1975), pp. 18–21.

Horngren, Charles T., "The Marketing of Accounting Standards," *Journal of Accountancy*, (October 1973), pp. 61–66.

———, "Setting Accounting Standards in the 1980's," in Norton Bedford (ed.), *Accountancy in the 1980's—Some Issues*, (The Council of Arthur Young Professors, 1977).

Hoxsey, J. M. B., "Accounting for Investors," *Journal of Accountancy* (October 1930), pp. 251–284.

Ijiri, Yuji, *The Foundations of Accounting Measurement* (Prentice-Hall Inc., 1967).

———, "Logic and Functions in Accounting," in Robert Sterling and William Bentz (eds.), *Accounting in Perspective*, (South-Western Publishing Co., 1971).

———, *Theory of Accounting Measurement* (American Accounting Association, 1975).

Interstate Commerce Commission, *Accounting for Federal Income Taxes*, 318 I.C.C. 803, U.S. Government Printing Office.

Jensen, Michael C., "Towards a Theory of the Press," unpublished paper, Graduate School of Management, University of Rochester, June 1976.

——— and William H. Meckling, "Theory of the Firm: Managerial Behavior, Agency Costs and Ownership Structure," *Journal of Financial Economics*, (October 1976), pp. 305–360.

——— and William H. Meckling, "On 'The Labor Managed' Firm and the Codetermination Movement," Public Policy Working Paper Series GPB 77-2, Center for

Research in Government Policy and Business, Graduate School of Management, University of Rochester, February 1977.

Johnson, Arthur M., *Government-Business Relations* (Charles E. Merrill Books, 1965).

Kehl, Donald, *Corporate Dividends* (The Ronald Press Company, 1941).

Kester, Roy B., "Sources of Accounting Principles," *Journal of Accountancy*, (December 1942), pp. 531–535.

Leake, P. D., *Depreciation and Wasting Assets and Their Treatment in Assessing Annual Profit and Loss* (1912), reprinted by Arno Press, 1976.

Leffler, Keith and Jerold Zimmerman, "A Theory of Municipal Government Agency Costs, Organizational Form, and Scale," working paper, Graduate School of Management, University of Rochester (July 1977).

Litherland, D. A., "Fixed Asset Replacement a Half Century Ago," reprinted in Michael Chatfield (ed.), *Contemporary Studies in the Evolution of Accounting Thought* (Dickenson Publishing Co., Inc., 1968), pp. 167–175.

Littleton, A. C., *Accounting Evolution to 1900* (1933), reprinted by Russell & Russell, 1966.

Matheson, Ewing, *The Depreciation of Factories, Mines and Industrial Undertakings and Their Valuation* (1893), reprinted by Arno Press, 1976.

Mattessich, Richard, "Towards a General and Axiomatic Foundation of Accountancy; with an Introduction to the Matrix Formulation of Accounting Systems," *Accounting Research*, (October 1957), pp. 328–355.

Mautz, Robert K., "The Role of the American Accounting Association in Accounting Research," *Research in Accounting Measurement*, Robert Jaedicke, Yuji Ijiri and Oswald Nielsen (eds.) (American Accounting Association, 1966).

——— and Jack Gray, "Some Thoughts on Research Needs in Accounting," *The Journal of Accountancy*, (September 1970), pp. 54–62.

McCraw, Thomas K., "Regulation in America: A Review Article," *Business History Review*, (Summer 1975), pp. 159–183.

Meckling, William H., "Towards a Theory of Representative Government," presented at the Third Annual Conference on Analysis and Ideology, Interlaken, Switzerland, June 4, 1976 (1976a).

———, "Values and the Choice of the Model of the Individual in the Social Sciences," *Revue Suisse d' Economic Politique et de Statistique* (December 1976b), pp. 545–560.

Moonitz, Maurice, "Accounting Principles—How They are Developed," in Robert Sterling (ed.), *Institutional Issues in Public Accounting*, (Scholars Book Company, 1974a), pp. 143–171.

———, *Obtaining Agreement on Standards in the Accounting Profession* (American Accounting Association, 1974b).

Mueller, Dennis C., "Public Choice: A Survey," *The Journal of Economic Literature* (June 1976), pp. 395–433.

Mundheim, Robert H., "Foreword, Symposium on Securities Regulation," *Law and Contemporary Problems* (Summer 1964), pp. 647–652.

Nash, Luther R., *Anatomy of Depreciation* (Public Utilities Reports, Inc., 1947).

Niskanen, William A., *Bureaucracy and Representative Government* (Aldine-Atherton, 1971).

Paton, William A., *Accounting Theory—With Special Reference to the Corporate Enterprise* (New York: The Ronald Press Company, 1922). Re-issued in 1962 by A.S.P. Accounting Studies Press, Ltd. Reprinted by Scholars Book Co., 1973.

———, *Accounting* (Macmillan Company, 1924).

——— and A. C. Littleton, *An Introduction to Corporate Accounting Standards* (American Accounting Association, 1940).

Peltzman, Sam, "Towards a More General Theory of Regulation," *Journal of Law and Economics*, (August 1976), pp. 211–240.

Pichler, Joseph A., "An Economic Analysis of Accounting Power," in Robert Sterling (ed.), *Institutional Issues in Public Accounting* (Scholars Book Co., 1974), pp. 45–73.

Pollins, Harold, "Aspects of Railway Accounting Before 1868," reprinted in A. Littleton and B. Yamey (eds.), *Studies in the History of Accounting* (Richard D. Irwin, Inc., 1956), pp. 332–355.

Posner, Richard A., "Theories of Economic Regulation," *Bell Journal of Economics and Management Science* (Autumn 1974), pp. 335—358.

Prakash, Prem and Alfred Rappaport, "Information Inductance and Its Significance for Accounting," *Accounting Organizations and Society*, Vol. 2, No. 1, (1977), pp. 29–38.

Rappaport, Louis H., *SEC Accounting Practice and Procedure*, Third Edition (Ronald Press, 1972).

Riggs, Henry E., *Depreciation of Public Utility Properties* (McGraw Hill Book Co., 1922).

Ripley, William Z., "Stop, Look, Listen!", *The Atlantic Monthly* (September, 1926), pp. 380–399.

Saliers, Earl A., *Depreciation; Principles and Applications*, Third Edition (Ronald Press Company, 1939).

Sanders, Thomas H., "A Review of Reviews of Accounting Progress," *Journal of Accountancy* (January 1946), pp. 9–26.

———, Henry R. Hatfield, and Underhill Moore, *A Statement of Accounting Principles* (American Institute of Accountants, 1938).

Scott, DR, "The Basis for Accounting Principles," THE ACCOUNTING REVIEW (December 1941), pp. 341–349.

Shackleton, Ken, "Government Involvement in Developing Accounting Standards: The Framework," *Management Accounting* (U.K.), (January 1977), pp. 17–21.

Smith, Clifford, "On the Theory of Lending," unpublished paper, Working Paper Series No. 7635, Graduate School of Management, University of Rochester, 1976.

Sprouse, Robert T. and Maurice Moonitz, "A Tentative Set of Broad Accounting Principles for Business Enterprises," *Accounting Research Study No. 3* (American Institute of Certified Public Accountants, 1962).

Sterling, Robert R., "Accounting Research, Education and Practice," *Journal of Accountancy* (September 1973), pp. 44–52.

——— (ed.), *Institutional Issues in Public Accounting* (Scholars Book Co. 1974).

Stigler, George J., "The Theory of Economic Regulation," *Bell Journal of Economics and Management Science* (Spring 1971), pp. 3–21.

———, "Do Economists Matter?", *Southern Economic Journal* (January 1976), pp. 347–363.

Storey, Reed K., "Revenue Realization, Going Concern and Measurement of Income," THE ACCOUNTING REVIEW (April 1959), pp. 232–238.

———, *The Search for Accounting Principles* (American Institute of Certified Public Accountants, 1964).

Sweeney, Henry W., *Stabilized Accounting* (Harper & Bros. Publishers, 1936).

U.S. Congress, Senate, Subcommittee on Antitrust and Monopoly of the Committee on the Judiciary, Hearings, *The Petroleum Industry*, Part I, 94th Congress, 1st Session, 1975.

U.S. Congress, Senate, Subcommittee on Reports, Accounting and Management of the Committee on Government Operations, *The Accounting Establishment: A Staff Study* (Metcalf Staff Report), 94th Congress, 2nd Session, 1976.

U.S. Department of Commerce, Bureau of the Census, *Historical Statistics of the United States, Colonial Times to 1970* (U.S. Government Printing Office, 1975).

U.S. Securities and Exchange Commission, "Administrative Policy on Financial Statements," *Accounting Series Release No. 4,* (April 25, 1938).

U.S. Securities and Exchange Commission, *Tenth Annual Report of the Securities and Exchange Commission: Fiscal Year Ended June 30, 1944* (1945).

Watts, Ross L., "Accounting Objectives," working paper series no. 7408, Graduate School of Management, University of Rochester, April 1974.

———, "Corporate Financial Statements, A Product of the Market and Political Processes," *Australian Journal of Management* (April 1977), pp. 53–75.

——— and Jerold L. Zimmerman, "Towards a Positive Theory of the Determination of Accounting Standards," THE ACCOUNTING REVIEW (January 1978), pp. 112–134.

Wilcox, E. B. and R. H. Hassler, "A Foundation for Accounting Principles," *Journal of Accountancy* (October 1941), pp. 308–314.

Zeff, Stephen A., *Forging Accounting Principles in Five Countries: A History and an Analysis of Trends*, Arthur Andersen Lecture Series (Stipes Publishing Co., 1972).

# I-A 3  *An "Events" Approach to Basic Accounting Theory*

GEORGE H. SORTER

In 1966, after two years work, a committee of the American Accounting Association issued *A Statement of Basic Accounting Theory*.[1] Undoubtedly, the most startling recommendations were the sanctioning of current costs and the advocacy of two column (historical and current) reports. To this member of the committee, however, even more startling was that the near unanimous agreement on the recommendations was arrived at by following two very divergent paths originating from two very dissimilar basic concepts about accounting. This split is not confined to committee members but rather seems representative of a more widespread and pervasive difference in the world outside. The majority view of the committee and the predominant faction outside believes in what I here define as the "value" approach to accounting. The minority view, of which I am sometimes the only member, I describe as the "events" approach. This view although implied by some in the past[2] has never to my knowledge been explicitly stated but might have far-reaching implications. This paper seeks to describe and contrast the two schools, present arguments for and illustrate the consequences of an "events" approach to accounting theory; and examine the logic leading to the conclusions embodied in the *Statement of Basic Accounting Theory*. Hopefully, this will provide not only insights and help for the analysis and evaluation of the committee's monograph but perhaps also stimulate discussion and criticism of a new approach and suggest new avenues of research and experimentation to make accounting more responsive to present day conditions.

George H. Sorter, "An 'Events' Approach to Basic Accounting Theory," *The Accounting Review*, January 1969, pp. 12–19. Reprinted by permission of *The Accounting Review*.

[1] American Accounting Association, *A Statement of Basic Accounting Theory*, A Report Prepared by the Committee on Basic Accounting Theory (American Accounting Association, 1966).

[2] This idea, like so many others had its origin primarily in the writings and thought of Professor William J. Vatter whom I hasten to absolve from any of its shortcomings.

## TWO VIEWS—VALUE AND EVENTS

### The Value Theory

The "Value" school within the committee, or as they would probably prefer to be termed the "User need" school, assumed that users' needs are known and sufficiently well specified so that accounting theory can deductively arrive at and produce optimal input values for used and useful decision models. Most of the value theorists visualize accounting's purpose as producing optimum income and capital value or values.[3] This leads to the popular sport of proper matching of costs and revenue. The assumption is that "proper matching" associates costs and revenue to produce the right income figure or figures—the figure or figures optimal for users' decision models.

Several criticisms may be leveled at this value approach.

1. There are many and varied uses of accounting data and it is therefore impossible to specify input values that are optimal for the wide range of possible uses.

2. For each specified use different users utilize a wide range of different decision models, that they have so far been unable to describe, define, or specify. Further, neither economists nor accountants have been able to advance the theoretically correct decision models.

3. The value theory is unnecessarily restrictive. Thus, events such as leases or commitments have, until recently, tended to be excluded from the accounting universe, partially at least, because they did not affect income or net asset values.

    The orientation of accounting toward producing income and asset values which are nothing but simple attempts to adjust for the lag between cash outflows and cash inflows has impeded the development of more sophisticated lag models made possible by more sophisticated techniques.

4. The value theory is not useful in explaining many current developments in accounting. Income theory, for instance, does not provide a basis for the current sub-aggregates that are utilized in the income statement such as sales, cost of sales, etc. It has also not been helpful in explaining the advocacy of the Fund Statement or in helping the conglomerate and a host of other current problems.

### The Events Theory

Proponents of the "Events" theory suggest that the purpose of accounting is to provide information about relevant economic events that might be useful in a variety of possible decision models. They see the function of accounting at one level removed in the decision-making process. Instead of producing input values for unknown and perhaps unknowable decision models directly, accounting provides information about relevant economic events that allows individual users to generate their own input values for their own individual decision models. In other words, given the state

---

[3] Not all value theorists are income oriented. Chambers for example can be considered a "value" but certainly not an "income" theorist.

of the arts, less rather than more aggregation is appropriate and the user, rather than the accountant, must aggregate, and assign weights and values to the data consistent with his forecasts and utility functions. "Events" proponents suggest that the loss of information generated by aggregation and valuation by the accountant is greater than the associated benefit. While they would agree that the accountants' suggested weights and values deserve to be communicated, they would insist that these weights be communicated in disaggregated form so that users always had the non-weighted raw data available as well.

This viewpoint seems particularly appropriate today when little is known about how accounting data is used but may even be preferred when more knowledge about decision models becomes available. It is possible to visualize reasonable decision models that are consistent with an "events" approach rather than a "value" approach. An investor, for instance, attempting to forecast the value of a firm at some future point may utilize two methods: (1) He may base his estimate of future values on the trend, size, and variability of current income or other aggregated values. (2) Alternatively, he may wish to use current accounting data to predict specific future events and then base his estimate of future values on these predicted events. In other words, he may wish to predict income or he may wish to predict sales, cost of sales, taxes, etc. The first model is more consistent with a value approach, the second with an events approach.

The criticism must be met that the "events" approach relies just as heavily upon knowledge of users' models as does the "value" approach. The argument goes as follows. Decisions as to what events are relevant (surely not all events can be recorded) must be made and can only be made with users' needs in mind. Thus, the users' needs must still be known. This is correct. But it seems clear that less need be known about decision models to decide whether or not an event might be relevant for a model than to have to decide how the data fits a specific decision model and what specific weights should be assigned.[4] In the lease example, under an "events" approach, it is only necessary to decide that information about leases, commitments or orders are relevant to a host of decision models for such information to be included in accounting reports. It is unnecessary to justify how, if at all, this information should be weighted in an income valuation model.

### To Aggregate or Not to Aggregate

As has been indicated, the real difference between the two schools lies in what level of aggregation and valuation is appropriate in accounting reports and who is to be the aggregator and evaluator. The question as to who is to aggregate or value is not unique to accounting. As Ijiri points out "... any aggregation generally involves loss of information in that the resulting total 'value' may be composed of many—possibly infinitely many—different *components*."[5] It is interesting to note that in two widely different areas there have recently been thrusts toward presenting less aggregated data. In modern statistics it is no longer considered good form to merely report

---

[4] "...a goal which by itself may not be so capable of definition as to determine a single perfect solution may nevertheless be clear enough and important enough to rule out some solutions..." from: Guido Calabresi, "Fault, Accidents, and the Wonderful World of Blum and Kalven," *Yale Law Journal* (December 1965), p. 222.

[5] Yuji Ijiri. *The Foundations of Accounting Measurement* (Prentice-Hall, Inc., 1967), p. 120.

confidence intervals. Instead the plea is for full presentation of the underlying data or distributions.[6] Only the user can decide what is or is not significant, given his loss function. In weather forecasts, we are no longer told that it will or will not rain or snow. Instead we are given probability estimates and must ourselves decide whether or not to carry umbrellas or to send out work crews. We are given the underlying raw data and must assign values consistent with our individual utility functions.

Accounting income has variously been thought of as a measure of how much can be spent and still be as well off as before, as a measure of managerial efficiency or as a basis for forecasting future values. But each of these depends on individual expectations, individual preference functions and individual decision models, not on some never clearly defined concept of "proper matching of costs and revenues." Unfortunately this attempt to match, the assigning of weights to generate values, the attempt to aggregate into an income figure, destroys potentially useful information about important underlying events and increases possible measurement errors and biases. Every item on an income statement is the result of at least two processes—the underlying event and the accountants' allocation of the event to a particular time period. This allocation has the purpose of matching in order to derive a "true" income figure or figures. Lifo and Fifo for example are used in an attempt to produce better income figures. Both, however, destroy information about the consumption event. If either Lifo and Fifo is used consumption of two identical units bought at different prices will necessarily be described differently. A user interested in comparing consumption activity for two periods is unable to distinguish between variations caused by the measurement process, be it Lifo or Fifo, and real differences in the consumption levels.

Deferred taxes attempts to secure proper matching of costs and revenues and thereby destroys information about current tax payments. Conventional absorption costing in an attempt to secure proper matching destroys information about production inputs and outputs since cost of goods sold and inventory become dependent on both the level of production and of sales.

The loss of information due to aggregation also holds for the balance sheet. Necessarily, every balance sheet account is an aggregation of two or more types of events (the events recorded on the debit and credit sides of the account). Very often the events so aggregated vary greatly in type, measureability and variability and therefore destroy much information about specific events. For instance, if current costs or values are used, acquisition and consumption activities as well as environmental changes are combined and the reconstructibility of each specific event is impaired. Acquisitions and amortizations or acquisitions and dispositions are events differing widely in possible measurement error. By combining them in asset and liability accounts information about each is destroyed.

As already indicated, income and capital valuations are attempts to deal with lags between cash outflows and cash inflows. These appear to be unnecessarily crude and primitive given current advances in methodology and measurement technique. The presentation of less aggregated data suggested by the "events" approach might stimulate investigation of more complicated but more useful lag and forecast models that could vary for different industries, firms, time periods, or individuals.

---

[6] See Howard Raiffa and Robert Schlaifer, *Applied Statistical Decision Theory* (Harvard University, Division of Research, Graduate School of Business, 1961), p. 68.

## SOME CONSEQUENCES OF AN EVENTS APPROACH

This is not the proper medium in which to describe some possible long-range consequences of the "events" approach. In a subsequent manuscript, I intend to speculate on the type of accounting reports appropriate to this approach. Even under the existing accounting framework there are several implications of "events" theory which might help to explain this point of view.

### The Balance Sheet

It is currently the fashion to say that the balance sheet or position statement has lost most, if not all, of its significance. But not for event theorists. We view the balance sheet not as a value statement nor as a statement of financial position but rather as an indirect communication of all accounting events that have occurred since the inception of the accounting unit. This indirect communication is provided by summing the effect of all events on the names used in describing these events and then recording the subsequent balances. Inventory, thus, does not report either value or costs but rather describes the acquisition and consumption activities that have occurred. This view has several advantages. It does not purport to report something that is not achieved (i.e., value) and it does facilitate the understanding and analysis of what is described. If the inventory figure, for instance, is visualized as a representation of the inventory, under value theory the accountant must somehow rationalize the particular costs or value figure that he uses. If historical cost is used, the validity of a representation of inventory that ignores value inevitably crops us. If value is used the argument centers about the justification of this rather than some other value. It is certainly difficult to justify either historical costs or any one representation of value. This difficulty does not create so grave a problem for the "event" theorist. Suppose original cost is used. Under an events notion this means simply that acquisition and consumption events, but not environmental changes, are recorded. Original costs need not be justified. One may certainly deplore the absence of information about environmental events (i.e., value changes) but one accepts information about the events that are described (i.e., acquisition and consumption) and uses them in whatever fashion is appropriate.

An "events" approach to the balance sheet could lead to operational rules about balance sheet construction and presentation. The following represents a possible rule. *A balance sheet should be so constructed as to maximize the reconstructability of the events being aggregated.* Various users may thus generate information about particular events they are interested in. One purpose of the balance sheet is to facilitate the preparation of Funds Statements and like reports that provide information about important events.

### The Income Statement

For value theorists the purpose of an income statement quite simply is to report income value or values. Under an "events" approach the purpose of the income statement is to provide direct communication concerning the operating events or activities of the firm. Accounting utilizes two forms of communication: an indirect or effect communication of all events (the Balance Sheet) and direct, specific or event communication of certain critical events (Income Statement, Cash Statement, Production Statement, Funds Statement, etc.). The concern of event theorists is not primarily with the final income figure but rather with describing critical operating activities of a firm. The preferred title would be "Statement of Operating Events." Events theory can suggest an operational rule for income statements. For instance, *each event should be described in a manner facilitating the forecasting of that same event in a future time period given exogenous changes*. The deferred tax question would then be resolved by investigating which quantification more reliably forecasts future tax payments. Both Lifo and Fifo would be rejected because they impede the ability to forecast acquisitions and consumptions of inventory in the future.

The "events" school can justify the present organization of the income statement which reports several sub-aggregates such as sales, cost of sales, etc., because these are considered critical operating events. Perhaps this is one instance when an events orientation has already affected the accounting structure.

### The Funds Statement

Value theorists, rigidly faithful to their doctrine, have the most difficulty in justifying this statement. They state rather feebly that "...the basic purpose of the Funds Statement is to account for the change in working capital during the period covered by the statement."[7] Such a concept certainly underrates the utility of this statement and leads to trivial discussions as to the proper definition of working capital. The "events" school thinks of this statement as "A Statement of Financial and Investment Events." The Working Capital account merely represents a useful technique to organize the events and prepare the statement. The important consideration is whether a financing or investment event is relevant and should be reported, not whether working capital is affected by a given event. This again demonstrates the flexibility of an "events" approach. Different financing or investment events may or may not be relevant for specific firms or at specific times. The content of the Funds Statement thus need not remain invariate for all times or for all firms.

### "A STATEMENT OF BASIC ACCOUNTING THEORY" AND THE EVENTS THEORY

Most of the recommendations contained in *A Statement of Basic Accounting Theory* flow more logically from an "events" rather than from a "value" orientation. Why are standards or guidelines necessary at all if a "value" approach is adopted? If users' needs are in fact well specified then accounting should provide the values that make the decision models operate optimally. The only relevant standard than would be the ability of the data to perform in the model. There would be no need for values to be verifiable or free from bias if they work well in a specified model. If, however, users' needs are not well specified suggesting an "events" approach, then it is necessary to employ standards that limit the range and define the description of relevant events.

The need for two-column reporting under a "value" approach is not clear. Presumably, the need arises because different columns are useful for different users; that is, historical cost data is useful for the stewardship function and current cost

---

[7] Perry Mason, "'Cash Flow' Analysis and The Funds Statement," *Accounting Research Study No. 2* (American Insitute of Certified Public Accountants, 1961).

data for the investment function. This rather inadequate rationale has led to the assumption that the historical costs column was only advocated as a stop-gap measure until current value could sweep the day. This was not the intent of the committee.

Multi-column reporting seems eminently compatible with an "events" view of accounting. The two column reports advocated by *ASOBAT* is a step in that direction. As the monograph states, "The historical information reflects market transactions, the current cost information reflects market transactions plus 'unrealized' market influences, and the difference shows the effect of unrealized environmental influences."[8] Since the historical cost column includes descriptions of events other than market transactions (i.e., depreciation, amortization, and other significant accruals) and because market transactions and environmental changes are not the only events that have relevance to the firm, the two columns advocated do not go far enough, but they represent a start.

Separate events should be reported in separate columns because (1) they vary in measurability, (2) they vary in controllability, and (3) they vary in importance from period to period. There is no question that market transactions and environmental changes, for instance, vary in measurability. Market transactions can be relatively satisfactorily described by single numbered quantifications (with relatively little measurement error). There is apt to be little variance around that single number. The same, however, cannot be said about environmental changes or forecasts where description by ranges or distributions could be more appropriate and where measurement errors could be material. As long as a single column is used there will be a tendency to continue to measure events by a single measurement process which is inappropriate for certain types of events and we shall continue to be faced with troubles in assessing measurement biases or errors.

These events also vary in controllability by the managers of a firm. Clearly, market transactions are more controllable than environmental changes but less controllable than conversions. If accounting reports are to be useful in evaluating management then a separation of events by controllability should help in fulfilling this objective.

Finally, the importance of the different classes of events may vary from period to period. An investor may predict a period of stability where certain environmental changes are expected to be minimal and in order to forecast adequately from accounting data he must then be able to separate the effect of environmental changes from market transactions. This he can do in multi-column reporting. As the importance of different types of events vary, users, according to their estimate of the future, can attach different weights to the different types of events.

At first blush, multi-column reporting seems a drastic departure from current practices—but is it really? Presently we use multi-row reporting. We break down the income statement into many sub-aggregates such as sales, cost of sales, S&A expenses, taxes, etc. We break down the balance sheet into many rows by classes of equities and assets. Very little research has been done as to what explains the current level of sub-aggregation and extreme proponents of the "value" school would have a hard time rationalizing the present format of the income statement. Presently the income statement is organized around a functional event structure, and the balance sheet around a functional effect structure. Multi-column reporting would add a

[8] American Accounting Association, *op. cit.*, p. 31.

"source of events" classification to both reports and instead of accounting reports consisting of a 7 by 1 matrix they would consist of a 7 by 5 matrix. This move from one matrix to another does not seem that revolutionary, and would be facilitated by an events approach.

## CONCLUSION

Admittedly, the above represents only a rough and underdeveloped first approach toward a new orientation for accounting theory. Why, then, is it presented here and now? Only in the hope of encouraging the research activities suggested by this approach and also in the further hope that it might stimulate a reexamination of some essential if rarely expressed implicit tenets of present accounting thought. The areas of possible research opportunities indicated by an events approach are many. The following represent a few:

1. Test whether line by line predictions of events, i.e., the prediction of sales, cost of sales, etc., are more efficient in explaining the future value of a firm than the use of more aggregated figures such as income.
2. Investigate the present format of accounting reports to see how useful these formats could be, i.e., to what extent do the various subcategories of the income statement and balance sheet covary? To what extent do they provide additional information?
3. Attempt to develop more sophisticated models to explain the lag between cash outflows and cash inflows, i.e., utilizing fund statements, production statements, and others in an attempt to predict cash flows.
4. Investigate the information loss due to the aggregations presently used by accountants. How much information is lost by aggregating and combining events to produce one income figure or to produce the different balance sheet amounts? A subsequent extension of this would be an investigation of the information loss due to expressing all economic activities in dollar terms.
5. Construct useful accounting reports based on an events approach.

Ultimately this paper will find its justification if what is presented here as the conclusion will serve as an introduction to the research activities and the reexamination advocated.

# I-A 4 *FASB's Statements on Objectives and Elements of Financial Accounting: A Review*

NICHOLAS DOPUCH AND SHYAM SUNDER

The Financial Accounting Standards Board (FASB) issued an exposure draft of the proposed statement on Objectives of Financial Reporting and Elements of Financial Statements of Business Enterprises on December 29, 1977. The first part of the Exposure Draft, dealing with the objectives of financial reporting, was issued in revised form a year later as the Statement of Financial Accounting Concepts No. 1 (SFAC 1)[FASB, 1978]. A final statement on the elements of financial statements has not yet been issued. In this paper we review the FASB's statement on objectives (as contained in SFAC 1) and on elements (as contained in the Exposure Draft). Though many of our comments could also be applied to other aspects of the project on the conceptual framework undertaken by the FASB, we shall limit our discussion to the two documents mentioned above.[1]

Few general criteria, other than internal consistency, have been proposed for evaluating conceptual frameworks. The approach taken in the reviews by Littleton [1962; 1963] of the Moonitz [1961] and the Sprouse and Moonitz [1962] monographs; by Ijiri [1971] of the APB *Statement No. 4* [AICPA, 1970]; by a subcommittee of the American Accounting Association (AAA) to respond to the FASB's Discussion Memorandum of the Conceptual Framework [AAA, 1977b]; by Sterling [1967] of the AAA's *A Statement of Basic Accounting Theory* [1966]; by Vatter [1963], Hanson [1940], and Kester [1940]; and by Deinzer [1964] of various statements sponsored by the AAA [1936; 1941; 1948; 1957; 1964a; 1964b] seem too diverse to provide common criteria

---

We have benefited from many helpful comments, in particular those by Professors Raymond J. Chambers, William W. Cooper, Sidney Davidson, Rashad Abdel-khalik, William R. Scott, Stephen A. Zeff, and the anonymous reviewers.

Nicholas Dopuch and Shyam Sunder, "FASB's Statements on Objectives and Elements of Financial Accounting: A Review," *The Accounting Review*, January 1980, pp. 1–21. Reprinted with the permission of *The Accounting Review*.

[1] These documents were preceded by two Discussion Memoranda [FASB 1974; 1976a]; the latter was accompanied by a statement of tentative conclusions on objectives of financial statements [FASB, 1976b].

for evaluating a conceptual framework. We decided, therefore, to use two criteria in our review: (1) To what extent do these statements differ from previous attempts of this nature; and, regardless of the answer to (1), (2) to what extent will these statements, if adopted, yield the benefits expected by the FASB? Since we arrive at pessimistic answers to both questions, we are led to consider two further questions: (a) What are the fundamental difficulties in developing a set of objectives of financial accounting, and (b) why do authoritative bodies persist in trying to develop a conceptual framework? The final section of the paper contains the summary and concluding remarks.

## COMPARISON WITH PREVIOUS ATTEMPTS TO DEVELOP A FRAMEWORK

### Objectives

The SFAC 1 is divided into two parts: Introduction and Background, followed by Objectives of Financial Reporting. The introductory section includes subsections on: (a) financial statements and financial reporting, (b) the environmental context of objectives, (c) the characteristics and limitations of information provided, (d) potential users and their interests, and (e) general-purpose external financial reporting. Financial statements are defined to be a subset of financial reporting, but no limits are provided on the number of elements of financial reporting that one may include in financial statements. The discussion of the environmental context of accounting bears a resemblance to the discussion by Moonitz [1961, Chapter 2] and by the Accounting Principles Board in Statement No. 4 (APBS 4) [AICPA, 1970, Chapter 3]. A discussion of the major characteristics of the U.S. economy in the statement of objectives would be justified if it were accompanied by a theory which linked the characteristics of various economies to alternative financial accounting systems. Since no such theory is provided, it is not clear how a vague description of the U.S. economy is useful for determining or understanding objectives.[2]

In the sections on potential users and general-purpose financial reporting it is stated that the specific objectives here refer to the general-purpose financial reports that serve the informational needs of external users who lack the authority to prescribe the financial information they want from an enterprise, a statement very similar to Objective No. 2 of the Trueblood Report [AICPA, 1973]. The FASB relies considerably on the Trueblood Report when it states that financial reporting "should provide information to help present and potential investors and creditors, and other users in assessing the amounts, timing, and uncertainty of prospective net cash receipts...." [FASB, 1978, para. 37]. The need for information on cash flows leads to the need for information on "the economic resources of an enterprise, the claims to those resources (obligations of the enterprise to transfer resources to other entities and owners' equity), and the effects of transactions, events, and circumstances that change resources and claims to those resources" (para. 40). After more discussion, the

---

[2] For example, paragraph 13 refers to efficient allocations of resources within a market economy, but there are several definitions of allocation efficiency which might be employed. In the absence of an agreed-upon definition, inefficiencies cannot be identified.

Board arrives at the conclusion that the

> primary focus of financial reporting is information about an enterprise's
> performance provided by measures of earnings and its components.... 
> Information about enterprise earnings and its components measured by
> accrual accounting generally provides a better indication of enterprise
> performance than information about current cash receipts and payments
> [FASB, 1978, para. 43–44].

This last statement is not an objective, but a means to an objective.

Although these paragraphs encompass many of the specific objectives of the
Trueblood Report, the emphasis and order of presentation are different. Other
departures from the Report are an omission of any reference to providing financial
forecasts and to non-profit and social accounting (Objectives 10, 11, and 12,
respectively, of the Trueblood Report).

In wording and substance, little is new or different in SFAC 1. Had the FASB
pointed out the parts of the existing reports,[3] such as APBS 4 and the Trueblood
Report, that it agreed with and emphasized its disagreements, its contribution would
have been easier to discern. Without such aid, we are hard-pressed to discern the
FASB's net contribution to these earlier efforts. Given that previous authoritative
efforts to write objectives are generally considered inadequate in helping to resolve
accounting issues, a basic test of the FASB's contribution is the extent to which
SFAC 1 may succeed where others have failed. We shall apply such a test after
discussing the elements of financial statements and characteristics of financial
information as provided in the FASB's Exposure Draft [FASB, 1977].

### Elements of Financial Statements

The second major section of the Exposure Draft [FASB, 1977], paragraphs 36
through 66, deals mainly with definitions of the main categories of accounts
appearing in financial statements: assets, liabilities, owners' equity, revenues,
expenses, gains, and losses. Supplementing these definitions are subsections containing discussions of the bases for definitions, the matching of efforts and accomplishments, and the need to provide financial statements which articulate with one
another. The elements of financial statements are integrated—revenues and gains
result in, or from, increases in assets, decreases in liabilities or combinations of the
two; expenses and losses result in, or from, decreases in assets, increases in liabilities,
*etc.*

A noteworthy feature of the FASB's definitions is their dependence on unspecified "accounting rules and conventions" [FASB, 1977, p. 19], again in the tradition of
the definitions provided by two previous authoritative bodies, the American Institute
of [Certified Public] Accountants' Committee on Terminology and Accounting

---

[3] Most and Winters [1977] analyzed the objectives promulgated by the Trueblood Study Group,
APBS 4, several of the Big Eight firms, the AAA, the National Association of Accountants, *etc.*
They found that of the ten main objectives issued by the Trueblood Study Group (Objectives 3
on cash flows, and 11 on non-profit accounting, were omitted), eight similar objectives could be
found in APBS 4. Similarly, Objectives 1, 2, 4, 5, 6, 7, and 8 in the Trueblood Report had
antecedents in from five to as many as eight other statements of objectives.

Principles Board.[4] This qualification appears to be inconsistent with the claim that conceptual frameworks can lead to the selection of appropriate principles and rules of measurement and recognition. How can a conceptual framework guide choices from among alternative principles and rules if the elements of the framework are defined in these very same terms?

The dependence of the FASB's definitions on unspecified rules and conventions leaves little basis on which to evaluate them, since a specific evaluation of these definitions would be speculative as long as we do not know what conventions will be adopted by the FASB at the subsequent stages of its project.

A second feature of the FASB's definitions is that they provide only the necessary conditions for a resource or obligation to be included in the asset or liability categories, respectively, rather than both the necessary and sufficient conditions. For example, a resource other than cash needs to have three characteristics to qualify as an asset:

> (a) the resource must ... contribute directly or indirectly to future cash inflows (or to obviating future cash outflows), (b) the enterprise must be able to obtain the benefit from it, and (c) the transaction or event giving rise to the enterprise's right to or interest in the benefit must already have occurred [FASB, 1977; para. 47].

Similarly, three characteristics are also necessary for an obligation to qualify as a liability:

> (a) the obligation must involve future sacrifice of resources—a future transfer (or a foregoing of a future receipt) of cash, goods, or services, (b) it must be an obligation of the enterprise, and (c) the transaction or event giving rise to the enterprise's obligation must already have occurred [FASB, 1977, para. 49].

Since these are only necessary characteristics, their presence does not imply that an obligation will qualify as a liability or that a resource will qualify as an asset. All of these conditions may be satisfied and an obligation still may not qualify as an asset or, alternatively, as a liability. In the absence of sufficient conditions, these definitions will be of limited use to accountants.

The definitions of revenues and expenses given by the FASB follow the traditional practice of defining these as increases and decreases in assets or decreases and increases in liabilities, respectively, provided that the changes in assets

---

[4] For example, the Committee on Terminology defined assets in Accounting Terminology Bulletin No. 1 [AICPA, 1953] as follows:

"Something represented by a debit balance that is or would be properly carried forward upon a closing of books of account according to the *rules or principles of accounting* ... on the basis that it represents either a property right ... or is properly applicable to the future" (para. 26, emphasis added).

The APB in its Statement No. 4 defined assets as "economic resources of an enterprise that are recognized and measured *in conformity with generally accepted accounting principles....*" [AICPA, 1970, para. 132] (emphasis added).

and liabilities relate to the earning activities of the enterprise (broadly defined). Gains and losses are defined as increases and decreases in net assets, *other* than revenues and expenses or investments and withdrawals by owners.

The definitions of revenue and expense in APB Statement No 4 [AICPA, 1970] are similar to the above except that the definitions there do not explicitly distinguish between revenues and gains nor between expenses and losses. A distinction between revenues and gains is also made by Sprouse and Moonitz [1962, p. 50] and by Paton and Littleton [1940, p. 60]. But while a distinction between expense and loss is made by Sprouse and Moonitz, Paton and Littleton do not do so. Indeed, they do not even provide an explicit definition of expense, which is consistent with their emphasis on *cost* rather than on the asset-expense distinction. It is not until their discussion of income that Paton and Littleton stress a distinction between costs matched against revenues (expenses) and those deferred to future periods (assets) [1940, Ch. V.].

On the whole, the differences between the FASB and the APB definitions are small and seem unimportant. An explicit discussion of the main sources of disagreement would have been more fruitful than a "new" set of definitions. Circular as they are, the conflict on definitions seems to us to be only a proxy debate whose principal, to which we return later, is the debate about the accounting rules themselves.

### Characteristics and Limitations of Financial Information

A part of the last major section of the Exposure Draft has been included in the introductory section of SFAC 1. There we find statements about: (a) the reliance of accounting on monetary transactions, (b) the emphasis of financial reports on individual enterprises and not on individual consumers or on society as a whole, (c) the role of estimation in accounting, (d) the fact that much of financial information reflects past events, (e) the coexistence of other sources of financial information, and (f) the costs of financial reporting.

The more well-known desirable "qualities" of accounting information, such as relevance, freedom from bias, comparability, consistency, understandability, verifiability, etc., are also referenced in the Exposure Draft, but are excluded from SFAC 1. The FASB acknowledges that trade-offs among these qualities are not easily accomplished in practice. The objectives and definitions of the elements of financial statements are expected to guide the Board in future phases of the conceptual framework project when these trade-off issues arise in more concrete form.

The characteristics and desirable "qualities" of accounting information discussed in the Exposure Draft are familiar to accountants and appear as "qualitative" objectives in APB Statement No. 4 and as components of accounting concepts or as postulates in other conceptual frameworks.

The above review of SFAC 1 and of certain parts of the Exposure Draft reveals little that is new on the objectives of financial reporting and definitions of the elements of financial statements. Lack of novelty, of course, does not imply worthlessness. It is quite possible that the FASB's effort may yet have the potential to yield some benefits. The FASB has suggested that the following benefits may manifest themselves as a result of achieving agreement on the conceptual framework [1976c, pp. 5–6]:

1.  Guide the body responsible for establishing standards,
2.  Provide a frame of reference for resolving accounting questions in the absence of a specific promulgated standard,

3. Determine bounds for judgment in preparing financial statements,
4. Increase financial statement users' understanding of and confidence in financial statements, and
5. Enhance comparability.

In reviewing this early part of the conceptual framework, it is probably fair to ask how reasonable it is to expect that the above-mentioned benefits will actually be realized. Of course, this evaluation may have to be changed when all the pieces of the conceptual project are in place. However, the evaluation of this part of the project, tentative as it is, should not await completion of the project.

In the following section we examine the degree to which the first two benefits stated by the FASB, *viz.*, guidance for establishing standards and resolution of accounting questions in the absence of standards, are likely to be attained on the basis of the given objectives and definitions. The effect of the project on users' understanding of, and confidence in, the financial statements is an empirical question and is beyond the scope of this review paper.[5] We are not sure what precisely is meant by (3), determination of the bounds of judgment in preparation of financial statements, and by (5), enhancement of comparability. Since the empirical or analytical contents of these benefits are not clear, it is difficult to evaluate, beyond purely subjective opinion, whether and to what extent these benefits will be derived from the FASB's objectives and definitions. We shall, therefore, confine ourselves to an evaluation of the first two benefits stated by the FASB.

## RESOLUTION OF THREE ACCOUNTING ISSUES

As a means of evaluating the potential benefits the FASB's objectives and definitions may provide in resolving accounting issues, we selected three which have been debated for some time and which have received much attention from accountants and others. The issues are: (1) deferred credits, (2) treatment of costs of exploration in the oil and gas industry, and (3) reports on current values of assets and liabilities.

### Deferred Credits

The FASB defines liabilities as "financial representations of obligations of a particular enterprise to transfer economic resources to other entities in the future as a result of a past transaction or event affecting the enterprise" [FASB, 1977, para. 49]. No specific reference to deferred credits appears in this section, although reference is made to liabilities arising from the collection of cash or other resources *before* providing goods or services, or from selling products subject to warranty. It is also stated that "legal enforceability of a claim is not a prerequisite to representing it as a liability" if future transfer is probable.

The APB, in Statement No. 4, is more direct:

> Liabilities—economic obligations of an enterprise that are recognized and measured in conformity with generally accepted accounting principles. Liabilities also include certain deferred credits *that are not obligations* but that are recognized and measured in conformity with generally accepted accounting principles [AICPA, 1970, Para. 132, emphasis added].

---

[5] The FASB may wish to commission such a study now, so that a preconceptual framework measure of confidence and understandability can be taken before this opportunity is lost.

A footnote to the last sentence specifically singles out deferred taxes as an example of liabilities which are not obligations!

Neither Paton and Littleton [1940] nor Sprouse and Moonitz [1962] refer to deferred credits arising from differences between financial and tax reporting, with both concentrating on the obligations of enterprises to convey assets or to perform services in the future.[6]

The FASB's definition of liabilities is so general that at this stage we cannot predict the Board's position on deferred taxes. However, those who favor the recognition of deferred taxes can adopt a somewhat broad interpretation of the FASB's definition of liabilities to justify the inclusion of deferred taxes as an element of financial statements, particularly at the individual asset level. In contrast, those who do not could take the FASB's statements literally and just as easily argue against the inclusion of deferred taxes. Hence, these broad definitions will not help resolve the issue.

### Accounting for Oil and Gas Exploration Costs

Bitter controversy still surrounds the issue of how to account for petroleum exploration costs. The issue surfaced in the petroleum industry some two decades ago when the full-cost method was introduced. But the essence of the issue has an earlier precedent.

Hatfield [1927, Chap. 2] considers the problem of whether the acquisition costs of successful experiments should be limited to the costs of the successful experiments themselves or whether they should also include the costs of unsuccessful experiments. Hence, the full-cost versus successful-efforts debate is part of a more general issue of what constitutes the costs of assets when the acquisition process is risky.

The issue reflects a difference of opinion regarding the level of aggregation at which the historical acquisition cost principle is applied to record assets for subsequent amortization. But there is no reference in the Exposure Draft to alternative levels of aggregation for asset recognition and measurement. The only explicit statement bearing on this problem is that "[i]nformation about enterprise earnings and its components measured by accrual accounting generally provides a better indication of enterprise performance than information about current cash receipts and payments" [FASB, 1978, para. 44]. However, both full-cost and successful-efforts accounting are forms of accrual accounting, so that proponents of the former (*e.g.*, the Federal Trade Commission) have the same support for their position as do proponents of the latter (*e.g.*, the FASB). The fact that the framework supports two opposing principles of accounting is preliminary evidence that the framework is unlikely to be a useful guide in resolving this issue.

### Selecting the Valuation Basis for Assets and Liabilities

Alternative theories of valuation and income were discussed in accounting texts published 50 years ago. For example, Hatfield [1927] states:

> Having accepted the principle that the original valuation of assets is normally their cost price, and having noticed the practical and theoretical

---

[6] The issue of deferred taxes did not appear in the accounting literature until about 1942. See AICPA [1942].

difficulty in determining the exact cost price, there remains the more important question as to subsequent revaluations of assets.... Shall the accountant base revaluation on (1) the original cost ... (2) on the estimated present cost of acquiring a similar asset ... or (3) on what the asset might be expected to bring if thrown upon the market in the process of liquidation [p. 73]?

Similar discussions appear even earlier in Paton [1922], in Hatfield [1909], and in a much more detailed fashion in Canning [1929].

Liquidation values were generally ruled out in such discussions because they seemed inconsistent with the going-concern notion, and since discounted values had not yet achieved popularity then, the choice between alternative valuation bases was usually limited to historical or replacement costs.

With respect to these alternatives, it might be informative to quote some statements from Paton and Littleton [1940], who, some accountants believe, had no tolerance for valuation bases other than historical cost accounting. On pages 122–123, they state:

With the passing of time, however, the value of the particular productive factor—as reflected in the current cost or market price of like units—is subject to change in either direction, and when a change occurs it becomes clear that the actual cost of the unit still in service or still attaching to operating activity is not fully acceptable as a measure of immediate economic significance.

Later, on page 123, they ask the question:

[W]ould accounting meet more adequately the proper needs of the various parties concerned if, in the process of separating the charges to revenue from the unexpired balances, the estimated replacement costs or other evidence of current values were regularly substituted for recorded costs incurred? There seem to be no convincing reasons for an affirmative answer. Recorded costs are objectively determined data; estimated current values are largely matters of opinion and for some types of cost factors are conspicuously unreliable.

In the section on "Limitations of Estimated Replacement Cost," they comment: "In the first place continuous appraisals at the best are costly, and can be used only if the benefits to be derived clearly justify the additional cost incurred" (p. 132). They then suggest that in periods of price stability and situations involving complex enterprises, such benefits are unlikely to exceed the costs of implementation. Finally,

The fair conclusion is that the cost standard of plant accounting holds up well, as compared with any alternative plan, when faced with typical business needs and conditions.... At the same time it would be going too far to hold that under no circumstances can any useful purpose be served by introducing into the accounts and reports, by appropriate methods, data designed to supplement the figures of actual cost [Paton and Littleton, p. 134].

The latter statement led them to recommend that alternative valuations be limited to supplementary schedules.

The above are practical, no theoretical, arguments and are probably representative of the views of many accountants who have expressed a reluctance to accept current costs in published financial statements. No conceptual framework, however logically conceived, can counter practical issues regarding the reliability of *estimates* of, say, replacement costs. The "true" replacement costs of assets are not observed until those assets are actually replaced (nor are "true" exit prices observed unless the assets are sold). So the issue is not whether current costs are useful "in making economic decisions"; rather, the issue is what criteria may be used to alternative estimates of unknown parameters. Unfortunately, neither SFAC 1 nor the Exposure Draft addresses this problem of estimation.

On the basis of the above analysis, we conclude that the results of the FASB's effort to write objectives and definitions are hardly different from previous attempts of this nature and, as such, are unlikely to help resolve major accounting issues or to set standards of financial reporting as the FASB had expected. Pessimistic as our conclusions are, they should not surprise those familiar with the standard-setting process during the past 30 years. The charge of the Trueblood Study Group was very similar to the first two benefits expected by the FASB:

> The main purpose of the [Trueblood] study is to refine the objectives of financial statements. Refined objectives should facilitate establishment of guidelines and criteria for improving accounting and financial reporting [AICPA, 1973, p. 67].

Both the supporters and the critics expressed doubts that this purpose of the study would be met. Bedford [1974, p. 16], while largely supporting the report, said, "I refer to the extremely difficult task of logically deriving accounting standards from objectives—not that I think it can be done but because I fear some will think it is appropriate." Miller [1974, p. 20], a critic of the report, stated, "The greatest shortcoming of the Trueblood Report is, it seems to me, that the accept/reject criteria are not sufficiently precise. I wish Professor Sorter and his associates had been less subtle." Sprouse stated, "I have no illusions about the use of such a document to prove that a particular accounting standard is 'right'" [1974, p. 28]. These doubts about the accomplishments of the Trueblood Report are very similar to our reservations about the fruits of the FASB's labors.

Since our conclusion about the potential value and effect of the FASB's objectives and definitions is pessimistic, we are led to inquire into the very nature of objectives of financial accounting and the fundamental difficulty of defining them in a social setting. The inability of different authoritative drafts of objectives produced in the last decade to achieve general acceptance on a conceptual framework is hardly due to the lack of diligence on the part of their authors; it may stem from addressing the wrong problem.

## THE NATURE OF OBJECTIVES OF FINANCIAL ACCOUNTING

> An objective is something toward which effort is directed, an aim or end of action, a goal [FASB, 1974, p. 13].

Financial accounting is a social or multiperson activity. Members of society engage in financial accounting or in other activities when they are motivated by their individual goals and objectives. We shall assume that the meaning of the terms "goal" and "objective," as they apply to individuals or homogeneous groups of individuals, is self-evident for the purpose of the present discussion. Given a clear definition of the objectives that motivate each individual to engage in an aspect of a social activity, what meaning can we assign to the term "objective" when it is applied not to individuals or groups, but to the activity itself? In what sense can a social activity be said to have an objective?

We suggest three different interpretations of the meaning of the objectives of a social activity: functional objectives, common objectives, and dominant group objectives. In this section we shall first explain the meaning and implications of each interpretation and then examine the nature of the objectives of financial accounting in light of these interpretations.

### Functional Objectives

The union of individual objectives could be referred to as the objective of the social activity in a *functional sense*. A functional explanation of social phenomena assumes that the consequences of a social arrangement or behavior are essential elements of the *causes* of that behavior (see Stinchcombe [1968], esp. pp. 80–100). Objectives that motivate individuals to engage in an activity on a continuing basis must also be the consequences of the activity; otherwise the individuals will not continue to engage in it. Thus, the functional explanation implies that the union of individual objectives can be identified without probing into the motivations of individuals by simply observing the set of consequences of the social activity. These consequences themselves therefore can be regarded as the objectives of the social activity. Since the consequences are observable phenomena, they can be objectively determined. However, the set of consequences may be so large that a complex and lengthy description may be the result. Nevertheless, a statement of consequences is one possible interpretation of the objective of a social activity.

### Common Objectives

A second possibility is to define the intersection of individual objectives, *i.e.*, the subset of objectives common to all individuals, as the objective of the social activity. By definition, common objectives are equal to or fewer in number than the functional objectives. If all individuals are motivated by an identical set of objectives, common objectives are the same as the functional objectives; if each individual is motivated by different objectives, the intersection is null and there are no common objectives.

### Dominant Group Objectives

A third possible interpretation of the objectives of a social activity is the objectives of an individual or subset of all individuals in the society who are able, through whatever mechanism, to impose their will on all others involved in the activity. In the presence of such a dominant group, the objectives of individuals not included in the group become irrelevant, since the dominant group objectives become the objectives of the social activity. Obviously, this interpretation cannot be used if the dominant group does not have the power to impose its will on the society.

### Accounting as a Social Activity

Accounting is a social activity engaged in by (1) corporate managers who perform in activities that are recorded by the accounting system; (2) corporate accountants who gather the data and compile the reports; (3) auditors who scrutinize and attest to the fairness of the reports; (4) outside government and private agencies, investors, employees, customers, *etc.*, who read these reports; and (5) college and university personnel who train their students in accounting. Each group of individuals engaged in financial accounting possesses its own private motives or objectives leading to this involvement. In the light of the three possible interpretations of the objectives of a social activity discussed above, what meaning can we assign to the objectives of financial accounting?

### Functional Interpretation of Accounting Objectives

Since all consequences of accounting are included in the functional interpretation of objectives, consider the following sample of objectives that would qualify under this interpretation:

1.  Increase employment of accountants, auditors, and teachers of accounting;
2.  Help companies market their securities to creditors and investors;
3.  Help outsiders monitor the performance of management;
4.  Maximize the wealth of the present owners of the company;
5.  Minimize income tax burdens of companies;
6.  Aid in controlling inflation;
7.  Disclose the impact of enterprise operations on the quality of the environment;
8.  Help management avoid hostile takeover attempts;
9.  Systematically record, classify, and report data on the business transactions of the enterprise;
10. Aid in enforcing anti-trust laws.

Each of the objectives listed above could be viewed as legitimate by one or more sets of individuals involved in financial accounting. Note that a complete description of the consequences of financial accounting will include not only "facts" but what is regarded as "fiction" by specific individuals. For example, a manager may regard the avoidance of hostile takeover attempts as a valid objective of financial statements while a shareholder may believe that the effect of financial accounting practices on avoidance of hostile takeovers is non-existent. In order to be included in the set, it is sufficient that someone involved in financial accounting believe in that consequence or use it as a personal objective. Note also that this set includes contradictory objectives and consequences. For example, management may believe that one accounting method for inventory accounting will help market the firm's securities, whereas shareholders may believe that an alternative inventory method is more revealing of management's competence. Similarly, the objective of accountants to increase the demand for their services may be in conflict with the objective of corporate managers to maximize their own or the shareholders' wealth.

Although probably not intended as such, the objectives stated by the FASB may be viewed as functional objectives. For example, the first objective given by the

FASB is:

> Financial reporting should provide information that is useful to present and potential investors and creditors and others users in making rational investment, credit, and similar decisions. The information should be comprehensible to those who have a reasonable understanding of business and economic activities and are willing to study the information with reasonable diligence [FASB, 1978, para. 34].

If "should" is removed from each sentence, this objective is reduced to a mere statement of an empirically verified and a widely accepted consequence of financial accounting. Financial accounting does, indeed, provide information useful to investors and creditors, and it is comprehensible to those willing to study the reports with reasonable diligence. But, being purely descriptive, functional objectives themselves cannot serve as normative goals to guide policy making. Nevertheless, if they are reasonably complete, they can serve to improve the understanding of the role of financial accounting in society.

There is reason to believe that the FASB did not intend to offer its statement as one of functional objectives. First, the statement is far from complete, concentrating on a few facts and a few unverified theories about the consequences of financial accounting, without any effort to present, for example, the motivations behind the supply side of financial accounting services. And the normative tone of the statement precludes the possibility that the FASB has attempted to provide a statement of the union of individual objectives of all persons involved in financial accounting.

## Common-Objectives Interpretation of Accounting Objectives

A second possible interpretation of the objectives of accounting is the subset of individual objectives which are common to all individuals involved in accounting. Cyert and Ijiri's [1974] model of heterogeneous interests can be modified to apply to the objectives. Cyert and Ijiri use a Venn diagram to illustrate their point. The elements of the sets considered by them are *pieces of information* which various interest groups—users, managers, and auditors—may be willing to use, provide, or attest, and the intersection of the three sets is the actual information provided by the financial statements. The choice problem posed by Cyert and Ijiri could be moved to a higher level of abstraction by considering the sets of *accounting principles* that each group would prefer to be used in the preparation of financial statements. A still higher level of abstraction would involve specific sets of objectives that each group would seek to fulfill through its involvement in financial accounting.

It is conceivable that the intersection of the three sets will become progressively smaller as we move to higher levels of abstraction from pieces of information to accounting principles to objectives, in which case the Venn diagrams at the three levels of abstraction might appear as in Figure 1.

We do not know whether the intersection of the sets grows larger or smaller as we move from items of information to principles to objectives and vice versa.[7] Generally, agreement on principles and objectives will be easier to obtain if such statements are

---

[7] The question is subject to debate; see, for example, the analysis of responses of various parties to the FASB's pronouncements by Coe and Sorter [1977–78] and Watts and Zimmerman [1978].

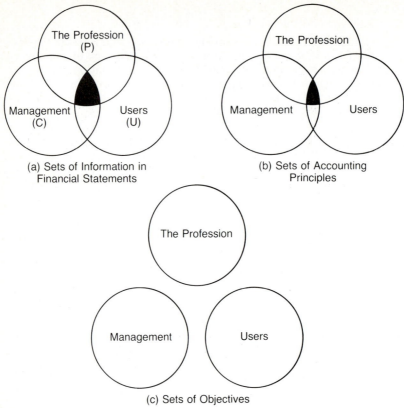

(a) Sets of Information in Financial Statements

(b) Sets of Accounting Principles

(c) Sets of Objectives

**FIGURE 1**

**Accounting Information, Principles and Objectives Preferred by Various Parties**

sufficiently vague so as to allow room for various interest groups to adopt their own interpretations. But vagueness, while necessary to obtain initial agreement, will reduce the usefulness of a statement of objectives in setting accounting standards. The proposition is borne out by the statements of objectives we have seen thus far. The vagueness of statements of this nature is consistent with the level of generality at which agreement is sought. It allows enough room for each interested party to maneuver to protect its own interest when actual accounting standards and rules are written.

Some empirical evidence is available on the non-overlapping nature of accounting objectives. In 1976, when the FASB carried out a survey to determine how many people involved in various aspects of financial accounting agreed with the Trueblood objectives, the Board was surprised to learn that only 37 percent of the respondents believed that providing information useful for making economic decisions was an objective of financial accounting:

> Let me point this up for you. In our first discussion memorandum on the conceptual framework of accounting, . . . we sought an expression of opinion

from respondents on the following as a basic objective of financial statements; it is taken directly from the Trueblood Report:

> The basic objective of financial statements is to provide information useful for making economic decisions.

> Could there be disagreement with a statement such as this? I am sure you will be astounded to learn that only 37 percent of our respondents were able to recommend the adoption of this objective. Twenty-two percent recommended that it be rejected out of hand; and 10 percent insisted that it needed further study. It is difficult to believe that only 37 percent can agree that the basic objective of financial statements is to provide information useful for making economic decisions. I think this suggests the problem quite clearly [Armstrong, 1977, p. 77].

We are puzzled at the Board's puzzlement. Why should we believe all groups of interested parties would adopt the provision of information useful for making economic decisions as their motivation for being involved in the financial reporting process? For example, we should not be surprised if auditors, like everyone else, seek to maximize their own wealth through participation in the accounting process. If the provision of economically useful information implies greater exposure to the risk of being sued without corresponding benefits of higher compensation, they will not see the provision of economically useful information (however defined) as *their* objective of the financial accounting process. Similar arguments could be made about any other interested party who might have been surveyed by the FASB. The members of each group probably stated what they believed were their objectives for being involved in the process.

At present, we do not have data to determine which, if any, objectives are actually common to all participants in accounting. Consequently we cannot yet determine whether the common-objectives approach is a feasible interpretation of the objectives of accounting.

## Dominant Group Interpretation of Accounting Objectives

Unlike the Trueblood Study Group, the FASB has not stated explicitly how it selected its subset of objectives from a much larger set of potential objectives. But from the objectives which the FASB did select, we can infer that it has followed the Trueblood Study Group in relying on the notion of user-primacy in financial accounting.[8] This notion represents the dominant-group approach to defining the objective of a social activity that we identified above.

Most of the discussion appearing in the literature on the objectives of financial accounting during the past ten years tends to rely on the notion of user-primacy. Beaver and Demski [1974], for example, concentrated their attention on the problems generated by the heterogeneity of tastes among the users of financial statements, on

---

[8] "While mindful of the importance of the audit function, the Study Group has been primarily concerned with the nature of information and not its attestability" [AICPA, 1973, p. 10]. The Trueblood Study Group left the problem of attestation and the interests of the management to "implementation" and did not consider these interests worthy of consideration within the set of objectives of financial reporting.

the assumption that this group would be the primary group whose interests would be reflected in the objectives of financial statements officially adopted by the authoritative agencies:

> There seems to be a consensus that the primary purpose of financial reporting is to provide information to financial statement users. Yet, the basic, fundamental role of objectives within this utilitarian, user-primacy framework remains obscure—largely we speculate because the problem of heterogeneous users has not been forcefully addressed.... A basic purpose of this summary and synthesis, then, is to offer a view of the nature and role of financial accounting objectives that explicitly rests on heterogeneous users [p. 170].

Cyert and Ijiri [1974] considered the heterogeneity of preferences for *information sets* among three diverse groups (assuming that the intragroup heterogeneity is unimportant) and analyzed the problem of determining accounting standards under the assumption that the user interest is primary. Referring to 1(a) of our Figure 1, they stated:

> This is a logical, if not a unique approach since in many user-corporate relationships the corporation is *accountable* to the users for its activities. If the users are in a position to demand information from the corporation based on a contractual or statutory relationship between them, it makes sense to define what Circle U is and then attempt to move Circle C toward it. Furthermore, in the interaction of the three groups, the profession's purpose is to help keep a smooth flow of information from the corporation to the users. Hence, Circle P is clearly subordinate to Circles C and U. Thus, it is perhaps the most practical way to state as objectives the need to move Circles C and P toward the goal of a newly defined Circle U [p. 32].

If the user group had the power to enforce its preferences at no cost to itself, the objectives of this group could be called the objectives of financial accounting. This would simplify the problem of setting objectives. Indeed, if the user group were homogeneous, the problem would be trivial. However, there is little evidence that the user group has the power to impose its preferences on financial accounting.

A considerable amount of confusion about the objectives of financial accounting has been generated by comparing them to the objectives of the firm. For example, Bedford [1974] notes, "The basic objective of financial statements is to provide information useful for making economic decisions. This statement is as direct as the statement that 'the basic objective of private enterprise is to make a profit' *and it is equally operational*" [p. 15; emphasis is added]. Few would dispute that, as stated, the profit-maximizing objective of the firm is merely a shorthand way of stating the objectives of the *shareholders* of the firm under the assumption of homogeneous shareholder preferences; it does not represent the specific objectives of the managers, employees, creditors or of any other parties inside or outside the firm. Besides, profit is a net concept in the sense that it is the difference between revenues and expenses, and its use as an objective implies that additional revenue should not be generated beyond the point at which the additional cost exceeds it. Provision of information for decision making, unlike profit, is a gross concept and cannot provide guidelines as to how far the firm should go in providing information for economic decisions.

The analogy to the theory of the firm is more apparent than real. In that theory, if the objective is to maximize the owners' wealth, production-investment variables can be chosen in view of the cost and revenue functions which serve as the environmental variables. What is the FASB (or any other agency entrusted with the task of writing accounting standards) supposed to maximize or optimize? When the FASB recommends that the objective of financial statements is to provide information useful for making rational credit and investment decisions, should we understand that the provision of such information should be maximized without regard to the cost and other consequences of making such information available? What are the variables over which to optimize, and what is the trade-off among these variables? Unless these trade-offs are defined, a statement of objectives that will be useful in arriving at the most satisfying accounting standards cannot be said to have been laid down, nor can there be a way of determining if the recommended objectives have been achieved by a given accounting standard.

The extraordinary emphasis of the recent pronouncements regarding objectives of financial accounting on user primacy can probably be traced to inappropriate applications of single-person decision theory in a multi-person context. In single-person decision theory, the generation of information is regarded as a more-or-less mechanical process which remains unaffected by its ultimate uses. The person making the choice of an information system out of the available alternatives calculates the expected present value of the benefits to be derived from the use of information produced by each system and makes the choice on the basis of the excess of these benefits over the respective costs. The same underlying event-generating mechanism is assumed to be common to all information systems, and it remains unaffected by the choice of information system made. This model, developed by the physical scientists and engineers for the control of mechanical or inanimate systems, is inappropriate for social systems, where the object of control is not an unchanging chemical process but a human being with learning capabilities. In control systems where human beings stand at both the sending and receiving end of the information channel, the flow of information affects behavior at both ends. We cannot choose an information line on the assumption of a constant behavior pattern of the persons at the other end. Indeed, the two-way effect of the information makes the designation of one party as user and the other as sender somewhat ambiguous. A user-primacy notion in the selection of objectives of financial accounting which ignores how firm managers are likely to adjust their behavior to the new information system (and how this adjustment in management behavior will affect the interests of the so-called users) represents a very short-sighted view of the whole problem. As such, solutions derived from this simplified approach will not work. A similar argument could be offered regarding the exclusion of the auditors from the "primary" groups whose interests must be explicitly considered in any realistic set of objectives of financial accounting.

To summarize, we have examined three possible interpretations of objectives of social activities in general and financial accounting in particular. We have concluded that the union of individual objectives, being too diverse and contradictory, cannot serve to guide policy; intersection of individual objectives may be null; the dominant-group objectives, assuming user primacy, do not reflect the economic reality of the power of suppliers in the accounting marketplace and are, therefore, unworkable. Fundamental to an understanding of the nature of financial accounting as they are, these difficulties in interpreting the objectives of financial accounting have received little attention in the literature. This lack of attention stands in sharp contrast to the repeated efforts to prepare a statement of objectives and definitions and leads us to examine the possible reasons that may stand behind the efforts to prepare an authoritative statement of objectives and definitions.

## WHY SEARCH FOR A CONCEPTUAL FRAMEWORK?

In the first section of the paper, we compared the SFAC 1 and Exposure Draft to the previous attempts of this nature and found little substantive difference. In the second section, we examined whether the first two of the five benefits claimed by the FASB may reasonably be expected to flow from these statements and reached a negative conclusion. Then we probed the very meaning of the term "objectives" as applied to financial accounting and found that term too ill-defined. These conclusions led us to inquire into reasons why authoritative bodies have continued to search for objectives and a conceptual framework of accounting. We consider several of these.

The first reason could be that our negative conclusions in section two regarding the usefulness of these statements in resolving accounting issues and standard-setting problems are wrong. If so, it should be easy for someone to illustrate, possibly using issues other than the three we selected, that these objectives and definitions will indeed help resolve the accounting issues. We are not aware of any such illustrations.

A second reason for the search for conceptual frameworks could be provided in terms of the three potential benefits claimed by the FASB and not examined in this paper. It may turn out that the issuance of the conceptual framework increases the users' confidence in, and understanding of, financial statements. Someone may also give workable definitions of "bounds for judgment" and comparability and show that the issuance of conceptual frameworks may have desirable consequences in these respects. Again, neither the theoretical arguments nor the empirical evidence that bears on these issues is available.

Two further reasons are possible: One lies in the form in which accounting problems are brought to the authoritative bodies, while the second lies in the attempts of the accounting profession to keep the rule-making power in its own hands.

Repeated efforts of authoritative bodies to define the conceptual framework of accounting in general and the elements of financial statements in particular may arise from the genuine belief that a determination of precise definitions of certain terms will somehow help resolve accounting controversies.[9] Such belief is reinforced each time an accounting controversy surfaces and the proponents of alternative methods present their arguments in the established terminology of accounting so as to convince the policy makers that the weight of tradition, so highly prized in accounting, is on their side. Given a strong motivation to have an accounting standard accepted which is favorable to one's interests, it is not difficult to devise an argument as to why a given transaction should be recorded in a certain way under the currently accepted definitions of accounting terms.[10] Since the views of various parties are presented to the policy-making bodies not in the form of conflicting private interests, but in the form of conflicting interpretations of accounting definitions, it may appear that a clearer definition of each accounting term will solve the problem. A frank discussion of the private interests of various contending groups may be

---

[9] See Zeff [1978, pp. 57–58] for a typology of the arguments offered in accounting controversies.
[10] See Kitchen [1954] for a stimulating discussion of the problems of definition in accounting.

tactically disadvantageous in open public discourse.[11] Hence, the overblown emphasis on authoritative definitions. However, definitions, no matter how carefully worded, cannot bear the burden of the struggle for economic advantage between various interest groups. Legal definitions survive in a similar environment only because their interpretations by the courts are backed by the power of the state to enforce them, a power not available to the FASB.

The conceptual framework-seeking behavior of the FASB and its predecessors can also be explained in terms of a self-interest perceived by the public accounting profession. The profession has long argued that its interests are best served if it can maintain control over prescription of accounting standards. This is revealed in its protests against any hint that the control of the profession over the standard-setting process may be weakened. Fear of governmental intervention has long been, and continues to be, the major reason for calls for action in the profession.[12] Consider, for example, the following:

> If the practitioners, after sufficient time has elapsed, have not come to some substantial agreement as to what are or should be considered accepted accounting principles and practices, we may well expect the Commission's [SEC's] staff accountants to prepare, and the Commission to publish what it shall demand in the way of such practices... [Smith, 1935, p. 327].

Appropriate as it is today, note that the above statement appeared in an article published almost 45 years ago. Disagreements centering on diverse accounting standards continue to attract much of the criticism leveled at the accounting profession and are the source of the greatest threat to the profession's control over the standard-setting process. The presence of diverse accounting practices hurts the credibility of the standard-setting bodies in two ways. First, the existence of alternative accounting methods is taken as *prima facie* evidence that the accounting standard-setting body is not doing its work properly and is simply allowing firms to record transactions in an arbitrary fashion. Second, whenever the standard-setting body proscribes the use of all but one of the alternative accounting methods, the advocates of the methods were no longer permitted to criticize the agency for being arbitrary in not protecting their interests. No matter what it does, a body like the FASB can expect to find itself criticized by powerful interest groups. A good example is provided by the debate on accounting for oil and gas exploration costs. The FASB was instructed to develop a uniform accounting standard for the oil and gas industry or face the threat of having such a standard written by a government agency. When the FASB chose the successful-efforts over the full-cost method, it found, aligned against it, a powerful industry group as well as some government departments and

---

[11] Since everybody is assumed to be serving the interests of the information user, proponents of all accounting methods argue their case because it will benefit such user. Recall that in the heyday of the LIFO controversy, a major argument for LIFO was that it yields a better measure of income. Watts and Zimmerman [1979] have attempted to explain the existence of some normative theories in financial accounting, using a parallel argument.

[12] Of course, the auditors' fear of government intervention is asymmetric. Consistent with their self-interests, they do want the government to continue to require an audit of certain business firms to ensure demand for their services but want to keep the standard-setting process free of government control.

agencies. Being largely an offspring of the accounting profession, the FASB has (as did the APB) little defense against the criticism that it does not have legitimate authority to make decisions which affect wealth transfer among members of society.

Thus, a body like the FASB needs a conceptual framework simply to boost its public standing.[13] A conceptual framework provides the basis for arguing that: (1) the objective of its activities is to serve the users of the financial statements (it is easier to use the public-interest argument for the user group than for any other group), and (2) it selects among accounting alternatives on the basis of broadly accepted objectives and not because of pressures applied by various interest groups seeking a favorable ruling from the Board. The ability, intelligence, ethical character, and past services, *etc.*, of the members of the FASB are not sufficient to convince the parties adversely affected by its rulings that it makes social choices through an impartial consideration of conflicting interests in society. Rather, a conceptual framework is needed to provide the rationalization for its choices.

If a more representative body were to take over the function of setting accounting standards, perhaps there would be less of a need for a conceptual framework. Indeed, the demand to develop a conceptual framework may be inversely related to the power of enforcement which the standard-setting agency can command. For example, the Securities and Exchange Commission, which has the legal power to enforce its Accounting Series Releases, has not been hampered by the fact that it has not yet enunciated a conceptual framework of accounting.

## CONCLUDING REMARKS

There is little evidence that official statements of objectives of financial accounting have had any direct effect on the determination of financial accounting standards. Whenever the APB or the FASB has had to consider a financial accounting standard, various interest groups presented arguments to support the methods that each perceived to be in its own best interests. The standards issued had to be compromises among the contending interests.[14] Whether the standard-setting process stays in the private sector or is transferred to some public agency, this feature is unlikely to change. What, then, will likely be the effect of the FASB's Conceptual Framework Project on the development of financial accounting stardards in the future?

Our initial guess is that the objectives selected by the Board will be ignored in future rule-making activities, just as were those from previous authoritative attempts. Following the publication of these objectives, the Board will probably feel obliged to pay lip service to them in its future pronouncements, but these pronouncements will not be affected in any substantive way by what is contained in the present documents.

It might have been a more fruitful exercise for the FASB to develop a set of objectives for itself and not for the entire social activity called financial reporting. A few examples of such objectives are provided for consideration:

First, the Board could explicitly recognize the nature of financial accounting as a social activity which affects a varied set of interests, both of those who actively

---

[13] A discussion of this public-interest argument appears in AAA[1977b].

[14] See, for example, Horngren [1973, p. 61], "My hypothesis is that the setting of accounting standards is as much a product of political action as of flawless logic or empirical findings."

participate and those who do not.[15] As the interests of each group are affected by the actions of the Board, it must expect to hear arguments in support of, and against, its decisions. The representations made by these parties could be viewed in the context of their own private interests. In the past, accountants in public practice (*i.e.*, auditors) have tended to be more vocal in their reactions to the Board's actions than have other parties. But perhaps accountants in public practice should have less direct influence on the rule-making process in the future. In its statement of objectives, the Board could define mechanisms for arriving at a compromise ruling after a hearing has been given to all affected groups in society. The Board's primary objective would simply be to arrive at a compromise ruling after considering various points of view on each issue.

A second objective for the FASB might be to limit the detail and specificity of its accounting standards. The pressure to write increasingly detailed and specific accounting standards is great and, in recent years, the resistance of the Board to such pressures seems to be weakening. In this connection, we might note that one of three conditions laid down by the Council of the Institute of Chartered Accountants in England and Wales for approving recommendations on accounting principles to its members was simply that the document be reasonably concise in form (see Zeff [1972, p. 11]).[16] Judging from the length and detail of some of its recent pronouncements (*e.g.*, those dealing with leases and oil and gas exploration costs), the FASB seems to have abandoned an attempt to keep its Statement of Financial Accounting Standards concise.

A third objective of the Board could be to abstain from issuing an accounting standard unless the pronouncement could command a substantial majority. The recent move to lower the minimum voting requirement for issuing an FASB recommendation to a simple majority of seven members will probably increase the frequency of FASB pronouncements which are widely opposed by large segments of interested parties and therefore undermine the basis of its support.

In short, the FASB could assume that various functions of financial statements are well established and known generally by those who produce, audit, and use accounting information. Its task would be essentially one of trying to appease conflicting interests in the presence of disagreements over accounting rules, measurements, disclosures, *etc.* But once this role were recognized, what would be the advantages and disadvantages of allowing a private board like the FASB to make compromise decisions? Is this not a function essentially similar to that performed by the courts, and, if so, are we now back to the proposal for an accounting court?[17]

These questions appear to offer fruitful areas of research, more so than trying to deduce *the* objectives of financial accounting. Perhaps we can achieve more progress by developing and testing theories regarding why a major part of the responsibility for standard setting continues to lie with a private agency, and why members of the profession and corporate managers continue to contribute time and money to the process of developing a conceptual framework. It is unlikely that a general fear of government regulation alone can account for the latter. And, finally, to conclude with

[15] An explicit objective along these lines was also proposed in AAA [1977b, pp. 10–11].

[16] Of course, there is no government agency in the UK which serves an enforcement role like that of the SEC in this country. This factor may allow broader statements in the UK.

[17] First proposed by Littleton [1935].

Baxter [1962, p. 427]:

> Recommendations by authority on matters of accounting theory may in the short run seem unmixed blessings. In the end, however, they will probably do harm. They are likely to yield little fresh knowledge. . . . They are likely to weaken the eduation of accountants; the conversion of the subject into cut-and-dried rules, approved by authority and not to be lightly questioned, threatens to reduce its value as a subject of liberal education almost to *nil*. They are likely to narrow the scope for individual thought and judgment; and a group of men who resign their hard problems to others must eventually give up all claim to be a learned profession.

## REFERENCES

American Accounting Association (1936), Executive Committee, "A Tentative Statement of Accounting Principles Affecting Corporate Reports," *The Accounting Review* (June 1936), pp. 187–91.

————, Executive Committee, "Accounting Principles Underlying Corporate Financial Statements," *The Accounting Review* (June 1941), pp. 133–39.

————, Executive Committee, "Accounting Concepts and Standards Underlying Corporate Financial Statements, 1948 Revision," *The Accounting Review* (October 1948), pp. 339–44.

————, Committee on Concepts and Standards Underlying Corporate Financial Statements, "Accounting and Reporting Standards for Corporate Financial Statements, 1957 Revision," *The Accounting Review* (October 1957), pp. 536–46.

————, Committee on Concepts and Standards—Long-Lived Assets, "Accounting for Land, Buildings and Equipment ," Supplementary Statement No. 1, *The Accounting Review* (July 1964a), pp. 693–99.

————, Committee on Concepts and Standards—Inventory Measurement, "A Discussion of Various Approaches to Inventory Measurement," Supplementary Statement No. 2, *The Accounting Review* (July 1964b), pp. 700–14.

————, Committee to Prepare a Statement of Basic Accounting Theory, *A Statement of Basic Accounting Theory* (AAA, 1966).

————, Committee on Concepts and Standards for External Financial Reports, *Statement on Accounting Theory and Theory Acceptance* (AAA, 1977a).

————, Subcommittee on Conceptual Framework for Financial Accounting and Reporting, *Elements of Financial Statements and Their Measurement: Report to the Financial Accounting Standards Board* (AAA, June 1977b).

American Institute of [Certified Public] Accountants (1942), Committee on Accounting Procedure, *Unamortized Discount and Redemption Premium on Bonds Refunded (Supplement)*, Accounting Research Bulletin No. 18, (AICPA, 1942).

————, Committee on Accounting Terminology, *Accounting Terminology Bulletin*, No. 1 (AIA, 1953). Reprinted in FASB [1977b].

American Institute of Certified Public Accountants (1970), Accounting Principles Board, *Basic Concepts and Accounting Principles Underlying Financial Statements of Business Enterprises*, Statement No. 4 of the APB (AICPA, 1970).

————, Study Group on the Objectives of Financial Statements, *Objectives of Financial Statements* (AICPA, 1973).

Armstrong, M. S., "The Politics of Establishing Accounting Standards," *Journal of Accountancy* (February 1977), pp. 76–79.

Baxter, W. T., "Recommendations on Accounting Theory," in W. T. Baxter and S. Davidson, eds., *Studies in Accounting Theory* (Sweet & Maxwell, 1962), pp. 414–27.

Beaver, W. H. and J. S. Demski, "The Nature of Financial Accounting Objectives: A Survey and Synthesis," *Studies on Financial Accounting Objectives, 1974*, supplement to the *Journal of Accounting Research* (1974).

Bedford, N. M., "Discussion of Opportunities and Implications of the Report on Objectives of Financial Statements," *Studies on Financial Accounting Objectives, 1974*, Supplement to the *Journal of Accounting Research* 12 (1974), p. 15.

Canning, J. B., *The Economics of Accountancy* (The Ronald Press, 1929).

Coe, T. L. and G. H. Sorter, "The FASB Has Been Using an Implicit Conceptual Framework," *The Accounting Journal* (Winter 1977–78), pp. 152–69.

Cyert, R. M. and Y. Ijiri, "Problems of Implementing the Trueblood Objectives Report," *Studies on Financial Accounting Objectives: 1974*, Supplement to the *Journal of Accounting Research* 12 (1974).

Deinzer, H. T., *The American Accounting Association-Sponsored Statements of Standards for Corporate Financial Reports: A Perspective* (Accounting Department, University of Florida, 1964).

Financial Accounting Standards Board, FASB Discussion Memorandum, *Conceptual Framework for Accounting and Reporting: Consideration of the Report of the Study Group on the Objectives of Financial Statements* (FASB, 1974).

———, FASB Discussion Memorandum, *Conceptual Framework for Financial Accounting and Reporting: Elements of Financial Statements and Their Measurement* (FASB, 1976a).

———, *Tentative Conclusions on Objectives of Financial Statements of Business Enterprises* (FASB, 1976b).

———, *Scope and Implications of the Conceptual Framework Project* (FASB, 1976c).

———, *Objectives of Financial Reporting and Elements of Financial Statements of Business Enterprises*, Exposure Draft of Proposed Statement of Financial Accounting Concepts (FASB, 1977).

———, *Objectives of Financial Reporting by Business Enterprises*, Statement of Financial Accounting Concepts No. 1 (FASB, 1978).

Hanson, A. W., "Comments on 'An Introduction to Corporate Accounting Standards'," *Journal of Accountancy* (June 1940), pp. 440–42.

Hatfield, H. R., *Modern Accounting* (D. Appleton and Company, 1909).

———, *Accounting: Its Principles and Problems* (D. Appleton-Century Company, 1927).

Horngren, C. T., "The Market of Accounting Standards," *Journal of Accountancy* (October 1973), pp. 61–66.

Ijiri, Y., "Critique of the APB Fundamentals Statement," *Journal of Accountancy* (November 1971), pp. 43–50.

Kester, R. B., "Comments on 'An Introduction to Corporate Accounting Standards'," *Journal of Accountancy* (June 1940), pp. 442–45.

Kitchen, J., "Costing Terminology, *Accounting Research* (February 1954). Reprinted in W. T. Baxter and S. Davidson, eds., *Studies in Accounting Theory* (Sweet & Maxwell, 1962), pp. 399–413.

Littleton, A. C., "Auditor Independence," *Journal of Accountancy* (April 1935), pp. 283–91.

———, Review of Moonitz, *The Basic Postulates of Accounting, The Accounting Review* (July 1962), pp. 602–05.

———, Review of R. T. Sprouse and M. Moonitz, *A Tentative Set of Broad Accounting Principles for Business Enterprises, The Accounting Review* (January 1963), pp. 220–22.

Miller, H. E., "Discussion of Opportunities and Implications of the Report on Objectives of Financial Statements," *Studies on Financial Accounting Objectives: 1974*, supplement to *Journal of Accounting Research* 12 (1974).

Moonitz, M., *The Basic Postulates of Accounting*, Accounting Research Study No. 1 (AICPA, 1961).

Most, K. S. and A. L. Winters, "Focus on Standard Setting: From Trueblood to the FASB," *Journal of Accountancy* (February 1977), pp. 67–75.

Paton, W. A., *Accounting Theory* (The Ronald Press, 1922).

Paton, W. A. and A. C. Littleton, *An Introduction to Corporate Accounting Standards*, Monograph No. 3 (AAA, 1940).

Smith, C. A., "Accounting Practice under the Securities and Exchange Commission," *The Accounting Review* (December 1935), pp. 325–332.

Sprouse, R. T., "Discussion of Opportunities and Implications of the Report on Objectives of Financial Statements," *Studies on Financial Accounting Objectives: 1974*, Supplement to the *Journal of Accounting Research* 12 (1974).

Sprouse, R. T. and M. Moonitz, *A Tentative Set of Broad Accounting Principles for Business Enterprises*, Accounting Research Study No. 3 (AICPA, 1962).

Sterling, R. R., "A Statement of Basic Accounting Theory: A Review Article," *Journal of Accounting Research* (Spring 1967), pp. 95–112.

Stinchcombe, A. L., *Constructing Social Theories* (Harcourt, Brace, and World, 1968).

Vatter, W. J., " $\sum_{i=1}^{i=22} (M_3)_i$ —An Evaluation," *The Accounting Review* (July 1963), pp. 47–77.

Watts, R. L. and J. L. Zimmerman, "Towards a Positive Theory of Determination of Accounting Standards," *The Accounting Review* 53 (January 1978), pp. 112–34.

———, "The Demand for and Supply of Accounting Theories: The Market for Excuses," *The Accounting Review* (April 1979), pp. 273–305.

Zeff, S. A., *Forging Accounting Principles in Five Countries* (Stipes Publishing Co., 1972).

———, "The Rise of 'Economic Consequences'," *Journal of Accountancy* (December 1978), pp. 56–63.

# I-A 5 *The Conceptual Framework: Myths and Realities*

PAUL B. W. MILLER

No endeavor in financial accounting has attracted more attention and criticism than the effort to create a comprehensive set of concepts for theory and practice. The attempts number in the dozens, beginning in the 1930s. The most recent and the most elaborate, of course, has been the work done on a conceptual framework by the Financial Accounting Standards Board, a project that had its inception in 1973, when the board was established.

With the issuing of FASB Concepts Statement no. 5, *Recognition and Measurement in Financial Statements of Business Enterprises*—the last originally scheduled building block of the framework—it seems worthwhile to explore the realities and the myths surrounding the endeavor.

Given the background and importance of the undertaking, it isn't surprising that several myths have sprung up about conceptual frameworks in general and about the FASB project in particular. This article, intended to lay to rest some of these misperceptions, explains what a conceptual framework might accomplish, sheds light on eight prevalent myths (see exhibit 1) and describes the real nature of the project.

## GOALS OF A CONCEPTUAL FRAMEWORK

Much has been said and written about a conceptual framework for accounting, so the focus here will be on the three paramount reasons to establish one:

1. To describe existing practice.
2. To prescribe future practice.
3. To define key terms and fundamental issues.

Conflicts among these goals, because they have contributed to the mythmaking, will also be explored.

*Existing practice.* One reason for bringing together accounting concepts is to provide an overview of what is done in practice. The basic objective of the description is to make understandable, in as cogent and simple a form as possible, what accounting is all about. A few broad principles generally are more comprehensible than a multitude of specific details.

*Future practice.* In the course of developing descriptive concepts, theorists generally become aware of inconsistencies and other deficiencies in practice. One result of these discoveries is the desire to develop another type of conceptual framework, one that goes beyond mere description and prescribes what ought to be done. These frameworks are often called normative because they reflect the values, or norms, of their compilers.

*Key terms and fundamental issues.* Another major purpose of a conceptual framework is to lay down broad definitions of basic terms to be used in debates about what ought to be done in practice. (In this limited sense a conceptual framework is like a constitution or other form of social contract that establishes basic principles.) These terms, moreover, help the profession and other interested parties identify the issues to be debated.

It is important to remember that having definitions doesn't eliminate the need for debates, nor does it predetermine an outcome. The need for discussion is continuous, and any given outcome depends on the powers of the participants at the time of the debate.

*Conflicts among goals.* No single framework, however, can satisfy more than one of these three objectives. In fact, there are barriers to setting up a framework that will meet even one of them.

First, it is difficult to establish a descriptive conceptual framework because not everyone agrees about what actually exists. Among accountants there is disagreement on, for example, the basic issue of whether the initial cost measurement of an asset is intended to be a description of the amount sacrificed to acquire it or a reliable estimate of its value at the date of acquisition. In most cases there is little difference between these two numbers; at other times, however, the difference is material, so the issue takes on importance.

Other limitations of a description of current practice are that it doesn't always help accountants cope with a new situation—say, a research and development partnership or an in-substance defeasance—or provide much help in improving existing practice.

Attempts to establish prescriptive frameworks have been unsuccessful, however, because of the near impossibility of reaching agreement between even two people, let alone among the seven members of the FASB or the hundreds of thousands of people who are involved in accounting. But even if a prescriptive conceptual framework could be achieved, practical impact would be unlikely if it lacked consensus and authoritative support. When, for example, the American Accounting Association published *A Statement of Basic Accounting Theory* in 1966, the document didn't influence practice because it didn't receive enough support from powerful interests.

It's no easier to set up a framework that merely defines basic terms and issues because control of the definitions contributes to control of the debates and, eventually, of the selection of which practices are changed or left unchanged. Accordingly, a consensus on even seemingly obvious points may be elusive.

There can also be significant difficulty in interpreting the definitions and making them operational. Accountants are likely to thoroughly debate, for example, the

---

**EXHIBIT 1**

**EIGHT MYTHS ABOUT CONCEPTUAL FRAMEWORKS**

1. The Accounting Principles Board failed because it didn't have a conceptual framework.
2. The Financial Accounting Standards Board can't succeed unless it has a conceptual framework.
3. A conceptual framework will lead to consistent standards.
4. A conceptual framework will eliminate the problem of standards overload.
5. The FASB's conceptual framework captures only the status quo of accounting practice.
6. The FASB's conceptual framework project has cost more than it should have.
7. The FASB will revise the existing standards to make them consistent with the conceptual framework.
8. The FASB has abandoned the conceptual framework project.

---

meaning of the phrase *probable future economic benefits*, which is part of the definition of an asset in FASB Concepts Statement no. 3, *Elements of Financial Statements of Business Enterprises*. Finally, conflicts arise in developing this type of framework if the definitions don't describe existing practice or allow for flexibility in coping with new situations.

Because the task of creating a conceptual framework is so complex, it isn't surprising that accountants have encountered so much resistance to their efforts. Perhaps even more resistance has been directed toward the FASB because it plays a highly visible and central role in the process.

## EIGHT MYTHS ABOUT CONCEPTUAL FRAMEWORKS

Those who have followed the recognition and measurement phase of the conceptual framework project know that there are many myths about such frameworks, especially the FASB's.

The eight most common myths, shown in exhibit 1, fall into four categories:

1. The political role of a conceptual framework (myths 1 and 2).
2. The technical role of a conceptual framework (myths 3 and 4).
3. The FASB's existing conceptual framework (myths 5 and 6).
4. The future of the FASB's conceptual framework (myths 7 and 8).

In each case, as is true of most myths, there is an element of truth, but there has been distortion over time, through telling and retelling.

### Myth no. 1

One problem with the myth that the Accounting Principles Board failed because it didn't have a conceptual framework is its premise—that the APB did, indeed, fail. For the sake of argument, let's accept the definition of failure as the inability to stay in existence.

From the perspective of the 1980s, it seems more likely that the APB stopped operating because it had an apparent structural bias that favored the interests of auditors and their clients to the detriment of users of financial statements. Part of the problem arose from the fact that the APB was a committee of the American Institute of CPAs and thus was seen to be within the auditing profession. With one exception, there were no users among the members of the APB, and users generally weren't included directly in its procedures of due process.

Most important, the Securities and Exchange Commission didn't send a clear, unambiguous signal about its attitude toward the APB's pronouncements. As a result of all these factors, the APB's failure can more appropriately be attributed to its apparent neglect of users than to the absence of a conceptual framework.

### Myth no. 2

The second myth is that the FASB can't succeed unless it has a conceptual framework. Again, it is easy to be sidetracked into a debate on what should be considered success. It can be argued, for example, that the FASB will succeed only if capital resources are allocated more efficiently as a result of its standards.

A more practical assumption can also be made, however—that mere continued existence constitutes success.

The FASB will survive if and only if it can maintain a mandate that reflects the interests of the beneficiaries of the capital market, who are, in effect, the participants in the national economy. To obtain this broad power base, the strong support of the SEC is essential. Specifically, some visible SEC action is needed to establish that the FASB has the best interests of the economy in mind, not just the interests of the preparers and auditors of financial statements.

By endorsing the FASB as the authoritative body for setting standards—in its Accounting Series Release no. 150, *Statement of Policy on the Establishment and Improvement of Accounting Principles and Standards*—the SEC has provided the needed visible support. Additional credibility is provided by the commission's continuing oversight activities.

From a political perspective, then, a conceptual framework isn't crucial to the FASB's viability, but the board may be able to operate more efficiently if some key terms and issues can be defined and identified.

### Myth no. 3

The validity of the myth that a conceptual framework will lead to consistent standards hinges on the process by which standards are created. If standards were handed down by a higher authority strictly on the basis of their conceptual soundness, a conceptual framework would, of course, lead to consistency.

But standards don't descend. Rather, they emerge from a nested set of political processes that create inconsistencies as the search for a consensus continues.

The core process is the negotiating among the seven members of the FASB. Like everyone else, individual board members have different ideas and want to get their views incorporated into the final pronouncements. But to put together a majority, compromises must be made, with the result that some conceptual consistency is often lost. (Of course, inconsistency is also created as individual board members change their views or are replaced.)

Inconsistencies are also created through the board's highly visible procedures of due process. When common themes are heard in constituents' objections to proposed standards, it behooves the board to compromise and make some changes, with the result that consistency can be lost.

Broader political pressure, especially from the SEC, also plays a part in generating inconsistencies among standards. Because the commission has so much power, it is unlikely that the FASB can resist the pressure from Washington to produce compromise standards that meet the needs of the SEC and its constituents merely by arguing that the result isn't perfectly compatible with the published concepts.

Given the reasonably balanced powers that exist, then, it's clear that consensus can be reached only through compromise. In turn, these compromises are governed by the priorities different groups have for different issues. Many users of financial statements may not care much about accounting for futures contracts, for example, but they may be intensely interested in accounting for pensions. Thus, they may be willing to accept virtually any answer on futures but will hold the line on the pension issues.

### Myth no. 4

To accept the myth that a conceptual framework will eliminate the problem of standards overload, one must first agree that there is an overload problem. This question won't be debated here.

Also implicit is the idea that the responsibility for decisions about accounting standards can be decentralized by shifting it to the auditor in the field. Doing so, it is argued, would mean that practitioners would be less burdened by detailed rules.

But it can also be argued that such decentralization isn't politically feasible because it would place power in the hands of one group (auditors) to the potential detriment of other groups (statement users and preparers). Giving so much control to auditors would be unacceptable to the other participants in the political processes by which standards are created.

Where, moreover, has the thrust for publishing more standards come from? It is likely that many auditors want them in order to have more leverage when facing down "creative" and perhaps stubborn clients who try to push the existing standards to their limits. As long as this situation exists, the FASB will be equally pressured to translate its broad concepts into authoritative and detailed standards rather than leave the interpretation to individual auditors, who are subject to client pressure.

### Myth no. 5

Those who believe the myth that the FASB's conceptual framework captures only the status quo of accounting practice tend to want the framework to go further in prescribing future standards. In effect, they are complaining that its present structure makes change less likely to happen.

A variation on this myth is that the conceptual framework has captured only the obvious and left out the more difficult points. Who could disagree, for example, with the idea that useful information should be provided? Who would disagree with the notion that information must be both relevant and reliable to be useful?

In response to these criticisms, it can be pointed out that the results of the early phase of the framework project are useful for defining the terms used by the board members and their respondents. At the very least, the existing framework lays some groundwork that makes the deliberative process more efficient, even if it doesn't provide an exact description of current practice or a clear prescription for future practice.

In sharp contrast is an opposing myth—that the conceptual framework is revolutionary. It has been argued that the framework emphasizes the statement of financial position over the income statement. It must be acknowledged that the framework has, in fact, cast doubt on some of the long-standing practices associated with so-called good matching and in this sense may be considered revolutionary. FASB Concepts Statement no. 3, for example, points out that a credit balance in the deferred tax account created under APB Opinion no. 11, *Accounting for Income Taxes*, doesn't meet the definition of a liability or of any other of the FASB's elements.

But this tendency to evaluate practice in terms of its effects on the income statement and the statement of financial position isn't revolutionary in the light of long-standing trends. It is now considered inappropriate, for example, to capitalize operating losses of development stage companies, to recognize self-insurance reserves and not to capitalize leases that are in-substance purchases of assets. Each change was made with the idea of improving both financial statements.

Perhaps the proponents of this contrasting myth think that additional emphasis on the balance sheet demotes income reporting. If so, they are mistaken. Rather, as was suggested, the shift is better interpreted as an equalization of the importance of the two statements.

This conclusion is supported by the growing interest in reporting non-articulated changes in owners' equity, as seen in accounting for long term investments in marketable securities (FASB Statement no. 12, *Accounting for Certain Marketable Securities*) and the foreign currency translation adjustment (FASB Statement no. 52, *Foreign Currency Translation*). (In its most basic form non-articulation is the reporting of an income number that doesn't include all changes in owners' equity other than investments by owners and distributions to them.)

Nonarticulation of at least one income statement is clearly favored in FASB Concepts Statement no. 5, which proposes a statement of "earnings" (which wouldn't articulate with the statement of financial position) and a statement of "comprehensive income" (which would articulate).

### Myth no. 6

The myth that the FASB's conceptual framework project has cost more than it should have is based on two premises: (1) the cost of the project is knowable; (2) the cost that should have been incurred is knowable. Both assumptions are questionable.

First, it's impossible to know precisely what the project has cost; there are simply too many joint costs. Any given board or staff member works on a number of projects at the same time. Further, the work on the framework has spilled over into other projects. There are also many hidden, hence unmeasurable, costs incurred by constituents in preparing responses to discussion documents.

To determine how much the project should have cost would require extraordinary insight, for no one has ever completed a conceptual framework under the circumstances that the FASB has faced. And any other method of estimating an appropriate cost would depend on individual evaluations of the goal of the project.

A parallel argument is that the costs have exceeded the benefits. One weakness of this view is, of course, the difficulty of measuring the costs and benefits. Another is the basic assumption that there are no further significant benefits to be derived from the framework. Although such an assertion may be true, it is premature at this point. Time and more evidence are needed.

Some have even contended that the project has produced no benefits. This view may be held by those who wanted the framework to be purely descriptive of existing practice or who preferred a purely prescriptive framework, one not bound by existing practice.

Of course, neither camp got what it wanted and thus may be unwilling to acknowledge that there are any positive elements in what the board has published.

### Myth no. 7

Some subscribe to the myth that the FASB will revise the existing standards to make them consistent with the conceptual framework. This belief may have been encouraged by the FASB's sweeping generalizations early in the project and, later, by the board's specific declarations in certain standards that it would review and amend these standards, as needed, to make them conceptually sound.

But for most exciting standards there is insufficient interest in revising them to justify putting the issues back on the agenda. It is unlikely, for example, that anyone would want to reconsider the treatment of troubled debt restructurings or foreign currency translations solely to bring them into compliance with a conceptual framework.

Perhaps more significant is the fact that interactions among compromises on different issues make it unlikely that some of them can be overturned. That is, the board's ability to resolve future issues would be reduced by any action that would make it harder to generate a consensus among board members or the board's constituents.

If every hard-won consensus is to be thrown open for renegotiation because of the conceptual framework, a board member would be reluctant to compromise. The politics of the situation simply demand that a consensus be left intact as long as possible.

If, however, enough powerful people—including the board, the Financial Accounting Standards Advisory Council, the SEC and other constituent organizations—do want a standard to be changed, it will be changed; if they want it to be left alone, it will be.

### Myth no. 8

The last widespread myth is that the FASB has abandoned the conceptual framework project. The nature of FASB Concepts Statement no. 5, issued in December 1984 after more than three years of effort, is one basis for this belief.

The overall strategy adopted was to draft and issue a less prescriptive and more descriptive statement. In effect, the board could claim a victory because the members did, at last, reach a consensus. Because this "victory" came about only because the board retreated from the unresolved substantive issues, the strategy has often been called the "Vietnam solution."

The statement reflects this strategy because it doesn't go far beyond earlier concepts statements and certainly doesn't tackle the measurement issue, on which the board was so deeply divided.

In particular, paragraph 66 of the statement says: "Items currently reported in financial statements are measured by different attributes, depending on the nature of the item and the relevance and reliability of the attribute measured. The Board expects the use of different attributes to continue." The question of which factors should be considered in making the choice among these attributes was, of course, the issue that the board members couldn't resolve.

The board's adoption of this strategy may indeed be an abandonment of the conceptual framework project. On the other hand, it may simply be an expedient action to allow other, more immediate issues (such as accounting for pension costs) to be addressed. Inevitably, the delay also provides an opportunity for power to shift in such a way that the previously intractable conceptual issues might be tackled and resolved more definitely in the future.

But it is also probably accurate to say that the board has indeed abandoned some of the original goals of the project, a step far different from abandoning the project itself.

## Realities of the Conceptual Framework

The conceptual framework is better understood as a political document than as a purely conceptual effort. The concepts statements have emerged from the same political processes—with the same need to compromise—that are used for setting standards. Inevitably, then, the framework lacks the conciseness of some other conceptual structures. But this potential shortcoming must be considered in light of the fact that the framework enjoys much more authoritative support and potential for affecting practice than any of its predecessors.

Another reality about the framework is that it is neither a complete description of existing practice nor a highly specific prescription for future practice. Yet it does broadly define a number of key terms and concepts that can be used in identifying and debating the issues.

Now for a warning of a lurking danger: the profession shouldn't consider the framework as the ultimate authority for resolving issues. The definitions are nonauthoritative enough to allow the board to work around them when seeking a consensus.

Further, the definitions aren't sufficiently precise to preclude debates about their meanings and applications. The framework isn't going to stop arguments—witness the pension project–but it may determine the ground rules for these arguments and the shape of the debates.

Finally, it must be remembered that the framework is still in its infancy. The profession is just starting to use it, and difficulties are inevitable. There are many more conceptual issues to tackle in the future, of course, and there are also many more benefits to be reaped from the existing concepts statements.

**The Framework and the Profession**

At the very least, the framework seems to have helped the board itself. Now that the members and their constituents are using the definitions, clearer communication is a likely result. And this improved communication will benefit the profession and the financial world in general as the effects of the framework make themselves felt.

The most prudent strategy for the profession to adopt is to try to work with the conceptual framework. Accountants can use it, try to change it—and certainly criticize it. But no one is well served by perpetuating the myths that have arisen around it.

# I-A 6   *The Function of a Conceptual Framework for Corporate Financial Reporting*

K. V. PEASNELL

## INTRODUCTION

The purpose of the present article is to examine ways in which a statement of financial reporting objectives (hereinafter referred to as 'conceptual framework', or CF for short) can be expected to improve the quality of company financial reporting. It is argued here that there is considerable confusion surrounding the function of a CF, especially over the ways in which a CF can be expected to assist a financial accounting policy-making body such as the Accounting Standards Committee (ASC) or the Financial Accounting Standards Board (FASB); there seems little prospect of developing a CF of value to policy makers without first clarifying the powers and responsibilities of the policy makers themselves.

In the American literature in particular, there is a marked tendency to treat the problems of the development of a conceptual framework separately and independently of the determination of suitable institutional arrangements for standard setting; and yet they both have the same end in mind, namely the promulgation and improvement of accounting standards. More to the point, it is the standard setters who have to make use of a CF, so it is important that their circumstances be considered first.

The plan of the paper is as follows. First the history of the search for a CF is briefly outlined and recent literature on the subject is summarised. Next, attention is

I am greatly indebted to my Lancaster colleagues, Professor Edward Stamp and Mr. Simon Archer, for many hours of discussion on the subject matter of this paper. The contribution of Eddie Stamp, in particular, has been especially significant. Whilst I have not hesitated to plunder the ideas of both colleagues, it should not be supposed that either individual subscribes to the views contained in this paper. Embryonic versions of the paper were presented at the Universities of Glasgow and Manchester, and thanks are due to the participants in those seminars for their helpful comments.

K. V. Peasnell, "The Function of a Conceptual Framework for Corporate Financial Reporting," Accounting and Business Research, Autumn 1982, pp. 243–256. Reprinted with the permission of *Accounting and Business Research*.

directed to the standard-setting process currently in operation in the UK. Use is made here of a simple way of viewing social conflict resolution mechanisms devised by Boulding (1965). Section four develops the premise that whether or not a CF has anything major to contribute depends on the ways in which corporate financial reporting is organised and policed. Reference is made there to three different accounting environments—laissez-faire, state control, and delegation to the profession. The final section contains a summary and concluding comments.

## THE QUEST FOR A CONCEPTUAL FRAMEWORK

### A Brief History of the Quest

Over the years, numerous attempts have been made to define the nature and purposes of corporate financial reporting—to develop a conceptual framework. Of course, most of these efforts are the works of individual scholars concerned to put the teaching of the subject on a sound theoretical footing; academic committees have also attempted to do the same, and for similar reasons in the main (e.g. see AAA, 1936, 1966, 1977). Only relatively recently have the professional accounting bodies shown any inclination to take part in this process. The concern in this subsection is with these officially commissioned studies; accounting theory development in the broad sense is of coincidental interest only. Attention is further restricted to developments in the USA, the UK and Canada.

The professional accounting bodies in these countries have taken the opportunity, from time to time, to issue statements about the nature, purposes and limitations of published financial statements of companies. No one has ever seriously suggested that any of these statements merited the title 'conceptual framework'. This is not to say that the statements were without influence or dealt with trivial matters— consider, for example, the English Institute's Recommendation N15, 'Accounting in Relation to Changes in the Purchasing Power of Money' (ICAEW, 1952)—merely that the objective in issuing them was much more limited.

Five attempts to develop a CF are worthy of special comment.[1] The first was a study commissioned by the American Institute of Certified Public Accountants (AICPA) some twenty years ago which saw the light of day as two interrelated monographs, one by the then AICPA Director of Accounting Research, Maurice Moonitz (1961), and the other by Sprouse and Moonitz (1962). The next study was explicitly charged by the AICPA with the development of a set of financial statement objectives intended to 'facilitate establishment of guidelines and criteria for improving accounting and financial reporting' and emerged as the Trueblood Report (AICPA, 1973). The third effort was commissioned in the UK in October 1974 by the (then styled) Accounting Standards Steering Committee; the report was eventually published as a discussion paper, *The Corporate Report* (ASC, 1975). The fourth and most extensive is that by the FASB, which was charged with trying to make the Trueblood Report operational. Following a lengthy review process that started as long ago as 1974 with a public hearing, an exposure draft was issued in December 1977

---

[1] A sixth study is now completed. ASC commissioned Professor Richard Macve of the University of Wales to study the feasibility of developing a conceptual framework in Britain (published 1981).

(FASB, 1977). The first part of the exposure draft, dealing with the objectives of financial reporting, was issued as Statement of Financial Accounting Concepts No. 1 (SFAC1) a year later (FASB, 1978). The second part, outlining the elements of financial statements of business enterprises, was issued as SFAC3 in late 1980 (FASB, 1980b); SFAC2, 'Qualitative Characteristics of Accounting Information' (FASB, 1980a) was issued earlier in 1980.[2] The fifth study, also of very recent origin, was written by an academic, Edward Stamp, on behalf of the Canadian Institute of Chartered Accountants (CICA, 1980).

A common pattern can be seen both in the circumstances surrounding the commissioning of the first four of these five research studies and in the reactions of the accounting and business community to the proposals and arguments contained in the subsequent reports. First, they were established at a time when the standard-setting programme was running into trouble. Secondly, the reports were greeted with a mixture of cries of disappointment and anger.

All the AICPA's efforts at influencing the development of generally accepted accounting principles met with considerable criticism. The first really major effort in this direction was itself the result of mounting professional and legal criticisms both of the quality of corporate reporting practices and of the early attempts of the AICPA to remedy matters (Zeff, 1972, pp. 140–167). The Accounting Principles Board (APB) was established in 1959 as a direct result of these criticisms. The APB gave top priority to the launching of a study into the 'basic postulates' and 'broad principles' of accounting, the study which resulted in the Moonitz and Sprouse–Moonitz monographs.

The profession's reactions to the two monographs were most interesting. Moonitz's 1961 study of basic postulates caused almost no reaction. The reason seems to have been that it operated at too high a level of abstraction and generalisation; with hindsight, one can see that readers were holding fire, waiting for the follow-up study on principles (Zeff, 1972, pp. 174–175). When the second monograph was published all hell broke loose. Indeed, the Sprouse-Moonitz monograph itself contained 24 pages of comment and dissent by no less than 9 of the 12 members of the project advisory committee. Hardly an auspicious start! Needless to say, the study had little positive impact on the subsequent accounting practice pronouncements of the APB. The problem was that the 'broad principles' enunciated by Sprouse and Moonitz required that assets be shown at their current values, and the profession was not ready to endorse principles so at variance with then accepted practice.

How could this be? After all, the broad principles were deduced from the basic postulates identified in the first of the two monographs. There were few serious criticisms made of the soundness of the authors' deductions, and the publication of the basic postulates had passed largely without comment. The postulates were subjected to scrutiny and criticism only *after* it was realised what the postulates together logically entailed.

The critics won the day and the APB seemed to abandon hope that fundamental research might provide a logical foundation for pronouncements on accounting principles. But the Board's problems continued to grow. Several APB Opinions ran into difficulty during preparation and in the period immediately following publica-

---

[2] A fourth Statement, SFAC4 has also been issued by the FASB (1980c); but as it deals with the 'objectives of financial reporting by nonbusiness organisations', it falls outside the scope of the present article.

tion. Something had to be done. In 1965 a committee was established and charged with developing the fundamentals of financial reporting. Five years later, the Board approved APB Statement No. 4 (APBS4), 'Basic Concepts and Accounting Principles Underlying Financial Statements of Business enterprises' (AICPA, 1970). The charge was to produce a document which would serve two purposes: (a) to provide a rationale for currently accepted practices, one which would be useful in reducing alternative practices in accounting to those justified by substantial differences in factual circumstances; (b) to enhance understanding of the purposes, potential and limitations of financial statements in providing needed information. APBS4: (i) sets out a framework describing the environment in which accounting exists, the present objectives of financial accounting and financial statements and the basic features and elements of financial accounting and (ii) describes presently generally accepted accounting principles (Zeff, 1972, pp. 196–198).

Not surprisingly, APBS4 did little to quell criticism of the profession. Although a lengthy and impressive piece of work, APBS4 does not really amount to a Conceptual Framework. At best, it is essentially a defensive, descriptive document. It was widely criticised as an inadequate response to the problems facing the profession. There were those, including some of the members of the Board, who argued that a prescriptive statement was needed to complement APBS4's description of currently accepted practice. The idea of putting standard-setting on a sound footing by going back to first principles, looking at the basic issues of standard-setting, was revived.

The result was twofold: the establishment of FASB as recommended by the Wheat Report (AICPA, 1972) and the publication of the Trueblood Report (AICPA, 1973). It is noted that these reports were the work of two study groups, working independently. *It was assumed that one could 'refine' the objectives of financial statements without regard to the policy-making procedures.*

The Trueblood Report was, in effect, handed over to the newly-created FASB. The FASB acted quickly, putting the Report near the top of its agenda, issuing a discussion memorandum (FASB, 1974), inviting comments and arranging a public hearing. However progress from this point on was very slow, so slow that the standard-setting programme could not await finalisation of the objectives study. Thus the FASB was in a very similar position to that which the APB had found itself in, in that the FASB had to develop accounting standards without benefit of a formal framework.

Although the Trueblood Report received far greater support from within the profession than did the ill-fated Moonitz-Sprouse study, it was not without its critics. The public hearings arranged by the FASB showed that there was considerable opposition from industry to the Report's emphasis on user needs and to some of the forms of disclosure mentioned in the Report. In particular, criticism was directed at Objectives 10, 11, and 12 in the Report, dealing with financial forecasts, non-profit accounting and social accounting; SFAC1 omits any reference to these items.

The FASB has little to show for its four years of hard work on the CF project. As Dopuch and Sunder (1980, p. 3) point out:

> In wording and substance, little is new or different in SFAC1. Had the FASB pointed out the parts of the existing reports, such as APBS4 and the Trueblood Report, that it agreed with and emphasized its disagreements, its contribution would have been easier to discern. Without such aid, we are hard-pressed to discern the FASB's net contribution to these earlier efforts.

Of course, the proof of the pudding is in the eating: 'a basic test of the FASB's contribution is the extent to which SFAC1 may succeed where others have failed' (Dopuch and Sunder, 1980, p. 3). On this point, Dopuch and Sunder make two observations which are worth noting. First, they point out that the definitions of the main categories of accounts appearing in financial statements—assets, liabilities, owners' equity, revenues, expenses, gains, losses—depend on unspecified rules and conventions. 'How can a conceptual framework guide choices from among alternative principles and rules if the elements of the framework are defined in these very same terms?' (p. 4). They argue that the definitions 'provide only the necessary conditions for a resource or obligation to be included in the asset or liability categories, respectively, rather than both the necessary and sufficient conditions' (p. 4). The necessary conditions are conventional ones and as such are unlikely to be too restrictive.

Second, Dopuch and Sunder argue that nothing in the FASB's CF seems to be of much help in resolving contemporary disclosure issues. They support this assertion by selecting three issues—deferred tax credits, treatment of costs of exploration in the oil and gas industry, reports on current values of assets and liabilities—for detailed consideration. They conclude: (i) 'The FASB's definition of liabilities is so general that at this stage we cannot predict the Board's position on deferred taxes' (Dopuch and Sunder, 1980, p. 6). (ii) 'The fact that the framework supports two opposing principles of accounting [for oil and gas exploration costs—full costs and successful efforts] is preliminary evidence that the framework is unlikely to be a useful guide in resolving this issue' (p. 7). (iii) Neither SFAC1 nor the Exposure Draft addresses the problem of estimation; yet it is on the practical issue of reliability of estimates that past efforts to encourage publication of current costs have foundered (p. 8).

Not all commentators are as pessimistic as Dopuch and Sunder about the benefits that might flow from the FASB's CF programme. Scott and De Celles (1980) take the view that a *virtue* of SFAC1 is that it avoids establishing a definite association between accounting objectives and specific financial reports because it leaves room for future development. This appears to be the FASB's thinking on the matter.

The only UK attempt to date to develop a CF was the 1975 ASC discussion paper, *The Corporate Report*. The discussion paper was produced in a very short time. The working party began work in October 1974 and its report was published in July 1975— several weeks before the report of the government-appointed Inflation Accounting Committee (Sandilands, 1975) was presented to the Chancellor of the Exchequer and the Secretary of State for Trade. (For comparison purposes, the Sandilands Report took 17 months to complete, the Trueblood Report 30 months, and *The Corporate Report* some 9 months.) *The Corporate Report* caused great controversy within the business community and the accounting profession. In particular, the emphasis placed in the discussion paper on greater disclosure, including statements of 'future prospects' and 'corporate objectives', was the subject of much criticism. Also, the more or less simultaneous publication of the Sandilands Report drew attention away from *The Corporate Report*—a possibility that was in effect acknowledged by the (then) chairman of the ASSC, Sir Ronald Leach, in his Foreword to the discussion paper when he specifically drew attention to the contribution of both documents to 'the fundamental problem of measurement of profit'. The 'great inflation accounting debate' has occupied the centre of the stage ever since, and the far more fundamental issues concerning the scope and nature of financial reporting dealt with in *The Corporate Report* have received scant attention. The discussion paper has faded away into history—one suspects to the profession's great relief.

Meanwhile, the Accounting Standards Committee (ASC) has had to get on with its business without the benefit of a CF. Its difficulties are considerable, if the controversies surrounding its attempts to produce a generally acceptable inflation accounting standard, for example, are anything to go by.

The latest attempt to develop a CF comes from Canada (CICA, 1980). The contents of *Corporate Reporting* are similar to those of *The Corporate Report* in a number of respects—which is not particularly surprising bearing in mind that its sole author, Edward Stamp, was a member of the committee which produced the ASC discussion paper. Also, like *The Corporate Report* and unlike either the Trueblood Report or the FASB conceptual framework programme, *Corporate Reporting* was produced very quickly at negligible cost. Unlike either of its predecessors, *Corporate Reporting* attempts to deal with the subject of what a CF is for and how it is intended to assist standard setters; attention is devoted to the Canadian business and accounting environment. Stamp opts for an evolutionary approach, as distinct from the FASB's normative approach, and sees the function of a CF as providing objectives and criteria which CICA's Accounting Research Committee can use not in a strictly deductive fashion but as tools in developing standards in a manner analogous to common law.

It is too early to form a view on the profession's reactions to Stamp's proposals. Initial reactions have focussed, in the main, on the case made by Stamp that Canada needs a CF appropriate to its particular cultural and institutional needs; some commentators take the view that the most cost-effective line for the Canadian profession and business community to take is simply to adopt the FASB's standards except when clear and compelling local concerns dictate otherwise. This particular issue is peculiar to Canada and is beyond the scope of the present article.

### A Brief Review of the Academic Literature

Academics have not neglected the subject of financial accounting standard setting and theory development. Perhaps the research most compatible with the type of programme being undertaken by the FASB, for example, is what is sometimes referred to as 'a priori theorising': the development and rationalisation, by means of deductive and inductive methods of reasoning, of systems of business accounting valuation and profit measurement. Certain types of empirical research can be and have been of direct and obvious value as well. The information economics approach, however, opens up a much wider perspective, one that brings the standard setting machinery and specific measurement and disclosure issues into one common framework.

Two consequences of the information economics approach to accounting theory development are worth noting. First, there is wider appreciation now in academic circles of the problems and pressures which quasi-official standard-setting bodies such as the FASB and the ASC have to deal with. This is the most positive result of the new approach. The tendency among academics to judge the output of the accounting policy-making process by some absolute standard of truth or private utility has greatly diminished as a result of this research. Second, there is a great deal of scepticism nowadays among academics about the worthwhileness of attempting to base accounting standard setting on a 'generally agreed' CF.

The information economics approach assumes that the various parties involved in standard setting (managers, the profession, users, etc.) are concerned with furthering their own interests and objectives, and not with ensuring that financial accounting standards meet the 'basic objectives of financial reporting'. Following this line of thought, Dopuch and Sunder (1980, p. 18) argue that

> There is little evidence that official statements of objectives of financial accounting have had any direct effect on the determination of financial accounting standards. Whenever the APB or the FASB has had to consider a financial accounting standard, various interest groups presented arguments to support the methods that each perceived to be in its own best interests. The standards issued had to be compromises among the contending interests.

Support for this pessimistic view is provided by Watts and Zimmerman (1978) who examined the corporate submissions made to the FASB concerning its Discussion Memorandum on 'Reporting the Effects of General Price-Level Changes in Financial Statements'.

It is not only managers, auditors and users whose views and submissions are subject to this sceptical evaluation; accounting theorists are given the same treatment. They are concerned with the pursuit of their own self-interest, in the sense of being active participants in the 'market for excuses'. Watts and Zimmerman (1979) argue that, in a regulated economy, financial accounting statements can have important and varying effects on the welfare of individuals and organisations affected by rate settings, anti-trust, labour negotiations, etc; therefore different parties want 'respectable' (in the sense of appealing to the 'public interest') accounting theories which will serve their cause.

Cushing (1977) suggests that the theorists who reject the possibility of finding an unobjectionable social welfare function (i.e. social goals which everyone is bound to accept) may be overstating the problem. In practice, society *is* able to reach decisions about the provision of 'collective' goods (which financial statements can be viewed as being) by the use of a partial, piecemeal approach. (This, in fact, is how accounting standard setters are proceeding—the continuing 'search' for a CF notwithstanding.) Cushing's suggestion, in effect, is that accounting policy makers should take a leaf out of the cost-benefit analyst's book and tackle problems one at a time, holding constant the welfare principles of concern in other areas of controversy.

Bromwich (1980) considers some of the conditions necessary for Cushing's partial standards approach to maximize the welfare of an individual using published financial reports for decision-making purposes. Bromwich shows that the individual's preferences (utility function) have to be somewhat unusual. This leads him to conclude that accounting policy makers, if they are to employ a partial standards approach in an unobjectionable manner, need to consider simultaneously accounting standards which display any significant element of interdependence. Although not despairing, Bromwich offers little comfort to those who would like to see standard setting put on a 'sound' basis secured upon a generally accepted CF.

## A MODEL OF THE UK STANDARD-SETTING PROCESS

The above review of professional and academic developments hardly does justice to past and current thinking. However, it sketches out salient aspects of the present state-of-the-art and background developments. In this section an attempt will be

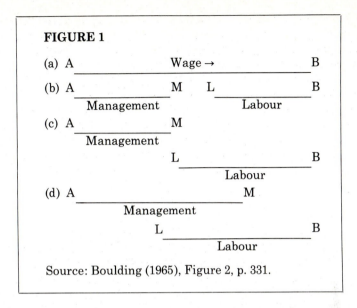

FIGURE 1

(a) A ———————————— Wage → ———————— B

(b) A ——————— M    L ——————————— B
     Management       Labour

(c) A ——————— M
     Management

         L ————————————— B
              Labour

(d) A ——————————————— M
       Management

     L ————————————— B
         Labour

Source: Boulding (1965), Figure 2, p. 331.

made to put some flesh on the bones of the earlier arguments in such a way that the essentially political nature of the standard-setting process will be brought out.

Standard-setting mechanisms such as the SEC, the FASB and the ASC have been brought into existence in order to deal with the conflicts of interest which exist in corporate reporting. The SEC, of course, is a government agency and, as such, has residual powers of enforcement denied to the FASB and the ASC. However, as the SEC has, by and large, delegated the setting of accounting standards to the FASB the distinction need not detain us. FASB and ASC have to deal with a variety of conflicts of interest and pressures, balancing one against the other. This is what is of interest here.

Use is made below of a model of conflict resolution devised by Kenneth Boulding (1965), an economist noted for his contributions to the literature on peace and conflict. The model is intended to throw light on the *dynamics* of bargaining and conflict such as in wage negotiations. It is helpful to go through the model with this application in mind and then to apply the model to standard setting.

Figure 1 concerns labour-management bargaining to fix a wage. A wage increases from A to B. In (b), labour will agree to any wage above L, and management will agree to any wage below M. But, as M is less than L, no agreement is possible. Negotiations will take place aimed at changing the positions of M and/or L. Management will try to persuade labour to lower L; labour will try to persuade management of the justice of L and that the firm can afford a greater wage, all in the hope of raising M. In the event of deadlock, there may be recourse to threats of strikes and lockouts. However, if such threats have to be carried out, both management and labour can be the losers. In the Figure, (c) represents a point where the gap between M and L has dropped to zero and a bargain can be struck. But, even where both parties recognise the dangers of conflict, there are difficulties in getting from (b) to (c). As Boulding (1965, p. 331) points out: 'Many of the difficulties in conflict situations arise out of the fact that in the actual division of the spoils of the bargaining process, victory tends to go to the recalcitrant.'

The parallels with management-labour negotiations are far from obvious but, nevertheless, often instructive. No longer is the conflict of the classical 'us' and 'them' variety. Instead, there are several parties involved; the mixture depends on the particular issue at stake, although corporate managements and the auditing profession are invariably interested in the outcome. Sometimes the unions, public interest pressure groups, government departments, and the investment community have an interest as well. On occasion, different corporate managements may be on opposite sides of the fence (e.g. over the proposal to include a monetary items adjustment in a current value accounting standard). In terms of Figure 1, 'management' remains as management (generally); 'labour' becomes the variety of parties with an interest in the particular accounting issue (e.g. investors and the Bank of England); for 'wage' now read 'the accounting issue in question' (e.g. 'accounting for foreign currency transactions', or 'current value accounting'). One can view the ASC as an arbitrator in a labour negotiation: the objective is somehow to bring M and L together.

To this point, the analogy between wage bargaining may seem uninteresting if not downright fanciful. After all, (b) in Figure 1 hardly represents most standard-setting disputes. The problem is usually not that different interest groups take up wholly incompatible positions, but that there is a variety of options open, each of which is acceptable to many (if not all) of the groups, the difficulty being to choose between the options. In other words the analogy is more often likely to be with the situation depicted in (d).

Figure 1(d) depicts what on first sight appears to be a non-conflict case: the minimum payoff required, L, is less than the opposition's maximum, M. In terms of the wage negotiation example, the minimum wage which labour will settle for is less than the maximum wage management is willing to pay. What could be better? The issue, though, is the whereabouts of the final settlement in the range of ambiguity, LM. If the wage is struck near L, management will obtain the bulk of the gains; conversely, if the wage bargain is struck near M, labour will take the lion's share. As Boulding (1965, p. 332) notes, 'a great deal depends upon the realism of the perception of the parties'. If labour appreciates the existence and extent of the LM overlap, but management does not, labour will have a very strong incentive to raise its L to near M, thereby securing gains that it previously could not have hoped for, and thus moving from (d) to (c). However, if management also comes to appreciate the extent of the LM overhang, it will be inclined to pull back M to near L. A consequence of *both* labour and management coming to appreciate the bargaining gains to be made can therefore be to change a situation full of opportunities for cooperation to one of conflict (b).

The same thing can happen in disputes over accounting standards. Different groups interested in a particular standard may start out with helpful attitudes, such as a strong desire to reach agreement, and with no very demanding or controversial requirements to be met. In this case they are likely to be in a situation like (d). Let us examine an hypothetical dispute over how best to take account of price changes in a period of rapid inflation. In particular, suppose that the business community is concerned about the destructive effects on business investment of taxation based on historical cost accounts and of wage claims based on 'inflated' profit figures. However, managers of businesses that are not capital-intensive are not greatly exercised over the subject and may well be sympathetic to the pleas of their less fortunate brethren. The unions are indifferent to the whole subject, regarding it as a 'technical' accounting matter of little relevance to wage negotiations. Furthermore, the government is concerned to maintain its tax revenue base but is mindful of the fact that punitive taxation that results in a rash of bankruptcies, falling investment and losses of industrial output is not likely to achieve this end in all but the very short run. A government Committee of Enquiry is set up and produces a set of Current Cost Accounting (CCA) proposals much like those contained in the Sandilands Report. All in all, the conditions of this hypothetical example might well be like (d) (with 'labour' representing the hardpressed industrial companies and 'management' signifying the government and managers of unaffected types of businesses such as banks). All seems to be set for the introduction of a CCA standard. Everything points to a solution very close to L in (d).

Matters do not rest there, however. Managers of the 'unaffected' financial institutions come to realise that all the benefits of this accounting standard are accruing to industrial companies and that the financial institutions gain nothing. Indeed, research studies suggest that, under the terms of the proposed CCA standard, the reported profits of industrial companies will be slashed; at the same time, inflation and accompanying high nominal interest rates have pushed up the profits of 'unaffected' financial institutions to record levels. Far from being unaffected by the new standard, banks, other financial institutions, retail stores, and the like now appear to be making huge profits relative to industrial companies. There is even a likelihood that the government will try to maintain its flow of tax revenues from the corporate sector by shifting more of the burden to the financial institutions. It would be surprising in these circumstances if financial businesses did not clamour for some kind of 'relief' as well—perhaps by the inclusion of 'money items adjustments' in the standard. At the same time, industrial companies with large net money indebtedness can be expected to object to these departures from the 'pure' CCA system. The overall result might be that the situation changes from one like that depicted in (d) to that in (b).

Consider what happens when the parties are deadlocked as depicted in (b). The observations of Boulding (1965, p. 330) on how deadlock can be broken are of interest:

> An important principle which is often overlooked is that the parties that have reached a conflict set relevant to a state of the world defined by only a few variables can frequently break the impasse and open up opportunities for further trading and further benign moves by *widening the agenda*, that is, by introducing new variables into the relationship. We notice this phenomenon, for instance, in collective bargaining in industrial relations where *there is a strong tendency to proliferate clauses in the contract, partly at least because this opens up further opportunities for bargaining*. An impasse in bargaining about wages and hours may be broken if various other fringe benefits, job security, procedural relationships, and so forth are thrown into the bargaining process. (Emphasis added.)

In terms of Figure 1, a settlement is obtained such that (b) is changed to (c) by the parties doing business on something other than wages, i.e. on an aspect of their relationship not in dispute. Examples of such behaviour are commonplace in the wider political arena. In accounting, progress might be made by the parties involved in the dispute *obscuring the issues* at stake. To a 'negotiator' trying to find common ground, theoretical clarity need not be a virtue; logical consistency might be unattainable.

This brings us back to the search for a Conceptual Framework from which 'generally acceptable' accounting standards can be derived in a logical manner. If the analysis of this section is at all near the mark, it is difficult to avoid concluding that a CF is largely irrelevant to the needs of the ASC as presently constituted. *In a system highly dependent on the cooperation and goodwill of reporting companies, the ASC needs to preserve its freedom to bargain and hence to obfuscate points in dispute. Viewed from the ASC's perspective, a CF might be more of a hindrance than a help. Flexibility is all important; but flexibility seems to be what a CF is intended to eliminate.*

Accounting standards are produced in Britain by what is, in essence, a bargaining process. The ASC is the more or less private property of the professional accounting bodies and has little or no power which it can employ to enforce its standards. Therefore, the ASC has no choice but to try to obtain the cooperation of the companies affected by its pronouncements and the agreement of the bulk of practising accountants. The weakness of the ASC's position was illustrated in dramatic fashion by the revolt of the members of the ICAEW to ED18 (ASC, 1976). There is little that the ASC can do when faced by a determined opposition. Experience has shown that the ASC has no powerful friends to whom it can look for support in times of trouble.

The FASB is in a somewhat different position. It is true, of course, that the FASB lacks power and often seems to be without influential friends. But in the final analysis the FASB derives its authority from the power which the 1933 and 1934 Securities Acts confer on the SEC. Indeed, the American accounting profession's involvement in the setting of disclosure standards can be directly traced to political pressures. Prior to 1930, auditing procedures and terminology were the dominant concerns of the accounting profession (Zeff, 1972, p. 119). But the 1933 and 1934 Acts changed all that. The Acts are concerned with the issue and trading of companny securities, and confer on the SEC broad authority to determine the accounting and auditing practices used by companies in the preparation of reports required under the Acts. Nowadays, the SEC largely delegates these powers to the FASB; the SEC exercises control on a 'management by exception' basis, there remaining the very real possibility that it would intervene whenever the FASB issues a standard which arouses opposition sufficient to muster political support of the kind likely to cause difficulties for the SEC itself or which contradicts a firmly-held SEC view.[3] (The SEC's introduction of a replacement cost disclosure requirement of 10-K registrants is a recent example.) The SEC has influence over the behaviour of registrant companies denied to the FASB. Therefore the FASB's freedom to bargain is somewhat circumscribed; it has the SEC (and sometimes *ad hoc* committees of the Senate) to contend with.

In Britain, government departments play a small part in standard setting. Of course, the government of the day is a force to be reckoned with, as the intervention of the Heath Administration over inflation accounting demonstrated. Nevertheless, government is just another of the parties that the ASC has to take account of and bargain with. In the United States, accounting policy making is an inherently

---

[3] Needless to say, the SEC often does accept standards of which it does not approve, e.g. the standard on capitalisation of interest. SEC disapproval is a necessary but not sufficient condition for its intervention in standard setting. Another necessary (perhaps sufficient) condition appears to be the build-up of political pressure of the kind we have tried to model above.

political activity as a consequence of the SEC's involvement in and overseeing of corporate financial disclosure; in Britain, it is largely a matter of bargaining between interest groups.

Whether the differences in the circumstances of the FASB and the ASC are greater than the similarities is an interesting question; but it is not one on which we need dwell. For our purposes it is sufficient to note that the FASB seems to have a greater yearning for a CF than does the ASC: the FASB has accorded the highest priority to its 'Objectives and Elements' study, avowedly setting great store in the possibilities a CF will afford for putting its standards programme on a sound footing; whereas the ASC seems to be very sceptical about the possibilities of a substantial pay-off from such efforts (ASC, 1978). This difference of opinion may be due to variations in temperament, education, etc., between the two countries, or it might be due to the different needs and pressures faced by standard setters in a political regulatory environment versus those in a largely unregulated one. It is to this latter possibility that we now turn.

## THE ALTERNATIVES

Whether or not a CF has anything major to contribute to corporate financial disclosure in general, and to accounting standard setting in particular, depends on the ways in which financial reporting is organised and policed. There are many different ways of organising and policing corporate disclosure. Three seem worthy of special attention:[4] (1) more or less complete *laissez-faire*; (2) state control and supervision; (3) delegation of power to the profession. These forms of organisation have been widely discussed in the literature. Each is considered briefly below.

### Laissez-faire

One way of organising corporate disclosure is not to attempt to organise it at all. In the extreme, there would be no legal disclosure rules of any kind, not even rules governing disclosure to shareholders in general meeting of the kind set out in the British Companies Acts and in the corporation laws of most American states. A modified form of *laissez-faire* is where statutory provision is made for the disclosure of information (financial and otherwise) to clearly defined parties, such as shareholders of record and creditors, who have legal property rights in the enterprise; the information ('right to know') provisions are made part and parcel of the granting of limited liability.

---

[4] Perhaps a fourth could be added: where accounting is 'regulated' by setting up an Accounting Court to which dissatisfied parties could appeal against corporate accounting practices which offend them. As, strictly speaking, an Accounting Court does not provide an alternative regulatory means or environment but is an addition to one of the three models discussed above, it is not treated separately. The only country which seems to have anything resembling an Accounting Court is the Netherlands, where, in a largely unregulated environment similar in many (but not all) respects to the British one, there was established in 1971 the Enterprise Chamber which is a special section of the Court of Justice. The main role of the Enterprise Chamber seems to be that of providing some kind of lower bound to reporting standards and, in particular, to put pressure (via publicity) on the auditing profession. Klaassen (1980, p. 340) argues that the court cases he has examined 'demonstrate that a company court is not a proper institution to produce accounting standards'.

It is likely that information will be provided to investors in excess of that demanded in law (assuming, of course, that the legal provisions are not particularly onerous). Promoters and managers of companies have financial incentives to contract to supply audited financial statements. If they do not incorporate, in the articles of association and in private lending contracts, provisions governing such supply then they will encounter great difficulty in raising finance at low cost (Jensen and Meckling, 1976). The various contracting parties (i.e. managers and owner-managers, outside investors, creditors, and union negotiators) will presumably weigh the costs and benefits of various alternative contractual arrangements in order to ascertain which disclosure and 'bonding' package has the best pay-off for each.

The purpose of disclosure agreements in an unregulated economy is to reduce *agency costs*. As Watts and Zimmerman (1979, p. 276) point out:

> Agency costs arise because the manager's (the agent's) interests do not necessarily coincide with the interests of shareholders or bondholders (the principals). For example, the manager (if he owns shares) has incentives to convert assets of the corporation into dividends, thus leaving the bondholders with the "shell" of the corporation. Similarly, the manager has incentives to transfer wealth to himself at the expense of both the shareholders and bondholders (e.g., via perquisites).

As agency costs may vary in amount and character from firm to firm, it follows that disclosure practices may vary between firms (and within a firm over time) *and with very good reason* (Watts, 1977). In fact, comparability may be desired by none of the parties involved. This is because what appears to be chaotic accounting practices or debenture-bonding arrangements may be, on the contrary, an equilibrium set of contractual devices which minimises the agency costs associated with the separation of management from control and with conflicts of interests between different classes of investors.

Auditing is an important activity in an unregulated economy. Indeed, it is one of the main ways of reducing agency costs: agency costs will not be reduced if the financial disclosures of management are not deemed credible and, as Stamp and Moonitz (1978, p. 23) point out, 'it can be said that the function of auditing is to lend credibility to financial statements.' Of course, there are those who view external auditing as a largely useless legal imposition which would (presumably) not come about (in present form) in an unregulated economy. Consider, for example, the views of Briston and Perks (1977, p. 48):

> We contend that neither the shareholder nor management derives obvious substantial benefit from the external audit process. The management of the company suffers disruption of its accounting and internal control systems as a result of the audit investigation and pressure upon its cash flow due to the monetary cost of the audit.... The auditor is not at all concerned that the published accounts are largely irrelevant to shareholders, whose information needs relate to future plans and forecasts of the company and assessments of its past and present efficiency.

There is no evidence known to the present author to support these assertions of Briston and Perks. On the contrary, auditing of much less impressive financial statements compiled on similar bases to those published nowadays was commonplace *before* statutory provision was made for mandatory audits (Watts and Zimmerman, 1979; Mumford, 1980). Moreover, agency theory suggests that published accounts are far from being 'largely irrelevant' to shareholders nor are audits of the same. Auditing is a 'contract compliance' cost (Demski and Feltham, 1976, p. 203).

Returning to the more general question of disclosure, even in an unregulated economy one can expect pressures to grow for professional accounting institutes to give some kind of 'guidance' or 'lead' in financial accounting matters. It is very difficult (if not impossible) to spell out, in the articles of association and in lending contracts, in sufficient detail the kinds of disclosures which will achieve the desired savings in agency costs. Recourse will almost certainly have to be had to poorly-specified terms such as 'profit' and 'financial position'; auditors will be asked to express a general 'opinion', such as whether or not the disclosures present a 'true and fair view'. It will, very probably, be cost-effective if the auditing profession pools its resources and sets up central agencies to provide guidance in these matters. There is a very great likelihood of a body along the lines of the ASC being set up even in an entirely unregulated economy. Indeed, the British standard-setting arrangements are largely the creation of the auditing profession and the business community, with the government playing a very minor role.

### State Control

It is instructive to pass to the opposite extreme, to consider what might happen in a totally regulated economy (i.e., totally regulated as far as the production and dissemination of corporate financial statements are concerned).

An unregulated economy does not necessarily produce economic 'goods' of the type, quantity and frequency which all—or even any—of the parties involved agree is optimal. With certain types of goods it can happen that the productive outcome brought about by all the parties bargaining and transacting on an individual basis is universally agreed to be inferior to the outcome that they collectively prefer. This can arise with a 'social good', that is good with the characteristic, *inter alia*, of being able to be consumed by more than one person and where other consumers cannot easily be excluded from consumption. In such a case, where free-riders are a problem, a collusive outcome can be superior for all or some and not worse for any if, but only if, it can be ensured that all the parties will cooperate. In general, a non-cooperative outcome involves less output of the good than does the collusive optimum (Van den Doel, 1979, ch. 2). Regulation of the output of social goods may be the only way of achieving the generally desired outcome. The difference between the non-cooperative and the collusive solutions corresponds to Rousseau's distinction between 'the will of all' and 'the general will' (Sen, 1967).

Published financial statements of companies can usefully be viewed as social goods. Of course, to managements interested in reducing agency costs and to actual and prospective investors they are private goods. But to the wider public which is interested, for example, in investing in rival companies or in assessing the extent of monopoly power, published accounting information is a social good.

Some would argue that published financial statements are social goods as far as the investing public is concerned, although the issue is the subject of great dispute (Benston, 1976). Certainly this line of thinking underlay the establishment of the SEC in the United States: 'full' disclosure is needed to reduce the incentives to insider trading the occurrence of which is a disincentive to external investment. Investment is important not only to the investors and firms directly involved but also to the public at large; the general will is involved.

State control and supervision of production is one frequently proffered solution to the social goods problem; another is to impose taxes and provide grants and other incentives to encourage the socially optimal level of output. In the case of accounting in Britain and America, the former solution has been adopted *in part*. Companies are compelled by law to make publicly available certain kinds of information. Legal provision is made for compulsory audit of the published data. In addition, in the USA, the SEC has a responsibility to ensure proper financial disclosure and has considerable powers (over 10-K filings) to this end. (State control in the sense of the state taking over the production of the social good is not really feasible in accounting.) But the amount of control over accounting exercised by government in Britain and America is not very great. In the USA the amount of control actually exercised by the SEC is rather small: the regulators take a watching brief, in the main, intervening very little, and effectively delegating day-to-day responsibility to the profession.

Another reason sometimes advanced for government regulation and control (of part or the whole) of the economy is to effect a change in the distribution of income and wealth in society. In a limited sense, the SEC's concern with protecting the 'lay' investor can be explained in these terms. As this is a concern of a strictly political nature, it is clear that responsibility and control must reside in the political arena. There seems to be no real role for professional accounting standard setters here, and hence no obvious reason for incorporating such considerations into a CF.

Consider the hypothetical situation in which private sector corporate financial accounting is under the strict control of a state regulatory agency. Regulations and accounting standards are laid down in considerable detail by the agency's officials. There might well be a scale of penalties for non-compliance with the regulations and standards; at a minimum, auditors will be expected to express their opinion (as to whether a true and fair view is being shown) in terms of compliance with the regulations and standards. What role is there for a CF along the lines of say SFAC1? The answer must surely be: precious little. The situation described is very much like that in the government—particularly the local government—sector of the economy. Standards are developed internally by the government bureaucracy, modified on occasion as a consequence of external pressures made effective through the political process.

### Delegation to the Profession

Delegation can take one of three forms. There can be a delegation by the regulatory agency of responsibility to the accounting profession but with power being retained by the agency. This is the arrangement in the USA, the FASB and the AICPA together being charged with responsibility for the governance of corporate reporting standards, but real power residing in the hands of the SEC and the other government agencies. Alternatively, power can reside in the hands of the accounting profession and responsibility in those of a government agency. (This is a somewhat implausible alternative and is included here only for completeness.) A third alternative is for both responsibility and (*de facto* and *de jure*) power to be put in the hands of the profession. An example of this is to be found in Canada. Canadian Federal law requires that accounting standards, as laid down from time to time in the

Canadian Institute's Handbook, *must* be used by Canadian corporations (incorporated under the Federal Act) in producing their published financial reports (Stamp, 1979, p. 23).

The lot of the profession in America is not a happy one. The FASB and the AICPA are being urged more or less continually by the committees of the House and the Senate, sundry government agencies and interested politicians to 'do something'. There is the ever-present threat that, if the FASB does not improve the state of company reporting, then the SEC will take over the setting of accounting standards. The business community and constituent parts of the profession all agree that this would be undesirable—it would, after all, reduce their influence on and control of the standard-setting process. On the other hand, particular business corporations and audit firms individually have strong incentives, on occasion, to disregard their acknowledged common interests and pursue their private interests—especially as the FASB is without power to stop them doing so. In the absence of coercion, the will of all (consisting of the separate wills of autonomous, independent individuals) does not correspond to the general will. The FASB can, of course, appeal to the SEC for help in enforcing its standards; but the results of such an appeal are by no means certain to be in the FASB's favour.

Companies and audit firms in conflict with the FASB can also appeal to the SEC both directly and via the wider political process. These other appellants may be able to muster powerful political support, say by 'log-rolling', i.e. conjoining the issue in question with another perhaps distant matter of considerable importance to the politicians (e.g. by offering financial and other support in a coming election). In such a case, the FASB might well find the SEC declining to help or even actively intervening against it. The result of such failure of the SEC to support the FASB is great damage to the prestige and hence the effectiveness of the FASB, thereby making the latter body reluctant to take on determined flouters of its accounting standards. An inevitable consequence of this kind of defeat is the public emphasis of the powerlessness of the standard-setting organisation. Thus, the FASB is in the worst of all worlds. Generally speaking, it is as dependent as is the ASC on the cooperation of business firms and their auditors, and hence has to do a great deal of wheeling and dealing; but it also has criticisms from the SEC and most other branches of government as well. All in all, the main beneficiary of the American responsibility-without-power form of delegation seems to be the SEC which can discharge its statutory obligations in a virtually risk-free manner.

It is not surprising that the FASB places so much emphasis on the importance of developing a CF; by doing so the FASB provides a (partial) answer to its critics: all will be well when the 'objectives and elements' of financial statements are determined. A cynic might argue that the CF programme is nothing more than a delaying tactic. Such cynicism is surely misplaced; if this had been the motive, the FASB would not have been so foolish as actually to *produce* (in parts) its conceptual framework. A more likely explanation for the FASB's professed faith in its CF programme is that, given its obvious lack of power (or powerful friends), it perceives a need to show that its heart and mind are in the right place: to demonstrate that it is trying by logical means to develop accounting standards based on principles of general appeal. More will be said on this point below.

The Canadian arrangement, whereby both responsibility and power are delegated to the profession, seems to have more to commend it as far as the profession and the business community in general are concerned. After all, the Canadian

Institute is likely to be more responsive to the needs and concerns of those it exists to serve, and less whimsical and better informed on business matters than is the wider polity. Power is located where responsibility lies; hence accounting policy decisions are likely to take account of all the issues currently dealt with in divided fashion by the FASB and the SEC in the USA.

It could be argued, of course, that the Canadian Institute is likely to be too influenced by the narrow self-interest of accountants and auditors (and of the business community they serve); that the wider public interest is badly served by such an arrangement; that power rightly belongs in and only in the hands of the government and its agencies. May be this is so. However, sight should not be lost of the fact that the medical profession gets by with delegated powers of this kind without exciting too much hostility. As Stamp (1979, pp. 23–24) points out:

> Anyone who believes that such a system of legislative backing is objectionable, and who thinks that Parliament should be actively involved in the standard setting process, should reflect upon how he would feel if the same attitude were to be adopted by Parliament towards the setting of standards of medical practice.

Besides, the conjoining of power *and* responsibility in the hands of the profession leaves it wide open to public criticism if it is insensitive to the interests and needs of groups affected by its pronouncements. In any event disaffected parties still have access to the general political process: in the same way that legislation puts power in the hands of the Canadian Institute, disabling legislation can also be enacted at a future date.

The Canadian Institute would appear to have a great need of a CF. How can it show that its efforts at developing (and enforcing) accounting standards are proceeding in a fair, logical and highly professional manner other than by setting out the framework within which it is operating? As the main argument offered for delegating power to the profession is that accountants have essential technical skills denied to legislators and civil servants, it follows that the standard setters will have to produce standards which are seen not to conflict with this central assertion.

## CONCLUDING REMARKS

The preceding sections can be summarised as follows:

1.  There have been a number of attempts by the profession to develop a CF. All were undertaken at a time when the standard setting programme had run into trouble. None of them seems to have been of obvious value to the standard setters.
2.  Academic researchers have tried in a variety of ways to throw some light on the issues and problems involved. Recently, considerable emphasis has been placed on what might be called the 'public choice' dimensions of financial accounting. Generally, the conclusions of such research have been discouraging to those in the profession interested in developing a CF that is capable of putting the accounting standards programme on a 'sound' footing.

3. British accounting has been analysed in terms of a bargaining model on the (not unrealistic) assumption that the ASC has little power and has to negotiate with groups whose interests may be in conflict. Little prospect is held out of a CF being of much direct help in such an environment.

4. Three different accounting 'environments' were examined. In only one did there appear to be an obvious role for a CF: where both responsibility and power is delegated to a body such as the ASC, as in Canada.

It has been assumed throughout that the purpose of developing a CF is to provide a basis for the creation of accounting standards. It has been tentatively concluded that only where both responsibility and power is delegated to the ASC is it likely that a CF has much to contribute. However, there is another way of viewing the role of a CF. Rather than providing a framework or platform for the standards programme, the CF could be intended to do no more than provide very broad general objectives for financial reporting to which no one could take serious objection; the aim would be to 'raise the moral tone' of the profession. The pressures and conflicts which the ASC has to handle would then cause no serious difficulty, as the CF would be expressed in sufficiently general terms as to avoid cramping the ASC's style. Indeed, to the extent that the documents which are currently in existence are statements of broad goals, they well serve this general purpose. Goals are achieved to a greater or lesser extent; they do not necessarily imply a moral or political imperative.

The role of such a tone-raising CF could be a valuable one. After all, much of the preceding analysis takes a somewhat dismal view of the motivations and interests of the people and organisations affected directly and indirectly by accounting standards. Conflicts of interest are seen to be a serious problem which the ASC has to deal with. One way of dealing with conflicts of interest is to try to encourage a feeling of common destiny and thereby reduce those conflicts (the siege syndrome). There is, after all, some evidence to suggest that accountants and businessmen do share beliefs about what is and is not good accounting. Perhaps these shared sentiments could be nurtured and strengthened. In which case, the purpose of a CF should be to encourage what might be called a 'professional' attitude.

Perhaps this is what the FASB's Conceptual Framework programme will yield. Needless to say, sceptics abound who suggest that, when enlightenment and self-interest are in conflict, enlightenment is the first to yield. There is more chance of success when self-interest is itself enlightened; i.e. when individuals are motivated by enlightened self-interest. This seems most likely to occur when there is a mechanism for ensuring that all parties keep to the (enlightened) bargain. The ASC needs power. For arguments on similar lines see Stamp (1979).

The problem of conflict has been stressed throughout. There are two main sources of conflict: conflict due to differences of opinion about consequences, and conflicts of interest. There is a need to distinguish between these two sources of conflict, wherever possible. This article has concentrated on the problem of conflicts of interest. However, many of the conflicts of opinion in accounting are due to lack of concrete knowledge about the consequences of various kinds of disclosures. A CF cannot eliminate consequence conflicts. Research is the only likely source of an answer.

It is appropriate to conclude by suggesting the appropriate structure for a 'real' CF designed to provide a base for the standards programme. If a CF is to serve as a guide to the standard setters then it should, in effect, provide them with a set of objectives and constraints. (Strictly speaking, accounting cannot have objectives; only people can (Chambers, 1976).) At a minimum, it seems essential to provide the elements of a 'constitution'. The framework should therefore set out: the basic principles of and sources of authority for 'accountability' and 'rights to know'; the consequences which financial reports are intended to have (and to avoid); the trade-offs which have to be made.

## REFERENCES

Accounting Standards (Steering) Committee (1975), *The Corporate Report: A Discussion Paper*.

Accounting Standards Committee (1976), Exposure Draft 18, *Current Cost Accounting*.

Accounting Standards Committee (1978), *Setting Accounting Standards: A Consultative Document*.

American Accounting Association (1966), Committee to Prepare a Statement of Basic Accounting Theory. *A Statement of Basic Accounting Theory*.

American Accounting Association (1977), Committee on Concepts and Standards for External Financial Reports, *Statement on Accounting Theory and Theory Acceptance*.

American Institute of Certified Public Accountants (1970), Accounting Principles Board, APB Statement No. 4, *Basic Concepts and Accounting Principles Underlying Financial Statements of Business Enterprises*.

American Institute of Certified Public Accountants (1972), Report of the Study Group on Establishment of Accounting Principles, *Establishing Financial Accounting Standards*.

American Institute of Certified Public Accountants (1973), Report of the Accounting Objectives Study Group (chairman, R. M. Trueblood), *Objectives of Financial Statements*.

Benston, G. J. (1976), *Corporate Disclosure in the UK and the USA* (Saxon House).

Boulding, K. E. (1965), 'The Economics of Human Conflict', in E. B. McNeil (ed.), *The Nature of Human Conflict* (Prentice-Hall), pp. 172–191; reprinted in K. E. Boulding and F. R. Glake (eds), *Collected Papers. Volume Two: Economics* (Colorado Associated University Press, 1971), pp. 325–344.

Briston, R. and R. Perks, 'The External Auditor—His Role and Cost to Society', *Accountancy* (November 1977), pp. 48–52.

Bromwich, M. (1980), 'The Possibility of Partial Accounting Standards', *Accounting Review* (April 1980), pp. 288–300.

Canadian Institute of Chartered Accountants (1980), *Corporate Reporting: Its Future Evolution*.

Chambers, R. J. (1976), 'The Functions of Published Financial Statements', *Accounting and Business Research* (Spring 1976), pp. 83–94.

Cushing, B. E. (1977), 'On the Possibility of Optimal Accounting Principles', *Accounting Review* (April 1977), pp. 308–321.

Demski, J. S., and G. A. Feltham (1976), *Cost Determination: A Conceptual Approach* (Iowa State University Press).

Dopuch, N. and S. Sunder (1980), 'FASB's Statements on Objectives and Elements of Financial Accounting: A Review', *Accounting Review* (January 1980), pp. 1–21.

Financial Accounting Standards Board (1974), FASB Discussion Memorandum, *Conceptual Framework for Accounting and Reporting: Consideration of the Report of the Study Group on the Objectives of Financial Statements.*

Financial Accounting Standards Board (1977), Exposure Draft of Proposed Statement of Financial Accounting Concepts, *Objectives of Financial Reporting and Elements of Financial Statements of Business Enterprises.*

Financial Accounting Standards Board (1978), Statement of Financial Accounting Concepts No. 1, *Objectives of Financial Reporting by Business Enterprises.*

Financial Accounting Standards Board (1980a), Statement of Financial Accounting Concepts No. 1, *Qualitative Characteristics of Accounting Information.*

Financial Accounting Standards Board (1980c), *Objectives of Financial Reporting by Non Business Organizations.*

Her Majesty's Government (1977), Secretary of State for Trade, Cmnd. 6888, *The Future of Company Reports: A Consultative Document* (HMSO).

Institute of Chartered Accountants in England and Wales (1952), Recommendation on Accounting Principles No. 15, *Accounting in Relation to Changes in the Purchasing Power of Money.*

Jensen, M. C. and W. H. Meckling (1976), 'Theory of the Firm: Managerial Behavior, Agency Costs and Ownership Structure', *Journal of Financial Economics* (October 1976), pp. 305–360.

Klaassen, J. (1980). 'An Accounting Court: The Impact of the Enterprise Chamber on Financial Reporting in the Netherlands', *Accounting Review* (April 1980), pp. 327–341.

Moonitz, M. (1961), Accounting Research Study No. 1, *The Basic Postulates of Accounting* (AICPA).

Mumford, M. J. (1980), 'Accounting Information and Bargaining: An Historical Study of Some Early American Accounts' (unpublished working paper, University of Lancaster).

Sandilands, F. E. P., chairman (1975), Report of the Inflation Accounting Committee, Cmnd. 6225, *Inflation Accounting* (HMSO).

Scott, G. and M. Decelles (1980), 'United States: Objectives of Financial Reporting Revisited', *Accountant's Magazine* (February, 1980).

Sen, A. K. (1967), 'Isolation, Assurance and the Social Rate of Discount', *Quarterly Journal of Economics*, Vol. 81, pp. 112–24.

Sprouse, R. T. and M. Moonitz (1962), Accounting Research Study No 3, *A Tentative Set of Broad Accounting Principles for Business Enterprises* (AICPA).

Stamp, E. and M. Moonitz (1978), *International Auditing Standards* (Prentice-Hall).

Stamp, E. (1979), ICRA Occasional Paper No. 18, *The Future of Accounting and Auditing Standards* (International Centre for Research in Accounting, University of Lancaster).

Van den Doel, H. (1979), *Democracy and Welfare Economics* (Cambridge University Press).

Watts, R. L. (1977), 'Corporate Financial Statements: A Product of the Market and Political Processes', *Australian Journal of Management* (April 1977), pp. 53–75.

Watts, R. L. and J. L. Zimmerman (1978), 'Towards a Positive Theory of the Determination of Accounting Standards', *Accounting Review* (January 1978), pp. 112–134.

Watts, R. L. and J. L. Zimmerman (1979), 'The Demand for and Supply of Accounting Theories: The Market for Excuses', *Accounting Review* (April 1979), pp. 273–305.

Zeff, S. A. (1972), *Forging Accounting Principles in Five Countries: A History and Analysis of Trends* (Stipes Publishing Co.).

# I-A 7 *Predictive Ability as a Criterion for the Evaluation of Accounting Data*

WILLIAM H. BEAVER, JOHN W. KENNELLY, AND
WILLIAM M. VOSS

T he evaluation of alternative accounting measurements is a problem of major concern to the accounting profession. With respect to this problem, Ijiri and Jaedicke have stated:

> Accounting is plagued by the existence of alternative measurement methods. For many years, accountants have been searching for criteria which can be used to choose the best measurement alternative.[1]

One criterion being employed by a growing body of empirical research is *predictive ability*. According to this criterion, alternative accounting measurements are evaluated in terms of their ability to predict events of interest to decision-makers. The measure with the greatest predictive power with respect to a given event is considered to be the "best" method for that particular purpose.

The criterion has already been applied in several different contexts. Brown has investigated the ability of models using alternative income measures (i.e., with and without tax deferral) to predict the market value of the firm. Green and Segall evaluated interim reports in terms of their usefulness in the prediction of future annual earnings. Horrigan has examined the predictive content of accounting data, in the form of financial ratios, with respect to bond rating changes and ratings on

William H. Beaver, John W. Kennelly, and William M. Voss, "Predictive Ability as a Criterion for the Evaluation of Accounting Data," *The Accounting Review*, October 1968, pp. 675–683. Reprinted with the permission of *The Accounting Review*.

[1] Yuji Ijiri and Rober K. Jaedicke, "Reliability and Objectivity of Accounting Measurements," *The Accounting Review*, (July 1966), p. 474.

newly issued bonds. One of the authors has studied accounting measures as predictors of bankruptcy and bond default.[2]

Because the predictive ability criterion is currently being used and is likely to experience even greater use in the future, this paper examines its origin, its relationship to the facilitation of decision-making, and the potential difficulties associated with its implementation. In order to illustrate the issues under discussion, the paper will refer to a hypothetical research project. The project proposes to evaluate the merits of alternative methods of reporting financial leases in terms of the prediction of loan default.

Loan default was chosen as the dependent variable for two reasons. A large body of literature in financial statement analysis suggests loan default is an event of interest to decision-makers (e.g., bankers), and *a priori* arguments can be advanced that will relate accounting measurements to the prediction of loan default. A cash flow model of the firm, such as that developed by Walter, implies that the probability of loan default is a function of the ratio of total debt to total assets.[3] However the model does not specify how debt and assets are best operationally measured. The financial lease controversy provides two measurement alternatives—capitalization and noncapitalization.

*A priori* arguments have been advanced, supporting each alternative as the more meaningful.[4] Empirically testable implications can be drawn from these arguments if they are interpreted in the light of the cash flow model. If the capitalization of leases does provide a "more meaningful" measure of debt and assets, then a debt-asset ratio that includes the capitalized value of leases in its components ought to be a better predictor of loan default than a debt-asset ratio that ignores capitalization.

The empirical part of the hypothetical study would involve the collection of financial statement data for a sample of default and nondefault firms. The debt-asset ratio would be computed for each firm, under each of the two lease treatments. The object would be to see which debt-asset ratio was the better predictor. An index of predictive ability is provided by the dichotomous classification test, which classifies the firms as default or nondefault based solely on a knowledge of the debt-asset ratio. The classifications are compared to the actual default status of the firms to determine the percentage of incorrect predictions—the lower the error, the higher the predictive power. The lease assumption that resulted in a lower percentage error

---

[2] Philip Brown, "The Predictive Abilities of Alternative Income Concepts" (an unpublished ˙anuscript presented to the Conference for Study of Security Prices, Graduate School of Business, University of Chicago, November 1966); David Green, Jr. and Joel Segall, "The Predictive Power of First-Quarter Earnings Reports: A Replication"; James Horrigan, "The Determination of Long-Term Credit Standing with Financial Ratios"; William H. Beaver, "Financial Ratios as Predictors of Failure," The last three papers appear in *Empirical Research in Accounting: Selected Studies, 1966* (Institute of Professional Accounting, Graduate School of Business, University of Chicago, 1967), pp. 21–36, 44–62, and 71–102, respectively.

[3] James E. Walter, "The Determination of Technical Solvency," *Journal of Business* (January 1957), pp. 30–43. Extension of the Walter model as applied to financial ratios appears in Beaver, *op. cit.* The lease study need not restrict itself to only the debt-asset ratio. Other ratios affected by capitalization could also be studied.

[4] Arguments for and against capitalization appear in John H. Myers, *Reporting of Leases in Financial Statements* (American Institute of Certified Public Accountants, 1962); and Donald C. Cook, "The Case Against Capitalizing Leases," *Harvard Business Review* (January-February 1963), pp. 145–155.

would tentatively be judged the better, the more meaningful, measurement alternative for the purpose of predicting loan default.[5]

## THE ORIGIN OF THE PREDICTIVE ABILITY CRITERION

Knowing the origin of the predictive ability criterion is important in understanding what is meant by predictive ability and why it is being used in evaluating accounting data. The criterion is well established in the social and natural sciences as a method for choosing among competing hypotheses.[6] It is our belief that alternative accounting measures have the properties of competing hypotheses and can be evaluated in a similar manner. Consider the following common features of competing hypotheses and alternative accounting measures:

1. Both are abstractions, which disregard aspects of reality deemed to be irrelevant and retain only those few crucial elements that are essential for the purposes at hand. Because there are many ways to abstract from reality, an unlimited number of mutually exclusive alternatives can be generated. Hence there is a need for a set of criteria for choosing among them.

2. Tests of logical propriety are one basis for evaluation. Conformity to these tests is a necessary but insufficient condition for selecting the "best." Two or more alternatives may pass the tests, and in that event it is futile to argue which is the "more logical." Ultimately, the choice must be made on the basis of which abstraction better captures the relevant aspects of reality. There is a need for an additional criterion that evaluates the alternatives in terms of the *purpose* for which they are being generated.

3. A primary purpose is the prediction of events, and hence comparison of alternatives according to their relative predictive power is a meaningful basis for evaluation. Predictive power is defined as the ability to generate operational implications (i.e., predictions) and to have those predictions subsequently verified by empirical evidence. More precisely, a prediction is a statement about the probability distribution of the dependent variable (the event being predicted) conditional upon the value of the independent variable (the predictor). Typically, the prediction asserts there is an association between $x$ and $y$ such that the outcome of $y$ is dependent upon the

[5] The sample design described here parallels that used in the Beaver study. A more complete description of the classification test is discussed in that study (pp. 83ff.). Another index of predictive power is provided by an analysis of Bayesian likelihood ratios. In many respects, the likelihood ratio analysis is superior to the classification test. However, the classification test was used because it can be more briefly stated and more easily understood. Also both indices ranked accounting measures virtually the same in the Beaver study.

[6] This section relies heavily upon the literature in scientific methodology, especially the following works: Morris R. Cohen and Ernest Nagel, *An Introduction to Logic and the Scientific Method* (Harcourt Brace, 1934); Ernest Nagel, *The Structure of Science* (Harcourt Brace, 1961); C. West Churchman, *Prediction and Optimal Decision* (Prentice-Hall, 1962); Abraham Kaplan, *The Conduct of Inquiry* (Chandler, 1964); and several articles appearing in Sherman Krupp's *The Structure of Economic Science* (Prentice-Hall, 1966). Additional bibliographic references appear in Carl Thomas Devine's "Research Methodology and Accounting Theory Formation," *The Accounting Review*, (July 1960), pp. 387–399.

value of $x$ [i.e., $P(y/x) = f(x)$].[7] But merely asserting the prediction does not make it "true." It must be verified by investigating the empirical correspondence between what the prediction asserts and what is in fact observed. Thus the determination of predictive ability is inherently an empirical question.

4.    The use of the predictive ability criterion presupposes that the alternatives under consideration have met the tests of logic and that each has a theory supporting it. The determination of predictive ability is not an indiscriminate search for that alternative which will maximize the $R^2$ (or any other index of predictive power). Theory provides an explanation why a given alternative is expected to be related to the dependent variable and permits the investigator to generalize from the findings of sample data to a new set of observations. Consequently, a complete evaluation involves both *a priori* and empirical considerations.

The lease study reflects each of the points listed above. Each measurement system (i.e., with and without capitalization) is an abstraction. One basis for choosing between them would be to subject the underlying *a priori* arguments to the tests of logical propriety, but in this case neither argument is inherently illogical. Hence it is impossible to resolve the controversy on solely *a priori* grounds. Note also it would be erroneous to prefer the capitalization of leases merely because noncapitalization abstracts from certain aspects of the lease event. To say one measurement system is more abstract than another is not an indictment of that system. The additional data provided by capitalizing leases may be irrelevant for the purposes at hand or may even be harmful in the sense of contributing only "noise" to the system. A choice can only be made by applying some purposive criterion. In the lease study, the purposive criterion chosen was predictive ability—in particular, the ability to predict loan default.

It is possible to generalize beyond the context of the lease controversy. Most, if not all, accounting controversies can be viewed as disputes over the relative merits of one measurement alternative versus another. The inadequacy of relying solely upon *a priori* arguments is generally recognized by the accounting profession. Several recent articles have drawn attention to this inadequacy and have called for more empirical research in accounting.[8] One factor that has impeded a movement in this direction is the inability to specify what the nature of the empirical research should be, although there is a consensus that the research ought to relate alternative measures to the purposes of accounting data. The predictive ability approach provides a method for

---

[7] Occasionally, a hypothesis may specify an independent relationship among the variables [i.e., $P(y/x) = P(y)$]. For example, the random walk theory of security price movements asserts that the probability distribution of the price change in a given time period is independent of the price change in any previous period. See Eugene F. Fama, "The Behavior of Stock Market Prices," *Journal of Business*, (January 1965), pp. 34–105. In comparing competing predictors, the relative strength of association with the dependent variable becomes the relevant consideration. Strength of association can be measured in many ways, which will vary with the nature of the data and the inferences to be drawn from the data. In the lease study, the percentage error in classification was chosen as the index of association.

[8] For example, R. J. Chambers, "Prospective Adventures in Accounting Ideas," *The Accounting Review*, (April 1967), p. 251.

drawing operational implications from the *a priori* arguments such that the measurement controversies become empirically testable according to a purposive criterion.

## RELATIONSHIP TO THE FACILITATION OF DECISION-MAKING

A key issue in accepting this approach is the contention that predictive ability is a purposive criterion. This section will examine that contention in more detail and will relate predictive ability to what is generally regarded as the purpose of accounting data—the facilitation of decision-making.

The idea that accounting data ought to be evaluated in terms of their purposes or uses is one of the earliest and most prevalent thoughts in accounting. In 1922 Paton concluded:

> Accounting is a highly purposive field and any assumption, principle, or procedure is accordingly justified if it adequately serves the end in view.[9]

Recently the American Accounting Association's *A Statement of Basic Accounting Theory* stated:

> In establishing these standards the all-inclusive criterion is the usefulness of the information.[10]

In spite of the obvious appeal to the idea that accounting data ought to be useful, the utilitarian approach has lacked operationality. Chambers has noted:

> For, if accounting is utilitarian there must have been some concept or some theory of the tests which must be applied in distinguishing utilitarian from nonutilitarian procedures.... It is largely because the tests of "utilitarian-ness"... have not been made explicit that the body of accounting practices now employed contains so many divergent and inconsistent rules.[11]

One reason for the inability to specify tests of usefulness is the manner in which usefulness is interpreted. Almost without exception, the literature has related usefulness to the facilitation of decision-making. The primacy of decision-making has been stressed by both Paton and *A Statement of Basic Accounting Theory*:

> The purpose of accounting may be said to be that of compiling and interpreting the financial data ... to provide a sound guide to action by management, investor, and other interested parties.[12]

---

[9] William A. Paton, *Accounting Theory* (The Ronald Press, 1922), p. 472.

[10] American Accounting Association, *A Statement of Basic Accounting Theory* (American Accounting Association, 1966), p. 3.

[11] Raymond J. Chambers, "Why Bother with Postulates?" *Journal of Accounting Research*, (Spring 1963), p. 3.

[12] William A. Paton, *Essentials of Accounting* (The Macmillan Company, 1949), p. 2.

> The committee defines accounting as the process of identifying, measuring, and communicating economic information to permit informed judgments and decisions by users of the information.[13]

However, the use of the decision-making criterion faces two problems. The first is to define the decision models (or processes) of potential users of accounting data. This problem has been noted by both Anton and Vatter.

> If we assume an operationalist view—that is, that information ought to be for decision-making purposes—the criteria [sic] is based upon an extension of significance, i.e., for what is the information significant.... While this is a purposive criterion it also gives us the dilemma noted above as to who will be the decision-maker and the uncertainty of his context.[14]

> Observation, analysis, and projection should be aimed at decision-making. This implies a view of the past and present that permits and facilitates decisions, without making them. How this fine line can be established depends upon what the decisions are, who makes them, and what data are relevant for those purposes. These questions still remain unanswered.[15]

Most business decisions currently are not made within the framework of a formally specified decision model. That is, in most decision-making situations, no model is available with which to evaluate alternative accounting measurements. Consider the lending decision faced by a loan officer in a bank. The specification of his decision model would require a knowledge of what the decision variables are, what weights are assigned to each decision variable, and what constraints, if any, are binding on the loan officer. It is unlikely that even the decision-maker would produce a formal model that would describe the process he went through in making lending decisions. Rules of thumb, such as "do not loan to any firm with a current ratio below 2," can be found, but it would be extremely difficult to determine the decision model implied by such rules. Specification of decision models, for the most part, is beyond the current state of knowledge. Although operations research and other quantitative techniques offer promise of greater specification in the future, it is not clear how soon, or to what extent, such specifications will be possible.[16]

The second problem is, even after the decision model is specified, it is not sufficient for determining which accounting measure produces the better decisions. Many, if not all, of the decision variables are capable of being measured in more than one way. For example, assume that a loan officer's objective function for the lending decision is a known function of promised return and probability of default on the

---

[13] American Accounting Association, *op. cit.*, p. 1.

[14] Hector R. Anton, "Some Aspects of Measurement and Accounting," *Journal of Accounting Research*, (Spring 1964), p. 6.

[15] William J. Vatter, "Postulates and Principles," *Journal of Accounting Research*, (Autumn 1963), p. 197.

[16] The difficulties encountered in attempting to specify the decision processes of loan officers are well documented in several articles appearing in the text by Kalman J. Cohen and Frederick S. Hammer, *Analytical Methods in Banking* (Irwin, 1966). Of special interest is the article by Kalman J. Cohen, Thomas C. Gilmore, and Frank A. Singer, "Bank Procedures for Analyzing Business Loan Applications," pp. 219–249.

loan. The lease controversy provides two operational measures for assessing the probability of loan default. The decision model can indicate whether different decisions are produced by using different definitions of the debt-asset ratio as a surrogate for the probability of default, but it cannot indicate which definition (i.e., with or without capitalization) will lead to the better decisions. Additional information is needed as to which ratio provides the better assessment of probability of default (i.e., which ratio is the better predictor of loan default).

At this point the relationship between predictive ability and decision-making becomes evident. Note the distinction between a prediction and a decision. In the context of the bank's lending decision, a prediction states the probability of loan default if the bank loans to a firm with a set of financial ratios. The decision is whether or not the bank should grant the loan, which also involves additional decision variables such as the promised return. The illustration points out an important relationship between predictions and decisions. A prediction can be made without making a decision, but a decision cannot be made without, at least implicitly, making a prediction.

In a world where little is known about the decision models, evaluating alternative accounting measures in terms of their predictive ability is an appealing idea, because it requires a lower level of specificity regarding the decision model. To evaluate alternative lease treatments in terms of their ability to predict loan default, we assume only that the probability of loan default is a parameter of the decision process, even though we may know little about how the bank's loan officers use the assessments of probability of default in reaching their decisions. Hence the predictive ability of accounting data can be explored without waiting for the further specification of the decision models.[17]

Because prediction is an inherent part of the decision process, knowledge of the predictive ability of alternative measures is a prerequisite to the use of the decision-making criterion. At the same time, it permits tentative conclusions regarding alternative measurements, subject to subsequent confirmation when the decision models eventually become specified. The use of predictive ability as a purposive criterion is more than merely consistent with accounting's decision-making orientation. It can provide a body of research that will bring accounting closer to its goal of evaluation in terms of a decision-making criterion.

## DIFFICULTIES OF IMPLEMENTATION

The purpose of this paper is to present the difficulties as well as the benefits of the predictive ability approach. However, none of the potential problems to be discussed are inherent to this approach. They are merely "facts of life" that are likely to be encountered in any meaningful attempt to evaluate alternative accounting measures.

1.  One difficulty of implementation will be the specification of what events constitute parameters of decision models and the specification of a theory that will link those events to the accounting measures in some sort of predictive relationship. The studies cited earlier suggest some of the events

---

[17] The relationship between predictions and the decision model is further discussed in the next section.

that could be predicted.[18] Also, portfolio theory appears to be a productive area for providing dependent variables, although as yet the relationships between the parameters of the portfolio models and the accounting data have not been explored.[19] However, a brief survey of the disciplines from which the dependent variables and the predictive theory are likely to originate indicates that much remains to be accomplished. In large part then the evaluation of accounting data, using the predictive ability criterion, will occur in conjunction with development and testing of predictive relationships in related disciplines, such as economics and finance.

2.   The findings of a predictive ability study are conditional on how the predictive model is specified. The construction of the prediction model involves a specification of the functional form of the relationships (e.g., linearity) and also how the variables are operationally defined. In the financial lease study, the findings would be conditional upon the rates used to discount the lease payments and the particular set of financial ratios used in the study. If no difference in predictive ability is found between the two sets of ratios (capitalized, noncapitalized), the finding may be attributed to (a) the particular discount rates chosen were not the appropriate rates, (b) the ratio form is not a meaningful way to express relationships among financial statement items, (c) the particular ratios chosen were not the optimal ratios for the prediction of default, or (d) capitalization does not enhance predictive ability. Additional research regarding the possibility of (a), (b) and (c) must be explored before inference (d) can be drawn. The accounting measure and the prediction model are being jointly tested. Positive results constitute a joint confirmation, while negative results may be due to a flaw in either or both factors. In practice it may be difficult to isolate the source of the negative results.

Another problem arises when positive results are obtained (i.e., when a "significant" difference between alternative measures is observed). For example assume the debt-asset ratio computed under the capitalization assumption predicts better than the noncapitalized debt-asset ratio in a single ratio prediction model. If additional ratios were included in the prediction model, the noncapitalized form of the debt-asset ratio might contribute more to the predictive power of the multivariate model than the capitalized form. If different models suggest contrary conclusions regarding the relative predictive power of the two lease assumptions, additional research will be needed to explain the reason for the conflicting results. Even if consistent results are observed for all of the models tested, there is always the possibility of an untested model which possesses greater predictive power and yet suggests the opposite conclusion regarding the relative predictive power of the alternative measures under study.[20]

---

[18] See footnote 2 for the bibliographic references.

[19] Harry M. Markowitz, *Portfolio Selection: Efficient Diversification of Investments* (Wiley, 1959). William F. Sharpe, "Capital Asset Prices: A Theory of Market Equilibrium Under Conditions of Risk," *Journal of Finance* (September 1964), pp. 425–42.

[20] There are two other related qualifications regarding a predictive ability study. (1) The findings are conditional upon the population from which the sample is drawn. (2) The findings are conditional upon the alternative measures chosen for study. For example, a third unspecified and untested measure may be better than the two measures under consideration.

3.  A third difficulty occurs because accounting data are currently being used as decision variables. There are two possible reasons for observing an association between the accounting measures and the event being predicted. (a) There is a "true" causal relationship between the measures and the event. (b) Decision-makers perceive there to be a causal relationship, and this perception is sufficient to produce an observed relationship. In the lease study a relationship between financial ratios and loan default may be observed because there is a causal relationship such that a "poor" ratio increases the probability of default. However, a relationship may also be observed merely because bankers believe there is causal relationship and use the ratios as decision variables. The bank may sever a line of credit because a firm fails to improve its ratios to a respectable level. The severing of the line of credit forces the firm into default. Similarly, the efficacy of capitalizing leases may be diminished or eliminated if loan officers do not incorporate the capitalization of leases into their credit analysis. Any observed relationship may be due to either (a) or (b) or both. It may be impossible to tell from the sample data the extent to which factor (b) is present.

    If the objective is predictive ability, do we care what its source is? Yes, if source (b) is not expected to be permanent. Decision-makers' use of accounting data as decision variables may change over time. In fact, the findings of a predictive ability study may cause them to change, and this might change the predictive relationships observed in the future.

4.  The evaluation of relative predictive power may require an assumption about the loss function associated with the prediction errors, which in turn involves additional knowledge of other variables in the decision model. Without this knowledge it may be impossible to conclude which measure is the better predictor.[21]

    For example, suppose the capitalized debt-asset ratio predicts the default status of a sample of default and nondefault firms with a lower number of total misclassifications. Can we conclude that capitalization is preferable? Not necessarily. Suppose the noncapitalized debt-asset ratio has more total misclassifications of both default and nondefault firms but fewer errors with respect to the classification of default firms. Since the loss of misclassifying a default firm is likely to be greater than the loss associated with misclassifying a nondefault firm, the latter measure may be the better predictor in terms of minimizing expected loss. More would have to be known about the loss function before one measure could be chosen over the other.

    Moreover, even if the capitalized debt-asset ratio performed better with respect to both type errors, additional analysis is needed before capitalization of leases could be recommended, because capitalization involves a greater cost to collecting additional data and making the necessary computations. Capitalization might lead to better predictions, but are they sufficiently better to warrant the additional cost? The answer involves a cost-

---

[21] Every index of predictive ability involves some assumption regarding the loss function of the prediction errors and/or the distribution of prediction errors. If different indices suggest different measures are better, the inability to select which index is appropriate implies the inability to select which accounting measure is the better predictor, until the loss function can be specified.

benefit analysis, which requires a knowledge of the loss function and hence the other decision variables.

The amount of additional knowledge of the decision model that will be required can only be assessed within the context of the empirical results of each predictive ability study. The margin of superiority of one measure over another may be so great that it is obviously the better predictor regardless of the form of loss function. In other situations, perhaps only the general form of the loss function (e.g., linear or quadratic, symmetric or asymmetric) need be specified. In instances where a greater knowledge of the loss function is needed than is available, the role of the predictive ability study may be to present the distribution of prediction errors for each measure and let the reader apply his own loss function in choosing among the measures. In any event the researcher must be constantly aware of this relationship to avoid drawing unwarranted inferences from the data.

5.   The findings of a predictive ability study are conditional upon the event being predicted. Even if a measure is a better predictor of one event (e.g., loan default), it is not necessarily a better predictor of other events. Additional research would be needed to investigate the predictive power of the measure for other purposes. If different measures are best for different predictive purposes, the problem of satisfying competing user needs arises.[22] If this problem exists, it would be difficult to resolve, although the use of multidimensional and special purpose statements offers a tentative solution.[23]

## CONCLUDING REMARKS

Two implications emerge from the previous discussion: (1) The preference for an accounting measure may apply only within the context of a specific predictive purpose or prediction model. It may be impossible to generalize about the "best" measurement alternative across different contexts. (2) Even within a specific context, the conclusions must be considered as tentative.

The inability to generalize is a possibility, but not an inevitability. We have cited only *potential* difficulties, whose relevance can only be assessed empirically, not by *a priori* speculation. What is important is to know to what extent we can generalize across purposes, and the only hope of acquiring this knowledge is to conduct the predictive studies. If we discover that different measures are best for different purposes, it would be erroneous to believe that the predictive studies are any less important because of that discovery. The inability to generalize, if it does exist, is not a flaw of the predictive ability methodology. It merely reflects the state of the world or the state of accounting theory, but in neither case is it an indictment of the methodology that exposes that fact.

Even within a specific context, the preference for one measure over another is tentative. A measure that performed poorly may not be permanently rejected in the sense that the researcher may refine the measure (and its theory) or redesign the study

[22] The decision-making criterion also faces the same potential problem. See comments made by both Devine and Moonitz. Carl Thomas Devine, *op. cit.*, p. 397. Maurice Moonitz, *The Postulates of Accounting* (American Institute of Certified Public Accountants, 1961), p. 4.

[23] For suggestions regarding multidimensional reporting see American Accounting Association, *op. cit.*

in the hope that future research will demonstrate that the measure is really better. Also there is always the possibility of an unknown or untested measure that performs even better than the best measure tested. Theory construction in other disciplines is an evolutionary process, where the hypotheses are continuously being revised, redefined, or overturned in the light of new theory and new evidence. There is no reason to believe that accounting theory will be different.

Although it is important that a general awareness of these factors exists, neither the potential inability to generalize nor the tentative nature of the conclusions should be regarded as a deterrent to conducting the predictive studies. Extension of research efforts into the predictive ability of accounting data is necessary for the fulfillment of accounting's decision-making orientation and for the meaningful evaluation of alternative accounting measures.

# I-A 8  *A Revolution in Accounting Thought?*

## M. C. WELS

Although the decade of the 1960s has been described by Carl Nelson as a "golden age in the history of a priori research in accounting" [Nelson, 1973, p. 4], the works cited as examples of that kind of research also have been severely criticized.[1] Nelson states that, "impressive as the scholarship is, we are not significantly advanced from where we were in 1960" [Nelson, 1973, p. 15]. He also is reported as having "contended that the existing a priori studies are of doubtful value" [Dopuch and Revsine, 1973, p. 32]. In similar vein, Gonedes and Dopuch are critical because, they allege, the same works are theoretically deficient, and it is possible "to declare the superiority of just about any set of accounting procedures, depending on the particular a priori model adopted" [Gonedes and Dopuch, 1974, pp. 49–50].

It will be argued here that those criticisms are based on a misunderstanding of the role of so-called *a priori research* in the overthrow of outdated ideas and practices. Far from being unproductive, the works referred to were a necessary step in the revolution currently underway in accounting thought. Far from being of doubtful value, those works have helped to place us in a significantly different position from that of 1960. Whether the works were theoretically deficient is, to some extent, irrelevant in this context, and the circularity implied by Gonedes and Dopuch's second criticism is a normal and healthy characteristic of theoretical works of that kind.

## SCIENTIFIC REVOLUTIONS

The notion of a revolution in accounting is taken from Kuhn's *The Structure of Scientific Revolutions* [1970].[2] His thesis is that science does not progress through accumulation. Rather, a series of tradition-shattering revolutions occur in which one "time-honored scientific theory is rejected in favour of another incompatible with it"

M. C. Wells, "A Revolution in Accounting Thought?" *The Accounting Review,* July 1976, pp. 471–482. Reprinted by permission of *The Accounting Review.*

[1] The examples given were, "the writings of Chambers, Edwards and Bell, Sterling, and Ijiri" [Nelson, 1973, p. 3].

[2] Kuhn's exposition has been subject to widespread criticism. See for example Shapere [1964] and Lakatos and Musgrave [1974]. However, references in this paper are to the enlarged edition of Kuhn's monograph. The postscript to that edition contains Kuhn's reply to his critics.

[Kuhn, 1970, p. 6]. The new theory, or set of ideas, is unique in that it is not derived from the previously accepted dogma. It is "seldom or never just an increment to what is already known" [Kuhn, 1970, p. 7], and in the process of moving from the old set of ideas to the new, the community of scientists follows a number of identifiable steps:

1. Recognition of anomalies
2. A period of insecurity
3. Development of alternative sets of ideas
4. Identification of schools of thought
5. Domination of the new practices or ideas

The first step is a precursor to the whole process; it initiates the period of crisis which follows. During that period, scientists became increasingly dissatisfied with the existing theoretical framework, and a search for alternatives begins. Therefore, the second and third steps are mutually interactive. As dissatisfaction grows, the search for alternatives gains impetus; as alternatives are discerned and discussed, the dissatisfaction is heightened. Schools of thought emerge, and one set of ideas gradually gains ascendency over the alternatives.

Because these steps involve such fundamental changes in the outlook and practices of the community of scholars, Kuhn applies the political metaphor of revolution to the process. He argues that the change takes place only after a serious malfunction has occurred in the sense that "existing institutions [or practices] have ceased adequately to meet the problems posed by an environment that they have in part created" [Kuhn, 1970, p. 92]. Just as political revolutions "aim to change political institutions in ways that those institutions themselves prohibit" [Kuhn, 1970, p. 93], so do scientific revolutions change previously held concepts of the field of enquiry in a way which is incompatible with those concepts. Such a fundamental change cannot take place within the existing institutional or conceptual framework. The challenger in incompatible with the incumbent. "The parties to a revolutionary conflict must resort to the techniques of mass persuasion" [Kuhn, 1970, p. 93], and, "like the choice between competing political institutions, that between competing paradigms proves to be a choice between incompatible modes of community life" [Kuhn, 1970, p. 94].

The process, or revolution, is unlikely to be completed quickly. The assimilation of new ideas will not be complete until previously accepted theories have been reconstructed and previously held facts have been re-evaluated. This is "an intrinsically revolutionary process that is seldom completed by a single man and never overnight" [Kuhn, 1970, p. 7].

There is, of course, no necessary reason why the pattern of developments in science (and particularly the physical sciences from which Kuhn derives most of his examples) should be found also in accounting. Kuhn does consider the possibility of his thesis being applicable in other fields, despite some obvious differences [p. 208]. Nevertheless, just as scientific theories may both describe and prescribe physical phenomena, so may accounting theories describe and prescribe financial phenomena. Furthermore, if the pattern of events in accounting can be seen to be following the pattern of successful revolutions described by Kuhn, then we will be able to explain the reasons for and the importance of the "golden age of a priori research" referred to above. In doing that, we also will answer the criticisms made of the works which appeared during that golden age.

It should be emphasized that the analogy here is to accounting thought.[3] Given the political difficulties of initiating change in accounting practices, that may well be an evolutionary rather than a revolutionary process. But it will not, I suspect, take place until the revolution described here is complete.

However, to apply the analogy to accounting thought, one initial condition must be satisfied: a community of scholars must be identified. This was emphasized by Kuhn in his postscript. He pointed out that "scientific communities can and should be isolated without prior recourse to paradigms" [Kuhn, 1970, p. 176]. Accordingly, I will specify the community to which this paper relates as comprising the members of academic and research organizations such as the American Accounting Association, the Association of University Teachers of Accounting of the United Kingdom, the Accounting Association of Australia and New Zealand, the Research Division of the AICPA and the Australian Accountancy Research Foundation.

### The Accounting Disciplinary Matrix

The basic techniques used for keeping accounting records can be traced back more than 500 years, but the information conventionally stored within those records is largely a product of this century. Only within the last 75 years did the historical cost doctrine crystallize and come to dominate the literature and practices of accounting. More recently still, during the 1930s and the 1940s, attempts were made to formalize the framework underlying the rules for recording and reporting financial matters. The works of Gilman (1939), Sanders, Hatfield and Moore (1938), Paton and Littleton (1940)[4] and others[5] attempted to rationalize existing practices and to set the framework within which alternative ideas and procedures might be evaluated.

The framework of ideas which emerged during this period has characteristics of a paradigm. However, note that Kuhn used the term *paradigm* in a number of different ways. As this was a cause of considerable confusion and a matter he dealt with at length in the postscript appended to the 1970 edition of his essay, we will avoid the use of the term here. Instead, substitute terms introduced in the postscript will be used as far as possible. For the general set of ideas that binds together a community of scientists, Kuhn uses the term *disciplinary matrix* [p. 182]. There are several features which distinguish a disciplinary matrix (disciplinary because it refers to the common possession by the members of a particular discipline; matrix because it comprises ordered elements of various sorts, each requiring further specification) [Kuhn, 1970, p. 182]. There are: (1) symbolic generalizations—readily understood and undisputed symbolic representations common to the discipline [p. 182]; (2) shared commitments— beliefs which help determine what will be accepted as explanations or solutions

---

[3] Other attempts to apply Kuhn's thesis to financial accounting may be seen in Chambers [1966, pp. 373–376] and to cost accounting in Wells [forthcoming].

[4] Paton and Littleton were also both members of the Executive Committee of American Accounting Association which in 1936 produced *A Tentative Statement of Accounting Principles Underlying Corporate Financial Statements.* This was "one of the first major attempts to develop a framework which might be regarded as representing a structure of the fundamental principles of accounting" [Bedford and Ziegler, 1975, p. 438].

[5] In their review of the influence of Littleton on accounting thought and practices, Bedford and Ziegler [1975] also identify the late 1930s as "the era to which the roots of much contemporary accounting practice may be traced" [p. 437]. Coincidentally, it was not until 1940 that the U.S. Securities and Exchange Commission brought together all of its various rules on the form and content of financial statements in one document—Regulation S-X [Zeff, 1972, p. 151].

p. 184]; (3) values—the various qualities which members of the community expect in the work of their colleagues [pp. 184–186]; and (4) exemplars—the concrete problem—solutions which students entering the community encounter and which show by example how they are to go about seeking solutions [p. 187].

Following these descriptions, the disciplinary matrix of accountants which emerged during the 1940s may be described as follows: (1) The symbolic generalization included accepted notions and formulations such as the double entry equation, representations of income, current asset/fixed asset classifications and calculations of working capital, rate of return and debt/equity ratios. (2) The shared commitments included the so-called realization and matching principles, the notion of going concern and the cost basis of valuation. (3) The values included conservatism, consistency, materiality, etc.[6] (4) Finally, the exemplars were seen in the textbooks and expositions of the period. There was (and still is) a remarkable similarity in the contents of most texts—so much so that the content of academic courses and examinations had become almost completely predictable.

Once a student has absorbed the elements of a disciplinary matrix, he or she views all problem situations in the same way as other members of his or her specialist group. Writers and researchers have a common standard of practice, and problems tend to have common solutions, or shared examples [Kuhn, 1970, p. 187]. Thus, we have the commonality of training and outlook which helps to bind together a community of scholars.

However, the existence of a disciplinary matrix does not imply that a rigid, inviolable set of rules also exists. Rather, and because members of the community have been trained in problem-solutions (or as Kuhn expresses it "learning by finger exercises or by doing," p. 471), they do not need a full set of rules. Accounting was in this position prior to 1930. Writers took for granted, or simply explained, general principles.[7] Only after the criticisms of the 1920s and early 1930s were efforts made to formalize the framework of accounting ideas and were authoritative bodies set up for that purpose.[8] This development, too, is foreseen by Kuhn who suggests that only when accepted procedures come under attack, does consideration of the rules become important [p. 47].

However, the formalization of rules did not eliminate all of the contradictions and conflicts that had plagued accounting expositions in the past. Neither accounting writers nor practitioners apparently saw any conflict in certain departures from a strict application of the historical cost rule, such as the valuation of inventory at the lower of cost or market or the deduction of depreciation charges from the cost of fixed assets.[9] Even this is to be expected, according to Kuhn. Because the rules are learned through their application in specific contexts, any diversity either is not apparent or

---

[6] Notice the similarity of symbolic generalizations, shared commitments and values to the conventions, doctrines and standards described by Gilman [1939], especially pp. 4, 41–43; 254; and 186, respectively.

[7] "There is, it is believed, a corpus of principles of accounting which are generally accepted. It is true that they are not "written law", they have not been codified; they must be sought in accounts and financial statements," [Sanders, Hatfield and Moore, 1938, p. 5]. For this reason, "the search for rules [is] both more difficult and less satisfying than the search for paradigms" [Kuhn, 1970, p. 43].

[8] For examples of this kind of reaction, see Zeff [1972, pp. 119–140].

[9] The first writer to pay particular attention to these conflicts, without resolving them, was Gilman [1939, pp. 128–130, 174, 235].

may be explained away by the different facts of each case. Therefore, what the rules serve to do is to "limit both the nature of acceptable solutions and the steps by which they are obtained" [Kuhn, 1970, p. 38].

## ANOMALIES AND PROFESSIONAL INSECURITY

> Discovery commences with the awareness of anomaly, i.e., with the recognition that nature has somehow violated the paradigm-induced expectations that govern normal science [or conventional practice] (Kuhn, 1970, pp. 52–53).

There have long been critics of conventional accounting practices and of solutions to problems proposed within the conventional framework [Brief, 1975; and Chatfield, 1974, pp. 273–276]. Outstanding examples in the period before the historical cost disciplinary matrix crystallized were Paton [1922], Sweeney [1936] and MacNeal [1939]. However, their criticisms appear to have had little impact on the subsequent ascendancy of the historical cost model. Recognition was not given in the literature of accounting to the great number of anomalies which defied resolution and which brought the accounting profession into public opprobrium until the 1960s and early 1970s. During this period, and since, the fundamental defects in the historical cost model repeatedly were identified and criticized by scholars, by businesspersons and in the courts.[10] The criticisms culminated in the most simultaneous publication of Briloff's *Unaccountable Accounting* [1972] and Chambers' *Securities and Obscurities* [1973]. Leasco, Westec, Lockheed, Four Seasons, I.O.S., Rolls Royce, Reid Murray, Minsec and a host of other companies which were involved in cases which highlighted the "gap in GAAP" [Briloff, 1966, p. 484; 1972, pp. 31–33] became almost household names.

The reaction by theorists to the evidence thrust before them precisely follows that predicted by Kuhn; it corresponds to the period of *professional insecurity* [Kuhn, 1970, pp. 67–68] wherein the rules are subject to increasing scrutiny and occasional amendment. The disciplinary matrix is questioned, but not abandoned:

> ... when confronted by anomaly [scientists] will devise numerous articulations and *ad hoc* modifications of their theory in order to eliminate any apparent conflict [Kuhn, 1970, p. 78].

During the 1960s and 1970s, the Accounting Principles Board in the United States and equivalent committees in other countries and innumerable authors proposed

---

[10] See, for example, the statement by the Inspectors of the Reid Murray Group of Companies, "... we believe that we are accustomed to the use of common sense, and common sense has compelled us to reject a number of accounting practices used in the group and, apparently regarded as acceptable by accountants," *Interim Report* ... [1963, p. 107]. This case was commented upon by Stamp [1964]. This and similar comments by other inspectors provoked a Report by the General Council of the Australian Society of Accountants. See "Accounting Principles and Practices Discussed in Reports on Company Failures," *Members' Handbook*, Item 401 (January 1966). See also, Greer [1963]; "Unaccountable CPA's," [1966]; Louis [1968]; "Accounting—Profits Without Honor" [1970]; Raymon [1970]; Stamp and Marley [1970]; Birkett and Walker [1971]; Spacek [1969 and 1973]; de Jonquieres [1973]; and Bedford [1973].

amendments to the rules to cope with the anomalies and criticisms.[11] Pronouncements, monographs and journal articles on problem areas such as purchase versus
poolings, equity accounting, tax effect accounting and materiality followed. There
were even attempts to increase the solidarity of the practicing profession. Carey
wrote disparagingly of CPAs who gave evidence against their professional brethren
[Briloff, 1972, p. 351], and the professional bodies issued statements requiring stricter
conformance with official pronouncements [Zeff, 1972, pp. 76, 180–182, 294–295; 1973,
pp. 22–23].

The ad hoc solutions which emerge during a period of crisis have a far-reaching
consequence; they make it possible to contemplate rules which previously would have
been unacceptable. That is, "... by proliferating versions of the [disciplinary matrix],
crisis loosens the rules of normal puzzle-solving in ways that ultimately permit a new
[disciplinary matrix] to emerge" [Kuhn, 1970, p. 80]. For example, the purchase versus
pooling debate provoked discussion of asset values which were not original costs;
equity accounting involved revaluing investments in associated companies; tax effect
accounting extended the acceptance of nontransaction-based debits and credits. If
accounting follows the revolutionary sequence of events, the acceptance of the
techniques adopted in response to these problems will have hastened the ultimate
acceptance of an alternative disciplinary matrix.

However, there is one class of anomaly which has proved to be intractable. The
historical-cost based system fails to take account of changes in asset prices and
changes in the purchasing power of the monetary unit. That failure has been a source
of criticism, particularly during periods of inflation. It is anomalous in that, despite
the going concern values in the financial statements, those statements no longer
represent the state of affairs of the corporation. There have been numerous instances
of the abuse of privilege by people in possession of current price data which have been
denied to others [Chambers, 1973, Chapter 10]. Yet, accounting for the effects of
inflation requires a substantial revision of the conventional thought in accounting.
Partial solutions, such as equity accounting or, in the U.K. and Australia, occasional
revaluations, are only partially successful.[12] The specific price and price-level
problems are the sorts of anomalies which lead, finally, to the overthrow of the
existing set of rules. Their "characteristic feature is their stubborn refusal to be
assimilated to existing paradigms. This type alone gives rise to new theories" [Kuhn,
1970, p. 97].

There is one further feature of the periods of crisis described by Kuhn for which
we may find a parallel in accounting:

> It is, I think, particularly in periods of acknowledged crisis that scientists
> have turned to philosophical analysis as a device for unlocking the riddles of
> their field.... To the extent that normal ... work can be conducted by using
> the paradigm as a model, rules and assumptions need not be made explicit....
> But that is not to say that the search for assumptions (even for non-existent
> ones) cannot be an effective way to weaken the grip of tradition upon the
> mind and to suggest the basis for a new one [Kuhn, 1970, p. 88]:

---

[11] See Zeff [1972, pp. 173–224] and the Australian Society of Accountants' Item 401, referred to
above.
[12] For further examples, including the switches to and from accelerated depreciation and to and
from LIFO inventory values, see Chambers [1973, pp. 93–103].

Again, there has long been concern for the theoretical foundations of accounting practices [Chatfield, 1974, Chapter 16; Hendriksen, 1970, Chapter 2]. However, it is possible to discern two related developments like those referred to in the quotation above. The first is the search for assumptions. Of particular interest here are Littleton's *The Structure of Accounting Theory* [1953], Moonitz's *The Basic Postulates of Accounting* [1961], the American Accounting Association's *A Statement of Basic Accounting Theory* [1966], Ijiri's *The Foundations of Accounting Measurement* [1967] and various shorter contributions and comments.[13] These were, in varying degrees, attempts to define the underlying assumptions of accounting. Yet they did not lead to a widely recognized set of basic ideas. Rather, as Kuhn suggests, they served to highlight the defects of the disciplinary matrix and loosen the grip of tradition. Therefore, perhaps we should not be surprised to find that, despite the vast expenditure of time and money, the AICPA belatedly (in 1971) recognized a need for a statement of, and initiated a study of, the "objectives" of financial statements.[14] That the Trueblood Study fits the pattern of events is evident; the report includes discussion of both objectives and alternatives to generally accepted accounting principles. Those alternatives would have been rejected out of hand even 10 years previously.[15]

The other development which is particularly noticeable throughout this period is the concern with principles and theory construction generally. Commencing, perhaps, with Chambers' "Blueprint for a Theory of Accounting" [1955], notable contributions or comments by Mattessich [1957], Devine [1960], Chambers [1963], Vatter [1963] and Sterling [1970] followed. These philosophical discussions have served to increase the rigour of the discipline,[16] but hopefully, they also have helped to unlock the riddles of the field.

## ALTERNATIVE PROPOSALS AND THEIR EVALUATION

One direct consequence of the philosophical discussions has been the emergence and refinement of alternatives to the disciplinary matrix of, e.g., asset values based on historical costs. There have been various attempts to derive logically consistent systems which overcome the defects of the historical cost system. Some of the authors proposing these systems which appeared during the golden age already have been identified—Edwards and Bell [1961] and Chambers [1966]; others include Sprouse and Moonitz [1962], Mattessich [1964] and Mathews [1965]. The works of these authors were debated throughout the 1960s, and that debate served to clarify and identify the alternatives. Without that identification, the next step of the revolutionary process could not proceed. It *has* proceeded, as shown by the published evaluations of the alternatives. The Trueblood Study report contained some discussion. More comprehensive evaluations have been undertaken by Chambers [1970], Macdonald [1974], McDonald [1972], Hanna [1974] and others, while the Price Waterhouse Study

---

[13] For a useful summary and list of references, see [Hendriksen, 1970, Chapter 4].

[14] Report of the Study Group on the Objectives of Financial Statements [the Trueblood Study] (1973). The study was commissioned in May 1971.

[15] See the alternatives listed [Trueblood Study, 1973, p. 41]. Notice also Sterling's observation of the change in attitudes [1970, p. vii].

[16] See Nelson [1973, p. 15] for a comment on the contribution of logic and other philosophical techniques to the accounting problem.

[Mueller, 1971] gives attention to the need for introducing consideration of the alternatives into regular teaching programmes.[17]

The fact that the evaluation process has taken place, and is continuing, is evidence of the importance of the so-called a priori works; hence, our disagreement with Nelson's comment that these works are of doubtful value. In the pattern of events described here, the works fulfill a critically important role; they are both a natural reaction to the recognition of anomalies and a vital step in the selection of a new disciplinary matrix. Furthermore, having those works to consider, and having the alternatives thus laid out, we are in a fundamentally different position from that of 1960. For while schools of thought embracing the various alternatives might now appear, that would not have been possible in 1960.

However, before discussing that possibility, there are some other characteristics of the evaluative stage which were described by Kuhn and which may be seen also in accounting. Kuhn drew attention to the similarities of the evaluative stage to the pre-paradigm period. It is the stage at which "frequent and deep debates over legitimate methods, problems, and standards of solution" take place, although "these tend to define schools rather than to produce agreement" [Kuhn, 1970, p. 48].[18] In accounting, this stage has been marked by debates about the admissability of data relating to events external to the firm and data based on managers' intentions; on the presentation of cash flow statements, earnings per share calculations, etc.; the raisings of problems, such as the translation of holdings of foreign currencies, the reporting for diversified companies, long-term contracts and land development projects; the legitimacy of cost allocations; and reconsideration of the standards which the solutions must meet such as objectivity, independence and freedom from bias.

It is also because of the importance of these debates, and the evaluative process generally, that we contended that the alleged theoretical defects in the works published in the 1960s were, in a sense, irrelevant. This is not to suggest that "anything goes." On the contrary, tightly reasoned and empirically valid theoretical prescriptions have a greater chance of being adopted than do loosely constructed sets of ideas. However, theoretical defects will, presumably, be discovered during the evaluation process, and their existence may even add to the extent and heat of the debate, thus aiding this part of the revolutionary process.

Yet another characteristic of this step in the process identified by Kuhn and found in accounting is the diversity of activity:

> In the absence of a paradigm or some candidate for a paradigm, all of the facts that could possibly pertain to the development of a given science are likely to seem equally relevant. As a result early fact-gathering is a far more random activity than the one that subsequent scientific activity makes familiar [Kuhn, 1970, p. 15].

---

[17] It is for the reason outlined here that Chambers was able to refer to Macdonald's book as a product of its time. See Chambers [1975]. The same comment might be made of May, Mueller and Williams [1975].

[18] Notice that Dopuch and Revsine saw a similar result emerge at the Conference on Accounting Research held at the University of Illinois in 1971: "As is true in the literature, many contributors were quite convinced that their approach was correct but were unable to persuade those who disagreed" [Dopuch and Revsine, 1973, p. 34].

This perhaps, is the reason why so many proposals have emerged in recent years. They include suggestions for publication of multicolumn financial statements and forecasts; the development of human resource accounting; and, on a different level, the far-ranging research into share price movements and their information theory and cost benefit analyses to the provision of financial information.

## SCHOOLS OF THOUGHT

It may be possible to identify schools of thought in respect of some or all of the matters of interest just referred to. However, one example will suffice—asset measurement alternatives. Four schools may be identified:[19]

1. Price-Level Adjusted (or Current Purchasing Power) Accounting
2. Replacement Cost Accounting
3. Deprival Value Accounting
4. Continuously Contemporary (or Net Realizable Value) Accounting.

Strong or widespread support for these schools is not yet discernible,[20] which is understandable. For, as Kuhn points out:

> The man who embraces a new paradigm at an early stage must often do so in defiance of the evidence provided by problem solving. He must, that is, have faith that the new paradigm will succeed with the many large problems that confront it, knowing only that the older paradigm has failed with a few. A decision of that kind can only be made on faith [Kuhn, 1970, p. 158].

Accounting researchers are not likely to rely on faith or make that decision lightly. But there are sufficient examples of dispute in the literature for us to identify

[19] A fifth proposal—present value accounting—is not listed here. Although it has been argued cogently by Hansen [1966], it does not appear to have won support as an operational alternative. It has been discussed rather as an ideal against which alternatives might be evaluated. See, for example, Solomons [1961] and Lemke [1966].

[20] The following is an example of one attempt at identifying members of schools of thought in relation to generalized theories of accounting based on alternative asset measurement systems. Some people undoubtedly will want finer distinctions; some will object to being linked with others with whom they disagree in some respects; some will object to having been omitted. Nevertheless, at the risk of offending some or all of the people concerned, I would identify the following on the basis of their published work:

| | |
|---|---|
| 1. Price-Level-Adjusted: | Jones [1956] |
| | Mason [1971] |
| 2. Replacement Cost: | Edwards & Bell [1961] |
| | Mathews [1965] |
| | Gynther [1966] |
| | Revsine [1973] |
| 3. Deprival Value: | Baxter [1970] |
| | Wright [1970] |
| | Stamp [1971] |
| | Whittington [1974] |
| 4. Continuously Contemporary (Net realizable value) | Chambers [1966] |
| | Sterling [1970] |
| | McKeown [1971] |

For a slightly different version of these schools, see Sterling [1970, pp. 7–19].

some of the characteristics of "paradigm debates" [Kuhn, 1970, p. 110]. For example, "each group uses its own paradigm to argue in that paradigm's defense" [Kuhn, 1970, p. 94]. The Provisional Statement of Accounting Practice, No. 7, issued by the I.C.A. in England & Wales, refers to the need for a method which shows the "effect of changes in the purchasing power of money on accounts prepared on the basis of existing conventions" [para. 3] in arguing for Constant Purchasing Power Accounting; the Replacement Price School relies on the notion of "maintenance of productive capacity" which implies the need to replace assets in kind, in support of replacement cost accounting [Edwards and Bell, 1961, p. 99]; Wright [1971, pp. 60–61] refers to the possible loss which a firm might suffer if deprived of an asset when arguing for deprival value (or value to the owner) accounting; and Chambers [1966, p. 190] stresses the importance of adaptive behaviour when arguing for a measure of assets which is indicative of the firm's capacity to adapt.

These examples of apparent circularity are not intended as criticisms. Obviously, different systems of ideas can be evaluated only in the context to which those systems apply[21]; hence, the comment at the beginning of this paper that the charge of circularity by Gonedes and Dopuch is misplaced. The point is that arguments of this sort are a necessary and inevitable part of the process of trying to win support for the competing points of view [Kuhn, 1970, p. 94]. Like Nelson, Gonedes and Dopuch's error lies in their failure to identify the place of a priori research works in the transition to a new disciplinary matrix.

These debates have other characteristics. Adoption of a new disciplinary matrix will, normally, require a fundamental shift in the view which theorists have of the world. Thus, in accounting there have been changes: the view that the value of the monetary unit is stable has changed to acceptance of the view that it is variable; the view that the point of realization should be the point of recognition of gains is giving way to the view that other evidence of gains is admissible; and the view that only actual transactions give rise to objective data is giving way to a less restricted notion of objectivity.

Similarly, members of competing schools will have different views of the phenomena which are the subject of their discipline:

> Practicing in different worlds, the two groups of scientists see different things when they look from the same point in the same direction. Again that is not to say that they can see anything they please. Both are looking at the world, and what they look at has not changed. But in some areas they see different things, and they see them in different relations one to the other. That is why a law cannot even be demonstrated to one group of scientists, and may occasionally seem intuitively obvious to another [Kuhn, 1970, p. 150].

Hence Gynther's view of firms is of ongoing nonadaptive organizations while Chambers sees organizations as being fluid and constantly adapting to environmental changes.[22] And, it seems, debate between them serves only to convince each of the validity of his own argument.

[21] Sterling and Harrison [1974, pp. 144] draw attention to the universality of this factor in their comments on the Gonedes and Dopuch paper.

[22] Compare Gynther [1966, pp. 46–48] and Penman [1970, p. 338]: "Companies ... just do not adapt": with Chambers [1966, p. 190].

## A NEW DISCIPLINARY MATRIX?

The analysis presented here suggests that financial accounting thought is undergoing a revolution. If that is so, then the criticisms of a priori research cited at the beginning of this paper are misplaced. The criticisms fail to recognize the importance of research which leads to the delineation of alternative sets of ideas. Those alternatives are candidates for a new disciplinary matrix; they are the basis of competing schools of thought.

If the analogy presented above is correct, i.e., if Kuhn's notion of a revolution can be applied to accounting, then it appears that accounting is emerging from a state of crisis [Kuhn, 1970, Chapter VIII]. Alternative sets of ideas have been proposed and debated, and schools of thought are beginning to emerge. Admittedly, the analysis does not enable us to identify neat periods of time which correspond with Kuhn's steps in the revolution. Yet, the characteristics of an accepted disciplinary matrix, the period of insecurity and the development of alternative sets of ideas appear to be well recognizable in accounting.

What will be the outcome? In accounting it is too soon to say. Researchers cannot be observed rushing to adopt any of the alternative sets of ideas. Continued debate, primarily amongst academics but increasingly involving the research organizations of the professional bodies is, however, serving to identify schools of thought. The next stage, according to Kuhn, will be "an increasing shift in allegiances" [p. 158] in favor of one of the alternatives. However, this is a process which takes time. After all, it involves the assimilation of a new theory, and that in turn involves a "reconstruction of prior theory and the reevaluation of prior fact"; i.e., "an intrinsically revolutionary process." But note, "it is seldom completed by a single man and never overnight" [Kuhn, 1970, p. 7].

## REFERENCES

"Accounting: Profits Without Honor," *Time* (March 1970), p. 70.

American Accounting Association, "A Tentative Statement of Accounting Principles Affecting Corporate Reports," *The Accounting Review* (June 1936), pp. 87–91; reprinted as a Tentative Statement of Accounting Principles Underlying Corporate Financial Statements (1936).

Baxter, W. T., "Accounting Values: Sale Price Versus Replacement Cost," *Journal of Accounting Research* (Autumn 1967), pp. 208–214.

Bedford, Norton M., "The Need for an Evaluation of Accounting Research" in Dopuch and Revsine, eds., *Accounting Research 1960–1970: A Critical Evaluation,* Monograph 7 (Center for International Education and Research in Accounting, University of Illinois, 1973).

———, and Richard Ziegler, "The Contributions of A. C. Littleton to Accounting Thought and Practice, *The Accounting Review* (July 1975), pp. 435–443.

Birkett, W. P. and R. G. Walker, "Response of the Australian Accounting Profession to Company Failures in the 1960's," *Abacus* (December 1971), pp. 97–136.

Brief, Richard P., "The Accountants' Responsibility in Historical Perspective," *The Accounting Review* (April 1975), pp. 285–297.

Briloff, Abraham J., "Old Myths and New Realities in Accountancy," *The Accounting Review* (July 1966), pp. 485–495.

———, *Unaccountable Accounting* (Harper and Row, 1972).

Chambers, R. J., "Blueprint for a Theory of Accounting," *Accounting Research* (January 1955), pp. 17–25.

———, "Why Bother with Postulates?", *Journal of Accounting Research* (Spring 1963), pp. 3–15.

———, *Accounting, Evaluation and Economic Behavior* (Prentice-Hall, 1966).

———, "Methods of Accounting," Parts I–VI, *The Accountant* (February 1970), pp. 299–303; (March 1970), pp. 341–345; (March 1970), pp. 408–412; (April 1970), pp. 483–486; (April 1970), pp. 551–555; (April 1970), pp. 643–647.

———, *Securities and Obscurities: A Case for the Reform of the Law of Company Accounts* (Gower Press; 1973).

———, "Profit Measurement, Capital Maintenance and Service Potential: A Review Article," *Abacus* (June 1975), pp. 98–104.

Chatfield, Michael, *A History of Accounting Thought* (The Dryden Press, 1974).

de Jonquieres, Guy, "U.S. Firms Under Fire," *The Financial Times* (June 1973), p. 44.

Devine, Carl T., "Research Methodology and Accounting Theory Formation," *The Accounting Review* (July 1960), pp. 387–399.

Dopuch, Nicholas and Lawrence Revsine, eds., *Accounting Research 1960–1970: A Critical Evaluation*, Monograph 7 (Center for International Education and Research in Accounting, University of Illinois, 1973).

Edwards, Edgar O. and Philip W. Bell, *The Theory and Measurement of Business Income* (University of California Press, 1961).

Gilman, Stephen, *Accounting Concepts of Profit* (The Ronald Press, 1939; reprinted 1956).

Gonedes, Nicholas J. and Nicholas Dopuch, "Capital Market Equilibrium, Information Production and Selecting Accounting Techniques: Theoretical Framework and Review of Empirical Work," *Studies on Financial Accounting Objectives: 1974* (Supplement to Volume 12), *Journal of Accounting Research* (1974).

Greer, Howard C., "How to Succeed in Confusing People Without Really Trying," *The Journal of Accountancy* (March 1963), pp. 61–65.

Gynther, R. S., *Accounting for Price-Level Changes: Theory and Procedures* (Pergamon, 1966).

Hanna, John R., *Accounting Income Models: An Application and Evaluation* (The Society of Industrial Accounts of Canada, 1974).

Hansen, Palle, *The Accounting Concept of Profit* (North-Holland, 1966).

Hendriksen, Eldon S., *Accounting Theory* (Irwin, 1970).

Jones, Ralph Coughenour, *The Effects of Price Level Changes* (American Accounting Association, 1956).

Kuhn, Thomas S., *The Structure of Scientific Revolutions,* International Encyclopedia of Unified Science, 2nd enlarged edition (University of Chicago Press, 1970).

Lakatos, Imre and Alan Musgrave, eds., *Criticism and the Growth of Knowledge* (Cambridge University Press, 1974).

Lemke, Kenneth W., "Asset Valuation and Income Theory," *The Accounting Review* (January 1966), pp. 33–41.

Louis, Arthur M., "The Accountants are Changing the Rules," *Fortune* (June 1968), p. 177.

Macdonald, Graeme, *Profit Measurement: Alternatives to Historical Cost* (Accountancy Age, 1974).

MacNeal, Kenneth, *Truth in Accounting* (Ronald Press Co., 1939).

McDonald, Daniel L., *Comparative Accounting Theory* (Addison-Wesley, 1972).

McKeown, James C., "An Empirical Test of a Model Proposed by Chambers," *The Accounting Review* (January 1971), pp. 12–29.

Mason, Perry, *Price Level Changes and Financial Statements* (American Accounting Association, 1971).

Mattessich, Richard, "Toward a General and Axiomatic Foundation of Accountancy," *Accounting Research* (October 1957), pp. 328–356.

———, Richard, *Accounting and Analytical Methods* (Irwin, 1964).

Mathews, R. L., "Price-Level Accounting and Useless Information," *Journal of Accounting Research* (Spring 1965), pp. 133–155.

May, Robert G., Gerhard G. Mueller and Thomas H. Williams, *A New Introduction to Financial Accounting* (Prentice-Hall, 1975).

Mueller, Gerhard G., ed., *A New Introduction to Accounting* (The Price Waterhouse Foundation, July 1971).

Nelson, Carl L., "A Priori Research in Accounting" in Dopuch and Revsine, eds., *Accounting Research 1960–1970: A Critical Evaluation,* Monograph 7 (Center for International Education and Research in Accounting, University of Illinois, 1973).

Paton, W. A., *Accounting Theory—with Special Reference to the Corporate Enterprise* (Ronald Press Co., 1922; reprinted, Accounting Studies Press, 1962).

——— and A. C. Littleton, *An Introduction to Corporate Accounting Standards* (American Accounting Association, 1940, reprinted 1965).

Penman, Stephen H., "What Net Asset Value?—An Extension of a Familiar Debate," *The Accounting Review* (April 1970), pp. 333–346.

Raymon, R., "Is Conventional Accounting Obsolete?" *Accountancy* (June 1970), pp. 422–429.

Report of the Study Group on the Objectives of Financial Statements, *Objectives of Financial Statements* (American Institute of Certified Public Accountants, October 1973).

Revsine, Lawrence, *Replacement Cost Accounting* (Prentice-Hall, 1973).

Sanders, T. H., H. R. Hatfield, and U. Moore, *A Statement of Accounting Principles* (The American Institute of Accountants, 1938, reprinted 1959).

Shapere, Dudley, "The Structure of Scientific Revolutions," *Philosophical Review* (July 1964), pp. 383–394.

Solomons, David, "Economic and Accounting Concepts of Income," *The Accounting Review* (July 1961), pp. 374–383.

Spacek, Leonard, *A Search for Fairness* (Arthur Andersen & Co., 1969 and 1973).

Sprouse, Robert T. and Maurice Moonitz, *A Tentative Set of Broad Accounting Principles for Business Enterprises*, Accounting Research Study No. 3. (American Institute of Certified Public Accountants, 1962).

Stamp, Edward, "The Reid Murray Affair," *Accountancy* (August 1964), pp. 685–690.

———, "Income and Value Determination and Changing Price-Levels: An Essay Towards a Theory," *The Accountants' Magazine* (June 1971), pp. 277–292.

———, and Christopher Marley, *Accounting Principles and the City Code* (Butterworth, 1970).

Sterling, Robert R., "On Theory Construction and Verification," *The Accounting Review* (July 1970), pp. 444–457.

———, and William Harrison, "Discussion of Capital Market Equilibrium, Information Production, and Selecting Accounting Techniques: Theoretical Framework and Review of Empirical Work" in *Studies on Financial Objectives: 1974*, supplement to Vol. 12 of *Journal of Accounting Research*, pp. 142–157.

Sweeney, Henry W., *Stabilized Accounting* (Harper Bros., 1936; reprinted, Holt Rinehart & Winston, 1964).

"Unaccountable CPA's," *Forbes* (October 1966), p. 15.

Vatter, William J., "Postulates and Principles," *Journal of Accounting Research* (Autumn 1963), pp. 179–197.

Wells, M. C., *Accounting for Common Costs* (International Center for Education and Research in Accounting, University of Illinois, forthcoming).

Whittington, Geoffrey, "Asset Valuation, Income Measurement and Accounting Income," *Accounting and Business Research* (Spring 1974), pp. 96–101.

Wright, F. K., "A Theory of Financial Accounting," *Journal of Business Finance* (Autumn 1970), pp. 51–79.

———, "Value to the Owner: A Clarification," *Abacus* (June 1971), pp. 58–61.

Zeff, Stephen A., *Forging Accounting Principles in Five Countries* (Stipes Publishing Co., 1972).

———, *Forging Accounting Principles in Australia* (Australian Society of Accountants, March 1973).

## I-A 9 *The Establishment and Enforcement of Accounting Standards: Methods, Benefits and Costs*

GEORGE J. BENSTON

### INTRODUCTION

In one important respect, accounting standards exist simply because there are public accountants; each person and firm decides the standard by which they want themselves known. Therefore, when one speaks for a mechanism by which uniform accounting standards can be established and enforced, the call necessarily is for imposing them on people who might prefer to behave otherwise. Uniform standards, though, may be imposed voluntarily, as when a group of accountants or firms agree to follow the same standards and to accept penalties if they violate their pledges. This generally describes the situation in the UK. Or the power of government may be invoked to enforce adherence to standards, as in the USA.

Whether one system of standard setting and enforcement is 'best' cannot be determined. Not all users have the same requirements for accounting data. Some want data that reflect cash flows, others would accept accruals, but not adjustments to the numbers that cannot be verified by reference to actual market transactions, while still others prefer estimates of economic values, but disagree about the basis on which

This paper was prepared during and as a consequence of my appointment to a Deering Fellowship at the London Graduate School of Business Studies in 1979. I am grateful to the John J. Deering International Scholarship Fund of The Arthur Young Foundation and to Arthur Young McClelland Moores & Co. for their support, to Professor Walter Reid for many discussions on the subject, and to Alice Benston, Michael Bromwich, Andrew Christie and Harold Edey for valuable comments and suggestions.

George J. Benston, "The Establishment and Enforcement of Accounting Standards: Methods, Benefits and Costs," *Accounting and Business Research*, Winter 1980, pp. 51–60. Reprinted with the permission of *Accounting and Business Research*.

these estimates are made.[1] These and other preferential differences make it conceptually impossible to demonstrate that one system is better than all others for all users. As Joel Demski's application of Arrow's Impossibility Theorem demonstrates, 'no set of standards (applied to the accounting alternatives *per se*) exists that will always rank accounting alternatives in relation to consistent individual preferences and beliefs.'[2] Michael Bromwich analyses the less ambitious task of constructing less than all-inclusive (partial) accounting standards and shows that even this limited task is fraught with conceptual difficulties.[3] However, the likely benefits and costs to groups of similarly affected individuals can be indicated and perhaps measured, the results of which should aid those interested in making judgments about the desirability of alternative types of accounting standards and methods of enforcement.

First, I delineate three types of accounting standards, after which three types of enforcement are described. These brief descriptions provide a framework for analysing the benefits from and costs of accounting standards to investors (who include some employees), public accountants, government, and society. Then the benefits and costs of a government mandated, regulatory commission system like the US Securities and Exchange Commission (SEC) are considered and contrasted with those from a private sector system, such as the standards set in the UK. A government sanctioned accounting court also is considered. The paper closes with my own conclusions and suggestions.

## ACCOUNTING STANDARDS—DEFINITION AND DELINEATION

For present purposes, the three types of accounting standards delineated are disclosure, presentation and content.[4] The first two are relatively non-controversial, which may obscure their importance. The last type is the most troublesome, and hence receives most discussion. Though the types are not mutually exclusive, and hence fail as clearly defined categories, I believe that the delineation is useful for the discussion.

*Disclosure.* This standard requires only an explicit description of the accounting methods and assumptions on which the numbers presented are based. For example, the financial statements could be limited to reports of cash flows derived from market transactions or could include accrued assets and liabilities. Price level adjustments or current costs could be employed in addition to or in place of other numbers. Different

---

[1] Possible citations abound. For example, see Colin J. Jones, 'Accounting Standards—A Blind Alley?' *Accounting and Business Research*, Autumn 1975, pp. 273–279 for arguments in support of cash flow reporting, and the many publications of Raymond J. Chambers for arguments calling for 'economically relevant' numbers.

[2] Joel Demski, 'The General Impossibility of Normative Standards,' *Accounting Review*, October 1973, p. 722. For a contrary view see R. J. Chambers, 'The Possibility of a Normative Accounting Standards', *Accounting Review*, July 1976, pp. 646–652 and for a reply see Joel Demski, 'An Economic Analysis of the Chambers' Normative Standard', *Accounting Review*, July 1976, pp. 653–656.

[3] Michael Bromwich, 'The Possibility of Partial Accounting Standards,' *Accounting Review*, April 1980, pp. 288–300.

[4] See Harold Edey, 'Accounting Standards in the British Isles,' in W. T. Baxter and S. Davidson, ed., *Studies in Accounting, 3rd edition*, London: Institute of Chartered Accountants in England and Wales, 1977, pp. 294–305, for an excellent discussion and similar delineation from which I have borrowed.

depreciation methods could be followed, but each would have to be described. However, there is no requirement that any particular number or variable (such as sales turnover) be reported.[5]

Although such a disclosure standard would seem to permit anything, it actually implies generally accepted definitions and requires an explicit statement of changes in the methods and assumptions followed. The use of generally accepted definitions, such as 'cash basis' and 'accrual accounting', increases the efficiency of communication and prevents disclosures from being confusing or misleading to users. Efficiency in communication is enhanced when common definitions are agreed to. For example, if 'sales' are defined by an adopted standard as meaning that 'the legal title to goods produced or held for exchange in the normal course of business have passed from the enterprise to a customer', and if this were the case, no further description is required. But if 'sales' included the values of goods transferred on consignment, the disclosure standard would require that the definition be made explicit. Should this disclosure practice not be followed, the financial statements are likely to be misleading to users who expect the standard definition. For similar reasons, the disclosure standard requires reporting of changes in the accounting methods or assumptions followed.[6]

I should note that the disclosure standard implies, though it does not require, some agreement among financial statement preparers of what the content of the statements should be. The fact that a standard definition of particular items is accepted and adhered to indicates some agreement that these items should be disclosed. But there is no requirement to report anything, though reporting is likely to avoid costs imposed by statement users (an important factor that I discuss further below). All that is required is that the items presented are not identified in a manner that is likely to mislead knowledgeable users.

*Presentation.* Standards can be adopted that specify the form and type of numbers presented. For example, it could be required that balance sheets list assets and liabilities in a particular order. Income statements also could follow a particular order. And fund or cash flow or other types of statements could be required. Presentation standards could differ for specific groups of companies (e.g., industries). The purpose of this type of standard is a reduction in the cost to users of recording and perhaps using financial statement data. It is not inconsistent with the disclosure standard, and may be applied in conjunction with it. As is the case for the disclosure standard, this standard implies some agreement about the content of the statements. However, this agreement is minimal, since it would be acceptable for some companies to report on the cash basis, others on the accrual basis, and others on historical cost,

---

[5] In this important sense, the meaning of the term, 'disclosure', differs from its use by advocates of government mandated reporting. Thus, though the US Securities Acts speak of disclosure as the keystone concept, the SEC's Accounting Series Release No. 4 (1938) declares that '... where financial statements filed ... are prepared in accordance with accounting principles for which there is no substantial authoritative support, such financial statements will be presumed to be misleading or inaccurate despite disclosures contained in the certificate of the accountant or in footnotes to the statements provided the amounts involved are material.'

[6] The Accounting Standards Steering Committee's (ASSC) 'explanatory foreword' to the Statements of Standard Accounting Practice (1975) is in the spirit of the disclosure standard described. Members of the Institute are expected to 'use their best endeavours to ensure that standards are observed or, if they are not observed, that significant departures should, if material, be disclosed unless this would be impractical or misleading in the context of giving a true and fair view.'

replacement costs, current costs, or general price-level-index-adjusted historical cost.

*Content.* Content standards specify what numbers are to be published rather than how they are to be published. Three aspects of content standards should be distinguished: disclosure, specific-construct, and conceptual.

A *disclosure-content* standard simply specifies the items that must be included in financial statements. The Companies Acts are examples of this standard. For example, the Companies Act 1967 requires disclosure of such items as debentures of the company which may be reissued, the basis of conversion of foreign currencies, and turnover (sales) unless the company is neither a holding company nor subsidiary and the amount does not exceed £25,000.

A *specific-construct-content* standard refers to the basis upon which individual items are to be reported, such as a rule requiring that research and development expenditures not be capitalised. The rule may be adopted by reference to a more general concept, such as only assets that have clearly measurable market (exit) values should be capitalised at no more than these amounts. But this is not necessarily the case. Rather, the rule may be the product of a solution to a particular problem, such as accountants' reaction to criticism when, in a well-publicised case, capitalised intangibles turned out to be overstated.

A *conceptually-based-content* standard requires a theory from which operational rules can be derived which can be referenced to adjudicate between alternative procedures. Thus a strict cash-flow concept of accounting provides rules or standards that can be applied to define how transactions should be recorded, aggregated and presented, e.g., an event that can be reported in an accounting statement has not occurred until the asset, cash, has been exchanged. General application of a conceptually-based-content standard assumes the existence of a coherent and complete framework or theory that governs accounting. Though some people believe that such a framework exists, or should exist, it is clear that they are far from agreement as to what it should be. Some people would want economic, present value concepts to be the basis for the measurement of values, some opt for exit values, others current replacement costs, others price-level adjusted historical costs, while some prefer a more consistently applied market transaction based, historical cost system.[7] As is mentioned above, there is no way to determine which of these theories is best for all. Hence the difficulty, if not the undesirability, of imposing a general content standard on external financial statements.

## METHODS OF ESTABLISHING AND ENFORCING ACCOUNTING STANDARDS

The accounting standards delineated above may be established and enforced by the following methods: evolution and voluntary individual compliance, private accountancy bodies, and governmental stricture. Not all of these methods are applicable to each of the three types of standards discussed, nor are the methods mutually exclusive, as is discussed next.

1) *Evolution and Voluntary Individual Compliance.* Though consistent with all three types of standards, this method is applicable principally to the first standard — disclosure. What is disclosed will be determined by individual enterprises. One aspect

---

[7] References to the numbers of papers and books that have been written in support of various theories on procedures would fill many pages.

of their decisions about disclosure is the cost to others of using the disclosed numbers. As a result of experience which reveals the cost and benefits of disclosing and not disclosing specific numbers, a consensus is likely to be reached such that particular accounting rules and methods become 'generally accepted'. (The incentive for companies to disclose financial data is discussed below.)

Included in this method are accounting rules adopted by trade associations and other voluntary organisations, such as stock exchanges. They may find it desirable to impose disclosure, presentation or content standards on their members because of their belief that they will jointly benefit thereby. For example, the transaction costs to creditors or other investors may be lower if all members of the group follow standards that define specific assets and liabilities. Another example is the common disclosure of sales or expenditures on advertising.

2) *Private Accountancy Bodies.* Organisations such as the Institute of Chartered Accountants in England and Wales and the American Institute of Certified Public Accountants may impose standards to which their members must adhere. These standards may specify minimum reporting requirements or procedures for determining that the data reported meet minimum levels of quality (reliability). They may apply to any of the types of standards discussed above and, to date, have in some measure been concerned with all three types.

3) *Governmental Stricture.* Unlike the other methods, the force of law can be applied to compel performance. Three facets of this method are distinguished. One is government agencies, such as a utilities or banking commission, that require all members of a regulated industry to report or publish specified data. The rules on which these reports are based may be specified in whole or in part; usually the form of reporting (the presentation standard) is specified exactly. Included in this sub-group are income tax rules that define taxable income. Another is a law, such as the UK Companies Acts, that requires companies to prepare financial statements to be filed with a governmental agency, or in which specific items (such as director's emoluments) must be disclosed. The third is determination and policing of accounting standards by a regulatory agency, such as the US Securities and Exchange Commission. The Commission is given the legal authority to define accounting standards that may be imposed on all corporations that are subject to the Commission's jurisdiction.

## THE BENEFITS AND COSTS OF ESTABLISHING AND ENFORCING ACCOUNTING STANDARDS

Though the benefits (net of costs) of accounting standards to society, cannot, in principle, be measured, they can be specified for individuals. For the purpose of this analysis, people are aggregated into the following groups: investors, public accountants, government, and consumers. Each of these categories is discussed next, in turn.

*Investors.* Investors include present shareholders and other investors (including creditors and customers who rely on the position and prospects of the company), prospective shareholders and other investors, top managers, and other employees. The interests of shareholders, as residual owners of the firm, are considered first. In the course of the discussion, it should become clear that the owners have an overwhelming incentive to serve the interests of the other investors. It is assumed initially that they determine the financial information to be disclosed, from which they receive the benefits and incur the costs. Later, the role of managers of diffusely owned companies is considered.

Financial statements are produced for reasons which include communicating with creditors and other prospective investors and, possibly, for dealing with labour unions and/or employees directly. These parties (particularly creditors and other investors) assess the risk and return from investments in the company (compared to alternatives). Any costs they expect to incur, either from obtaining information or from assuming some possibility of loss, are, in effect, charged to the owners (present shareholders) of the company. Therefore, it pays the owners to provide these parties with financial statements and other information that will reduce the costs these users otherwise would incur.

Furthermore, financial data will be voluntarily disclosed because owners expect potential investors to fear the worst about their companies. Hence, these potential investors will reduce the returns they expect to obtain from investing in (or dealing with) the company to offset the losses associated with their fears. Therefore, the companies with 'good things' to reveal will disclose them and those that do not disclose are likely to be thought to have something to hide. Among the remaining (non-disclosing) companies are those that have less to hide than the others. For these 'better' companies, disclosure is preferable to the suspicion generated from no disclosure. The same process continues for the companies remaining. Finally, the companies that choose not to disclose items that other companies disclose evidently have decided that the negative aspects of disclosure (such as helping competitors) exceed the costs imposed by suspicious investors.

The company's owners, therefore, have an incentive to choose the accounting procedures and form of presentation of financial numbers that would be acceptable to users, since any costs imposed by poor or incomplete information on the users who want information about the company actually would be borne by the owners. Because the users may be a diverse group whose requirements, expertise, and tendency towards suspicion differ, the owners must attempt to achieve a balance between the overall costs of and benefits from disclosure. This calculation is similar to that undertaken for other business decisions, such as which products to produce and which distribution methods to use.

It should be noted that potential investors have reason to believe that the owners might mislead them (though perhaps not intentionally). After all, owners (like other people) tend to maximise their own welfare, which is not the same as the welfare of others. An important means by which owners can convince users of the veracity of accounting statements, and overcome the problems of moral hazard and adverse selection, is by having the statements attested to by people whose expertise and integrity is acceptable to the users. This role is played by independent public accountants. As I discuss in greater detail elsewhere,[8] public accountants have a comparative advantage over the company's employees in providing the attestation service.

Accounting standards would be valued if they reduced the cost of evaluating the statements to users. But the standards and their enforcement are costly, in several important regards. First, recording, transforming, and presenting data that a

[8] See George J. Benston, 'The Market for Public Accounting Services: Demand, Supply, and Regulation,' *The Accounting Journal*, vol. 3, 1980.

company would not disclose were it not required to do so is costly. Second, the more complicated and extensive the data base and presentation, the more costly is an audit and attestation by a public accountant. Third, for some companies, providing the information specified by the standards to investors may be exceeded by the costs of informing competition. Fourth, the specific numbers that the owners of one company believe will best inform investors are likely to differ from the numbers that another company finds most useful to investors (net of costs), because the circumstances of companies differ. In addition, inappropriate standards impose costs on users (and hence on company owners) because the users have to learn about the standards in order to know what to disregard. Therefore, for many individual companies, the costs from standardisation may well exceed the benefits. However, those companies that would produce the data required by a standard even in its absence would benefit from reduced costs to users and from obtaining the data from other companies.

I believe that most companies are likely to find a content standard based on economic concepts more costly than beneficial. The problem is that it is conceptually impossible for the numbers, to which public accountants would be willing to attest, to provide, in themselves, valid measures of economic value or changes in value until fitted into a user's model. In addition, the measurement of economic values requires use of an implicit discount rate, which is likely to differ among individuals. Therefore, any set of numbers reported is unlikely to meet all (perhaps even most) users' requirements. Even worse, numbers that purport to report economic values are likely to be incorrect when events are other than as predicted. These numbers then may be misleading to investors, who consequently may charge the companies and their accountants with negligence or fraud. Therefore, an economic value based content standard would decrease rather than increase investors' confidence in the company's owners' veracity.

In contrast, minimal disclosure and presentation standards are likely to yield greater benefits than costs for most companies. These standards tend to reduce the costs to users of interpreting and processing the data presented. In addition, investors may find useful the data published by companies other than the one in which they are contemplating an investment. Companies also may find other companies' data useful. But if these benefits cannot be captured by the companies individually, their owners will not individually have an incentive to publish the numbers. They may benefit jointly, however, by agreeing to standards that govern the presentation, quantity and quality of financial data. For example, they could voluntarily form groups, such as stock exchanges or trade associations, which impose standards on their members. They also might be in favour of governmentally enforced standards, particularly where the government could employ more effective sanctions against cheating. Companies that would find disclosure by others beneficial to them also have reason to favour government imposed standards. However, they probably will not benefit when the government officials' objective functions differ substantially from their own. As is discussed further below, this is likely to be the case.

Consider now the incentives for voluntary disclosure by the top managers of companies, the owners of which are diffuse. The owners of these corporations are not in a position to make or enforce disclosure policies. This is the situation for most publicly owned corporations. But before ownership becomes diffuse, the promotors and owners of these companies are likely to realise that, once they have ceded control to professional managers, the managers might choose not to disclose data that the owners want. Furthermore, if these data are not disclosed, the owners would be paid a lower price for their shares by other investors, who discount the expected cost of not getting the desired data. Therefore, the original promotors and owners have incentives to establish a system of reporting that managers would find difficult to drop or reduce. For this purpose, they arrange for control by an elected board of directors, for auditing by a recognised firm of independent public accountants, and often for subjecting the company to requirements enforced by an outside organisation, such as a stock exchange. Government mandated reporting also might be useful for this purpose.

Another, and probably no less important factor working for adequate voluntary disclosure, is the managers' and other employees' incentives for establishing and maintaining a public reporting system. They also are investors in the company, since they incur transactions costs when they change jobs, and since the ability of the enterprise to reward them for their performance is a function of how others in the company perform. As in the case for most persons, managers and other employees tend to maximise their own welfare. Hence they realise (as do owners and other investors) that they will be suspected of misusing company resources (that is, of using the resources in ways that do not maximise the owners' wealth). Their salaries and other rewards, therefore, are likely to reflect this expected behaviour. Thus they benefit from a control and reporting system that is cost effective in reducing this sub-optimal behaviour. But, as is true for the owners, the managers would not want to disclose information that would harm the company (e.g., by benefiting competitors) more than it reduces costs to investors.

Where non-management employees consider themselves or are considered partners of the managers and owners, in the sense that they work for a share of the wealth created, the accounting system may provide a means of establishing the amount of wealth that is to be divided. For this purpose, generally accepted accounting standards would be desirable, since these workers are likely to distrust accounts that are subjectively determined by management. It is in the owners' and managers' interest, therefore, to establish an accounting system that is trusted by those who use its output. As is discussed next, public accountants provide the service of assuring these people and others that the company's resources have not been misused and that the financial statements published are not designed to mislead users.

*Public Accountants.* Public accountants sell their expertise and integrity in auditing companies' records and attesting to the validity (in some sense) of their financial statements. A major reason for their employment in this capacity is that it is generally recognised that they stand to lose much should they be sloppy or dishonest in performing an audit or in agreeing to the publication of misleading figures. No doubt it is true that some accountants are people of such superior personal moral standards that users are satisfied simply to know that these people have attested to a company's statements. (I believe that the founders of the profession were successful because they were known for holding high personal standards.) Thus individuals and firms of accountants take their reputations for integrity very seriously. But users tend to rely on these and other public accountants, not only because of their personal integrity, but because the economic (and psychic) value of the integrity would be diminished, if not destroyed, were the accountants to perform badly or dishonestly; therefore the accountants have strong incentives not to do so.

Though individuals and firms are concerned primarily with their own reputations, the failings of other public accountants are likely to be costly if the public considers all public accountants to be of a class. Therefore, it is beneficial for like-minded public accountants to define themselves as a particular class identified by a form of trademark, such as chartered and certified public accountant, in addition to their identification as firms, such as Arthur Young McClelland Moores. While members of firms can police their fellow partners, it is difficult to monitor the performance of other chartered or certified public accountants. For this purpose, the establishment of standards to which all chartered or certified accountants subscribe is useful.

In particular, disclosure and auditing standards serve this requirement, since they can be achieved by experts who exercise due care and independence. Content standards also are desirable if they make audits more effective, and work against companies using financial statements to mislead investors. However, a content standard that called for assessments of economic values would endanger the reputation of public accountants, since it cannot be achieved and requires subjectively-based estimates that might mislead investors, or that appear, *ex post*, to have misled investors.

Public accountants may desire that accounting standards be enforced by government, for several reasons. One is the fear that competition among accountants may lead some to chance compromising their integrity. Another is the desire (common to most sellers of goods and services) to increase the demand for their products by legal requirements. A third is derived from the specialist's belief that the laity would benefit from a higher quality product, but does not recognise the benefits therefrom because of ignorance; consequently a legal requirement should be imposed. As is discussed further below, this requirement is likely to have unpleasant concomitant effects for public accountants when the authority for accounting standards is vested in government agents.

*Government.* Four aspects of the government's interest in accounting data and standards may be distinguished: taxation, regulation of enterprises, planning and regulation of the economy, and enhancement of economic efficiency and other social goals. Each is discussed briefly.

*Income taxation* requires a definition of income that is administratively efficient. If the government (by which I mean the collective will of the people or of those in power, as expressed by laws and regulations) wants the tax system to be economically neutral, the definition of taxable income should reflect the real economic activities undertaken by taxpayers. For example, if income is defined by historical costs, and an inflation is expected but depreciation rules are not changed, the net (after tax) costs of assets is greater because the deductible depreciation understates the economic sacrifice involved. In this situation, taxpayers will shift their resources to other assets and to consumption. If the government wants the tax system to be biased in favour of, say, investment over consumption, it might subsidise the purchase of productive assets by permitting higher rates of depreciation. Equity considerations may also be a desired outcome. For example, when an unexpected inflation occurs, resources are shifted from creditors to debtors (unless their contracts are price-level indexed). Government might want to mitigate these windfalls with taxes. In any event, it would seem preferable (from the government's point of view) that the definitions of taxable income yield the desired, as compared to other, outcomes.

Administrative efficiency also is an important aspect of taxation. Two costs of collecting taxes might be delineated. One is the resources used by taxpayers to avoid taxes. Since a tax is an expense that is equivalent to any other expense for the individual taxpayer, it pays taxpayers to organise their affairs to the point where the marginal value of resources used to avoid taxes equals the marginal amount of taxes avoided. But for society, these resources are wasted, since, given a legislated level of government expenditures, someone must pay the taxes. The other expense is the resources used by the government to assess and collect the taxes.

For administrative efficiency, it is useful to base taxable income on the records designed for a business' control and reporting requirements. These records are audited and, since they are maintained in any case, using them reduces the cost of the tax system to society. Both types of administrative expense can be reached by presentation and content accounting standards, since they tend to make the tax incidence more certain. But, because the measurement of economic values necessarily is subjective, and hence difficult to administer, a compromise between the goals of taxation must be made.

In deciding the specific accounting standards that will achieve its goals, government is not well advised to rely completely on the standards developed for financial statement reporting. As is discussed above, internal control and public reporting are determined by the costs and benefits to the enterprise. The government, though, is likely to want other net benefits. For example, immediate write-off of assets may be permitted for tax purposes as a means of subsidising investment. Whether or not company owners and managers believe that the benefits from using price-level adjusted data or current cost data are worth the cost, the government nevertheless could base taxes on these data if it believes that historical cost-determined taxable income results in misallocated resources, the cost of which exceeds the cost of change. Because companies individually cannot capture fully the benefits from a better tax assessment system, the government should not expect them voluntarily to adopt the 'best' accounting system from its viewpoint.

*Regulation of enterprises* often is based on accounting data. For example, the rate that US public utilities can charge is determined by the rate of return they earn on their assets. Insurance companies and banks report financial data that inspectors use to evaluate their operations. As is the case for income taxation, the required accounting procedures tend to be those that impose the least costs on the regulated and the regulator. Hence, presentation and content standards are imposed, with the emphasis on administrative efficiency. For this reason, the standards may be (and usually are) somewhat different and more highly specified than are the standards that individual enterprises adopt for other purposes.

It is important to note an inherent problem when government agencies attempt to use accounting reports for economic planning purposes. Because of the subjective nature of economic value, accounting numbers are poor and often misleading indications of the current or past status and periodic economic changes of the enterprises in the economy. Furthermore, should government want to obtain numbers that can be collected and aggregated with reasonable efficiency, it must specify exact and complete accounting content standards. But the result of this specification necessarily is less economically meaningful numbers. Rather than impose data preparation and collection costs on enterprises and (probably of greater importance) costs on the economy of decisions based on inappropriate data, government would be well advised to recognise the accounting system's limitations and look elsewhere for numbers or question the advisability of much economic planning and control.

The enhancement of economic efficiency and other social goals might be achieved if the optimal publication of accounting data by companies could be obtained by means of government action. One action might be the specification of presentation standards to facilitate the recording and comparison of data among companies. Content standards also might serve this purpose, subject to the important limitation that economic content generally cannot be standardised. As is discussed above, companies may not publish data because they cannot capture the full benefits to users (the externality) of the data, such as evaluations of investment opportunities in other companies. Another possible benefit is more accurate evaluation by the public of enterprises generally. For example, publication only of historical cost-based income figures in an inflationary period may result in the public's or labour unions' overestimation of business profits and their consequent demand for higher taxes or wage settlements. The government also has the power to enforce standards by punishing cheating with fines and other sanctions.

Two important limitations of the possible benefits from government imposed standards should be emphasised. One is that individual companies have incentives for publishing data that are in relatively easy-to-use forms and that do not give the public and labour unions a potentially damaging perception of the company's economic position. (These incentives include joining together with other companies to follow common standards.) The second is that government mandated standards are costly and the costs can exceed the benefits. Because these costs differ importantly depending on the type of system of government mandation adopted, a further discussion is undertaken in which the UK's essentially passive system is contrasted with USA's active system.

## A COMPARISON AND EVALUATION OF ALTERNATIVE METHODS OF ENFORCING ACCOUNTING STANDARDS[9]

*Government Mandated Rules—The Securities and Exchange Commission (SEC).* The SEC was created in 1934 to administer the Securities Act of 1933 and the Securities Exchange Act of 1934. Five full time commissioners, appointed by the President, preside over a large staff of professional and other employees. The Commission is given the responsibility and authority to prescribe accounting standards and rules for reports filed pursuant to the Securities Acts. All corporations with over 500 shareholders and $1,000,000 in assets are legally obligated to file periodic reports with the Commission conforming to the accounting rules and standards that it promulgates and including the items that it specifies. Furthermore, the Commission defines the conditions under which public accountants who attest to the statements are considered 'independent', and disciplines attesting accountants who violate these conditions.

Those who believe that accounting standards are desirable and are upset because evolutionary, voluntary developments are too slow and, in any event, appear to be incomplete, might favour an SEC type of enforcement. The advantages claimed for such a commission include the following: (1) the rules can be adapted to changing circumstances by experts who are in continual contact with the reporting problems of companies and with users' changing requirements; (2) the SEC has the legal authority

---

[9] A more complete comparison of the administration of accounting disclosure laws in the UK and the USA may be found in George J. Benston, *Corporate Financial Disclosure in the UK and the USA*, Saxon House/Lexington (DC Heath) and the Institute of Chartered Accountants in England and Wales, 1976, especially Chapter 5.

to enforce standards, and thus can provide a goad to the accounting profession to develop standards and prevent 'free riders' from not complying with the standards; and (3) the SEC has the resources (financial and experiential) to develop and design standards in an attempt to optimise social net benefits. However, these expectations have not been met in the USA. Furthermore, I believe that such a commission is inherently unlikely to act other than as the SEC has acted over its history.

A regulatory commission, such as the SEC, necessarily is staffed with people, who (like others) tend to maximise their own welfare. When a commission is given power and responsibility, it generally uses them because its officers will be criticised if they fail to have put a regulation in force that, at least in appearance, might have prevented or mitigated a real or apparent crisis. (It is important to emphasise that appearance is as important as, perhaps even more important than, reality, since public criticism often is based on appearance alone.) Unlike a private enterprise, though, the commission does not benefit from resources saved when unnecessary regulations are removed. Therefore, the commission tends to be conservative, in the sense that it continues old regulations even when they appear to be no longer useful, and adds new regulations in response to each problem, real or presumed. Furthermore, the commission prefers administratively efficient regulations, regulations that can be described by written rules and that protect the commission from public criticism of its administration. Thus the accounting standards adopted and enforced need not be (indeed, are unlikely to be) those that would capture for society the externalities of non-mandated financial reporting.

Throughout most of its 45 years' history, the SEC has operated in a manner similar to that sketched briefly above. Though it delegated much of its authority to promulgate accounting standards to the organised accounting profession, it early established a strong, conservative, historical-cost bias. In particular, it acted vigorously in insisting that intangible assets (especially goodwill), and similar items that are not likely to be objectively determined, be written off as expenses. Other types of 'soft information' also were excluded from documents filed pursuant to the law. These included sales and profit forecasts and asset revaluations (including price-level adjustments). Thus the Commission acted to make its task administratively convenient and defensible, even though the result was that financial statements tended to provide less information to users. As problems and minor crises occurred new regulations were added; almost none were withdrawn. When activism among US regulatory agencies and legislatures became popular in the 1960s, the SEC also changed its policies in that it added a relatively large number of new regulations and other requirements, including adoption of mandatory fixed asset replacement cost estimates for large corporations. However, the SEC has not attempted to establish 'new' accounting standards directly, with a few exceptions.[10] But it has promulgated very detailed rules that govern the items that must be reported.

In summary, the SEC has not acted to establish overall accounting content standards that reflect economic values, despite its legislated power to do so. The Commission's reluctance, I suggest, stems from its realisation that the political costs

---

[10] Recently, the SEC overturned an accounting standard adopted by the Financial Accounting Standards Board (FASB) that would have required oil and gas exploration and development companies to use successful-efforts accounting, and substituted an as yet not implemented requirement that present value accounting be used to value fuel reserves. As a consequence the FASB withdrew its standard.

potentially incurred would exceed the benefits to it as an agency. The costs include disagreements among the constituents (e.g., accounting practitioners, security analysts and brokers, companies, the press, and legislators) as to which standards to apply. But perhaps of greater importance is the Commission's recognition that general content standards that purport to provide economic measurements open it to potentially damaging criticism. However, the Commission has not been inactive. It has established presentation standards and a very large number of specific rules that attempt to govern almost every situation that has come to its attention. Thus companies and public accountants are faced with the expense of learning and following these regulations, while it is doubtful that users have achieved much in the way of benefits.[11]

*Private Sector Standard Setting—The UK Method.* The Companies Acts specify that financial statements are to be produced by companies, which items are to be disclosed therein, and rules governing measurement of some of these items. In this important regard, accounting standards are not privately determined. The accounting bodies, through the Statements of Standard Accounting Practice, specify standards that qualified accountants should follow. However, auditors can accept statements that are based on other methods, if they quantify the difference and explain why the alternatives are more consistent with 'a true and fair view'. Or auditors can object to the use of other alternatives and qualify their attestations. The Stock Exchange also can demand that certain additional reporting standards be followed, but, as in the USA, they tend to follow and support the accounting profession's pronouncements.

Some critics object to the UK system because only the Companies Acts can require strict adherence to standards. Aside from the provisions of the Acts and some Stock Exchange requirements (which apply only to listed companies), these critics complain that only a disclosure standard is in force, particularly since companies can and do accept qualified attestations.

*An Accounting Court as a Means of Enforcing Standards.* A statutory accounting court has been suggested, to which companies that do not follow accounting standards established by the Accounting Standards Committee (or similar body) could be brought.[12] The companies charged would have to demonstrate that the procedures they used are preferable to those described in the adopted standards for presenting 'a true and fair view'. The function of the court would be to adjudicate disputes and therefore enforce accounting standards and establish a body of case law to which future decisions could be referred. A review of the activities of such a court in the Netherlands, however, provides reasons to believe that it would not serve this purpose well. After reviewing the court's case history, Jan Klaassen concludes: 'Only the issues put forth by the plaintiff are judged by the court. It does not take a position

---

[11] See Benston, *ibid*, Chapter 5, for the reasoning and evidence on which this conclusion is based.

[12] As best I could learn, an accounting court was proposed first in the USA by Leonard Spacek, who outlined the procedures under which it would operate in 'Draft of a Bill That Would Create a United States Court of Accounting Appeals,' in *A Search for Fairness in Financial Reporting to the Public* by Leonard Spacek, Chicago: Arthur Andersen & Co., 1969, pp. 576–582. Edward Stamp also called for the creation of an accounting court that would be empowered to accept accounting statements (in one version) or rule on disputes (in another version). See 'The Public Accountant and the Public Interest,' *Journal of Business Finance*, vol. 1 (1969), pp. 32–42, reprinted in Edward Stamp and Christopher Marley, *Accounting Principles and the City Code: The Case for Reform*, London: Butterworths, 1970, pp. 168–187.

on other issues. It makes its judgments only on the specific circumstances of each case. This makes the Enterprise Chamber an inadequate vehicle for the development of accounting standards.'[13]

## CONCLUSIONS

The establishment and enforcement of accounting standards requires, as a minimum, a clear and accepted idea of what the standards should reflect. I suggest that such standards include the following: (1) the accounting statements presented should disclose any material deviation from the expected stewardship of a company's directors and top management (as defined by the statutes and the courts); it should report on the outcome of an audit carried out under generally accepted auditing standards; (2) the statements should report data that are objectively determined from market transactions; adjustments made to the data (such as accruals, allocations, revaluations, and price-level adjustments) should be described either by reference to generally known procedures (if these were established) or with sufficient descriptions; and (3) changes from previous periods in the reporting procedures followed should be explained so that users are not misled. I believe that it is theoretically impossible for financial statements on accounting measurements to report the economic value of the enterprise as a going concern. Therefore, content standards that attempt to bring this about are not operational.

The question as to how accounting standards should be established and enforced is answered by reference to the net benefits of the externalities involved and the costs of administration. I believe that the magnitude of the externalities that could be gained from mandating accounting standards is small. This conclusion is based on the assumption that the private producers of accounting statements presently have incentives that result in their individually publishing close to the optimal amount and type of data, or in creating voluntary organisations that compel the members to disclose close to the optimal. On the other side of the equation, the USA's experience with the SEC leads me to conclude that it is not likely that such an agency will or even can determine the optimal set of information to be disclosed or the 'best' accounting standards to be followed. To the contrary, the agency has incentives to add considerable costs and few benefits to the disclosure process, and tends to do so. Similarly, I expect that if an accounting court evolved into a standard setting agency, it would be subject to the same behavioural forces, and these would result in its degeneration into an administrative agency such as the SEC.

In any event, before changes in the present system in the UK are considered further, I suggest that the objections to the present system of setting and enforcing standards be examined more closely. In what ways is it deficient? What reason is there to believe that these deficiencies are not inherent and are best recognised as such? Have the costs of improving the system (including the costs of making and interpreting changes) to companies, accountants, and users been fully considered and compared with the expected benefits? If change appears desirable, can an educational process rather than mandatory standards be used as a means of improving reporting? Until these and other questions are resolved, or at least considered, I suggest that caution is the wise policy.

[13] Jan Klaassen, 'An Accounting Court: The Impact of the Enterprise Chamber on Financial Reporting in the Netherlands,' *Accounting Review*, April 1980, p. 337.

# I-A 10 *Research for Accounting Policy: An Overview*

ROBERT G. MAY AND GARY L. SUNDEM

A significant amount of accounting research is devoted to questions of accounting (financial reporting) policy. Such research is addressed to the alternative models, measurement rules and disclosure requirements that are or might be applied in current financial reporting by business enterprises. Such research accounts for much of the combined research efforts sponsored or undertaken by institutions such as the AICPA and FASB as well as for much of the independent academic research in accounting.

The purpose of this paper is to offer a model for organizing one's thoughts and efforts directed toward the process of accounting policy making and related research strategies. The motivation for attempting such a task is a conviction that results from individual accounting research studies must be interpreted as interrelated building blocks for accounting policy decisions. As Gonedes and Dopuch [1974] showed, virtually no research strategy used by accounting researchers to date is capable of selecting the most socially desirable accounting alternative. However, because Gonedes and Dopuch applied such a demanding performance criterion to accounting research (i.e., achieving a social ranking of alternatives), they leave an impression of great pessimism. Yet, as will be evident later, the most promising use of any given research strategy (data source) in the area of financial reporting policy is not in selecting optimal alternatives; rather, it is in contributing, *along with all other available strategies*, to developing theories that then may be used by policy makers to settle specific issues.

The paper begins with a description of accounting policy making as a social choice process. This discussion contains a brief enumeration of certain implications of the social choice dimension of accounting policy making; the second section presents a model for interpretation of research for accounting policy making; and the third section discusses the potential contributions of various research strategies.

The authors would like to thank the participants of the accounting colloquia at the University of Washington and Oklahoma State University for their helpful comments on earlier drafts.

Robert G. May and Gary L. Sundem, "Research for Accounting Policy: An Overview," October 1976, pp. 747–763. Reprinted by permission of *The Accounting Review*.

## ACCOUNTING POLICY DECISIONS AS SOCIAL CHOICES

For nearly half a century, the accounting profession has been concerned with forming accounting policy, i.e., deciding which measurement and reporting alternatives are acceptable and which are not. From the time the first standard audit report in 1933 referred to "accepted principles of accounting" [Rosenfield, 1964], the profession has taken upon itself the task of deciding what is acceptable. The Committee on Accounting Procedure (1939–1950), The Accounting Principles Board (1959–1973) and the Financial Accounting Standards Board (1973–) have had major policy-making responsibility. Yet, after all of these years of policy making, the procedures for policy formulation are not always well understood.

Before proceeding to a detailed discussion of policy decisions, it is necessary to distinguish between accounting theories and accounting policy [Ijiri, 1975, pp. 9–11]. An accounting theory is a descriptive or predictive model whose validity is independent of the acceptance of any goal structure. Though *assumed* goals may be part of such a model, research relating to a theory or model of accounting does not require acceptance of the assumed goals as necessarily desirable or undesirable. On the other hand, accounting policy requires a commitment to goals and, therefore, requires a policy maker to make value judgments. Policy decisions presumably are based on *both* an understanding of accounting theories *and* acceptance of a set of goals. Research relating to accounting policy decisions must recognize and discern the aspect of the policy-making process at issue.

For the moment, we will discuss the unique aspect of accounting policy, namely, goal formulation. Several recent attempts have been made to delineate the goals or objectives of financial accounting [e.g., Arthur Anderson & Co.; 1972; Study Group on the Objectives of Financial Statements, 1973; Defliese, 1973; and Accounting Standards Steering Committee, 1975]. Since the selection of a set of goals is inherently a value judgement, most debate about sets of goals is a debate about whose value judgments are best. This is an insoluable problem, as value judgments are neither right nor wrong, true nor false. The resolution of the problem of selection of goals must be solved by general agreement, not by proof of correctness. Therefore, the first step in a logical process of policy formulation is to obtain general agreement on the goal of financial accounting.

The statements of goals of financial accounting made to date suffer from two major problems: (1) they have not received general acceptance and (2) they do not provide a basis for selecting among alternative policies. For instance, a recent statement of goals asserts that "the basic objective of financial statements is to provide information useful for making economic decisions" [Study Group of the Objectives of Financial Statements, 1973, p. 13]. However, this is not a statement of a goal of financial statements, but merely a delineation of the domain of accounting policy decisions. That is, it states *what* accounting policy makers are to be concerned with, but it does not state *how* comparisons among alternative policies are to be made.

We suggest that an objective of maximization of social welfare (which may be implied, though not stated, in the above objective) is a necessary addition to the above goal statement.[1] While this is admittedly our value judgment, such a goal seems to provide a criterion for policy decisions and, to our knowledge, no one has expressed

---

[1] See Committee on Concepts and Standards; External Financial Reports [1975, pp. 42–44] for more details.

disagreement with it as an objective. In a letter to the AICPA, the SEC has expressed concern that accounting policy decisions be "consistent with the public interest" [Burton, 1973, p. 271]. Indeed, the Securities Acts clearly were motivated by a desire to prevent recurrence of the socially deleterious events surrounding the crash and ensuing Great Depression. Moreover, the U.S. Congress has intervened in accounting policy decisions at least once, in the investment tax credit decision, when it felt that an accounting policy decision was not in the public interest. Since accounting policy decisions that apparently are not consistent with the public interest can be reversed by a higher authority, it is apparent that either accounting policy makers (the SEC-FASB) at least must appear to pursue a social welfare criterion or have their power consistently preempted by the legislature, which presumably applies such a criterion. Thus, the political environment of accounting policy formulation implies acceptance of a social welfare criterion for accounting policy decisions as social choices.

It is possible for accounting policy decisions to be made by each individual or firm producing a financial statement, in the same way that policy decisions concerning any other economic commodity are made. A demand for accounting information exists because individuals wish to improve their investment decisions. This private demand would lead to production and sale of financial statements.

Although general public policy would apply (e.g., general antitrust policy would apply to the industry structures that evolved in the production and sale of private financial information about business enterprises), no special public accounting policy would be necessary to satisfy demand for financial information on the part of individuals. Research in financial accounting could contribute to such a laissez-faire environment by producing microeconomic information (e.g., predicting individual costs and benefits), similar to cost and market research relevant to the production and distribution of other goods and services.

But accounting information may have public value apart from its private value [Fama and Laffer, 1971; Hirshleifer, 1971; and Demski, 1974a]. Because accounting information may influence individual investor's assessments and, through these assessments, the structure of security prices, therefore the information may influence the distribution of costs of capital among firms and, through that distribution, the allocation of capital to various uses in the economy. The possibilities of both production and consumption externalities in information generation imply that regulation of accounting information production may lead to an allocation of resources that is pareto superior to that achieved by a free-market equilibrium allocation. Moreover, changes in information production induced by regulation may alter the value of securities portfolios and, through those values, the distribution of wealth among individuals. Either one or both of these potential influences adds a social value dimension to the regulation of financial accounting information.

A necessary (but not sufficient) condition for regulation to create a socially *better* allocation of resources and/or distribution of wealth is that it *at least* be capable of producing a *different* allocation and/or distribution than would be attained in a free market.[2] There are several reasons that this condition may be met. First, regulation

---

[2] The social desirability of any piece of *regulation* will depend on the amount of and ownership of resources used to decide on and enforce the regulation as well as the reallocation of resources and redistribution of wealth brought about by the regulation. Henceforth, we will not be concerned about the desirability of any particular regulation, but we will accept the result that regulation is potentially desirable. The dilemma of comparing the social desirability of alternative *allocations* is discussed in Demski [1974a, pp. 227–228].

can impose production of information on entities with comparative advantages in producing the information (usually perceived to be the business enterprise in the case of financial accounting information). However, these entities do not necessarily have a private incentive to do so. In this way, it may be possible to alter the information set employed privately by investors in forming their preferences for various securities by altering the distribution of costs of information [May and Sundem, 1973]. Such alterations may affect resource allocation and wealth distribution directly by changing the production opportunities of other (external) information suppliers, even though their effect on the security price structure is minimal. Second, since optimal investment strategies imply interfirm comparisons, some external economies in information processing may be achievable through imposition of certain unifor-mities in financial accounting information produced. This may mean lower costs of acquiring information for investors and other decision makers. Third, to the extent that a policy apparatus lessens the probability of major financial scandals, it may contribute to the general perception of risk *over a vast number of risky investments* and, therefore, the level of savings and investment in the economy as a whole.

Accounting information is like many other commodities produced in our economy today: the private market for such information is modified by explicit public policy (regulation) decisions. The decisions to produce and consume accounting information are influenced by the FASB, SEC and other regulatory bodies. As noted earlier, in practice as well as in theory, the social welfare impact of accounting reports apparently is recognized. Therefore it is no surprise that the FASB is a political body and, consequently, that the process of selecting acceptable accounting alternatives is a political process. If the social welfare impact of accounting policy decisions were ignored, the basis for the existence of a regulatory body would disappear. Therefore, the FASB must consider explicitly political (i.e., social welfare) aspects as well as accounting theory and research in its decisions.

In a democratic-capitalist society, it is virtually unassailable in principle that social policy should be sensitive to individual preferences.[3] However, Demski [1973] has shown that, in general, the characteristics of accounting information per se (e.g., relevance, objectivity) do not reflect the preferences of individuals affected by the use of the information. This implies that policy makers must go beyond comparing alternative policies regarding the degree to which their outputs conform to certain purely technical or aesthetic standards, e.g., "true economic value," "true income," relevance and objectivity. That is, accounting policy makers must employ a decision model that is sensitive to individual preferences. Such a decision model is called a collective choice rule.

Unfortunately, selection of a collective choice rule is complicated by two very formidable difficulties. First, it has been proven that it is impossible to construct a collective choice rule that satisfies even a minimal set of general conditions.[4] Second, notwithstanding the impossibility of constructing a completely satisfactory collec-tive choice rule, it seems reasonable to assert further that it is extraordinarily costly, if not impossible, to construct a social decision-making system that could assess the

---

[3] This notion was expressed most succinctly by Quirk and Saposnik as follows:

"In principle, one could conceive of a whole host of theories of welfare economics, based upon differing sets of value judgments concerning the manner in which the term "desirable" state of the economy or economic system should be defined; in practice, essentially all of modern welfare economics is based upon one fundamental ethical postulate. To borrow Samuelson's phrase: In evaluating states of the economy, *individuals' preferences are to count.*" [1968, p. 104].

consequences for and preferences of every individual who might be affected by a given accounting policy decision.[5]

Clearly, the above discussion presents a paradox. On the one hand, we would like to have a systematic way for accounting policy makers to choose among alternatives based on individual preferences. At the same time, no such systematic way exists that satisfies even a relatively few desirable properties. Moreover, as a practical matter only limited knowlege of individual preferences is feasible.

One way to face this challenge is to explore applications to accounting of the concepts of social choice that have evolved in welfare economics and decision theory. Some initial efforts in this direction were Demski [1974a and 1974b], Gonedes and Dopuch [1974] and May and Sundem [1976], but the issues are far too formidable to resolve here. Research into the selection of an appropriate collective choice rule for accounting policy decisions is one of the most difficult tasks facing accounting researchers. We will proceed on the assumption that no satisfactory resolution of the issues will abandon completely the ethical judgment that *individuals' preferences are to count* in accounting policy decisions.

## A MODEL FOR ACCOUNTING POLICY DECISIONS

Our model of accounting policy decisions now has a goal—maximization of social welfare—and a social decision process employing some collective choice rule (currently, the FASB with their operating procedures) for selecting among accounting alternatives. This section completes the model by describing the framework for research in accounting theories to support the accounting policy decisions. This framework is shown in Figure 1; this figure provides the basis for the subsequent discussion of potentials for and limitations of accounting research.

Notice that Figure 1 is subdivided (by the dotted lines) into several sectors, including (1) business firms and auditors, (2) individuals, (3) markets and (4) accounting policy makers. These sectors are not meant to be mutually exclusive in the sense that no individual may be represented in more than one. Rather, they are intended to represent individuals in various distinguishable roles relevant to the discussion. Notice that there is a counterclockwise flow in the figure. This represents the general direction of impetus or influence in the accounting policy-making process, at least in principle, and necessarily abstracts from the many potential counter-currents and forces. We will discuss each of the four sectors individually, indicating briefly some of the kinds of research that are appropriate for that part of the policy process. Then we will discuss the overall framework of accounting research for policy decisions.

Sector I represents the formal accounting policy decision system. Accounting policy makers are shown explicitly, but there is no implication that they must exert an influence on the choice of accounting practices allowed. They could allow a laissez-

---

[4] Arrow's original proof, which applies to collective choice rules that represent orderings of social states, first appeared in Arrow [1951]. Arrow's theorem was first cited in the accounting literature by Demski [1974a]. The conditions, the proof and its implications are described in very readable style in the unstarred (non-mathematical) chapters of Sen [1970] and in Quirk and Saposnik [1968, Chapter 4].

[5] A social decision-making system, as the term is used here, is intended to include a collective choice rule plus the necessary institutional apparatus to implement the rule.

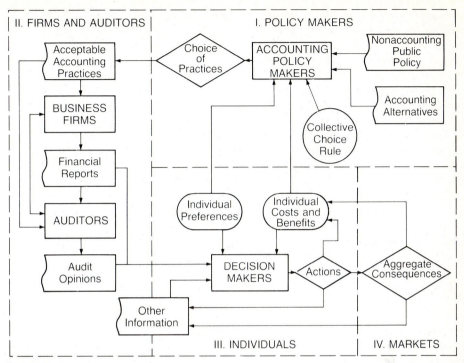

**FIGURE 1**
**The Accounting Policy-Making Process**

faire environment to exist, with financial accounting statements treated as a nonregulated commodity. However, the potential social welfare impacts of these statements and the current institutional structure suggest that some regulation is likely, so the framework is more consistent with the existence of specific accounting policy makers with some power to enforce their policy decisions. It is also consistent with the current political environment within which the FASB and SEC operate—one in which accounting policy decisions must be acceptable to a broad set of individuals and not merely consistent with "accounting theory."

Accounting policy makers must specify the set of acceptable accounting practices, which depends on the collective choice rule and social decision system they use (which were discussed in the previous section). It also depends on the accounting alternatives available; development and refinement of these alternatives is an important area for research. Nonaccounting public policy is also an important input. An often neglected area of research is how accounting policy fits into an overall public policy framework. (See, e.g., Committee on Concepts and Standards: External Financial Reports [1975], p. 43.) Other inputs relate to feedback on the impacts of policy decisions on individuals which will be discussed in more detail later.

Section II of Figure 1 traces through the effect of policy decisions on financial statements, including auditors' opinions. A first step in predicting ultimate consequences of policy decisions is to predict their effect on financial statements.

Therefore a priori research, which predicts the financial statement effects of alternative measurement and reporting rules, can be an important research contribution. And, where possible, empirical research confirming or describing actual financial statement effects is probably even more helpful.

Sector III consists of all individuals in society, each of whom makes consumption and investment decisions. We arbitrarily could divide these individuals into three categories: (1) those who produce and/or audit financial statements or other information, (2) those who use financial statement and other data in their decision making and (3) those who do not use any investment-relevant information. Most accounting research makes these divisions and concentrates only on *users* of financial statement data. This is a major simplification that is not necessarily desirable. Only if the extra cost of a complete analysis is greater than the benefit achieved is such simplification desirable. So, in our general framework we include *all* individuals whose welfare can conceivably be affected by accounting policy in this sector. Thus, this sector may include individuals who act in the capacities of enterprise management and independent auditors or, for that matter, public policy makers in the other sectors.

Individuals use information, including, but by no means limited to, financial statements and auditors' opinions, in making consumption and investment decisions. Tracing through the effect of financial reports on individual actions is an important area of accounting research. Such research may examine directly the influence of financial reports on actions. Or, it may assess the influence on predictions of the feasibility and consequences (costs and benefits) of various courses of action, and perhaps to a lesser extent, any influence on preferences. Further, the effects of financial reports cannot be restricted to their influence on only traditional investment decisions. For example, one effect of available financial reports may be to stimulate decision makers to produce other information, either for their own or others' consumption.

Direct effects of financial reports on individual actions may be assessed by examining the decisions of users of the data. But secondary effects, some due possibly to the presence of information or decision alternatives that would not exist in the absence of financial reports, may affect the action of nonusers as well.

Section IV, markets, highlights even more effects on nonusers of financial reports. Individual consumption and investment decisions in the aggregate generate equilibrium market prices. These, in turn, influence the allocation of resources and distribution of wealth in the economy. While virtually all investment decision makers may act rationally on the assumption that their individual transactions cannot affect prices, in the aggregate many such decision makers, taking similar actions, may change prices. Similarly, a decision by one individual to seek or produce information to supplement or complement what appears in financial reports supplied by firms may only affect that individual. On the other hand, many decision makers making similar conclusions may create sufficient demand to stimulate the emergence of a new firm or industry specializing in production of such information.

When such aggregate effects take place, not only are they not necessarily taken into account (predicted) by the many individual decision makers whose collective actions cause them, but also they may touch the lives of many individuals whose actions did not contribute in the least to their occurrence. For example, when the relative price of a security changes, the wealth levels of all holders of that security change, even though some holders chose to hold the security at both the former and the present prices.

Three primary areas of research are relevant in the market sector: (1) determine the method by which individual actions combine to yield equilibrium prices, (2) develop descriptive models of equilibrium prices with accounting numbers among the explanatory variables and (3) determine the effects of different sets of equilibrium prices on resource allocation and wealth distribution. Researchers in finance and economics probably have a competitive advantage over accounting researchers in areas 1 and 3, but it is still necessary for accountants to be aware of research in these areas and to apply that research to accounting problems. Moreover, area 2 may not stimulate much interest among researchers in finance and economics.

Combining the individuals and markets sectors, we can see the ultimate consequences of accounting policy decisions. If a social welfare criterion is accepted, these policy decisions ideally should be judged on (1) their aggregate consequences, (2) the effect on individual costs and benefits implied by these consequences and (3) the preferences of individuals for alternate possible consequences. Prediction of these elements is part of the policy-making process and completes the circle in Figure 1.

An overview of Figure 1 gives several insights into potential directions for accounting research. Most important is the fact that with our current state of knowledge about decision processes, markets and collective choice, it is impossible to derive a definitive social ordering (or partial ordering) of accounting alternatives. No one piece of research can do that, and none should claim to. Gonedes and Dopuch [1974] correctly criticize many studies for making such a claim. Yet, research studies do not have to provide a social ranking to be helpful to policy makers. Any research that increases our understanding of any of the relationships in Figure 1 can provide a benefit. We should not despair because accounting research cannot provide conclusive evidence about the optimal set of allowable accounting practices. Rather, we should focus our research effort on producing information that is useful to policy makers in their decision process, including information that may help them revise their process.

Given the present political and institutional structure (including an implied but not necessarily well-specified collective choice rule and sensitivity to non-accounting public policy), the two primary inputs to policy decisions are: (1) forecasts of the *consequences to individuals* of policy alternatives and (2) forecasts of *individual preferences* over those consequences. The role of research in support of actual policy decisions is *not one of selecting the best alternatives*. Rather, it is one of forecasting or producing information for forecasting consequences for and preferences of individuals. It is generally impossible to construct a social decision-making system that possesses all of even a minimal set of desirable characteristics: therefore, it is also impossible to construct *conclusive* accounting research strategies (methods) for determining optimum accounting policies—without first assuming away the collective choice dimension. (See Beaver and Demski, [1974], pp. 175–176; or Gonedes and Dopuch, [1974], pp. 78–80).

To forecast consequences and preferences, researchers must specify the level of analysis. Demski [1974a, pp. 222] has suggested use of a complete general equilibrium analysis of alternative accounting policies, specified in terms of the individual "... consumptions schedules to which they give rise." However, the suggestion would seem to apply only to the general theoretical level rather than the specific policy-decision (operational) level. Under present technology, it is clearly infeasible to consider the consequences and preferences over those consequences of each possible variation on accounting policy for each individual in society who is potentially affected. Moreover, it is doubtful that policy makers could comprehend the full set of tradeoffs of costs and benefits over all affected individuals. Yet, if it is generally accepted that a market (laissez-faire) system for accounting information is inadequate, policy decisions must be made. This implies that although a sensitivity to individual preferences may be desirable, it is one of the things that inevitably will be traded off to some degree in favor of tractability and efficiency in any practicable policy-making process.[6] Most likely, information (research) produced for accounting policy decisions will consist of evidence relevant to predictions of consequences of various policy alternatives for various groups of *similarly affected individuals*, along with evidence relevant to predictions of the preferences (or at least the direction of preferences) *of the same groups* for such consequences.

In considering the sources and methods of obtaining such data, another important implication of the accounting policy-making process (as depicted in Figure 1) should be emphasized. The introduction of aggregate effects of direct individual actions (sector IV of Figure 1) is a reminder that not all consequences can be predicted at the individual decision-maker level. Aggregate or market effects (e.g., price changes) are spillover effects of direct actions taken by individuals. Such spillover effects may have consequences for other individuals who have not contributed directly to their occurrence. Thus, for instance, the set of relevant expected consequences and preferences for a given accounting policy decision includes the expected consequences for and preferences of *non-users as well as users* of accounting information.[7]

## RESEARCH STRATEGIES: SOME EXAMPLES

We have used the framework in Figure 1 to point out some potentially fruitful areas for accounting research. In this section we use the framework to examine some specific existing research strategies. The framework will allow us to assess both the potential and limitations of these strategies.

The inability of research strategies generally to provide conclusive evidence for significant policy problems takes us back to Figure 1 with the question: "What avenues are available to help policy makers predict consequences, particularly aggregate consequences, of major policy alternatives?" It is of considerable importance that Figure 1 depicts a *linked process* from the use of acceptable accounting alternatives in financial reporting (sector II) through the aggregate consequences of the use of the resulting information by individual decision makers (sector IV), finally leading to the individual costs and benefits associated with those aggregate consequences (upper right of sector III.).

---

[6] Demski seems to agree implicitly with this implication in acknowledging the value of research efforts that may help "...simplify the consequence domain..." in Beaver and Demski [1974, p. 176].

[7] In essence, this is a rejection of the approach used, in part, in Study Group on the Objectives of Financial Statements [1973], pp. 17–20, where the objectives of financial statements are referenced to their presumed usefulness to typical investors and creditors.

In principle, policy makers should be able to trace the implications of any given policy alternative through each link in the process. In practice, of course, this is hardly possible to any satisfactory degree because of the lack of a comprehensive and cohesive theory or set of theories descriptive of the behavior of the process in each stage. Of particular significance are: (1) the absence of a theory of individual investment decision making, based, at least in part, on accounting information and (2) the absence of a theory which explains equilibrium market prices, at least in part, in terms of accounting variables and which is consistent with the theory of individual decision behavior. Mutually consistent theories of individual equilibria and market equilibria have been put forth in the finance literature in recent years (i.e., portfolio theory and capital asset pricing theory), but these theories are nonspecific as to how observable forms of information, such as available accounting information, influence individual decisions and the structure of market equilibrium prices.

The challenge of developing such accounting-specific theories of individual and market behavior is formidable. Moreover, the demands of the task probably cannot be met without employment of virtually all research tools and methods presently in use by accounting researchers (and, perhaps, some yet to be developed). This is the basic theme of the remainder of the paper.

Before reviewing several potentially productive research strategies, an additional comment is in order. Some people may argue that the individual investment decision level is irrelevant for accounting policy making since the latter inherently is oriented toward aggregate consequences. For instance, in a recent critique of various research strategies (vis-a-vis accounting policy decisions), Gonedes and Dopuch [1974, p. 106] made the following statement specifically aimed at lab/field research studies:

> Specifically, given an efficient capital market, studies of the behavior of particular types of investors (e.g., 'average' investors or 'financial analysts') are not likely to lead to reliable generalizations about the relationship between the production of accounting information and capital market equilibrium. To see this, recall that, within a competitive market, market behavior is a function of the interaction among rivalrous price takers. The attainment of equilibrium in such a market is induced by the workings of the system as a whole, or *aggregate* market behavior, and not by the actions of particular individuals.

We do not disagree with this description of how market equilibria obtain—which perhaps makes it appear paradoxical that previously we pinpointed as significant the absence of a theory of *individual* investment decision making incorporating accounting variables. Actually, we see no inherent conflict as long as theories of individual behavior are not themselves taken to be ideal predictors of market behavior. A predictive theory of capital market equilibria could, of course, be constructed without regard to individual decision making, but there is no intrinsic superiority to such an approach. Moreover, although individual actions are not necessarily one-for-one with competitive market phenomena, there is no inherent reason suggesting that theories predicting market phenomena *cannot* be constructed based on theories of individual "rivalrous price-taking" behavior. Indeed, precisely because market equilibria are established (at least as manifest by observable exchange prices) by the interactions of individuals, this approach would seem to be very promising a priori. Yet another reason to pursue a theory of individual decision making is that, as Figure 1 depicts, the consequences for individuals of altering accounting policy are jointly a function of individual action and aggregate or market actions.

## A Priori Research

Before accounting policy makers can choose among alternatives in accounting, alternatives must exist from which to choose. So, an important precedent to accounting policy decisions is research that specifies alternative measurement and reporting possibilities. Included in this research is the development of accounting models such as price-level-adjusted models, replacement cost models and exit value models. Also included is research into methods of measurement and reporting that are potentially applicable within any of these models. While this research itself cannot provide evidence on the desirability of various models or measurement methods, it can direct empirical investigations into the most promising areas.

A priori research also may be useful in constructing potential models of behavior at all major points in Figure 1. Such a priori models will be especially helpful in developing testable hypotheses regarding the effects of accounting variables on individual decisions and on market equilibria.

## Predictive-Ability Research

One specific potentially fruitful avenue for accounting research is investigation into the relationship between accounting signals and the distributional properties of future returns from investments in firms' securities to which decision makers' preferences are presumably sensitive. The types of investigations include such things as studies of the time-series properties of accounting numbers and tests of predictive ability.

Early in the history of empirical research in accounting, Beaver, Kennelly and Voss [1968] introduced the predictive ability criterion. Hakansson [1973, p. 160], among others, expressed a belief that the criterion was well suited to research problems in accounting—particularly as a building block in a decision theoretic approach.

However, the predictive-ability criterion is not without its faults. Greenball [1971] pointed out: (1) that studies of predictive ability are really joint tests of the outputs of alternative accounting methods and the particular prediction model(s) selected and (2) that such tests are irrelevant for assessing the potential of various accounting methods to serve nonprediction-oriented decisions (e.g., performance measurement). Similarly, Gonedes and Dopuch [1974, p. 109] observe that there "... remains the question about whether ... predictive ability is a sufficient basis for selecting from alternative accounting techniques."

However, these limitations should not be taken as fatal flaws, since, as pointed out earlier, no research technique consistently will produce conclusions as to the relative social "desirability" of accounting alternatives. If the predictive-ability criterion and other criteria for examining the time-series properties of accounting alternatives are used and interpreted judiciously, they offer a potential contribution, albeit a limited one, to research for accounting policy making. This potential is present because, as is evident in Figure 1, all consequences of accounting policy (other than the direct production-related consequences of imposing the policy on firms and auditors) come through the use of the outputs in decisions—some of which inevitably will hinge on *predicted* values of relevant variables.

### Sensitivity of Accounting Time-Series to Policy Alternatives

A largely neglected (in recent times), but potentially profitable, avenue of accounting research is investigating the degree to which actual accounting time series may be expected to differ under various accounting alternatives, given observable or even assumed or simulated environmental conditions under which firms operate. Although unappealing as a sole basis of choices among accounting alternatives, such investigations can make a potentially important, though perhaps prosaic, contribution—particularly when integrated with the predictive ability and basic time series approaches mentioned in the preceding section. In the linked sequence leading to predictions of consequences of policy alternatives depicted in Figure 1, every link contributes to the ultimate objective. Moreover, since predictions of the effects of alternatives on accounting outputs is the first substantive step in predicting consequences, it has special implications for the efficiency of the *applied policy-making process.* That is, considerable savings potentially may be realized if the prediction process stops at this point in those cases where the alternatives being considered show no potentially significant differences in accounting outputs. However, again we must emphasize the importance of a cohesive theory covering the entire chain. "Significance" must be gauged in terms of possible ultimate consequences of the alternatives at the end of the chain in order for a cutoff decision to be appropriate at the accounting output prediction stage.[8]

### Modeling Individual Decision Making

Upon reflection, the most serious limitation of studies of time-series properties and/or predictive ability is the lack of criteria within those research strategies for determining (1) what constitutes variables worthy of prediction and (2) what constitutes significantly different predictive ability (or other characteristic) of accounting outputs under different policy alternatives.[9] This again emphasizes the importance of employing such strategies within the fuller context depicted in Figure 1. The principal direct source of criteria for time-series and predictive-ability studies is a theory or model of individual investment decision making under uncertainty—specified, at least in part, in terms of accounting variables.

The central method in deriving such a model would be the application of decision theory similar to the way it has been applied in finance in recent years. However, there is an important distinction. Since the investment decision essentially boils down to a tradeoff between present and future consumption (usually in the form of claims to the intermediate good, cash), it is obvious that present and future consumption (cash) streams are the variables of interest to an investor—not historical accounting variables per se. Thus the challenge to accounting in modeling

---

[8] This is another way of saying that statistical significance and behavioral or economic significance are not the same.

[9] A third major limitation pointed out by Greenball [1971] is the dependence of predictive-ability tests on prediction models selected. However, this limitation can be ameliorated by fairly exhaustive replications over the set of plausible prediction models available under a given state of technology.

the investment decision is to specify how and which accounting variables that satisfy the constraints of a public reporting environment in which management and investor goals are potentially incongruent relate to the variables to which investor preferences are sensitive. Of course, this is precisely the problem implied by time-series and predictive-ability research—which brings out a virtually unavoidable interaction between model building and time-series and predictive-ability efforts.

### Behavioral Research

To date, most behavioral research aimed at financial accounting has been oriented toward testing the so-called functional fixation hypothesis [Ijiri, Jaedicke and Knight, 1966] in lab or field environments controlled to various degrees, i.e., testing subjects' decision sensitivity to alternative accounting measurement rules, e.g., FIFO versus LIFO [see Gonedes and Dopuch, 1974, Exhibit 1, p. 107 for a list of such studies through 1973]. Such studies are in general highly susceptible to criticism, particularly for lack of external validity, i.e., failure to sufficiently simulate conditions under which actual investment decisions are made so that few, if any, valid generalizations can be drawn from the results [Gonedes and Dopuch, 1974, pp. 104–106]. Aside from such methodological problems, there are also the issues of whether the way individuals actually use information should influence financial reporting policy and, therefore, whether actual information processing is a fruitful subject for research aimed at policy making.

Clearly if research for accounting policy making were aimed strictly at constructing normative theory, the relevance of such studies could be questioned quite legitimately. However, if our earlier conclusion is accepted that the purpose of research for accounting policy is aimed at constructing theories enabling policy makers to predict consequences of policy alternatives, then studies concerned with how individuals process information, and, specifically, how they process accounting-type signals, take on considerable potential relevance. Of course, this potential relevance is also dependent upon acceptance of the relevance of a theory of individual, as opposed to purely aggregate, investment decision making for which we made a case earlier. Its importance is limited by the fact that nonusers as well as users of financial statements are affected by accounting policy decisions.

### Modeling Aggregate Market Behavior

Moving to sector IV, the market sector, from sector III, the individual decision sector, in Figure 1 we can observe that general equilibrium analysis, or even more limited theoretical work into equilibrium in the capital markets, has a potential contribution to make. For even if a satisfactory theory of individual decision making based on accounting information can be developed, there remains the problem of predicting the aggregate effects of individual decisions, which are also conditional on accounting information.

Bearing in mind that presumably "individual preferences are to count" in accounting policy choices, general equilibrium analysis, in which aggregate phenomena, e.g., equilibrium prices and quantities traded, are derived from a model in which individuals and their preferences are represented, would seem to be a preferred methodology [Demski, 1974a]. However, due to the dimensionality problem noted earlier associated with representing each individual, firm, etc., in one model, as a practical matter traditional macroeconomic methods, which typically operate only on aggregate variables and, often, in a partial equilibrium mode, may be more promising.

### Security Price-Based Research

Recently, much hope was placed in the security price structure as a source of direct evidence for determining optimum accounting policy, based on the apparent fair-game efficiency [Fama, 1970] of the market with respect to publicly available information. The basic objective of this research was to identify the set of accounting practices that would produce financial reports that were most highly associated with the security price structure. Most methods of measuring association may be described in general terms by (1), where $R_{jt}$ is the observed rate of return for security $j$ over time period $t$. $R_{mt}$ is the corresponding rate of return on the market portfolio (usually represented by some broad-gauged index), $A_{jt}$ is the cumulative record of accounting data about firm $j$ as of time $t$ and $g'$ is the selected measure of association (e.g., the now-familiar API) between unexpected increments in firms' accounting records and unexpected changes (not explained by market changes) in firms' securities prices:

$$R_{jt} - E(R_{jt} | R_{mt}) = g'[A_{jt} - E(A_{jt} | A_{jt-1})]. \tag{1}$$

In terms of Figure 1, this measure of association relates the output of sector II, financial reports, with the aggregate consequences of sector IV. But Figure 1 highlights some potential problems with this research strategy.

First, this method can be applied only when the effect of accounting alternatives on financial reports is known (i.e., when $A_{jt}$ is known for each alternative). Research identifying accounting alternatives and predicting the effects of these alternatives on financial reports is a necessary adjunct to security price-based research.

A second concern is the measurement problems caused by "leapfrogging" from accounting outputs to aggregate market consequences; this treats the territory between (i.e., individual decision making and the process or phenomenon of aggregation) as a "black box." Any alleged association is based on a chain of causation: (1) from unanticipated accounting signals (new information) through their impact on individual expectations, (2) from individual expectation changes through individual actions and (3) from individual actions to their impact on aggregate supply and demand for securities which would imply price changes. Confidence in the associations developed, especially predicting continuing associations of the same type, would be much greater if there were a well-developed theory describing at least some of these links. Research into opening up the black box in sector III of Figure 1 seems to be an important supporting factor for security price-based research.

A third class of problems, closely related to the black-box aspects of security price research to date, relates to the treatment and effects of "other information." The effect of nonaccounting information on prices is surrogated by $R_{mt}$, so that the effects of the data in individual firms' financial reports can be isolated. This created two potential problems: (1) other information may have an impact not adequately reflected by $R_{mt}$ and (2) market-wide effects of accounting reporting practice may be reflected in $R_{mt}$ and thus not identified as an effect of the accounting policy. In addition, accounting policy may affect the economic availability of other in-formation; thus, the full impact of accounting policy cannot be reflected in the association between accounting outputs and security prices [May and Sundem, 1973].

This is especially true if data from a nonextant accounting policy is being associated with extant prices.

The fourth major problem with security price-based research is that it stops at aggregate consequences, not relating these consequences to individual costs and benefits or preferences. Gonedes and Dopuch [1974, pp. 48–75] show that only under various combinations of very limiting assumptions do the prices of firms' securities reflect the ex ante values to investors of information production decisions of management. Since it is hard to conceive of any real situations where these assumptions hold, security price-based research has little potential for assessing the desirability of accounting alternatives.

Despite these limitations, security price-based research does have some potential value by providing a measure of the relative effects on prices of alternative accounting policies (see Gonedes and Dopuch [1974, p. 76]). However, even to provide this benefit, security price-based research must overcome the several measurement problems mentioned earlier. Most important is the bias present in association measures when accounting policy decisions involve choices between the status quo and potentially costly alternatives [May and Sundem, 1973]. Unfortunately, the majority of nontrivial accounting policy decisions involve such choices. In those cases, the only way presently available to divine information about the potential relative effects on security prices of heretofore undisclosed costly alternatives is to experiment—a strategy most policy makers would be loathe to attempt.

On a more positive note, not all accounting policy decisions involve highly costly but previously unreported alternatives. For instance, there may be questions of whether the status quo policy of requiring costly reporting under multiple alternatives by certain firms should be continued, e.g., whether firms should continue to be required to report fully diluted earnings per share as well as primary earnings per share figures. The apparent marginal contribution to market estimates of securities' expected returns and risks of one such alternative, given that extant reporting policy requires reporting of both alternatives, conceivably can be tested using security price data (see Sundem, Felix and Ramanathan [1975]). Similar strategies apply to alternatives that are not all included in current mandatory reporting requirements— *provided* excluded alternatives are known to be available to market participants at virtually zero acquisition costs (as in Beaver and Dukes [1972]).

On an additional positive note, it should be pointed out that measures of the effects of accounting changes have potential value in ex post evaluation of actual policy decisions. Since accounting policy decisions, like other decisions, involve uncertain future consequences, knowledge of errors in prediction in one case may lead to refinements of predictions in other cases. That is, if an alteration in accounting policy is adopted based on policy maker's predictions of expected changes in relative securities' prices, confirmation of whether such changes take place subsequently as expected is potentially valuable in refining policy makers' models for predicting consequences of policy alternatives. In effect, what holds for policy makers' predictions holds as well for theory verification, i.e., the security price structure is a potentially valuable source of data for verification of proposed theories of equilibrium prices, specified in terms of accounting variables.

In conclusion, security price-based research encompasses only part of the policy-making process. As such, it cannot provide a social ranking of alternatives. But it does make an important link in the process. If measurement problems can be overcome so that confidence can be placed in that link, this type of research potentially has a contribution to make.

## CONCLUSION

We could continue with additional examples of research methods that by themselves will not yield results that directly bear on the desirability of accounting alternatives but can serve as building blocks in a complete view of accounting policy decisions. However, by now our main point should be clear. With our present state of technology in accounting research, there is no research method that will identify the most desirable accounting policy alternative. Nor is there any great likelihood that such a method will emerge, given the social choice dimension of accounting policy making. But there are many research methods that can provide data useful to accounting policy makers who must predict consequences of accounting alternatives and preferences over those consequences. The results of such research should not be put forth as conclusive support for any accounting alternative; neither should it be rejected because it is not able to provide such conclusive support.

This paper does not support the usefulness of any piece of accounting research that might be attempted. Such research still must be carefully designed and carried out. We do not propose any methods of judging the internal validity of research designs. But, given that a research study has internal validity, we propose a framework in which its external validity can be examined. By identifying the aspects of the accounting policy-making process in Figure 1 that are being examined, both the potential contributions and the limitations of research projects readily can be identified. We hope this provides an interpretative framework for accounting research, such that: (1) contributions are not ignored, (2) unwarranted generalizations are minimized because they are no longer perceived as necessary to justify the research effort and (3) accounting research will be more productive in general due to greater complementarity among individual research efforts.

## REFERENCES

Accounting Standards Steering Committee. *The Corporate Report* (Accounting Standards Steering Committee, 1975).

Arrow, K. J., *Social Choice and Individual Values* 1st edition (John Wiley and Sons, 1951: 2nd edition Yale University Press, 1963).

Arthur Andersen & Co., *Objectives of Financial Statements for Business Enterprises* (Arthur Andersen & Co., 1972).

Beaver, W. H. and J. S. Demski, "The Nature of Financial Accounting Objectives: A Summary and Synthesis," *Studies on Financial Objectives 1974.* Supplement to Volume 12 of the *Journal of Accounting Research.*

————, and R. E. Dukes, "Interperiod Tax Allocation, Earnings and Expectations, and the Behavior of Security Prices," *The Accounting Review* (April 1972), pp. 320–332.

————, J. W. Kennelly and W. M. Voss, "Predictive Ability as a Criterion for the Evaluation of Accounting Data," *The Accounting Review* (October 1968), pp. 675–683.

Burton, J. C., "The SEC and the Accounting Profession: Responsibility, Authority, and Progress," in R. Sterling, *Institutional Issues in Public Accounting* (Scholars Book Co., 1973), pp. 265–275.

Committee on Concepts and Standards: External Financial Reports, "Objectives of

Financial Statements: An Evaluation," Supplement to *The Accounting Review* (1975), pp. 41–49.

Defliese, P. L., *The Objectives of Financial Accounting* (Coopers and Lybrand, 1973).

Demski, J. S., "The General Impossibility of Normative Accounting Standards," *The Accounting Review* (October 1973), pp. 718–723.

———, "The Choice among Financial Reporting Alternatives," *The Accounting Review* (April 1974a), pp. 231–232.

———, "The Value of Financial Accounting" (Unpublished paper, Standford University, Graduate School of Business, 1974b).

Dopuch, N., and L. Revsine, eds., *Accounting Research 1960–1970: A Critical Evaluation* (University of Illinois, 1973).

Fama, E. F., "Efficient Capital Markets: A Review of Theory and Empirical Work," *Journal of Finance* (May 1970), pp. 383–417.

———, and L. Laffer, "Information and Capital Markets," *Journal of Business* (July 1971), pp. 289–298.

———, and M. H. Miller, *The Theory of Finance* (Holt, Rinehart and Winston, 1972).

Gonedes, N., and N. Dopuch, "Capital Market Equilibrium, Information Production, and Selecting Accounting Techniques: Theoretical Framework and Review of Empirical Work," *Studies on Financial Accounting Objectives: 1974*, Supplement to Volume 12 of the *Journal of Accounting Research*.

Greenball, M., "The Predictive Ability Criterion: Its Relevance in Evaluating Accounting Data," *Abacus* (June 1971), pp. 1–7.

Hirshleifer, H.: "The Private and Social Value of Information and the Reward to Inventive Activity," *American Economic Review* (September 1971), pp. 561–574.

Ijiri, Y., *Theory of Accounting Measurement* (American Accounting Association, 1975).

———, R. Jaedicke and Kenneth E. Knight, "The Effects of Accounting Alternatives on Management Decisions," in Jaedicke *et al.*, eds., *Research in Accounting Measurement* (American Accounting Association, 1966), pp. 186–199.

May, R. G. and G. L. Sundem, "Cost of Information and Security Prices: Market Association Tests and Accounting Policy Decisions," *The Accounting Review* (January 1973), pp. 80–94.

———, "Cost of Information and Security Prices: A Reply," *The Accounting Review* (October 1974), pp. 791–793.

———, "Accounting Policy Decisions as Social Choices" (Unpublished paper, University of Washington, Seattle, 1976).

Quirk, J. and R. Saposnik, *Introduction to General Equilibrium Theory and Welfare Economics* (McGraw-Hill, 1968).

Rosenfield, P. H., "The Auditors Standard Report Can Be Improved," *Journal of Accountancy* (October 1964), pp. 53–59.

Sen, A. K., *Collective Choice and Social Welfare* (Holden-Day, 1970).

Study Group on the Objectives of Financial Statements. *Objectives of Financial Statements* (AICPA, 1973).

Sundem, G. L., W. L. Felix and K. V. Ramanathan, "The Information Content of Earnings Per Share" (Unpublished paper, University of Washington, 1976).

# I-B    Agency Theory

## I-B 1    *Positive Research in Accounting*

JEROLD L. ZIMMERMAN

The last fifteen years have witnessed an emerging interest in positive research in accounting. In the last five years the attention of some researchers has turned to developing a positive theory of the determination of accounting standards. That is, a theory, that can explain managers' voluntary choice of accounting procedures and how the regulated standards have changed over time. If and when constructed, a positive theory of the determination of accounting standards will be able to *explain* the existing set of generally accepted accounting standards and *predict* how that set will be altered with changes in the underlying variables. Such a positive theory will allow us to explain and predict the actions of the various parties to the standard setting process, including the actions of managers, auditors, accounting policy makers, politicians and other regulators. The purpose of this paper is to discuss what positive research in accounting is and how it has evolved (section A), to present a capsule summary of the current research (section B), and to offer some predictions of what is likely to be learned from this inquiry (section C).

## A. POSITIVE RESEARCH

Milton Friedman's monograph entitled, *Essays in Positive Economics* (1953), discusses in detail positive research in economics. A positive science[1] is described as "a body of systematized knowledge concerning *what is*" (J. M. Keynes, *The Scope and Method of*

Research support was provided by the Center for Research in Government Policy and Business and the Managerial Economics Research Center, University of Rochester. Many of the thoughts and views expressed in this paper are the product of a prolonged and fruitful collaboration with Ross Watts. The comments of Phil Meyers, Subrata Sen, Jerold Warner and in particular Michael Jensen and Ross Watts are gratefully acknowledged.

Jerold L. Zimmerman, "Positive Research in Accounting," in *Perspectives in Research*, ed. R. Nair and T. H. Williams, University of Wisconsin, Madison, May 1980, pp. 107–128. Reprinted with the permission of the University of Wisconsin, Madison.

[1] For a discussion of the difference between positive and normative research see Friedman (1953), Jensen (1976), and Zimmerman (1978).

*Political Economy* cited by Friedman). That is, positive research seeks to develop a theory that can explain observed phenomena. A positive theory of the determination of accounting standards seeks to answer such questions as:

1. Why do some firms choose straight-line and others accelerated depreciation for financial reporting?
2. Why do some oil companies choose full-cost accounting and others successful-efforts accounting for exploration costs?
3. Why do public accountants support a quasi-private as opposed to a government-operated accounting standards board?
4. Why does the Securities and Exchange Commission (SEC) continue to subcontract (with veto power) to the accounting profession the overt policy-making role?

Answers to these questions, in terms of a set of empirically tested hypotheses, form a positive theory of accounting. Such a theory can address such questions as:

1. Is the Financial Accounting Standards Board (FASB) likely to alter generally accepted accounting standards for financial reporting if a 10–5–3 depreciation system is adopted for tax purposes?
2. Is the SEC's Reserve Recognition Accounting (RRA) proposal likely to be implemented?
3. Is the FASB likely to survive a major financial debacle involving financial reporting?

A positive theory is of the form, "If A then B," that is capable of being refuted. A positive theory of the manager's choice of depreciation accounting would be—"If bond covenants (written in terms of accounting numbers) become binding, then managers are more likely to switch from accelerated to straight-line depreciation for book purposes" (Holthausen, 1980). Notice that this statement can be refuted by the evidence. Furthermore, this theory, if not refuted, explains why managers switch depreciation methods.

The nature of positive research in accounting has changed over the last fifteen years. The best way to illustrate this change is to use three of the more widely cited empirical accounting papers:

1. Ball and Brown (1968), that examines the information content of annual earnings.
2. Ball and Watts (1972), that examines the time series properties of annual earnings.
3. Kaplan and Roll (1972), that tests the stock price reaction to accounting procedure changes [see also Ball (1972) and Sunder (1975)].

All of these classic papers do not address the question of why managers (or policy makers) choose the accounting standards that they do. All of them examine "what"-type questions. What is the association between stock prices and earnings, stock prices and accounting changes, etc. Ball and Watts (1972) did not address the positive question of why earnings follow a random walk. Kaplan and Roll (1972) did not address the positive question of why managers change accounting procedures, although the Kaplan and Roll findings suggest that managers probably do not change accounting standards to "fool" the market.

Two other examples will serve to illustrate how positive research in accounting is changing. Dyckman and Smith (1979), Collins and Dent (1979) and Lev (1979) addressed the question of whether there was a security price reaction to the FASB's proposed elimination of full costing for oil and gas in 1977. Basically, these papers did not address the question of why some firms used full cost and others successful efforts. Collins and Dent and Lev found a stock price reaction which, in turn, led them to ask why it occurred.[2] Subsequent research by Collins, Rozeff and Dhaliwal (1981) is starting to probe the question of why, in an efficient capital market, oil and gas producers care about whether exploration costs are deferred or written off for financial accounting.

Another example concerns inflation accounting (ASR 190 and SFAS 33). The research findings to date have not found any evidence that replacement cost disclosures in 1977 contained information (see *Journal of Accounting and Economics*, 2:2). Primarily, these studies have not addressed the positive question of why the SEC and FASB adopted the form of inflation accounting that they did.

Both of these examples, oil and gas and inflation accounting, illustrate how positive research is evolving. The earlier empirical research on capital market efficiency and the time series behavior of earnings provides the basic foundation upon which the current positive propositions are being constructed. For example, the research on capital market efficiency has formed the basis for the current positive research in accounting by providing evidence on the ability of the capital markets to adjust for "cosmetic" changes in accounting procedures.

Another distinguishing feature between the earlier and later research is the nature of the questions addressed and the propositions tested. The earlier research usually did not seek to develop and test a model of an individual's choice of accounting standards (an exception is the income smoothing literature, discussed below). Often, the early studies sought to establish if an association did (or did not) exist between two variables and did not seek to explain why such an association did (or did not) exist. Often, straw men were tested. For example, Ball (1972) tested whether the "monopolistic hypothesis" (i.e., the market is misled by accounting changes) was consistent with the evidence.

The more recent research, on the other hand, seeks to develop models of accounting choice. Starting with the assumption of individual rationality (i.e., expected utility maximization), this research seeks to identify the relevant costs and benefits of alternative accounting procedures. For example, in addressing the question of why managers expend resources lobbying before standard setting boards on proposed accounting standards, Watts and I started with the assumption that managers, shareholders, and regulators/politicians are rational (see Watts and Zimmerman, 1978). We then tried to identify how accounting standards affect the firm's cashflows and hence shareholder wealth.[3]

The same approach was used in Zimmerman (1979). Given individual rationality, I sought to explain why cost allocations are such a pervasive phenomena in virtually all organizations. That is, how do cost allocations affect the firm's cashflows? What

[2] Dyckman and Smith (1979) did not find a statistically significant stock price reaction.
[3] Note that maximizing shareholders' expected wealth is not strictly equivalent to maximizing shareholders' expected utility.

benefits are derived from allocating costs over direct costing for internal reporting purposes?

Besides assuming individual rationality, the recent research makes assumptions regarding the alternatives faced by the individual which includes assumptions about relative costs and benefits. For example, constructing a model of how compensation plans affect the manager's choice of depreciation methods requires the researcher to make assumptions regarding (1) the set of available depreciation models, (2) the bookkeeping costs of making the change, (3) the costs borne by the outside directors in monitoring manager's behavior, (4) the effects of alternative depreciation methods on the time series properties of reported earnings and management compensation payments, etc. The research then proceeds to derive testable implications, which if empirically supported, tell us something about the incentives of individuals and the costs and benefits of the alternatives.

Although the earlier empirical research in accounting (except the income smoothing literature) did not seek to develop and test models of an individual's choice of accounting standards, the current positive research draws heavily upon the earlier findings, in particular, the capital market studies. The next section illustrates how the early attempts to develop a positive theory of accounting choice were thwarted by making assumptions about capital market efficiency that were later refuted by positive research. In particular, some early attempts to develop a positive theory will be contrasted with current positive research efforts.

## B. A CAPSULE SUMMARY OF THE RECENT POSITIVE RESEARCH IN ACCOUNTING[4]

### 1. Income Smoothing Hypothesis

The first serious attempt to construct a positive theory of the manager's choice of accounting procedures was undertaken by Gordon (1964), and Gordon, Horowitz, and Meyers (1966) at the University of Rochester. In my opinion, these papers were the first two papers in a line of inquiry that sought to develop a systematic explanation of the manager's choice of accounting procedures. For the first time, a model of managerial choice was formulated *and* subsequently tested.[5] But more important, these authors understood the role of data is constructing a positive theory and subjected their hypothesis to the rigors of empirical testing. Gordon's original work (1964) and the paper by Gordon, Horowitz and Meyers (1966) became the seminal papers on the income smoothing hypothesis.

Unfortunately, the income smoothing hypothesis was based on the faulty positive proposition (discovered by subsequent research) that capital markets are inefficient (Watts and Zimmerman, 1980c, chap. 5). In particular, Gordon (1964) assumed that a firm's stock price is a direct, mechanical function of the growth and variance of reported earnings. That is, the extreme form of the Gordon assumption would say that firms with identical future cashflow distributions would *not* have the same market

---

[4] Due to space limitations, this section cannot be complete nor totally representative of the literature.

[5] On a historical note, Hepworth (1953) speculated that managers would smooth income for tax reasons and to placate shareholders. Hepworth did not propose smoothing as a general phenomena nor did he propose to test his ideas.

values if they had different growth rates and/or variances of reported earnings. Accounting procedures can affect both of these parameters. Using two other assumptions: that managers maximize utility and their utility depends on the stock price, Gordon deduced that managers choose accounting procedures that maximize the growth but minimize the variance in reported earnings, thereby maximizing share price.

Numerous other researchers have attempted to extend and test the smoothing model but have met with mixed results (see Gonedes and Dopuch, 1974, pp. 109–110). Ex post, the major problem with building a positive theory on the Gordon assumptions has been that one of his key, underlying assumptions is inconsistent with the evidence.

## 2. Positive Theories of Managers' Choices of Accounting Procedures

Ross Watts and Michael Jensen in a 1973 working paper re-examined the positive question of why managers choose the accounting procedures that they do. But their work, unlike the smoothing literature, assumed that the stock price depends on the firm's future cashflows and not mechanically on reported earnings. Based on the then current research into the efficiency of capital markets, they assumed that the market would value two firms with identical future cashflow distributions identically, even though they used different accounting procedures. Hence, the search for a positive theory of accounting focused on how accounting procedures affect the firm's cashflows. Watts (1974) further elaborated the beginnings of such a theory. The ideas in Watts (1974) in conjunction with the insights provided in Jensen and Meckling (1976) on agency theory formed the foundation for the current positive research in accounting of which Watts (1977) and Watts and Zimmerman (1978) are representative.

The current state of the positive theory of the manager's choice of accounting procedures can be briefly summarized as:

1. The production process of the firm requires the combination of various factors of production which are usually owned by different parties (capital, labor, management, etc.). The self-interest of each of these parties gives rise to a set of agency problems and hence the view of the firm as "a nexus of contracts" which is the least cost solution to the agency problem (Jensen and Meckling 1976, and Fama 1980).

2. Accounting numbers are useful devices in some of the contracts that are written to reduce the agency costs of certain conflicts (Jensen and Meckling 1976; Watts 1977; Watts and Zimmerman 1978, 1979; and Smith and Warner 1979). In particular, accounting numbers are used in debt contracts (Leftwich 1980 and Holthausen 1980) management compensation contracts (Watts and Zimmerman 1978) and corporate by-laws (Watts and Zimmerman, 1979).

3. Besides being used in some of the private contracts among the factor input owners of the firm, accounting numbers are also used by government to regulate and tax the firm (Watts 1974, 1977; and Watts and Zimmerman 1978, 1979). Government regulation takes two forms. Direct regulation, usually of the rates charged by public utilities, is the more commonly thought of form. (See Jarrell (1979) for tests of how accounting numbers were initially used by the first state public utility commission). Besides direct regulation, individuals using the powers of the state can transfer wealth from the firm via

affirmative action, OSHA, EPA, antitrust, price controls, etc. These latter activites impose what we call "political costs" on the firm which managers attempt to reduce via lobbying, public relations, and lower reported earnings. Accounting numbers are often used in these struggles to transfer corporate wealth (see Benston, 1980, for a more complete review of this literature).

Accounting numbers affect the firm's cashflows and hence stock prices by altering agency costs (which include bookkeeping costs), taxes, the effects of regulation, and political costs (e.g., antitrust, price controls, etc.). That is, changes in accounting procedures (e.g., switching from accelerated to straightline depreciation for financial accounting only) affect the firm's net cashflows beyond the bookkeeping costs of making the changes. In particular, the firm's net cashflows are affected if the accounting change alters the numbers in debt and management compensation contracts, the firm's revenues if it is a regulated utility, and the costs incurred by the firm from increased government investigative and regulatory activities if the change increases government scrutiny of the firm.

Since reported accounting numbers are used for different purposes simultaneously, it is unlikely that a single accounting procedure is optimum for all purposes. For example, higher reported profits relax prior constraints in lending agreements but at the same time draw the attention of regulators. Managers must then make trade-offs and compare the potential costs of additional regulation and bookkeeping against the benefits of less binding debt covenants.

The set of accounting procedures that result are those that maximize the value of the firm (Gordon 1964 and Watts 1974).[6] Also, the choice of the optimum set of accounting procedures is conceptually no different from the manager's choice of the optimum financing policy, production mix, advertising policy, etc.

The difficult aspect and the role played by positive research is to delineate and measure the costs and benefits of alternative accounting procedures. Yet, it is the knowledge of these costs and benefits and how they vary across the firms that makes a positive theory valuable. In essence, the manager chooses a portfolio of accounting procedures (e.g., straight-line depreciation, flow-through for the investment tax credit, LIFO, etc.) that, in his best judgment at the time, maximizes the manager's welfare. By observing the cross-sectional and time series variation in manager's choices of accounting procedures, inferences can be made regarding the relative costs and benefits of alternative procedures. Knowledge of these costs and benefits will allow us to construct a positive theory that not only explains the manager's current choice of accounting procedures, but can then be used to predict the manager's future accounting choices and reactions to proposed accounting standards. For example, a positive theory of accounting informs policy makers of the likely costs individuals will incur from the elimination of a currently accepted accounting procedure. A positive theory would also suggest to auditors and managers whether the firm is currently using the optimum set of accounting procedures.

The beginnings of such a positive theory are starting to emerge. Besides the paper already cited, Hagerman and Zmijewski (1979) and Zmijewski and Hagerman (1980)

---

[6] Some readers may question the conclusion that managers choose financial accounting procedures that maximize firm value. Yet, few would question the proposition that *tax* accounting procedures are chosen to minimize the net present value of the firm's tax liability and thereby maximize the value of the firm.

derive and test a cross-sectional model of managers' choice of four accounting policies (depreciation, inventory, pension amortization and investment tax credit). Although they did not include the effects of accounting numbers on bond covenants as independent variables in their model, they still find proxies for political costs and the existence of management compensation plans to be statistically significant predictors of the manager's choice of accounting procedures.

Watts (1977) and Watts and Zimmerman (1980a) hypothesize that if accounting numbers are useful in reducing agency costs, then we should observe that the earliest firms (e.g., firms in the twelfth and thirteenth century) voluntarily provided financial numbers and provisions for auditing these numbers. Watts and Zimmerman (1980a) find evidence that the early English firms (the merchant guilds) voluntarily kept accounts that were routinely audited by the owners in the thirteenth century. Furthermore, the evidence in Watts and Zimmerman (1979) suggests that accounting procedures changed in response to major institutional changes (e.g., utility regulation, taxation, the securities acts).

Holthausen (1980) attempts to explain why firms would *voluntarily* switch back to straight-line depreciation for financial reporting purposes. He hypothesizes that bond indentures and management compensation plans are likely to be affected by the switchback and hence provide managers with the incentive to make this voluntary change. In particular, if the contraints in these contracts start to become binding, managers are likely to switch back. His empirical tests do not support these hypotheses.[7]

Leftwich (1980) develops the hypothesis that *mandatory* changes in accounting procedures affect the firm's lending agreements and hence the value of the firm. He tests this hypothesis using the Accounting Principles Board Opinion on Business Combinations and a sample of actively merging firms that would most likely be affected by this mandatory ruling. The tests are consistent with his hypothesis.

Collins, Rozeff and Dhaliwal (1981) use a multiple regression methodology similar to Leftwich's (1980) and Holthausen's (1980). Collins, Rozeff, and Dhaliwal are able to explain a statistically significant proportion of the cross-sectional variation in the abnormal returns of the full-cost oil producers around the release of the exposure draft to SFAS 19 that proposed the elimination of full costing. Their independent variables include information on debt and management compensation contracts as well as other firm-specific variables such as size, the effect of the proposed elimination of full costing on stockholder equity, etc.

These studies, taken as a whole, provide encouraging support for the development of a positive theory of the manager's choice of accounting procedures—a theory that ultimately will be able to explain the cross-sectional and time series variation in managers' choices of accounting procedures. Besides understanding how accounting numbers affect shareholder wealth, a positive theory should explain how accounting numbers affect auditors and regulators, the other major participants in the standard setting process. The next section briefly reviews some of the positive research analyzing the auditors' and regulators' incentives to participate in the standard setting process.

---

[7] Holthausen relies on stock price changes at the time of the switchback to test his hypotheses. If the magnitude of the wealth effects of the switchback are small or anticipated by the market prior to the change, then his tests are likely to be weak.

### 3. A Positive Theory of Accounting that Incorporates Auditors and Regulators

Turning first to positive research on auditing, Watts and Zimmerman (1980a) trace the historical development of auditing from the thirteenth century in England to the present day.[8] By using agency theory to examine the market forces that give rise to auditing, we are able to reject the null hypothesis that auditing arose because the government required audits. The evidence is consistent with the hypothesis that auditing arose to reduce the agency costs from the conflicts of interests among the parties to the firm. Furthermore, the evidence is consistent with the hypothesis that professional auditors, as opposed to part-time auditors, arose in part to solve the moral hazard problem (see Benston 1975).

In another paper, Watts and Zimmerman (1980b), a model of auditors' lobbying behavior was developed and tested. In particular, the model suggests that accounting standards affect the auditor's wealth directly by altering the quantity of auditing mandated by the regulatory process and indirectly by altering the wealth of the auditor's clients. The wealth of the auditor's clients are affected (see subsection 2 above) by altering the accounting numbers used in the client's existing contracts, political costs, bookkeeping costs, etc. Given that the auditor maximizes his wealth, he has incentives to lobby for/against a proposed accounting standard. Tests of the model are consistent with its predictions.

Benston (1980) presents an analysis of the market for accounting and auditing services and summarizes the relevant literature. The primary purpose of his paper is to analyze the Congressional proposal to increase government regulation of auditing and accounting. While no hypotheses are derived or empirical tests conducted, the incentives of auditors, politicians, and regulators are discussed.

Benston also has written extensively on the incentives of government officials to regulate financial disclosure (Benston (1980) reviews much of this previous work; also see Benston, 1969, 1973, 1975 and 1976). His analysis and empirical tests primarily are directed at the public policy question of whether the benefits of the SEC exceed its costs. While Benston does not formulate or test hypotheses regarding why the regulators do what they do, important insights and inferences emerge from this work. For example, based on Benston's findings (along with the expanding research in the economics of regulation [Posner, 1974] future positive research on the incentives of regulators to regulate accounting should *not* be based on the assumption that regulators are operating in the "public interest" (i.e., there is no evidence to support such an assumption).

Finally, DeAngelo (1979) develops and tests a model of the incentives of the auditor and his client. Based on her analysis, she is able to explain the form of the contract between the auditor and client. Preliminary tests appear consistent with her hypothesis.

In summary, there has been some positive research into the demand for auditor services and the incentives of auditors to participate in the process by which accounting standards are determined. However, our knowledge of these incentives is far less than the current state of knowledge of the manager's incentives. Part of the difference in our state of knowledge is likely due to the wealth of data on corpora-

---

[8] The books by Zeff (1972), Carey (1969, 1970) and Moonitz (1974) are among the most complete historical accounts of the U.S. standard setting process. They provide useful descriptive material on the actual behavior of auditors and regulators in the standard setting process.

tions (stock prices, COMPUSTAT, 10-Ks, etc.) and the corresponding lack of data on auditors.

If our understanding of auditors' incentives is miniscule, then our understanding of the policy makers' and regulators' incentives is virtually non-existent.[9] Part of the problem in developing testable implications regarding policy makers/regulators is that the economic theory of the political process is still in its embryonic stage. For example, economists are unable to explain why the SEC exists in the U.S. and not in the U.K., why farmers get farm subsidies while extractive industries get tax breaks (i.e., the form of the government subsidy), or why the airlines were "deregulated" when they were and not the railroads. Answers to the preceding questions require an economic theory of regulation, a theory that can explain existing institutions—why they exist and take the forms they do. The economic theory of the firm (e.g., Alchian and Demsetz 1972; Jensen and Meckling 1976; Fama 1980, etc.) is much further developed. Hence it can provide a better foundation for developing positive propositions regarding how accounting affects the manager's wealth than the economic theory of regulation can provide regarding how accounting affects the regulator's/politician's wealth.

## C. The Future of Positive Research in Accounting

This brings me to the final topic. What progress towards developing a positive theory of accounting choice are we likely to achieve and what payoffs will this line of inquiry produce given this progress?

Projecting research progress over the next five to ten years is a precarious business. Progress will depend on the quantity and quality of research efforts devoted to this pursuit. I expect the quantity of research to expand. There are a growing number of high quality, empirically trained, accounting researchers tiring of conducting event studies of information content. Some of these individuals are starting to apply the event-study methodology to address policy questions. For example, Collins and Dent (1979), Dyckman and Smith (1979), and Lev (1979) examined SFAS 19. Gheyara and Boatsman (1980); Ro (1980); and Beaver, Christie, and Griffin (1980) examined ASR 190 replacement cost disclosures. Questions regarding why accounting procedures are chosen naturally arise out of such event studies. The following two questions arise from SFAS 19 and ASR 190: (1) why were the full cost firms affected by SFAS 19, and (2) given no evidence that investors used the replacement cost disclosures, why did the SEC mandate ASR 190? Such positive questions lead other researchers to attempt to answer them. For example, Collins, Rozeff, and Dhaliwal (1981) try to explain why the full cost firms were affected by SFAS 19.

Given the low-cost availability of "good" data (e.g., CRSP and COMPUSTAT) and a fairly robust technique (see Brown and Warner 1980; e.g., security price research), positive research in accounting will continue to address why various accounting procedures are chosen and accounting standards sanctioned.[10]

---

[9] See Watts (1977) and Zimmerman (1977) for a review of the "Crisis Hypothesis" of political actions. One of the earliest references to this crisis theory is in James Madison's Federalist Paper No. 47, 1788 (see Cooke 1961, pp. 333–4).

[10] For example, instead of examining the information content of management forecasts (Patel 1976; and Gonedes, Dopuch, and Penman 1976), some researchers will ask the question—why do some managers release forecasts while others do not?

The quality of future positive research also is likely to improve. Accounting researchers' econometric skills are generally quite good and getting better. In my opinion, the average quality of the empirical work in the leading accounting journals is not significantly below the average quality of the empirical work in the leading finance and economics journals.

Besides better econometric skills, accounting researchers' finance and economics training is improving. If the past is any guide to the future, then it will be out of economics and finance that future positive propositions in accounting are most likely to emerge. Thus, if an individual wants to conduct positive research in accounting, he should maintain a working knowledge of finance and microeconomics (primarily industrial organization, property rights, and managerial economics).

Based on the increasing quantity and quality of positive research in accounting, I expect the current research to continue to expand. Within the next five to ten years we should have a fairly detailed model of how accounting numbers affect the firm's cashflows. This will increase our understanding of why managers choose the accounting procedures that they do and why they lobby on proposed standards as they do.

Our understanding of how accounting standards affect auditor wealth will not be as well developed as our understanding of how accounting affects the manager's wealth, but will certainly be further along than it is now. We will have a better idea of why auditors tend to specialize by industry and why they provide the non-audit services (tax, management advisory services, etc.) that they do. That is, our understanding of the economics of the audit firm will be greater than it is today. However, due to the lack of data and small sample sizes, I do not expect that positive models of the auditor's lobbying behavior on accounting standards will ever achieve the predictive ability that positive models of mangers' lobbying behavior will achieve.

Over the next five or ten years, a positive model incorporating politicians and policy makers is likely to emerge. But again, due to small sample sizes and the lack of a theory of the political process, the explanatory power of models of politicians' actions will not achieve the same predictive ability as models of managers' or even auditors' choice of accounting standards. For example, I do not expect to see a model that predicts why the SEC required replacement costs and not price level adjustments in the near future, or a model of why the SEC promulgated RRA and did not affirm SFAS No. 19. As previously discussed, answers to such questions require a theory of the political process and the answers to some very difficult theoretical questions.

Besides a lack of theory of the political process, there are other obstacles that retard the development of positive propositions in accounting. Three of the more difficult problems are outlined. First, a theory of finance is not as fully developed as one would like. If accounting numbers are used in contracts to control capital structure and dividend payments (see Smith and Warner 1979), questions of optimal capital structure and dividend policy have important implications for accounting. Hence progress in accounting will depend on progress in finance (and economics) and to some extent vice versa.

Second, most accounting standard changes and voluntary changes in accounting procedures by managers are likely not to be of sufficient magnitude to affect stock prices for most listed firms. This reduces the usefulness of the event study technique and requires the researcher to devise alternative test procedures.

Third, developing testable implications in accounting requires the researcher to make simplifying assumptions regarding (unobservable) *relative costs*. As discussed earlier, accounting numbers are used for multiple purposes, forcing managers to trade-off the costs and benefits of the different purposes. The accounting researcher, who cannot observe the costs and benefits but only the outcome of the manager's decision process, must make assumptions about the *relative costs* of the various purposes in order to derive testable implications. For example, in Watts and Zimmerman (1978), we had to make assumptions about the relative magnitudes of the costs price-level accounting would impose vis-a-vis management compensation plans, compared to the costs price-level accounting would impose vis-a-vis political costs. That is, would managers (whose earnings are lower under price-level accounting) favor the proposed standard because of the lower political costs or oppose the standard because of the adverse effect on compenation plans? We *assumed* the political cost effects would dominate for larger firms. This assumption was justified using a relative transactions cost argument. Without this assumption no predictions could be made regarding how managers would lobby on the price-level issue. It is important to recognize that assumptions regarding relative costs must be made to derive testable implications. At times these assumptions appear arbitrary and ex post. But if they yield testable implications that are consistent with the evidence in replications, then progress towards a positive theory of accounting is achieved and our understanding of the relative magnitudes of the costs and benefits enhanced.

Given the modest progress towards a positive theory of accounting that I expect, what payoffs are we likely to receive? There are basically three groups who might benefit from progress towards a positive accounting theory. First, students will be better equipped to deal with the problems they will face. For example, after teaching the flow-through and deferral methods of the investment tax credit, how do we inform our students as to the relative advantages of the two methods? Some instructors argue that the choice doesn't matter if you adopt an extreme form of the efficient markets hypothesis. Other instructors argue one method is better than the other because it is more conservative, or better matches revenues to expenses, etc. That is, they try to rationalize one method using some combination of the standard normative litany. A positive theory will allow us to explain how these two methods affect the firm's cashflows and hence how the manager should make the choice.

The second group that one would like to believe would benefit from a positive theory of accounting are policy makers. To the extent it allows policy makers to form better estimates of the costs (and benefits) firms incur due to the policy makers' actions, the policy makers could make more "informed" choices. However, until we have a better understanding (i.e., a positive theory) of how policy makers select the actions they do, it is difficult to speculate on what they would find useful.

The third beneficiary of a set of empirically tested positive propositions are economics and finance researchers. Finance researchers have found the explanation of firms' capital structures to be an elusive problem. The firm's accounting procedures and capital structure are both endogenous decision variables and are likely to be interrelated if agency costs are an important determinant of both. To the extent that positive propositions of accounting choice are formulated and tested, they will have implications regarding the firm's capital structure and finance theory.

Positive propositions in accounting will also be of interest to economists. Agency theory, problems of moral hazard, and the theory of the decentralized firm—all managerial economics topics—are likely to be better understood to the extent that the manager's choice of accounting procedures can be explained. Any progress in explaining how the accounting policy makers behave will be of interest to economists working on a theory of regulation. Numerous other examples can no doubt be constructed of how a positive accounting theory can contribute to answering more general economic questions.

To conclude, I am optimistic and excited about the future positive research possibilities in accounting. There is virtually an unlimited supply of interesting positive research questions that can be addressed with our existing methodology due to the rate at which the SEC and FASB continue to promulgate standards. Furthermore, this research is of interest not only to academics in accounting, finance, and economics but to our students and the accounting profession (even though the profession may find some of the results disturbing).

## REFERENCES

Alchian, Armen and Harold Demsetz, 1972, Production, information costs, and economic organization. *American Economic Review* LXII: 777–795.

Ball, Ray, 1972. Changes in accounting techniques and stock prices. Empirical Research in Accounting: Selected Studies, 1972, Supplement to *Journal of Accounting Research* 10: 1–37.

Ball, Ray and Phillip Brown, 1968. An empirical evaluation of accounting income numbers. *Journal of Accounting Research* 6: 159–177.

Ball, Ray and Ross L. Watts, 1972. Some time series properties of accounting income. *Journal of Finance* XXVII: 663–682.

Beaver, William H., Andrew A. Christie, and Paul A. Griffin, 1980. The information content of SEC accounting series release No. 190. *Journal of Accounting and Economics* 2:2.

Benston, George J., 1969. The effectiveness and effects of the SEC's accounting disclosure requirements. In *Economic Policy and the Regulation of Corporate Securities*, Henry Manne (ed.), Washington: American Enterprise Institute for Public Policy Research.

Benston, George J., 1973. Required disclosure and the stock markets: An evaluation of the securities and exchange act of 1934. *American Economic Review* LXIII (March): 132–155.

Benston, George J., 1975. Accountants' integrity and financial reporting. *Financial Executive* XLIII (August): 10–14.

Benston, George J., 1976. *Corporate Financial Disclosure in the U.K. and the U.S.A.* Saxon House/Lexington Books (D.C. Heath) and the Institute of Chartered Accountants in England and Wales (London).

Benston, George J., 1980. The market for public accounting services: Demand, supply & regulation. *Accounting Journal* 3: forthcoming.

Brown, Stephen J. and Jerold B. Warner, 1980. Measuring security price performances. *Journal of Financial Economics*, 8:3 (September): 205–258.

Carey, J. L., 1969. *The rise of the accounting profession, from technician to professional 1896–1936.* New York: American Institute of Certified Public Accountants.

Carey, J. L., 1970. *The rise of the accounting profession to responsibility and authority 1937–1969.* New York: American Institute of Certified Public Accountants.

Collins, Daniel W. and Warren T. Dent, 1979. The proposed elimination of full cost accounting in the extractive petroleum industry. *Journal of Accounting and Economics* 1 (March): 3–44.

Collins, Daniel W., Michael S. Rozeff, and Dan S. Dhaliwal, 1981. The economic determinants of market reaction to proposed mandatory accounting changes in the oil and gas industry: A cross-sectional analysis. *Journal of Accounting and Economics*, forthcoming.

Cooke, Jacob E., 1961. *The Federalist*. Middletown, CT: Wesleyan University Press.

DeAngelo, Linda, 1979. The market for audit services and the economic determinants of the auditor-client contractual form, unpublished working paper, University of Washington.

Dyckman, Thomas R. and Abbie J. Smith, 1979. Financial accounting and reporting by oil and gas producing companies: A study of information effects. *Journal of Accounting and Economics* 1 (March): 45–75.

Fama, Eugene F., 1980. Agency problems and the theory of the firm. *Journal of Political Economy* 88 (April): 288–307.

Friedman, Milton, 1953. *The methodology of positive economics, Essays in Positive Economics*. Chicago: University of Chicago Press.

Gheyara, Kelly and James Boatsman, 1980. Market reaction to 1976 replacement cost disclosures. *Journal of Accounting and Economics*, 2:2.

Gonedes, Nicholas and Nicholas Dopuch, 1974. Capital market equilibrium, information production, and selecting accounting techniques: Theoretical framework. Studies on Financial Objectives: 1974. *Journal of Accounting Research* Supplement: 48–129.

Gonedes, Nicholas, Nicholas Dopuch, and Stephen Penman, 1976. Disclosure rules, information production, and capital market equilibrium: The case of forecast disclosure rules. *Journal of Accounting Research* 14 (Spring): 89–137.

Gordon, Myron J., 1964. Postulates, principles and research in accounting. *Accounting Review* 39 (April): 251–263.

Gordon, Myron J., Bert N. Horowitz, and Phillip T. Meyers, 1966. Accounting measurements and normal growth of the firm. In *Research in Accounting Measurements*, Jaedicke, Ijiri and Nielsen (eds.), American Accounting Association, 221–231.

Hagerman, Robert L. and Mark E. Zmijewski, 1979. Some determinants of accounting policy choice. *Journal of Accounting and Economics* 1: 141–162.

Hepworth, S. R., 1953. Smoothing periodic income. *Accounting Review* 28 (January): 32–39.

Holthausen, Robert W., 1980. Theory and evidence on the effect of bond covenants and management compensation contracts on the choice of accounting techniques: The case of the depreciation switch-back. Unpublished Ph.D. dissertation, University of Rochester.

Jarrell, Gregg A., 1979. Pro-producer regulation and accounting for assets: The case of electric utilities. *Journal of Accounting and Economics* 1: 93–117.

Jensen, Michael C., 1976. Reflections on the state of accounting research and the regulation of accounting. Presented at the Stanford Lectures in Accounting, May 1976, Stanford University, Palo Alto, California.

Jensen, Michael C., and William H. Meckling, 1976. Theory of the firm: Managerial behavior, agency costs and ownership structure. *Journal of Financial Economics* 3:4 (October): 305–360.

Kaplan, Robert S. and Richard Roll, 1972. Investor evaluation of accounting information: Some empirical evidence. *Journal of Business* 45 (April): 225–257.

Leftwich, Richard, 1980. Private determination of accounting methods in corporate bond indentures. Unpublished Ph.D. dissertation, University of Rochester.

Lev, Baruch, 1979. The impact of accounting regulation on the stock market: The case of oil and gas companies. *Accounting Review* 54 (July): 485–503.

Moonitz, Maurice, 1974. *Obtaining agreements on standards in the accounting profession.* SAR #8, Sarasota, FL: American Accounting Association.

Patell, James M., 1976. Corporate forecasts of earnings per share and stock price behavior: Empirical tests. *Journal of Accounting Research* 14 (Autumn): 246–276.

Posner, Richard A., 1974. Theories of economic regulation. *Bell Journal of Economics and Management Science* 5:2 (Autumn): 335–358.

Ro, Byung T., 1980. The adjustment of security returns to the disclosure of replacement cost information. *Journal of Accounting and Economics* 2:2.

Smith, Clifford and Jerold Warner, 1979. Financial contracting: An analysis of bond covenants. *Journal of Financial Economics* 7: 117–162.

Sunder, Shyam, 1975. Stock price and risk related to accounting changes in inventory valuation. *Accounting Review* 50: 305–315.

Watts, Ross L., 1974. Accounting objectives. Unpublished working paper No. 7408, University of Rochester.

Watts, Ross L., 1977. Corporate financial statements, a product of the market and political processes. *Australian Journal of Management* 2: 53–75.

Watts, Ross L. and Michael C. Jensen, 1973. Outline of theory, policy and accounting. Unpublished manuscript, University of Rochester.

Watts, Ross L. and Jerold L. Zimmerman, 1978. Towards a positive theory of the determination of accounting standards. *Accounting Review* 53: 112–134.

Watts, Ross L. and Jerold L. Zimmerman, 1979. The demand for and supply of accounting theories: The market for excuses. *Accounting Review* 54 (April): 273–305.

Watts, Ross L. and Jerold L. Zimmerman, 1980a. The markets for independence and independent auditors. Unpublished manuscript, University of Rochester.

Watts, Ross L. and Jerold L. Zimmerman, 1980b. Auditors and the determination of accounting standards. Unpublished working paper GPB 78–06, University of Rochester.

Watts, Ross L. and Jerold L. Zimmerman, 1980c. Notes on empirical research in accounting. Unpublished manuscript, University of Rochester.

Zeff, Stephen A., 1972. *Forging accounting principles in five countries.* Champaign, IL: Stipes Publishing Company.

Zimmerman, Jerold L., 1977. The municipal accounting maze: An analysis of political incentives. *Journal of Accounting Research* Supplement: 107–144.

Zimmerman, Jerold L., 1978. On the 'statement of accounting theory and theory acceptance.' Proceedings of the 1978 American Accounting Association Annual Meetings, Denver, Colorado.

Zimmerman, Jerold L., 1979. The costs and benefits of cost allocations. *Accounting Review* 54 (July): 504–521.

Zmijewski, Mark E. and Robert L. Hagerman, 1980. An income strategy approach to the positive theory of accounting standard setting/choice. Unpublished manuscript, State University of New York at Buffalo.

# I-B 2 *The Development of a Positive Theory of Corporate Management's Role in External Financial Reporting*

LAUREN KELLY

## INTRODUCTION

Recent attention has been given to developing a positive theory of management's role in the selection of accounting methods and formulation of accounting standards.[1] These efforts seek explanations for management's concern with the accounting procedures used in preparation of the firm's external financial reports. Attention is directed to management's motivations for choosing alternative accounting methods and for reacting to proposed and enacted standards. A positive theory seeks to explain observed phenomena by searching for the reasons that events occur. This orientation differs from descriptive research, which focuses on depicting what actually occurs, and normative theory, which focuses on prescribing what should occur. In the accounting context, positive research seeks to explain and predict the existence of an observed set of procedures rather than to identify solely what procedures managers actually use or should use in financial reporting.

The author is grateful for the comments received from Doug Moses.

Lauren Kelly, "The Development of a Positive Theory of Corporate Management's Role in External Financial Reporting," *Journal of Accounting Literature*, Spring 1983 pp. 111–150. Reprinted with the permission of the *Journal of Accounting Literature*.

[1] The development of a positive theory of the determination of accounting standards is more broad in that it encompasses all parties affected by external financial reporting: management, auditors, policy makers, regulators [Zimmerman, 1980]. The purpose of this paper is to study only corporate management, focusing on both its discretionary choice of accounting procedures and its role in the policy-setting process.

On a general level, a positive theory asks why management is concerned with the accounting procedures used in preparing financial reports. Underlying recent research efforts is the assumption that managers (and other parties to the process) act rationally, seeking to maximize their personal wealth. In addition, informational efficiency in the stock market is presumed.[2] Agency cost theory is the economic model underlying these efforts, wherein the firm is viewed as a set of contracts mitigating the conflicts of interest among management, shareholders, and bondholders.

Management's involvement in external financial reporting may be categorized as (1) the selection of alternative accounting methods and levels of disclosure, or (2) a reaction to proposed or enacted standards in the form of lobbying, discretionary accounting changes, and changes in financing, production, or investment activities of the firm. Initial research focused on identifying differences in accounting procedures and reactions across firms at one point in time and changes in procedures and reactions for a given firm over time. Subsequent research has addressed the effect of alternative accounting procedures on management's wealth, and thus management's incentives to influence the standard-setting process, choose among acceptable accounting alternatives, and change the firm's financing, production, or investment activities. Fuller knowledge concerning these incentives will assist policy makers in assessing the impact of a proposed standard and anticipating reactions to alternative policy resolutions.

Impeding progress in the development of a positive theory is the lack of a fully developed model which explains the cash flow implications to the firm of alternative accounting procedures, the concomitant effect on management's wealth, and thus management's choices from allowable alternatives or reactions to proposed and enacted standards. The purpose of this paper is to present a model of management's choices and reactions based on the relationship between external financial reporting and management's wealth.

In the next section, management's actions in the selection of accounting procedures and reaction to accounting standards are defined. The incentives or determinants of these actions are then addressed by identifying the components of management's wealth and how they are affected by the firm's financial reports. In the fourth section, measurement aspects of the model developed in the prior sections are reviewed. Previous research is reviewed in the fifth section and is related to the model of management's choices and actions. The final section contains implications and suggested avenues for future research.

## MANAGEMENT'S ACTIONS IN THE SELECTION OF ACCOUNTING PROCEDURES AND REACTION TO STANDARDS

To study management's choices and reactions, it is necessary to assess the costs and benefits of alternative accounting procedures in terms of their cash flow implications. This process involves identifying the points at which the selection of accounting methods and reactions to policy prescriptions occur. At any point in time, it may be

---

[2] As pointed out by Zimmerman [1980, pp. 112–13], earlier efforts at the development of a positive theory were based on disbelief in stock market efficiency (e.g., the income smoothing hypothesis). This presumption contradicts research findings that cash flows rather than accounting numbers are used in setting security prices.

assumed that management has chosen from alternative procedures and disclosures to establish the original set of accounting methods which maximizes its wealth, based on the economic conditions confronted by the firm and the accounting alternatives allowed. As depicted in Figure 1, economic events and changes in acceptable accounting alternatives have an impact on the firm's financial reports. Three reactions to this situation can be observed. First, management may lobby policy makers to initiate a change in allowable procedures or to express support or opposition to a proposed or enacted accounting standard. Second, discretionary accounting changes can be made to mitigate the financial statement effect of the economic event or accounting standard. And, last, management may change the financing, production, or investment activities of the firm, also in an attempt to assuage the financial statement's effect.

Examples can be given of the points at which management makes decisions regarding or because of accounting procedures. At any given time, the firm is assumed to possess an optimal mix of accounting procedures, for example, depreciation policies and inventory methods.

Lobbying activities may arise if a change in the economic environment leads firms to prefer accounting methods not currently allowed. For example, corporate pressure to drop last-in-first-out tax conformity rules arose during periods of higher inflation levels. Similar reactions to accounting standards occurred when the elimination of full cost accounting was proposed for the oil and gas industry. This action incited vociferous reaction by affected firms, which lobbied their positions with policy makers and Congress in opposition to the proposal. A change in economic conditions influences discretionary changes in accounting policies; thus higher inflation rates encourage the use of accelerated depreciation methods. Discretionary changes also can be made to mitigate the effect of a mandated accounting change; for example, firms might use longer pension cost amortization periods to assuage the negative impact on earnings from the required expensing of research and development costs. Changes in financing, production, or investment activities occur with changes in economic events, such as disinvestment of foreign subsidiaries in politically unstable countries. However, such changes also may occur in reaction to mandated accounting changes, for example, the increased use of hedging which accompanied the requirement to recognize currently all realized and unrealized foreign exchange gains and losses.

The choices and reactions that arise because of accounting policies must be isolated from those which are due to economic events, since only the former are relevant to a positive theory of management's role in external financial reporting. Additionally, the differential costs and benefits involved with alternative accounting procedures and corporate reactions must be recognized. For example, it is probably less costly for a firm to lobby than to change financing, production, or investment activities in response to an accounting policy. Offsetting these costs, and providing the incentives for management's choices and reactions, are benefits in terms of the effect of alternative accounting policies on management's wealth. These benefits are influenced by the probability of success of the various reactions. Thus lobbying, while less costly, may be less effective in mitigating the impact of an accounting change on a financial statement. Additional complications arise regarding whether the same variables universally explain management's motivations and whether the same decision processes are used by management in reaching its choices and reactions.

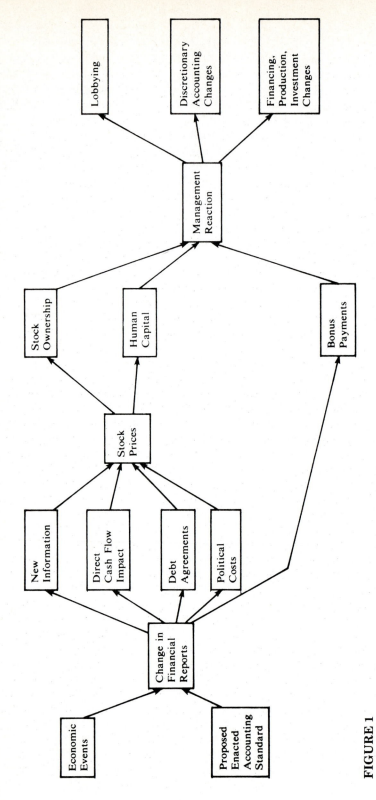

**FIGURE 1**
**Wealth Effects and Reaction to Accounting Changes**

## INCENTIVES FOR MANAGEMENT'S ACTIONS

Intervening between a change in the firm's financial reports and management's reaction are the wealth effects of the change. The avenues for such effects, and thus the incentives for reacting, are depicted in the center of Figure 1 and are discussed in this section.

### Components of Management's Wealth

Understanding management's concern with the accounting policies used in external financial reporting requires identifying the manner by which accounting methods affect management's wealth. Managers are assumed to maximize their wealth, which is a function of current and future compensation. Components of managerial compensation include salary, incentive remuneration such as cash bonuses and stock or stock options, perquisites or nonpecuniary rewards, and enhancement to the value of managerial human capital. (See Smith and Watts [1981] for a review of executive compensation schemes.) Incentive remuneration and the value of human capital are affected by the firm's financial reports, both directly and via the stock market. These effects may occur through changes in the level of bonus payments, the disclosure of new information, direct cash flow effects (e.g., tax effects, bookkeeping costs), and expected cash flow impacts (e.g., debt covenants, political costs).

Positive theory research focuses on the cash flow effects of accounting procedures, and the resulting impact on management's wealth, as the motivation for management to choose from alternative accounting methods and react to accounting standards. Management's decisions regarding accounting procedures are intended to enhance the level of bonus payments or the firm's stock prices (thereby increasing the value of stock, stock options, and human capital).

### Contracting Theory

Conceptualizing the firm as a nexus of contracts among the various factors of production was suggested first by Coase [1937, 1960]. Attention then turned to property rights, in which contracts create certain rights for each of the parties within a firm. Alchian and Demsetz [1972] viewed these contracts as necessary for team production by the various inputs. Since each member of the team is motivated by self-interest, Alchian and Demsetz are concerned with shirking or the need to monitor team production to reduce malfeasance. Jensen and Meckling [1976] studied contracts between bondholders and shareholder-management and between shareholders and management. These contracts arise to minimize the costs associated with shirking or the inherent conflicts of interest between the parties. An alternative view has been proffered by Fama [1980]. The internal and external managerial labor markets are suggested as sufficient for "full ex post settling up," thus eliminating the need for contracts to ajudicate the various conflicts.

Viewing the firm as a nexus of contracts gives rise to issues regarding how such agreements are affected by accounting policies. How they are affected, in turn, has cash flow implications to the firm and thus wealth implications to management. Since accounting measurements are used to enforce many of the contracts, agency theory is used to explain reactions of the contracting parties to changes in methods of accounting measurements. To determine how accounting procedures affect management's compensation, the nature of the agreements that arise in the agency theory relationship is examined.[3]

### Agency Theory

An agency relationship is defined as "a contract under which one or more persons (principal(s)) engage another person (the agent) to perform some service on their behalf which involves delegating some decision making authority to the agent" [Jensen and Meckling, 1976, p. 308].[4] In the context of the firm, management acts as agent for the equity suppliers (shareholders and bondholders) who represent the principals. Two potential conflicts of interest exist: the shareholder/manager conflict, giving rise to the agency cost of equity, and the bondholder/shareholder-management conflict, giving rise to the agency cost of debt. These agency costs are composed of a residual loss, bonding expenditures by the agent, and monitoring expenditures by the principal.

Acting in their own self-interest, managers do not always make decisions that are optimal for the principal. Assuming rational expectations, shareholders and bondholders anticipate this divergence and reduce the price they are willing to pay for the firm's stock or bonds. This reduced price is the residual loss, or the decrease in market value of the firm's equity due to the discrepancy between decisions made by the agent and those the principal would make. Ultimately, the manager bears this loss in the form of a higher cost of capital. To reduce this cost, the agent may contract to ensure that the principal's interests will not be harmed or to provide for retribution if such harm occurs. These contracts represent bonding costs that are borne by the agent. Additionally, the principal may incur expenditures in attempts to restrict the manager's actions. These monitoring costs are also borne by the agent, as they reduce the price received for the firm's equity. In equilibrium, the benefits from the bonding and monitoring contracts (the reduction in the residual loss) equal the costs of contracting and management's lost utility from placing restrictions on its actions (e.g., the reduction in shirking or perquisites taken from the firm).

### Management Compensation

The form of management's compensation is determined by the contracts that arise to mitigate the shareholder/manager conflict of interest. Jensen and Meckling [1976] illustrate this conflict as the tendency for management to procur increasing amounts of perquisites as its proportional ownership falls. In their theory, management gains full utility from nonpecuniary income but bears only its proportion of ownership in the cost. Monitoring and bonding agreements arise to tie the manager's interest to shareholders, and reduce the manager's tendency to appropriate non-pecuniary benefits.[5] Common forms of incentive compensation schemes are bonus

---

[3] For the moment, less than full ex post settling up is assumed. Fama's conceptualization will be discussed more fully in a subsequent section.

[4] This section draws from Jensen and Meckling [1976].

[5] Other monitoring and bonding agreements include audits of the accounting records, formal control systems, budget restrictions, explicit bonding against malfeasance, limits on the manager's decision making power, etc. They are not discussed here since they are not affected by accounting procedures.

plans dependent upon accounting earnings and stock ownership and stock option plans which lessen the conflict of interest by making management shareholders.

Fama [1980] suggests that these conflicts are eliminated through the managerial labor market. If management fails to act in the best interest of the shareholders (i.e., firm value is not maximized), the labor market revises the future wages of managers, thus reducing the value of their human capital. Bonding and monitoring contracts are needed to resolve the shareholder/management conflict only if this adjustment mechanism is imperfect (i.e., there is less than full ex post settling up). Even in the case of full ex post revisions, the managerial labor market is presumed to be sophisticated and to use cues from the stock market and other indications of the firm's performance for valuing management's human capital. This presumption provides an additional incentive for management to be concerned with the level of the firm's share prices and the cash flow effects of accounting alternatives.

### Stock Prices

Compensation agreements arising from the agency relationship, and management's concern with the value of its human capital, can be used to explain the role of share prices in management's wealth. To understand management's concern with the impact of accounting procedures on the firm's stock prices, it is necessary to identify the avenues for obtaining a stock market effect. Efficient market research has shown that a stock market reaction to accounting standards or discretionary accounting changes results only when new information is disclosed or when there is a direct cash flow effect (e.g., from use of the new method for income tax purposes, the effect of the method on bookkeeping costs, a change in management's bonus payment). (See Fama [1976] for a review of the efficient market theory and research.) This leaves a large number of seemingly cosmetic or neutral accounting changes that are not expected to impact the firm's share prices. Recently, researchers have gone beyond direct cash flow effects to consider changes in expectations regarding future cash flows due to the impact of an accounting change on the firm's debt covenants or its political costs.

Securing outside equity through debt financing gives rise to agency costs from the conflict of interests between bondholders and shareholder-management. In this analysis, it is assumed the manager acts to maximize the value of the firm's stock rather than the value of the firm (debt plus stock). Actions that transfer wealth from bondholders to shareholders can arise from discrepancies between the dividend, financing, or investment policies that were expected when the debt was originally issued and those policies that are actually followed. For example, management may increase dividend payments to shareholders by selling the firm's assets, issue additional bonds of equal or higher priority, undertake investment projects with a variance of return higher than indicated when the debt was issued, or reject projects with positive returns if the benefits would accrue to the bondholders. Rational expectations on the part of bondholders should lead them to price the debt lower in order to compensate for these potential wealth transfers. This reduction in the value of the firm is the residual loss from the issuance of debt.

Since this agency cost is borne by the shareholder-manager, incentives for monitoring and bonding agreements arise. Monitoring contracts are represented by bond covenants, defined as provisions in the indenture which place restrictions on specific management actions after the bonds are sold. The costs relating to such restrictions are assessed by bondholders in pricing the debt and thus ultimately are borne by the shareholder-manager. Bonding agreements arise if management can perform the monitoring activities more effectively by agreeing to the restrictions in advance. (See Smith and Warner [1979] for a review of the monitoring and bonding agreements commonly found in debt contracts.)

Monitoring contracts often concern the firm's production and investment policies, with restrictions on investments in other businesses (including mergers) and the disposition of assets. Limits frequently are placed on the firm's ability to pay dividends. Subsequent financing activities may be affected by restrictions on the issuance of additional debt and the incurrence of fixed claims such as leases. Sinking funds, conversion, and callable provisions often are found in bond indentures. Bonding agreements include requirements to issue financial reports, provide certificates of compliance, or purchase insurance against malfeasance. Since production and investment policies are difficult to monitor, most restrictions relate to the firm's dividend and financing activities. The common basis for measuring restrictions is the set of generally accepted accounting procedures used to prepare the firm's current financial statements, primarily because it is costly to require specific accounting methods.

Violation of the firm's debt covenants places the firm in technical default, which might accelerate maturation of debt or renegotiation of the indenture. Bond trustees do not adjust for the effect of an accounting change on the firm's financial statements if they lack the needed accounting expertise, or if they do not find such adjustments cost effective. Default on covenants clearly represents a cost to the firm, and the stock market's anticipation of this situation affects the firm's share prices negatively. Thus management is concerned about the effect of an accounting standard or a discretionary accounting change on the restrictiveness of the firm's covenants, on stock market reactions, and, ultimately, on the value of management's stock ownership and human capital.

Costs to the firm relating to political events come from several sources. Accounting numbers may be used in the direct regulation of certain industries, for example, in setting rates for public utilities or in distributing the income of banks.[6] Changes in accepted accounting procedures may affect the methods used in tax accounting, giving rise to potential cash flow effects. The political sector uses the firm's financial reports to affect wealth transfers from the corporate sector. For example, the appearance of high profits can invoke antitrust activities, selected taxation of profits, higher union demands, or price controls.[7] Management may attempt to avoid these situations through the use of accounting procedures. Anticipation of such costs by the stock market can lead to share price movements, with an impact on the value of management's stock ownership and human capital.

As has been seen, accounting numbers are used in a variety of contexts, requiring management to consider the alternative costs and benefits that arise from various uses. The costs involved in the choice of an accounting alternative or reaction to a proposed or enacted standard depend upon the nature of the action: lobbying, discretionary accounting change, or changes in financing, production, or investment

---

[6] Jarrell [1979] has shown empirically that regulated electric utilities use the accounting system to revalue upward their asset base, allowing them to earn supracompetitive returns.

[7] As with debt contracts, these parties are either unsophisticated in their ability to adjust for nonsubstantive accounting changes or do not find such adjustments cost effective.

activities. The costs of inaction arise from the impact of the discretionary or mandatory accounting change on management's wealth. The avoidance of a negative effect, and the probability of success from a specific reaction, comprise the benefits of management's action. In any specific accounting change, management must make tradeoffs, for example, the increased political costs but decreased debt restrictions that arise from higher income. Given the current state of knowledge, it is impossible to determine a priori which effect will dominate.

## MEASUREMENT OF THE IMPACT OF MANAGEMENT'S WEALTH

While the previous section identified the components of management's wealth, attention now is directed to how the constructs are measured. The forms of the contracts that affect management's wealth are scrutinized to determine the ways by which an accounting change can impact a contract and thereby management's wealth. This process necessitates defining the terms of bonus payments, stock ownership plans, and debt covenants, as well as the influence of accounting disclosures on the value of management's human capital and the firm's political costs. Exhibit 1 outlines the dimensions of wealth changes as a function of (1) the financial statement effect of an accounting change, (2) determinants of stock price reactions, and (3) avenues for affecting management's wealth. The measurements discussed in this section are largely those suggested by previous research.

### Financial Statement Effect

The magnitude of the impact of an accounting change must be considered separately for each specific change and each particular contract. This process requires identifying the terms of the contract (i.e., the accounting measurements used to enforce the agreement) and the effect of the accounting change on those measurements. For example, in assessing the likelihood of management's reaction to an accounting change that affects bonus payments, the specific income effect of the change must be considered. For any particular bonus agreement, the greater the impact on accounting income, the larger the effect on management's wealth.

An accounting change can impact the level and/or variability of earnings. Management's risk attitude may influence its reaction to an increase in income variability (i.e., more intense peaks and troughs). A highly risk averse manager would be expected to react negatively to an increase in the variability of income, preferring to avoid the negative consequences from lower earnings on bonus payments and debt covenants and from higher earnings on political costs. Less risk averse managers would tend to favor greater variability in income due to the potential positive effects on bonus payments, debt covenants, and political costs.

Surrogates often are used to assess the degree of the impact on the accounting numbers. For example, the potential income effect of expensing research and development costs might be measured as a function of the firm's involvement in innovative activities, or the potential working capital effect of capitalizing leases might be assessed as a function of the firm's leasing activities.

### Stock Price Effect

Efficient market research has provided empirical support for the presence of stock price reactions to accounting changes that result in the disclosure of new

**EXHIBIT 1**

**Effects of Accounting Changes**

  I. Financial Statement Effect
 II. Stock Price Effect
    A. New Information
    B. Direct Cash Flow Impact
      1. Recordkeeping costs
      2. Tax effects
    C. Bond Covenants
      1. Closeness to constraints
      2. Renegotiation
        a. public/private debt
        b. callable/noncallable debt
      3. Leverage
          debt/equity ratio
      4. Covenant restrictions
        a. Net tangible assets
        b. Capitalization
        c. Working capital
        d. Unrestricted retained earnings
        e. Long-term debt
        f. Fixed charges
        g. Leases
    D. Political Costs
      1. Direct regulation
          membership in a regulated industry
      2. Indirect regulation
        a. Size
           i. total assets
          ii. sales revenue
         iii. market capitalization
        b. Membership in politically-sensitive industry
        c. Market share
           i. firm
              sales/total industry sales
          ii. industry concentration
              sales of largest firms/total industry sales
        d. Capital intensity
          gross fixed assets/sales
        e. Systematic risk and variability of accounting earnings
          beta coefficient
      3. Tax changes
III. Management Wealth Effect
    A. Human Capital
      1. Management's percentage ownership
      2. Changes in management

**EXHIBIT 1 (*Continued*)**

    B.  Stock Ownership
        1.  Existence of stock appreciation rights
        2.  Existence of stock option plans
        3.  Management's percentage ownership
        4.  Proportionate wealth from stock ownership market valuation of proportionate ownership
    C.  Bonus Payments
        1.  Existence of bonus plan
        2.  Proportionate wealth from bonus payments
            incentive compensation/total remuneration

information or in a direct cash flow effect. However, the lack of direct cash flow effects is not a sufficient condition for the absence of a stock price reaction. Positive theory research has considered potential cash flow effects from debt agreements and political costs.

*Bond Covenants*  Discretionary accounting changes may be used by management to loosen the restrictions contained in debt agreements. Mandated changes in accounting procedures also affect the distance from constraints, and violation of the covenants may become imminent. Assessment by the stock market of future cash flow effects from these situations is dependent on (1) the magnitude of the impact of the accounting change on measurement of the covenants, (2) the closeness of the firm to its constraints, and (3) the likelihood for renegotiation of the bond contract.

As shown by Kalay [1982], the potential for transfer of wealth from bondholders to manager-shareholders increases with greater amounts of leverage. Since higher debt levels result in more wealth per share to transfer, bondholders reduce bond prices accordingly. To avoid this residual loss, manager-shareholders may agree to more debt restrictions. In this manner, the agency costs of debt increase as the firm's leverage rises, such that higher debt-to-equity ratios indicate a greater likelihood for violation of debt covenants.

The restrictions found in debt agreements are specific to the individual covenants. However, generalizations regarding the nature of the restrictions can be made for the more common forms. Investments in other businesses often are permitted only when the debtor's net tangible assets exceed a minimum or are limited to a percentage of the firm's capitalization. Management's operating decisions are restricted by covenants that require the maintenance of a minimum working capital or current ratio. Dividend payments, as well as restrictions on redemptions, purchases, retirements, partial liquidations, or capital reductions, are limited to an amount of available funds. In the case of dividends, this amount is the firm's unrestricted retained earnings (accumulated earnings plus proceeds from the issuance of new equity minus any dividends paid). New debt issues are restricted by requirements to maintain financial leverage as measured by ratios such as net tangible assets to long-term debt, capitalization to long-term debt, tangible net worth to long-term debt, working capital, and net income to fixed charges (including interest). Limitations on leasing obligations are enacted by including leases within debt restrictions, that is, defining the present value of leases as long-term debt and lease payments as fixed obligations.

Enforcement of debt covenants depends on the definition of accounting measures such as net tangible assets, capitalization, current assets, current liabilities, retained earnings, net income, long-term debt, leases, and fixed charges. These definitions can be specified within the debt agreement or stated in terms of generally accepted accounting principles either at the time the bonds are originally issued or when the firm's current financial reports are prepared. Most covenants use current accounting procedures due to the expense of keeping separate accounting records and monitoring compliance with specified procedures. Thus, management usually is accorded discretion in choosing from allowable accounting alternatives to measure debt restrictions. In addition, mandated changes in accounting procedures arising from the issuance of an accounting standard often are allowed to affect the measurement of constraints. Covenants may become more restrictive as a result of policies which reduce net income or net tangible assets or increase the level of debt. Such effects can result in technical default that might lead to renegotiation, redemption, or difficulty in acquiring additional equity.

Management could attempt to renegotiate the terms of the debt contract to eliminate the effect of a mandated accounting change. Since amendments to bond contracts typically require concurrence of at least two-thirds of the lenders, renegotiation is easier for private placements with a small number of institutional lenders than for public debt issues. Private debt does not need to be registered with the Securities and Exchange Commission and does not come under the Trust Indenture Act; thus the terms in such agreements can be more specific. For example, the debt agreements could specify accounting procedures that deviate from generally accepted accounting principles. (See Leftwich [1983] for evidence on these issues.) The degree of public versus private debt held by the firm is used as an indicator of (1) management's tendency to use discretionary accounting procedures to loosen restrictive covenants or (2) management's reaction to a mandated change via lobbying, discretionary accounting changes, or changes in financing, production, or investment policies. Difficulties arise in delineating criteria that distinguish public from private debt.

Management's preferences may be for accounting procedures that would increase income and asset values, thereby loosening the restrictiveness of bond covenants. Management's accounting choices and reactions to standards would then be a function of the firm's leverage, slack in debt restrictions, amount of public and private debt, number of accounting measures used to enforce debt agreements, and impact of the accounting change on the covenants. These measures comprise the costs of management's failure to react either with or because of an accounting change; that is, they represent the costs of operating within the confines of the debt constraints. These costs can be compared with alternatives such as renegotiation or repurchase of the debt to determine management's actions. Future cash outflows may be expected to result from having debt restrictions adversely affected by an accounting change. These changes could also yield share price adjustments. As a result, management would be concerned with the effect on the value of its holdings of stock and stock options (including stock appreciation rights), as well as the value of its human capital. Thus managers may be motivated to operate within loose debt constraints.

*Political Costs*    Political costs arise from both direct and indirect regulation of the firm. Some governmental agencies stipulate the accounting methods to be used in reporting to regulatory bodies. These agencies often require the use of generally accepted accounting principles or are influenced by them in the formation of their reporting requirements. The management of utilities, banks, insurance firms, and transportation companies may be motivated to use discretionary accounting changes and react to proposed and enacted standards to favorably influence regulation. This aspect of political costs has been measured by a dichotomous variable reflecting membership in an industry regulated with accounting disclosures.

Indirect regulation arising from antitrust investigation, union demands, price controls, social responsibility, or other interventions into the activities of the firm is a second aspect of political costs. Financial reports often are used to scrutinize the firm, thus influencing the likelihood of adverse intrusion. In general, management could fear that higher accounting earnings imply abnormal returns, increasing the chance of government actions. Several measures of this potential cost have been suggested. If large firms are scrutinized more closely than smaller companies, firm size would lead to increased exposure to government actions.[8] Ceteris paribus, the larger the firm's size, the greater the potential for future cash outflows from political intervention during periods of high profits. Firm size has been measured by total assets, sales revenue, or market value of common equity.

Potential government intrusion also is related to the firm's membership in an industry considered politically sensitive. For example, in the oil and gas industry, windfall profits, combined with national goals to find alternative energy sources, motivated the decision to enact higher taxes. This aspect has been measured as a dichotomous variable for membership in such an industry.

Market share, or the firm's individual concentration and the level of competition within the industry, also has been used to measure political vulnerability. In addition to antitrust proceedings, higher earnings encourage potential entrants into the industry, thereby reducing returns to firms already in the industry. If an individual firm has a high market share, or if there is a high concentration of market power in a few firms, the firm is more likely to earn abnormal profit and be exposed to increased competition. The firm's market share is measured by the proportion of its sales to total industry sales, while market power is measured by concentration ratios such as the proportion of total industry sales accounted for by a specified number of the largest firms in the industry.

The appearance of abnormal profit also may be related to the firm's capital intensity. If capital-intensive firms do not incorporate the opportunity cost of capital into net income, accounting earnings will exceed those of labor-intensive firms with the same economic profit. Capital-intensive firms thereby may be more likely to incur political costs. Capital intensity has been measured by the ratio of total fixed assets to sales revenue.

Analogously, the firm's risk and variability of earnings may give rise to the appearance of excess profits. The risk/return relationship implies that higher risk firms earn larger returns. Unless adjustments are made for risk characteristics, such firms appear to earn abnormal income. Greater variability of earnings gives rise to periods of high profits, which may be misinterpreted as excess returns. Both risk and

---

[8] Siegried [1975] and "Curse of Bigness" [1969] are often cited as evidence for the association between firm size and antitrust proceedings. See Ball and Foster [1982], who discuss the serious construct validity issues that arise from using firm size to operationalize the concept of political costs.

variability of earnings have been measured by the beta coefficient of the firm's earnings, derived from the market model.

Management's reaction to an accounting standard might be affected by the expectation that the policy will influence future taxation of the firm. Measurement of this aspect of potential political costs requires specifying the firm's exposure to a tax effect from the specific policy. For example, the expectation of an impact on the firm's taxes from expensing research and development costs is greater for companies more heavily involved in innovative activities.

Underlying the potential for political costs from direct and indirect regulation and taxes is the belief that regulators, politicians, and other users do not incorporate the substantive effect of an accounting change into their decisions. Failure to adjust for accounting changes could result because such parties either lack the ability to make adjustments or perceive few personal benefits from doing so. Management's belief that accounting changes will affect political costs might explain the use of discretionary accounting methods and reactions to accounting standards.

In summary, the management of firms under direct regulation appear to favor accounting methods that increase their cash flows. For example, firms in an industry subject to rate regulation could prefer accounting standards that reduce reported earnings, since lower profits increase the likelihood of a rate increase. Indirect regulation might lead firms that are politically vulnerable to use accounting procedures and prefer accounting standards that lower net income. Thus firms seem more likely to shun income-increasing procedures if they belong to a regulated industry, are relatively larger in size, belong to a politically sensitive industry, possess larger market share or are in a highly concentrated industry, are highly capital intensive, and/or exhibit high systematic risk or earnings variability. Expectation of increased cash outflows resulting in adverse stock price reaction is greater in these situations. The management of these firms might be expected to select accounting methods and react to accounting standards to counteract such adverse consequences.

### Management Wealth Effect

*Human Capital*   The effect of changes in the firm's stock prices and reports of the firm's performance on the value of management's human capital is a difficult concept to make operational. This factor encompasses the impact on management's future wages and employment opportunities. Professional managers may be more concerned than owner-managers about the value of their human capital. An owner-manager could feel relatively secure in future employment, since some control over the firm is possessed. A professional manager, however, may be more dependent upon the external labor market and its use of stock prices for future wealth. The degree of management ownership can be measured by the percentage of the firm's common stock owned by corporate management. An ex post measure of the influence of the external labor market may emerge from measuring the number of management personnel who leave the firm in a given time period. This wealth effect results from more long-run considerations than those that arise from management's explicit compensation contracts with the firm.

*Stock Ownership*   Jensen and Meckling's [1976] agency theory of the firm suggests that lower management proportional ownership of a firm leads to increases in the optimum amount of monitoring. Stock ownership and stock option plans have been used to reduce these agency costs by associating management's wealth (the value of their personal assets) with that of shareholders. Management's remuneration also is affected by the firm's stock prices when management is granted stock appreciation rights, incentive schemes that provide for cash payments as a function of appreciation in the firm's stock prices.

Measuring the importance of stock ownership in management's accounting choices and reactions to accounting standards is complicated by the need to assess the manager's total wealth and then the relative importance of the value of management's stock ownership to that wealth. For any given firm, the larger management's proportional ownership, the greater should be the manager's concern with share price movements. While management's proportional share of the market valuation of the firm (and changes therein) can be measured, it is difficult to relate this value to each individual manager's total wealth. Thus management's proportional ownership of the firm, or the market valuation of those shares, is at best a surrogate for the magnitude of management's concern with the firm's stock prices.[9]

*Bonus Payments* The influence of incentive bonus plans on management's decisions regarding accounting policies depends upon the relative importance of such compensation to management's total wealth. Ideally, measurement of this proportionate influence would consider all sources of management's income during the period. However, management's total wealth is very difficult to operationalize. To measure the degree of impact on bonus income from an accounting change, the form of the compensation agreement must be scrutinized. Oftentimes bonus payments are a function of accounting earnings, with stipulations that earnings exceed a minimum level (usually determined as a percentage of capitalization) or constraints on the bonus to a maximum amount (determined as a percentage of dividends to stockholders, management's salary, or a fixed dollar amount). In these cases, a minimum level of income must be earned before bonuses are paid, and a ceiling is set to bonus payments.

Management's compensation agreements frequently are written using accounting numbers from the firm's financial reports prepared with current generally accepted accounting procedures, since constraints on management's choice from allowable procedures are costly to enforce. Incentive agreements could specify the use of accounting methods that existed when the contracts were written. This restriction too would necessitate the extra expense of two separate sets of records. Without constraints on accounting procedures, management's discretionary accounting changes and changes mandated through accounting standards impact the manager's income. The effect of such accounting changes could be mitigated by renegotiation of compensation agreements. Renegotiation itself is a costly process, and management's

---

[9] The difficulties faced by smaller firms in acquiring outside equity financing have been cited as an additional reason for managment's concern with the effect of accounting changes on the firm's stock prices (see Deakin, [1979] and Horwitz and Kolodny, [1980]). These allegations presume inefficiencies in the market for securities of smaller firms, and thus concern with accounting earnings per se. This assumption is not relevant to the present model, which focuses on the cash flow implications of accounting changes rather than the direct manipulation of stock prices through accounting procedures. Negative cash flow effects (and depressed stock prices) that arise because of the firm's industry or size are captured in the political cost construct.

actions probably are influenced by its assessment of the likelihood of such adjustments.

The ownership structure of the firm has been used as an indirect measure of the importance of incentive compensation schemes for reducing agency conflicts of interest. In owner-controlled firms with closely held stock, shareholders may exercise more active control, directly monitoring the actions of management. The outside owners of manager-controlled firms appear more dependent on incentive contracts to protect their interests. Ceteris paribus, assuming more diffuse ownership results in a greater use of monitoring devices, management should evidence greater concern with accounting standards in manager-controlled firms.

At the simplest level, it appears that management may use discretionary accounting changes to increase the level of accounting earnings, or react favorably to accounting standards that enhance the firm's income. This tendency would be stronger in situations where management's proportionate wealth from bonus payments is large. However, such accounting choices or reactions seem unlikely if the firm's income would not exceed the minimum level necessary for bonus payments. Nor should management be concerned with accounting changes if the maximum bonus allowed is already being earned. In fact, in this situation, management may attempt to decrease current earnings and enhance future periods' income.

The measurement problems discussed here have complicated the operationalization of this construct. In most cases, firms have been categorized by whether such incentive plans exist.[10] To measure the relative influence of bonus income, incentive payments have been related to the total remuneration received by management from the firm in a given time period. The ownership structure of the firm has been used to measure indirectly the likelihood that incentive compensation schemes are used.

## PREVIOUS RESEARCH ON FACTORS INFLUENCING MANAGEMENT'S CHOICES AND REACTIONS

To date, fourteen studies have been published that focus on management's discretionary accounting choices and reaction to accounting standards from the vantage of the effect of accounting methods on management's wealth. These studies are categorized into those that concern management's voluntary choice of accounting methods to establish the optimal mix of accounting policies and those that concern corporate reaction to mandated accounting changes. The evidence from these studies is summarized in Table 1 and discussed in this section. (See Holthausen and Leftwich [1982] for a different categorization and review of this research.)

### Discretionary Accounting Choices

The central question addressed in this group of studies is whether the voluntary selection of accounting procedures is used as a means of influencing the level of executive incentive compensation or to reduce the restrictiveness of debt covenants or exposure to political costs and thereby enhance the firm's stock prices. The researchers have focused on (1) the selection by management of the set of accounting

---

[10] Ball and Foster [1982] discuss the serious construct validity problems that arise from using the 0-1 dummy variable to represent compensation plans. This simplification ignores other forms of remuneration and the implicit use of accounting disclosures to set compensation levels.

procedures to be used at a point in time; (2) the decision to disclose information voluntarily or engage an external auditor; (3) stock market reaction to a discretionary change in accounting procedures.

*Accounting Procedure Selection*   Dhaliwal [1980] examined the influence of the firm's leverage on management's choice of successful efforts versus full cost accounting for oil and gas exploration costs prior to the issuance of FAS No. 19.[11] The restrictive debt covenants found in most debt agreements led Dhaliwal to expect highly levered firms to avoid accounting methods that result in lower and/or more volatile accounting earnings or in lower net tangible assets. Compared with full cost accounting, successful efforts reduce income and equity and increase the variability of earnings. Thus, Dhaliwal hypothesized that the average debt/equity ratio of firms using full cost was larger than that for firms using successful efforts. The 1976 debt/equity ratios of 33 pairs of firms were compared, where the firms were matched on sales revenue to control for firm size. A statistically significant difference was found between the average debt/equity ratio of companies using full cost and those using successful efforts. This finding provides some support for the contention that the firm's leverage influences management's selection of accounting methods.[12]

Dhaliwal extended his study by adjusting the asset position of nineteen of the full cost firms to a successful efforts basis. He found that the asset size of the full cost firms was statistically significantly larger than that of the successful efforts firms. This finding is contrary to predictions derived from the political cost variable, which imply that larger firms prefer accounting methods that decrease earnings. Dhaliwal interprets this finding as evidence that the leverage factor dominates political costs considerations. However, larger firms may be avoiding the increased variability of earnings under successful efforts (i.e., the intensified peaks in their earnings stream), which is consistent with the political cost factor.

Hagerman and Zmijewski [1979] attempted to identify the economic motives underlying management's voluntary selection of accounting methods for inventory (LIFO versus FIFO), depreciation (accelerated versus straight line), investment tax credit (flow through versus deferral), and the amortization period of past service pension costs. Their sample consisted of 300 randomly selected firms which disclosed their choice of accounting methods in their 1975 annual reports and 10Ks. Five factors were hypothesized as influencing whether the firms used income-increasing or income-decreasing accounting methods: (1) political costs measured by (a) size (sales and total assets), (b) industry concentration (sales of largest eight firms/total industry sales), (c) capital intensity (gross fixed assets/sales), and (d) systematic risk and variability of accounting earnings (beta coefficient); and (2) bonus payments measured by the existence of a bonus plan. Hagerman and Zmijewski hypothesized that large, risky, capital-intensive firms in highly concentrated industries use income-reducing methods, while the existence of bonus plans explains income-increasing procedures.

Probit analysis was used to estimate separate models of the four accounting choices. Only the models explaining the choice of inventory and depreciation

---

[11] Dhaliwal claims he studies management's attitude toward FAS No. 19, but his tests are on the use of the alternative accounting methods prior to the standard.
[12] Dhaliwal also found that full cost firms have statistically significant greater amounts of total long-term debt than successful efforts firms.

**TABLE 1**

**Evidence on Factors Explaining Management's Choices and Reactions Discretionary Accounting Choices**

| | *Accounting Procedure Selection* | | | | |
|---|---|---|---|---|---|
| | Dhaliwal | Hagerman and Zmijewski[1] | Zmijewski and Hagerman | Bowen, Lacey and Noreen | Dhaliwal, Salamon and Smith |
| Financial Statement Effect | | | | | |
| Impact or earnings | | | | | |
| Impact or stockholder's equity | | | | | |
| Level of activity | | | | | |
| Bond Covenants | | | | | |
| Closeness to constraints | | | | | |
| dividends paid/unrestricted retained earnings | | | | S | |
| unrestricted retained earnings/market value | | | | | |
| common stock | | | | | |
| income/interest expense | | | | S | |
| net tangible assets/long-term debt | | | | S | |
| Renegotiation | | | | | |
| public/private debt | | | | | |
| callable debt | | | | | |
| Leverage | | | | | |
| debt/equity | S | | | | |
| preferred stock/equity | | | S | | |
| Covenant restrictions | | | | | |
| existence of covenants | | | | | |
| number of accounting measures | | | | | |
| Conversion costs | | | | | |
| convertible debt | | | | | |

| Political Costs | | |
|---|---|---|
| Direct regulation | | |
| membership in regulated industry | | |
| Indirect regulation | | |
| size | | |
| total assets | S | |
| sales revenue | N,S | N,S |
| market capitalization | S[2] | |
| membership in politically sensitive industry | S | |
| market share | | |
| firm | | |
| sales/total industry sales | | |
| industry concentration | S,N | S |
| sales of largest firms/total industry sales | S | |
| capital intensity | | |
| gross fixed assets/sales | S,S | N |
| systematic risk and variability of | | |
| accounting earnings beta coefficients | N,S | N |
| Tax changes | | |
| Management Wealth Effect | | |
| Management's stock ownership | | |
| Incentive plans | | |
| existence of a bonus plan | N,S | |
| incentive compensation/total remuneration | S | N |
| ownership control | | S |

S   Supported
N   Not supported

[1] The first symbol represents factors for inventory methods, while the second symbol represents factors for depreciation policy
[2] The direction of influence was opposite of that hypothesized
[3] This variable was intended to capture both political costs and misspecification in the return generating model
[4] The first symbol represents factors for lobbying, while the second symbol represents factors for financing or operating changes

TABLE 1 (*Continued*)

**Evidence on Factors Explaining Management's Choices and Reactions Discretionary Accounting Choices**

| | Voluntary Disclosure and Auditing | | | Stock Market Reaction |
|---|---|---|---|---|
| | Salamon and Dhaliwal | Leftwich, Watts and Zimmerman | Chow | Holthausen |
| **Financial Statement Effect** | | | | |
| Impact or earnings | | | | N |
| Impact or stockholder's equity | | | | |
| Level of activity | | | | |
| **Bond Covenants** | | | | |
| Closeness to constraints | | | | |
| dividends paid/unrestricted retained earnings | | | | |
| unrestricted retained earnings/market value | | | | |
| common stock | | | | N |
| income/interest expense | | | | |
| net tangible assets/long-term debt | | | | |
| Renegotiation | | | | |
| public/private debt | | | | |
| callable debt | | | | N |
| Leverage | | | | |
| debt/equity | | N | S | S$^2$ |
| preferred stock/equity | | N | | |
| Covenant restrictions | | | | |
| existence of covenants | | | | |
| number of accounting measures | | | S | |
| Conversion costs | | | | |
| convertible debt | | | | |

| Political Costs | | |
|---|---|---|
|   Direct regulation | | |
|     membership in regulated industry | | |
|   Indirect regulation | | |
|     size | | |
|       total assets | | |
|       sales revenue | | |
|       market capitalization | $N^3$ | |
|     membership in politically sensitive industry | N | |
|     market share | | |
|       firm | | |
|       sales/total industry sales | | |
|       industry concentration | | |
|       sales of largest firms/total industry sales | | |
|     capital intensity | | |
|       gross fixed assets/sales | | |
|     systematic risk and variability of accounting earnings beta coefficients | | |
|   Tax changes | | |
| Management Wealth Effect | | |
|   Management's stock ownership | S | N |
|   Incentive plans | | |
|     existence of a bonus plan | S | N |
|     incentive compensation/total remuneration | | |
|     ownership control | | |

S  Supported
N  Not supported

[1] The first symbol represents factors for inventory methods, while the second symbol represents factors for depreciation policy
[2] The direction of influence was opposite of that hypothesized
[3] This variable was intended to capture both political costs and misspecification in the return generating model
[4] The first symbol represents factors for lobbying, while the second symbol represents factors for financing or operating changes

**TABLE 1 (Continued)**

**Evidence on Factors Explaining Management's Choices and Reactions Mandated Accounting Changes**

| | Lobby and Financing, Production or Investment Changes | | | Stock Market Reaction | |
| --- | --- | --- | --- | --- | --- |
| | Watts and Zimmerman | Dhaliwal | Kelly[4] | Collins, Rozeff and Dhaliwal | Leftwich |
| **Financial Statement Effect** | | | | | |
| Impact or earnings | | | N,N | N | |
| Impact or stockholder's equity | | | | S | |
| Level of activity | | | | N | |
| **Bond Covenants** | | | | | |
| Closeness to constraints | | | | | |
| dividends paid/unrestricted retained earnings | | | | | |
| unrestricted retained earnings/market value | | | | | |
| common stock | | | | | |
| income/interest expense | | | | | |
| net tangible assets/long-term debt | | | | | |
| Renegotiation | | | | | |
| public/private debt | | | | N | N |
| callable debt | | | | | S |
| Leverage | | | | | |
| debt/equity | | S | S,N | N | S |
| preferred stock/equity | | | | | |
| Covenant restrictions | | | | | |
| existence of covenants | | | | S | |
| number of accounting measures | | | | | |
| Conversion costs | | | | | |
| convertible debt | | | | | N |

Political Costs

| | Col 1 | Col 2 | Col 3 | Col 4 | Col 5 |
|---|---|---|---|---|---|
| **Direct regulation** | | | | | |
| membership in regulated industry | N | | | | |
| **Indirect regulation** | | | | | |
| size | | | | | |
| total assets | S | N | S,S | | |
| sales revenue | S | | | | |
| market capitalization | | | | $S^{2,3}$ | $S^{3}$ |
| membership in politically sensitive industry | | | | | |
| market share | | | | | |
| firm | | | | | |
| sales/total industry sales | N | | | | |
| industry concentration | | | | | |
| sales of largest firms/total industry sales | | | | | |
| capital intensity | | | | | |
| gross fixed assets/sales | | | | | |
| systematic risk and variability of | | | | | |
| accounting earnings beta coefficients | | | | | |
| Tax changes | N | | | | |
| **Management Wealth Effect** | | | | | |
| Management's stock ownership | | | S,N | | |
| Incentive plans | | | | | |
| existence of a bonus plan | N | | N,N | | |
| incentive compensation/total remuneration | | | S,N | S | |
| ownership control | | | | | |

S   Supported
N   Not supported

[1] The first symbol represents factors for inventory methods, while the second symbol represents factors for depreciation policy
[2] The direction of influence was opposite of that hypothesized
[3] This variable was intended to capture both political costs and misspecification in the return generating model
[4] The first symbol represents factors for lobbying, while the second symbol represents factors for financing or operating changes

methods were statistically significant. For inventory, capital-intensive firms in highly concentrated industries were found to use LIFO, an income-decreasing method. Accelerated depreciation was used to decrease income by large firms with relatively higher risk and more capital intensity. The existence of a profit-sharing plan was negatively related to the use of accelerated depreciation. Hagerman and Zmijewski were troubled to find that the important explanatory factors depended upon the accounting method, since this finding implies the use of different variables to make each decision. The question then became why managers are motivated by different economic factors in selecting accounting procedures.

In an extension of their study, Zmijewski and Hagerman [1981] developed an income strategy approach in which the firm's accounting choices were viewed as a part of an overall financial reporting policy rather than as independent decisions. Under this view, management selects accounting procedures to achieve a long-run income strategy. Using the same sample of 300 companies, firms were placed into one of sixteen possible categories based on whether their inventory, depreciation, investment tax credit, and pension plan amortization period were income-increasing or income-decreasing. (For example, one category contained firms using all income-decreasing procedures for the four accounting choices, a second category contained firms using an income increasing method for inventory only, etc.) The categories were further aggregated, then ranked in terms of the most income-decreasing to the most income-increasing. The ranks were predicted using the same five independent variables from the previous study, plus the firm's debt/equity ratio as a measure of leverage. The resulting model was statistically significant, with larger firms in highly concentrated industries using income-decreasing strategies and highly levered firms with profit-sharing plans using income-increasing strategies. These results were much stronger than those when the accounting choices were modeled independently. Thus Zmijewski and Hagerman concluded that firms act as though they choose accounting policies relative to an income strategy decision process.[13]

Bowen, Lacey, and Noreen [1981] studied the voluntary choice of capitalizing interest costs related to assets under construction prior to the policy prescriptions issued by the SEC and FASB. Since the propensity to capitalize interest was influenced by the firm's industry, the sample consisted of 91 pairs of firms matched on industry. Six variables were hypothesized as influencing management's decision to capitalize interest in 1974: (1) bonus payments measured by the existence of a bonus plan; (2) bond covenants and the closeness to the firm's constraints measured by (a) the pool of retained earnings available for dividends (dividends paid/unrestricted retained earnings), (b) tightness of interest coverage ratios (income/interest expense), and (c) limits on leverage (net tangible assets/long-term debt); and (3) political costs measured by (a) size and membership in a politically sensitive industry (oil and gas), and (b) size of nonpetroleum firms (total sales). Bowen, Lacey, and Noreen expected firms not to have capitalized interest due to political costs but to

---

[13] Zmijewski and Hagerman also partitioned their sample into low and high political cost groups (based on the median size and concentration ratio) to determine if the same factors were important to both groups. They found the model was statistically significant only for high political cost firms and concluded that further research is needed to identify the economic factors motivating managers of firms not subject to high political costs. This analysis is suspect, however, since there is no basis for asserting that the median firm size of concentration ratio represents the threshold distinguishing low and high political cost firms.

have capitalized interest because of bonus plans and the tightness of debt covenants. Univariate and multivariate tests reveal that firms capitalizing interest faced more restrictive bond covenants: the dividend constraints, interest coverage ratios, and limits on leverage were statistically significant. While the largest firm in the oil and gas industry expensed interest costs, the size factor for firms in all other industries indicated that larger companies capitalized interest.

Dhaliwal, Salamon, and Smith [1982] studied the relationship between the ownership control status of the firm and the choice of depreciation methods for financial reporting. They defined an owner-controlled firm as one in which one party owned 10 percent or more of the voting stock and exercised active control or one party owned 20 percent or more of the voting stock. No single block of stock greater than 5 percent owned by any party defined a manager-controlled firm. The authors allege that diffuse ownership means that outside owners rely more heavily on incentive compensation schemes to monitor management, while the owners of a closely held firm can observe managers' behavior more directly. Dhaliwal, Salamon, and Smith posit that manager-controlled firms more frequently use income-increasing accounting methods, since incentive compensation schemes that depend on reported income are more likely to occur in this ownership structure. Thus, ownership control is used to surrogate for the presence of incentive compensation schemes. The alternative view is the Fama thesis that the managerial labor market acts as a sufficient disciplining mechanism, such that there are no differences in the accounting procedures used in different ownership structures.

To test their hypothesis, Dhaliwal, Salamon, and Smith examined the use of straight-line versus accelerated depreciation for financial reporting purposes by 83 firms in 1962. One of their concerns was that systematic differences in the size and leverage of owner-controlled versus manager-controlled firms would confound the analysis. Univariate tests of the differences in these characteristics revealed that manager-controlled firms were larger than owner-controlled firms but there was no statistically significant difference in debt-to-equity ratios. No attempt was made to interpret these results using agency theory arguments. Since prior research has shown that larger firms tend to choose income-decreasing accounting methods, the correlation of size with ownership structure reduces the power of the test of the main hypothesis.

Univariate tests of the difference in the proportion of manager-controlled versus owner-controlled firms using straight-line depreciation indicated a statistically significant difference, with the former group using the income-increasing method. A probit analysis was used to include the effect of size and leverage. The model was statistically significant, with the debt-to-equity ratio significant and positively related to the use of straight-line depreciation and firm size insignificant. Ownership control was significant, with manager-controlled firms using straight-line depreciation. These results supported the hypothesis that the selection of accounting methods is influenced by the firm's ownership structure. The authors interpreted their findings as evidence against Fama's thesis that the managerial labor market is a sufficient disciplining mechanism.

*Voluntary Disclosure and Auditing*  Salamon and Dhaliwal [1980] studied management's discretionary choices regarding the level of monitoring, focusing on the voluntary disclosure of segmental information. The basic premise of their study is the agency theory contention that the costs of external monitoring are borne either directly by the firm or indirectly as a lower price received for its stock. If it is more cost effective for management rather than external parties to provide information, an increase in the level of disclosure should reduce the firm's cost of capital. Salamon and Dhaliwal posit that firms with less need for public external financing will have a lower level of voluntary disclosures. If small firms rely less heavily on external capital sources, their disclosures will be less extensive then those of large firms.

Salamon and Dhaliwal's sample was 25 diversified firms that did not provide segmental sales and profit information from 1967 through 1970 and 26 companies that disclosed this information prior to 1968 when the SEC announced that it was considering requiring segmental disclosures. The Mann-Whitney U test was used to determine if the voluntary disclosure of segmental information was related to company size. The tests indicated that total assets of firms making these disclosures were statistically significantly larger than of the nondisclosure firms.[14] Salamon and Dhaliwal interpreted these results as indication that the requirement to report segmental information is more onerous for smaller firms, since such firms are not currently making or do not need to make these disclosures.

The disclosure of interim reports as a discretionary choice of monitoring levels was studied by Leftwich, Watts, and Zimmerman [1981]. Variations in the frequency of external reporting were posited as related to agency theory constructs arising from differences in the firms' capital structures, asset structures, and use of other monitoring devices. Seven variables were studied. First, assets in place (total assets/firm value) controlled for asset structure. For a given level of fixed claims, agency costs were posited as lower if the firm has fewer growth opportunities (a higher ratio of assets in place), because it is more costly to shift the risk of existing assets. Thus interim reporting was expected for firms with high growth opportunities. Second, size (market value of the firm) controlled for the agency costs of outside capital (larger firms depend on more outside capital) and proxied for the firm's industry, exchange listing, political costs, etc. Two variables measured the agency costs of outside capital: debt (book value of debt/size) and preferred stock (book value of preferred equity/size). Two variables measured the package of monitoring devices available to management: outside directors and the firm's exchange listing. Finally, the historical reporting frequency of the firm measured inertia.

The relationship between these variables and the frequency of reporting (quarterly, semiannually, or annually) was examined empirically for 165 firms. Probit analysis was used to model the relationships both cross-sectionally during 1948 and for the 61 firms that changed reporting frequency during the period 1937 to 1948. The results indicated that firms on the New York Stock Exchange reported with a higher frequency and that there was an inertia effect. Results regarding the capital and asset structures were largely anomalies which did not support agency theory predictions regarding monitoring.[15]

Chow [1982] used an agency theory framework to study management's incentives to employ external auditors voluntarily. To reduce the monitoring costs arising from agency conflicts of interest, management may offer to have the firm's records

---

[14] These results are contained in Table 1 under management's wealth effect from stock ownership, since a higher cost of capital lowers the firm's value.

[15] The results on the assets in place variables and the first interpretation of firm size are included in Table 1 as affecting management's wealth through stock ownership. The results concerning alternative monitoring devices and inertia are omitted from Table 1.

independently audited. Firm-specific characteristics are posited as influencing the expected costs and benefits, and thus the probable use of, external auditing. Jensen and Meckling [1976] proposed an inverse relationship between management's ownership of the firm and the shareholder/management conflict of interest. This proposal implies a greater likelihood for external auditing with lower proportional management ownership. Chow proxied this effect using the average percentage common stock owned by officers and directors for the firm's industry. In addition, the firm's leverage was posited as influencing the use of auditing, since larger proportions of debt allow for greater potential wealth transfers from bondholders to shareholders. Greater numbers of accounting measures used in the firm's debt covenants led Chow to expect that an outside auditor would be employed. Finally, auditing was posited as more probable for larger firms (measured as market value of the firm), since there is a greater total potential wealth transfer.[16]

Chow studied the use of external auditing by a sample of 165 firms using the year 1926. A univariate analysis using the nonparametric Mann-Whitney U test indicated that audited firms had statistically significantly larger size, greater debt, more accounting measures used in debt covenants, and larger proportional management ownership. These results varied somewhat, depending upon the firm's stock exchange listing. Multivariate tests were conducted using logit analysis, and the resulting models were statistically significant. The findings were generally consistent with those of the univariate tests. Chow concluded that, consistent with agency theory predictions, there was strong evidence that higher debt levels resulted in voluntary audits, moderate to strong support that more accounting measures in debt contracts led to external auditing and moderate evidence that larger firms were audited.[17] The firm's exchange listing influenced the strength of these relationships. Chow was reluctant to interpret the statistically significant positive relationship between management ownership proportions and auditing, since this result contradicted his a priori expectation. Instead, the finding may provide support for a direct wealth effect arising from management's stock ownership. That is, the use of auditing to lower monitoring costs and the firm's cost of capital may be influenced by the amount of personal wealth that management has invested in the firm's stock.

*Stock Price Reaction*   Holthausen [1981] related stock market reactions to a change in depreciation procedures with agency theory variables to study the rationale for management's discretionary accounting changes. His sample was 125 firms which voluntarily switched during the period 1955 to 1978 from accelerated depreciation to straight-line depreciation for financial reporting purposes only. This accounting change increases net tangible assets, stockholder's equity, and net income. Holthausen expected share prices to be more positively affected when firms were more highly levered, were closer to their covenants, and experienced a significant impact from the change on the restrictiveness of their constraints. He posited that cross-sectional differences in the abnormal performance of stock prices at the time of the announcement of the depreciation switch-back would be explained by firm specific factors related to debt restrictions and management compensation contracts.

---

[16] Also, the marginal costs of auditing decrease for larger firms.
[17] As in the previous two studies, this interpretation of size is embodied in the managerial wealth effect from stock ownership.

Positive abnormal performance was hypothesized to be a function of (1) the financial statement effect as measured by the impact of the change in depreciation methods on earnings per share/the price of the firm's stock (2) leverage as measured by book value of public debt/market value of common stock and book value of private debt/market value of common stock (3) closeness to debt constraints as measured by inventory of funds available for dividends/market value of common stock, and (4) renegotiation costs as measured by comparing the coefficients of the private debt and public debt variables. Negative abnormal performance was expected for firms with management compensation contracts as measured by the existence of a bonus plan, because of the increased cash outflow associated with higher incentive payments. Firm size was included as a variable, measured by book value of debt plus market value of common stock, intended to capture misspecification in the return-generating model as well as political costs.

Holthausen's results revealed little significant abnormal performance in the month preceding or immediately surrounding the announcement of the depreciation switchback. Only the relationship between the firm's leverage and abnormal performance was statistically significant. Contrary to expectations, greater amounts of debt were related to negative abnormal performance, with the effect strongest in the period surrounding the announcement date. Holthausen suggested that this result might occur if management changed depreciation methods when it expected debt restrictions to become tighter, thus signaling its expectations to the stock market. To examine further whether leverage proxied the restrictiveness of the debt constraints, Holthausen modeled the time series of the firm's inventory of payable funds standardized by dividends, earnings, and size. The analysis did not reveal that this constraint became more binding seven years before or three years after the accounting change. Holthausen suggested that the methodological problems in assessing the stock market's expectations were the primary reason for the overall lack of results. He also suggested that these results would occur if full ex post settling up characterized the managerial labor market, rendering the choice of accounting techniques unimportant to bond covenants and management compensation contracts.

### Mandated Accounting Changes

The central question addressed in this group of studies is the impact on the firm of mandated changes in the accounting procedures used to prepare external financial reports. This research has focused on (1) management's lobbying and financing, production or investment changes in response to the wealth effect of an accounting standard, and (2) stock price reaction to a mandated accounting change due to the effect on agency theory contracts. Management's use of discretionary accounting procedures to mitigate the effect of the mandated change has not been studied.

*Lobbying and Financing, Production or Investment Changes*    Watts and Zimmerman [1978] suggested that the effect of a proposed accounting standard on management's wealth would explain support or opposition to the change. Lobbying positions on the FASB's discussion memorandum on general price-level adjusted financial statements were studied for those firms that submitted comments, with 33 opposing and 18 supporting the change. Each firm was classified by whether income would be increased or decreased by the price-level adjustments. Studying only the effect of political costs measured by firm size (total assets), Watts and Zimmerman found that large firms whose earnings would be reduced supported the proposal. A discriminant function was estimated to predict corporate positions on general price-level adjustments based on bonus payments (a dichotomous variable for the existence of a bonus plan) and political costs including (1) direct regulation (a dichotomous variable for utilities), (2) indirect regulation (sales revenue for firm size and ratio of sales to total industry sales for market share at the firm level) and (3) tax effects (depreciation and net monetary assets for the potential financial statement effect). Firm size emerged as the only statistically significant variable which explained corporate lobbying positions, with large firms opposing general price-level adjustments when income was increased.

In an attempt to study the relative costs of alternative reactions to mandated accounting changes, Zmijewski and Hagerman [1981] predicted that the Watts and Zimmerman firms that lobbied with the FASB were more likely to have extreme income strategies (all income-increasing or -decreasing). In this situation, firms are less able to counteract the effect of an accounting policy by using discretionary accounting changes. Zmijewski and Hagerman found that Watts and Zimmerman's sample had statistically significantly more firms with extreme income strategies than could be expected by chance.

Lobbying positions on the FASB's discussion memorandum regarding accounting for interest costs were studied by Dhaliwal [1982]. Prior to the FASB's involvement, firms had been allowed to choose between capitalization or expensing of interest costs on funds borrowed to construct assets not yet producing revenue. Changing from capitalization to expensing interest costs reduces the firm's earnings. Dhaliwal posited that agency theory variables and political cost considerations would explain corporate positions on the interest cost issue. Firms with higher leverage (book value of debt/total assets) were expected to support capitalization, thus minimizing the likelihood of default due to debt covenants. Larger firms (total assets) were posited as opposing capitalization, since lower earnings could yield tax, political, and regulatory benefits. Finally, the existence of management compensation plans tied to accounting data implied support for capitalization.

Dhaliwal's sample was 30 firms opposing capitalization and 14 firms opposing expensing of interest costs. Financial data were obtained for 1977, the year of the discussion memorandum period. Univariate tests were conducted using the nonparametric Mann-Whitney U test and Chi Square analysis. The results indicated statistically significant differences only for the debt variable, with more highly levered firms against expensing. A multiple discriminant analysis resulted in a statistically significant model, and the leverage factor accounted for most of the discriminatory power. As in the univariate analysis, firms with proportionately greater amounts of debt opposed expensing interest costs.

Both corporate lobbying and changes in financing or operating activities were studied by Kelly [1982] for the FASB standard on foreign currency translation.[18] Firms alleged that this accounting change made their profits more volatile. Agency theory constructs were used to explain management's opposition to the exposure

---

[18] Other studies have examined the effect of accounting policies on financing, production, and investment decisions (e.g., Dukes, Dyckman, and Elliott, 1980 and Horwitz and Kolodny, 1980). However, these effects were not related to contracting theory variables.

draft for the standard and subsequent financing or operating decisions to overcome the impact of the accounting change. Kelly's first hypothesis was that the two types of reactions would be related; that is, the firms that lobbied against the standard would also make financing or operating changes after its passage.

Five economic variables were used to characterize the firms that reacted. Incentive compensation was hypothesized as being related to a reaction due to the enhanced troughs in income. This variable was measured as both the existence of a bonus plan and the ratio of incentive compensation to total management remuneration. More highly levered firms were posited as reacting, due to the effect of lower income on debt covenants. Enhanced peaks in income could mean higher expected political costs and a reaction against the standard. This effect was surrogated by firm size, measured as total assets. Management's percentage ownership of the firm was included to test Jensen and Meckling's [1976] theory that high proportional ownership increases management's concern with changes in the firm's value due to debt and political costs against Fama's contention that the managerial labor market renders this monitoring device unimportant. Finally, the potential financial statement effect was assumed as the firm's foreign asset percentage of total consolidated assets, to gauge management's expectation of greater income variability.

Kelly's sample was 52 firms responding to a questionnaire regarding changes in financing or operating activities following passage of the standard. Fourteen of the firms lobbied against the standard; 26 firms made financing or operating changes. A Chi Square analysis indicated no statistically significant relationship between the two reactions. The financial data were collected for 1976, consistent with the time period of management's reaction. T-tests and probit analysis were used to examine the univariate and multivariate relationship between the economic variables and corporate reaction. Lobbying activities occurred for firms that had greater proportions of incentive compensation, greater leverage, larger asset size, and lower proportional management ownership. This last result was interpreted as evidence supporting the importance of a managerial labor market. Only large size was related to financing or operating changes. Firms that engaged in both reactions were characterized by greater leverage, larger asset size, and lower management ownership.

*Stock Market Reaction*   Negative abnormal stock market returns had been observed for full cost oil and gas firms following the FASB's issuance of an exposure draft mandating the use of the successful efforts method. Collins, Rozeff, and Dhaliwal [1981] examined the contracting cost theory as one possible explanation for this finding. The elimination of full cost accounting would reduce income and stockholder's equity and increase the volatility of earnings. For a sample of 47 full cost firms and 10 successful efforts firms, they hypothesized that negative cumulative abnormal returns would be positively related to (1) the financial statement effect from use of full cost (percent change in earnings per share, percent change in stockholder's equity, and ratio of exploration expenditures to total revenue for the proportion of the firm's operations in exploration and production activities), (2) the possession of contracts (a dichotomous variable for the existence of debt and/or management compensation agreements), (3) leverage (debt to equity ratio), and (4) renegotiation costs (a dichotomous variable for the existence of public or private debt). Firm size also was hypothesized as related to abnormal returns; however, Collins, Rozeff, and

Dhaliwal suggested that this relationship was a comprehensive variable proxying for leverage, public debt, political costs, and misspecification of the return-generating model. No a priori directional effect was specified. Firm size was measured by book value of debt plus market value of common stock.

A statistically significant relationship was found between cumulative abnormal returns and the financial statement effect measured by the impact on stockholder's equity, the possession of contracts, and, to a lesser degree, firm size. While the financial statement effect and contract variables were related to negative abnormal returns, larger firm size was related to positive abnormal returns. This relationship contradicted expectations formulated under the political cost theory, where accounting changes that decrease income were expected to yield positive benefits to larger firms.

Leftwich [1981] was concerned with the impact on stock prices of the accounting policy that restricted the use of pooling of interest accounting for business combinations. His hypotheses focused on the market value of the firm's equity following a mandated accounting change that tightens the restrictions in debt agreements. The abnormal performance of 338 firms using pooling of interests at least once between November 1968 and December 1972 was calculated for 21 events occurring during the policy-making deliberation period. Statistically significant cumulative prediction errors indicated nine events with negative abnormal returns and one with positive abnormal returns. For each event, Leftwich examined debt-related variables to explain the abnormal returns cross-sectionally. The average prediction error was hypothesized as a function of (1) leverage, where greater amounts of debt result in more negative abnormal returns (book value of public debt/market value of common stock and book value of private debt/market value common stock) (2) renegotiation, where greater amounts of public debt result in more negative abnormal returns (the relative difference in size and direction on the public debt and private debt variables) and where callable debt results in lower negative abnormal returns (book value callable debt/market value common stock), (3) convertible costs, where greater amounts of convertible debt result in lower negative abnormal returns (book value convertible debt/market value common stock),[19] and (4) firm size due to model misspecification and political costs (book value debt plus market value common stock).

Variables measuring leverage and renegotiation costs associated with callable debt were statistically significant in the hypothesized direction. A statistically significant relationship was found between large firms and lower negative abnormal returns. While this result is consistent with political cost arguments, Leftwich felt that size probably proxied for some omitted variable.[20]

### Generalizations from Previous Research

Comparison of these studies does not yield resounding conclusions, largely because the studies focus on different management choices and reactions and because

---

[19] This result occurs because of lower conversion costs from the reduced probability of conversion when debt covenants are tightened.

[20] Leftwich also examined distance from debt constraints and time to maturity (hypothesizing that a shorter time to maturity made financing, production or investment changes to loosen debt restrictions easier). Neither of these variables was significant in explaining abnormal performance.

different models, constructs, and variables are used in each study. Generalizations are offered from comparison of the similarities and differences of the studies based first on the economic variables and second on management's actions.

*Economic Variables*   The financial statement effect of an accounting change was included in three studies, and in general this factor was not supported. Two studies found that the direct effect of the accounting change on earnings was not significant, suggesting that management is not driven by bottom-line fixation (i.e., sole concern with the earnings figure and disbelief in market efficiency).

In examining the determinants of a stock market effect from expected cash flow changes, the bond covenant factor received the greatest attention and the most empirical support. Leverage was included in nine studies and was largely supported. The existence of covenants and the number of accounting measures used to enforce restrictions were each tested once and supported. Three measures of a firm's closeness to its debt constraints were statistically significant in a study of voluntary choice of accounting methods, while restrictiveness of the dividend covenant was unrelated to the stock market reaction to a discretionary accounting change. Renegotiation costs were not supported in the three studies that measured this factor by public versus private debt proportions but were supported by the one measuring this variable as callable debt. Conversion costs were not supported in the study that included this aspect of the firm's debt as a factor in stock market reaction to a mandated accounting change.

Political costs produced mixed results. Only the study concerning lobbying on general price-level accounting examined direct regulation, and no support for this industry-related factor was found. This result may have occurred because the adjustments were not proposed for the primary financial statements. Indirect regulation as measured by firm size has received moderate support for all types of management choices and reactions. In the studies of stock market reaction, results on this variable are confounded by model misspecification. One study included membership in a politically sensitive industry as a variable and found it to be statistically significant with the voluntary choice of interest capitalization. Several studies attempted to capture other aspects of political costs from indirect regulation (e.g., market share, capital intensity, and systematic risk and earnings variability), with inconsistent and inconclusive results. The potential tax effects of general price-level adjustments were not supported for lobbying positions.

The managerial wealth effect from stock ownership was examined directly in two studies as management's proportional ownership. Both studies yielded results that contradicted the authors' interpretation of Jensen and Meckling's thesis. All the studies on voluntary disclosure and auditing included firm size as a measure of the potential wealth transfer or cost of capital from changes in the level of monitoring. Monitoring affects shareholder wealth and thus management's wealth in the form of stock ownership. All three studies found firm size to be statistically significant.

Compensation contracts as a component of management wealth measured as the presence of a bonus plan, have received little empirical support. For discretionary accounting choices, this variable was significant twice but also insignificant twice. This factor was not supported in the stock market reaction to voluntary accounting changes. None of the studies on lobbying and financing, production, or investment changes found empirical support for this dichotomous variable. In a refinement of the bonus payment factor, one study found moderate statistical significance for the proportional effects, measured as the ratio of incentive compensation to total remuneration. A firm's ownership structure was used as an indirect measure of the importance of incentive contracts in the selection of accounting procedure by one researcher and was statistically significant.

*Management's Actions*   The five studies of management's discretionary choice of accounting procedures focused on incentive plans, debt covenants, and political costs. Bonus payments were a factor in two of the three studies that examined their direct influence and were supported when measured as ownership control. Bond covenants were supported in three studies but not tested in a fourth. Political costs as measured by size were included in four studies and yielded mixed results. Other conceptualizations of political costs from indirect regulation also gave inconsistent findings. Thus, debt contracts and, to a lesser extent, management compensation appear to be important variables in management's voluntary selection of accounting procedures.

Research on changes in the level of monitoring through discretionary disclosures or external audits focused on management's stock ownership, debt covenants, and political costs. Only the study on the use of independent auditors included the direct percentage of management's ownership. This factor was found significant to the use of auditing, although its directional influence contradicted the author's hypothesis. Two of the three studies supported size as an indirect test of the potential impact of changes in the value of the firm on management's personal wealth. Frequency of reporting was not related to the firm's leverage, while potential debt costs were important to the use of auditing. The one study that interpreted firm size as a measure of political costs found this variable to be insignificant. These inconsistent results render it impossible to make generalizations concerning the factors that influence voluntary disclosures and auditing.

Only the leverage factor was statistically significant in the study on stock market reaction to a discretionary accounting change. Its direction, however, was the opposite of the hypothesis. The financial statement effect and political costs (firm size) were significant variables. The results were confounded by the general lack of stock market reaction to the accounting change studied.

Three research studies concerned lobbying activities with the FASB in response to a proposed change in accounting procedures. Only one included the potential financial statement effect, and no support was found for this factor. The managerial wealth effect was important when measured as management's percentage stock ownership. Incentive compensation was insignificant for the existence of a bonus plan but significant for the magnitude effect. Two of the researchers included the effect of debt covenants as the firm's leverage, and both studies supported the role of this factor in lobbying positions. Political costs were measured by the firm's size, with two studies finding statistically significant results. Other aspects of political costs could not be supported in the study that used alternative measures of this factor. Thus debt contracts and, to a lesser extent, political costs and managerial wealth factors appear to be important in management's lobbying activities. The one study on changes in financing or operating activities found only firm size to be statistically significant.

The two studies of stock market reactions to mandated accounting changes showed limited support for the financial statement effect. The existence of a bonus plan was related to abnormal performance in one study. Costs from renegotiation, conversion of debt, and the existence of debt covenants received mixed support. Both studies included leverage, and only one found this factor statistically significant to abnormal performance. Political costs were measured solely by size, and they were intended to capture model misspecification. The variable was supported in both studies, but in one case its directional influence was opposite to that hypothesized. The mixed results indicate that no one factor dominated explanations of stock market reaction to an involuntary accounting change.

### Conclusion

The purpose here was to present a model of management's accounting choices and reactions by reviewing and synthesizing the available theory and research evidence on the relationship between external financial reporting and management's wealth. The cash flow effects of alternative accounting procedures and the impact on management's wealth are viewed as the incentives for management to choose from alternative accounting methods and disclosures and react to accounting standards. Both theoretical and methodological problems in the development of a positive theory will be addressed in this section.

While contracting and agency theories provide a model for management's concern with the firm's accounting procedures, there is little basis for assuming that all the factors enter into management's choices and reactions in the same manner. For example, the impact of bonus payments may be weighed more heavily by management in its decision to lobby against a proposed standard than in its decision to change financing, production, or investment activities once the standard has been enacted. Nor is there any means for determining, a priori, which of the factors will dominate. For example, under what conditions will the lower-debt related costs dominate the higher political costs of an income-increasing accounting change? Analogously, there is no model of the relative costs of the various reactions to mandated accounting changes. While it seems correct that, intuitively, the least costly means for counteracting the effect of a policy will be chosen, there has been no specification of the costs of the reactions or how these costs change with the specific situation. For example, it is not known when, if ever, changes in the firm's financing, production, or investment activities are more feasible, less costly, and more effective than discretionary accounting changes to mitigate an accounting standard.

Additional conceptual development is needed on each of the economic factors as well. There is considerably more theory on the bondholder/shareholder-management conflict of interest, which may explain why, empirically, this factor has been more fully explored and positively supported. However, there is no reason to expect this variable to be the most important one. The shareholder manager conflict has received less attention. Further theoretical development is needed before adequate empirical tests can be devised. This gap may explain why, for example, the bonus payment factor has been difficult to measure and largely unsupported empirically. The components of political costs have yet to be specified. The dimensions of direct and indirect regulation and expected tax effects have not been systematically considered, which probably accounts for most empirical studies having used ad hoc measures of the political cost variable.

The nature of the firm's stock prices as an intervening variable has not been considered either theoretically or empirically. It is conceivable that changes in the firm's stock prices have different effects on management's wealth in the form of stock and stock options, stock ownership, and the value of human capital. This last factor particularly is in an embryonic stage of development. Finally, while the effect on stock prices of the firm's contracts and expected political costs arising from an accounting change has been considered empirically, theoretical problems have plagued the development of an adequate methodology. Little theory exists on the impact of information and direct cash flow changes on the valuation of the firm. Additional empirical problems arise due to difficulties in determining the time when a revision in expectations occurs and in controlling for changes in economic conditions that confound the effect of accounting changes.

Methodologically, observation error pervades this area of research, due largely to the difficulties in isolating the effect of changing economic conditions on accounting methods. Thus it may be difficult to assert that financing, production, or investment changes are a reaction to an accounting standard as opposed to an economic event.

Major problems also arise from the large amount of measurement error in operationalizing the variables. The definition of the constructs must be kept distinct from their measurement. Some of these operational problems have been mentioned, for example, the difficulties in measuring management's total wealth to assess the relative importance of changes in bonus payments or the firm's stock prices, or in measuring the value of human capital.

Furthermore, the constructs and their measurement must be specific to the firm and the accounting changes. This requirement involves such considerations as the following: Does the firm have a bonus plan dependent upon accounting earnings? Is the firm currently at the minimum or maximum income constraint? Will the plan be renegotiated? What are the components of management's wealth and the nature of its compensation contracts, including stock incentive plans? How restrictive are the firm's debt covenants, and will the debt agreements be renegotiated? Specifically, what kinds of political costs confront the firm? Are generally accepted accounting principles used or ignored by direct regulators? Are all firms in a "politically sensitive" industry threatened by the same costs? How are heterogeneous expectations of political costs measured? In the final analysis, it may be that the effect of accounting changes is so firm-specific that generalizations from empirical research are not possible.

Methodological problems and the lack of theoretical development could lead to a pessimistic assessment for future prospects of this line of research. However, the current status is not unlike the initial development of efficient market research, in which an interplay between empirical studies and conceptual foundations leads to steady progress. Ideally, a well-developed model of management's role in the accounting choice and standard-setting process would be available for empirical verification. Lacking such a model, however, advancements can be made through theoretical and empirical refinements as research continues.

## REFERENCES

Alchian, A. and H. Demsetz, "Production, Information Costs, and Economic Organization," *American Economic Review* (December 1972), pp. 777–95.

Ball, R. and G. Foster, "Corporate Financial Reporting: A Methodological Review of Empirical Research," *Journal of Accounting Research, Supplement* (1982), forthcoming.

Bowen, R., J. Lacey and E. Noreen, "Determinants of Corporate Decision to Capitalize Interest," *Journal of Accounting and Economics* (August 1981), pp. 151–79.

Chow, C., "The Demand for External Auditing: Size, Debt, and Ownership Influences," *Accounting Review* (April 1982), pp. 272–91.

Coase, R., "The Nature of the Firm," *Economica* (November 1937), pp. 386–405.

Coase, R., "The Problem of Social Costs," *Journal of Law and Economics* (October 1960), pp. 1–44.

Collins, D., M. Rozeff, and D. Dhaliwal, "The Economic Determinants of Market Reaction to Proposed Mandatory Accounting Changes in the Oil and Gas Industry: A Cross-Sectional Analysis," *Journal of Accounting and Economics* (March 1981), pp. 37–71.

"Curse of Bigness," *Barron's*, June 30, 1969.

Deakin, E., "An Analysis of Differences Between Non-Major Oil Firms Using Successful Efforts and Full Cost Methods," *Accounting Review* (October 1979), pp. 722–34.

Dhaliwal, D., "The Effect of the Firm's Capital Structure on the Choice of Accounting Methods," *Accounting Review* (January 1980), pp. 78–84.

Dhaliwal, D., "Some Economic Determinants of Management Lobbying for Alternative Methods of Accounting: Evidence from the Accounting for Interest Costs Issue," *Journal of Business, Finance and Accounting* (1982), pp. 255–65.

Dhaliwal, D., G. Salamon, and E. Smith, "The Effect of Owner Versus Management Control on the Choice of Accounting Methods," *Journal of Accounting and Economics* (July 1982), pp. 41–53.

Dukes, R., T. Dyckman and J. Elliott, "Accounting for Research and Development Costs: The Impact on Research and Development Expenditures," *Journal of Accounting Research, Supplement* (1980), pp. 1–26.

Fama, E., *Foundations of Finance.* New York: Basic Books, 1976.

Fama, E., "Agency Problems and the Theory of the Firm," *Journal of Political Economy* (April 1980), pp. 288–307.

Hagerman, R. and M. Zmijewski, "Some Economic Determinants of Accounting Policy Choice," *Journal of Accounting and Economics* (August 1979), pp. 141–61.

Holthausen, R., "Evidence on the Effect of Bond Covenants and Management Compensation Contracts on the Choice of Accounting Techniques: The Case of the Depreciation Switch-Back," *Journal of Accounting and Economics* (March 1981), pp. 73–109.

Holthausen, R. and R. Leftwich, "The Economic Consequences of Accounting Choice: Implications of Costly Contracting and Monitoring," unpublished working paper, University of Chicago, 1982.

Horwitz, B. and R. Kolodny, "The Economic Effects of Involuntary Uniformity in the Financial Reporting of R & D Expenditures," *Journal of Accounting Research, Supplement* (1980), pp. 38–74.

Jarrell, G., "Proproducer Regulation and Accounting for Assets," *Journal of Accounting and Economics* (March 1979), pp. 93–116.

Jensen, M. and W. Meckling, "Theory of the Firm: Management Behavior, Agency Costs and Ownership Structure," *Journal of Financial Economics*, vol. 3 (1976), pp. 305–60.

Kalay, A., "Stockholder-Bondholder Conflict and Dividend Constraints," *Journal of Financial Economics* (July 1982), pp. 211–33.

Kelly, L., "Corporate Lobbying and Changes in Financial or Operating Activities in Reaction to FAS No. 8," *Journal of Accounting and Public Policy* (Winter 1982), pp. 153–73.

Leftwich, R., "Evidence of the Impact of Mandatory Changes in Accounting Principles on Corporate Loan Agreements," *Journal of Accounting and Economics* (March 1981), pp. 3–36.

Leftwich, R., "Accounting Information in Private Markets: Evidence from Private Lending Agreements," *Accounting Review* (January 1983), pp. 23–42.

Leftwich, R., R. Watts, and J. Zimmerman, "Voluntary Corporate Disclosure: The Case of Interim Reporting," *Journal of Accounting Research, Supplement* (1981), pp. 50–77.

Salamon, G. and D. Dhaliwal, "Company Size and Financial Disclosure Requirements with Evidence from the Segmental Reporting Issue," *Journal of Business, Finance and Accounting* (1980), pp. 555–68.

Siegried, J., "Determinants of Antitrust Activity," *Journal of Law and Economics* (October 1975), pp. 559–81.

Smith, Jr., C. and J. Warner, "On Financial Contracting: An Analysis of Bond Covenants," *Journal of Financial Economics*, vol. 7 (1979), pp. 117–61.

Smith, Jr., C. and R. Watts, "Incentive Tax Effects of U.S. Executive Compensation Plans," unpublished working paper, University of Rochester, 1981.

Watts, R. and J. Zimmerman, "Towards a Positive Theory of the Determinants of Accounting Standards," *Accounting Review* (January 1978), pp. 112–34.

Zimmerman, J., "Positive Research in Accounting," *Perspective on Research*, edited by R. Nair and T. Williams (May 1980), pp. 107–128.

Zimmerman, J., "Political Costs, Taxes and Firm Size," unpublished working paper, University of Rochester, 1982.

Zmijewski, M. and R. Hagerman, "An Income Strategy Approach to the Positive Theory of Accounting Standard Setting/Choice," *Journal of Accounting and Economics* (August 1981), pp. 129–49.

# I-B 3 *Towards a Positive Theory of the Determination of Accounting Standards*

ROSS L. WATTS AND JEROLD L. ZIMMERMAN

Accounting standards in the United States have resulted from a complex inter-action among numerous parties including agencies of the Federal government (notably the Securities and Exchange Commission and Treasury Department), state regulatory commissions, public accountants, quasi-public accounting standard-setting boards (the Committee on Accounting Procedures (CAP), the Accounting Principles Board (APB), and the Financial Accounting Standards Board (FASB)), and corporate managements. These parties have, in the past, and continue to expend resources to influence the setting of accounting standards. Moonitz [1974], Horngren [1973] and [1976], Armstrong [1976] and Zeff [1972] document the sometimes intense pressure exerted on the "private" accounting standard-setting bodies (i.e., CAP, APB, FASB). These pressures have led to several reorganizations of the standard-setting boards.

Ultimately, we seek to develop a positive theory of the determination of accounting standards.[1] Such a theory will help us to understand better the source of the pressures driving the accounting standard-setting process, the effects of various accounting standards on different groups of individuals and the allocation of

We wish to thank members of the Finance Workshop at the University of Rochester, members of the Accounting Seminar at the University of Michigan and, in particular, George Benston, Ken Gaver, Nicholas Gonedes, Michael Jensen, Keith Leffler, Martin Geisel, Cliff Smith and an anonymous referee for their helpful suggestions.

Ross L. Watts and Jerold L. Zimmerman, "Towards a Positive Theory of the Determination of Accounting Standards," *The Accounting Review*, January 1978, pp. 112–134. Reprinted with the permission of *The Accounting Review*.

[1] See Jensen [1976] and Horngren [1976].

resources, and why various groups are willing to expend resources trying to affect the standard-setting process. This understanding is necessary to determine if prescriptions from normative theories (e.g., current cash equivalents) are feasible.

Watts [1974] and [1977] has started to develop such a theory. This paper expands on this initial work by focusing on the costs and benefits generated by accounting standards which accrue to managements, thereby contributing to our understanding of the incentives of management to oppose or support various standards. Management, we believe, plays a central role in the determination of standards. Moonitz supports this view:

> Management is central to any discussion of financial reporting, whether at the statutory or regulatory level, or at the level of official pronouncements of accounting bodies. [Moonitz, 1974, p. 64]

Hence, it seems appropriate that a precondition of a positive theory of standard-setting is understanding management's incentives.

The next section introduces those factors (e.g., tax, regulatory, political considerations) which economic theory leads us to believe are the underlying determinants affecting managements' welfare and, thereby, their decision to consume resources trying to affect the standard-setting process. Next, a model is presented incorporating these factors. The predictions of this model are then tested using the positions taken by corporations regarding the FASB's Discussion Memorandum on General Price Level Adjustments (GPLA). The last section contains the conclusions of the study.

## FACTORS INFLUENCING MANAGEMENT ATTITUDES TOWARDS FINANCIAL ACCOUNTING STANDARDS

In this paper, we assume that individuals act to maximize their own utility. In doing so, they are resourceful and innovative.[2] The obvious implication of this assumption is that management lobbies on accounting standards based on its own self-interest. For simplicity, (since this is an early attempt to provide a positive theory) it could be argued that we should assume that management's self-interest on accounting standards is congruent with that of the shareholders. After all, that assumption has provided hypotheses consistent with the evidence in finance (e.g., the risk/return relationship of the various capital asset pricing models). However, one function of financial reporting is to constrain management to act in the shareholders' interest. (For example, see Benston [1975], Watts [1974], and Jensen and Meckling [1976a].) Consequently, assuming congruence of management and shareholder interests without further investigation may cause us to omit from our lobbying model important predictive variables. To reduce this possibility, we will examine next the

---

[2] Many economic models assume a rather limited version of economic man. In particular, they assume that man maximizes his own welfare when he is constrained to play by certain rules and in certain institutional settings, ignoring his incentives to avoid or change the rules, setting, etc. Meckling [1976] analyzes this issue.

effects of accounting standards on management's self-interest without the con-gruence assumption. The purpose of the examination is to identify factors which are likely to be important predictors of lobbying behavior so that we can include them in our formal model.

The assumption that management selects accounting procedures to maximize its own utility is used by Gordon [1964, p. 261] in an early attempt to derive a positive theory of accounting. There have been several attempts to test empirically Gordon's model, or variants of it, which we call the "smoothing" literature.[3] Problems in the specification of the empirical tests in the smoothing literature leave the Gordon model essentially unconfirmed.[4] Also, certain aspects of the Gordon model contribute to the model's lack of confirmation. Essentially, Gordon [1964] assumed that shareholder satisfaction (and, presumably, wealth) is solely a positive function of accounting income. This assumption avoids the conflict between shareholders and management by implying that increases in stock prices always accompany increases in accounting income. However, recent research casts serious doubt on the ability of management to manipulate directly share prices via changes in accounting procedures.[5]

We assume that management's utility is a positive function of the expected compensation in future periods (or wealth) and a negative function of the dispersion of future compensation (or wealth). The question is how do accounting standards affect management's wealth?[6] Management's total compensation from the firm consists of wages, incentive compensation (cash bonuses and stock or stock options), and nonpecuniary income, including perquisites (discussed in Jensen-Meckling, 1976a). Since it is unclear what role accounting standards play in the level of nonpecuniary income, we exclude it and focus on the first two forms of compensation. To the extent that management can increase either the level of incentive com-pensation or the firm's share price via its choice of accounting standards, they are made better off.

This analysis distinguishes between mechanisms which increase management's wealth: 1) via increases in share price (i.e., stock and stock options are more valuable) and 2) via increases in incentive cash bonuses. The choice of accounting standards can affect both of these forms of compensation indirectly through i) taxes, ii) reg-ulatory procedures if the firm is regulated, iii) political costs, iv) information production costs, and directly via v) management compensation plans. The first four factors increase managerial wealth by increasing the cashflows and, hence, share price. The last factor can increase managerial wealth by altering the terms of the incentive compensation. Each of these five factors are discussed in turn.

---

[3] Ball and Watts [1972]; Barefield and Comiskey [1972]; Barnea, Ronen and Sadan [1975]; Beidleman [1973]; Copeland [1968]; Cushing [1969]; Dasher and Malcom [1970]; Gordon [1964]; Gordon, Horwitz and Meyers [1966].

[4] For these defects see Ball and Watts [1972], Gonedes [1972] and Gonedes and Dopuch [1974].

[5] Fama [1970] and Gonedes and Dopuch [1974]. Further, the results of studies by Kaplan and Roll [1972], Ball [1972] and Sunder [1975] which address the specific issue support the hypothesis that the stock market can discriminate between real events and changes in accounting procedures. Given that the market can on average discriminate, then it must be concluded that managers (on average) expect the market to discriminate. Obviously, managers do and will attempt to influence their share price by direct accounting manipulation, but if these attempts consume resources, then incentives exist to eliminate these inefficient allocations.

[6] For earlier discussions of this question see Watts [1974] and Gonedes [1976].

### Factors Affecting Management Wealth[7]

*Taxes.* Tax laws are not directly tied to financial accounting standards except in a few cases (e.g., the last-in-first-out inventory valuation method). However, the indirect relationship is well documented Zeff [1972] and Moonitz [1974]. The adoption of a given procedure for financial accounting does not decrease the likelihood of that procedure's being adopted in future Internal Revenue codes, and more likely, will increase the chance of adoption. To the extent that management expects a proposed financial accounting procedure to influence future tax laws, their lobbying behavior is affected by the future tax law effects.

*Regulation.*[8] Most public utility commissions base their rate-setting formulas on accounting determined costs. A new accounting standard which reduces a utility's reported income may provide its management with an "excuse" to argue for increased rates. Whether the utility commission grants the increase depends on whether groups opposed to the rate increase (e.g., consumer groups) are able to exert political pressure on the commission.[9] This depends on such factors as information costs (to be discussed later). However, to the extent that there is some probability of a rate (and hence cashflow) increase (either temporary or permanent) as the result of an accounting standards change, utilities have an incentive to favor that change. Similarly, they have an incentive to oppose changes in accounting standards which might lead to a rate decrease.

*Political Costs.* The political sector has the power to effect wealth transfers between various groups. The corporate sector is especially vulnerable to these wealth redistributions. Certain groups of voters have an incentive to lobby for the nationalization, expropriation, break-up or regulation of an industry or corporation.[10] This in turn provides an incentive for elected officials to propose such actions. To counter these potential government intrusions, corporations employ a number of devices, such as social responsibility campaigns in the media, government lobbying and selection of accounting procedures to minimize reported earnings.[11] By avoiding the attention that "high" profits draw because of the public's association of high reported profits and monopoly rents, management can reduce the likelihood of adverse political actions and, thereby, reduce its expected costs (including the legal

---

[7] We have purposefully excluded from the set of factors being examined the information content effect of an accounting standard on stock prices. We have done this because at present the economic theories of information and capital market equilibrium are not sufficiently developed to allow predictions to be made regarding the influence an accounting standard on the capital market's assessment of the distributions of returns (see Gonedes and Dopuch, 1974). We believe that a theory of the determination of accounting standards can be developed and tested ignoring the information content factor. If at some future date, the information content factor can be specified and included in the theory, then the predictions and our understanding of the process will be improved. But we see no reason to delay the development of a theory until information content is specified.

[8] We deal in this paper with public utility regulation and the forms of rate regulation employed. Other industries (e.g., banking and insurance) are regulated differently and these industries are ignored in this paper to simplify the analysis.

[9] For the economic theory of regulation upon which this discussion is based see Stigler [1971], Posner [1974] and Peltzman [1975]. Also, Horngren [1976].

[10] Stigler [1971], Peltzman [1975], and Jensen and Meckling [1976b]. An example of an industry facing such action is the oil industry.

[11] For an alleged example of this, see Jack Anderson, Syndicated Column, United Features (New York, April 10, 1976).

costs the firm would incur opposing the political actions). Included in political costs are the costs labor unions impose through increased demands generated by large reported profits.

The magnitude of the political costs is highly dependent on firm size.[12] Even as a percentage of total assets or sales, we would not expect a firm with sales of $100 million to generate the same political costs (as a percentage of sales) as a firm with $10 billion of sales. Casual empiricism suggests that Superior Oil Company (1974 sales of $333 million) incurs considerably less costs from anti-trust, "corporate responsibility," affirmative action, etc., than Exxon with sales of $42 billion.

*Information Production (i.e., bookkeeping) Costs.* Changes in accounting procedures are not costless to firms. Accounting standard changes which either increase disclosure or require corporations to change accounting methods increase the firms' bookkeeping costs (including any necessary increases in accountants' salaries to compensate for additional training).[13]

*Management Compensation Plans.* A major component of management compensation is incentive (bonus) plan income (Conference Board [1974]), and these plans are based on accounting income. Our survey of 52 firms in our sample indicates that the majority of the companies formally incorporate accounting income into the compensation plan.[14] Hence, a change in accounting standards which increase the firm's reported earnings would, *ceteris paribus*, lead to greater incentive income. But this would reduce the firm's cashflows and share prices would fall. As long as the per manager present value of the after tax incentive income is greater than the decline in each manager's portfolio, we would expect management to favor such an accounting change.[15] But this assumes that the shareholders and nonmanager directors do not oppose such an accounting change or do not adjust the compensation plans for the change in earnings.[16] In fact, the increased cashflows resulting from the political costs, regulatory process and tax effects of an accounting change assumes that

---

[12] Several studies document the association between size and anti-trust [Siegfried 1975]. In proposed anti-trust legislation, size *per se* has been mentioned specifically as a criterion for action against corporations. See the "Curse of Bigness," *Barron's*, June 30, 1969, pp. 1 and 8. Also see a bill introduced into the Senate by Senator Bayh (U.S. Congress, Senate, Subcommittee on Anti-trust and Monopoly (1975), pp. 5–13) would require divesture for oil firms with annual production and/or sales above certain absolute numbers. In the hearings on that bill, Professor Mencke of Tufts University argued that absolute and not relative accounting profits are the relevant variable for explaining political action against corporations.

Menke said, "Nevertheless, precisely because the actions of large firms are so visible, the American public has always equated absolute size with monopoly power. The major oil companies are among the very largest and most visible companies doing business in the United States.

Huge accounting profits, but not high profit rates, are an inevitable corollary of large absolute firm size. This makes these companies obvious targets for public criticism." (U.S. Congress, Senate, Subcommittee on Anti-trust and Monopoly (1976), p. 1893).

[13] We are assuming that any change in accounting standards does not reduce the firm's information production costs. Although there may be cases where a firm is using a costly procedure which is eliminated by a simpler, cheaper procedure, information production costs in this case may decline, but we expect these situations to be rare.

[14] The frequency is 69 percent.

[15] At this early stage in the development of the theory, we assume that management of the firm is composed of homogeneous (i.e., identical) individuals to simplify the problem.

[16] Our examination of the description of 16 management compensation plans indicated that all the plans were administered by the nonmanaging directors.

various politicians/bureaucrats (i.e., the electorate) do not fully adjust for the change. A crucial assumption of our analysis is that the shareholders and nonmanaging directors have more incentive to adjust for and control increases in reported earnings due to changes in accounting standards than do politicians and bureaucrats.

### Incentives for Various Groups to Adjust for a Change in Accounting Standards

An individual (whether a shareholder, nonmanaging director, or politician) will adjust a firm's accounting numbers for a change in accounting standards up to the point that the marginal cost of making the adjustment equals the marginal benefits. Consider the incentives of the outside directors to adjust bonus compensation plans due to a change in accounting standards. If these directors do not adjust the plans, management compensation rises and share price falls by the full discounted present value of the additional compensation.[17] Each outside director's wealth declines to the extent of his ownership in the firm and there is a greater chance of his removal from the board.[18]

If nonmanaging directors did not control management (including adjusting the compensation plans for changes in accounting standards), the decline in firm value offers incentives for an outsider or group to tender for control of the firm and install outside directors who will eliminate those managerial activities which are not in the best interest of the shareholders.[19] This group would then gain a proportionate share of the full capitalized value of the eliminated abuses (e.g., the present value of the incremental compensation resulting from the change in accounting standards). Therefore, the benefits for shareholders and nonmanaging directors to adjust compensation plans for changes in accounting standards are immediate and direct, if there is an efficient capital market for equity claims.

However, for the politicians and bureaucrats, our analysis suggests that the lack of a capital market which capitalizes the effects on the voters' future cashflows reduces the benefits accruing to the politicians of monitoring accounting standards, and the result is that they will perform less adjustments for changes in accounting standards.[20] For example, what are the benefits accruing to a utility regulator for adjusting a utility's accounting numbers for a change in standards? In the previous case of an outside director, the share price will fall by the discounted presented value

---

[17] Likewise, we would expect the outside directors to adjust the incentive compensation targets in those circumstances when it is in the shareholders' interest to report lower earnings (e.g., LIFO), thereby not reducing the managers' incentive via bonus earnings to adopt LIFO.

[18] Our analysis indicates that outside (nonmanaging) directors are "efficient" monitors of management, Watts [1977]. If this were not the case, the capital market would quickly discount the presence of outside directors. As far as we can determine, firms are not required by the New York Stock Exchange listing requirements or Federal regulations to have outside directors. Paragraph 2495G of Commerce Clearing House, Volume 2, New York Stock Exchange encourages listed firms to appoint outside directors. "Full disclosure of corporate affairs for the information of the investing public is, of course, normal and usual procedure for listed companies. Many companies have found this procedure has been greatly aided by having at least two outside directors whose functions on the board would include particular attention to such matters." This listing statement is consistent with our observation that outside directors provide monitoring benefits.

[19] This assumes, of course, that such takeovers earn a fair rate of return net of transactions costs.

[20] See Zimmerman [1977] and Watts [1977] for further discussion of this issue.

of the increased compensation resulting for an incomplete (or inaccurate) adjustment of the compensation plan. But if the regulator does not completely adjust for a change in accounting standards and allows the utility's rates to increase (resulting in a wealth transfer from consumers to the utility's owners), then the only cost the regulator is likely to incur is removal from office due to his incomplete adjustment. He incurs no direct wealth change. For small rate increases, the *per capita* coalition costs each consumer (or some group of consumers) would bear lobbying for the regulator's removal would vastly outweigh the small *per capita* benefits they would receive via lower regulated rates. Hence, rational consumers would not incur large monitoring costs of their regulators and other politicians (Downs [1957]; Alchian [1969]; and Alchian and Demsetz [1972]). Knowing this, it is not in the regulators' and politicians' interests to adjust changes in accounting standards as fully as if they were confronted with the same change in accounting standards in the role of outside directors or shareholders in the firm. The benefits of adjusting for changes in accounting standards are lower in the political sector than in the private sector.[21] Hence, there is a greater likelihood that a given accounting standard change will result in increased tax, regulatory, and political benefits than will the same change result in increased management compensation. For a given accounting standard change, managers should expect their own shareholders and outside directors to make a more complete adjustment than politicians.

Given this analysis, we predict that managers have greater incentives to choose accounting standards which report lower earnings (thereby increasing cashflows, firm value, and their welfare) due to tax, political, and regulatory considerations than to choose accounting standards which report higher earnings and, thereby, increase their incentive compensation. However, this prediction is conditional upon the firm being regulated or subject to political pressure. In small, (i.e., low political costs) unregulated firms, we would expect that managers do have incentives to select accounting standards which report higher earnings, if the expected gain in incentive compensation is greater than the foregone expected tax consequences. Finally, we expect management also to consider the accounting standard's impact on the firm's bookkeeping costs (and hence their own welfare).

The next section combines these five factors into a model of corporate lobbying standards.

## A POSITIVE THEORY OF MANAGEMENT LOBBYING ON ACCOUNTING STANDARDS

Given a proposed accounting standard, management's position depends on the size of the firm (which affects the magnitude of the political costs) and whether the proposed standard increases or decreases the firm's reported earnings.[22] Figure 1 separates the

---

[21] It could also be argued that politicians and regulators have a higher marginal cost of adjusting than do shareholders, nonmanaging directors, and other capital market participants since the former group does not necessarily have a comparative advantage of adjusting financial statements, whereas, existing capital market participants probably have a comparative advantage at such activities.

[22] The expected effect of an accounting standard could vary over time (i.e., it could increase current reported income and decrease some future reported income). In that case, the analysis is slightly more complex, but the criterion is still the same (i.e., the effect on the manager's wealth). However, for simplicity, the remainder of the paper refers to standards increasing or decreasing reported income as though the whole time series of future income shifts up or down.

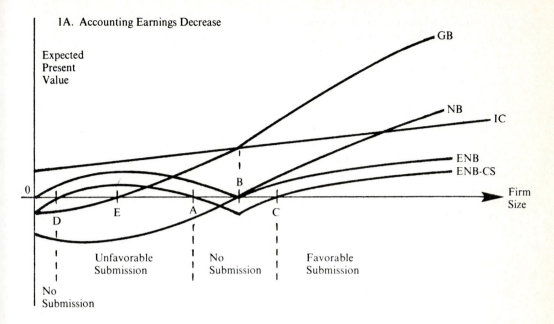

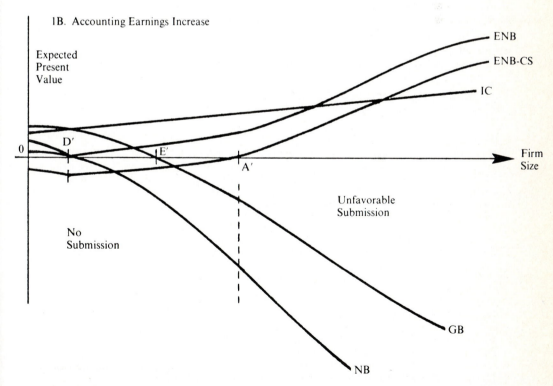

**FIGURE 1**
**A Model of Firms' Submissions to the FASB**

standard's impact on earnings into decreases (1A) and increases (1B). The curve GB in Figure 1A (earnings decrease) denotes the proposed accounting standard's present value to management including the tax, regulatory, political, and compensation effects as a function of firm size. For small firms (below size E), not subject to much political pressure, these managers have an incentive to oppose the standard since their bonus compensation plans will have to be adjusted (a costly process), if their incomes are to remain unchanged by the new standard. Above size E, the political, regulatory, and tax benefits of reporting lower earnings due to the new standard are assumed to dominate the incentive compensation factor.

The benefits (costs) of a proposed accounting standard are expected to vary with the firm's size. This relationship can exist for two reasons: (1) the magnitude of the reported income change may be larger for larger firms and (2) for an income change of a given magnitude, the benefits (costs) vary with firm size.[23] Hence, the present value of the stream of benefits (or costs) to the firm, GB, are an increasing function of firm size.[24]

Information production costs, curve IC, are also expected to vary to some extent with firm size due to the increased complexity and volume of the larger firm's accounting system. The difference between the gross benefits, GB, and the additional information costs, IC, yields the net benefits curve, NB.

If the firm size is in the region OB, the net benefits curve, NB, is negative, and the firm will consider making an unfavorable submission to the FASB. Before the firm makes a submission, management holds beliefs regarding the likelihood the FASB will adopt the standard and the likelihood the FASB will adopt the standard if the firm makes an opposing submission.[25] The difference between these beliefs is the change in the adoption likelihood if management makes a negative submission. The product of this difference and the negative net benefits, NB, (i.e., the present value[26] of the cashflows arising from the five factors) is the expected present value of the net benefits curve, ENB. For example, a firm will incur negative net present value benefits

---

[23] Whether the magnitude of the income change does vary with firm size depends on the particular accounting standard in question. For certain accounting standards (e.g., requiring all firms to report depreciation based on current replacement costs) it is apparent *a priori* that there will be a correlation between the income change and firm size. For other standards (e.g., general price level accounting) *a priori*, it is not obvious that a relationship will exist (e.g., net monetary gains may offset depreciation in larger firms). However, since political costs depend on firm size then we expect the benefits (costs) of standard changes to vary with firm size. For example, if all firms' earnings decline by $1 million (due to a standards change) then we would expect larger firms to incur larger benefits since the likelihood of anti-trust actions are expected to be associated with firm size.

[24] We would expect firms in different industries to be subject to different political pressures, tax structures, and regulation. Hence, Figure 1 is developed for firms in the same industry that only differ by size.

[25] In this situation, it is possible that management will lobby on an accounting standard because of secondary (or gaming) effects (i.e., vote trading thereby influencing subsequent FASB pronouncements). We chose not to introduce gaming because it complicates the model and such complication is only justified if it improves or is likely to improve the empirical results. We are able to predict corporate behavior without considering gaming, and we do not consider it likely to improve these results.

[26] The firm is discounting the future cashflows with the appropriate, risk-adjusted discount rate. Furthermore, we are assuming that this discount rate is not increasing in firm size which is consistent with the available evidence.

of \$100,000 if the standard is adopted. They believe the likelihood of adoption is .60. By making a negative submission to the FASB the likelihood falls to .59. The expected net present value of the benefits of the submission is then +\$1000.

Firms larger than size B face positive net benefits if the standard is adopted. They will consider supporting the standard to the FASB, thereby increasing the standard's likelihood of adoption.[27] Hence, the expected net benefits curve is also positive beyond point B since it is the product of a positive net benefit and a positive change in the FASB's likelihood of adoption given a favorable submission.

If the cost of the submission is \$CS, consisting primarily of the opportunity cost of the manager's time, then the total expected net benefits of a submission given the submission cost is a vertical downward shift in the ENB curve by the amount CS, ENB—CS. A firm will make a submission if ENB—CS is positive. This occurs in the regions DA, where opposing submissions occur, and beyond C, where favorable submissions are made. Between O and D and between A and C no submissions are made.

In Figure 1B, the proposed standard increases reported income. This case is similar to the previous one except the gross benefits are only positive for small firms where the management compensation plans are expected to dominate the tax, political, and regulatory factors. Beyond size $E'$ gross benefits are negative since, for those firms, the income increases are expected to increase governmental interference (political costs), raise future tax payments, and lead the public utility commission to reduce the firm's revenues (if the firm is regulated). The net benefits curve is again the algebraic sum of GB (gross benefits) and IC (information costs) and the submission's expected net benefits less submission costs, ENB—CS, cuts the axis at $A'$. Accordingly, firms with asset sizes in the interval $OA'$ make no submissions and firms of sizes beyond $A'$ make unfavorable submissions.

When we consider the implications of both figures, we see that larger firms (firms larger than size C in Figure 1) will make favorable submissions if their incomes are decreased by the accounting standard, and unfavorable submissions if their incomes are increased. Smaller firms (firms smaller than size C in Figure 1) will either not submit or make unfavorable submissions.

While Figures 1A and 1B reflect the general tendency of costs and benefits of an accounting standard to vary with firm size, there will be exceptions to this relationship. We have omitted variables, some of which we recognize. In particular, regulation costs borne by utilities depend not only on net income but also on operating earnings.[28] The effect of an accounting standard on operating earnings may vary with firm size.

The increment to a regulated firm's value of an accounting change which reduces operating earnings is increasing in firm size. Most public utility commissions set

---

[27] We are assuming that the likelihood of the FASB adopting the standard, if the firm makes a submission, is independent of firm size. This is unrealistic since large firms, we expect, would have more influence with the Board. However, inclusion of this additional dependency does not change the results; in fact, it strengthens the predictions.

[28] Operating earnings, although explicitly defined by each public utility commission, are generally, utility revenues less operating expenses, including depreciation but excluding interest and taxes. We assume that the adoption of GPLA would mean that price-adjusted depreciation would affect operating earnings while the gain or loss on monetary assets would be treated like interest and would only affect net income.

revenues according to the following type of equation:

$$\text{Revenues} = \text{Operating Expenses} + \text{Depreciation} + \text{Taxes} + r \cdot \text{Base} \qquad (1)$$

where $r$ is the accepted rate of return allowance on the investment base (usually the historic cost of net plant and working capital) [Haskins and Sells 1974.] Interest is not directly included in the rate-setting formula. The approach is to work on a return to total assets. Since all the terms on the right-hand side of equation (1) are highly correlated with firm size, any accounting standard that increases reported operating expenses, depreciation, or the recorded value of the asset base proportionally will, in general, result in an increase in the utility's revenues. And these increments to the utility's cashflows will, in general, be increasing in firm size.

When an accounting standard increases net income and decreases operating earnings of utilities, as does price-level adjustments [See Davidson and Weil, 1975b], we would not necessarily expect the relationship between management's attitude to the standard and firm size to be as we specified above (i.e., larger firms favoring or opposing the standard depending upon the effect on net income and smaller firms opposing the standard). As a consequence, we concentrate on testing that relationship for unregulated firms.

Another omitted variable is the political sensitivity of the firm's industry which clearly affects the political cost of an accounting standard change. We do not have a political theory which predicts which industries Congress singles out for wealth transfers (For example, why was the oil industry subject to intensive Congressional pressure in early 1974 and not the steel industry?)[29] Consequently, we do not consider it formally in our model. As we shall see, political sensitivity has an impact on our results (only one steel company submitted on price-level accounting compared to seven oil companies submitting), but it does not eliminate the general relationship between firm size and management's accounting lobbying behavior.

## EMPIRICAL TESTS

### Data

On February 15, 1974, the FASB issued the discussion memorandum "Reporting the Effects of General Price-Level Changes in Financial Statements" and scheduled a public hearing on the topic for April 25, 1974. Public comments and position papers were solicited. One hundred thirty-three accounting firms, public corporations, industry organizations, and government agencies filed written comments.

We assume the submission indicates the position of corporate management. Clearly, this assumption could introduce some error into our tests. For example, some controllers of corporations may submit not because of corporate effects, but because they receive nonpecuniary income from the submission (e.g., if they are officers in their local chapter of the National Association of Accountants). However, we expect

---

[29] This does not mean we do not have any ideas as to which variables are important. For example, in the case of consumer goods industries, we suspect that the relative price change of the product is important.

the error to be random. Ignoring this error biases our tests of management's attitudes on accounting standards towards rejecting the theory.

Almost all the corporations making submissions (49 out of 53) were New York Stock Exchange firms. Of the remaining four firms, one was listed on the American Stock Exchange, one was traded over the counter, and the other two were not traded. Of the 53 firms, 18 submitted opinions expressing favorable views on general price level adjustments whereas 34 expressed opinions ranging from strong objection to discussions of the merits of current costing to skepticism and feelings that GPLA was premature. These 34 were classified as opposing GPLA. For one firm, Transunion, an opinion could not be ascertained, and this firm was subsequently dropped from the sample. The firms making submissions and their position on the issue are listed in Table 1.

Once the sample of firms was identified from their submissions to the FASB, 1972 and 1973 financial data was obtained from the COMPUSTAT tape and the 1974 Moody Manuals. In addition, data on the existence of management incentive compensation plans was obtained by a questionnaire mailed to the chief financial officer of each firm. Missing data on the nonresponses (30 percent of the firms) was obtained from the firms' proxy statements and annual reports. If no mention of an incentive plan was found, we assumed the firm did not have one. Firms classified as having management incentive compensation plans based on accounting earnings[30] are denoted by an (M) in Table 1.

The precise impact of reported earnings on executive incentive compensation is difficult to estimate simply because the firm has such a plan. The most common procedure companies use is to take some fraction of reported earnings after deducting a return on invested capital as a pool out of which incentive compensation is paid. However, most companies do not pay out all of this pool each year. The important point, though, is that managers in firms with management compensation plans which report higher adjusted earnings will not suffer a decline in their incentive compensation and it may actually increase their compensation (depending on the monitoring by the outside directors).

### Methodology

The FASB's General Price Level Adjustment (GPLA) standard would require supplementary price adjusted statements. Even though the supplementary statements will not replace conventional reports, users of the information will obviously make comparisons [See Ijiri, 1976] and if adjusted income is above (below) unadjusted income, we expect our previous reasoning to hold, and we assume the effect is the same as an increase (decrease) in reported income.

A price-level adjusted income figure does not exist for all firms in our sample. Since only a few firms voluntarily published GPLA statements, income proxies must be constructed. Fortunately, a previous series of studies by Davidson and Weil (1975a and 1975b) and Davidson, Stickney, and Weil (1976) developed an adjusting procedure which relies solely on published financial statements and GNP deflators. Using either their published figures for 1973 financial statements or using their procedures, we

---

[30] If the firm had an incentive plan, but it was not tied to reported earnings then this firm was coded as not having an incentive plan (Gillette).

TABLE 1

Firms Making Submissions to the FASB on General Price Level
Adjustments*

| Firms Advocating GPLA | Firms Opposing GPLA |
|---|---|
| *Regulated Firms* | |
| AT&T | Aetna Life & Casualty (M) |
| Commonwealth Edison | Commerce Bank of Kansas City |
| Consumer Power (M) | Liberty Corporation (M) |
| Detroit Edison | Northeast Utilities |
| Duke Power | People Gas |
| Indiana Telephone | Southern Natural Resources (M) |
| Iowa Illinois Gas & Electric | Pennzoil |
| Northwestern Telephone | Texas Eastern Transmission (M) |
| Southern Company | Texas Gas Transmission |
| *Unregulated Firms* | |
| Exxon (M) | Continental Oil (M) |
| Gulf Oil (M) | Standard Oil of Indiana (M) |
| Shell Oil (M) | Texaco (M) |
| Standard Oil of California (M) | Rockwell International (M) |
| Caterpillar Tractor | United Aircraft (M) |
| Dupont E. I. DeNemours (M) | Automated Building Components |
| General Motors (M) | Copeland Corporation (M) |
| Ford Motor Company (M) | General Electric (M) |
| Marcor (M) | General Mills (M) |
| | Gillette |
| | W. R. Grace (M) |
| | Harsco (M) |
| | Inland Steel (M) |
| | International Harvester (M) |
| | American Cyanamid (M) |
| | IT&T (M) |
| | Eli Lilly & Co. (M) |
| | Masonite (M) |
| | Merck (M) |
| | Owens-Illinois, Inc. (M) |
| | Reliance Electric (M) |
| | Seagrams Sons, Inc. (M) |
| | Sears Roebuck (M) |
| | Texas Instruments (M) |
| | Union Carbide (M) |

* Transunion Corporation made a submission, but they did not state a position on
  GPLA. It made two technical comments.
  M denotes the firm has a management compensation plan.

were able to obtain estimates of the direction of change in reported price-level income.[31]

In addition to using the Davidson and Weil results or procedures, we constructed proxy variables based on unadjusted depreciation and net monetary assets. Both of these variables have a direct negative impact on GPLA earnings (i.e., the larger depreciation or net monetary assets, the lower the adjusted income and the smaller or more negative the difference between GPLA adjusted income and unadjusted income). If we assume that our sample of firms has the same age distribution of depreciable property, then (cross-sectionally) depreciation and net monetary assets can serve as a surrogate for the effect of GPLA earnings.[32] Those numbers are readily available for our sample.

Davidson and Weil [1975c] also estimate the effect of GPLA on income for 1974 (which was in the future at the time of the submissions). Even though the adjustment procedure was slightly different, only two of our 19 firms in the combined samples reverse the direction of the income effect between 1973 and 1974. Similarly, all of the utilities (24), and 35 of the 50 other companies in their sample have income effects of the same sign in both years. Since the effects of income changes in the immediate future are less heavily discounted, these results suggest that the error introduced by our assumption of stationary income changes is not likely to be severe.

### Tests of the Theory

In the reported tests, we use asset size as the surrogate for firm size.[33] Based on our model, we can make predictions about the relationship between asset size and firm submissions. We predict that firms whose earnings are increased by GPLA will oppose GPLA regardless of their size (i.e., there will be no association between size and submission). However, for firms whose earnings are decreased by GPLA, we predict

---

[31] 1973 was a period of high inflation. If firms based their FASB lobbying position on the price adjustments produced by high unexpected inflation without considering more "typical" years, then this would introduce errors into the data and finding a statistically significant result becomes more difficult. If these errors are systematic with respect to firm size, then our results could be biased. We do not expect this to be the case. To control partially for this, statistical tests are performed which are independent of the magnitude of the price change. Net monetary assets in 1973 may still be abnormally small (large) due to the high rate of inflation, but these preliminary tests suggest that our results are not dependent upon 1973 being atypical.

[32] The assumption that the age distribution of depreciable property is the same across our firms is reasonable. The firms who submitted to the FASB on the GPLA issue, generally, were large, capital-intensive and long-established firms. Moreover, the results using these surrogates are consistent with the results using Davidson and Weil's estimates.

[33] In this case, firm size is measured by the firm's *Fortune* 500 rank in assets. The results are identical when rank in sales is used. Furthermore, the intent of government intervention depends on the metric used by the courts, legislators, and regulators. Market share, concentration and size are among the commonly used indicators. Absolute size is important in explaining government regulation for both theoretical and empirical reasons. An implication of Peltzman's (1975, p. 30) theory of regulation is that the amount of wealth redistributed from firms by government intervention is a positive function of economies of scale. Since we expect large firm size to indicate the presence of economies of scale, implication of Peltzman's theory is that government intervention will be greater for larger firms. Empirically, we observe numerous cases of politicians and regulators echoing the conventional wisdom of certain segments in society, that big business is inherently bad. (See "Curse of Big Business," *Barron's* June 16, 1969 and footnote 12).

that they will either support GPLA or will not make a submission depending on where asset size C (Figure 1) occurs in their industry. Since we cannot determine the asset size corresponding to point C, we are in a position analogous to being able to predict the sign of a regression coefficient but not its magnitude. Consequently, our test of the model does not include asset size C (analogous to the magnitude of the coefficient). The test is only of the prediction that there is a positive relationship between asset size and submission for firms with income decreases.

Firms making submissions were classified according to the direction of change in their net income and ranked by their asset size (Table 2). Of the 26 firms with income decreases, eight voted yes and 18 no.[34] The eight yes votes came from the larger firms, thus supporting our prediction. To test the null hypothesis that the eight firms which voted yes are drawn from the same population of firms (with respect to size) as the 18 that voted no, we performed a Mann-Whitney U test. Our tables indicate that we can reject the null hypothesis at the .001 level.[35]

Of the eight firms with income increases or no changes in net income, seven voted no. Thus, the general tendency of these firms is to vote no as predicted by our model.

The results in Table 2 are consistent with the implications of our model including our assumption that the management compensation factor is dominated by political and tax considerations. Of the 31 unregulated firms with management compensation plans, eight had increases or no change in income and 23 had decreases in income as a result of price-level adjustments. If management compensation dominates tax and political factors, then firms with increases in income would be more likely to support price-level adjustments than firms with decreases. In fact, the reverse is true. The frequency of firms with income decreases which support price-level adjustment is seven out of 23 (30 percent) while the frequency of firms with income increases that support price-level adjustments is one out of eight (12.5 percent).

The above results support the relationship between management's attitudes on GPLA and firm size for the 23 unregulated firms. However, if we assume that firm size and the direction of the income change are independent (Table 2 supports this assumption), then (if there is no size effect) the average size of firms supporting GPLA should be the same as the average size of firms opposing. Thus we can use the voting behavior of all 52 firms in our sample to test the size relationship.

Table 3 presents the median rank on asset size for both regulated and unregulated firms favoring and opposing GPLA. The median rank in the *Fortune* 500 of the nine unregulated firms supporting GPLA is 10. The median rank of the 25 unregulated firms opposing GPLA is 92.

---

[34] We use the term "vote" to mean responding to a discussion memorandum by issuing a corporate opinion.

[35] Siegel [1956], p. 274. Even after any reasonable adjustment for the degrees of freedom lost due to previous statistical analysis, this result is still significant.

An intuitive idea of the strength of the relationship between management's attitude and firm size can be obtained by considering an analogy. Suppose we put 26 balls in an urn representing the firms with earnings decreases; eight red balls representing the firms that voted yes; and 18 black balls, representing the firms that voted no. Now, we randomly draw 13 balls out of the urn without replacement representing the largest 13 firms (out of the 26). The probability that we draw eight red balls (analogous to the probability of the eight firms voting yes being the "large" firms if the null hypothesis of no association between votes and size is correct) is .001. If the votes of firms are not independent, as in the case of gaming, this analogy is inappropriate. But we do not have any evidence of vote dependence (via gaming or otherwise).

**TABLE 2**

**Asset Size, Direction of Earnings Effect and Corporate Position on GPLA**

| Rank on Asset Size | Firm | Rank in Fortune 500 (1973) | Corporate Position, Classified by Earnings Change[†] | |
| --- | --- | --- | --- | --- |
| | | | Increase or no change | Decrease |
| 1 | Exxon | 1 | | Yes |
| 2 | General Motors | 2 | | Yes |
| 3 | Texaco | 3 | No | |
| 4 | Ford | 4 | | Yes |
| 5 | Sears Roebuck (Rank 1 in retail sales) | 7 | | No |
| 6 | IT&T | 8 | No | |
| 7 | Gulf Oil | 9 | | Yes |
| 8 | Standard Oil of California | 10 | | Yes |
| 9 | General Electric | 11 | No | |
| 10 | Standard Oil of Indiana | 12 | | No |
| 11 | Shell Oil | 16 | | Yes |
| 12 | Dupont E. I. Nemours | 18 | | Yes |

Point C*————————————————————————————

| Rank on Asset Size | Firm | Rank in Fortune 500 (1973) | Increase or no change | Decrease |
| --- | --- | --- | --- | --- |
| 13 | Union Carbide | 22 | | No |
| 14 | Continental Oil | 26 | | No |
| 15 | Marcor (Rank 2 in retail firms) | 33 | Yes | |
| 16 | International Harvester | 34 | | No |
| 17 | Caterpillar Tractor | 47 | | Yes |
| 18 | Rockwell International | 54 | No | |
| 19 | W. R. Grace | 55 | No | |
| 20 | Owens-Illinois | 80 | No | |
| 21 | Inland Steel | 85 | | No |
| 22 | American Cyanamid | 92 | | No |
| 23 | United Aircraft | 107 | | No |
| 24 | Seagrams Sons Inc. | 108 | | No |
| 25 | Eli Lilly & Co. | 135 | | No |
| 26 | Merck | 143 | | No |
| 27 | General Mills | 156 | No | |
| 28 | Texas Instruments | 164 | | No |
| 29 | Gillette | 167 | | No |
| 30 | Reliance Electric | 332 | | No |
| 31 | Harsco | 368 | | No |
| 32 | Masonite | 386 | | No |
| 33 | Automated Building Components | Not Ranked | | No |
| 34 | Copeland Corporation | Not Ranked | | No |

* Point C in Figure 1 is determined by minimizing the number of misclassifications.
† Yes = Favored GPLA
  No = Opposed GPLA

**TABLE 3**

**Median Ranks of Firm Size by Regulation and Position on GPLA***

|  | Regulated (N = 18) | | Unregulated (N = 34) | |
| --- | --- | --- | --- | --- |
|  | In Favor (9) | Against (9) | In Favor (9) | Against (25) |
| Median Rank | 13 | 38 | 10 | 92 |

* *Fortune* [May and July, 1974].

For regulated firms, there also appears to be a relationship between size and management attitudes. The net incomes for all the utilities investigated by Davidson and Weil [1975b] are increased by GPLA suggesting none of the utilities should favor GPLA. However, as noted in the preceding section, operating earnings are relevant to rate determination. Those earnings fall for all the utilities investigated by Davidson and Weil [1975b] and this could explain why relatively larger regulated firms favor GPLA.

If we assume our model is correct and that asset size C is the same for all industries, we can estimate C by minimizing the number of prediction errors (analogous to estimating a regression coefficient by minimizing the sum of squared errors). This estimate provides information on the relative importance of political and/or tax costs for different size firms. Given the data, C is between the 18th and 22nd largest firms in the *Fortune* 500 in 1973 (see Table 2). This suggests that reduced political and/or tax costs outweigh information production and/or management compensation factors in determining management's position on GPLA only for very large firms. For most other firms, information production costs dominate.

Are the major benefits of reporting lower adjusted incomes derived from tax or political considerations? It is very difficult to differentiate between these two factors, but one possible way is the following. Is the change in adjusted income proportional to firm size? If it is, then both the tax and political factors may be operating. But if there is no association between firm size and the magnitude of the income change, then the tax effect cannot explain why larger firms favor GPLA. Therefore, this result could only be due to political costs. We can obtain estimates of the income effect of GPLA for 11 of the firms whose incomes would be reduced by GPLA (six supporting, five opposing).[36] The average reduction in income for the six firms which supported GPLA is $177.7 million, while the average reduction for the five which opposed GPLA is $38.5 million. Thus, it appears that the income change does vary with size and the preceding results are consistent with both the tax and political costs affecting management's attitudes.

The preceding results test only whether the size effect exists for firms which did submit to the FASB. It is interesting to examine the effect of GPLA on firms which did

---

[36] This test was performed on 11 firms with income decreases which Davidson and Weil reported 1973 adjusted earnings. Firms which were manually adjusted by us for Table 2 were excluded from this test since only the sign of the earnings change was calculated.

not submit. In particular, the firms of asset size above our estimated C which did not submit are of interest since our model predicts they would submit on the basis of the income effect. Dupont is the last firm above asset size C in Table 2 to vote. It is ranked 18th in the *Fortune* 500 in 1973. There are seven firms ranked higher than 18th which did not make a submission to the FASB. They are IBM (ranked 5th), General Telephone (6th), Mobil Oil (7th), U.S. Steel (13th), Chrysler (14th), Tenneco (15th), and Atlantic Richfield (17th).

The size of the income change is crucial to determining why these seven firms did not submit. If changes are not associated with firm size, the expected benefits of a submission could be very small and may not exceed the submission costs. Unfortunately, Davidson and Weil only estimated the change in earnings in 1973 for three of these seven firms: IBM, U.S. Steel, and Chrysler. All three have income reductions with GPLA and their average reduction is $88 million. This is less than the average reduction for the six firms with income reductions which did submit ($177 million), but it is not trivial. Further, the reductions for two of the three nonsubmissions (IBM and General Telephone) exceed the reductions for four of the six submissions. Consequently, it is difficult to attribute the fact that the three firms did not submit to the lack of an income effect.[37]

In summary, these tests confirm the relationship between size and management attitudes on GPLA. Political costs and, perhaps, tax effects influence management's attitudes on accounting standards. Although we are not able to explain some of the notable nonsubmitting firms' decisions, we would point out that most of the firms submitting are large, and the likelihood of submission increases with asset size (12 of the 18 firms ranked 1–18 in the *Fortune* 500 submitted, four of the 18 firms ranked 19–36 submitted, two of the 18 firms ranked 37–54 submitted, one of the 18 firms ranked 55–72 submitted, etc.).

### Discriminant Analysis

The preceding tests were based on the direction of the earnings change, not the magnitude of the change. A discriminant analysis is conducted including management compensation, depreciation, and net monetary assets as independent variables, and using data on 49 of the 53 firms making submissions to ensure consistency of the Davidson and Weil procedures.

The change in price-adjusted income is correlated with the magnitudes of depreciation and net monetary assets. The larger both of these variables in unadjusted terms, the larger will be the decline (in absolute dollars) in adjusted net

---

[37] A more likely explanation of U.S. Steel's failure to submit is the fact that the steel industry was not as politically sensitive as the oil industry (for example) at the time. In other words, a given earnings effect has less political cost or benefit. This possibility is not included in our model. This could also explain Chrysler's failure to submit. As number three after General Motors and Ford they may be subject to less political pressure (and hence cost). In addition, the "free rider" effect may explain some of these nonsubmissions.

While we can only expect a positive theory to hold on average, the failure of IBM to submit is puzzling. That firm has anti-trust suits outstanding and some economists allege that it earns monopoly profits. For a discussion of one of these suits and statements by economists that IBM earns monopoly profits, see "The Breakup of IBM" *Datamation*, October 1975, pp. 95–99.

income. We do not perform an actual price-level adjustment, but rely on the unadjusted magnitudes of depreciation and net monetary assets.

The general form of the discriminant function we estimate is[38]

$$p_i = \alpha_1 + \alpha_2 \frac{DEP_i}{MKTVL_i} + \alpha_2 \frac{NMA_i}{MKTVL_i} + \alpha_3 (SALES_i) CHG_i$$

$$+ \alpha_4 \left( \frac{SALES_i}{TSALES_i} \right) CHG_i + \alpha_5 MCOMP_i + \alpha_6 REG_i \qquad (2)$$

where

$$p_i = \begin{cases} \dfrac{\text{Number of opposing firms}}{\text{Total firms in sample}} & \text{if the } i^{\text{th}} \text{ firm favored GPLA} \\[2ex] \dfrac{\text{Number of supporting firms}}{\text{Total firms in sample}} & \text{if the } i^{\text{th}} \text{ firm opposed GPLA} \end{cases}$$

$MKTVL_i$ = the market value of the firm's equity (number of common shares outstanding × average share price)

$$REG_i = \begin{cases} 1 & \text{if the } i^{\text{th}} \text{ firm was regulated} \\ 0 & \text{otherwise} \end{cases}$$

$$MCOMP_i = \begin{cases} 1 & \text{if the } i^{\text{th}} \text{ firm had a management incentive scheme} \\ 0 & \text{otherwise} \end{cases}$$

$DEP_i$ = unadjusted depreciation expense in 1973 for the $i^{\text{th}}$ firm

$NMA_i$ = net monetary asset position in 1973 for the $i^{\text{th}}$ firm

$$CHG_i = \begin{cases} +1 & \text{if price-level adjusted income is below unadjusted income or if} \\ & \text{the firm is regulated} \\ -1 & \text{if price-level adjusted income is above unadjusted income} \\ 0 & \text{otherwise} \end{cases}$$

$SALES_i$ = Sales of the $i^{\text{th}}$ firm

$TSALES_i$ = Total sales of the COMPUSTAT firms with the same SIC code as firm $i$.

$\dfrac{SALES_i}{TSALES_i}$ = a proxy variable for market share

Table 4 presents the results of various functional forms of equation (2) fitted over various subsets of the data.[39] The first two terms,

$$\frac{NMA}{MKTVL} \quad \text{and} \quad \frac{DEP}{MKTVL},$$

---

[38] Northwestern Telephone, Commerce Bank of Kansas City, and Indiana Telephone were dropped from the sample due to a lack of data.

[39] The discriminant function is estimated using ordinary least squares. $t$-statistics on the coefficients are reported. The usual $t$-tests cannot be performed since the dependent variable is not normally distributed nor can asymptotic properties of large samples be used. However, the $t$-statistic is still useful as an index of the relative importance of the independent variable.

## TABLE 4

**Discriminant Analysis Coefficients ($t$-statistics)**

| Model Number | N | Sample | Constant | DEP/MKTVL | NMA/MKTVL | SALES × CHG | $\frac{SALES}{TSALES}$ × CHG | MCOMP | REG | $R^2$ | Yates Adjusted Chi Square* |
|---|---|---|---|---|---|---|---|---|---|---|---|
| 1 | 49 | total | −.0241 | 122.6 | −38.9 | .000044 | −.4131 | −.2355 | −.3443 | .358 | 9.25 |
|   |    | sample | (−.12) | (.60) | (−1.62) | (3.67) | (−1.11) | (−1.42) | (−1.29) |   |   |
| 2 | 49 | total | −.0855 | 160.4 | −14.2 | .000043 | −.4381 | −.1619 |   | .332 | 9.25 |
|   |    | sample | (−.44) | (.79) | (−.98) | (3.53) | (−1.17) | (−1.03) |   |   |   |
| 3 | 49 | total | −.0973 | 143.0 | −15.6 | .000034 |   | −.1601 |   | .311 | 9.25 |
|   |    | sample | (−.50) | (.70) | (−1.07) | (3.58) |   | (−1.02) |   |   |   |
| 4 | 34 | unregulated firms | .0431 | 74.0 | −36.5 | .000044 | −.3271 | −.2186 |   | .366 | 19.96 |
|   |    |   | (.19) | (.27) | (−1.06) | (3.58) | (−.89) | (−.89) |   |   |   |
| 5 | 34 | unregulated firms | .0412 | 86.2 | −35.3 | .000038 |   | −.2335 |   | .347 | 13.16 |
|   |    |   | (.18) | (.32) | (−1.03) | (3.73) |   | (−.96) |   |   |   |
| 6 | 49 | total | −.0079 | 215.3 |   | .000033 |   | −.2365 | .0077 | .293 | 11.74 |
|   |    | sample | (−.04) | (1.09) |   | (3.44) |   | (−1.39) | (.05) |   |   |
| 7 | 49 | total | −.0662 |   |   | .000033 |   |   |   | .201 | 5.98 |
|   |    | sample | (−1.03) |   |   | (3.44) |   |   |   |   |   |

* The Yates correction for continuity is useful in establishing a lower bound on the $\chi^2$ statistic.

normalize the unadjusted figures by the market value of the equity[40] and the estimated coefficients measure the extent to which an increase in relative depreciation or net monetary assets affect voting behavior. These coefficients, which should capture the tax effects, are predicted to be positive under that hypothesis (the larger the depreciation and net monetary assets the greater the decline in adjusted income and the greater the tax benefits).

The sign on normalized depreciation is as predicted, but normalized net monetary assets is of the wrong sign. One of the following three hypotheses explain this result: the tax effect is only operating via depreciation;[41] depreciation and net monetary assets, being inversely related (correlation coefficient ranging from $-.41$ to $-.55$), are entering the regression with opposite signs; or the tax effect is not an explanatory factor. Since our sample is very small, it is not possible to use a holdout subset to distinguish between these hypotheses.

The next two variables,

$$(\text{SALES}) \text{ CHG and } \left(\frac{\text{SALES}}{\text{TSALES}}\right) \text{CHG},$$

are proxies for political costs. These two variables, assume that political costs are symmetric for both earnings increases and decreases. The multiplicative dummy, CHG, is positive if earnings decline (based on the Davidson-Weil [1975a] results) or if the firm is regulated.[42]

The sign on SALES $\times$ CHG is as predicted, positive, and in addition has the highest $t$-statistic of all the independent variables. In addition, the coefficient on SALES $\times$ CHG is the most stable coefficient across various realizations and sub-samples which leads us to conclude that firm size is the most important variable. The sign of

$$\frac{\text{SALES}}{\text{TSALES}} \times \text{CHG}$$

is of the wrong sign. But this is probably due to the crude metric of market share,

$$\frac{\text{SALES}}{\text{TSALES}},$$

this variable is attempting to measure.[43] When the market share proxy is eliminated, the model's predictive ability is not impaired.

---

[40] Normalizing by the market value of the common stock introduces some error since we are not including the market value of the debt or preferred stock. However, since the market value of the common is highly correlated with total market value of the firm, we do not expect serious problems except that there may be some systematic, negative understatement of normalized net monetary assets.

[41] That is, this sample of firms does not expect the tax laws to be changed to include in taxable income gains/losses on net monetary assets.

[42] Since the regulatory commission bases rates on depreciation, net monetary assets are not expected to be an important consideration, hence operating earnings decline for regulated firms.

[43] Our measure of industry sales does not include firms in the industry not on the COMPUSTAT tape and furthermore all the firm's sales are assumed to be in the firm's dominant SIC category.

MCOMP, a dummy variable for management compensation schemes is expected to have a negative sign regardless of the change in earnings. Prior research indicates that executive compensation is more highly associated with operating income (which includes depreciation) than net income (which includes gains/losses on monetary assets).[44] Therefore, MCOMP is not multiplied by CHG. The sign of MCOMP being negative is consistent with our predictions.

If the firm is regulated, the dummy variable, REG, is one. Regulated firms' price-level adjusted operating incomes decline, unambiguously, and therefore these firms should tend to favor GPLA if the regulatory factor is operating. Yet, the sign of the coefficient of REG is negative in Model 1. This sign is negative because REG is inversely related to

$$\text{MCOMP and } \frac{\text{NMA}}{\text{MKTVL}}$$

(correlation coefficients of $-.60$ and $-.86$ respectively). When

$$\frac{\text{NMA}}{\text{MKTVL}}$$

is deleted from the model (Model 6), the sign of REG reverses, the importance of

$$\frac{\text{DEP}}{\text{MKTVL}}$$

increases, and the discriminatory power of the model improves from a Chi-Square of 9.25 to 11.74. However, the multicolinearity between

$$\text{REG, MCOMP, and } \frac{\text{NMA}}{\text{MKTVL}}$$

precludes our drawing any conclusions regarding the impact of management compensation or regulation on lobbying behavior.

Models 4 and 5 are fitted using only the unregulated firms (N = 34). REG and then

$$\frac{\text{SALES}}{\text{TSALES}} \times \text{CHG}$$

have been deleted. The $R^2$ statistic still remains high and the Yates adjusted Chi

---

[44] Our examination of management compensation plans indicates that although the minimum and maximum amounts transferred to the bonus pool depend on the final net income number, we find that the actual bonus paid is most highly associated with operating or current income (depreciation is included, but extraordinary gains and losses are excluded). We correlated the change in management incentive compensation expense for 271 COMPUSTAT firms with changes in operating income and changes in net income after extraordinary items. The correlation coefficient for changes in operating income exceeded that for changes in net income after extraordinary items for over two-thirds of the firms. Gains or losses on monetary assets are not included in operating income. Consequently, only adjusted depreciation (ignoring inventory adjustments) are expected to affect management compensation and the effect is to reduce management pay.

Square is significant at the 1 percent level. In fact, Model 4 correctly classifies the voting behavior for 32 out of the 34 firms.

The constant should be capturing the partial effect of information production costs after controlling for the other factors. When the total sample is used in the estimation, the constant is negative as expected. When the regulated firms are excluded, the constant is positive. But in all models the constant is close to zero.

The estimated discriminant functions are consistent with the tests of the theory. All of the discriminant functions are statistically significant and the intervening variable driving these findings is firm size. In fact, firm size explains over half the explained variance in voting behavior (Model 7).

These results are consistent with those using the Davidson and Weil findings. The discriminant functions indicate that the political cost factor is more important than the tax factor in affecting management's attitudes.

The major empirical problem in the discriminant analysis is the rather small sample size which precludes using a hold-out sample and, furthermore, does not allow more sophisticated econometric techniques to control for the multicolinearity. Hence, it is difficult to control for the interaction between the underlying factors. However, these preliminary results are encouraging and suggest that additional research in this area is warranted.

## SUMMARY AND CONCLUSIONS

We have focused in this paper on the question of why firms would expend resources trying to influence the determination of accounting standards. The histories of the Committee on Accounting Procedures, the Accounting Principles Board, and FASB are replete with examples of managements and industries exerting political pressure on the standard-setting bodies.

A possible answer to this question is provided by the government intervention argument, namely, that firms having contact (actual or potential) with governments, directly through regulation (public utility commissions, Interstate Commerce Commission, Civil Aeronautics Board, etc.) or procurement, or indirectly through possible governmental intervention (antitrust, price controls, etc.), can affect their future cashflows by discouraging government action through the reporting of lower net incomes. The empirical evidence with respect to the position 52 firms took before the FASB on price level restatements is consistent with respect to this hypothesis.

The single most important factor explaining managerial voting behavior on General Price Level Accounting is firm size (after controlling for the direction of change in earnings). The larger firms, *ceteris paribus*, are more likely to favor GPLA (if earnings decline). This finding is consistent with our government intervention argument since the larger firms are more likely to be subjected to governmental interference and, hence, have more to lose than smaller corporations.

The existence of costs generated by government intervention may have more fundamental and important effects on the firm's decisions than just its lobbying behavior on financial accounting standards. Not only would we expect the firm to manage its reported earnings, but also to alter its investment-production decisions if the potential costs of government interference become large. For example, government intervention costs may lead the firm to select less risky investments in order to eliminate the chance of high returns which then increase the likelihood of government intervention. If the total risk of these less risky investments tends to be positively correlated with the systematic risk of the firm, then we would expect the beta (the estimate of the covariance between the return on the stock and the market return normalized by the variance of the market) on the common stock to be significantly below one (average risk) for those firms facing large government intervention costs. The evidence from the sample of firms making submissions to the FASB on GPLA is consistent with this hypothesis. The average $\beta$ is .67. Furthermore, firms favoring GPLA tend to have lower betas than the firms in opposition.[45]

Our findings, in a preliminary extension of these results, tend to confirm the decline in systematic risk as firm size increases and as government intervention costs rise. These tentative findings are suggestive of fertile research possibilities of examining the effects of politically motivated factors on the maximizing behavior of firms' managements and shareholders.

We believe that the general findings in this paper, if confirmed by other studies, have important implications for the setting of financial accounting standards in a mixed economy. As long as financial accounting standards have potential effects on the firm's future cashflows, standard setting by bodies such as the Accounting Principles Board, the Financial Accounting Standards Board, or the Securities and Exchange Commission will be met by corporate lobbying. The Committee on Accounting Procedures and the Accounting Principles Board could not withstand the pressure. The former Chairman of the FASB also has complained of the political lobbying, and the FASB has been forced to defer the controversial GPLA topic. The SEC has, until recently, avoided direct involvement in the setting of accounting standards. One could hypothesize that this was in their own interest. By letting the American Institute of Certified Public Accountants be the scapegoat, the Securities and Exchange Commission could maintain their "credibility" with Capitol Hill and the public.

## REFERENCES

Alchian, A. A., "Corporate Management and Property Rights," *in Economic Policy and the Regulation of Corporate Securities* (H. Manne, ed.), (American Enterprise Institute, 1969).

———— and H. Demsetz, "Production, Information Costs and Economic Organization," *American Economic Review* (December 1972), pp. 777–795.

Armstrong, Marshall S., "The Politics of Establishing Accounting Standards," A speech before the Third Annual Securities Regulation Institute in San Diego, California, January 16, 1976, as reported in Arthur Andersen & Co., *Executive News Briefs*, (February 1976), p. 1.

Ball, R., "Changes in Accounting Techniques and Stock Prices," *Empirical Research in Accounting: Selected Studies, 1972.* Supplement to *Journal of Accounting Research* (1972), pp. 1–38.

[45] The average betas of various subclasses are:

|  | Regulated | Unregulated | Combined |
|---|---|---|---|
| Firms opposing GPLA | .67 | .72 | .71 |
| Firms favoring GPLA | .50 | .65 | .59 |
| Combined | .59 | .70 | .67 |

Note that as a firm grows via diversification its beta should tend to one.

——— and Ross Watts, "Some Time Series Properties of Accounting Income," *Journal of Finance* (June 1972), pp. 663–82.

Barefield, R. M., and E. E. Comiskey, "The Smoothing Hypothesis: An Alternative Test," THE ACCOUNTING REVIEW (April 1972), pp. 291–298.

Barnea, A., J. Ronen, and S. Sadan, "The Implementation of Accounting Objectives— An Application to Extraordinary Items," THE ACCOUNTING REVIEW (January 1975), pp. 58–68.

Beidleman, C. R., "Income Smoothing: The Role of Management," THE ACCOUNTING REVIEW (October 1973), pp. 653–667.

Benston, George J., "Accountants Integrity and Financial Reporting," *Financial Executive* (August 1975), pp. 10–14.

The Conference Board, *Top Executive Compensation* (Conference Board, 1974).

Copeland, Ronald M., "Income Smoothing," *Empirical Research in Accounting: Selected Studies*. Supplement to *Journal of Accounting Research* 1968, pp. 101–116.

Cushing, B. E., "An Empirical Study of Changes in Accounting Policy," *Journal of Accounting Research* (Autumn 1969), pp. 196–203.

Dasher, B. E. and R. E. Malcom, "A Note on Income Smoothing in the Chemical Industry," *Journal of Accounting Research* (Autumn 1970), pp. 253–259.

Davidson, Sidney, Clyde P. Stickney and Roman L. Weil, *Inflation Accounting* (McGraw-Hill, 1976).

——— and Roman L. Weil, "Inflation Accounting: What Will General Price Level Adjusted Income Statements Show?" *Financial Analysts Journal*, (January— February 1975a) pp. 27–31; 70–81.

——— and Roman L. Weil, "Inflation Accounting: Public Utilities," *Financial Analysts Journal*, (May—June 1975b), pp. 30–34; 62.

——— and Roman L. Weil, "Inflation Accounting: Some 1974 Income Measures," *Financial Analysts Journal*, (September—October 1975c), pp. 42–54.

Downs, A., *An Economic Theory of Democracy*, (Harper and Row, 1957).

Fama, Eugene F., "Efficient Capital Markets: A Review of Theory and Empirical Work," *Journal of Finance*, (May 1970), pp. 383–417.

Gonedes, N., "Income-smoothing Behavior Under Selected Stochastic Processes," *Journal of Business* (October 1972), pp. 570–584.

———, "Class Discussion Notes: Section 8," unpublished manuscript, University of Chicago (January 1976).

——— and N. Dopuch, "Capital Market Equilibrium, Information Production, and Selecting Accounting Techniques: Theoretical Framework and Review of Empirical Work," *Studies on Financial Accounting Objectives: 1974*. Supplement to *Journal of Accounting Research* (1974).

Gordon, M. J., "Postulates, Principles and Research in Accounting," THE ACCOUNTING REVIEW (April 1964), pp. 251–263.

———, B. N. Horwitz, and P. T. Meyers, "Accounting Measurements and Normal Growth of the Firm," *Research in Accounting Measurement*, eds. Jaedicke, Ijiri and Nielsen (American Accounting Association, 1966), pp. 221–231.

Haskins and Sells. *Public Utilities Manual* (New York, 1974).

Horngren, Charles T., "The Marketing of Accounting Standards," *Journal of Accountancy* (October 1973), pp. 61–66.

———, "Setting Accounting Standards in 1980," unpublished speech before the Arthur Young Professors Roundtable (March 30–31, 1976).

Ijiri, Yuji, "The Price-Level Restatement and its Dual Interpretation," THE ACCOUNTING REVIEW, (April 1976), pp. 227–243.

Jensen, Michael C., "Reflections on the State of Accounting Research and the Regulation of Accounting," Presented at the Stanford Lectures in Accounting, May 21, 1976.

———, and William H. Meckling, "Theory of the Firm: Managerial Behavior, Agency Costs and Ownership Structure," *Journal of Financial Economics* (October 1976a), pp. 305–360.

———, and William H. Meckling, "Can the Corporation Survive?" Public Policy Working Paper Series, PPS76–4, Graduate School of Management, University of Rochester, (April, 1976b).

Kaplan, R. S., and R. Roll, "Investor Evaluation of Accounting Information: Some Empirical Evidence," *Journal of Business* (April 1972), pp. 225–57.

Meckling, William H., "Values and the Choice of the Model of the Individual in Social Sciences," *Revue Suisse d' Economic Politique et de Statistique* (December 1976).

Moonitz, Maurice, *Obtaining Agreement on Standards*. Studies in Accounting Research No. 8 (Sarasota, Florida: American Accounting Association, 1974).

Peltzman, S., "Toward a More General Theory of Regulation," *Journal of Law and Economics*, (August 1976), pp. 221–240.

Posner, Richard A., "Theories of Economic Regulation," *The Bell Journal of Economics and Management Science*, (Autumn 1974), pp. 335–358.

Siegel, Sidney, *Nonparametric Statistics* (McGraw-Hill, 1956).

Siegfried, John, "Determinants of Antitrust Activity," *Journal of Law and Economics* (October 1975), pp. 559–581.

Stigler, G. J., "The Theory of Economic Regulation," *The Bell Journal of Economics and Management Science*, (Spring 1971), 3–21.

Sunder, S., "Empirical Analysis of Stock Price and Risk as They Relate to Accounting Changes in Inventory Valuation," THE ACCOUNTING REVIEW (April 1975), pp. 305–315.

U.S. Congress, Senate, Subcommittee on Antitrust and Monopoly of the Committee on the Judiciary, *Hearings, The Petroleum Industry*, Part I, 9th Congress, 1st Session, 1975.

U.S. Congress, Senate, Subcommittee on Antitrust and Monopoly of the Committee on the Judiciary, *Hearings, The Petroleum Industry*, Part III, 9th Congress, 1st Session, 1976.

Watts, Ross, "Accounting Objectives," Working Paper Series No. 7408, Graduate School of Management, University of Rochester, (April 1974).

Watts, Ross, "Corporate Financial Statements: Product of the Market and Political Processes," *Australian Journal of Management* (April 1977), pp. 53–75.

Zeff- Stephen, *Forging Accounting Principles in Five Countries: A History and an Analysis of Trends*, Arthur Andersen Lecture Series (Stipes Publishing Company, 1972), pp. 110–268.

Zimmerman, Jerold, "The Municipal Accounting Maze: An Analysis of Political Incentives," Supplement to the *Journal of Accounting Research* (1977).

# I-C  Capital Market Efficiency

## I-C 1  *What Should Be the FASB's Objectives?*

WILLIAM H. BEAVER

W as the acrimony out of the investment tax credit much ado about nothing? Does it matter whether special gains and losses are reported in the ordinary income or in the extraordinary item section? When firms switch from accelerated to straight-line depreciation, what is the effect upon investors? Did the Accounting Principles Board allocate its resources in an appropriate manner? If its priorities needed reordering, where should the emphasis have been shifted? What objectives should be adopted for financial accounting standards?

To answer such questions, the Financial Accounting Standards Board plans to sponsor a sizable research program.[1] For this reason, now is an appropriate time to take stock of the current body of knowledge and assess its implications for the setting of financial accounting standards. This article summarizes the results of recent research that has explored several facets of the relationship between financial statement data and security prices. The findings have a direct bearing on the questions raised at the outset and suggest that our traditional views of the role of policy-making bodies, such as the APB, SEC and FASB, may have to be substantially altered.

Currently we have far too little evidence on important issues in accounting. However, given this paucity of knowledge, it would be unfortunate if we ignored the evidence that we do have. Aspects of this research have already had a considerable effect on the professional investment community. Yet there has been no awareness of this research in accounting at the practical level or in the setting of past standards, as

The author wishes to acknowledge financial assistance provided by the Dean Witter Foundation. The conclusions expressed here are those of the author and do not necessarily reflect those of the foundation or any of its members.

William H. Beaver, "What Should Be the FASB's Objectives?" *The Journal of Accountancy*, August 1973 pp. 49–56. Copyright © 1973 by the American Institute of Certified Public Accountants, Inc. Opinions expressed in the *Journal of Accountancy* are those of editors and contributors. Publication in the *Journal of Accountancy* does not constitute endorsement by the AICPA or its committees.

[1] "Recommendations of the Study on Establishment of Accounting Principles," *Journal of Accountancy*, May 72, pp. 66–71.

reflected in the APB Opinions. If the hopes for success of the FASB are to be realized, it is imperative that we lead, no lag, in incorporating the current state of knowledge into the setting of standards. Regulating financial accounting standards in ignorance of this evidence makes the prospects for success dim.

## THE EVIDENCE

The behavior of security prices with respect to financial statement data is a widely discussed and hotly debated topic. The financial press is replete with articles of alleged effects of financial statement data on prices. In most cases, such allegations are not supported by any evidence. In a few cases, evidence of an anecdotal nature is offered. For example, the price of the stock of the ABC Company changed dramatically at approximately the same time the firm changed its method of depreciation to straight-line. Therefore, the cause was the change in accounting method. Such stories, while often entertaining, hardly constitute convincing evidence for several reasons. First, such an approach may select only those cases which are favorable to the hypothesis of the author while ignoring those instances that would refute it. For example, an examination of the price changes of only one firm or a few hand-picked firms that changed depreciation methods is insufficient. An examination must be made for all firms that changed depreciation methods or at least a large, randomly selected sample. Second, the analysis explains price changes after-the-fact on the basis of a single factor. There may be many factors that cause a price change. Usually, little or no care is taken to account for these other factors.

Unfortunately, until recently such evidence was the only type available. However, the issue is far too serious to be left to casual empiricism. Security prices are of obvious importance because of their impact upon the wealth, and hence the welfare, of investors. This importance is formally recognized in SEC legislation. Recent cases arising out of Section 10b-5 testify to the fact that accounting practices are evaluated in terms of their effect on security prices.[2] Moreover, it is inconceivable that the FASB could set optimal financial accounting standards without assessing the impact of their actions on security prices.

The prevailing opinion in the accounting profession is that the market reacts naïvely to financial statement information. This view is reinforced by the anecdotal data of the sort described earlier, and by the obvious fact that the market is populated with several million uninformed, naïve investors, whose knowledge or concern for the subtleties of accounting matters is nil. However, in spite of this obvious fact, the formal research in this area is remarkably consistent in finding that the market, at least as manifested in the way in which security prices react, is quite sophisticated in dealing with financial statement data. One rationale for the observed sophistication of security prices is that the professional investors "make the market" and competitive bidding among one another for securities effectively makes the prices behave in such a manner that they reflect a considerable amount of sophistication. In

---

[2] For example, litigation is currently under way in the cases of *Memorex* and *Occidental Petroleum Corp.*, pursuant to SEC action under Section 10b-5. Brief summaries of issues appear in the June 25, 1971, and March 5, 1971, issues of *The Wall Street Journal*, respectively. In both cases, measures of damages being discussed are directly related to the effect of the firms' accounting practices on security prices.

any event, regardless of what the actual causal mechanism may be, there is considerable evidence that security prices do in fact behave in a sophisticated fashion. In the terminology of this literature, the securities market is said to be "efficient" with respect to financial statement data.[3]

A market is said to be efficient if security prices act as if they "fully reflect" publicly available information, including financial statement data. In other words, in an efficient market the investor is playing a "fair game" with respect to published information. Specifically, this means no investor can expect to use published information in such a way as to earn abnormal returns on his securities. Each investor can expect to earn a return on a security commensurate with its risk.[4] All securities of the same degree of riskiness will offer the same expected return, regardless of what accounting methods are used and no matter how much time is spent gleaning the secrets of the financial statements hidden in the footnotes. Hence, no amount of security analysis, based on published financial statement data, will lead to abnormal returns. There are obvious implications for the community of professional investors, among others. However, there are also equally dramatic implications for the accounting profession. For this reason, the evidence, which has examined several aspects of market efficiency with respect to financial statement data, is summarized below.[5]

One aspect of efficiency is the speed with which security prices react to public information when it is announced. Empirical evidence indicates that prices react quickly and in an unbiased fashion to a variety of events, including announcements of stock splits, stock dividends, secondary offerings and rights issues, as well as both annual and interim earnings announcements. This finding is exactly what one would expect in a market where the security prices at any point in time fully reflect the information released. Moreover, the studies of earnings announcements find security

---

[3] Three forms of efficiency have been delineated: (1) the weak form, which deals with efficiency with respect to the past sequence of security prices (e.g., the random-walk hypothesis), (2) the semistrong form, which concerns efficiency with respect to published information, and (3) the strong form, which involves all information including inside information. This article deals with efficiency in the semistrong form. There is also considerable evidence with respect to the weak form of efficiency, but it is beyond the scope of this article. For a summary of this literature, see W. Beaver, "Reporting Rules for Marketable Equity Securities," *Journal of Accountancy*, Oct. 71, pp. 57–61.

[4] A detailed discussion of security risk and how it relates to expected returns is beyond the scope of the article. However, there has been a substantial amount of research in the portfolio theory and capital asset pricing literature dealing with this relationship. Briefly, the literature suggests that expected return must be commensurate with the risk incurred, in that securities with greater risk must offer higher expected return. Of course, the actual return in a given period may differ from expected return. For a more complete discussion of this issue in a nontechnical manner, see C. Welles, "The Beta Revolution: Learning to Live With Risk," *The Institutional Investor*, September 1971, pp. 21–64; W. Sharpe, "Risk, Market Sensitivity and Diversification," *Financial Analysts Journal*, January-February 1972, pp. 74–79.

[5] A more detailed summary of the literature is provided in the article by Eugene Fama, "Efficient Capital Markets: A Review of Theory and Empirical Work," *Journal of Finance*, May 1970, pp. 383–417. The implications of this literature for accounting also have been discussed in the following articles: W. Beaver, "The Behavior of Security Prices and Its Implications for Accounting Research Methods," *The Accounting Review* (Supplement, 1972), pp. 407–37; R. Ball, "Changes in Accounting Techniques and Stock Prices" (unpublished paper, University of Chicago, 1972); and N. Gonedes, "Efficient Capital Markets and External Accounting," *The Accounting Review*, January 1972, pp. 11–21.

prices anticipate earnings for several months prior to the announcement.[6]

Another aspect is this: Does the market look behind accounting numbers or is it fooled by them? Does the market act only on reported accounting numbers or does it adjust for other information, such as the accounting method used to calculate those numbers? In other words, does the market use a broader information set than merely the reported accounting numbers? In this respect, there have been several studies of changes in accounting methods and the subsequent behavior of security prices.[7] All of these studies show essentially the same result. There is no increase in price by changing to an accounting method that reports higher earnings than would have been reported had no change been made. The market, as reflected in price behavior, is not so naïve as many people claim. Instead, it acts as if it looks beyond accounting numbers and takes into account the fact that earnings are being generated by a different method.

Further evidence compared the price-earnings ratios of firms that use accelerated methods of depreciation for both tax and reporting purposes (A/A group) with the price-earnings ratios of firms that use accelerated methods for tax purposes but straight-line for reporting purposes (A/S group).[8] The price-earnings ratio for the A/A group was larger than the price-earnings ratio for the A/S group. This finding is consistent with a market which recognizes that firms will report lower earnings under accelerated methods of depreciation than they would have under straight-line methods. Further analysis suggested that risk and growth could not explain the difference in the price-earnings ratios. In fact, the average riskiness and average growth rates were the same for both depreciation groups. However, when the earnings of the A/S group were converted to the earnings that would have been reported had they used an accelerated method for reporting, the price-earnings ratios of the two depreciation groups were essentially equal. In other words, when the firms were placed on a uniform accounting method, the price-earnings differences disappeared. Thus, the market appears to adjust for differences in depreciation methods among firms and, in effect, looks behind reported accounting data. Moreover, further testing found that changes in security prices more closely follow changes in certain

[6] The studies referred to here are E. Fama, L. Fisher, M. Jensen and R. Roll, "The Adjustment of Stock Prices to New Information," *International Economic Review*, February 1969, pp. 1–21; M. Scholes, "The Market for Securities: Substitution Versus Price Pressure and the Effects of Information on Share Prices," *Journal of Business*, April 1972, pp. 179–211; R. Ball and P. Brown, "An Empirical Evaluation of Accounting Income Numbers," *Journal of Accounting Research*, Autumn 1968, pp. 159–78; P. Brown and J. Kennelly, "The Informational Content of Quarterly Earnings: An Extension and Some Further Evidence," *Journal of Business*, July 1972, pp. 403–21; G. Benston, "Published Corporate Accounting Data and Stock Prices," *Empirical Research in Accounting: Selected Studies, 1967, Journal of Accounting Research* (Supplement, 1967), pp. 1–54; and W. Beaver, "The Information Content of Annual Earnings Announcements," *Empirical Research in Accounting: Selected Studies, 1968, Journal of Accounting Research* (Supplement, 1968), pp. 67–92.

[7] The empirical studies referred to here include R. Kaplan and R. Roll, "Investor Evaluation of Accounting Information: Some Empirical Evidence," *Journal of Business*, April 1972, pp. 225–57; R. Ball, *op. cit.*; T. R. Archibald, "Stock Market Reaction to Depreciation Switchback," *The Accounting Review*, January 1972, pp. 22–30; and E. Comiskey, "Market Response to Changes in Depreciation Accounting," *The Accounting Review*, April 1971, pp. 279–85.

[8] W. Beaver and R. E. Dukes, "Interperiod Tax Allocation and Depreciation Methods: Some Empirical Results," *The Accounting Review*, July 1973.

nonreported forms of earnings than they do changes in reported earnings. This finding is consistent with a market where a broad information set is used in assessing price changes in contrast to one where there is sole, unquestioning reliance upon reported earnings.

In sum then, the evidence, across a variety of contexts, supports the contention that the market is efficient with respect to published information.

## IMPLICATIONS

This evidence, together with the evidence on the performance of mutual funds, has led to changes in the investment community.[9]

Many portfolio managers and their clients have moved away from a "beat-the-market," high-turnover philosophy to one where the emphasis is placed upon risk management and the minimization of operating costs. The Samsonite pension fund contract is but one recent example. Wells Fargo Bank has agreed to manage the Samsonite pension fund where the agreement stipulates the maintenance of a given level of risk within prespecified limits, a lid on the maximum amount of turnover that can occur and a restriction on the minimum number of securities comprising the fund.[10]

Given the practical impact that this research has had on the investment community, one might suspect that there are implications for the practice of accounting as well. In fact, there are several important implications for accounting in general and for the FASB in particular. However, there has been virtually no reaction on the part of the accounting profession. One reason is a general lack of awareness of this research, because its dissemination has essentially been restricted to academic journals. Another reason is that the anecdotal form of evidence discussed earlier continues to carry considerable weight among many members of the accounting profession. As a result, many readers may refuse to accept the evidence in support of market efficiency. But what if the mounting evidence in support of an efficient market finally becomes so overwhelming and compelling that it is accepted by all seven members of the FASB, all SEC Commissioners and staff, and all congressmen? What are the implications for the FASB? There are at least four major implications.

*First.* Many reporting issues are trivial and do not warrant an expenditure of FASB resources. The properties of such issues are twofold: (1) There is essentially no difference in cost to the firm of reporting either method. (2) There is essentially no cost to statement users in adjusting from one method to the other. In such cases, there is a

---

[9] The empirical evidence finds that mutual fund returns fail to cover even research costs and brokerage commissions (let alone loading charges). After deducting these expenses, the net return to the mutual fund shareholder is below the return that could have been obtained from a simple strategy of buying and holding a portfolio of the same degree of riskiness. In fact, only after all such costs were added back in computing the return is the average mutual fund performance approximately equal to (but not greater than) the return from random portfolios of the same degree of riskiness. Moreover, these results not only apply to the average performance of all mutual funds but additional tests also indicate that no individual funds were able to produce superior returns consistently. For example, past performance by a fund appeared to be of no value in predicting superior performance in the future. See M. Jensen, "Risk, the Pricing of Capital Assets, and the Evaluation of Investment Portfolios," *Journal of Business*, April 1969, pp. 167–247. See also M. Zweig, "Darts, Anyone? As Market Pickers, Market Seers, the Pros Fall Short," *Barron's*, February 19, 1973, pp. 11–25.

[10] C. Welles, *op. cit.*

simple solution. Report one method, with sufficient footnote disclosure to permit adjustment to the other, and let the market interpret implications of the data for security prices.

Unfortunately, too much of the resources of the APB and others has been devoted to issues that warrant this straightforward resolution. For example, the investment credit controversy belongs in this category, as do the issues regarding the definition of extraordinary items, interperiod tax allocation, earnings per share computations involving convertible securities, and accounting for marketable equity securities. By contrast, the FASB should shift its resources to those controversies where there is nontrivial additional cost to the firms or to investors in order to obtain certain types of information (for example, replacement cost accounting for depreciable assets). Whether such information should be a required part of reporting standards is a substantive issue.

*Second.* The role of financial statement data is essentially a preemptive one— that is, to prevent abnormal returns accruing to individuals by trading upon inside information. This purpose leads to the following disclosure policy: If there are no additional costs to disclosure to the firm, there is prima facie evidence that the item in question ought to be disclosed.

This relatively simple policy could greatly enhance the usefulness of financial statements. Many forms of information are currently being generated internally by the firm and could be reported with essentially no additional cost (e.g., the current market value of marketable equity securities). Such information, if not publicly reported, may constitute inside information. Merely because prices reflect publicly available information in no way implies that they also fully reflect inside information. One information cost that investors may be incurring currently is abnormal returns earned by those who have monopolistic access to inside information. Opponents of greater disclosure bear the burden of proof of showing that individuals can be prevented from earning excess returns with the undisclosed information or that the cost of disclosure exceeds the excess returns. Given the private incentives to trade on inside information, such a condition is very difficult to ensure.

Incidentally, efficient securities markets also have some important implications regarding the accountants' growing concern over legal liability. Accountants can be held legitimately responsible for insufficient disclosure. However, they should not be held responsible for using a "wrong" method (e.g., flow-through v. deferral) as long as they disclose the method that was used and sufficient data to permit adjustment to the nonreported method.

*Third.* The FASB must reconsider the nature of its traditional concern for the naïve investor. If the investor, no matter how naïve, is in effect facing a fair game, can he still get harmed? If so, how? The naïve investor can still get harmed, but not in the ways traditionally thought. For example, the potential harm is not likely to occur because firms use flow-through v. deferral for accounting for the investment credit. Rather, the harm is more likely to occur because firms are following policies of less than full disclosure and insiders are potentially earning monopoly returns from access to inside information. Harm is also likely to occur when investors assume speculative positions with excessive transactions costs, improper diversification and improper risk levels in the erroneous belief that they will be able to "beat the market" with published accounting information.

This implies that the FASB should actively discourage investors' beliefs that accounting data can be used to detect overvalued or undervalued securities. This also implies that the FASB must not attempt to reduce the complex events of multimillion dollar corporations to the level of understanding of the naïve, or, perhaps more appropriately labeled, ignorant investor. We must stop acting as if all—or even most—individual investors are literally involved in the process of interpreting the impact of accounting information upon the security prices of firms.

An argument often advanced against fuller disclosure is that the increased disclosure will befuddle and confuse the naïve investor. A specific manifestation of this argument is that earnings under market value rules are more volatile and hence may lead to more volatile security prices. For example, the insurance industry currently opposes the inclusion of such information on marketable securities in the income statement, even though market values are already reported on the balance sheet. Given that market values on the balance sheet are already part of public information, it is absurd to think that there is going to be any further effect on security prices because of the income statement disclosure. Yet considerable resources of the APB, the insurance industry and others have been wasted on an attempt to resolve this issue. In the more general case where there is no reporting of market values, the efficient market evidence implies that the market is not reacting naïvely to the currently reported numbers but, rather, is forming "unbiased" assessments of the market values and their effects on prices. Since the market is currently being forced to assess the effects of market values indirectly, they are probably estimating the values with error. Hence, if anything, reporting the actual numbers may eliminate the estimation errors which may be one source of volatility in security prices.

Moreover, one message comes through loud and clear from finance theory. The investor is concerned with assessing risk as well as expected return. In this context, one role of financial statement data is to aid the investor in assessing the risk of the security. But presenting less volatile numbers, we may be doing him a disservice by obscuring the underlying riskiness of his investment. Hence, it is impossible to argue that less volatile numbers per se are better than more volatile numbers. Taken together with the evidence in the efficient market, this suggests that the market can decide for itself how it wishes to interpret a given piece of information. The same sort of reasoning should be applied to the currently hot topic of reporting and attesting to forecasts. In an efficient market, a paternalistic attitude is unwarranted; furthermore, operationally, if it is used to rationalize lesser disclosure, it is much more likely to result in the protection of management than in the protection of investors, which is its ostensible purpose.

*Fourth.* Accountants must stop acting as if they are the only suppliers of information about the firm. Instead, the FASB should strive to minimize the total cost of providing information to investors. In an efficient market, security prices may be essentially the same under a variety of financial accounting standards, because, if an item is not reported in the financial statements, it may be provided by alternative sources. Under this view, which is consistent with the evidence cited earlier, the market uses a broad information set, and the accountant is one—and only one— supplier of information. One objective is to provide the information to investors by the most economical means. In order to accomplish this objective, several questions must be addressed: What are the alternative sources of information to financial statements? What are the costs of providing a given piece of information via the alternative source vis-à-vis the financial statements? Most importantly, do financial statement data have a comparative advantage in providing any portion of the total information used by the market, and, if so, what portion?

The nature of the costs has already been alluded to. One set of costs is the "cost" of abnormal returns being earned by insiders because of monopolistic access to information. A second set of costs is excessive information costs. They can occur in two situations:

1. When the accountant fails to report an item that must be conveyed to the investing public through some other, more expensive source.

2. When the FASB requires firms to report an item that has a "value" less than its cost or items that could have been reported through other, less expensive sources of information. A third set of costs is incurred when investors erroneously believe that they can "beat the market" using published financial statement information. This set includes excessive transaction costs stemming from churning their accounts, improper diversification because of disproportionately large investment in "underpriced" securities and the selection of improper risk levels.[11]

## NATURE OF FUTURE RESEARCH

One of the objectives the FASB must face is the establishment of a research program. Several areas should be explored:

1. Although the evidence in favor of market efficiency with respect to published information is considerable, the issue is by no means closed and further work on the particular types of accounting information items is needed.

2. Much more research is needed regarding market efficiency with respect to inside information. Such research will help to specify what the costs of nondisclosure are.

3. Evidence is needed on how individual investors, as opposed to the aggregate prices, react to information. Specifically, what is the process or mechanism by which information reaches individuals and is subsequently impounded in prices? What evidence is there of excessive transactions costs' being incurred by investors who act on information that already has been impounded in prices? Research into volume activity, as opposed to price activity, may be particularly insightful here. What evidence is there that individuals incur improper selection of risk levels by taking speculative positions based on

[11] The costs of holding erroneous beliefs regarding market efficiency extend beyond investors. For example, consider the recent decision by Chrysler to change inventory methods because of alleged inefficiencies in the capital markets (both debt and equity markets). Even though Chrysler had reported supplemental statements in its previous annual reports, this was judged to be inadequate to overcome the inability of the capital market to look behind the reported numbers. The initial effect of a switch in inventory methods for both book and tax purposes was an incremental tax bill of approximately $50 million spread over a 20-year period. The efficient market evidence suggests that such a decision was a serious misallocation of resources. In fact, if anything, Chrysler is in worse economic position now because it is paying higher tax bills. For a summary of facts, see "Chrysler Posts $7.6 Million Loss for the Year," *The Wall Street Journal*, February 10, 1971.

accounting data? There are currently research methods available in finance that can provide at least a partial answer to these questions. The application of behavioral science also offers promise here.

4.  More research is needed regarding the association between certain specific financial statement items and security prices. For example, are there certain items that are now being reported which do not seem to be used by the market as reflected in security prices? Conversely, are there certain types of information which are not currently reported but, in spite of that fact, are reflected in security prices? In the former instance, such items are candidates for being considered for possible exclusion from currently reported items. With respect to the latter, such items are candidates for being considered part of currently reported items.

5.  Further research is needed to examine to what extent financial statement data are helpful to individual investors assessing the risk of a security. In an efficient market, the usefulness of financial statement data to individual investors is not to find mispriced securities, since they are nonexistent. What then is the value, if any? The value lies in the ability of financial statement data to aid in risk prediction. Some recent findings in the area by Beaver, Kettler and Scholes are encouraging, but much more research is needed.[12]

## ERRONEOUS INTERPRETATIONS

The implications of market efficiency for accounting are frequently misunderstood. There are at least two common misinterpretations.

The first belief is that, in an efficient market world, there are no reporting issues of substance because of the "all-knowing" efficient market. Taken to its extreme, this error takes the form of asserting that accounting data have no value and hence the certification process is of no value.[13] The efficient market in no way leads to such implications. It may very well be that the publishing of financial statements data is precisely what makes the market as efficient as it is. As I was careful to point out earlier, merely because the market is efficient with respect to published data does not imply that market prices are also efficient with respect to nonpublished information. Disclosure is a substantive issue.

---

[12] W. Beaver, R. Kettler and M. Scholes, "The Association Between Market Determined and Accounting Determined Risk Measures," *The Accounting Review*, October 1970, pp. 654–82.

[13] In this regard it is imperative to distinguish between two important aspects of information: (1) The first is to aid the market in arriving at a given set of security prices. One aspect of this role is to provide a market where the investors are playing a fair game with respect to some given information set (e.g., accounting data). (2) The second is to aid individual investors, who face a given set of prices, to select the optimal portfolio. One aspect of this role is the use of financial statement data in risk prediction. It is entirely possible that future research will discover that financial statement data have no role to play at the individual investor level and that the sole role is a social one. In any event, the social level is of paramount concern to a policy-making body such as the FASB. The distinction is made particularly clear in E. Fama and A. Laffer, "Information and Capital Markets," *Journal of Business*, July 1971, pp. 289–98; and J. Hirshleifer, "The Private and Social Value of Information and the Reward to Inventive Activity," *American Economic Review*, September 1971, pp. 561–74; see also, W. Beaver, *op. cit.*, pp. 424–25.

A second erroneous implication is simply to find out what method is most highly associated with security prices and report that method in the financial statements. As it stands, it is incorrect for several reasons. One major reason is that such a simplified decision rule fails to consider the costs of providing information. For example, a nonreported method may be less associated with security prices than the reported method because the cost of obtaining the nonreported numbers via alternative sources is too high. Yet such information may be provided via financial statements at substantially lower costs. In another context, suppose the nonreported method showed the higher association with security prices; does it follow that the nonreported method should be reported? No, not necessarily. Perhaps the market is obtaining the information at lower cost via the alternative sources.[14]

Moreover, the choice among different accounting methods involves choosing among differing consequences, as reflected in the incidence of costs and security prices which affect individuals differently. Hence, some individuals may be better off under one method, while others may be better off under an alternative method. In this situation, how is the optimal method to be selected? The issue is one of social choice, which in general is an unresolvable problem because of the difficulty (impossibility) of making interpersonal welfare comparisons.[15]

There are certain specific issues (e.g., similar to those discussed in this article) which closely suggest a policy decision, if one is willing to accept the mild ethical assumption of Pareto-optimality.[16] However, such situations must meet a fairly specific set of conditions.

Regardless of the final resolution by the policymaker, it is still possible to specify the types of evidence that are relevant to choosing among alternatives. In simplest terms, although evidence cannot indicate what choice to make, it can provide information on the potential consequences of the various choices. Without a knowledge of consequences (e.g., as reflected in security prices), it is inconceivable that a policy-making body such as the FASB will be able to select optimal financial accounting standards. In spite of the importance of a knowledge of consequences, currently too little is known about price behavior and virtually nothing is known about the magnitude of the three types of costs outlined earlier.

## CONCLUSION

Financial statement information is inherently a social commodity. However, it is clear that decisions regarding its generation and dissemination are of a much different nature than we have traditionally thought them to be. This change in the way we view the FASB is conditioned upon the assumption of market efficiency. While there is need for further research in this area, there is sufficient credibility in

---

[14] These issues are discussed at greater length in R. May and G. Sundem, "Cost of Information and Security Prices: Market Association Tests for Accounting Policy Decision," *The Accounting Review*, January 1973, pp. 80–94.

[15] K. Arrow, *Social Choice and Individual Values* (Yale University Press, 1968). The issue has been discussed in an accounting context in J. Demski, "Choice Among Financial Accounting Alternatives" (unpublished, Stanford University, 1972).

[16] The concept of Pareto-optimality states that a society prefers one alternative to another, if at least some people are better off and no one is worse off.

the evidence to date that we should be prepared to face its implications:

1. Many reporting issues are capable of a simple disclosure solution and do not warrant an expenditure of FASB time and resources in attempting to resolve them.
2. The role of accounting data is to prevent superior returns' accruing from inside information and can be achieved by a policy of much fuller disclosure than is currently required.
3. Financial statements should not be reduced to the level of understanding of the naïve investor.
4. The FASB should strive for policies that will eliminate excessive costs of information.
5. The FASB should sponsor a full-scale research program in the areas indicated, so that it may have some evidence of the consequences of their choices among different sets of financial accounting standards.

# I-C 2 *Efficient Market Theory: Its Impact on Accounting*

ARTHUR R. WYATT

As a practitioner who tries to keep up with the musings of accounting academicians (with only limited success), I have found that the efficient market hypothesis (EMH) can be both tantalizing and frustrating. It is fascinating because, if its validity becomes better established and more widely acknowledged, accounting standard setters will have to take notice. EMH is frustrating, however, because few accountants in practice are aware of the concept and a lot fewer understand it.

Even though EMH has had significant exposure in the accounting literature and elsewhere, practitioners and businessmen seem largely uninformed about its basic tenets. Nevertheless, many current considerations in accounting standard setting have relationships to the efficiency of market behavior—the Financial Accounting Standards Board's focus on economic consequences and cost-benefit concerns, the American Institute of CPAs' ongoing concern about accounting standards overload and the historical thrust of standard setters to "narrow the range of accounting alternatives." This article should provide some insight, from a practitioner's perspective, on the promise and frustrations of EMH.

After providing a brief description of EMH, the article considers three practice-oriented aspects of EMH. First is a description of some transactions that appear to deny the propriety of EMH in some respects. This discussion suggests the following question: If EMH is valid, why do profit-motivated businessmen frequently enter into forms of transactions that aren't very profitable (when compared with alternatives) solely or primarily because those forms will produce financial statement results they believe will make their companies look better? Second are some observations on the ramifications of EMH for financial accounting standard setters. Finally, observations are made on some of the troubling aspects of the research on EMH to date and possible avenues for additional research.

One caveat is necessary at the outset, however. Because I have done no substantive research on EMH, I am somewhat skeptical about EMH, even in the face of the significant research results that have been reported in this area in the last 10 or

15 years. I am not skeptical about this research to date, but I am somewhat skeptical about researchers' speculations about and views on the ramifications of EMH drawn from reported research results. This skepticism reflects, no doubt, the fact that I deal far more with nonbelievers in EMH than with believers. But it also results from my awareness of business activities that seem to deny the validity of EMH. Researchers may look down on my evidence as being merely anecdotal in nature. However, much accounting research is merely an aggregation of anecdotes crammed into mathematical formulas to produce results that have apparent statistical measurability. As long as an anecdote has a factual basis, it most likely reflects the real world and, therefore, shouldn't be rejected by researchers.

## WHAT IS EMH?

My understanding of EMH is that this theory holds that capital markets are efficient in the sense that they process information instantaneously and that prices fully reflect all available information. Stated differently, one can't systematically beat or fool the market using only publicly available information. I also recognize that EMH doesn't carry any inference that accountants, managers or others need to believe that the market is efficient, nor do their actions need to be consistent with the notion of market efficiency. EMH holds that, regardless of the beliefs of or actions taken by those who make transactions, the securities market will process the publicly available information in such a manner that security prices will fully reflect that information.

Now to some observations that frustrate one who appreciates the rigor of the EMH research to date but who is puzzled by the contrary real world evidence.

## TRANSACTIONS THAT DISPUTE THE VALIDITY OF EMH

As the first example of transactions that appear to deny the validity of EMH, let's consider the problem arising in the Lifo area. We have here a threshold question: Why haven't a substantial number of companies in the U.S. adopted Lifo? The answer frequently given is that the income tax conformity rules in the Lifo area place those companies reporting on Lifo in a disadvantageous financial statement income position compared with the position they would be in on a Fifo basis and that the cash savings arising from adopting Lifo for tax purposes are inadequate to offset the perceived financial statement disadvantages.

Within the last year the Internal Revenue Service has significantly relaxed its conformity requirements. It is now acceptable to have book-tax differences within certain constraints. Certain possible differences between book and tax haven't yet been accepted by the IRS, however; this means that if the given procedure is acceptable to the IRS it also has to be followed for financial statement purposes until such time as the conformity requirements are relaxed further.

To illustrate, let's assume that a company has been on Lifo for several years and has at this date the same inventory amount for both financial statements and the income tax return. In the current year the company adds several new items to inventory. The tax law permits new items to be priced in the dollar value Lifo inventory pool either at current costs or at reconstructed base-year costs. Let's assume that under the current cost approach the new items would result in a Lifo increment of $12 million; under a reconstructed base-year cost approach the new items would result in a Lifo increment of $8 million. Thus, the current cost approach results in a higher inventory and a higher pretax book income of $4 million. Either of these approaches is acceptable insofar as the IRS is concerned, but the service hasn't yet approved a book-tax nonconformity status for this aspect of Lifo pricing. The issue facing management is which approach to adopt.

From the income tax perspective, the issue is clear. Management should adopt the reconstructed base-year cost approach since it results in $4 million less pretax income and approximately $2 million less income tax to pay. In effect, the company would be legitimately permitted to borrow the $2 million from the government, without interest, until such time as a Lifo layer liquidation occurred or the inventory was otherwise disposed of.

From a financial statement perspective, the issue is also clear. Management would elect to use the current cost approach since it results in $4 million more pretax income than would result under the reconstructed base-year approach. After providing income taxes, the company would report $2 million additional net income as compared with that under the alternative approach.

If the book-tax conformity rules had been relaxed in this area, management could elect to follow the reconstructed base-year cost approach for the tax return and the current cost approach for the financial statements. However, the IRS hasn't yet approved book-tax nonconformity for the pricing of new items.

What does the company decide to do? Most frequently, companies decide to adopt the current cost approach for both book and tax purposes. In effect, management makes the decision to pay $2 million more in taxes in the current year to get $2 million more in reported income than if it followed the alternative approach. Such a conclusion seems to be both uneconomic and either a denial of EMH (i.e., managements believe the market will give them credit for the additional income reported) or evidence of a lack of understanding of the concepts involved.

Probing further, we find that many managements are told by investment bankers that the stock market benefit that a company gets from being on Lifo is obtained simply from the disclosure that the company is on Lifo. The investment bankers seem to indicate that analysts aren't sophisticated enough to determine whether the Lifo methods the company uses are those that provide the optimum tax savings available to them under the law or whether the procedures adopted provide only a portion of the advantages available under the law. The investment bankers tell managements that the market will believe that the new $2 million reported increment in earnings, if the current cost method is adopted, is part of real earnings from operations and that the company will get credit both for this increased earnings level as well as credit for having reported as a Lifo company.

If the management involved was a believer in EMH, it seems clear that it would adopt the reconstructed base-year cost and obtain the maximum tax savings available. It would be unconcerned about, or indifferent to, the fact that adoption of such an approach would produce $2 million less reported earnings than adoption of an available alternative. As long as management-disclosed information about the method of Lifo calculation followed, EMH would hypothesize that the market wouldn't give the company reporting the $2 million additional earnings a benefit for that increment because it was solely the result of an accounting election and not the result of an economic event.

Off-balance-sheet financing is a second example of a transaction form that seems to deny EMH. Here the threshold question is, Why do so many U.S. companies enter into expensive financing arrangements when less expensive financing is available?

One effect of the accelerating inflation in the U.S. over the past several years has been a deterioration in the traditional debt-to-equity relationships for many companies. The cost of new and replacement assets has risen rapidly; the stock market has been weak and an expensive means of raising capital; and debt borrowing has been much more widely used, resulting in higher debt levels. Since in times of rising prices historical cost accounting fails to recognize the increased values of inventory and property (and this value differential for inventory can be substantial when a company has been on Lifo for many years), the shareholders' equity of most companies is substantially understated in terms of economic values. With borrowing levels up and shareholders' equity understated, the debt-to-equity ratio appears to be very weak for many companies. One might even postulate that the debt-to-equity ratio appears weak in many instances when in fact it isn't.

As debt-to-equity ratios deteriorate, the credit ratings of companies' debt instruments become downgraded. Thus, management faces severe pressures in its decisions on how to finance plant expansion and replacement. Raising equity capital is too costly. Continuing to go to the debt markets becomes increasingly costly as the debt-to-equity ratio deteriorates in a progressive fashion.

One way to resolve this dilemma is to try to find a way to finance plant acquisitions and replacements so that a liability won't have to be recognized. Many such vehicles exist. What has evolved, in fact, is an accounting device to try to compensate for the substantial underevaluation of assets under the historical cost method. Since the accounting profession has been unwilling to move toward a current value approach for its accounting model, the business community has found a way for companies to borrow and not present the debt in the balance sheet. Thus, we have achieved a measure of compensation for the defects of historical cost accounting. The undervalued assets are offset by understated liabilities. Whether this phenomenon enhances or diminishes the credibility of audited financial statements is a matter of opinion.

Let's consider as a specific example the leasing of airplanes. For example, Boheed may sell a plane to Village Bank, which arranges for some nonrecourse debt financing for a portion of the purchase price and invests its own equity funds in the balance of the purchase price. Village Bank then leases the aircraft to Trans American Airlines. The lease terms look very favorable. Trans American will pay rentals that involve an aftertax financing cost of, say, 5 percent. This relatively favorable rate arises because the lessor, Village Bank, obtains the tax benefits associated with owning the aircraft—the investment tax credit and the timing benefits of accelerated depreciation. The lease also provides that Trans American has a fair market value purchase option at the expiration of the lease, say, 14 years hence. A more favorable purchase option might require the lessee to capitalize the lease under the rules set forth in FASB Statement no. 13, *Accounting for Leases*.[1]

Let's assume further that Trans American uses the plane for the full lease term of 14 years and, when that term expires, it still needs the plane. The plane is in remarkably good shape because aircraft maintenance is regular and recurring, and, in fact,

---

[1] Financial Accounting Standards Board Statement no. 13, *Accounting for Leases* (Stamford: FASB, 1976).

at the end of 14 years few if any component parts of the original aircraft are still part of the plane that is flying. As the lease expiration date approaches, Trans American finds that the fair market value of the 14-year-old aircraft is just about equal to the original price paid by Village Bank to Boheed. Thus, if Trans American decides to exercise its purchase option, it will need to pay Village Bank an amount equal to the original price for the plane.

What has Trans American accomplished through the lease vehicle? First, it kept the plane off its balance sheet for 14 years and also kept the related financing obligation off the balance sheet. As a cost of doing this, it has, in fact, paid for the airplane twice, although the original purchase price was financed on a relatively favorable basis. The question is, Is the market fooled by the lease financing vehicle, the off-balance-sheet-financing approach? Apparently the management of Trans American thought it was and may even continue to think so. I leave to speculation one of the reasons that some believe many U.S. airlines are currently facing earnings problems.

To generalize, leasing or other forms of off-balance-sheet financing are more costly than traditional means of financing. That doesn't mean, of course, that the additional cost isn't compensated either fully or in part by other perceived benefits. But the fees paid to investment bankers, lawyers and accountants are always higher for nontraditional financing forms than they are for traditional financing forms. Frequently, the market extracts a higher interest rate for a nontraditional financing vehicle. Maybe it is only one thirty-second or one-sixteenth or one-eighth of a point, but on big amounts over a long period of time such differentials can be costly. Finally, the purchase option price needs to be negotiated at a much higher level than the lessee often would prefer if the lessee is to be successful in keeping the financing off the balance sheet.

Assuming that off-balance-sheet financing methods are disclosed adequately, and in general the adequacy of disclosures hasn't been seriously questioned, why is it that these methods of financing have grown so much in recent years? Wouldn't EMH clearly demonstrate that, whether the obligation incurred is placed within the body of the balance sheet or in the footnotes, the market price of the company shares will be unaffected? Why is it that the credit-rating agencies appear to be ignorant of or nonbelievers in EMH?

The FASB published a research report entitled *The Economic Effects on Lessees of FASB Statement No. 13, Accounting for Leases.*[2] That research found that a majority of the companies surveyed were structuring the terms of new lease contracts to avoid capitalization. The results also showed an apparent conflict between what some bankers and financial analysts said they did and what they actually might have done. For example, the majority answered that they didn't downgrade their evaluations of companies that capitalize leases. But when asked to evaluate financial statements of companies that differed only in their method of accounting for leases, more than 40 percent of the bankers and analysts considered the noncapitalizing entity more profitable. That research report seems to me to contain food for thought for EMH advocates.

As a third example that disputes the validity of EMH, let's consider the area of business combinations. Here the threshold question is, Why do U.S. companies labor

---

[2] A. Rashad Abdel-khalik, *The Economic Effects on Lessees of FASB Statement No. 13, Accounting for Leases* (Stamford: FASB, 1981).

so hard to achieve satisfaction with the pooling-of-interests accounting rules when EMH suggests that the marketplace won't be fooled by whether the transaction is recorded by the purchase method or by the pooling-of-interests method?

Business combinations continue to be common, and significant efforts are expended to meet the 12 pooling criteria of Accounting Principles Board Opinion no. 16, *Business Combinations*.[3] In one recent, relatively modest combination proposal of $300 million in value, several problems arose. If the transaction was accounted for as a purchase, the excess cost over book value would be about $120 million, or about $.04 a share on a 40-year amortization basis or $.10 a share if the excess was allocated to the assets. The buyer had reported $1.40 in earnings in the prior year.

In this case the buyer incurred significant legal, accounting and investment banker fees in negotiating a transaction, restructuring it and so on to meet the pooling requirements. The buyer contended the deal wouldn't be made if it had to be accounted for by the purchase method. The buyer asserted that his earnings couldn't stand the dilution, that the marketplace would knock down the market value of his securities to an unacceptable degree. In addition to the above costs, meetings were held with the Securities and Exchange Commission staff, and these meetings don't take place without some incurred cost.

Ultimately, the transaction was abandoned. No way could be found to overcome the pooling rule defects and achieve agreement between the buyer and the seller. An analysis led to the conclusion that the transaction appeared to make economic sense and that abandonment of it was in no way a reflection of economic unsoundness. This result isn't atypical. If EMH is valid, why do businessmen continue to act as if it isn't?

Some have hypothesized that decision makers in business have compensation arrangements that are primarily tied to short-term earnings reports and that for this reason decisions are made that may appear to be irrational in the long run but are rational when evaluated from the perspective of the compensation arrangements of those in the decision-making role. Admittedly, this can be a factor. However, many compensation arrangements of managements are fixed or relatively fixed, and I have seen no particular correlation between the types of compensation arrangements that managements have and the structuring of transactions to meet particular accounting objectives. While that hypothesis may have validity, additional research is needed before such validity can be established.

Before moving on to some of the ramifications of EMH for the financial accounting standard setters, let's consider the recent FASB project on foreign currency translation. Under FASB Statement no. 8, *Accounting for the Translation of Foreign Currency Transactions and Foreign Currency Financial Statements*,[4] a company has reported a noncash loss or gain in its income statement. This loss or gain has increased the variability of reported earnings, but disclosures have generally been good, so that one who analyzes the financial statements is able to determine the portion of reported earnings that is attributable to the foreign currency translation loss or gain. Presumably, EMH would hold that the effects of applying Statement no. 8 would be trivial on stock market prices because the disclosures are sufficient to permit adjustments to various alternatives.

---

[3] Accounting Principles Board Opinion no. 16, *Business Combinations* (New York: AICPA, 1970).
[4] FASB Statement no. 8, *Accounting for the Translation of Foreign Currency Transactions and Foreign Currency Financial Statements* (Stamford: FASB, 1975).

Even so, the evidence is substantial that many managers altered their foreign cash management and hedging operations to hedge "accounting risks" and not only to hedge the economic risks hedged before the adoption of Statement no. 8. Many managements ended up with new policies that reduced accounting risks and, at the same time, may have reduced economic risks. If, in fact, the stock market is efficient, i.e., isn't fooled by the difference in reported accounting results from adoption of a new hedging policy, the stock market price would remain unaffected. But if the new hedging policy does, in fact, mitigate economic risks as well, and if the stock price remains unchanged, is the market for that stock really efficient?

## EMH AND THE STANDARD-SETTING PROCESS

Many commentators on EMH have concluded that EMH supports dispensing with accounting standard setting; that all the effort expended to date by the APB and the FASB has been principally a waste because, regardless of the conclusions reached, the market would adjust; and that disclosure was the factor of overriding significance in the accounting process. Such comments are obviously disturbing for accounting standard setters and those interested in the day-to-day processes of reaching accounting judgments on emerging transactions.

Even those who accept EMH, however, should recognize that management decisions appear to be affected by accounting rules and by management's perception of how a transaction form will affect reported earnings. Under these circumstances, a better observation may be that EMH supports and enhances the importance of an accounting standard-setting process based on soundly conceived standards as compared with one based on politically compromised standards.

The following hypothesis seems to have some merit: If financial statements are to be issued, the information should be as relevant, as reliable and as representationally faithful as possible. For example, if a balance sheet is to be presented and is to include the liabilities of the entity, this hypothesis would hold that all the liabilities should be reported in the balance sheet. Under this notion, the argument that disclosure of any omitted liabilities will cure any defect from the omission of a liability in the body of the balance sheet is without merit. Either the balance sheet should report all liabilities or financial statements should be dispensed with completely and financial reporting should be limited to narrative disclosures.

At this stage of accounting evolution I am unpersuaded that financial statements are an unnecessary and uneconomic business phenomenon. Thus, my observation is that neither discontinuance of the current standard-setting process nor total reliance on disclosure for financial reporting is an appealing alternative. Periodic reporting in a systematized manner does serve a purpose in our society. It permits an evaluation of the credibility of periodic news release data. It permits entity-to-entity comparisons. It permits comparisons with expectations and evaluations of forecasts and of management forthrightness. It provides a basis for assessing management performance.

It seems to me that an alternative view of those who are believers in EMH, therefore, could well be that accounting standard setting is of even greater significance if the hypothesis is valid, and it should rest far more heavily than in the past on a conceptual framework. The objective should be to develop a conceptually tight system subject to as few political or economic pressures as possible.

To me, the evidence is overwhelming that accounting alternatives do affect managements' business decisions. So, even if the stock market isn't fooled, accounting standards development may still be of substantial importance to the efficient functioning of our economy. If EMH is valid, it seems that the case for standard setting based on a conceptual framework is at least as valid as the case for abandoning the standard-setting effort. Likewise, it seems that the case for standards that have been heavily influenced by economic consequences is lessened. If the hypothesis isn't valid, the case for a conceptual framework foundation is still strong, but the case for the influence of economic consequences is relatively greater.

## SOME THOUGHTS ON FUTURE RESEARCH

Finally, I'd like to put forth some thoughts, naive though they may be, about future research in this area. While I am tempted to say that to date far more research has been done in this area than any real world influence can justify, I will resist drawing such a conclusion.

My anecdotes have tried to establish the proposition that managers do act as if the market weren't efficient. Isn't more research needed into factors affecting manager behavior? If managers' reactions to proposed accounting changes lead to fundamental changes in entity decisions, and if the market price doesn't react to those decisions, is the market really efficient?

My anecdotal evidence seems to support a hypothesis that managers who make decisions don't act as if they understand or accept EMH. Since they are the structurers of transactions, and they act as if EMH doesn't exist, dilemmas are created. Is the market really efficient or does the research supporting it have fundamental defects that haven't been recognized to date? If the market is really efficient, what can be done to better educate managers about the ramifications of the hypothesis? If, in fact, one hypothesizes that managers act as they do because of current profit incentives, why is it that managers may engage in transactions that cost more than they are worth in the short run?

Finally, I note that some researchers in the area have questioned prior research on the basis that the necessary constraints imposed may introduce an artificiality that is difficult to measure and identify. Those with real expertise in research in the EMH area may need to reconsider approaches taken in the past to determine if the research designs have been defective.

## IS THE REAL WORLD IGNORING EMH?

In summary, while EMH research to date appears to provide substantial support for the hypothesis, it seems equally clear that the real world of accounting either ignores or disputes the validity of the hypothesis and thus of the research. Some may believe that my criticisms are inappropriate because my perception of EMH appears far more encompassing than the proponents of the hypothesis contend. However, I do recognize that proponents of EMH have taken great pains to emphasize the narrow constraints of the hypothesis—that it pertains only to efficiency in the processing of information and reflection of this information in security prices.

Of far greater consequence, it would appear, is the efficient functioning of the economy—the avoidance of transactions that lack economic rationality even though they produce favorable accounting results. Can EMH provide a basis for evaluating motivations for seemingly economically unsound transactions? Does the hypothesis contain the seeds of ideas that could provide new stimulus to the accounting standard-setting process?

Those believers who have asserted that the role of standard setters should be less important than it was in the past—and that standard setters should act only when absolutely necessary—really seem to presume that the current state of accounting standards is optimal. If accounting alternatives exist and if a Gresham's law[5] of accounting standards prevails, doesn't EMH suggest that action is needed to eliminate those alternatives that lead to less sound economic decisions? Isn't it possible that there is a close tie between EMH and the thrust of standard setting which is oriented toward the elimination of accounting alternatives and reliance on a sound conceptual framework?

Those are heavy questions, but, for those of us in the real world, research that would lead to answers to some of these questions would, at a minimum, reduce frustrations and improve the efficiency of those who market accounting hypotheses.

[5] An observation in economics that, when two coins are equal in debt-paying value but unequal in intrinsic value, the one having the lesser intrinsic value tends to remain in circulation and the other to be hoarded or exported as bullion.

# I-C 3 *EMH, CMR and the Accounting Profession*

JAMES W. DEITRICK AND WALTER T. HARRISON, JR.

Accountants should be aware of the efficient market hypothesis (EMH) because it has important implications for accounting practice. This article, therefore, identifies EMH-related issues of concern to accountants and brings to light the practical importance of EMH research.

First, some background information about EMH may be needed. The term *efficient market* may be interpreted in different ways. To some, it may mean a market in which resources are allocated to the most efficient entities. This is "allocational efficiency." However, in EMH parlance, the term *efficient* refers to the way information is reflected in security prices and the term *market* refers to the market for securities (e.g., the New York Stock Exchange or the over-the-counter stock market).

In an efficient market, security prices behave as if they fully incorporate all existing information quickly and without bias. This implies that information, old and new, has been impounded into security prices as a result of the analysis and collective wisdom of investors and their advisers. In this context, the term *efficiency* pertains to the securities market as a whole. Efficiency doesn't suggest that every, or any, investor has knowledge of all information. It doesn't mean that all information has been properly presented by a company or correctly interpreted by individual decision makers. Nor does it imply that managers make optimal management decisions. Rather, market efficiency in the context of EMH simply means that security prices reflect the aggregate impact of relevant information in an unbiased way and that the adjustment to new information is very rapid.

To accommodate different types of information, EMH has been described in three forms, as follows:
- The "weak form" of market efficiency implies that a security's price at a particular time fully reflects the information contained in its sequence of past prices.
- The "semistrong form" asserts that a security's price fully reflects all publicly available information.
- The "strong form" suggests that a security's price fully reflects all information including information that isn't publicly available, for example, inside information.

Of the three, the semistrong form is of most direct interest to the accounting

James W. Deitrick and Walter T. Harrison, Jr., "EMH, CMR and the Accounting Profession," *Journal of Accountancy*, February 1984, pp. 82–94. Copyright © 1984 by the American Institute of Certified Public Accountants, Inc. Opinions expressed in the *Journal of Accountancy* are those of editors and contributors. Publication in the *Journal of Accountancy* does not constitute endorsement by the AICPA or its committees.

profession because accountants produce financial statement information that is disclosed publicly.

Numerous studies support the weak and the semistrong forms of EMH. This means that publicly available information alone can't be used to select securities that will yield abnormal returns on average and over long periods of time.[1] This doesn't mean that investors can't earn above-normal rates of return. Over any particular period, some investors will earn abnormal returns by chance, others may correctly identify mispriced securities[2] and some may benefit from inside information. On the other hand, the research evidence shows that the strong form of EMH doesn't hold. Inside information isn't quickly impounded into security prices and, therefore, can be used to develop trading strategies that will yield abnormal returns.

The vast majority of EMH research has been based on the prices of common stocks, as opposed to the prices of preferred stocks, bonds, bank loans or privately placed debt. Therefore, our references to market efficiency are limited to the market for common stocks.

Given that information is quickly impounded into stock prices, it is empirically possible to examine the change in a company's stock price within a "window period" surrounding public release of new information. A window period generally ranges from a date briefly before the release of new information to a date when the company's stock price is believed to fully reflect the new information. Such an investigation reveals what effect, if any, the information had on the stock price. This kind of analysis is called capital market research (CMR).[3]

While EMH describes the pricing mechanism of the securities markets, CMR builds on the EMH foundation to examine actual market responses to various kinds of information. It is natural for companies and their accountants to be curious about how the stock market is likely to react to new disclosures. For example, companies frequently consider how a particular news item will affect their stock prices and whether certain disclosures are likely to confuse investors. Many of these concerns are now susceptible to empirical investigation via CMR. Since the late 1960s, CMR studies have examined stock price reaction to a variety of events and disclosures, including annual and quarterly earnings announcements, changes in dividends, forecasted earnings, accounting changes, business combinations, "subject-to" audit opinions and accounting for leases, among many others.

This research, which is based on actual stock price data, has provided some well-established conclusions. Perhaps the most conclusive finding is the importance of accounting income to investors. Numerous studies have found stronger correlations between stock price movements and accounting income than between stock price

---

[1] A stock or portfolio of stocks is said to have an abnormal stock return if its actual return (i.e., stock price appreciation plus dividends) during a given time period differs from its expected risk-adjusted return.

[2] It is possible to have mispriced securities in an efficient market. For example, the price of a security may not reflect its "true" underlying value because of several possible factors, including the widespread dissemination of false or misleading information about the company (e.g., Equity Funding). Market efficiency doesn't mean that the market is clairvoyant.

[3] Capital market research is based on the premise that security returns are made up of two informational components, one incorporating systematic information about the market as a whole (e.g., news about general political developments and economywide events) and another incorporating company-specific information. By eliminating from a company's stock return the influence of marketwide information, it is possible to focus on the effect of company-specific information.

movements and cash flow. This finding is an important validation of accrual accounting. On the surface, this finding might appear surprising because of analysts' widespread interest in cash flow data and the Financial Accounting Standards Board's belief that financial reporting should help decision makers assess "the amounts, timing, and uncertainty of prospective cash receipts...."[4] However, the FASB also believes that accrual accounting is superior to cash flow accounting as a means of reflecting a company's future cash flow generating ability.

Another interesting finding is that the stock market seems to price securities on the basis of economic reality rather than on cosmetic accounting appearances. This means that two companies that are identical in every way would have the same stock price even though they are using different accounting methods unless their accounting results affect their cash flows. Consequently, although accounting income is important, the CMR evidence suggests that the market does not naively or mechanistically establish prices from accounting income without first examining the company's underlying economic position.

EMH and CMR have brought rigorous, systematic empirical research to important accounting issues. Therefore, accountants can look to CMR for objective evidence that has been developed across many companies and over lengthy time periods. However, EMH and CMR say nothing about the desirability of particular accounting standards or procedures. Because accounting has an impact beyond security prices, accounting policy decisions involve issues of social choice and, to be politically viable, must consider the perspectives of all interested parties.

## CMR STUDIES COMMISSIONED BY THE FASB AND THE SEC

The FASB and the Securities and Exchange Commission have commissioned CMR studies to answer practical, real-world questions. To illustrate, companies that were forced to capitalize their leases to comply with FASB Statement no. 13, *Accounting for Leases*,[5] argued that capitalization would result in dire consequences, including downward pressure on their stock prices. To investigate this assertion, the FASB commissioned a CMR study.[6] The FASB also has commissioned studies of the stock price effects of its Statement no. 8, *Accounting for the Translation of Foreign Currency Transactions and Foreign Currency Financial Statements*;[7] Statement no. 33, *Financial Reporting and Changing Prices*;[8] and Statement no. 19, *Financial Account-*

---

[4] Financial Accounting Standards Board Concepts Statement no. 1, *Objectives of Financial Reporting by Business Enterprises* (Stamford: FASB, 1978), par. 37.

[5] FASB Statement no. 13, *Accounting for Leases* (Stamford: FASB, 1976).

[6] FASB Research Report, *The Economic Effects on Lessees of FASB Statement No. 13, Accounting for Leases* (Stamford: FASB, 1981).

[7] FASB Statement no. 8, *Accounting for the Translation of Foreign Currency Transactions and Foreign Currency Financial Statements* (Stamford: FASB, 1975). FASB Research Report, *An Empirical Investigation of the Effects of Statement of Financial Accounting Standards No. 8 on Security Return Behavior* (Stamford: FASB, 1981).

[8] FASB Statement no. 33, *Financial Reporting and Changing Prices* (Stamford: FASB, 1979). W. H. Beaver and W. R. Landsman, "The Incremental Information Content of FAS 33 Disclosures" (Working paper, Stanford University, December 1982); and J. W. Bartley and C. M. Boardman, "The Use of SFAS 33 Data to Identify Investment and Takeover Targets" (Working paper, University of Utah, February 1983).

*ing and Reporting by Oil and Gas Producing Companies.*[9] In addition, the SEC commissioned its own study of the stock price effect of FASB Statement no. 19.[10] In these instances the FASB and the SEC presumably identified stock price effects as an important economic consequence of their accounting standards.

Developments in the U.S. during the 1970s, such as the foreign payments scandal, the oil embargo, double-digit inflation and congressional hearings have brought accounting issues before the public as never before. As economic phenomena have become more complex, accounting has grown in importance and lobbying efforts by persons affected by accounting standards have intensified. Thus, it appears that the economic consequences of accounting standards have become a permanent fixture of the standard-setting arena. And CMR is a generally accepted means of measuring economic consequences.

## IS EMH VALID?

In the February 1983 *Journal*, an article on EMH by Arthur R. Wyatt was published.[11] Because we regard Wyatt's article as an articulate statement of practitioners' views on EMH, we believe it provides an excellent basis for continuing the dialogue between academicians and practitioners about this important but apparently misunderstood concept. In his article, Wyatt cited four incidents in which companies engaged in seemingly uneconomical transactions that "appear to deny the validity of the EMH."[12] They involve a company's preference for (1) the use of current cost for new items added to its Lifo pool, (2) expensive off-balance-sheet financing, (3) pooling-of-interests accounting and (4) hedging transactions to reduce its exposure to volatile foreign currency exchange rates. Wyatt asserted that these events are frustrating because the real-world evidence seems to be in conflict with the rigor of EMH. We plan to show that these examples do not indicate a conflict between real-world evidence and EMH and that they have no implications for the validity of the hypothesis.

*Lifo example.* Wyatt's first example concerns the election by companies using Lifo to value new layers of inventory at their current cost rather than at a lower reconstructed cost, which is permitted by the Internal Revenue Service. Wyatt argues that this uneconomical decision, which produces unnecessarily high tax payments, is either a denial of EMH or evidence that management doesn't understand EMH. He reasons that if management believed in EMH, it would adopt the reconstructed base-year cost to obtain the related tax savings.

This example doesn't deny the validity of EMH for two reasons. First, the stock market is either efficient or inefficient; what management believes about EMH is irrelevant. An analogy is the pre-Copernican belief that the earth was the center of the universe. The sun was, of course, the center of the universe regardless of what

---

[9] FASB Statement no. 19, *Financial Accounting and Reporting by Oil and Gas Producing Companies* (Stamford: FASB, 1977). T. R. Dyckman and A. J. Smith, "Financial Accounting and Reporting by Oil and Gas Producing Companies: A Study of Information Effects," *Journal of Accounting & Economics*, March 1979, pp. 45–75.

[10] H. Haworth, J. Matthews and C. Tuck, Securities and Exchange Commission Directorate of Economic Policy Research Report, *Full Cost versus Successful Efforts: A Study of a Proposed Accounting Change's Competitive Impact* (Washington, D.C.: SEC, 1978).

[11] Arthur R. Wyatt, "Efficient Market Theory: Its Impact on Accounting," JofA, Feb. 83, pp. 56–65.

[12] Ibid., p. 57.

people thought. It seems to us that Wyatt is confusing allocational efficiency with capital market efficiency in this example.

Second, the election to value new inventory at current cost suggests that managers don't believe in the strong form of EMH. Specifically, managers know it isn't standard reporting practice to disclose the specific costs used to value a new Lifo layer of inventory. Further, they know the stock market won't learn of their uneconomical decision because the decision is inside information. Consequently, they have reason to believe their stock price won't suffer as a result of their pricing choice. In effect, the stock market isn't efficient in the strong form. But this says nothing about the validity of semistrong-form efficiency, which is of primary interest to accountants.

Wyatt's example can be interpreted to suggest that managers both understand and believe in semistrong-form efficiency. This may explain why companies don't disclose all the details of their Lifo election. If managers believe the market isn't semistrong-form efficient, they can disclose all the alternatives, costs and expected benefits without fear of market penalty because, in their view, the market won't impound this information into their stock price. However, companies don't reveal such details in real-world disclosures. We leave the reader to speculate why this is the case.

But, still, why did management make a decision that increased its tax burden? EMH can't answer this question for the reason given above: EMH and management beliefs are logically distinct. Therefore, in addressing the question, "Why did they do it?" we can only conjecture. Possible reasons include the following: (1) the book value effects may help the company secure additional financing at more favorable rates (e.g., due to an improved debt–equity ratio); (2) management's decision provides for a relatively larger amount of retained earnings, which may ease the payment of dividends or reduce the likelihood of a loan covenant violation; (3) management may believe the higher reported earnings will boost their stock price above what it would have been with the alternative method; or (4) management compensation, if based on reported earnings, would be increased. Wyatt mentions the last two possibilities. All four and perhaps others are possible in an efficient market.

While CMR can't tell us why managers behave as they do, it has provided us with clues about stock market reactions to different inventory valuation methods. For instance, companies that use Lifo generally have higher price-earnings ratios than companies that use Fifo, even though Fifo often results in higher reported income. Also, while the findings are somewhat conflicting, there is evidence that companies changing from Fifo to Lifo experience increased stock prices whereas changing to Fifo results in decreased stock prices.[13]

*Pooling example.* In this case, after incurring considerable costs, a company abandoned an economically sound merger because it couldn't be structured as a

---

[13] S. Sunder and A. R. Abdel-khalik and J. C. McKeown found positive market reactions to companies that changed to Lifo. W. E. Ricks, on the other hand, found negative reactions. See S. Sunder, "Stock Price and Risk Related to Accounting Changes in Inventory Valuation," *Accounting Review*, April 1975, pp. 305–315; A. R. Abdel-khalik and J. C. McKeown, "Understanding Accounting Changes in an Efficient Market: Evidence of Differential Reaction," *Accounting Review*, October 1978, pp. 851–868; and W. E. Ricks, "The Market's Response to the 1974 LIFO Adoptions," *Journal of Accounting Research*, Autumn 1982, Part I, pp. 367–387.

pooling of interests. Wyatt indicates that the decision to abort the combination was induced by management's belief that purchase accounting would dilute reported earnings and thereby cause the market to lower the price of the company's stock. He asks, "Why do U.S. companies labor so hard to achieve satisfaction with the pooling-of-interests accounting rules when EMH suggests the marketplace won't be fooled by whether the transaction is recorded by the purchase method or by the pooling-of-interests method?"[14] There are many possible answers.

As discussed above in conjunction with the Lifo example, EMH carries no implications about management beliefs. We would argue that, if the market were to discover that a company rejected an economically viable business combination merely for accounting reasons, the market may actually bid down the company's stock price due to decreased confidence in management. But because such information is seldom made public, companies that behave in this way probably suffer no adverse stock price consequences. And since Wyatt's question involved an empirical issue, we can look to a CMR study for an answer. Consistent with the hypothesis that the market isn't fooled by cosmetics, a group of researchers has found that pooling-of-interests accounting does not lead to higher stock prices vis-à-vis purchase accounting.[15] Again, management may have favored pooling for other reasons, such as to increase its own compensation, ease debt covenant restrictions or attempt to fool bankers and other decision makers operating outside of an efficient market.

*Off-balance-sheet financing example.* Wyatt raised several questions about companies that use off-balance-sheet financing when apparently less costly financing arrangements are available. Specifically, he asks if the market is fooled by off-balance-sheet lease financing and adds that lessee managers apparently think so. Whether the market is fooled by the accounting treatment is the fundamental issue. The FASB research report entitled *The Economic Effects on Lessees of FASB Statement No. 13, Accounting for Leases,* examined the stock price behavior of lessee companies that were required to capitalize leases formerly treated as operating leases. The report indicated that no significant price adjustments were found. This finding is consistent with an efficient stock market because no new information was provided by capitalization. The pre-Statement no. 13 financial statements generally disclosed sufficient detail in the notes for decision makers to compute the present values of the leases and adjust the financial statements if they so desired.

But why did management elect this "expensive" choice? Again, EMH can't provide the answer. It might have been an attempt to fool a lender whose decision involves a loan committee of, say, three or four persons and thus doesn't benefit from the collective wisdom of a broad aggregate such as the stock market. All management has to do is satisfy one bank to obtain financing. In those situations, the benefits to the company may exceed the higher costs, and the "more expensive" choice may prove to be the economical one.

*Foreign currency example.* Foreign currency translation was the subject of Wyatt's fourth example. Of particular interest were hedging activities to mitigate the

[14] Wyatt, "Efficient Market Theory," p. 60.
[15] H. Hong, R. S. Kaplan and G. Mandelker, "Pooling vs. Purchase: The Effects of Accounting for Mergers on Stock Prices," *Accounting Review,* January 1978, pp. 31–47.

volatility in earnings caused by fluctuations in foreign currency exchange rates. These hedging activities could be undertaken for two reasons: to reduce (1) real economic risk or (2) "accounting risk" (i.e., the volatility in reported accounting income).

We believe Wyatt is referring to the FASB Research Report, *An Empirical Investigation of the Effects of Statement of Financial Accounting Standards No. 8 on Security Return Behavior*, which found no significant market reaction to FASB Statement no. 8 disclosures. In this context Wyatt stated, "Many managements ended up with new policies that reduced accounting risks and at the same time, may have reduced economic risks. If, in fact, the stock market is efficient, i.e., isn't fooled by the difference in reported accounting results from adoption of a new hedging policy, the stock market price would remain unaffected. But if the new hedging policy does, in fact, mitigate economic risks as well, and if the stock price remains unchanged, is the market for that stock really efficient?"[16]

We caution against drawing any conclusions about market efficiency from this example for two reasons. First, the point of the example hinges on the word *if*. Second, how could the market know whether hedging activities undertaken to mitigate accounting risk also hedged economic risk? That information would be known only by a handful of company employees, and thus the market couldn't react to such inside information.

## WHY SHOULD PRACTICING ACCOUNTANTS BE AWARE OF EMH AND CMR?

We believe accountants should be aware of EMH and CMR because they have important applications to accounting practice. Four such applications follow:[17]

• Counseling clients. CMR results can be used by accountants as a basis for counseling clients. For example, a client contemplating making an accounting change that will increase its reported income for the purpose of supporting its stock price should be informed that such tactics don't fool the market. In fact, downward rather than upward stock price movements are generally associated with companies that make discretionary accounting changes when there is no underlying economic justification (e.g., a switch from accelerated to straight-line depreciation for financial statement purposes only).[18] One explanation for this result is that the market can see through such attempts to increase earnings artificially or to conceal an underlying negative shift in a company. Also, a client worried about a reduced stock price if it changes to Lifo to get a tax advantage could be advised that the stock market is likely to reward such a decision despite lower reported earnings. These findings are

---

[16] Wyatt, "Efficient Market Theory," p. 62.

[17] For a more detailed discussion of CMR implications, especially for standard setting, see W. H. Beaver, *Financial Reporting: An Accounting Revolution* (Englewood Cliffs, N.J.: Prentice-Hall, 1981), pp. 163–167.

[18] See for example, R. S. Kaplan and R. Roll, "Investor Evaluation of Accounting Information: Some Empirical Evidence," *Journal of Business*, April 1972, pp. 225–257; and W. T. Harrison, Jr., "Different Market Reactions to Discretionary and Non-discretionary Accounting Changes," *Journal of Accounting Research*, Spring 1977, pp. 84–107.

consistent with EMH assertions that the stock market reacts to underlying economic phenomena (e.g., cash flows) rather than to cosmetic accounting appearances.[19]

CMR gives accountants additional evidence and leverage when disagreements arise with clients about the disclosure or nondisclosure of certain information. The research indicates that security prices are affected by numerous sources (e.g., press releases, news conferences, industry publications, the financial press, etc.). Financial statements are but one source of information. Consequently, managers and accountants shouldn't naively believe that stock prices will be affected because of a financial statement disclosure (e.g., a lawsuit) that has already been reported publicly elsewhere. We aren't suggesting that clients will automatically acquiesce to accountants merely because of empirical evidence. We acknowledge that some of these implications of EMH and CMR are hard to sell because they often seem counterintuitive. However, by being well informed about CMR, accountants can assist clients in anticipating the reaction of the stock market to various types of financial disclosures.

• Disclosure. In a semistrong efficient market, publicly available information is impounded into stock prices, regardless of where it is reported. Thus, empirical research demonstrates that the substance of an accounting disclosure is more important than its form or location in the financial report. This means that the resolution of controversial issues such as the capitalization or expensing of a particular cost (e.g., research and development),[20] the question of balance sheet presentation or note disclosure (e.g., unfunded pension liabilities) or the choice of disclosure in a primary financial statement or in a supplementary report (e.g., the effects of inflation) isn't expected to affect security prices unless material economic consequences are based on reported financial statement amounts. As evidence of the market's sophistication in this regard, Moody's Investor Service includes off-balance-sheet pension obligations (disclosed in the notes) when computing its "adjusted debt ratios."[21] Consequently, it seems that both the stock market and the credit-rating agencies don't focus exclusively on the primary financial statements and are able to interpret complex note disclosures. The implication for accounting practice is this: It may be counterproductive to argue with a client over where in the financial statements an item is disclosed. Of greater importance is that the disclosure be adequate.

• EMH and CMR as legal evidence to establish claims for damages. It is common for legal proceedings involving rule 10b–5 lawsuits to examine claims for damages resulting from market transactions in a widely traded security.[22] Often EMH and CMR provide the framework and the quantitative methodology for estimating such

---

[19] After concluding from a CMR study that the market isn't fooled by accounting techniques, Kaplan and Roll indicated that "earnings manipulation may be fun, but its profitability is doubtful." Kaplan and Roll, "Investor Evaluation," p. 245.

[20] R. L. Vigeland, "The Market Reaction to Statement of Financial Accounting Standards No. 2," *Accounting Review*, April 1981, pp. 309–325.

[21] P. J. Regan, "Credit Ratings and Pension Costs," *Financial Analysts Journal*, March–April 1979, pp. 6–7.

[22] Rule 10b–5 of the Securities Exchange Act of 1934 is a broad prohibition of "manipulative and deceptive devices" in connection with the purchase on a sale of securities issued under the auspices of the act.

damages. The estimation techniques are fairly standard, and we know of specific instances in which an important element of a decision was the damage estimate provided by CMR. Not only is CMR evidence admissible in court but it also can play a key role in damage settlements.[23]

• EMH and CMR and standard-setting. In the standard-setting arena, it is common for the FASB, and to some extent, the SEC, to commission CMR projects. In addition, the American Institute of CPAs auditing standards board recently considered the stock price effects of the subject-to opinion in its deliberations to abolish or retain this type of opinion. Although we don't know the weight given CMR findings in the actual standard-setting process, it is obvious that EMH and CMR aren't being ignored.

What is the implication of this fact for accounting practice? It is this: EMH and CMR are influencing today's accounting and auditing standards. Recently, William H. Beaver critiqued FASB action relative to the five implications of EMH–CMR for standard setting he identified in 1973.[24] In brief, they were

1.  "A role of accounting data is to prevent superior returns accruing from inside information and can be achieved by a policy of fuller disclosure.
2.  "Accountants much stop acting as if they are the only suppliers of information about the [company]. Instead, the FASB should strive to minimize the total cost of providing information to investors.
3.  "The FASB should sponsor a full-scale research program in the areas indicated, so that it may have some evidence of the consequences of their choices among different sets of financial accounting standards.
4.  "Financial statements should not be reduced to the level of understanding of the naive investor.
5.  "Many reporting issues are capable of a simple disclosure solution and do not warrant an expenditure of FASB time and resources in attempting to resolve them."[25]

Beaver's conclusion was "I give the FASB full credit for the first four implications and half-credit for the fifth. That is a score of 90% to which I would give a grade of 'A'...."[26] Therefore, it would seem that accountants would want to keep abreast of the factors that are shaping the direction of accounting standards.

## SUMMARY AND CONCLUSIONS

EMH and CMR have been a part of the accounting environment since the 1960s. EMH is an aggregate concept describing the relationship between security prices and information. The empirical evidence implies that the stock market is reasonably efficient. In particular, the evidence shows that stock prices are more influenced by the disclosure of real economic events than by cosmetic accounting effects. This

---

[23] See for example, P. J. Leas, "The Measure of Damages in Rule 10b–5 Cases Involving Actively-Traded Securities," *Stanford Law Review*, January 1974, pp. 371–398.
[24] W. H. Beaver, "What Should Be the FASB's Objectives?" JofA, Aug. 73, pp. 49–56.
[25] W. H. Beaver, "The FASB: The Perspective of an Efficient Market Researcher" (Paper presented at the Eighth Arthur Young Professors' Roundtable, Harriman, N.Y., May 6, 1983), p. 2.
[26] Ibid., p. 7.

implies that the market isn't fooled by differences in accounting techniques that aren't accompanied by economic differences. CMR builds on the EMH foundation to examine the effects of actual accounting disclosures on stock prices. Thus, it helps us understand the economic environment in which we operate.

The issues discussed in this article demonstrate that EMH and CMR are an integral part of the real world of accounting. If Wyatt is correct that few practicing accountants are aware of EMH and even fewer understand it, there is reason for concern. This lack of awareness and understanding can bias perspectives and impair service to clients and to the public. In this vein, Wyatt asks, "What can be done to better educate managers [and accountants] about the ramifications of the hypothesis?"[27] This article is a step toward addressing that question.

---

[27] Wyatt, "Efficient Market Hypothesis," p. 65.

# I-D  Economic Consequences

## I-D 1  *The Politicization of Accounting*

DAVID SOLOMONS

There was once a time, not so many years ago, when accounting could be thought of as an essentially nonpolitical subject. If it was not as far removed from politics as was mathematics or astronomy, it was at least no more political than psychology or surveying or computer technology or statistics. Even in areas of accounting such as taxation, which might be thought to be most relevant to questions of public policy, practitioners were generally content to confine themselves to technical issues without getting involved as accountants in the discussion of tax policy.

Today, to judge from current discussions of the standard-setting process, accounting can no longer be thought of as nonpolitical. The numbers that accountants report have, or at least are widely thought to have, a significant impact on economic behavior. Accounting rules therefore affect human behavior. Hence, the process by which they are made is said to be political. It is then only a short step to the assertion that such rules are properly to be made in the political arena, by counting heads and deciding accounting issues by some voting mechanism.

There are several articulate spokesmen for this point of view. Dale Gerboth writes that "a politicization of accounting rule-making [is] not only inevitable, but just. In a society committed to democratic legitimization of authority, only politically responsive institutions have the right to command others to obey their rules."[1] And, in another passage from the same article, Gerboth says, "When a decision-making process depends for its success on public confidence, the critical issues are not

This article is adapted from a paper appearing in *Essays in Honor of William A. Paton—Pioneer Accounting Theorist*, edited by Stephen A. Zeff, Joel Demski and Nicholas Dopuch (Ann Arbor, Mich.: Division of Research, Graduate School of Business Administration, University of Michigan, 1978).

[1] Dale L. Gerboth, "Research, Intuition, and Politics in Accounting Inquiry," *Accounting Review*, July 1973, p. 481.

technical; they are political.... In the face of conflict between competing interests, rationality as well as prudence lies not in seeking final answers, but rather in compromise—essentially a political process."[2]

In the same vein, Charles Horngren writes that "the setting of accounting standards is as much a product of political action as of flawless logic or empirical findings. Why? Because the setting of standards is a social decision. Standards place restrictions on behavior; therefore, they must be accepted by the affected parties. Acceptance may be forced or voluntary or some of both. In a democratic society, getting acceptance is an exceedingly complicated process that requires skillful marketing in a political arena."[3]

Robert May and Gary Sundem take a similar position: "In practice as well as in theory, the social welfare impact of accounting reports apparently is recognized. Therefore it is no surprise that the [Financial Accounting Standards Board] is a political body and, consequently, that the process of selecting an acceptable accounting alternative is a political process. If the social welfare impact of accounting policy decisions were ignored, the basis for the existence of a regulatory body would disappear. Therefore, the FASB must consider explicitly political (i.e., social welfare) aspects as well as accounting theory and research in its decisions."[4]

Other voices that call for an explicit recognition of the probable economic and social impact of a new accounting standard are not always easily distinguished from those asserting that political considerations should determine what the standard should be.[5] However, these two views should not be confused.

The structure committee of the Financial Accounting Foundation grappled with the question of the political nature of the standard-setting task in *The Structure of Establishing Financial Accounting Standards*. On the nature of the standard-setting process, it says: "The process of setting accounting standards can be described as democratic because like all rule-making bodies the Board's right to make rules depends ultimately on the consent of the ruled. But because standard setting requires some perspective it would not be appropriate to establish a standard based solely on a canvass of the constituents. Similarly, the process can be described as legislative because it must be deliberative and because all views must be heard. But the standard setters are expected to represent the entire constituency as a whole and not be representatives of a specific constituent group. The process can be described as political because there is an educational effort involved in getting a new standard accepted. But it is not political in the sense that an accommodation is required to get a statement issued."[6]

There is something here to please everyone. Yet the committee does finally come out on the side of the angels: "We have used the word constituency to indicate that the FASB is accountable to everyone who has an interest. We are not suggesting that the

[2] Ibid, p. 479.

[3] Charles T. Horngren, "The Marketing of Accounting Standards," *Journal of Accountancy*, Oct. 73, p. 61.

[4] Robert G. May and Gary L. Sundem, "Research for Accounting Policy: An Overview," *Accounting Review*, October 1976, p. 750.

[5] John Buckley (in "FASB and Impact Analysis," *Management Accounting*, April 1976, p. 13) straddles this line most uncomfortably. His article has been thought to support politically slanted standards although he nowhere explicitly says that he does.

[6] Structure committee, *The Structure of Establishing Financial Accounting Standards* (Stamford, Conn.: FAF, April 1977), p. 19.

Board members are in place to represent them or that the standards must necessarily be based on a numerical consensus."[7]

That accounting influences human behavior, if only because it conveys information, is obvious enough, though research into the workings of "the efficient market" has cast doubt on some of the supposed results of accounting choices. There are, without question, political aspects of accounting. There are similarly political aspects of physics, which result in enormous expenditures on research into nuclear energy and weaponry. Geology, in its concern with the world's reserves of fossil fuels, obviously has political implications. Research into sickle cell anemia became a political question when the heavy incidence of this disease among black Americans came to light. There are very few areas of human knowledge which are devoid of political significance. But that does not mean that the processes by which knowledge is advanced or by which new applications are found for old knowledge are themselves political processes in the sense in which that term is usually understood. Political motives for asking a question may be entirely appropriate. A politically motivated answer may or may not be appropriate. It obviously depends on the nature of the question.

It may be useful to look more carefully at the part which politics should and should not play in accounting standard setting. The future of the FASB may depend on a better understanding of that issue. Indeed, the very credibility of accounting itself may be at stake.

## ACCOUNTING AND NATIONAL GOALS

The most extreme expression, so far as I am aware, of the view that political considerations should enter into the formulation of accounting standards—not merely into the choice of accounting questions to be studied but also into the formulation of the standards themselves—is to be found in a lecture given in New York in November 1973 by Professor David Hawkins. He noted that Congress and the executive branch of the federal government were "becoming more and more aware of the behavioral aspects of corporate reporting and its macro economic implications. Increasingly, I believe, these policy makers will demand ... that the decisions of those charged with determining what constitutes approved corporate reporting standards result in corporate reporting standards that will lead to individual economic behavior that is consistent with the nation's macro economic objectives. ... This awareness on the part of economic planners brings accounting standards setting into the realm of political economics."[8]

Events since 1973 have not shown any diminution in this awareness. The question is whether this is to be regarded as a threat to the integrity of accounting or as an opportunity, perhaps even an obligation, on the part of accountants to cooperate with government in furthering its economic policy. Hawkins left us in no doubt where he stood in this matter: "The [FASB's] objectives must be responsive to many more considerations than accounting theory or our notions of economically useful data. ... Corporate reporting standards should result in data that are useful for economic

---

[7] Ibid.

[8] David M. Hawkins, "Financial Accounting, the Standards Board and Economic Development," one of the 1973–74 Emanuel Saxe Distinguished Lectures in Accounting, published by the Bernard M. Baruch College, City University of New York, April 1975, pp. 7–8.

decisions *provided that the standard is consistent with the national macro economic objectives and the economic programs designed to reach these goals.*"[9] And, as if that were not enough, he added that "because the [FASB] has the power to influence economic behavior it has an obligation to support the government's economic plans."[10]

In that last passage, the word "because" is noteworthy, implying as it does that the power to influence economic behavior always carries with it an obligation to support the government's plans. Even if the matter under discussion were, say, pricing policy or wage policy or some aspect of environmental protection, the assertion would be open to argument. In relation to accounting, where the end product is a system of measurement, the position which Hawkins urges on the FASB could, I believe, threaten the integrity of financial reporting and deprive it of whatever credibility it now has.

There is no question as to the sensitivity of some, indeed most, of the issues that have been or are now on the agenda of the FASB or its predecessors, and of course this sensitivity stems from the fact that standards dealing with those issues have influenced or will influence behavior. This can only mean that there is widespread skepticism about the "efficient market" hypothesis. The financial community is not indifferent to the accounting rules imposed on it by the FASB. It is not the purpose of this article to explore the nature of this concern.[11] It will be enough to recognize that the FASB's constituents think it matters whether leases are capitalized or not, whether foreign currency transactions are accounted for by one method or another, whether contingencies are provided for by charges against income or by allowing retained earnings to accumulate. These questions do not affect the amount of information that is disclosed but simply the way in which these economic phenomena are reported; yet this fact does not desensitize them. Perhaps investors *are* naive. Only on the basis of such an assumption (and on the assumption that no new information will be disclosed by a politically motivated standard) is the impact of politics on accounting standards worth discussing at all.

## THE ECONOMIC IMPACT OF ACCOUNTING STANDARDS

Few if any accounting standards are without some economic impact. The requirement that U.S. companies write off purchased goodwill is said to give an advantage to foreign companies in bidding for American businesses because, not being subject to the same accounting requirement, they can afford to offer a higher price. FASB Statement no. 2, *Accounting for Research and Development Costs*, which requires that R&D be expensed as incurred, has been said to constitute a threat to technological

---

[9] Ibid, pp. 17, 9–10.

[10] Ibid., p. 11.

[11] Yet one cannot ignore the troublesome paradox posed by the numerous empirical studies which have shown "that the capital market does distinguish between [accounting] changes that appear to be reporting changes of no economic importance and those that appear to have substantive economic implications." (Nicholas J. Gonedes and Nicholas Dopuch, "Capital Market Equilibrium, Information Production, and Selecting Accounting Techniques: Theoretical Framework and Review of Empirical Work," *Studies on Financial Accounting Objectives: 1974*, supplement to vol. 12 of the *Journal of Accounting Research*.) If the market can "see through" accounting changes that result from changes in standards, why do they generate so much heat?

progress, especially by smaller companies that may be contemplating seeking access to the capital market and will therefore want to show good profits before doing so.[12] FASB Statement no. 5, *Accounting for Contingencies*, by greatly restricting the circumstances in which an estimated loss from a loss contingency can be accrued by a charge to income, is said to have caused U.S. insurance companies to reinsure risks for which previously they would have relied on self-insurance.

One of the most sensitive standards has been that dealing with foreign currency translation (Statement no. 8, *Accounting for the Translation of Foreign Currency Transactions and Foreign Currency Financial Statements*). Under the so-called temporal method mandated by the board, monetary assets and liabilities of a foreign subsidiary of a U.S. corporation have to be translated, for consolidation purposes, as the rate of exchange current at the balance sheet date. Assets which, in accordance with generally accepted accounting principles, are carried at cost or cost less depreciation have to be translated at the rate current at the time they were acquired. Exchange gains and losses, realized and unrealized, have to be brought into the income statement. For companies that formerly used a current/noncurrent classification, the important changes lie in the treatment of inventories and of long-term debt. Inventories, as current assets, were formerly carried at the current rate and are now carried at the historical rate; long-term debt, as a noncurrent liability, was formerly carried at the historical rate and now, as a monetary item, is carried at the current rate. Moreover, unrealized translation gains, formerly kept out of the income statement, now have to be brought in. The result has been greatly to increase the volatility of the reported earnings of companies with important foreign operations. Criticism of Statement no. 8 has focused on this increased volatility rather than on whether the new rules result in a better or worse representation of financial performance.

Whatever one may think about the merits of FASB Statement no. 19, *Financial Accounting and Reporting by Oil and Gas Producing Companies*, there can be little doubt that the Securities and Exchange Commission would not have acted as it did at the end of August to overrule this standard if there had not been political pressure from certain oil and gas companies which felt that they would be injured by the mandatory use of the "successful efforts" method of costing. It will be some time before the full effect of this action on the standard-setting process can be seen in its true light.

Numerous other politically sensitive accounting issues could be cited, but none has received as much attention as accounting for inflation, for none has such widespread potential repercussions throughout the business world. Each method which has been proposed to replace or to modify traditional methods would affect different companies differently, making some look more prosperous than they are under present methods and others less prosperous. For example, current purchasing power adjustments to historical cost accounting (general price level accounting) tend to make utilities with heavy debt capital look better off; replacement cost accounting tends to make companies with a large investment in depreciable assets, such as steel companies, look relatively less profitable. A system using exit values (e.g., continuously contemporary accounting, or COCOA) would make firms using assets that

---

[12] This argument, when the treatment of R&D was still on the FASB's agenda, led Hawkins to say, in his 1973 Emanuel Saxe Lecture (p. 14), "I do not believe the Board can eliminate the alternative capitalization." Events proved him wrong.

are not readily salable look bad. Though the protracted arguments about the relative merits of these and other rival systems have not generally overtly recognized the vested interests that stand to gain or lose by the way the argument goes, the political implications of inflation accounting have probably had as much responsibility for the difficulty in reaching agreement on the direction in which to move as have the technical problems involved.

In some of these instances, notably those concerning contingency reserves and foreign currency translations, critics of the FASB are asserting that economic behavior, such as reinsurance or hedging, which would not have been rational under the old accounting rules becomes rational under the new ones. Such an assertion is difficult to defend because the new rules have not changed the underlying cash flows or the risks attached to them. Only if significance is attached exclusively to "the bottom line," rather than to the present value of the enterprise, can the change in behavior be defended.

## MEASUREMENT AND POLITICS

The above examples will serve to illustrate some of the points of contact between accounting and politics. Many more could be cited. Indeed, because standards need to be set mainly in areas where there is controversy, it is highly probable that in every case someone will find the new treatment less favorable than the status quo and there is constantly a temptation for such people to rush off to their legislative representatives to get the government to interfere.[13] That sort of initiative represents the gravest threat on the horizon to the private control of standard setting.

If we are looking for ways to achieve political ends by tinkering with methods of measurement, there is plenty of scope outside the accounting field. Indeed, the danger has already been observed in other areas. For instance, the index of retail prices has a powerful effect on wage settlements in many industries. There is nothing absolute about a price index. The number obtained depends on the choice of base year, the items chosen for inclusion in the market basket and the weights attached to the items in constructing the index. A statistician who agreed with Hawkins about the responsibilities of those concerned with measurement could easily construct an index which would damp down price changes and could take credit for aiding in the fight against inflation.[14]

I have suggested elsewhere[15] that one way of reducing the traffic accident rate would be for highway authorities to lower the average speed by arranging to have all

[13] The letter dated October 6, 1977, addressed to the FASB chairman-designate by Senator William Proxmire (D-Wisconsin) and four Wisconsin congressmen and reported in the FASB *Status Report* no. 55, "Persons Opposing the FASB Exposure Draft on Oil and Gas Accounting Apparently Seek Support in Congress for Retention of Alternatives," October 14, 1977, is a case in point.

[14] There is nothing farfetched about this. In *The Final Days* (New York: Avon Books, 1977, p. 177), Bob Woodward and Carl Bernstein state that "late in 1971, Nixon had summoned the White House personnel chief, Fred Malek, to his office to discuss a 'Jewish cabal' in the Bureau of Labor Statistics. The 'cabal,' Nixon said, was tilting economic figures to make his administration look bad." Another example came to my notice when I was in Singapore in 1976. There the administration was accused of keeping the price index down by changing the grade of rice included in the collection of food items going into the index.

[15] In my Price Waterhouse lecture at Stanford University in 1972 entitled "Financial Accounting Standards: Regulation or Self-Regulation?"

speedometers consistently overstate speeds so that drivers would think they were driving faster than they actually were. Speedometers influence behavior. Why not influence it in a beneficient direction?

This last example will serve to lay bare the profound threat to accounting implicit in the propositions of Hawkins and of the others referred to above. If it ever became accepted that accounting might be used to achieve other than purely measurement ends, faith in it would be destroyed[16] just as faith in speedometers would be destroyed once it was realized that they were subject to falsification for the purpose of influencing driving habits.

Hawkin's view that "because the [FASB] has the power to influence economic behavior, it has an obligation to support the government's economic plans" is, I believe, not only destructive of accounting but it is also infeasible. Governments have a habit of changing their plans from year to year, and even from month to month. Are accounting standards to be changed with every change in the political climate? One has only to recall President Nixon's turnabout from a "no wage and price controls" stance to an espousal of rigorous controls in 1971–72—or President Ford's switch from proposals for tax increases to "whip inflation now" to an acceptance of tax cuts to stimulate employment in 1974—to see how futile it is to talk about supporting the government's economic plans or how impossible it would be for a standards board to keep up with the government.

## THE IMPORTANCE OF NEUTRALITY

Simply because information has an effect on human behavior does not mean that it should not seek to be neutral as between different desired modes of behavior. Unless it is as neutral as the accountant can make it, it is difficult to see how it can be relied on to guide behavior. As Chambers observes, "If the form of accounting is permitted to change with changes in policy, any attempt to scrutinize and to evaluate specific policies will be thwarted."[17]

Neutrality in accounting implies representational accuracy. Curiously, it has been little discussed, though other terms related to it have received more attention. The American Accounting Association's 1977 committee on concepts and standards for external financial reports gets near the heart of the matter when it says: "Users of financial information prefer that it have a high degree of reliability. Reliability is that quality which permits users of data to depend upon it with confidence as representative of what it purports to represent. But reliable information is not necessarily useful. It could, for example, be reliable but unrelated to the use at hand. Several relatively general terms are often used as synonyms for, or to cover parts of,

---

[16] Support for this view is to be found in Arthur R. Wyatt's article, "The Economic Impact of Financial Accounting Standards," *Arthur Andersen Chronicle*, September 1977, p. 49. Somewhat ironically in the circumstances, the same view has been espoused more recently by the chairman of the SEC. In his Statement of August 29 on accounting practices for oil and gas producers, setting aside FASB Statement no. 19, Harold M. Williams said: "If it becomes accepted or expected that accounting principles are determined or modified in order to secure purposes other than economic measurement—even such virtuous purposes as energy production—we assume a grave risk that confidence in the credibility of our financial information system will be undermined."

[17] Raymond J. Chambers, *Accounting, Evaluation and Economic Behavior* (Englewood Cliffs, N.J.: Prentice-Hall, Inc., 1966), p. 326.

the concept of reliability. Thus, verifiability, objectivity, lack of bias, neutrality, and accuracy all are related to reliability. Like relevance, reliability (above some minimal level) is a necessary but not a sufficient condition for usefulness of data."[18]

If the preceding sentence is true, these two qualities (relevance and reliability) together go far toward ensuring usefulness. Relevance comprehends subsidiary characteristics of information one might list, such as timeliness. And the essential element in the reliability of information (at least for our present purpose) is that it shall as accurately as possible represent what it purports to represent.[19] This implies neutrality.

Neutrality, in the sense in which the term is used here, does not imply that no one gets hurt. It is true, as the AAA 1977 committee on the social consequences of accounting information says, "Every policy choice represents a trade-off among differing individual preferences, and possibly among alternative consequences, regardless of whether the policy-makers see it that way or not. In this sense, accounting policy choices can never be neutral. There is someone who is granted his preference, and someone who is not."[20] The same thing could be said of the draft, when draft numbers were drawn by lot. Some people were chosen to serve while others escaped. It was still, by and large, neutral in the sense that all males of draft age were equally likely to be selected.

## ACCOUNTING AS FINANCIAL CARTOGRAPHY

Information cannot be neutral—it cannot therefore be reliable—if it is selected or presented for the purpose of producing some chosen effect on human behavior. It is this quality of neutrality which makes a map reliable; and the essential nature of accounting, I believe, is cartographic. Accounting is financial map-making. The better the map, the more completely it represents the complex phenomena that are being mapped. We do not judge a map by the behavioral effects it produces. The distribution of natural wealth or rainfall shown on a map may lead to population shifts or changes in industrial location, which the government may like or dislike. That should be no concern of the cartographer. We judge his map by how well it represents the facts. People can then react to it as they will.

Cartographers represent different facts in different ways and match the scale of their maps to their purpose. Every map represents a selection of a small portion of available data, for no map could show physical, political, demographic, climatological, geological, vegetational and numerous other kinds of data and still be intelligible. The need to be selective in the data that one represents does not normally rob the map of its neutrality, although it could.

As with the geographic features that cartographers map, different financial facts need to be represented in different ways, and different facts are needed for different

---

[18] Committee on concepts and standards for external financial reports, *Statement on Accounting Theory and Theory Acceptance* (Sarasota, Fla.: American Accounting Association, 1977), p. 16.

[19] This is close to Yuji Ijiri's statement that "in general, a system is said to be reliable if it works the way it is supposed to" (*The Foundations of Accounting Measurement: A Mathematical, Economic, and Behavioral Inquiry* [Englewood Cliffs, N.J.: Prentice-Hall, Inc., 1967], p. 137). But his more formal definition of reliability is couched more in terms of the predictive value of information, an aspect of the matter with which I am not here concerned.

[20] Committee on the social consequences of accounting information, *Report of the Committee on the Social Consequences of Accounting Information* (Sarasota, Fla.: AAA, 1978), p. 24.

purposes. It is perfectly proper for measurements to be selected with particular political ends in mind or to be adapted to a political end if it is made clear to users of the measurement what is being done. For example, the government is entitled, for taxation purposes, to define taxable income in whatever way suits it. It would be quite another matter for it to tell accountants that they were to use this definition for all purposes to which an income number might be put.

## SOME CONTRARY VIEWS

There have recently been some expressions of a different view of accounting from mine that deserve comment here. Sometimes the difference in the weight to be given to economic impact in standard setting is merely one of emphasis. Sometimes it is more fundamental in nature. Sometimes neutrality is dismissed on other grounds.

Probably no one argues that those who formulate accounting standards should do so with total unconcern for their economic consequences. Indeed, without some concern for such consequences, the selection of problem areas that call for standards could not be made. It was the economic consequences of not having a standard to deal with some particular problem which presumably directed attention in that direction in the first place. To require the FASB to report on the probable standard when an exposure draft is issued[21] — if it can be done, for the impact will often not be clear or unambiguous — is not at all objectionable, so long as the standard is designed to bring about a better representation of the facts of a situation, with whatever behavioral results flow from that, and not to promote some preselected economic objective or mode of behavior.

Some of those who would play down the value of neutrality in accounting standards do so because, they argue, the financial phenomena which accountants must report are not independent of the reporting methods selected. This view is expressed by the AAA 1977 committee on the social consequences of accounting information in the following passage from its report: "The view that measurement merely involves representing or describing stocks and flows is a static view. It assumes that the stocks and flows are history, fixed forever, no matter how you measure them. But what about tomorrow's stocks and flows? They are governed by the business decisions of enterprises — decisions which might change depending upon how you choose to measure the stocks and flows. The traditional framework fails to take this interdependence of measurement and decisional behavior into consideration."[22]

It is true that, where human beings are the subjects of measurement, behavior and measurements are not independent of each other. But this does not make neutrality a less desirable quality of measurement in such cases. If one substitutes speedometers for accounting and driving behavior for stocks and flows in the AAA committee's statement above, one can see that as an argument against neutrality it is quite unconvincing. There is nothing static about the relationship between the speed of a vehicle and the reading on the speedometer, and there is unquestionably feedback. The behavior of the driver is reflected on the dial, and what is on the dial affects the behavior of the driver. Speedometers still should register speed accurately

---

[21] As recommended by Prem Prakash and Alfred Rappaport in "The Feedback Effects of Accounting," *Business Week*, January 12, 1976, p. 12.

[22] Social consequences committee, p. 23.

and neutrally. The decision about how to react to the reading must be left to the driver.

A different criterion for the selection of approved accounting methods is put forward by William Beaver and Roland Dukes in a discussion of interperiod tax allocation: "The method which produces earnings numbers having the highest association with security prices is the most consistent with the information that results in an efficient determination of security prices. Subject to [certain] qualifications..., it is the method that ought to be reported."[23] And, having found that "deferral earnings are most consistent with the information set used in setting security prices," they conclude that "if one accepts market efficiency, the results suggest that the [Accounting Principles Board] made the 'correct' policy decision ... in the sense that it requires a method which is most consistent with the information impounded in an efficient determination of security prices."[24]

Beaver and Dukes themselves point out that any inferences to be drawn from their evidence are "conditional upon the prediction models used to test the accounting measures.... Any findings are the joint result of prediction models and accounting methods, and only appropriately specified joint statements are warranted."[25] In other words, the identification of the accounting method found to generate earnings numbers or cash flow numbers most closely associated with security prices depends on the way that "unexpected returns" are defined. The results of this analysis do not point unambiguously, therefore, toward a particular accounting method.

This could explain why, left to themselves, companies do not all choose the same accounting methods. They do not all use the same prediction models, and therefore the accounting method that has the most information content for one company is not the one with the most for another company. One moral that might be drawn from this is that we do not need accounting standards at all but, rather, that in an efficient market laissez-faire should prevail. A different conclusion about the Beaver and Dukes study is reached by Gonedes and Dopuch when they say that "under the contemporary institutional setting, captial market efficiency—taken by itself—does not imply that the prices of firms' ownership shares can be used in assessing the desirability of alternative information-production decisions."[26] In any case, whichever way the efficient market points us, it does not point us toward politically motivated accounting standards.

## LIMITATIONS OF THE ANALOGY WITH CARTOGRAPHY

There is a danger, with any analogy, of pushing it too far, and the analogy between accounting and cartography is no exception. Most maps represent external phenomena that have an independent existence of their own. The accountant is on safe ground only when he is doing the same thing—representing external phenomena such as cash flows, contractual rights, market values, etc. Of course, cartographers

---

[23] William H. Beaver and Roland E. Dukes, "Interperiod Tax Allocation, Earnings Expectations, and the Behavior of Security Prices," *Accounting Review*, April 1972, p. 321. They add, in a footnote, that "the criterion suggested above provides a simplified method for preference ordering of alternative measurement methods."
[24] Ibid, p. 331.
[25] Ibid, p. 332.
[26] Gonedes and Dopuch, p. 92.

have sometimes amused themselves by drawing maps of fictitious countries, like Erewhon or Atlantis, an activity which, too, has had its accounting counterparts.

Whatever limitations representational accuracy may have in pointing us toward right accounting answers, it will at least sometimes enable us to detect a wrong answer. For instance, FASB Statement no. 2, which requires all R&D expenditures to be expensed as incurred, is bad cartography because to represent the value of the continuing benefits of past research expenditures as zero will usually not be in accord with the facts of the situation, however expedient the treatment may be. Off-balance-sheet financing requires that certain unattractive features of the landscape be left off the map, so that again the map is defective. The criterion by which rules are to be judged is not the effect which they may or may not have on business behavior. It is the accuracy with which they reflect the facts of the situation.

## CONCLUSION

It is not at all palatable for accountants to be confronted by a choice between appearing to be indifferent to national objectives or endangering the integrity of their measurement techniques. But if the long-run well-being of our discipline is what matters, the right choice should be easy to make. It is our job—as accountants—to make the best maps we can. It is for others, or for accountants acting in some other capacity, to use those maps to steer the economy in the right direction. If the distinction between these two tasks is lost sight of, we shall greatly diminish our capacity to serve society, and in the long run everybody loses.

# I-D 2 *The Rise of "Economic Consequences"*

STEPHEN A. ZEFF

Since the 1960's, the American accounting profession has been aware of the increasing influence of "outside forces" in the standard-setting process. Two parallel developments have marked this trend. First, individuals and groups that had rarely shown any interest in the setting of accounting standards began to intervene actively and powerfully in the process. Second, these parties began to invoke arguments other than those which have traditionally been employed in accounting discussions. The term "economic consequences" has been used to describe these novel kinds of arguments.

By "economic consequences" is meant the impact of accounting reports on the decision-making behavior of business, government, unions, investors and creditors. It is argued that the resulting behavior of these individuals and groups could be detrimental to the interests of other affected parties. And, the argument goes, accounting standard setters must take into consideration these allegedly detrimental consequences when deciding on accounting questions. The recent debates involving foreign currency translation and the accounting for unsuccessful exploration activity in the petroleum industry have relied heavily on economic consequences arguments, and the Financial Accounting Standards Board and the Securities and Exchange Commission have become extremely sensitive to the issue.[1]

The economic consequences argument represents a veritable revolution in accounting thought. Until recently, accounting policy making was either assumed to be neutral in its effects or, if not neutral, it was not held out to the public as being responsible for those effects. Today, these assumptions are being severely questioned, and the subject of social and economic consequences "has become *the* central

This article is an abridged version of a paper presented on June 9, 1978, at the Stanford Lectures in Accounting, Graduate School of Business, Stanford University.

[1] Several articles have been written on "economic consequences." See, e.g., Alfred Rappaport, "Economic Impact of Accounting Standards—Implications for the FASB," *Journal of Accountancy*, May 1977, pp. 89–98; Arthur R. Wyatt, "The Economics Impact of Financial Accounting Standards," *Journal of Accountancy*, Oct. 77, pp. 92–94; and Robert J. Swieringa, "Consequences of Financial Accounting Standards," *Accounting Forum*, May 1977, pp. 25–39.

contemporary issue in accounting."[2] That the FASB has commissioned research papers on the economic consequences of selected standards and has held a conference devoted entirely to the subject[3] underscores the current importance of this issue.

Accounting policy makers have been aware since at least the 1960s of the third-party intervention issue,[4] while the issue of economic consequences has surfaced only in the 1970s. Indeed, much of the history of the Accounting Principles Board during the 1960s was one of endeavoring to understand and cope with the third-party forces which were intervening in the standard-setting process. In the end, the inability of the APB to deal effectively with these forces led to its demise and the establishment in 1973 of the FASB.

The true preoccupations of the intervening third parties have not always been made clear. When trying to understand the third-party arguments, one must remember that before the 1970s the accounting model employed by the American Institute of CPAs committee on accounting procedure (CAP) and the APB was, formally at least, confined to technical accounting considerations (sometimes called "accounting principles" or "conceptual questions") such as the measurement of assets, liabilities and income and the "fair presentation" of financial position and operations. The policy makers' sole concern was with the communication of financial information to actual and potential investors, for, indeed, their charter had been "granted" by the SEC, which itself had been charged by Congress to assure "full and fair disclosure" in reports to investors. Third-party intervenors, therefore, would have had an obvious incentive to appeal to the accounting model used by policy makers rather than raise the specter of an economic consequences model preferred by the third parties.

When corporate management began intervening in the standard-setting process to an increasing degree, therefore, its true position was probably disguised. An examination of management arguments suggests the following range of tactical rhetoric. Arguments were couched in terms of

1. The traditional accounting model, where management was genuinely concerned about unbiased and "theoretically sound" accounting measurements.
2. The traditional accounting model, where management was really seeking to advance its self-interest in the economic consequences of the contents of published reports.
3. The economic consequences in which management was self-interested.

If one accepts Johnson's dictum that it requires a "lively imagination" to believe that management is genuinely concerned with fair presentation when choosing

---

[2] *Report of the Committee on the Social Consequences of Accounting Information* (Sarasota, Fla.: American Accounting Association, 1978), p. 4.

[3] *Conference on the Economic Consequences of Financial Accounting Standards* (Stamford, Conn.: FASB, 1978).

[4] In this article, I am chiefly concerned with third-party intervention in the standard setting for unregulated industries. Accounting policy makers in this country have been alive for several decades to the accounting implications of the rules and regulations of rate-making in the energy, transportation and communication industries. See, e.g., George O. May, *Financial Accounting: A Distillation of Experience* (New York: The Macmillan Company, 1943), chs. 7–8, and William A. Paton, "Accounting Policies of the Federal Power Commission—A Critique," *Journal of Accountancy*, June 44, pp. 432–60.

between accounting alternatives,[5] it could be concluded that the first argument has seldom been employed in third-party interventions. In recent years, particularly since the early 1970s, management has become more candid in its dialogues with the FASB, insistently advancing the third argument and thus bringing economic consequences to the fore.

Two factors tend to explain why economic consequences did not become a substantive issue before the 1970s. First, management and other interested parties predominantly used the second argument cited above, encouraging the standard-setting bodies to confine themselves to the traditional accounting model. Second, the CAP and APB, with few exceptions, were determined to resolve, or appear to resolve, standard-setting controversies in the context of traditional accounting.

## EARLY USES OF ECONOMIC CONSEQUENCES ARGUMENTS

Perhaps the first evidence of economic consequences reasoning in the pronouncements of American policy makers occurred as long ago as 1941. In Accounting Research Bulletin no. 11, *Corporate Accounting for Ordinary Stock Dividends*, the CAP, in accordance with "proper accounting and corporate policy," required that fair market value be used to record the issuance of stock dividends where such market value was substantially in excess of book value.[6]

Evidently, both the New York Stock Exchange and a majority of the CAP regarded periodic stock dividends as "objectionable,"[7] and the CAP acted to make it more difficult for corporations to sustain a series of such stock dividends out of their accumulated earnings. As far as this author is aware, the U.S. is still the only country in which an accounting pronouncement requires that stock dividends be capitalized at the fair market value of the issued shares,[8] and this position was originally adopted in this country, at least in part, in order to produce an impact on the stock dividend policies of corporations.

A second evidence of economic consequences entering into the debates surrounding the establishment of accounting standards, this time involving management representations, occurred in 1947–48. It was the height of the postwar inflation, and several corporations had adopted replacement cost depreciation in their published financial statements.[9] Among the arguments employed in the debate involving the CAP were the possible implications for tax reform, the possible impact on wage bargaining and the need to counteract criticisms of profiteering by big business. Despite the pressures for accounting reform, the CAP reaffirmed its support of historical cost accounting for depreciation in ARB no. 33, *Depreciation and High Costs*, and in a letter issued in October 1948.

---

[5] Charles E. Johnson, "Management's Role in External Accounting Measurements," in Robert K. Jaedicke, Yuji Ijiri and Oswald Nielsen (editors), *Research in Accounting Measurement* ([n.p.], AAA, 1966), p. 91.

[6] Accounting Research Bulletin no. 11, *Corporate Accounting for Ordinary Stock Dividends* (New York: American Institute of Accountants, 1941), pp. 102–03.

[7] George O. May, letter to J. S. Seidman, dated July 14, 1941 (deposited in the national office library of Price Waterhouse & Co. in New York), p. 1.

[8] Price Waterhouse International, *A Survey in 46 Countries: Accounting Principles and Reporting Practices* ([n.p.], PWI, 1975), table 145.

[9] *Depreciation Policy When Price Levels Change* (New York: Controllership Foundation, Inc., 1948), ch. 14.

A clear use of the economic consequences argument occurred in 1958, when three subsidiaries of American Electric Power Company sued in the federal courts to enjoin the AICPA from allowing the CAP to issue a letter saying that the deferred tax credit account, as employed in the then-recently issued ARB no. 44 (Revised), *Declining-Balance Depreciation*, should be classified as a liability.[10] The three public utility companies were concerned that the SEC, under authority granted by the Public Utility Holding Company Act, would not permit them to issue debt securities in view of the unfavorable debt-to-equity ratios which the proposed reclassification would produce. The case reached the U.S. Supreme Court, where certiorari was denied. In the end, the clarifying letter was issued. Nonetheless, the SEC accommodated the public utility companies by consenting to exclude the deferred tax credit from both liabilities and stockholders' equity for purposes of decisions taken under the Public Utility Holding Company Act.[11]

Shortly after the creation of the APB, the accounting treatment of the investment tax credit exploded on the scene. The three confrontations between the APB and the combined forces of industry and the administrations of Presidents Kennedy, Johnson and Nixon have already been amply discussed in the literature.[12] The government's argument was not that the accounting deferral of the investment tax credit was bad accounting but that it diluted the incentive effect of an instrument of fiscal policy.

In 1965, the subject of segmental reporting emerged from a hearing of the Senate Subcommittee on Antitrust and Monopoly on the economic effects of conglomerate mergers. The aim of the senatorial inquiry was not to promote better accounting practices for investor use but to provide the subcommittee and other government policy makers with accounting data that would facilitate their assessment of the economic efficacy of conglomerate mergers. Company managements naturally looked on such disclosures as potentially detrimental to their merger ambitions. Pressure applied by this powerful subcommittee eventually forced the hand of the SEC to call for product-line disclosures in published financial reports. The repercussions of this initiative, which had its origin in a Senate hearing room, are still being felt.[13]

In 1967–69, the APB responded to an anguished objection by the startled Investment Bankers Association of America (today known as the Securities Industry Association) to a provision, once thought to be innocuous, in APB Opinion no. 10, *Omnibus Opinion-1966*, which imputed a debt discount to convertible debt and debt issued with stock warrants. The IBA was concerned about the impact of the

---

[10] *The AICPA Injunction Case—Re: ARB [No.] 44 (Revised)*, Cases in Public Accounting Practice [no. 1] (Chicago, Ill.: Arthur Andersen & Co., 1960).

[11] *SEC Administrative Policy Re: Balance-Sheet Treatment of Deferred Income-Tax Credits*, Cases in Public Accounting Practice [nos. 5 and 6] (Chicago, Ill.: Arthur Andersen & Co., 1961), pp. 35–59.

[12] See Maurice Moonitz, "Some Reflections on the Investment Credit Experience," *Journal of Accounting Research*, Spring 1966, pp. 47–61; John L. Carey, *The Rise of the Accounting Profession: To Responsibility and Authority 1937–1969* (New York: AICPA, 1970), pp. 98–104; and Stephen A. Zeff, *Forging Accounting Principles in Five Countries: A History and an Analysis of Trends* (Champaign, Ill.: Stipes Publishing Company, 1972), pp. 178–80, 201–2, 219–21 and 326–27.

[13] Charles W. Plum and Daniel W. Collins, "Business Segment Reporting," in James Don Edwards and Homer A. Black (editors), *The Modern Accountant's Handbook* (Homewood, Ill.: Dow Jones-Irwin, Inc., 1976), pp. 469–511.

accounting procedure on the market for such securities. In Opinion no. 14, *Accounting for Convertible Debt and Debt Issued With Stock Purchase Warrants*, the APB rescinded its action in regard to convertible debt while retaining the rest.[14]

From 1968 through 1971, the banking industry opposed the inclusion of bad-debt provisions and losses on the sales of securities in the net income of commercial banks. Bankers believed that the new measure would reflect unfavorably on the performance of banks. Eventually, through a concerted effort by the APB, the SEC and the bank regulatory agencies, generally accepted accounting principles were made applicable to banks.[15]

From 1968 through 1970, the APB struggled with the accounting for business combinations. It was flanked on the one side by the Federal Trade Commission and the Department of Justice, which favored the elimination of pooling-of-interests accounting in order to produce a slowing effect on the merger movement and on the other by merger-minded corporations that were fervent supporters of pooling-of-interests accounting. The APB, appearing almost as a pawn in a game of political chess, disenchanted many of its supporters as it abandoned positions of principle in favor of an embarrassing series of pressure-induced compromises.[16]

In 1971, the APB held public hearings on accounting for marketable equity securities, leases and the exploration and drilling costs of companies in the petroleum industry. In all three areas powerful industry pressures thwarted the board from acting. The insurance industry was intensely concerned about the possible effects on its companies' stock prices of including the unrealized gains and losses on portfolio holdings in their income statements.[17] The leasing initiative was squelched after senators, representatives and even the secretary of transportation responded to a letter-writing campaign by making pointed inquiries of the SEC and APB. The letter writers raised the specter of injury that the board's proposed action would supposedly cause to consumers and to the viability of companies in several key industries.[18] The petroleum industry was unable to unite on a solution to the controversy over full costing versus successful efforts costing, as it was alleged that a general imposition of the latter would adversely affect the fortunes of the small, independent exploration companies.[19] Using its considerable political might, the industry succeeded in persuading the board to postpone consideration of the sensitive subject.[20]

On each of the occasions enumerated above, outside parties intervened in the standard-setting process by an appeal to criteria that transcended the traditional questions of accounting measurement and fair presentation. They were concerned instead with the economic consequences of the accounting pronouncements.

---

[14] Zeff, pp. 202, 211.

[15] Carey, p. 134: Maurice Moonitz, *Obtaining Agreement on Standards in the Accounting Profession*, Studies in Accounting Research no. 8 (Sarasota, Fla.: AAA, 1974), pp. 38–39; Zeff, pp. 210–11.

[16] Robert Chatov, *Corporate Financial Reporting: Public or Private Control?* (New York: The Free Press, 1975), pp. 212–22; and Zeff, pp. 212–16.

[17] Charles T. Horngren, "The Marketing of Accounting Standards," *Journal of Accountancy*, Oct. 73, pp. 63–64.

[18] Leonard M. Savoie, "Accounting Attitudes," in Robert R. Sterling (editor), *Institutional Issues in Public Accounting* (Lawrence, Kan.: Scholars Book Co., 1974), p. 326.

[19] See the testimony and submissions in *APB Public Hearing on Accounting and Reporting Practices in the Petroleum Industry*, Cases in Public Accounting Practice [no.] 10 (Chicago, Ill.: Arthur Andersen & Co., 1972).

[20] Savoie, p. 326.

"Economic consequences" have been invoked with even greater intensity in the short life of the FASB. Such questions as accounting for research and development costs, self-insurance and catastrophe reserves, development stage companies, foreign currency fluctuations, leases, the restructuring of troubled debt,[21] domestic inflation and relative price changes, and the exploration and drilling costs of companies in the petroleum industry have provoked widespread debate over their economic consequences.[22] The list is both extensive and impressive, and accounting academics are busily investigating the empirical validity of claims that these and other accounting standards may be linked with the specified economic consequences.

## THE STANDARD-SETTING BODIES RESPOND

What have been the reactions of the standard-setting bodies to the intervention by outside parties and the claim that accounting standards should or should not be changed in order to avoid unhealthy economic or social consequences? In the 1940s and 1950s, the CAP enhanced its liaison with interested third parties through a wider circulation of exposure drafts and subcommittee reports. From 1958 to 1971, through appointments to key committees, joint discussions and symposiums, mass mailings of exposure drafts and formal public hearings, the Institute and the APB acted to bring interested organizations more closely into the standard-setting process. The hope was, one supposes, that these organizations would be satisfied that their views were given full consideration before the final issuance of opinions. These accommodations were, however, of a procedural sort, although it is possible that these outside views did have an impact on the substantive content of some of the resulting opinions. It would appear that the APB was at least somewhat influenced by economic

[21] At the FASB's public hearing, some bankers warned of the dire economic consequences of requiring banks to write down their receivables following restructurings. Walter Wriston, chairman of Citicorp, asserted that the restructuring of New York City's obligations might just not have occurred if the banks would have been required to write down the carrying value of their receivables. Walter B. Wriston, *Transcript of Public Hearing* on FASB discussion memorandum, *Accounting by Debtors and Creditors When Debt Is Restructured* (1977-vol. 1-part 2), pp. 69–70. Yet the FASB, in its lengthy, "Basis for Conclusions" in Statement no. 15, *Accounting by Debtors and Creditors for Troubled Debt Restructurings* (in which the feared write-downs were not required), did not refer to bankers' claims about the economic consequences of requiring significant write-downs. Does that omission imply that the FASB paid no attention to those assertions? Did the FASB conduct any empirical research (as it did concerning the economic consequences claims raised in connection with Statement no. 7, *Accounting and Reporting by Development Stage Enterprises*) to determine whether there was adequate ground to sustain such claims?

[22] See, e.g., Joseph M. Burns, *Accounting Standards and International Finance: With Special Reference to Multinationals* (Washington, D.C.: American Enterprise Institute for Public Policy Research, 1976); Committee on the Social Consequences of Accounting Information, pp. 9–12; Rappaport, pp. 90, 92; FASB, *Conference on the Economic Consequences of Financial Accounting Standards*; U.S. Department of Energy, comments before the Securities and Exchange Commission, "Accounting Practices—Oil and Gas Producers—Financial Accounting Standards," unpublished memorandum, dated April 3, 1978.

Evidence attesting to the attention given by the FASB to economic consequences issues may be found in the "Basis for Conclusions" sections of the applicable statements. In addition to companies and industry groups, government departments (such as the Department of Commerce, in Statement no. 7, and the Departments of Energy and Justice, in Statement no. 19, *Financial Accounting and Reporting by Oil and Gas Producing Companies*) were actively involved in the discussion of economic consequences.

consequences in its prolonged deliberations leading to the issuance of Opinions no. 16, *Business Combinations*, and no. 17, *Intangible Assets*.[23] During the public hearings in 1971 on marketable equity securities and the accounting practices of companies in the petroleum industry, management representatives on several occasions asserted economic consequences as relevant considerations. Yet members of the APB's subject-area committees neither asked for proof of these assertions nor, indeed, questioned their relevance to the setting of accounting standards.[24]

Since it was the APB's inability to cope with the pressures brought by outside organizations that hastened its demise, it is worth noting that the FASB included the Financial Executives Institute (FEI) among its co-sponsors. In my opinion, the incorporation of the FEI in the formal structure of the Financial Accounting Foundation (FAF, the FASB's parent) is one of the most significant advantages which the FASB possesses in relation to its predecessor.[25]

The procedural machinery established for the FASB is even more elaborate than that which existed in the final years of the APB. The object of these additional procedures has been to expand and intensify the interaction between the board and interested outside parties, notably companies, industry associations and government departments and agencies. A task force drawn from a broad spectrum of interested groups is appointed prior to the preparation of each discussion memorandum. The DM itself is much bulkier than the modest document the APB had issued before its public hearings; it contains a neutral discussion of the entire gamut of policy issues that bear on the resolution of the controversy before the board. A Financial Accounting Standards Advisory Council (FASAC), composed of representatives of a wide array of interested groups, was appointed to be a sounding board for the FASB. The board itself has been composed of members drawn from accounting practice, the universities, companies and government—again, so that it would be responsive, and would appear to be responsive, to the concerns of those "constituencies." In an effort to persuade skeptics of the merit of its recommendations, the board includes in its statements a lengthy explanation of the criteria, arguments and empirical considerations it used to fashion the recommended standards.

Following criticism from within the profession of the board's operations and procedures, the FAF conducted a study in 1977 of the entire FASB operation. Among the FAF's many recommendations were proposals that the board expand its formal and informal contacts with interested groups and that it include an economic impact analysis in important exposure drafts. On this latter point, the FAF's structure committee concluded: "The Board need not be unduly influenced by the possibility of an economic impact, but it should consider both the possible costs and the expected benefits of a proposal."[26] In addition, the structure committee recommended actions that would strengthen the roles of the task forces and the FASAC.[27] In 1978, under

[23] Wyatt, p. 92–93.

[24] *Proceedings* of Hearing on Accounting for Equity Securities, Accounting Principles Board (New York: AICPA, 1971), section A—Transcript; and *APB Public Hearing on Accounting and Reporting Practices in the Petroleum Industry*.

[25] The inclusion of the FEI could arguably become the undoing of the FASB. If the FEI were to lose confidence in the board, it is possible that many of the companies which now contribute to the Financial Accounting Foundation might decline to continue doing so, provoking a financial crisis that could threaten the board's viability.

[26] Financial Accounting Foundation structure committee, *The Structure of Establishing Financial Accounting Standards* (Stamford, Conn.: FAF, 1977), p. 51.

[27] Ibid., pp. 23–25.

pressure from Congress, the board began to conduct virtually all its formal meetings (including those of the FASAC) "in the sunshine."

The history of the APB and the FASB is one of a succession of procedural steps taken to bring the board's deliberations into closer proximity to the opinions and concerns of interested third parties. As in the case of the APB, it is possible that an effect of these more elaborate procedures has been a change in the substance of the FASB's conclusions and recommendations.

By the middle 1970's, however, it was decided that the FASB should add economic (and social) consequences to the substantive issues it normally addresses. The inclusion of "probable economic or social impact" among the other "qualities of useful information" in the board's conceptual framework DM,[28] the board's announcement of its interest in empirical studies of economic consequences,[29] and the recommendation of the FAF structure committee that the board inform itself adequately on the "various impacts its pronouncements might have"[30] collectively confirm this new direction. The issue of economic consequences has, therefore, changed from one having only procedural implications for the standard-setting process to one which is not firmly a part of the standard setters' substantive policy framework.

## ECONOMIC CONSEQUENCES AS A SUBSTANTIVE ISSUE

Economic consequences have finally become accepted as a valid substantive policy issue for a number of reasons:

- The tenor of the times. The decade of the 1970s is clearly one in which American society is holding its institutions responsible for the social, environmental and economic consequences of their actions, and the crystallized public opinion on this subject eventually became evident (and relevant) to those interested in the accounting standard-setting activity.
- The sheer intractability of the accounting problems being addressed. Since the mid-1960s, the APB and the FASB have been taking up difficult accounting questions on which industry positions have been well entrenched. To some degree, companies that are sensitive to the way their performances are evaluated through the medium of reported earnings have permitted their decision-making behavior to be influenced by their perceptions of how such behavior will be seen through the prism of accounting earnings. Still other such companies have tailored their accounting practices to reflect their economic performances in the best light—and the managers are evidently loathe to change their decision-making behavior in order to accommodate newly imposed accounting standards. This would also be a concern to managers who are being paid under incentive compensation plans.[31]

---

[28] Financial Accounting Standards Board discussion memorandum, *Conceptual Framework for Financial Accounting and Reporting: Elements of Financial Statements and Their Measurement* (Stamford, Conn.: FASB, 1976), par. 367.
[29] Financial Accounting Standards Board, *Status Report*, no. 45, February 7, 1977.
[30] Structure committee, p. 31.
[31] Alfred Rappaport, "Executive Incentives vs. Corporate Growth," *Harvard Business Review*, July–August 1978, pp. 81–88.

- The enormity of the impact. Several of the issues facing the APB and the FASB in recent years have portended such a high degree of impact on either the volatility or level of earnings and other key financial figures and ratios that the FASB can no longer discuss the proposed accounting treatments without encountering incessant arguments over the probable economic consequences. Particularly apt examples are accounting for foreign exchange fluctuations, domestic inflation and relative price changes and the exploration and drilling costs of companies in the petroleum industry.

- The growth in the information economics-social choice, behavioral, income smoothing and decision usefulness literature in accounting. Recent writings in the information economics-social choice literature have provided a broad analytical framework within which the problems or economic consequences may be conceptualized. Beginning with Stedry,[32] the literature on the behavioral implications of accounting numbers has grown significantly, drawing the attention of researchers and policy makers to the importance of considering the effects of accounting information. The literature on income smoothing has suggested the presence of a managerial motive for influencing the measurement of earnings trends. Finally, the decision usefulness literature, although it is confined to the direct users of accounting information, has served to lessen the inclination of accountants to argue over the inherent "truth" of different accounting incomes and, instead, to focus on the use of information by those who receive accounting reports.[33]

- The insufficiency of the procedural reforms adopted by the APB and the FASB. Despite the succession of procedural steps which both boards have taken to provide outside parties with a forum for expressing their views, the claims of economic consequences—and the resulting criticisms of the boards' pronouncements—have continued unabated. The conclusion has evidently been reached that procedural remedies alone will not meet the problem.

- The Moss and Metcalf investigations. By the middle of 1976, it was known that Congressman John E. Moss (D-Calif.) and the late Senator Lee Metcalf (D-Mont.) were conducting investigations of the performance of the accounting profession, including its standard-setting activities, and it could reasonably have been inferred that the responsiveness of the standard-setting bodies to the economic and social effects of their decisions would be an issue.

- The increasing importance to corporate managers of the earnings figure in capital-market transactions. Especially in the 1960s, when capital markets were intensely competitive and the merger movement was fast paced, the earnings figure came to be viewed as an important element of managerial strategy and tactics. This factor is of importance in today's markets, as the pace of merger activity has once again quickened.

- Accounting figures came to be viewed as an instrument of social control. The social control of American enterprise has been well known in the rate-regulated energy, transportation and communications fields, but in recent years the earnings figure has, to an increasing degree, been employed as a

---

[32] Andrew C. Stedry, *Budget Control and Cost Behavior* (Englewood Cliffs, N.J.: Prentice-Hall, Inc., 1960).

[33] Committee on concepts and standards for external financial reports, *Statement on Accounting Theory and Theory Acceptance* (Sarasota, Fla.: AAA, 1977), pp. 5–29.

control device on a broader scale.[34] Examples are fiscal incentives (such as the investment tax credit and redefinitions of taxable income that diverge from accounting income) that have an influence on debates surrounding financial reporting,[35] the price-control mechanism of Phase II in 1972–73[36] and the data base contemplated by the Energy Policy and Conservation Act of 1975.

- The realization that outsiders could influence the outcome of accounting debates. Before the 1960s, accounting controversies were rarely reported in the financial press, and it was widely believed that accounting was a constant, if not a fixed parameter, in the management of business operations. With the publicity given to the accounting for the investment credit in 1962–63, to the fractious dialogue within the AICPA in 1963–64 over the authority of the APB and to other accounting disagreements involving the APB, managers and other outside parties have come to realize that accounting may be a variable after all—that the rules of accounting are not unyielding or even unbending.

- The growing use of the third argument, advanced earlier in the article, in accounting debates. Mostly for the reasons enumerated above, outside parties began to discard the pretense that their objections to proposed changes in accounting standards were solely, or even primarily, a function of differences over the proper interpretation of accounting principles. True reasons came out into the open, and accounting policy makers could no longer ignore their implications.

It is significant that economic consequences have become an important issue at a time when accounting and finance academics have been arguing that the U.S. capital markets are efficient with respect to publicly available information and, moreover, that the market cannot be "fooled" by the use of different accounting methods to reflect the same economic reality.[37]

## THE DILEMMA FACING THE FASB

What are the implications of the economic consequences movement for the FASB? It has become clear that political agencies (such as government departments and congressional committees) expect accounting standard setters to take explicitly into consideration the possible adverse consequences of proposed accounting standards. This expectation appears to be strongest where the consequences are thought to be significant and widespread—and especially where they might impinge on economic and social policies being pursued by the government. In these instances, the FASB must show that it has studied the possible consequences but that the benefits from implementing the standards outweigh the possible adverse consequences. Where the

---

[34] DR Scott, though writing in a different context, nonetheless was prophetic in his prediction that accounting would increasingly be used as a means of social control. DR Scott, *Cultural Significance of Accounts* (New York: Henry Holt and Co., 1931), esp. ch. 14.

[35] The "required tax conformity" issue of the early 1970s (see Zeff, pp. 218–19) is another instance.

[36] Robert F. Lanzillotti, Mary T. Hamilton and R. Blaine Roberts, *Phase II in Review; the Price Commission Experience* (Washington, D.C.: Brookings Institution, 1975), pp. 73–77; and C. Jackson Grayson, Jr., and Louis Neeb, *Confessions of a Price Controller* (Homewood, Ill.: Dow Jones-Irwin, Inc., 1974), pp. 71–76.

[37] See, e.g., William H. Beaver, "What Should Be the FASB's Objectives?" *Journal of Accountancy*, Aug. 73, pp. 49–56.

claimed consequences have implications for economic or social policies of national importance, the FASB should not be surprised if a political resolution is imposed by outside forces.

To what degree should the FASB have regard for economic consequences? To say that any significant economic consequences should be studied by the board does not imply that accounting principles and fair presentation should be dismissed as the principal guiding factor in the board's determination. The FASB is respected as a body of accounting experts, and it should focus its attention where its expertise will be acknowledged. While some observers might opt for determining accounting standards only with regard to their consequences for economic and social welfare, the FASB would surely preside over its own demise if it were to adopt this course and make decisions primarily on other than accounting grounds.

The board is thus faced with a dilemma which requires a delicate balancing of accounting and nonaccounting variables. Although its decisions should rest—and be seen to rest—chiefly on accounting considerations, it must also study—and be seen to study—the possible adverse economic and social consequences of its proposed actions. In order to deal adequately with this latter function, the board may find it convenient to develop a staff of competent analysts from allied disciplines, notably economics.

Economic consequences bids fair to be the most challenging accounting issue of the 1970s. What is abundantly clear is that we have entered an era in which economic and social consequences may no longer be ignored as a substantive issue in the setting of accounting standards. The profession must respond to the changing tenor of the times while continuing to perform its essential role in the areas in which it possesses undoubted expertise.

# II Income Measurement

This part of the book is concerned with the nature of income and problems involved in income measurement.

Section A deals with a comparison of economic and accounting income concepts. In the introductory piece, Boulding (1977) discusses the relationship between accounting and economics in a "theory of the firm" context. His main argument is that communication between the two disciplines should become more open and that accountants should have a substantial knowledge of economics, and vice versa. According to Boulding, accountants are only interested in the past and present, emphasizing the earnings figure. Economists, however, are concerned with "profit maximization" and, as such, deal with the present and future. The information requirements for each are different, but not entirely different. Business managers are profit maximizers, and require information about future expectations. The accountant only provides some information to management. Other information must be gathered from the economists. Since decision-making at the firm level requires both sets of information, it is only natural that the two fields meld. In the second piece in this section, Solomons (1961) differentiates between the concepts of economic and accounting income and argues that accounting income is flawed as an indicator of the firm's success or failure due to its emphasis on realization rather than value changes. Economic income, on the other hand, requires highly uncertain data. Solomons foresees a decline in the significance of the income statement, with greater emphasis on the funds statement.

Section B is concerned with the allocation problem, and contains one article. Thomas (1975) discusses the thorny problem of allocating costs and revenues in income measurement. All such allocations are arbitrary, asserts Thomas, since they can be neither refuted nor verified. Because factors of production interact, generating joint benefits, any attempt to allocate such benefits among the inputs is bound to be unsuccessful. Thomas calls for an end to allocation and recommends two alternatives to accomplish that goal: the use of exit values or cash flow statements.

# II-A The Concept of Income

## II-A 1 *Economics and Accounting: The Uncongenial Twins*

K. E. BOULDING

Economics and accountancy are two disciplines which draw their raw material from much the same mines. From these raw materials, however, they seem to fashion remarkably different products. They both study the operations of firms; they both are concerned with such concepts as income, expenditure, profits, capital, value and prices. In spite of an apparently common subject-matter, however, they often seem to inhabit totally different worlds, between which there is remarkably little communication. When I studied economics at Oxford a generation ago, it was not considered necessary for an economist to know any accounting at all. Indeed, as far as I recall, not even the opportunity to study accounting was given. It was no doubt regarded as a pedestrian, commercial, workaday subject, quite unworthy of being admitted to those dignified halls. The situation, I am sure, is better at the newer institutions, both in Britain and the United States. Even in the United States, however, accounting is rarely integrated in any systematic or satisfactory way into an economist's education. The student of economics frequently has to pass a single required course in accounting, and that is the end of it. There is very little intellectual intercourse between economists and accountants at the professional level. The faults here may be more on the side of the economists than of the accountants. It is very rare to find an economist who reads the accounting journals. It is almost equally rare, however, to find an accountant who is well versed in economics.

K. E. Boulding, "Economics and Accounting: The Uncongenial Twins," in *Studies in Accounting*, 3rd ed., edited by W. Baxter and S. Davidson, Institute of Chartered Accountants of England and Wales, London, 1977. Reprinted with the permission of the Institute of Chartered Accountants of England and Wales.

This situation is all the more deplorable because many of the basic concepts of economics are, in fact, derived from accounting practice, and many accounting practices have been devised in an attempt to answer what are essentially economic questions. The concept of profit, for instance, is essentially an accounting concept. A large amount of the activity of accountants consists in the attempt to measure it. The concept of profit is likewise fundamental to economics. It is supposed to be the great motive power of a market system. It is supposed to account for the behavior of enterprises, and it is supposed to guide the allocation of resources among competing uses. The economist's concept of profit, however, and the accountant's concept often seem to have little in common. We do not, of course, have to have a single concept of profit for all purposes. The concept of profit will quite rightly differ depending upon the purpose for which we need it. The definition of profit for tax purposes, for instance, may differ considerably from the definition which is required for other forms of decision-making. What we need here is not a single definition of profit applicable to all cases, but a spectrum of definitions, in which the relationship of the various concepts is reasonably clear and in which the definition is fitted to the purpose for which it is to be used.

The point where accounting and economics come closest together is in what the economists call the theory of the firm. This is not surprising, as it is with a formalized and abstract description of the history of the firm that accounting is largely concerned, especially if we stretch the concept of the firm to include governmental and non-profit organizations of an economic character. The basic concept here both for accounting and for economics is that of the balance-sheet or position statement. This is essentially a description of the state of a firm or enterprise at a given moment of time. In its simplest form, what might be called the physical balance-sheet of an enterprise consists of a simple list of the values of all variables which are associated with it as they exist at a moment of time. This is a much larger concept, of course, than that of the accountant's balance-sheet. A great many variables which might be significant from the point of view of the state of the enterprise and especially from the point of view of its future, such as the quality of its management, or the morale of its work force, are quite rightly excluded from the accountant's balance-sheet. The accountant is interested in a limited aspect of the state of the enterprise, confined to those items which can be reduced by some rule or other to a value equivalent. What the accountant is doing, that is, when he constructs the balance-sheet, is essentially to make up a list of those items associated with the enterprise which can be valued, and he then proceeds to value them: he replaces the physical quantity of the item by so many dollars, pounds, or whatever the valuation unit may be. This he does by a variety of techniques, the end product of which is all the same—a sum of monetary values.

The ratio of the physical quantity of some item in the physical balance-sheet to the corresponding value equivalent may be called the "valuation coefficient." Frequently, the valuation process is performed by a rule which establishes a valuation coefficient, and then the value of a given physical quantity is obtained by simply multiplying the physical quantity by this coefficient. Thus, if an enterprise has a stock of a thousand bushels of wheat, we value this stock at some price or cost per bushel, say $2 per bushel, which is the valuation coefficient, and the total value of the stock is then $2,000. Some confusion may be caused by the fact that certain items in the physical balance-sheet are already expressed as a sum of money, for instance, a loan or a bond. In this case, of course, the valuation coefficient is unity, but it still exists.

The accountant gives some such name as net worth to the total net value of an enterprise. This is the sum of all the value items, both positive and negative (*i.e.*, assets less liabilities). The accountant may not seem to attach much significance to net worth by itself, but he is very interested indirectly in the size of this total, since—as we shall see on p. 90—the size of his profit figure depends on changes in net worth.

The difference in outlook of economists and accountants is perhaps one of emphasis rather than of principle. We may say, however, that accountants are primarily interested in the enterprise as it is now and as it has been in the past. The economist is interested in the "might have beens," as well as the actual situation. The accountant asks himself simply how profitable is the enterprise; the economist asks himself how profitable it might have been if it had done something different, and especially what it would have to do in order to make maximum profits.

Another possible difference, although the accountant might deny this, is that the accountant has a focus of interest in certain aggregates and totals, such as net worth or aggregate profit figures, whereas the economist is more interested in the structure of the enterprises. This interest in structure is admittedly soft-pedalled by many economists; it is a fair criticism of the theory of the firm, as set out in most economics textbooks, that the firm is depicted as acutely concerned with possible costs and revenues and, oblivious of asset structure—as having a profit budget but no balance-sheet.

To put the point in more mathematical language, the economist is interested in the balance-sheet as a vector in $n$-space. The accountant is interested in reducing this $n$-dimensional vector to a simple scalar, that is a single number. Unfortunately, even though rules can be applied, that is principles of valuation, for reducing an $n$-dimensional vector to a single number, these rules are inevitably somewhat arbitrary, and different rules may give entirely different results. This principle can be illustrated in Figure 1 in which we take an extremely simple enterprise, which has only two assets which we will call wheat, measured along OW, and money, along OM. A point P in this field represents a position or state of the enterprise, that is, its physical balance-sheet.

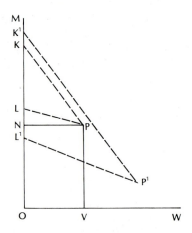

**FIGURE 1**

Thus, the point P represents an enterprise with NP bushels of wheat and VP shillings of money. If, now, we want to represent this position by a single figure, we have to value the wheat. If we suppose NK to be the value of the amount of wheat NP, then the valuation coefficient is $\dfrac{NK}{NP}$, which is the slope of the line KP. The net worth of the enterprise is then ON + NK, or OK. Consider now, two different positions of the enterprise, P and $P^1$ (the latter standing for more wheat and less money). The accountant wishes to know which of these two positions represents the larger value or net worth. If the valuation coefficient for wheat is the slope of KP and $K^1P^1$, then it is clear that $P^1$ represents the larger value, that is, the larger net worth, as $OK^1$ is larger than OK. Suppose, however, that we value the wheat at a lower price or coefficient equal to the slope of LP and $L^1P^1$. Now we see that the point P represents the higher value OL, whereas the point $P^1$ represents the lower value $OL^1$. Without knowing a set of valuation coefficients, therefore, we cannot tell whether the point P is "larger" or "smaller" than $P^1$. This is why the valuation procedure may properly be regarded as the heart of accountancy.

Both economics and accountancy are interested, not only in the state of an enterprise at a moment, but also in the course of the enterprise through time, that is, the sequence of position statements as they pass from one time period to the next. Suppose, for instance, that in figure 2, in which the axes have the same meaning as in figure 1, the point $P_0$ represents an initial position of the enterprise. Suppose now that the firm buys more wheat, moving from position $P_0$ to $P_1$. This means it gives up an amount of money equal to $P_0Q$ and acquires an amount of wheat equal to $QP_1$. The price at which the wheat has been bought is $\dfrac{P_0Q}{QP_1}$ which is the slope of the line $P_0P_1$. Now suppose the firm sells wheat following the line $P_1P_2$, *i.e.*, at a higher price. It is clear that in some sense a profit has been made. How much profit, depends on the valuation coefficients which are used. $P_2$ might even indicate smaller profit than $P_0$, if wheat were valued on both dates at a very high valuation coefficient, such as the slope of $K_0P_0$ and $K_2P_2$ (which reduces net worth from $OK_0$ to $OK_2$); but the accountant's bias towards conservatism will in general make for low coefficients, and so depress net worth where stocks of goods are high. In the course of successive periods, the enterprise will move to positions such as $P_3$, $P_4$, $P_5$, etc. If its operations have been successful, the result of these various transformations will be to move its position in some sense further "out" in the field. Exactly what constitutes "out," however, depends upon the system of valuation.

Profit can always be defined, in some sense, to mean an increase in net worth. The calculation of profit, that is to say, always involves the calculation of net worth from the position statements of two successive periods.[1] The rate of profit is the rate of increase of net worth in some sense or another. The problem is complicated somewhat by the fact that there may not only be asset transformations in the course of the history of the enterprise, there may also be withdrawals, that is, simple deductions

---

[1] This may not be obvious to accounting students trained to draft income statements *before* balance-sheets. But the costs and revenues in the former statement are all implicit in the changes in the latter, and are measured by these changes.

    The accountant on occasion isolates some gains, *e.g.*, windfalls may be shown separately from operating profit. But such technicalities do not affect the main argument.

from assets of one kind or another. Thus from the position $P_5$ in Figure 2, we could go directly downward to $P_6$ indicating a simple withdrawal of money from the enterprise. Yet a third event which may take place during the history of an enterprise is a revaluation—say, a change in the valuation coefficient by which physical assets are valued.

Virtually all events which are of significance to the enterprise can be classified in one of these three categories, either as an asset transformation, a revaluation, or a withdrawal. Asset transformations may be either through production or through exchange. When a miller grinds wheat into flour, for instance, he diminishes the quantity of wheat (raw materials) in the inventory shown in his position statement, and increases the quantity of flour (finished goods). When he exchanges flour, let us say, for accounts receivable, he diminishes the quantity of flour and increases the quantity of accounts receivable. The most fundamental concept of *cost* is that it represents the transformation ratio in *production*, that is, the ratio in which the input assets are transformed into the output assets. The most fundamental concept of *price* is that of the asset transformation ratio in *exchange*. If wheat costs $1·50 a bushel, this means on the whole that resources or inputs equivalent to $1·50 have to be used up or destroyed in order to increase the stock of wheat by one bushel. If the price of wheat is $2 a bushel, this means that wheat can be transformed into money through exchange at this rate.

Withdrawals may also be of two kinds, positive and negative. A negative withdrawal consists usually of simply putting money into the enterprise. The initial capital of an enterprise represents a negative withdrawal which is usually the first event in its history from the accounting point of view. Interest and dividend payments, of course, represent positive withdrawals.

In accounting practice, revaluations frequently occur at the moment of sale. Inventory, for instance, will be valued at cost in some sense until the moment of sale, when the article is revalued to the sale price. At the moment of sale (that is, in the

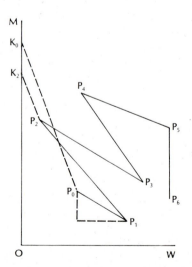

FIGURE 2

asset transformation) there is both a change of values from one item in the position statement to another, and an increase in values. The profit-making occurs essentially in the revaluation which takes place at the moment of sale. The fact that revaluation and exchange are bound up in a single transaction has often caused confusion, and it is necessary, analytically, to separate these two essentially dissimilar operations.

Another important difference between the accountant's and the economist's point of view, as we have seen, is that the accountant on the whole is interested in what is or what has been, whereas the economist is interested in what might be. In particular the economist is interested in the problem of what he calls "maximizing behavior." The accountant is interested, primarily, in what has happened to the enterprise in the past and in what is its position today; the economist is interested in the question of whether the enterprise could have done better. In accounting, for instance, price is largely treated as a datum and as a constant. In economics, price is usually treated as a variable. The economist asks himself what would have happened if there had been a different set of prices, exchanges, transformations, or withdrawals from that which actually occurred. Would the enterprise be better off now, or worse off? In particular, the economist is interested in the best pattern of behavior, that is, the pattern of behavior which places the enterprise in a position superior to that which can be reached by any other pattern of behavior. Achieving this best pattern is what the economist means by "maximizing behavior."

A good many of the propositions of price theory are based on the assumption that businessmen do, in fact, maximize profits. This is, of course, a highly dubious assumption. It is not only that there are always things for which businessmen are willing to sacrifice profits, such as security, respectability, liquidity, and so on, which means, of course, that they do not maximize profits. But a more fundamental difficulty is that the information which would enable a businessman to maximize his profits generally is not available to him. The difficulty here is a very fundamental one for the accountant and for the economist. Decisions are always made in the hope of the future, whereas information is always derived from the past. The theory of maximizing behavior assumes implicitly that we know all the possible patterns of the future and that we can select the best out of them. Our knowledge of the future, however, must be derived from our experience of the past, and our experience of the past is highly limited. Our image of the future or of the various possible futures is always dependent on some kind of projection of our past experience. These projections, however, are unreliable and they may be based on a very limited perception of the kind of dynamic system in which the enterprise operates. The basic difficulty here is that the future depends not only on the decisions of one person, but on the decisions of all the decision-makers of a society. A man can control his own decisions within limits, but he cannot control the decisions of others even though he may attempt to predict them. Because of this, there are bound to be inconsistencies in the images of the future of different individuals, which means that some of them must be falsified. Maximizing behavior, that is to say, is something which cannot be universally applied by its very nature.

In spite of the practical difficulties in the way of maximizing profit, the economist's theory of maximization, which is known usually as the marginal analysis, has a good deal of merit. Its merit lies perhaps in the questions which it raises rather than in the answers which it is able to give. It is always useful to take a given situation and to ask, "Could we have done better?" It is also useful to ask, "What do we need to know in order that we could do better?" It is perhaps because of pressure from the economist that the accountant has in many instances become interested in the concept of what he calls "incremental cost" and what the economist calls "marginal cost." These two concepts are not perhaps identical but they are closely related. The economist looks at a given situation and asks himself "Suppose we did something a little different? Would the increase in revenue be greater than the increase in cost?" If it is, then profits are clearly not being maximized now, and we shall do well to make the change. If, on the other hand, a given change increases revenue less than it increases cost, not only are we very sure that we should not make the change but we have evidence that we should make a change in an opposite direction. Even though, therefore, we can seldom be sure that we are actually at the point of maximum profit, we can frequently tell whether a proposed change is likely to move us toward that point or away from it. The economist recognizes, of course, that marginal costs or receipts are hard to measure. They represent a "might be" rather than an "is" and they are, therefore, not perhaps congenial to the accountant's insistence on the measurement of the actual. It is potentialities, however, rather than actualities which are most significant in the making of decisions, and in so far as we regard the whole process of information collection and processing in the organization as essentially an aid to the making of decisions, these potentialities are even more important than the actualities.

We shall notice also that the accountant himself is not altogether free from the necessity of considering potentialities, and in particular he cannot avoid making certain projections about the future. This is implicit, in fact, in any evaluation process. The act of valuation, Janus-like, has two faces. It faces back into the past and forward into the future. On the one hand, we value assets by past cost, sometimes compounded; on the other hand, we value them as discounted future net receipts. The former is what we can most easily find out; the latter, however, is the truly significant figure. The accountant is wise to take the past accounts as the basis for his evaluations. He may sometimes recognize the uncertainties of the present and of the future by making write-ups or write-downs, as the case may be—periodically adjusting past accounts to the present knowledge of the future. If he does not do this, the stock market will tend to do it for him. A firm, for instance, which has sunk a lot of money into assets in a country undergoing the fervors of a revolution is likely to find that the stock market values its shares on future expectations rather than past costs. In economics, as Jevons once said, "Bygones are bygones." For the accountant, bygones are not bygones without a struggle. It is probably just as well that he struggles. Sometimes, however, the struggle must be abandoned and bygone costs must be written down (or up) in the face of present realities.

The implication of the above is that even the accountant's calculation of profit is essentially based on some expectations about the future. Profit is not simply a matter of past performance; it always has in it an element of future expectation. This is because profit depends upon revaluations, and these revaluations may have to be made in the light of changes in expectations in the future. A firm which suffers a diminution of the value of its assets by a million pounds for whatever reason also suffers a diminution of its current profit—in our fundamental sense—by a million pounds. Profit, therefore, is not merely a matter of trying to sell again at a higher price. Many of the elements of cost in fact involve future expectations. It has been said that we should call no man happy until he is dead; likewise perhaps we should call no firm profitable until it has been finally liquidated. Nevertheless, the accountant must give some kind of an answer to the question "What profits have been earned?"

He must do this for legal as well as for decision-making reasons, for the law requires that, to some extent, the behavior of a firm conform to, or at least be limited by, its accounting results, especially for purposes of paying taxes or for distributing dividends.

The economist then looks on the accountant as a man who has to perform an impossible task. He has first to reduce what is essentially a multi-dimensional reality to a one-dimensional figure; and, in the second place, he has to do this on the basis of knowledge about the future which he cannot possibly have. Under these circumstances, it is not surprising that the economist regards much accounting procedure as in the nature of ritual. To call these procedures ritualistic is in no way to deny or decry their validity. Ritual is always the proper response when a man *has* to give an answer to a question, the answer to which he cannot really know. Ritual under these circumstances has two functions. It is comforting (and in the face of the great uncertainties of the future, comfort is not to be despised) and it is also an answer sufficient for action. It is the sufficient answer rather than the right answer which the accountant really seeks. Under these circumstances, however, it is important that we should know what the accountant's answer means, which means that we should know what procedure he has employed. The wise businessman will not believe his accountant although he takes what his accountant tells him as important evidence. The quality of that evidence, however, depends in considerable degree on the simplicity of the procedures and the awareness which we have of them. What the accountant tells us may not be true, but, if we know what he has done, we have a fair idea of what it means. For this reason, I am somewhat suspicious of many current efforts to reform accounting in the direction of making it more "accurate".

I am particularly suspicious of attempts to improve accounting by building into it an explicit recognition of the fact that the price level changes. It is easy to criticize accounting practice—and this is a criticism which economists have frequently made—on the ground that it assumes a monetary unit of constant value whereas in fact the monetary unit fluctuates constantly in purchasing power. The accountant's balance-sheet, it is argued, is reckoned in dollars of different ages, some of them perhaps of the year of the founding of the enterprise and others of last week. In the interim, however, the value of the monetary unit may have changed completely through the large social forces of inflation and deflation. This is almost as if we were trying to add feet to centimeters without reducing them to a common unit of length. A hundred feet plus ten centimeters is certainty not a hundred and ten anythings, and the acountant's balance-sheet total is not much better. It is argued also that because the accountant tends to perform valuation on the basis of historical cost, his measure of profit is inflated in a period of inflation and is correspondingly depressed in a period of deflation. Profits are made by selling things at a price greater than the cost. In an inflationary period, however, if the cost has been incurred at an earlier date, the price will reflect the general rise in prices as well as the relative price of a particular commodity. Hence, profits in accounts will be larger than they should be in terms of a dollar of constant purchasing power. Deflation destroys accounting profits in a similar way. An attempt is made to correct this distortion through valuing inventories by the last-in, first-out method, which is a more sophisticated substitute for the original first-in, first-out method.

The case for "constant dollar" accounting may be a strong one, but it is by no means invulnerable. The profits of inflation and the losses of deflation are not altogether illusory to the individual concern. Inflation, for instance, moves the real distribution of wealth away from those who hold liquid assets towards those who hold assets which are rising in price. Up to a point, the accounting profits of inflation reflect this, although they probably exaggerate it. Similarly, a deflation redistributes wealth towards those who simply sit tight with liquid assets, and the accounting losses therefore of those who trade and indulge in enterprise at such periods, again, are a partial reflection of this fact. There is something to be said also for a certain naïveté and simplicity in accounting practice. If accounts are bound to be untruths anyhow, as I have argued, there is much to be said for the simple untruth as against a complicated untruth, for if the untruth is simple, it seems to me that we have a fair chance of knowing what kind of an untruth it is. A known untruth is much better than a lie, and provided that the accounting rituals are well known and understood, accounting may be untrue but it is not lies; it does not deceive because we know that it does not tell the truth, and we are able to make our own adjustment in each individual case, using the results of the accountant as evidence rather than as definitive information.

My plea for naïveté, or at least for simplicity in accounting practice, does not preclude the hope that one day we may be able to set the whole information-collecting and processing operation of an organization on a somewhat more rational basis than now exists. At present one suspects that a great deal of information is collected and processed which actually is irrelevant to the making of decisions or the taking of any kind of action. The collection of such information is pure waste from the point of view of the organization even though it may have certain scientific value. Scientific information, however, is much better collected directly than as a by-product of other operations. By contrast, a great deal of information which is highly relevant to the making of decisions is neither collected nor processed. Nobody, to my mind, has yet developed an adequate theory of information collection and processing from the point of view of the decision-making process. When this is done, we may find that both accounting and economics may each lose their life in a larger science and a larger process. Until that day comes, one can only plead for more communication and understanding between the accountant and the economist for each has much to learn from the other, especially if each recognizes the autonomy of the other. Their concepts are often different because the purposes for which they are used are different. These differences must be borne in mind if fruitful communication is to take place.

# II-A 2 *Economic and Accounting Concepts of Income*[1]

DAVID SOLOMONS

In recent years, discussion of the measurement of income has been largely colored and dominated by problems created by changes in the value of money. Serious as these problems are, they are really secondary ones, for they presuppose some basic agreement about the nature and measurement of income during a period of stable prices. Between accountants and economists, it need hardly be said, no such agreement exists. My purpose in this paper is first to examine these differences—a task which has been performed, with greater or less thoroughness, many times before—and then to consider the only attempt known to me to work out a concept of income which would, like the accountant's, be capable of practical use and yet would stay close to the fundamental definition of income with which we begin. The attempt at reconciliation to which I refer is Sidney Alexander's concept of variable income, put forward in his monograph, "Income Measurement in a Dynamic Economy."[2] Alexander's suggestion deserves more discussion than it has received hitherto, whether we finally judge it to be a workable concept or not. It is for that reason that I shall have something to say about it here. My conclusion about the practical utility of the concept, as a matter of fact, will be adverse; and from that disappointing conclusion I am led on to the view that the time has come to develop other and more effective tools to do the jobs which periodic income so signally fails to do in the field of financial planning and control. As I shall suggest, there are signs that the central position which income occupies in accounting is already being usurped.

David Solomons, "Economic and Accounting Concepts of Income," *The Accounting Review*, July 1961, pp. 374–383. Reprinted with the permission of *The Accounting Review*.

[1] This paper was presented at the Northeast Regional Meeting of the American Accounting Association at the Massachusetts Institute of Technology on October 28–29, 1960.

[2] Published as the first of *Five Monographs on Business Income* by the Study Group on Business Income, 1950. Alexander's work in a slightly revised version, will shortly be republished in the 2nd edition of *Studies in Accounting*, to be edited by W. T. Baxter and Sidney Davidson.

## USEFULNESS OF THE INCOME CONCEPT

Any discussion of competing ideas of income ought, I think, to start with the question: "Do we really need an income concept, and if so, what for?" Only when we have asked and answered this question can we say whether there is anything we need to define, and whether one or more than one concept of income is necessary.

Let us consider income for taxation purposes first. It is really rather remarkable that income has become so universally accepted as a good measure of taxable capacity, for on closer inspection it seems to have grave defects. Command over capital resources would seem to be a much fairer guide to the subject's ability to pay taxes, and also to the demand made by the individual on various governmental services such as defense and law and order. Alternatively, as suggested by Mr. Kaldor, it might be more sensible to tax people according to what they spend rather than on what they earn. This is not a plea for the substitution of indirect for direct taxation, of course, but for the use of a computation of expenditure rather than of income as the basis of taxation. It is not necessary to go into this matter here. For my purpose, it is enough to note that our system of direct taxation could get along quite well, and, indeed, perhaps better, if we did not have a concept of income at all.

A second important purpose which the concept of income is said to serve is in the determination of corporate dividend policy. So long as dividends are paid out of income and not otherwise, it is asserted, the rights of creditors will not be prejudiced by the return of capital to stockholders. If this means, as it does in certain jurisdictions, that currently or recently earned net profits may be distributed without making good earlier losses of capital, it is clear that the rights of creditors are being very imperfectly protected. The payment of a legal dividend by no means implies, in such circumstances, that the stockholders' capital is intact. Moreover, a corporation may earn a profit and yet to be too short of cash to be able to pay a dividend without endangering its short-term solvency. The existence of current net income, therefore, may tell directors nothing about the dividend policy they ought to follow. It makes much more sense for the law to require, as it sometimes does, either that stockholders' capital should be intact before a dividend is paid out of any excess, or to require some defined margin of assets over and above those necessary to pay creditors' claims, before allowing the payment of dividends to stockholders. Either type of restriction is more effective in protecting the rights of creditors than one based on an income concept, while at the same time being free of the difficulties of defining and measuring net income.

A third major need served, or said to be served by the concept of income, is as a guide to investment policy. Prospective investors seek to maximize their return on investment, and their search will be guided by the income earned on existing investments. This is related to another argument—that income provides the best measure we have of success in the management of business enterprise in a competitive economy. These are important needs, and they both point in the same direction. That investment is most attractive which offers us the greatest present value of future receipts per dollar invested, when discounted at the going rate of interest, and insofar as historical data can help us in the choice of investments, it will be data about the growth in present value of existing investments. Again, that manager is most successful who, during a given period, increases the present value of the enterprise entrusted to him proportionately the most. In both of these cases, it is growth in present value which alone appears to be significant; and since it seems to carry out the function generally attributed to income, growth in present value must be what we had better understand income to mean.

## ECONOMIC INCOME

The concept of income to which we have been led corresponds of course, to Hicks's definition of income. For an individual, he defines income as the maximum amount a man can consume in a period and still be as well off at the end of the period as he was at the beginning. There is no doubt that when, as individual salary-earners and investors, we think of our personal income for a year, we commonly do not think of it in this way, but rather as a stream of prorated receipts, unaffected by any changes in the value of the tangible assets with which we started the year and certainly as having nothing to do with any change in our future prospects—in our "goodwill," in other words—which may take place during the year. But this does not lead me to conclude that "the income of a person or other entity is what he believes to be his income . . ."[3] for we can be mistaken about the nature of income just as men were once mistaken about the nature of combustion when they attributed it to phlogiston. Rather, I would say, "Income is as income does."

If we take Hicks's definition of income as applied even to an individual, it is easy to see, however we define our terms, income in Hicks's sense and income as the accountant measures it will only by accident ever be the same thing. As Hicks points out, the difficulty about this definition is in saying what we mean by "being as well-off" at one date as at another. He offers us three different measures of well-off-ness, which, however, come together, if we abstract from changes in the value of money and from changes in the rate of interest, to give us a single measure of well-off-ness command over money capital. If we accept constancy of money capital as representing constancy of well-off-ness, then income in Hicks's sense becomes the amount by which the individual's net worth has increased during the period, due allowance being made for the value of what he has consumed or given away during that time.

To use Hicks's definition for the income of a business entity rather than for that of an individual, we need only modify it slightly; the income of the business, whether it is incorporated as a separate legal entity or not, is the amount by which its net worth has increased during the period, due allowance being made for any new capital contributed by its owners or for any distributions made by the business to its owners. This form of words would also serve to define accounting income, insofar as net accounting income is the figure which links the net worth of the business as shown by its balance sheet at the beginning of the accounting period with its net worth as shown by its balance sheet at the end of the period. The correspondence between the two ideas of increased net worth is, however, a purely verbal one: for Hicksian income demands that in evaluating net worth we capitalize expected future net receipts, while accounting income only requires that we evaluate net assets on the basis of their unexpired cost.

It is hardly open to question that you cannot really assess the well-off-ness of an enterprise by aggregating the costs, or the unexpired costs, of its assets and deducting

[3] "Scope and Method of Theory and Research in the Measurement of Income and Wealth," by Myron J. Gordon (*The Accounting Review*, Oct. 1960), p. 608.

its liabilities. Any differences between the current value of its tangible assets and their book value based on cost will be excluded; and any value which the enterprise may have over and above the value of its tangible assets will also be excluded. We may sum up the relationship between these two different concepts of increase in net-worth, economic income and accounting income, by starting with accounting income and arriving at economic income thus:

- Accounting income
    - \+ Unrealized changes in the value of tangible assets which took place during the period, over and above value changes recognized as depreciation of fixed assets and inventory mark-downs,
    - − Amounts realized this period in respect of value changes in tangible assets which took place in previous periods and were not recognized in those periods,
    - \+ Changes in the value of intangible assets during the period, hereafter to be referred to as changes in the value of goodwill
    - = Economic income.

## THE REALIZATION PRINCIPLE

Obviously the main difference between these two income concepts lies in the accountant's attachment to realization as the test of the emergence of income. The Study Group on Business Income, in its 1952 report, rather surprisingly suggested that "the realization postulate was not accepted prior to the First World War,"[4] and supported this with quotations from both American and British sources. It seems to me, on the contrary, that the trend has, for a long time now, been away from, rather than towards, placing emphasis on the importance of realization. For a long time the relationship of income to capital was likened to the relation of the fruit to the tree. Just as there was no difficulty in separating the crop from the tree, so there need be no difficulty in distinguishing income from the capital which produced it. It was in line with this thinking that, for the first thirty-six years after Peel has re-introduced the income tax in Britain in 1842, no relief was given by the British tax code for the using up of fixed assets in the course of carrying on a business. The introduction of income tax depreciation allowances in Britain in 1878, and their growth in importance there and here since then, constitute a movement away from the idea that you can evaluate the fruit without giving thought to the value of the tree—that realized profits can be measured in disregard of what have sometimes been called "mere value changes" in the assets of the business. Another earlier step away from the pure realization principle was the "cost or market-price" rule for valuing inventory. You will not find this in accounting literature before the mid-nineteenth century, for before that time consistent valuation at cost seems to have been the rule. The recognition of unrealized losses on inventory is a clear recognition of "mere value changes," if only in one direction, as being relevant to the determination of income. As final evidence of the same tendency, I suppose we might cite the development of cash accounting into accrual accounting as itself a de-emphasizing of the importance of realization. For what it is worth, we can perhaps say that over the years accounting income and

---

[4] *Changing Concepts of Business Income* (Macmillan, New York, 1952), p. 23.

economic income have moved a little closer together. Yet of course, when everything has been said, accounting income is still substantially realized income.

The tableau set out above may make it easier for us to evaluate the two income concepts in terms of the two qualities which outweigh all others in importance, their usefulness and their practicality. It is because the results of this evaluation are what they are that it is natural to hanker after a compromise income concept which has a greater share of these qualities combined than either accounting or economic income has, taken by itself.

## THE CASE FOR AND AGAINST ACCOUNTING INCOME AND ECONOMIC INCOME

Whether we use one concept of income or another, or indeed whether we use any concept of income at all, clearly should depend, as I have already said, on the purpose we want to serve and the income concept which will best serve it. In what follows I shall concentrate my attention on one aspect of this matter only, namely, the measurement of business income for the purpose of assessing entrepreneurial success or failure in the profit-making sector of the economy. From this point of view it must be said that accounting income is seriously defective. By focussing attention on the result of current realization of assets and ignoring all other value changes except such as are covered by the "cost or market" rule, and by depreciation, it can lead to some rather ridiculous results. One such result is that described by Kenneth MacNeal.[5] Two investors each have $1,000 to invest. One buys $1,000 worth of stock A, the other buys $1,000 worth of stock B. By the end of the year both stocks have doubled in price. The first investor sells out just before Dec. 31, and reinvests the $2,000 he gets from the sale in stock B. The second investor continues to hold his block of stock, which is also worth $2,000 at the end of the year. Thus both start equal, with $1,000 each in cash: they also finish equal, both holding equal quantities of stock B worth $2,000. It is impossible to say that one investor has been more successful than the other. Yet one of them shows an accounting profit of $1,000 as the result of his realization, while the other shows no accounting profit at all.

Another absurd result is cited by Sidney Alexander, that of the manager of a large corporation who is considering a deal which will increase his accounting profit by a million dollars but which will result in the destruction of the firm's goodwill by forcing it out of business. By looking only at changes in tangible equity (and only at a part of that), while ignoring changes in goodwill, accounting income provides us with a very unsatisfactory measure of managerial success. Another way of putting this is to say that if maximizing profit is ever a rational business goal, it is rational only if profit means economic profit, not accounting profit.

It may be said, and with truth, that the differences between accounting income and economic income are only short-run differences, i.e. if we take a sufficiently long period in the life of an enterprise the changes in the value of equity which distinctively enter into economic income will also be reflected in accounting income. Thus MacNeal's second investor will have his wise investment reflected in his profit when eventually he sells his stock in a later period, if by then it has not fallen in value.

---

[5] In his article "What's Wrong with Accounting," *The Nation*, October 7–14, 1939, and reprinted in the 1950 edition of *Studies in Accounting*, ed. W. T. Baxter (London, Sweet & Maxwell, Ltd.).

That over the whole life of an enterprise its total accounting income and economic income must be identical cannot be gainsaid. But this is poor consolation for short-run defects in our measure of income. *All* the problems of income measurement are the result of our desire to attribute income to arbitrarily determined short periods of time. Everything comes right in the end; but by then it is too late to matter.

Having cast some doubt on the effectiveness of accounting income as a gauge of managerial success, we have to recognize that it emerges satisfactorily from the other test, that of practicality. Insofar as objectivity is regarded as an indispensible quality of an income concept which is to have any claim to being practical, accounting income is practical enough. But this is of little moment if it does not measure what we want to measure. Objectivity without relevance is not much of a virtue. The question is whether we can retain some or all the objectivity of accounting income while answering the question which accounting income palpably fails to answer: How much better off has the accounting entity become during the period?

In passing, we might notice a contrary point view on the relevance of the two income concepts we are comparing in a statement by Professors Hill and Gordon.[6] Rejecting the idea that unrealized profits should be included in income, they argue that "information as to what management *expects to make* on the things it *has not sold* is no substitute for information as to what management *has made* on the things it *has sold*." The answer to this is that neither is the second kind of information a substitute for the first, and it is only the second kind which accounting conventionally provides. Both kinds of information are necessary to assess managerial success. As I have already tried to show, to look at realized profits and losses only may be to ignore an important part of the total picture.

In advocating their particular brand of business income, economists have usually argued that the increase in net worth of the enterprise, which constitutes income, must be arrived at by valuing the whole enterprise at the beginning and the end of the period whose income we wish to measure. These valuations, they say, must be made by discounting, at each date, the expected stream of receipts less the expected stream of payments of the enterprise as far into the future as possible, to arrive at the present value of the net stream. Any amounts distributed by the enterprise to its proprietors during the period must, of course, be added back to give the increase in net worth which, in this view, is synonymous with income. Expressed in this way, the concept looks quite impractical, for it seems to demand a superhuman degree of foresight, not only about the broad sweep of events but also about the details of day-to-day transactions.

I do not think that too much should be made of this difficulty. We do not allow uncertainty about the future entirely to inhibit us from valuing property on the basis of expected net receipts, or at least on the best estimate we can make of them. Moreover, there are simplifying assumptions we could make which would render the valuation process more manageable. Nevertheless, the difficulties are still somewhat formidable.

A second difficulty about the concept of economic income is that in successive discounting of expected future receipts and payments, effect will have to be given not only to real foreseeable changes in the enterprise's future, but also to changes in

---

[6] *Accounting: A Management Approach*, by T. M. Hill and Myron J. Gordon (2nd edition, 1960, Irwin), p. 143.

human expectations about this future. Thus, suppose that at the beginning of the period a large receipt is foreseen as coming in in three years' time. At the end of the period (of, say, a year) the receipt is thought to be much less certain, and in any case probably smaller than was previously expected. The net worth of the enterprise will have apparently shrunk during the year, then, not because of a real change in the future but only because of a change in expectations about the future. Thus economic income will react both to real future changes and to changes in human expectations, and the effects of these two sets of factors will be inextricably combined.

## THE CONCEPT OF VARIABLE INCOME

The concept of "variable income" attempts to eliminate the effect of a change in expectations from our measure of economic income. Alexander, it will be remembered, approaches the problem of measuring business income by considering first the income from a bond, indeed from quite a variety of bonds. He starts with a perpetual bond which pays no interest in the ordinary sense, but whose owner annually receives $10 if, on the toss of a coin, it comes down heads and nothing if it comes down tails. As a matter of fact this example is hardly more bizarre than the British premium savings bonds which have been in issue since 1956 and which, while securing the investor's capital, pay no interest in the ordinary sense but offer the chance, after a qualifying period of six months, of a prize in a monthly lottery. The amount of the prize fund is determined by calculating interest, at the rate prescribed from time to time, on the bonds eligible for the draw. In the case of Alexander's perpetual bond, he argues that, assuming a 5% rate of interest, the bond would maintain a steady value of $100, whatever the results of the tosses from year to year, for an even chance of receiving $10 or nothing is equivalent to an expectation of receiving $5 each year, giving a capital value, at 5%, of $100. As a matter of fact, according to the strength of the gambling instinct in the community in question, the bond might just as easily be worth more or less than $100; but so long as its value is accepted as being unaffected by the results of each toss, it does not matter just what that value is. And of course, since each toss is a separate event, the chances of success next time are unaffected by past results, so there is no reason why the value of the bond should be affected by the incidence of heads or tails. The income from the bond in any year is then equal to its owner's receipts from it, $10 or nothing according to the result of the toss.

We get closer to real life with Alexander's second bond, which is like the first but has a life limited to 20 years. This bond at the outset will have a capital value of $62.70, this being the present value, at 5%, of a 20 year annuity of $5 annually (the expectation of receipts from the bond). A year later, regardless of the outcome of the toss, it should be worth only $60.42, the present value of a 19 year annuity of $5, and each year as the bond's expectation of life diminishes, its value will continue to fall. In this case the bond-holder enjoys an income which is always less than his receipts by the amount of the diminution in the value of his security. The loss of capital value in the first year was $2.28, so that if the coin came down heads his receipts were $10 and his income was $7.72, while if the coin came down tails his receipts were zero and his income was—$2.28. This illustration leads us straight to Alexander's first definition of variable income, at least as it applies to income from securities, which is that variable income is equal to the net receipts from the security plus or minus any change in its value which was, *at the beginning of the period*, expected to take place during the period.

This it must be noted, is a first approximation to the definition of variable income for the full definition has to provide for the possibility that the net receipts of the period may themselves cause future expectations of receipts to be modified during the period, as where a particularly large distribution to owners of a security during the present period is made at the expense of distributions to be made in future periods. In such a case, variable income has to be defined as the net receipts from the security plus or minus any change in its value during the period which was expected at the beginning of the period, plus or minus the discounted present value of any consequential change in expected future receipts brought about by the level of current receipts. This modification of the definition to take account of consequential change in the value of the security will be seen to be of some significance when shortly we consider the determination of the variable income of a business enterprise.

Because changes in the value of a security which result from changes in expectations which occur during the period are excluded from the definition of variable income, this does not mean that they must be neglected altogether. What it does mean is that they are considered to be best kept separate from income, to be reported separately as unexpected gains. Here, another of Alexander's illustrations makes the point clear. Suppose, he says, the amount paid on the perpetual bond is suddenly raised from $10 or nothing on the toss of a coin to $12 or nothing. At a 5% rate of interest this announcement will raise the value of the bond from $100 to $120. There is an unexpected gain of $20, quite apart from any variable income there may be during that year.

This is perhaps a suitable point at which to compare the informativeness of the three income concepts we can choose from in this case. Accounting income would be reported as $10 for the year if the coin came down heads. The change in the terms of the bond would not be regarded as having any relevance to the determination of current income. Economic income would be reported as $30, the receipts for the period plus the increase in the value of the bond. Alexander's proposal is that we should report a variable income of $10 and an unexpected gain of $20. There seems to me to be no room for doubt that this last method of reporting is more informative than either of the others, if our purposes is to assess the success of the bondholder's investment policy for the year.

Incidentally, the relationship between economic income and variable income can be expressed symbolically quite simply, if we write $V$ as the value of the asset whose income we are considering, $R$ for the net receipts from it, use the subscripts 0 and 1 for the beginning and end of period 1, and the further subscripts $a$ and $e$ for actual magnitudes and expected magnitudes respectively. Then:

$$\text{Economic income} = \text{Variable income} + \text{unexpected gain}$$
$$V_{1a} - V_{0a} + R_a = (V_{1e} - V_{0a} + R_a) + (V_{1a} - V_{1e})$$

However, it has to be admitted that this formulation is incomplete insofar as it excludes from variable income and leaves in unexpected gain the consequential changes in $V_{1a}$ which have already been referred to.

## THE VARIABLE INCOME OF A BUSINESS ENTERPRISE

It is easy enough to separate the receipts of the owner of a security from the security itself. When we turn to a business enterprise, we cannot use the amounts distributed by the enterprise to its proprietors to help us in determining the income of the enterprise; and the net receipts of the enterprise will include the proceeds of converting non-cash assets into cash, which proceeds we obviously cannot reckon as income. What corresponds to $R_a$, in the case of an enterprise, is the change in net tangible assets during the period, all assets being valued at cost. This is equal to accounting net income before charging depreciation or providing for inventory mark-downs, and it is the first element in enterprise variable income.

The second element, $V_{1e} - V_{0a}$, is the change in the ex dividend value of the enterprise during the year which can be predicted with more or less certainty at the beginning of the year. This predictable change in value is, I suggest, what we ought to be measuring when we provide for depreciation, that is to say, it is depreciation based more on the expected loss of market value through use or obsolescence of assets rather than on allocations of historical cost.[7] Of course, in a world from which uncertainty had been banished, these two concepts of depreciation would amount to the same thing.

The third and last element in the variable income of a business enterprise, corresponding to the consequential change in the value of a security resulting from the year's distribution to proprietors, could be of major importance. We must include in variable income any change in the value of the enterprise which is the result of managerial activity during the year over and above the predictable change just discussed. Such change may take the form of a change in the value of tangible assets or a change in the value of goodwill. To qualify for inclusion in variable income these value changes must be brought about by the activity of the firm. If they are purely the result of factors extraneous to the firm, such as a change in the law or a change in the market rate of interest, then they are not part of variable income but are unexpected gains.

The distinction which has to be drawn here is between value changes which are merely the result of a change in expectations and value changes which are the result of managerial activity. If variable income is to measure the firm's success in adding to its well-off-ness, value changes of the latter type must be included in it. In his original formulation of the way in which the variable income of a corporation might be determined, Alexander did not draw a distinction between internally and externally generated changes in the value of goodwill, but suggested that any change in its value might be included in variable income. However, this seems to me to be inconsistent with his earlier definition. The principal difference between variable income and economic income, as I understand it, is that while economic income includes all changes in the value of net worth which have taken place during the period, variable income includes only those changes which inevitably result from the passage of time or are the result of the activities of the period. To implement this idea, we have to try to distinguish changes in the value of goodwill which are the result of managerial activity, those which reflect, that is to say, changes in expectations brought about by the management and changes in the value of goodwill which cannot so be accounted for.

We have, then, these three constituents of variable business income:

1. The change in net tangible assets, valued at cost.
2. As a deduction, the expected loss of market value of assets through use or obsolescence.

---

[7] I must repeat here that I am assuming away changes in the value of money. Insofar as these must be reckoned with, some form of stabilization would have to be built into the above scheme.

3. Internally generated differences between the value of both tangible and intangible assets at the accounting data and their cost at date of acquisition (or their value at the previous accounting date), to the extent that these differences have not already been included in (2) above.

It is this third element, and especially the recognition of certain changes in the value of goodwill as constituting part of the firm's net income, which particularly distinguishes variable income from accounting income.

## CAN WE MEASURE VARIABLE INCOME?

Variable income is a valuable idea, I think, in clarifying our thinking about what an income concept should give us and in recognizing the limitations of accounting income. But can we, in practice, hope to make the distinction between those value changes which are to be included in variable income and those which are to be included in unexpected gain?

Regretfully, I do not think that we can. We must remember that we have two problems, one of valuation and one of attribution, if we want to implement the idea of variable income for a business enterprise. Even if we are prepared to ignore any but quite substantial divergences between the depreciated cost and the current value of tangible assets, we should as a minimum have first to revalue goodwill at the end of each accounting period and then to apportion any change in its value between that part which was the result of managerial activity and that part which was the result of good or bad luck. One has only to state this difficulty to see that there can never be any simple solution to it. Even in very simple domestic situations we know that we can rarely separate the results of good luck and good judgment. In a complex business situation, how much less likely are we to be able to do so!

This difficulty, which would confront us even if our accounts were kept in monetary units of constant purchasing power, is exacerbated when we have to allow for price level changes. When an asset is bought for $1,000 and prices in general rise so that a year later the asset, though then partly worn out, is worth more on the market than when it was first bought, is this value change to be regarded as an "unexpected gain" or are we to attribute it to the good judgment of management in purchasing the asset in anticipation of a price rise? If the use of the variable income idea requires us to answer questions like this, I conclude that we simply cannot use it, except, perhaps in simple non-business situations.

## CONCLUSION

Just as Hicks was led to the conclusion that income was not an effective tool of economic analysis, so it seems to me that we are led to the conclusion that periodic income is not an effective tool of financial planning or control. This conclusion seems to accord ill with the fact that income measurement has long been a central theme of accounting and the main preoccupation of the accounting profession. Yet this fact need not impress us. The practice of medicine once consisted largely of blood-letting. It may be that we are already witnessing a decline in the importance of income measurement. Certainly there is a livelier sense of short-comings of ascertained profit figures than there once was, for most of the purposes for which such figures have traditionally been used. There is a rather striking confirmation of this in the preamble to Recommendation XV of the Institute of Chartered Accountants in England and Wales. This Recommendation is concerned with the price-level problem, and the passage I have in mind (paragraph 312) reads as follows:

> The Council cannot emphasize too strongly that the significance of accounts prepared on the basis of historical cost is subject to limitations, not the least of which is that the monetary unit in which the accounts are prepared is not a stable unit of measurement. In consequence the results shown by accounts prepared on the basis of historical cost are not a measure of increase or decrease in wealth in terms of purchasing power; nor do the results necessarily represent the amount which can prudently be regarded as available for distribution, having regard to the financial requirements of the business. Similarly the results shown by such accounts are not necessarily suitable for purposes such as price fixing, wage negotiations and taxation, unless in using them for these purposes dues regard is paid to the amount of profit which has been retained in the business for its maintenance.

This seems pretty much to throw away the baby with the bath-water.

The fact is that, for several important purposes, periodic income, either historical or prospective, has already been or is being superseded. For decision-making purposes the idea of "contribution" has taken over from net income. In the field of taxation, we depart from income as the tax base every time we introduce special allowances for depletion, or provide for accelerated depreciation, or permit an anomalous treatment of capital gains. Even for reporting to stockholders, just as in the first half of this century we saw the income statement displace the balance sheet in importance, so we may now be de-emphasizing the income statement in favor of a statement of fund flows or cash flows. Each of us sees the future differently, no doubt. But my own guess is that, so far as the history of accounting is concerned, the next twenty-five years may subsequently be seen to have been the twilight of income measurement.

## II-B 1   *The FASB and the Allocation Fallacy*

ARTHUR L. THOMAS

Off to an impressively active start, the Financial Accounting Standards Board has already wrestled with a broad range of accounting issues. Topics on its active agenda or on which it has issued Standards include

1. Accounting for leases.
2. Accounting for research and development costs.
3. Contingencies and future losses.
4. Gains and losses from extinguishment of debt.
5. Interest costs and capitalization.
6. Accounting for pensions.
7. Segment reporting.
8. Business combinations.
9. Interim financial statements.
10. Reporting by development stage entities.
11. Reporting in units of general purchasing power.
12. Translation of foreign currency transactions and financial statements.
13. The recommendations of the Trueblood Report.[1]

All these topics involve some kind of *allocation*, which is the assignment of a total to one or more locations or categories. A thesaurus gives "division," "partition,"

I am grateful to Paul Rosenfield for his comments on an earlier draft of this article.

Arthur L. Thomas, "The FASB and the Allocation Fallacy," *The Journal of Accountancy*, November 1975, pp. 65–68. Copyright © 1975 by the American Institute of Certified Public Accountants, Inc.

[1] "Objectives of Financial Statements," Report of the Study Group on the Objectives of Financial Statements, Robert M. Trueblood, chairman (New York: AICPA, October 1973).

"slicing," "splitting" and "apportionment" as synonyms of "allocation." Accounting's allocations include assignment of a lease's costs to the individual years of its life, assignment of R&D costs to the single year of their expenditure and assignment of long term investment interest to successive annual revenues. All the FASB topics listed above fall into one of the following two classes of allocations, with items 7 through 9 falling into both:

1.   The first nine topics require deciding when to recognize revenues, expenses, gains or losses—that is, deciding to what periods they should be assigned. For example, the FASB may eventually specify how to allocate pension costs to successive annual pension expenses.
2.   The last seven topics involve ways of preparing financial statements composed mainly of allocated data. For example, this is implicit throughout the Trueblood Report and explicit in its position statement and income statement recommendations.

In fact, almost all of our revenue recognition and matching efforts require allocation.

## THE ALLOCATION PROBLEM

The foregoing is background to a problem that we accountants acknowledge, but whose severity we usually misjudge. To use a term from formal logic, recent research indicates that, unfortunately, our allocations must almost always be *incorrigible*—that is to say, they can neither be refuted nor verified.[2] Incorrigibility will be a central concept in this discussion, and it is well to give a few examples even if doing so may initially seem to be a detour.

Let's suppose that someone claims that beings live among us who look and act exactly like humans, but who actually are aliens, seeded on this planet by flying saucers. We ask: do they come equipped with authentic looking birth certificates? Yes. Would tests of their internal structure, chromosomes or the like expose them? No. Could psychiatrists unmask them? No. The horrible thing is that they have such good counterfeit memories that even the aliens themselves don't know their real nature—you may be one yourself.

Such claims are incorrigible, for no experiment could prove either that such aliens exist or that they don't. Here are some other incorrigible claims:

- Charles Dickens may not have been a greater author than Shakespeare, but he was more of a person.
- Our bourbon is mellower.
- The official state flower of Unicornia is the marsh mallow.
- Even if the colonists had lost their war of independence, by now America would be independent of Britain.
- Since I've lost weight, I've become more spiritual.

[2] Arthur L. Thomas, Studies in Accounting Research No. 9, *The Allocation Problem: Part Two* (American Accounting Association, 1974), hereafter SAR 9.

Now, if our allocations are incorrigible, practicing accountants should be deeply concerned. We attest that financial statements present fairly the positions of companies and the results of their operations. But if both our revenue recognition and matching are founded upon allocations that we can neither refute nor verify, *we have no way of knowing whether these attestations are true.*

*Are* they incorrigible? I'll begin with matching and for brevity will disregard extraordinary items (and other nonoperating gains and losses), lower-of-cost-or-market writedowns and the like. Our matchings assign costs of a firm's non-monetary inputs (inventories, labor, other services, depreciable assets, etc.) to the expenses of one or more accounting periods, temporarily reporting as assets costs assigned to future periods. We're all familiar with the theory behind these matching assignments: each input's purchase price should be allocated to successive periods in proportion to the contribution it makes to each period's revenues. Academics and most practitioners also know that an equivalent matching theory can be developed around contributions to net cash inflows.

The allocation problem has several dimensions, some of which are subtle. But one is easily described: to match costs with revenues, we must know what the contributions of the firm's individual inputs *are*. Unfortunately, as I'll illustrate below, there's no way that we can know this.

Seeing why this is so requires introducing a final concept, *interaction*. Inputs to a process interact whenever they generate an output different from the total of what they would yield separately. For instance, labor and equipment interact whenever people and machines working together produce more goods than the total of what people could make with their bare hands and machines could make untended. As this example suggests, interaction is extremely common. Almost all of a firm's inputs interact with each other—their failure to do so would ordinarily signal their uselessness.

Surprising as it may seem, it can be proved that whenever inputs interact, calculations of how much total revenue or cash flow has been contributed by any individual input are as meaningless as, say, calculations of the proportion of a worker's services due to any one internal organ: heart, liver or lungs. Thus, despite all textbooks and American Institute of CPAs or FASB releases to the contrary—despite what you've been trained to believe—our attempts to match costs with revenues must almost always fail. The next section tries to demonstrate this.


## A SIMPLE EXAMPLE

A complete demonstration, meeting all possible counterarguments, is very lengthy.[3] But a simple example reveals the kernel of the matter. What follows is offered in the same spirit as Robert Sterling's recent illustration in these pages that only price-level-adjusted current-value financial statements are fully relevant and interpretable:

"A highly simplified case will be considered in this article. The advantages of simplified cases are that they are easily understood by both the reader and the author and they are more easily solved. If we cannot solve the simplified cases, then we can be fairly certain that we also cannot solve the complex cases. Thus, if a particular

---

[3] See SAR 9, chapters 1–6, for the attempt.

approach fails to provide a solution for simplified cases, then we can avoid wasting effort by trying that approach on complex cases."[4]

However, instead of Sterling's cash, securities, bread and milk trading economy, I'll describe a production process for bread alone and confine the discussion to strictly physical measures (to avoid complications introduced by monetary valuations).[5] If individual contributions are necessarily incorrigible even in the following example, it's hard to imagine how they could be otherwise in the vastly more complex processes by which business enterprises generate their products, services, revenues and cash flows.

A prospector manufactures sourdough bread by a three-stage process:

1. He makes leaven by mixing flour, sugar and water in a crock, then keeps it in a warm place for about a week (until it bubbles).
2. He makes bread by transferring all but a cup of leaven to a large pot, where he mixes it with soda and additional flour, sugar and water, kneads it slightly and then lets it rise. He digs a shallow pit, fills it with coals from his camp fire, covers the pot, places it in the pit, buries it in hot coals and keeps it there until the bread is baked.
3. He replenishes the leaven (for the next baking) by adding enough flour and water to restore the crock to its original level.

Water, airborne yeasts and wood are free goods here. We accountants would be concerned with the following inputs to this process: flour, sugar, soda, labor, the crock, the pot and a shovel. Finally, part of the flour and sugar leaven for one loaf becomes included in the leaven for the next. The output of each baking is one loaf of bread.

Although its manufacture is simple, the moment we try to calculate the contributions of any individual input to this output we face a dilemma. Each input (except, perhaps, the soda and the shovel) is essential. Therefore, we could plausibly assign all of the output to any individual input. For example, we could assign all of the output to the flour, reasoning that were flour withheld from the process there would be no bread. Yet, we could equally well assign all of the output to the pot, since without it the loaf would have been incinerated.

Having assigned all output to any one input, we've implicitly assigned zero to each other input. But if either all or zero is appropriate for each input, any intermediate allocation will be equally appropriate—say, half the loaf to the flour and a sixth each to the pot, labor and the crock.

I'm unable to prove which of the infinitely many possible ways of allocating the loaf is correct. Therefore, I can't specify the individual contributions of the inputs; instead, all I'm entitled to say is that they generate the loaf jointly. Research shows that other writers on economics and accounting—even efficient-markets investigators—are equally unable to solve this problem. Perhaps the reader can. But until someone does, any contributions calculated for these inputs must be incorrigible:

---

[4] Robert R. Sterling, "Relevant Financial Reporting in an Age of Price Changes," *Journal of Accountancy*, February 75, p. 42.

[5] As a technical point, I've also simplified by discussing only incremental contributions of inputs. See SAR 9, especially pp. 32–40, 47–48 and 141–44, for the parallel problems that arise for their marginal contributions.

1.   One can't verify them, because any other calculation is just as good.
2.   One can't refute them, because their calculation is just as good as any other.

Therefore, any attempts at matching based on these contributions (say, depreciation of the pot or calculation of a value for the ending leaven inventory) will also be incorrigible. But the sourdough process is so much simpler than the productive processes of business enterprises, that *matching must necessarily be incorrigible for them, too*—unless, again, the reader can show how complications ease the calculations. To generalize, when a company tries to match costs with revenues there's no way either to refute or to verify the results. Instead, all possible ways of matching will be just as good—or bad—as each other.

If it's any consolation, I don't like this conclusion either, and have spent years trying to disprove it. Nor should you accept it without further inquiry. But I urge you at least to suspend disbelief in it (and in what follows) until you've read the detailed research, cited earlier, that backs it up.

And please notice that the difficulty here isn't one of being unable to allocate—there might be some way of getting around that problem. Instead, we're drowned in possible allocations, with no defensible way to choose among them. To be sure, since we must prepare reports, we eventually do pick one set of figures or another. Long before completing our training, we became accustomed to do this with few (if any) pangs. First, we narrow the possibilities by looking to generally accepted accounting principles and then select one of the survivors according to industry custom, apparent advantage to the company, apparent appropriateness of the method to the firm's circumstances or some other plausible rationale. But how can the incorrigible results be useful to decision makers?

Unless you (or someone) can suggest ways in which calculations that can neither be verified nor refuted assist decisions,[6] our allocations of the costs of depreciable assets, inventories, labor and other inputs are irrelevant to investor needs. Indeed, although it's painful to say this, they are mere rituals—solemn nonsense—and our beliefs in them are fallacies. This should trouble all of us, because practitioners spend much time conducting such rituals, and theorists much time elaborating on such fallacies.[7]

The Accounting Principles Board was well aware of this, but, underrating its severity, was satisfied to claim that exact measurements are seldom possible and that allocation often requires informed judgment.[8] With all due respect, acknowledging that few allocations are exact is like replying, "Few animals are ever completely healthy," in response to the statement, "Sir, your cow is dead."

Finally, since what's true of individual inputs also holds for groups of inputs, I'm forced to conclude that our revenue recognition practices are rituals, too. For revenue recognition allocates the firm's *lifetime* output to the groups of inputs that constitute its resources during the individual years of its life. Once again, the details of this appear in SAR 9.

---

[6] Assistance that goes beyond the unsatisfactory, short run utilities is described on pp. 8–9, 40–46, 65–70 and 163–74 of SAR 9.
[7] For examples of the latter, see SAR 9, pp. 94–110, 116–19 and 128–55.
[8] For examples, see APB Statement No. 4, pp. 11, 13–15, 21–22, 46–48 and 102.

## THE FASB'S RESPONSIBILITY

What, then, of the FASB? We've seen it worry, or propose to worry, about which allocations are most appropriate for various accounting situations. The FASB should stop doing this. Instead, whenever possible, it should *eliminate* allocations. Such incorrigible figures don't do readers of our reports any real good, and they

1.  Cost money.
2.  Strain relations between auditors and clients (when they disagree about which incorrigible figures to report).
3.  Cause many of the nonuniformity problems that plague us (since allocations are incorrigible, naturally GAAP conflict–there's no way to settle which rules are right).
4.  Thereby confuse individual readers, thus violating what the Trueblood Report designates as the basic objective of financial statements.
5.  Generally breed distrust in our profession.

When their elimination isn't possible, the FASB should keep allocations unsophisticated (if we must be incorrigible, at least let's be simple), choose allocation rules on expedient, political grounds (ceasing to worry about theory) and be candid about what it's doing. In particular, the FASB should actively

1.  Try to convert conventional reporting practices to allocation-free ones. There are two main allocation-free alternatives to conventional accounting: current value reporting and the type of funds statement reporting that defines "funds" as net quick assets.[9] Certainly, Sterling is correct that merely adjusting allocated historical costs for changes in purchasing power serves little purpose: adjusted ritual remains ritual. The same is true of foreign currency translations.
2.  Meanwhile, avoid launching any new incorrigible allocations in such areas as interim and segment reports, leases, contingencies, interest and pensions. And eliminate the more flagrantly incorrigible allocations that we now commit. A prime example of the latter (despite its being one of the APB's greatest political triumphs) is tax deferral: we take the difference between an incorrigible book allocation and an incorrigible tax allocation and allocate it, incorrigibly.

In conclusion, I would emphasize that none of these remarks is intended to disparage accounting practitioners. As SAR 9 points out (p. 157), practitioners have honestly believed that allocations are appropriate and have struggled to cope with them, while we academics saddled practitioners with a matching theory that requires such assignments, then failed to provide defensible ways for their calculation. But the hard fact remains that so long as we continue to certify that incorrigible allocations present fairly a firm's financial position and the results of its operations, we're making claims that we just can't back up. Professional responsibility urges that we, and the FASB, cease to tolerate this.

---

[9] See SAR 9, chapter 7.

# III Accounting for Changing Prices

This part of the book examines alternative accounting models and the concept of capital maintenance. Different models and accounting procedures have been proposed to deal with the problems of general inflation and specific price changes.

Section A consists of four papers. Chasteen (1984) classifies in an algebraic framework models dealing with price changes: historical cost, current cost, and current exit value—with and without constant dollar adjustments—providing an introduction to these models for comparative analysis. Sterling (1981) also distinguishes among the historical cost, current cost, and exit value models, but in so doing uses a specific example of purchasing and selling a security. Sterling concludes that all three models are plagued by problems of additivity and categorization, although exit valuation suffers less from these difficulties than the other two models. The third selection in Section A is Chambers' (1975) paper on "continuously contemporary accounting," which constitutes a combination of exit values with a constant dollar "capital maintenance" adjustment. Chambers compares the constant dollar, replacement cost, and exit value models, asserting that neither general price level accounting nor current value accounting is a complete method of accounting for changing prices. Continuously contemporary accounting is advocated to deal with both changes in particular prices and general price level changes.

Bell (1982) examines the response to inflation by the British in the Sandilands Report (1975) and the Americans in the FASB *Statement No. 33*, "Financial Reporting and Changing Prices" (1978). Bell observes two basic flaws in the Sandilands Report: Various gains or cost savings are ignored in the income measurement, and no attention is given to the changing value of the currency due to inflation. Bell is pleased with the current cost/constant dollar framework called for in FAS 33 and the income calculated in this framework, which includes not only current revenue less current costs at current prices but also real realizable cost savings.

Section B deals with the subject of capital maintenance. Lemke (1982) furnishes a critical comparison of physical versus financial capital maintenance, arguing that physical capital maintenance does not have a place in a dynamic business environment. In contrast to financial capital maintenance, physical capital maintenance is unable to deal with the issue of non-identical asset replacements. Lemke believes that the development of agency theory may help to resolve the capital maintenance debate.

Section C, which is concerned with monetary gains and losses, contains one article, Buckmaster (1982), explaining the "primitive state" of accounting for gains and losses from holding monetary items. Particular attention is given to the ideas set forth by Middleditch and Sweeney.

# III-A Valuation Models

## III-A 1 *A Taxonomy of Price Change Models*

LANNY CHASTEEN

Classification is an important element of any discipline. How theories relate to or compete with each other, how apparently competing theories contain common threads, and how some theories extend or build upon others contribute to a better understanding of that discipline.

The accounting literature is rich with models that deal with the effects of changing prices on a firm. The merits of the conventional historical cost model versus some form of current value have been debated. The effects of an unstable measuring unit for standards of comparison have been examined. More formal expositions have been couched in terms of a concept of capital maintenance for interpreting the nature of cash flows in income determination. The role of capital maintenance in long-run income determination and the roles of capital maintenance and asset valuation in periodic income determination have been examined [Shwayder, 1969; Gynther, 1970].

Dissatisfaction with a particular price change model which specifies either explicitly or implicitly (1) a valuation method (or a measured attribute) for assets and liabilities and (2) a capital maintenance concept has led to alternative models. In addition, variations or modifications have resulted when some aspect of a given theory appeared deficient. As a result, there exist many distinctly different price change models and variations thereof. Without proper classification these permutations make direct comparisons difficult.

This paper has a modest purpose: to classify the existing models so that analysis and comparison are more efficient. This taxonomy can be a useful instructional tool either by providing an overview prior to an in-depth study of the models or by providing closure after the various models have been studied. An algebraic approach, similar to that taken by Chambers [1966, 1978], Barton [1975], and others, is used for exposition. (A numerical example appears in the Appendix.) Apart from a brief

Lanny Chasteen, "A Taxonomy of Price Change Models," *The Accounting Review*, July 1984, pp. 515–523. Reprinted with the permission of *The Accounting Review*.

description of each model's rationale, no in-depth examination will be made. Adequate examination has appeared previously in the literature.

The first section of this paper gives the assumptions and price change data on which the models are based. The historical cost models, current cost models, and current exit value models are presented in the next three sections. A brief summary concludes the paper.

## ASSUMPTIONS AND PRICE CHANGE DATA

1.  A firm begins operations at a time $t = 0$ with monetary assets of $M$, nonmonetary assets acquired at a price of $N$, and monetary liabilities of $L$. Thus, at $t = 0$ the firm's financial position is given by $M + N = L + R$, where $R$ equals equity and $R > 0$.
2.  No transactions occur from $t = 0$ to $t = 1$.
3.  During the time interval from $t = 0$ to $t = 1$, the following price changes occur:

|  | At $t = 0$ | At $t = 1$ |
|---|---|---|
| General price index | 1 | $1 + p$ |
| Current cost of nonmonetary assets | $N$ | $N(1 + s_1)$ |
| Current exit value of nonmonetary assets | $N$ | $N(1 + s_2)$ |

where $p$ = proportional change in the general level of prices ($\div 100$), $s_1$ = proportional change in the asset's current cost ($\div 100$), and $s_2$ = proportional change in the asset's current exit value ($\div 100$).

4.  For simplicity, assume that $p$, $s_1$, and $s_2 > 0$ and that $p$, $s_1$, and $s_2$ are not necessarily equal.

The various price change models can be classified in one of two ways:

1.  The models may be grouped according to their capital maintenance (investment recovery) concept and the asset valuation methods may be varied. The three capital maintenance concepts which appear in the literature are the nominal dollar, constant dollar (general purchasing power), and physical capital concepts. The three asset valuation methods are historical cost, current cost, and current exit value.
2.  The models may be grouped according to their asset valuation method and the capital maintenance concepts may be varied.

The first approach is appealing in that, for a given capital maintenance concept, all models which use that concept give identical amounts of long-run earnings. The second approach, however, is used in this paper because it appears to be a better method of presenting variations or modifications to a given model. The two terms which describe each model—an attribute to be measured (an asset valuation method) and a capital maintenance concept—will appear as follows:

Attribute Measured/Capital Maintenance Concept

## HISTORICAL COST MODELS

### Historical Cost/Nominal Dollars (HC/N$)

The $t = 1$ financial position under the traditional HC/N$ model is represented as follows:

$$M + N = L + R \tag{1}$$

$$(t = 1 \text{ capital})$$

The model is a conceptual description of GAAP. If the nonmonetary asset was inventory or an equity security investment, the asset might be reported at $N(1 + s_1)$ or $N(1 + s_2)$, if $s_1$ or $s_2$ were negative.

### Historical Cost/Constant Dollars (HC/C$)

The traditional *HC/C$* model as developed by Sweeney [1936], *Accounting Research Study No. 6*, and APB *Statement No. 3* is as follows:

$$M + N(1 + p) = L + \underbrace{R(1 + p)}_{(t = 1 \text{ capital})} - \underbrace{-p(M - L)}_{(\text{income (loss)})} \tag{2}$$

This model also may be expressed in general purchasing power units other than $t = 1$ units. For example, SFAS *No. 33* permits average-for-the year dollars in the supplementary *HC/C$* disclosures. In terms of our one-period example, $t = 0$ dollars also could be used.

Two variations on this model are the Ijiri [1976] interpretation and the "one-line adjustment" approach. The Ijiri variation is:

$$M + N(1 + p) = L + \underbrace{R(1 + p)}_{(t = 1 \text{ capital})} + \underbrace{Np - Rp}_{(\text{income (loss)})} \tag{3}$$

Ijiri offers a different interpretation from the traditional *HC/C$* model. He describes $Np$ as a "price-level holding gain" and $Rp$ as a "price-level capital charge."

The one-line adjustment model was proposed as early as the mid-1950s [Chambers, 1978] and has been supported by Grady [1975] and Price Waterhouse [Agrawal and Rosenzweig, 1982]. It may be represented as follows:

$$M + N = L + \underbrace{R(1 + p)}_{(t = 1 \text{ capital})} - \underbrace{RP}_{((\text{loss}))} \tag{4}$$

This model may be interpreted as a surrogate for the traditional *HC/C$* model, and its primary rationale is based on simplicity.

All three of the above models incorporate a general purchasing power concept of capital maintenance and, therefore, report identical cumulative income over the life of a firm. The models in equations (2) and (3) also give identical periodic income amounts; thus they differ only in interpretation. The model in equation (4) in effect calculates a purchasing power loss from holding both net monetary assets *and* nonmonetary assets. By comparison, the traditional $HC/C\$$ model in equation (2) reduces this loss by the restatement of $N$ to $N(1 + p)$ by assuming that the asset's specific price increase is at least equal to $p$.[1]

## CURRENT COST MODELS

Three distinct current cost models appear in the literature: current cost/nominal dollars, current cost/constant dollars, and current cost/physical capital (productive capacity). Each of these current cost models adopts a different concept of capital maintenance, and, as discussed below, there are several additional variations for the physical capital model.

### Current Cost/Nominal Dollars (CC/N$)

The $CC/N\$$ model is as follows:

$$M + N(1 + s_1) = L + \underbrace{R}_{(t = 1 \text{ capital})} + \underbrace{Ns_1}_{(\text{income})} \qquad (5)$$

Two theories or hypotheses underlie this model. The first is the superiority of this model over the $HC/N\$$ model in evaluating firm management's operating activities and holding activities [Edwards and Bell, 1961]. Though not demonstrated with the present transactionless example, this model disaggregates a firm's replacement or current cost income into two elements: (1) current operating profit (revenues less the current costs of earning the revenues) and (2) holding gains $(Ns_1)$.[2] This model also has been described as the "cost-savings hypothesis" model [Samuelson, 1980].

The second hypothesis is based on prediction [Revsine, 1973]. Under certain circumstances, current operating profit may be a good predictor of future operating profit and future dividend-paying ability. The holding gain component may provide signals about increased future cash flows.[3]

### Current Cost/Constant Dollars (CC/C$)

This model, which conceptually underlies the supplementary current cost disclosures required by $SFAS\ No.\ 33$, is as follows:

$$M + N(1 + s_1) = L + \underbrace{R(1 + p)}_{(t = 1 \text{ capital})} + \underbrace{N(s_1 - p) - p(M - L)}_{(\text{income (loss)})} \qquad (6)$$

[1] To illustrate, $SFAS\ No.\ 33$ does not permit the restatement of nonmonetary assets to exceed realizable value. Said another way, the restated amount cannot exceed the amount of accessible general purchasing power embodied in the asset.

[2] In the transactionless example assumed in this paper, current cost measurements are made in end-of-period current cost. The use of average current cost also has been proposed and thus may be considered as a variation in the subsequent discussion of current operating profit and recognized holding gains. Unrealized holding gains on assets held at a financial position date, however, are measured at end-of-period current cost under the average current cost variation.

[3] Although not germane to this paper, the issue of current cost of assets presently owned versus current cost of technologically superior assets has been addressed in the literature, and thus variations on these themes exist with respect to current cost valuation.

In (6), $N(s_1 - p)$ is the holding gain (specific price increase), net of inflation, and $p(M - L)$ is the purchasing power loss.[4] The $CC/C\$$ model attempts to overcome criticisms of the $HC/C\$$ model's treatment of nonmonetary assets by using specific input prices. Furthermore, the model considers the effects of general price level changes on a firm's monetary assets and liabilities. Thus, this model incorporates the same current cost information reported in the $CC/N\$$ model with two additions: a general purchasing power gain or loss on monetary items and holding gains "net of inflation."[5]

### Current Cost/Physical Capital (CC/PC)

The basic $CC/PC$ model, sometimes referred to as a replacement value model, is as follows:

$$M + N(1 + s_1) = L + \underbrace{R + Ns_1}_{(t = 1 \text{ capital})} \tag{7}$$

The model's algebraic representation is similar to the above $CC/N\$$ model except that the holding gains are considered a capital maintenance adjustment instead of an element of income.

The $CC/PC$ model interprets current operating profit arising from earnings activities as "distributable income"—the maximum amount that can be distributed as a dividend each period and allow the firm to replace its productive capacity. Because a firm which uses this model and which pays periodic dividends equal to periodic earnings still may not be able to replace the assets used in its earnings activities when current costs continually rise over time, the issue of "backlog depreciation" [FASB, 1976] may be considered as a variation within the context of this model.

May [1976] has extended the distributable income notion to situations where the income calculation also incorporates increased costs of resources which may never appear on a financial position statement. May defines "current period residual income" as (a) year-end net assets (adjusted for dividends paid and additional paid-in capital) at year-end replacement costs, minus (b) beginning-of-year net assets (as reported) *plus* adjustments equal to the *difference* between (i) year-end costs and (ii) beginning-of-year costs *of the maximum investment required* in each resource employed in the business to sustain current levels of operations indefinitely. Whereas current operating profit provides an estimate of long-run average periodic cash flows and maximum average *future* periodic dividends, in nominal dollars, current period residual income provides an estimate of the maximum *current period* dividend consistent with maintaining current capacity to generate net cash flows [May, 1976; AAA, 1977].

Other variations on the $CC/PC$ model are an incorporation of purchasing power gains and losses on monetary items based on *specific* price changes [Gynther, 1966], "gearing adjustment," valuation of assets based on whether they are considered essential or nonessential to the continuing operations of a firm, and the "value to the business" or "deprival value" theory.

---

[4] In *SFAS No. 33*, these two elements are disclosed but are not included in income from continuing operations.
[5] Although Edwards and Bell [1961] and Revsine [1973] assume, for the most part, a stable general price level, they acknowledge the need to consider general price level changes.

Specific purchasing power gains and losses on monetary items also can be incorporated in the following model:

$$M + N(1 + s_1) = L + \underbrace{R + Rs_1}_{(t = 1 \text{ capital})} - \underbrace{s_1(M - L)}_{(\text{income (loss)})} \qquad (8)$$

Since a purchasing power gain or loss generally is calculated with reference to the assets that the firm normally purchases, $s_1$ is used in equation (8). Thus, the model in (8) considers the effect of specific price changes on both nonmonetary items and monetary items.

Proponents of the gearing adjustment maintain that current cost increases (holding gains) on operating assets represent income to equity holders to the extent that these assets are financed by long-term monetary liabilities. The gearing adjustment is calculated by allocating the holding gain (specific price increase) on nonmonetary assets between income and capital as follows:

$$\text{Income portion} = \frac{L}{L + R}(Ns_1)$$

$$\text{Capital maintenance portion} = \frac{R}{L + R}(Ns_1)$$

Thus, the income to be distributed allows the firm to maintain its present debt/equity ratio, given certain assumptions about additional financing.

The gearing adjustment causes difficulty in classification. Although the model is a variation on the current cost/physical capital theme, the gearing adjustment, in principle, results in a *mixed* concept of capital maintenance. That is, a portion of the holding gain is considered income (a nominal dollar concept of capital) and a portion is considered a capital adjustment (a physical capital concept).

*SSAP No. 16* sets forth current cost disclosure requirements for certain U.K. companies and incorporates both a specific price change adjustment (see equation (8)), and the gearing adjustment. Assuming that $M$ and $N$ are operating assets and that $L$ is long-term monetary debt, the current cost model under *SSAP No. 16* would be as follows:[6]

$$M + N(1 + s_1) = L + \underbrace{R + Ns_1\frac{R}{(L + R)} + Ms_1\frac{R}{(L + R)}}_{(t = 1 \text{ capital})} + \underbrace{Ns_1\frac{L}{(L + R)} - Ms_1\frac{R}{(L + R)}}_{(\text{income})}$$

$$(9)$$

Valuation of assets based on whether they are considered essential or nonessential to the continuing operations of a firm is another variation on the *CC/PC* model. Under this theory, essential assets are valued at current cost; holding gains on essential assets are considered capital maintenance adjustments. Assets not essential to continuing operations are valued at exit value [Australian Accounting Standards Committee, 1975]. This recommendation appears to be an extension of the use of

---

[6] Technically, *SSAP No. 16* limits the portion of $Ns_1(L)/(L + R)$ to be included in income to the portion realized. This realized portion is reported as a reduction in current cost expenses.

several valuation bases, depending on the particular financial statement element involved [MacNeal, 1970; Backer, 1974].

Under the "value to the business" or "deprival value" theory, assets are valued at current cost unless replacement is not desirable, in which case they are valued at the higher of value in use (present value) or value in exchange (current exit value). Since replacement would not be desirable if current cost exceeded the higher of present value or current exit value, the valuation rule simplifies to the lower of current cost or realizable value. Although this theory usually is associated with the CC/PC model, presumably it also could apply to the CC/N$ and the CC/C$ models. For example, *SFAS No. 33* requires that recoverable value—present value or current exit value, as appropriate—be used to measure assets if recoverable value is less than current cost.

One final point should be made about the CC/PC model. This model appears to have more variations than any of the others. One reason for this, according to Chambers, is that because the concept of physical capacity is hard to quantify in financial terms, no firm meaning can be assigned to the maintenance of physical capacity [Chambers, 1978]. Consequently, perceived deficiencies or shortcomings in the CC/PC model have resulted in "patchwork."

## CURRENT EXIT VALUE MODELS

The current exit value attribute may be combined with either a nominal dollar or a constant dollar concept of capital.

### Current Exit Value/Nominal Dollars (EV/N$)

The EV/N$ model is as follows:

$$M + N(1 + s_2) = L + \underbrace{R}_{(t\,=\,1\ \text{capital})} \qquad \underbrace{+\ Ns_2}_{(\text{income})} \qquad (10)$$

The holding gain ($Ns_2$) is similar to the holding gain under the CC/N$ model, except that it is based on exit prices instead of entry prices.

### Current Exit Value/Constant Dollars (EV/C$)

This model has been proposed by Sterling [1970, 1975] and Chambers [1966, 1978]. The Sterling model is:

$$M + N(1 + s_2) = L + \underbrace{R(1 + p)}_{(t\,=\,1\ \text{capital})} \quad \underbrace{+\ N(s_2 - p) - p(M - L)}_{(\text{income})} \qquad (11)$$

It is identical in formulation to the CC/C$ model except that the nonmonetary assets are valued at exit prices instead of current cost.

The Chambers model is:

$$M + N(1 + s_2) = L + \underbrace{R(1 + p)}_{(t\,=\,1\ \text{capital})} \quad \underbrace{+\ Ns_2 - Rp}_{(\text{income})} \qquad (12)$$

Since $Ns_2 - Rp$ in (12) equals $N(s_2 - p) - p(M - L)$ in (11), Chambers and Sterling, while in basic agreement on the propriety of exit value, arrive at income by different means [Chambers, 1975]. Sterling's income number is comprised of a holding gain, net of inflation, plus a purchasing power gain or loss on monetary items. Chambers, on the other hand, prefers to call $Ns_2$ a "price variation adjustment" and $Rp$ a "capital maintenance adjustment." Under Chambers' formulation, a purchasing power loss ($Rp$) is calculated on the firm's $t = 0$ net asset position.

## SUMMARY

The algebraic approach in this paper has classified most of the price change models that have appeared in the accounting literature. The classification scheme presented here would appear to be useful for identifying common threads and distinct differences among price change models as well as for identifying modifications or extensions to a particular model.

## APPENDIX

This Appendix presents a numerical example for each of the twelve model equations which appear in the body of this paper. Let

$$M = \$200 \qquad \frac{L}{L + R} = \frac{1}{3} \qquad s_1 = .24$$

$$N = \$1000 \qquad\qquad\qquad s_2 = .30$$

$$L = \$400 \qquad \frac{R}{L + R} = \frac{2}{3} \qquad C = \text{capital at } t = 1$$

$$R = \$800 \qquad p = .10 \qquad I = \text{income (loss)}$$

The beginning ($t = 0$) financial position statement is:

$$\$200 + \$1000 = \$400 + \$800$$
$$M \qquad N \qquad L \qquad R$$

Ending ($t = 1$) financial position statements for each price change model are:

(1) $\$200 + \$1000 = \$400 + \$800$
   $\qquad\qquad\quad C$

(2) $\$200 + \$1000(1.10) = \$400 + \$800(1.10) - .10(\$200 - \$400)$
   $\quad 200 + \$1100 = \$400 + \$880 + \$20$
   $\qquad\qquad\qquad\quad C \qquad I$

(3) $\$200 + \$1000(1.10) = \$400 + \$800(1.10) + \$1000(.10) - \$800(.10)$
   $\quad \$200 + \$1,100 = \$400 + \$880 + \$20$
   $\qquad\qquad\qquad\quad C \qquad I$

(4) $\$200 + \$1000 = \$400 + \$800(1.10) - \$800(.10)$
   $\quad \$200 + \$1000 = \$400 + \$880 - \$80$
   $\qquad\qquad\qquad\quad C \qquad I$

(5) $\$200 + \$1000(1.24) = \$400 + \$800 + \$1000(.24)$
   $\quad \$200 + \$1240 = \$400 + \$800 + \$240$
   $\qquad\qquad\qquad\quad C \qquad I$

(6) $200 + $1000(1.24) = $400 + $800(1.10) + $1000(.24 - .10) - .10($200 - $400)

$200 + $1240 = $400 + $880 + $\underbrace{$140 + $20}$

C    I

(7) $200 + $1000(1.24) = $400 + $800 + $1000(.24)

$200 + $1240 = $400 + $1040

C

(8) $200 + $1000(1.24) = $400 + $800 + $800(.24) - .24($200 - $400)

$200 + $1240 = $400 + $992 + $48

C    I

(9) $200 + $1000(1.24) = $400 + $800 + 2/3($1000)(.24) + 2/3($200)(.24)

+ 1/3($1000)(.24) - 2/3($200)(.24)

$200 + $1240 = $400 + $992 + $48

C    I

(10) $200 + $1000(1.30) = $400 + $800 + $1000(.30)

$200 + $1300 = $400 + $800 + $300

C    I

(11) $200 + $1000(1.30) = $400 + $800(1.10) + $1000(.30 - .10) - .10($200 - $400)

$200 + $1300 = $400 + $880 + $220

C    I

(12) $200 + $1000(1.30) = $400 + $880(1.10) + $1000(.30) - $800(.10)

$200 + $1300 = $400 + $880 + $220

C    I

## REFERENCES

Agrawal, S. and K. Rosenzweig (1982), "One-line Adjustment Methods of Accounting for the Effects of Inflation," *Collected Abstracts of the AAA Annual Meeting* (AAA, 1982), p. 29.

Accounting Principles Board (1969), *Financial Statements Restated for General Price-Level Changes*, Statement No. 3 (AICPA, 1969).

Accounting Research Division (1963), *Accounting Research Study No. 6*, "Reporting the Financial Effects of Price-Level Changes" (AICPA, 1963).

American Accounting Association (1977), Subcommittee on the Conceptual Framework for Financial Accounting and Reporting, *Response to Discussion Memorandum, Parts II and III of the FASB* (AAA, 1977).

Australian Accounting Standards Committee (1975), "A Method of Current Value Accounting," Preliminary Exposure Draft (AASC, 1975).

Backer, M. (1974), "A Model for Current Value Reporting," *CPA Journal* (February 1974), pp. 27–33.

Barton, A. (1975), *An Analysis of Business Income Concepts,* ICRA Occasional Paper No. 7, International Centre for Research in Accounting (University of Lancaster, 1975).

Chambers, R. J. (1966), *Accounting, Evaluation and Economic Behavior* (Prentice-Hall, 1966).

———(1975), "NOD, COG and PuPu: See How Inflation Teases," *Journal of Accountancy* (September 1975), pp. 56–62.

———(1978), "The Use and Misuse of a Notation: A History of an Idea," *Abacus* (December 1978), pp. 122–144.

Edwards, E. and P. Bell (1961), *The Theory and Measurement of Business Income* (University of California Press, 1961).

Financial Accounting Standards Board, (1976), *Conceptual Framework for Financial Accounting and Reporting: Elements of Financial Statements and Their Measurement,* FASB Discussion Memorandum (FASB, 1976).

———(1979), SFAS No. 33, *Financial Reporting and Changing Prices* (FASB, 1979).

Grady, P. (1975), "Purchasing Power Accounting," *Price Waterhouse Review* (1975), pp. 3–5.

Gynther, R. (1966), *Accounting for Price-Level Changes* (Pergamon Press, 1966).

———(1970), "Capital Maintenance, Price Changes, and Profit Determination," *The Accounting Review* (October 1970), pp. 712–730.

Ijiri, Y. (1976), "The Price-Level Restatement and Its Dual Interpretation," *The Accounting Review* (April 1976), pp. 227–243.

MacNeal, K. (1970), *Truth in Accounting* (Scholars Book Company, 1970).

May, R. G. (1976), "Some *A Priori* Properties of Conventional and Current-Cost Income Numbers Vis a Vis Security Analysis," *Proceedings of the Second Annual Duke University Accounting Symposium* (Duke University, 1976), pp. 92–114.

Peat, Marwick, Mitchell and Co. (1980), *Current Cost Accounting: A Guide to SSAP 16* (PMM & Co., 1980).

Revsine, L. (1973), *Replacement Cost Accounting* (Prentice-Hall, 1973).

Samuelson, R. A. (1980), "Should Replacement-Cost Changes Be Included in Income?" *The Accounting Review* (April 1980), pp. 254–268.

Schwayder, K. (1969), "The Capital Maintenance Rule and the Net Asset Valuation Rule," *The Accounting Review* (April 1969), pp. 304–316.

Sterling, R. R. (1970), *Theory of the Measurement of Enterprise Income* (University of Kansas, 1970).

———(1975), "Relevant Financial Reporting in an Age of Price Changes," *Journal of Accountancy* (February 1975), pp. 42–51.

Sweeney, H. (1936), *Stabilized Accounting* (Harper and Row, 1936).

# III-A 2 *Costs (Historical versus Current) versus Exit Values*

ROBERT R. STERLING

## INTRODUCTION

This essay is intended to be a contribution to the continuing quest for improved methods of accounting. It has three separable but related goals which are addressed to three problems. The primary goal is to differentiate clearly three alternative methods of accounting. The primary problem is that in previous discussions we have not sharply distinguished the alternatives and we have combined separable questions. The secondary goal is to consider a specific, simple case and try to demonstrate that one of the alternative methods is superior to the others. The secondary problem is that past discussions have utilized criteria that do not discriminate the alternatives and therefore do not aid in making a rational choice. The selection of the preferred alternative requires the identification and application of a criterion that will discriminate. The tertiary goal is to extend the application of the identified criterion to other specific cases. The tertiary problem is that there are many different kinds of firms and different kinds of assets for which the method of accounting is in dispute. The overall goal is to reach for the chalice of more general principles that has eluded us for so long. The overall problem is that we have too many specific, *ad hoc* principles.

The three related goals and problems constitute the three sections of this essay. A highly simplified case will be utilized to explain the nature of the alternatives in Section 1 and to identify and apply the criterion in Section 2. The advantage of simplified cases is that they are easily understood by both author and reader. The idea is to strip away the complexities so that we can concentrate on the conceptual differences and see which one best achieves the objectives of reporting. If we can be clear on the concepts and objectives, it should aid in the analysis of more complex cases which is the goal of Section 3.

Since this essay considers exit values that are beyond popular opinion, it has the double labour: first, making them understood and, second, proving and demonstrating. The sequence is important to my aspirations. I would be pleased if I could clear

Robert R. Sterling, Costs (Historical Versus Current) versus Exit Values, *Abacus*, Vol 17, No. 2, 1981, pp. 93–129. Reprinted with the permission of *Abacus*.

up the many misunderstandings which surround exit valuations whether or not the demonstrations withstand the readers' tests. Of course, I think that the demonstrations are correct, else I would not present them, but I would rather have them shown to be incorrect than to be misunderstood.

## 1. EXPLICATION

The purpose of this section is to explicate the two different kinds of exchangeable values which vie for inclusion in the accounts. The differences arise from frictions which cannot be avoided. A second source of differences is the temporal location of the two kinds of exchangeable values. In this section our purpose is to observe—to explain precisely and neutrally—and not to criticize.

### 1.1 The Problem

Rapidly changing prices caused many clients (users) and accountants to seek improvements to historical cost accounting. Many proposed that we begin to report current prices rather than (or in addition to) historical costs. At first the focus was on timing, on *current* prices versus *historical* costs, as was evidenced by the recurring theme that we should report more up-to-date information. It seems that almost all accountants, perhaps primarily because we are accustomed to recording costs, perceived the only alternative to historical costs to be current costs. For this reason, the focus narrowed, almost unnoticed, from current *prices* to current *costs*. The overwhelming majority of the research and discussion has been directed toward the question of current costs versus historical costs.

The narrowed focus caused us to overlook two important points: (1) there are two different kinds of current prices—current costs and exit values—as will be explained below, and (2) the pros and cons of reporting current information versus historical information are different from the pros and cons of the kind of information that should be reported. Overlooking these two points has caused much mischief.

First, it has prohibited the widespread recognition of the *existence* of an alternative. Most of the past discussion has been about the merits of alternative methods of accounting for costs, and the use of exit values has not been perceived as an alternative. Recognition of the existence of an alternative is a prerequisite for the rational choice of the preferred alternative. We may know that we prefer vanilla to strawberry but we cannot know that we prefer vanilla to chocolate if we do not know that chocolate exists.

Second, it has prohibited the widespread recognition of the *conceptual differences* between the two. Many have thought that since both are current prices, and since the difference in magnitude is often immaterial, the conceptual difference is immaterial. The fact is that the difference in magnitude is sometimes material and the conceptual difference is always material. The equality of the two has hindered resolution of the question of current costs versus historical costs because it has often been debated on the basis of the characteristics of exit values. In effect, such arguments say that we should adopt (reject) current costs and abandon (retain) historical costs because exit values are good (bad).[1] We may know that we like vanilla but we cannot know that we prefer vanilla to strawberry by tasting chocolate.

Third, it has prohibited the widespread recognition of the *nature* of the two alternatives. As a result, arguments are often based on a misunderstanding. We have witnessed spirited arguments that current costs are superior (inferior) to exit values because exit values are based on past (future) prices when in fact exit values are one kind of current price. We may know we like vanilla but we cannot know that we prefer vanilla to chocolate if we mistake pistachio for chocolate.

Fourth, current costs versus historical costs *combines* two separable questions. It is quite possible, for example, to favour reporting current prices but to oppose reporting costs, or vice versa. The dissenters' views in relation to Financial Accounting Standard 33 provides an example of a case where current information is favoured but a particular kind of current information is opposed. This suggests that we might make more progress if the question were divided. A menu that lists only vanilla ice cream and strawberry pie combines the choice of vanilla versus strawberry with the choice of ice cream versus pie. We may decide to forgo dessert even though we might have selected strawberry ice cream had it been offered.

### 1.2 The Price Distinction

Consider a marketable security with a price of $1,000 per share. If one were to purchase a share, one would pay $1,000 plus the commission of, say, $100 for a total of $1,100. If one owned a share and were to sell it, one would receive $1,000 minus the commission, or $900. The $1,000 is, of course, the familiar "cost" which is "historical" if it refers to the past date of purchase, "current" if it refers to the present, or "future." The $900 is the unfamiliar "exit value," which can also be modified by adding "historical," "current," or "future." Thus, there are figures representing three concepts:

Definition 1: Cost = cash paid or payable if purchased ($1,100).
Definition 2: Price = reference figure ($1,000).
Definition 3: Exit value = cash received or receivable if sold ($900).

The concepts refer to the same moment in time—the figures exist simultaneously. The ranking is important and constant. The historical cost was greater than the historical

---

[1] I must take my share of the blame for this. Many of my past efforts (see, for example, Sterling [1970]) have been primarily concerned with the current versus historical question and, in order to avoid becoming embroiled in the combined issues, I made some assumptions which equated current costs and exit values. As a result, my past work is interpreted as support for current costs about equally as often as it is for exit values. For example, Vancil and Weil [1976] introduced a reprint of my "Relevant Financial Reporting" with some very kind words which concluded: "He proved that using replacement costs to measure income produces a result which is interpretable and relevant" (p. 2). I appreciate what I consider to be a very high compliment since it is so difficult to prove anything in accounting, but I hasten to confess that I was trying to prove that exit values, not replacement costs, met those criteria.

It is enlightening to compare the interpretation of the works of others in similar situations. Revsine [1973], for example, presents an analysis of a perfectly competitive, frictionless market for the purpose of demonstrating some characteristics of replacement costs. In such a market the frictions of transaction costs are nonexistent and therefore replacement costs and exit values are identical. For this reason, every conclusion regarding replacement costs also applies to exit values yet no one interprets Revsine's work as support for exit values. I believe that the cost paradigm is so ingrained that we seldom perceive the existence of an alternative.

exit value, the current cost is greater than the current exit value, and the future cost will be greater than the future exit value. The difference is *always* twice the commission.[2]

## 1.3 The Questions

Now that we have drawn the distinction we can ask the first question.

Question 1: Should we adopt costs or exit values as the basis for reporting assets and income?

The question arises at purchase as well as at all interim balance sheet dates.

*1.31 Purchase*   The question initially arises at the moment of purchase. To record the cost we would write

| | | | |
|---|---|---|---|
| 1 Jan. | Marketable Securities | $1,100 | |
| | Cash | | $1,100 |

on the basis that the cost is determined by setting it equal to the amount of cash *paid*. By contrast, to record the exit value we would write

| | | | |
|---|---|---|---|
| 1 Jan. | Marketable Securities | $900 | |
| | Loss on Purchase | 200 | |
| | Cash | | $1,100 |

on the basis that the exit value is determined by setting it equal to the value of the cash *receivable*. Of course, we could record the cost of the share at $1,100 and then

---

[2] Terminology is difficult because the desire for precision conflicts with the desire for communication. Precision demands that different words be used for different referents and that often requires the use of jargon; but jargon requires that readers learn the new terms and that inhibits communication. The problem first arises here in the meaning of "cost." The way that I am using the term conforms with the instructions to capitalize all costs necessary to acquire the asset. Since commissions are necessary, $1,100 would be recorded as the cost. An alternative is to expense the commission on the basis of properly classifying costs or conservatism or tax considerations. This would result in recording the price of $1,000 as the cost. The lower of cost or market rule, if applied strictly, would require that it be recorded at the net realizable value of $900 and in subsequent years this would also be referred to as the cost. Thus, even in this simple case there are three possible meanings of "cost." For this reason, I toyed with the idea of using a more precise but less familiar jargon, such as "entry value", to refer to the $1,100 but rejected it since "current cost" is widely used and was recently distinguished from "replacement cost" in FAS 33 [1979].

The same problem plagues "exit value." Some refer to the $900 as the "sale price" and that terminology has the advantage of being widely known since all accountants deal with sales but it has the disadvantage of being widely misunderstood. In my experience most accountants associate sale price with the unknown price that will exist in the future when the sale is made. This differs from exit value both because it refers to the price—$1,100 instead of $900—and it refers to the future instead of the present. "Net realizable value" would require deducting the commission and therefore it refers to the $900 but it too is often associated with the future instead of the present as well as being part of the lexicon of "historical cost." Some define exit values, especially in regard to inventories, as the future proceeds from sale (cf., e.g., Edwards [1975], p. 240). For that reason, I toyed with the idea of using an even more unfamiliar term than "exit value" but decided instead to try to define precisely what *I* mean when I use the term.

draft another entry to write it down to $900 and we could call the $200 "commission expense." I drafted the entry in the form that would contrast the conceptual difference and I called the $200 "loss on purchase" for the same reason.

In the cost literature assets are defined as things that are expected to *benefit* the *future*. This immediately raises a question about the above entries. If assets benefit the future, why record the present price instead of the future price?

Question 2:  Should we record the present price or the future price (and future dividends)?

This question will not detain us long. I raise it for two reasons. First, to point out that it is separate from Question 1. To decide to record costs does not *ipso facto* answer the question of whether we should record present or future costs. And the same is true for exit values. The reason we do not record future prices is obvious: the future is unknown. We would be accused of hubris or worse if we attempted to record the future price since the best we could do is to record somebody's forecast of the future price. There have been a number of people who have recommended that we report forecasts because they would be useful. *If* we decide to accept those recommendations, we would still be faced with the question of the kind of forecasted future price that we should report. In this essay, I will consider the relevance of forecasted prices (and dividends) to decisions but I will not delve into the problems of reporting them.

Second, the response to the unknown future is a primary conceptual difference between costs and exit values. Assets are often defined as "*costs* that will benefit the future". To put it negatively, if a cost will not benefit the future, then it should not be capitalized, should not be recorded as an asset, should be expensed. The reason for the recording of cost is that the benefit is expected to be greater than the cost. The sacrifice, cash paid, is measured and the value of the share is set *equal* to that *sacrifice* because the *benefit* is expected to be *greater* than the sacrifice. Setting the value equal to the sacrifice precludes recording a gain or loss at purchase. By contrast, exit values focus on the *present benefit of the cash receivable*. The idea is that if the share were sold one moment after the purchase, the cash balance would be $900 which is compared to the cash balance of $1,100 one moment prior to purchase. The decline in the benefits of the cash balance is the $200 loss on purchase. To put the same idea in more familiar terms, the $1,100 is an expenditure and in that sense it is a cost; the $900 is a receivable and in the sense of debiting receivables and crediting revenues, it is a revenue; the "matching of costs and revenues" yields a $200 loss.

*1.32 Interim dates*   Question 1 arises again at each balance sheet date. Assuming the price to have increased to $1,050 at 31 January, adding and subtracting the commission yields a cost of $1,150 and an exit value of $950 at that date.

Historical cost accounting prohibits making an entry to record the price increase on the basis of conservatism or the realization convention or both. We could institute a similar prohibition in regard to exit values and call it "historical exit value accounting." Then we could return to Question 1 because the alternatives are to report the $1,100 historical cost or the $900 historical exit value on the 31 January balance sheet. The point is that deciding to report historical prices does not *ipso facto* answer the question of what kind of prices to report. Likewise deciding to report costs or exit values does not *ipso facto* answer the question of historical versus current. There is a third, separate question.

Question 3: Should we report the current price or the historical price at each
balance sheet date?

It seems that the combination of Questions 1 and 3 has hindered progress toward
resolution of both questions and I have separated them for that reason. Of course, no
one has ever suggested that we report historical exit values but that is merely
additional evidence of the fact that almost all accountants think in terms of costs.
Since I, too, do not want to put it forward as a serious contender, I will not discuss it
further except to say that "exit value" means "current exit value" unless specifically
indicated otherwise. This leaves us with the three alternatives of historical cost,
current cost and exit value.

The adjusting entry to record both the current cost and the exit value is:

| | | |
|---|---|---|
| 31 Jan. Marketable Securities | $50 | |
| Gain | | $50 |

Although the adjusting entry records the same amount for both, the concept is
different. For current costs the idea is to write the share up to the amount payable at
31 January, i.e., to record the cash that would be required to be paid if it were
purchased on that date. Since the amount payable is now $1,150 and the amount paid
was $1,100, there is a "holding gain" of $50.[3] By contrast, for exit values the idea is to
write the share up to the receivable amount at 31 January, i.e., to record the amount of
cash that would be received if it were sold on that date. Since the amount receivable is
now $950 and it was $900, there is a "value gain" of $50. Thus, there are two different
concepts:

Definition 4: Holding  Gain = sacrifice  change = cash  payable − prior  cash
payable (paid).

Definition 5: Value  Gain = benefit  change = cash  receivable − prior  cash
receivable (paid).

The conceptual difference is the same as at purchase. The future benefits were
expected to be greater than the sacrifice, cash paid, at purchase, and therefore the
value of the share was set equal to that sacrifice. At interim dates the increase in
future benefits is expected to be greater than (or equal to) the increase in the sacrifice,
cash payable, and therefore the value of the share is set equal to the present sacrifice
and the difference is a holding gain. By contrast, exit value is an attempt to record the
present benefit and it is considered to be a gain because that present benefit is greater
than the past benefit. Thus, the gains (or losses) are based on two quite different
concepts.

In the case at hand the difference in amount reported is $200. Current cost would
report net income of $50 consisting of the holding gain of that amount. Exit value
would report a net loss of $150 consisting of the value gain of $50 and the loss on
purchase of $200. Of course, historical cost would report a zero gain.

In subsequent months the same type of adjusting entry would be required to
record the change in the cash payable or cash receivable. Dividends would be
recorded in the usual way and therefore the net income for both current costs and exit

---

[3] I am aware that a number of professional versions of CCA do not recognize the $50 as a "gain."
The notion used here is that developed by Edwards and Bell [1964].

values would be the dividends plus or minus the holding gains or value gains, respectively. The net income for historical cost would be equal to the amount of the dividends since it records neither holding gains or value gains. Since dividends have the same effect on all three options, they are not pertinent to the distinction.

*1.33 Sale*    The questions do not arise at time of sale. Instead, all three methods debit the cash for the amount received, credit the share for its recorded value and take the difference to be a gain. For example, if the share were sold on 1 February and there had been no changes from 31 January, we would write

| | | | |
|---|---|---|---|
| 1 Feb. | Cash | $950 | |
| | Loss on Sale | 150 | |
| | Marketable Securities | | $1,100 |

for historical costs, or

| | | | |
|---|---|---|---|
| 1 Feb. | Cash | $950 | |
| | Loss on Sale | 200 | |
| | Marketable Securities | | $1,150 |

for current cost, or

| | | | |
|---|---|---|---|
| 1 Feb. | Cash | $950 | |
| | Marketable Securities | | $  950 |

for exit values.

As usual when the cycle of cash to cash is complete, there is no difference in valuations or in reported income for the entire period. In this case the net loss is $150 for the two months for all three options.

For costs, both historical and current, the idea is the familiar matching of costs and revenues. Since the future has now become the present, the benefits—cash receipts—are known and therefore it is no longer necessary to focus on the sacrifice. Instead, the benefits can be matched with the sacrifice. Both match the $950 with a past cost. The difference is that historical cost matches it with cash paid at purchase of $1,100 while current cost matches it with the cash payable of $1,150 at the last balance sheet date. Exit values, by contrast, continue to focus on the benefits by taking the difference between the cash received and the prior cash receivable.[4]

### 1.4 Summary

The case reveals that there are both similarities and differences. One similarity is that all three report the same total gain from purchase to sale. The major difference between current prices and historical costs is that a past amount is reported on the present balance sheet under historical costs while current prices report an amount of cash equivalents at the balance sheet date. Current costs and exit values are similar in that they both measure at the balance sheet date and in that they both measure cash equivalents. They differ only in that current cost measures the cash equivalents pay-

---

[4] In an unfortunately neglected article, Bedford and McKeown [1972] stated the distinction clearly in points (1) and (2), p. 337.

able if purchased while exit values measure the cash equivalents receivable if sold.

Since all three report the same amount of cash received and paid, as well as the ultimate gain after sale, the only deviation in reported values and gains occurs on interim financial statements. Exhibit 1 summarizes the characteristics of the three options.

Depending upon the predisposition, one will be struck by either the similarities or the differences. In the interim, when differences exist, I would characterize the differences in two ways: first, the measurement of a sacrifice attribute versus a benefit attribute, and, second, the measurement at a point in time versus measurement at purchase. Recognition that they are measurements of different attributes should dispel much confusion and assist in the analysis.

## 2. THE SPECIAL CASE

Now that the alternative methods have been distinguished and defined, we can attempt to answer the questions, to decide which method is best and on what grounds. As suggested in the quotation by Raiffa, I ask the reader to get involved in the decision instead of worrying about what information some unknown users may or may not want or understand.

### 2.1 The Problem

Recognition that the alternatives are different attributes and understanding the nature of each is a prerequisite to selection. An additional prerequisite is the specification of the criteria that are to be used in the selection. Understanding the nature of the alternatives will not permit selection in the absence of criteria but such understanding will permit us to recognize inappropriate criteria. The criteria (sometimes called "principles," "basic concepts," "conventions," etc.) that have been used in the past were inappropriate either because they did not discriminate among the alternatives or they confused definitions with criteria. To illustrate the nature of the problem I will present a few, but only a few, examples.

*2.11 Undiscriminating criteria*   Much of the criticism that has been levelled against the alternatives in the past was based on various criteria that did not discriminate. When all alternatives satisfy a criterion or all fail to satisfy it, the criterion does not discriminate, does not aid in making a choice.

One prevalent criterion is "economic reality" which has been used at one time or another to defend *and* to criticize *all* accounting practices and proposals. Such a broad and contradictory usage is ample evidence that the criterion is intolerably vague yet it continues to be used.[5] Historical cost proponents often criticize current price accounting because it records cash equivalents instead of the economic reality of cash. The argument is that we should record actual cash as opposed to the

---

[5] One reason that I have proposed the criterion of empirical testability in other works is to try to make "economic reality" operational. In the specific sense of empirical testability I think economic reality is a useful criterion that will discriminate alternatives but in its general sense it does not discriminate.

**EXHIBIT 1**

**Interim Balance Sheet**

| Focus | | Time | Numeraire | Flow Direction | | Event | | Accounting Method |
|---|---|---|---|---|---|---|---|---|
| Sacrifice | of | Past | Dollars | Paid | at | Past purchase | is | Historical cost |
| Sacrifice | of | Present | Dollars | Payable | for | Immediate purchase | is | Current cost |
| Benefit | of | Present | Dollars | Receivable | from | Immediate sale | is | Exit value |

**Interim Income Statement**

| Time Period | Accounting Method | | Gain |
|---|---|---|---|
| Past—Past | Historical cost | is | Zero |
| Present—Previous | Current cost | is | Holding gain |
| Present—Previous | Exit value | is | Value gain |

recording of hypothetical, unreal cash equivalents. The fact is that historical cost also records cash equivalents for all non-cash exchanges. If the share had been purchased on account, for example, the cost would have been set equal to the cash equivalent of the account payable. If the share had been sold for a note, for example, the cash equivalents of that note receivable would have been matched with the past cash equivalents of the account payable to determine the "actual" cash realized. Receivables and payables are not concepts foreign to historical cost accounting. The only difference is that historical cost records such cash equivalents at the event of exchange instead of at the balance date but that difference concerns the timing of the measurement, not its reality. The opposite is also true. Cash or cash equivalents paid at purchase are as economically real as cash equivalents receivable or payable at the balance sheet date. The only distinction is that one is past and the other is present, not that historical costs are unreal. Thus, the criterion of economic reality fails to discriminate.

It has often been said that both historical costs and current costs are consistent with the going concern assumption while exit values violate that assumption. Many say that exit valuation requires a liquidation assumption or that it implies that the firm is liquidating because it records "liquidation values." The fact is that a going concern both purchases and sells. In the case of marketable securities it is abundantly clear that from time to time the firm will sell some shares for their exit value as well as purchase some shares for their cost. To assign interim values on either basis does not imply anything at all about continuity or liquidation of the firm. To argue that we should adopt historical or current costs because a going concern purchases at cost has as little force as arguing that we should adopt exit values because it sells at exit value. Thus, the going concern criterion fails to discriminate. The criterion of management intent is similar. We often hear that the fact that management does not intend to sell proves that exit values are absurd. That criterion can be reversed. The fact that management does not intend, indeed cannot, purchase an asset that it already owns provides as much proof that costs are absurd. Thus, the criterion of management intent fails to discriminate.

It has been said that historical costs "provide a permanent record" of the activities of the firm while current prices "destroy that permanent record." A variant is that exit values destroy the permanent record but current costs do not because they are a "natural extension" of historical costs. It is difficult to know what this means but it must be based on some sort of misunderstanding. Current price accounting reports the amount paid as a use on the funds statement, the current prices on the balance sheets or statement of financial position, and the differences on the income statements. Historical cost accounting reports the amount paid as a use on the funds statement *and* as an asset on the balance sheet *and* it continues to report that amount on interim balance sheets, with the consequence of reporting a zero gain on interim income statements. The argument seems to be about what statement the amount paid should be reported on and how often it should be reported rather than about permanent records. The "natural extension" variant must mean that current costs are updated historical costs but that is an argument about what to put in the record, not its permanence. Since all three write the journal entries in indelible ink, the criterion of providing a permanent record fails to discriminate.

*2.12 Definitions vs criteria*   Many of the past debates have mistaken definitions for criteria. In effect, such debates have defined a rectangle as consisting of straight lines, pointed out that circles have curved lines and then concluded that rectangles are preferable to circles because rectangles meet the criterion of straight lines and circles do not. If the original question concerned straight versus curved lines, such arguments are restatements of the question, not criteria.

The conservatism principle has often been invoked in such debates. Since exit values are always less than current costs, we can say that exit values have the virtue of being more conservative. Although conservatism discriminates in this sense, it is merely a synonym for 'less than' and therefore the argument reduces to a consideration of whether less than is preferable to greater than. Since we have not resolved that issue, to argue that exit values should be reported because they are more conservative than current costs is merely a restatement of Definitions 1 and 3, not a criterion. We cannot say whether current prices are more or less conservative than historical costs since prices could go up or down. We can define "historical costs" as the lower of historical cost or current price and then say that "historical costs" have the virtue of being conservative. But to argue that "historical costs" are more conservative than current prices is merely a restatement of the definition of lower of cost or market, not a criterion. Hence, conservatism is a definition of a difference, not a criterion.

The realization convention is similar. The criticism that exit values record a gain at purchase is based on a misunderstanding since, as illustrated above, exit values record a loss on purchase. By contrast, both historical costs and current costs defer recognition of that loss until sale. Thus, the first question is whether the realization convention applies to losses as well as gains and, if so, do exit values violate that convention by recording a loss at purchase or do costs violate that convention by not recording a loss until sale? But this is merely a restatement of Question 1 since the definition of exit values requires recording a loss at purchase, and vice versa for costs. It is true that current price accounting violates the realization convention by recording gains prior to sale while historical cost accounting does not violate that convention. But this is merely a restatement of Question 3 since the definition of historical cost prohibits recording a gain prior to sale and vice versa for current prices. Hence, realization is a definition of a difference, not a criterion.

The stewardship or accountability objective is similar. What should the steward be accountable for? For example, we could make the steward accountable for dollars and adopt financial capital or make him accountable for physical units and adopt physical capital. What we make the steward accountable for determines what we account for. In this sense it is a criterion that does not discriminate. Sometimes those who employ stewardship implicitly define what the steward should be accountable for and therefore it is a definition, not a criterion. The objective of accounting for economic events is also similar. What events should we account for? Historical cost defines exchanges as accountable events and defines a price increase in the absence of an exchange a nonaccountable event. Current price defines a price increase as an accountable event. It is either a criterion that does not discriminate or those who employ it have some implicit events in mind and therefore it is a definition instead of a criterion.

There are a great many such criteria that have been utilized in the past. Space limitations, as well as tedium, prevent a consideration of all such criteria. The above examples should be sufficient to make the point: the criteria that have been utilized in the past do not aid in a rational choice and therefore we must seek other criteria.

## 2.2 The Criterion

Recognition that the alternatives are measurements of different attributes immediately suggests the criterion of relevance. Just as my height and weight are different attributes of the same object, the cost and exit value of the share are different attributes of the same object. Merely stating an objective permits a selection of the attribute. If my objective is to gain or lose weight, then I must measure my weight to see whether, and by how much, I have achieved that objective. Of course measurement of height is a perfectly legitimate activity and it will be relevant to decisions regarding other objectives but it is irrelevant to decisions regarding weight gains. That is, height and weight are both 'useful' in the sense that height will be relevant to some decisions but not to others and the same is true for weight. The point is that "usefulness" in the absence of a specific decision context is too general to allow us to decide which attribute should be measured: it is a criterion that will not discriminate among attributes.

The same is true for costs and exit values. If we can be clear on the objectives and the decisions regarding those objectives, it will allow us to decide which attribute(s) to measure and report. "Usefulness" is too general since costs will be relevant to some decisions but not to others and the same is true of exit values. It is this reason that causes me to state the relevance criterion in relation to a specified decision model.

Criterion 1: An attribute is relevant to a decision model if that attribute is specified by that decision model.

The corollary, of course, is that if an attribute is not specified by a decision model, it is irrelevant to that decision model.

## 2.3 Application of the Criterion

The objective of economic activity is said to be "profit maximization" but that begs the question since we are exploring alternative ways to measure profits. However, it is clear that humans prefer more net cash flows to less net cash flows. Thus, we can say that the objective of economic activity is to maximize future net cash flows. Since the cash balance is a summary measure of the cash inflows (debits) and outflows (credits), we can express the same idea by saying that the objective is to increase the cash balance, to obtain a future cash balance that is greater than the present cash balance. The task is to identify the decision model that is pertinent to that objective and then to examine that decision model to see which attributes are specified by that decision model, to see which attributes are relevant.

*2.31 Exchange decisions* One advantage of considering the simple case of marketable securities is that the decision model is well known. As every accountant and financial analyst knows, the decision to exchange requires the comparison of the current price with the future cash flows. Of course the future cash flows may require various adjustments, primarily for the time differences by discounting and also perhaps a separate adjustment for risk differences, but those are refinements which are explored in great depth in many finance and accounting textbooks and need not detain us here. The future cash flows consist of the future dividends and the terminal price, i.e., the price when the share is sold in the future. Thus, this well-known decision model specifies two attributes:

1. Future Cash Flows which consist of
   (a) Future Dividends, and
   (b) Future Terminal Price.
2. Current Price.

Some shares are bought for growth or "capital gains" rather than "current income" and this provides a convenient way to divide the question.

First, consider a growth share in which future dividends are expected to be zero. This reduces the relevant attributes to the (1b) future terminal price and (2) current price. If the future terminal price is expected to be less than the current price then a cash maximizer will not purchase an unowned share for the obvious reason that his future cash balance will be less than his present cash balance if he does purchase. A cash maximizer will sell an owned share under those conditions for the equally obvious reason that his present cash balance will be greater than his future cash balance if he does sell. There is *no* reason to purchase or not sell in this situation because it is, in effect, the exchange of, say, 1,000 present dollars for, say, 700 expected future dollars and that is not a cash maximizing decision even with zero discount rate, zero time differential, zero risk, etc. When the future terminal price is greater than the current price we can only say that a cash maximizer will *tend* to purchase or not sell because the decision also depends upon the date of the future price, the discount rate, and the existence of other alternatives which may be more cash maximizing.

It is rare to find universal agreement about anything, especially in accounting, but it does appear that the above decision model and its specified (relevant) attributes are undisputed.[6] The relevance of the two prices requires that we reconsider Question 2: should we report the current or the future price? As noted above, we cannot report the future price because it is unknown. The recommendations to report forecasts of future prices have been based on general "usefulness" and they often conclude that we should report forecasted prices (or discounted cash flows) *instead of* current prices. The relevance criterion, by contrast, clearly indicates that *if* we could accurately forecast future prices, we should report the forecasted prices *in addition* to current prices. That is, the relevance criterion does not discriminate future from current prices because both are specified by the decision model and there-

---

[6] I have tried very hard to state it in a form that is undisputed but perhaps I should explicitly disclaim normative decision models, intrinsic values, abnormal returns and the like. First, the decision model is not normative in that it can be applied to the objective of minimizing cash by reversing all the inequalities and defining 'better off' as a smaller cash balance. It is difficult to think of examples where that objective would be in force but perhaps a misanthropic manager of a philanthropic foundation illustrates the case. Since the tax regulations generally require that income be distributed in grants, the misanthrope can avoid such distributions by avoiding income and therefore the above decision model applies. Second, it does not matter whether the cash maximizer uses intrinsic value, inside information or a Ouija board to form the expectations. The basis for forming the expectations is not pertinent to my purpose. Third, the cash maximizer may earn abnormal returns from inside information or those returns may be due to accepting a high risk or it may not be possible to earn abnormal returns. The only thing required is that the cash maximizer be trying to earn some returns. Some of my past work has been misinterpreted and I apologize for not having been more explicit but I find it difficult to disclaim everything that I do not mean so I will ask the reader to take note of what I do not say as well as what I do say.

fore both are equally relevant. However, it does discriminate current from past prices because the decision model does not specify any past price, neither at a past event, such as purchase, nor at a past time. This does not mean that past prices are "useless" nor does it mean that they were not relevant to past decisions but it does mean that they are not relevant to present exchange decisions.

The decision model was stated above in terms of prices because it is usually stated that way. In the usual statement of the decision model the distinction between costs and exit values is either implicit or thought to be "negligible" in economic terminology or "immaterial" in accounting terminology. The demonstration of the conceptual difference requires that the distinction be explicit regardless of materiality. Thus, we must refine the decision model by substituting current cost or exit value as appropriate.

In deciding to purchase or not purchase, one must compare the current cost to the terminal exit value. To use the same figures as those in the journal entries, the current price at 1 January was $1,000 and the terminal price was $1,050 and therefore a cash maximizer would tend to purchase if the decision were based on prices. But that would be an error since the cash outflow would be the $1,100 current cost and the cash inflow would be the $950 terminal exit value. Thus, one must compare the current *cost*, not the current *price*, to the terminal *exit value*, not the terminal *price*, in making cash maximizing purchase decisions.

In deciding to sell or not sell, one must compare the current exit value to the terminal exit value. In terms of the journal entry figures, the $900 1 January exit value needs to be compared to the $950 terminal exit value. A cash maximizer would tend to not sell since the future cash balance is expected to be $50 greater than the present cash balance. Comparing the current price of $1,000 to the terminal exit value of $950 would indicate a sale that is an error.

The terminal exit value is relevant to both decisions but the current cost is relevant to the purchase or not purchase decision and the current exit value is relevant to the sell or not sell decision. To put it another way, the current cost is relevant to decisions regarding exchanges of *unowned* shares and the current exit value is relevant to decisions regarding exchanges of *owned* shares.

The current exit value of an owned share is relevant in another way that seems to be both obvious and difficult to grasp. (Perhaps the problem with grasping it is that it is too obvious.) Decisions are the choice between *mutually exclusive* alternatives. If one can own one share of GM and one share of GE, then one need not choose between them, no decision is required. Current exit values of owned shares, in comparison to current costs of unowned shares, specify the *available* mutually exclusive alternatives. Consider Exhibit 2. Since one must sell one share of GM for $900 and purchase one share of GE for $1,100, the purchase of one share of GE is *not* an available alternative. The available alternative to owning one share of GM is to own 900/1,100 or about 82 per cent of one share of GE. Of course one could add $200 cash to the exit value of GM and then purchase GE but that emphasizes the point since one cannot purchase GE without having the additional $200 cash.

Consideration of the second — current income — type of share will further clarify the point. Assume that the cash maximizer expects the future dividends to be as shown in Exhibit 2 in perpetuity. The effect of this assumption is to eliminate the terminal exit value as a future cash flow and reduce the relevant attributes to the (1a) future dividends and (2) current price. This again brings up Question 3 about reporting future dividends versus current prices and the answer is the same: both are relevant

**EXHIBIT 2**

|  | GM | GE |
|---|---|---|
| Current Cost | $1,100 | $1,100 |
| Price | 1,000 | 1,000 |
| Exit Value | 900 | 900 |
| Dividends | 55 | 66 |
| Rate of Return | | |
| on Current Cost | | |
| $55/$1,100 | 5% | |
| $66/$1,100 | | 6% |
| on Exit Value | | |
| $55/$900 | 6.1% | |
| $66/$900 | | 7.3% |
| Position | owned | unowned |

but the best we can do in regard to future dividends is to report somebody's forecast. It also again brings up the need to distinguish the kind of current price. In this case the decision is usually based on comparing rates of return. It has been vigorously argued that since we compute the rate of return on the current cost of unowned shares, we must also compute the rate of return on the current cost of owned shares in order to be consistent. Otherwise, so the argument goes, we will be comparing apples and oranges. On the basis of that consistent comparison, we should sell GM and purchase GE in order to earn 6 per cent instead of 5 per cent. But the purchase requires additional financing of $200 which, at the same interest rate of 6 per cent, would cost $12. The dividends from GE of $66 less the interest of $12 yields a net of $54 as compared to the $55 from GM. Thus, the result of a decision based on the consistent comparison is a decline in cash flows of $1. The $54 is, of course, 900/1,100 times the dividend of $66 which is another way of saying that the alternative to owning one share of GM is to own 900/1,100 shares of GE.

Another way to illustrate the point is to assume that the cash maximizer could invest any amount in a bank time deposit at 6 per cent. Since he now earns only 5 per cent on GM, he should sell GM and put the money in the bank in order to earn 6 per cent. But the result is the same since 6 per cent of the $900 exit value is $54. The difference, of course, is that GM is now earning 6.1 per cent *on exit value* and in order to make cash maximizing decisions one must compare that rate to the rates of return on the current cost of alternatives. Since the 6.1 per cent return on exit value for GM is greater than the 6 per cent return on current cost for either GE or a time deposit, the cash maximizing decision is to not sell GM. The 5 per cent return on current cost for GM may be consistent but it is also not relevant to cash maximizing decisions.

In summary, exit values are demonstrably relevant to exchange decisions of owned assets in regard to straightforward cash magnitude comparisons as well as in regard to rate of return comparisons. Since owned shares are listed on the balance sheet (and unowned shares are not listed), I conclude that, on the basis of relevance, exit values should be reported.

*2.32 Previous exchange decisions*    At various times in the past it was decided to purchase or not purchase or sell or not sell. This was made on the basis of the decision model identified above and required the forecasting of either future dividends or the terminal exit value. The future, or at least part of it, has now become the present and we want to look backward to see whether, and by how much, the cash maximizer has achieved the objective. In other words, we want to *evaluate* past decisions.

If the share has been sold, then all cash flows from this share have already occurred and the only thing required is to compare the present cash balance with the past cash balance. Since the original decision was made on the basis of a forecasted cash balance greater than the current cash balance, since the cash maximizer prefers larger to smaller cash balances, if the present cash balance is greater than the past cash balance, then the cash maximizer has achieved the objective of being "better off," the difference in magnitude is a measure of how much better off and the corresponding accounting term is "gain." The problem arises at interim dates when we need to make some sort of determination of whether, and by how much, the cash maximizer is better off than he was at some prior date. The choices are to report the historical cost and a zero gain, the current cost and a holding gain, or the exit value and a value gain.

Historical cost accounting does not address the problem. It repeats the report of the past cost on the present balance sheet with the consequent of a zero gain. Thus, in the best interpretation it does not provide an evaluation of the past decision at interim dates and in the worst interpretation it provides an erroneous evaluation since a zero gain is reported regardless of subsequent events. (The lower of cost or market version of historical cost provides an asymmetric evaluation.) By contrast, current price accounting does address the problem but it presents the choice of two attributes.

Current costs focus on cash outflow differences, sacrifice differences, and assert that one is better off from cost increases because future cash inflows parallel cost increases. Thus, a current cost increase heralds a future cash balance greater than the present cost. Exit values focus on cash inflow differences, the benefit difference, and assert that one is better off from exit value increases because the present cash balance if sold will be greater than a past cash balance. In the above case the price increased from $1,000 to $1,050 which resulted in reporting a holding gain and a value gain of $50. Since both current costs and exit values report that the cash maximizer is better off by the same amount, it appears that the distinction is semantic and of no consequence. Further inquiry, however, reveals that the two different concepts can lead to different amounts.

It is possible for current costs and exit values to change while the price remains constant. The occasional restructuring of commission rates is a real-world case of such a situation. Suppose that a share was owned when the commission increased from $100 to $150 but the price remained constant. Exhibit 3 contrasts the two cases.

When the price increases, column (b), the reported gain is the same under both options as shown in column (d). Whether we label that $50 gain a holding gain or value

**EXHIBIT 3**

|  | (a)<br>1 Jan. | (b)<br>31 Jan. | (c)<br>31 Jan. | (d)<br>(b)–(a) | (e)<br>(c)–(a) |
|---|---|---|---|---|---|
| Current Cost | 1,100 | 1,150 | 1,150 | 50 | 50 |
| Price | 1,000 | 1,050 | 1,000 | 50 | –0– |
| Exit Value | 900 | 950 | 850 | 50 | – 50 |

gain is of no consequence. However, when the commission increases, column (c), the amount of the reported gain differs by $100, a holding gain of $50 versus a value loss of $50 as shown in column (e). The simplicity of the case permits us to see that there are different kinds of holding gains. I will divide the growth (zero dividend) share from the current income (zero terminal exit value) share to distinguish the kinds of holding gains.

First, consider the current income share. This reduces the problem to the relation of increases in current costs to increases in future dividends. It is agreed that an increase in expected future dividends will result in an increase in the present price. If we reverse this reasoning and say that an increase in the present price will result in, and therefore is evidence of, an increase in future dividends, we have erred. All that we can legitimately conclude from an increase in the present price is that it is evidence of an increase in expectations. Since those expectations may or may not be realized, a holding gain based on a price increase is *conjectural*. If the current cost increase is due to a commission increase, it has no relation to expected future dividends, much less to actual future dividends. There is no evidence, neither logical nor empirical, that would allow us to conclude that either expected or actual future dividends parallel commission increases. It is unlikely that such a parallel would exist and therefore we can say that a holding gain based on a commission increase is *dubious*.

Second, consider the growth share with zero expected dividends. This reduces the problem to the relation of increases in current costs to increases in terminal exit values. Since prices can go up or down, the effect of a present price increase on the terminal exit value is unknown. Thus, holding gains based on price increases are *conjectural*. On the other hand, we can be certain that the effect of a commission increase is to decrease the terminal exit value. Whatever the terminal exit value turns out to be, it will be less by the amount of the commission increase. Thus, in regard to the future cash flows from the terminal exit value, a holding gain based on a commission increase is *detrimental*.

In summary, when we look at cost increases that are expected to benefit the future, we find that in regard to dividends they are at best conjectural and at worst dubious and in regard to terminal exit values they are best conjectural and at worst detrimental. When we divide the question the other way, we find that the benefit from a price increase on both types of cash flows is conjectural and the benefit from a commission increase is at best dubious and at worst contradictory. It is contradictory because it is a benefit that is detrimental, i.e., not beneficial.[7]

[7] My conjecture is that all cash maximizers would consider themselves worse off from a commission increase and therefore would think that it is contradictory to report it as a gain. I discussed the justification in its future benefit form rather than the past cost saving form because my conjecture is that most accountants, having been brought up in the historical cost tradition, look at current cost increases as future benefits. Those brought up in the economic tradition, such as Edwards and Bell [1974], think of it as a cost saving and explicitly disclaim it being a benefit increase or, in their terminology, an addition to "realizable income" (p. 93). My conjecture is that all cash maximizers would consider a commission increase to be a cost dissaving and therefore would think that it is contradictory to report it as a gain. See Rosenfield [1969] for an excellent discussion in general as well as a specific conclusion that holding gains are "unintelligible," which is similar to my conjecture. See Samuelson [1980] for a lucid exposition in general as well as a specific conclusion that cost savings have no natural zero point. See Revsine [1973] for a thorough analysis in general as well as the specific conclusion that some types of holding gains are not beneficial.

Current cost analysts recognize the existence of cost increases that are not beneficial but their proposed solution is "a selective elimination from income of those price [current cost] changes that do not reflect expected changes in [future cash] operating flows while including those that do correspond to expected flow changes" (Revsine [1973], p. 144). Implementation of this solution will present a dilemma: either inconsistent reporting of assets—some at current cost and others at historical cost—or the disposition of a deferred credit for those current cost increases that are not beneficial. But the more important question is if the objective is to measure benefits, why not measure benefits? Why measure the sacrifice and use it as a surrogate for benefits? My hypothesis is that we are so steeped in measuring costs or sacrifices that we do not perceive the alternative of measuring benefits. That is, Question 1—costs versus exit values—is never addressed because it is taken for granted that we will report costs and the only question is current versus historical costs. This *combines* Question 1 with Question 3—current versus historical—but it also *confuses* Question 1 with Question 2—future versus current—because the reason for measuring the current sacrifice is that it is expected to benefit the future.

The confusion of temporal locations has plagued accountants for a very long time. Earlier we were told that it was impossible to measure the present but that we could measure past costs and that we should report them because they will benefit the future. Now we are told that it is possible to measure current costs and that we should report them because they will benefit the future. Since current costs benefit the future, changes in current costs—holding gains—indicate changes in future benefits. But when it is discovered that some changes in current costs will not benefit the future, we are told to segregate them and report only those that will benefit the future. If the objective is to report forecasts of future benefits, why not report forecasts of future benefits? The usual answer is that the future is unknown and that forecasts are unreliable. But the proposed solution requires that we forecast the future in order to segregate those cost increases that benefit the future from those that do not. Thus, reporting the segregated cost increases as holding gains because they benefit the future is, in fact, a report of a forecast, albeit disguised. If forecasts are too unreliable to report, then the segregated holding gains are also too unreliable to report. That is, holding gains are at best conjectural.

Even if holding gains were reliable indicators of future benefits, it would not relieve us of the task of measuring the present. As noted above (Section 2.31), the decision model specifies *both* the present price and the future price (or future dividends). One cannot decide to purchase or not purchase from knowledge of the future exit value alone; it requires a comparison of the current cost with the future exit value. One cannot decide to sell or not sell on the basis of knowledge of the future exit value alone; it requires a comparison of the present exit value with the future exit value. Thus, if current costs were reliable forecasts of future exit values or holding gains were reliable forecasts of changes in future exit values, the relevance criterion would require that *both* be reported. The reason is that decisions require that the present be distinguished from the future. A cash maximizer purchases because he expects his future cash balance to be greater than his present cash balance. In the evaluation of previous exchanges the present must be distinguished from the past for the same reason. Reporting holding gains because they benefit the future mixes future expectations with past gains. In order to *decide* one must compare the *present* with the *future* and confusing the two will produce decision errors. In order to *evaluate* past decisions one must compare the *present* with the *past* and confusing the two will produce evaluation errors. We do distinguish the future, present and past at the event of sale. When the cash is collected, the present cash balance is compared with the past cash balance to determine the past gain and there is no notice taken of what the future cash balance may be. The present cash balance is likely to be used to purchase another share and therefore we could confound ourselves with questions about whether the present cash balance will benefit the future or not. But we do not so confound ourselves, we simply and straightforwardly measure the present benefits of the present cash balance, recognizing that it is both decision relevant (in comparison with future balances) and evaluation relevant (in comparison with previous balances).

Exit valuation is an attempt to measure the present benefits without regard to the future benefits or present or past sacrifices. Exit values are measures of what the present cash balance would be if the share were sold in the present. It is an attempt to determine the equivalent cash balance. Thus, exit values are simply an extension of the idea that humans are better off when their cash balances increase and worse off when they decrease. A value change *is* the difference between equivalent cash balances. For that reason, I conclude that value changes should be reported on the income statement.

## 2.4 Summary and Conclusions

A major impediment to resolving questions about alternative accounting methods has been the utilization of criteria (or principles) that either do not discriminate or mistake definitions for criteria. For this reason, we must seek other criteria. It is generally agreed that accounting reports should be useful but that criterion is too general to be of much help in choosing accounting methods. The criterion of relevance, by contrast, refers to a specific decision context and a specific decision model. Identification of the decision context and the decision model permit an unequivocal specification of the relevant attributes.

A well-known, universally accepted decision model regarding exchanges of shares was identified. It was assumed that the objective is to maximize net cash flows or balances. (Strictly speaking, that assumption is unnecessary because the identified decision model could also be used to minimize cash flows or balances.) Since that decision model and the specified attributes are undisputed it permits three unequivocal conclusions:

Conclusion 1:  Future cash flows are relevant to cash maximizing decisions regarding exchanges of shares.

Conclusion 2:  Costs are relevant to cash maximizing decisions regarding purchases of unowned shares.

Conclusion 3:  Exit values are relevant to cash maximizing decisions regarding selling of owned shares.

Since previously purchased—owned—shares are reported on the financial statements, the conclusions permit the elimination of costs, both current and historical. Only future cash flows and exit values are relevant to cash maximizing decisions regarding owned shares. Since the future is unknown, only forecasts of future cash flows can be reported. The problem of reporting forecasts is beyond the scope of this essay but if accurate forecasts can be made, the relevance criterion indicates that both should be reported. Until that issue is settled, exit values should be reported because they are necessary, but not sufficient, to cash-maximizing decisions regarding owned shares.

> Conclusion 4: Exit values of owned shares should be reported on the balance sheet.

The forward-looking decisions require the distinction of the present cash balance from the expected future cash balance. Backward-looking evaluations of past decisions require the distinctions of the present cash balance from the past cash balance. When the share is owned, when the cash has not been collected, the forward-looking decisions require the comparison of the present cash equivalent balance with a future cash balance. Backward-looking evaluations require the comparison of the present cash equivalent balance with the past cash balance. Thus, interim gains for owned shares should be measured as the difference between the present cash equivalent balance and the previous cash balance.

> Conclusion 5: Exit values of owned shares should be utilized as the basis for measuring past gains and those value gains should be reported on the income statement.

*2.41 Irrelevance*    I cannot extend the conclusions to say that costs should *not* be reported on the basis of irrelevance because there may be other decision models which specify costs. I cannot think of anything that one can do with owned shares except sell or not sell them so I do not believe that other decision models exist. But that is a test of a joint hypothesis since it is at least equally likely that my failure to find such a decision model is due to my limitations as it is to the nonexistence of such decision models. In either event, I cannot prove the nonexistence of such decision models. As every auditor knows, it is much easier to prove the existence of an asset than it is to prove the nonexistence of a liability. For this reason, the onus is on others to prove the relevance of costs. In order to stimulate the provision of that proof, I will offer a conjecture that goes much beyond what has been demonstrated.

> Conjecture 1: The cost of an owned share is irrelevant to all cash maximizing decisions regarding that share.

Note that it takes only *one* case of demonstrated relevance to prove that conjecture wrong since I have been so bold (or foolish) to say that costs are irrelevant to *all* cash maximizing decisions regarding an owned share. I challenge the reader to prove Conjecture 1 wrong.

*2.42 Ranking*    In previous works I have attempted to rank the various alternatives on the basis of relevance. The reason for that attempt was to allow other criteria to influence the decision. For example, a characteristic of relevance is timeliness which would permit a finer partitioning—a distinction between current costs and historical costs—resulting in the following:

1. Exit values
2. Current costs
3. Historical costs.

One other criterion has already influenced that array, namely, the unknown future eliminated the future terminal exit value and future dividends. Where forecasts should be ranked is an open question. But note that such questions need not conflict with this ranking. For example, Staubus [1977] has presented a well-reasoned case for the reporting of evidence of future cash flows. I happen to be sceptical of our ability to accomplish that but I would be the last to deny the relevance of evidence of future cash flows. Thus, Staubus's work is complementary to the ranking, not conflicting.

The proposal for additional disclosure is also not in conflict. We could decide to adopt two of the methods, use multi-column reports or supplementary statements, and this would require that other criteria be utilized to decide which of the two. For example, Bedford and McKeown [1972] present a well-balanced case for reporting both (1) and (2). It is conceivable that such a combination would be more relevant than any single category. I am sceptical of that but I have not done enough work on combinations to permit me to draw a conclusion one way or the other. Another version of disclosure is to present any one or a combination of the above at lower levels of aggregation or in more detail. Others want to report all three methods plus anything else that seems useful. But at some point other criteria must come into play. Unbridled disclosure cannot be the answer because constraints such as the marginal cost of producing the marginal information exceeding its marginal benefits or information overload must come into force at some point. (See Revsine [1973], pp. 14–18 for a clear, concise statement of the problem.) Perhaps the relevance criterion would allow us to eliminate the lower ranked methods as those constraints become binding. In addition, there may be other conflicting criteria that would result in different rankings which would force us to consider trade-offs. At one time the criterion of objectivity was thought to conflict with the ranking but the redefinition of objectivity by Ijiri and Jaedicke [1966] permitted empirical tests, e.g. by McDonald [1968], which indicate that the criterion of objectivity is not in conflict with the above ranking and therefore trade-offs are not required.

Some studies on user wants conflict with the ranking. For example, Benston and Krasney [1978] have reported that sophisticated users have a strong demand for historical costs. Other studies complement the ranking. For example, Tweedie [1977] has reported that naive users have a strong demand for cash flows and exit values. The combined test results serve only to refine the question: should we supply the information demanded by sophisticated users or naive users or naive users or both? In this sense, tests on user wants do not conflict with the ranking.[8] Since it is widely

---

[8] Of course, we could answer the question on the basis that sophisticated users know more than naive users, by definition, but I think that there is a more fundamental question involved. Namely, are we accountants passive suppliers of neutral information or are we a part of a milieu in which the kind of information that we supply influences the demand of the users? I have previously offered the conjecture ("hypothesis" overstates my feeble offering) that the latter is the case. Specifically, I conjectured that if we surveyed users the results would be that naive users would demand exit values and that sophisticated users would demand historical costs (Sterling [1970], pp. 54 and 343). The combined results of Benston and Krasney [1978] and Tweedie [1977] confirm that conjecture. Indeed the Benston and Krasney results show that less sophisticated users have a weaker demand for historical costs than do more sophisticated users. Tweedie's results show that naive users have a near zero demand for historical costs. Thus, the three data points suggest that demand for historical costs varies directly with sophistication.

In an attempt to explain the first conjecture, I offered a second conjecture that the issuance of a particular kind of information has a tendency to influence the users to demand that

recognized that a market is efficient with respect to a given information set, then the market would still be efficient with respect to (1) or (2) or (1) and (2) etc. so that the ranking does not conflict with the efficient market tests. There is nothing that I am aware of in any of the behavioural studies, information economics, or agency theory, that conflicts.

For all these reasons, I would like to say Q.E.D. in regard to the relevance of the exit value of an owned share. That is a small achievement but my aspirations are small. I would like to see us solve one problem in accounting, however trivial, instead of continuing to move from one unsolved problem to another, instead of continuing to accumulate unresolved issues.

## 3. EXTENSIONS

The reason for considering the special case in detail was the hope that it will provide insights into other special cases. The purpose of analysis—the breaking apart—is to discover commonalities which will permit a synthesis—the putting together—so that we have an understanding of all special cases. The ultimate goal is to weave a general principle that is founded on irreducible and stubborn facts.

### 3.1 The Problem

It often seems to me that we tend to view each type of exchange and each type of asset in isolation with the result that each type requires the application of a special principle. The problem with Generally Accepted Accounting Principles is that general refers to accepted instead of principles. Instead of there being a few general principles, there are a myriad of special principles. This, I believe, is what people mean when they say that there are *no* principles of accounting. What I think they are expressing is a desire for more general principles. I share that desire.

All general principles have limited application. That apparent paradox is illustrated by the general principles of plane geometry being limited to applications to flat surfaces. To show that a principle has a limited range of application is not sufficient reason to reject it since that is a characteristic of all principles. However, we prefer more general principles to less general principles for such reasons as simplicity, elegance and parsimony. The practical aspect of such a preference is that it aids in learning, reduces confusion and promotes consistency. A general principle is a powerful, practical tool in dealing with stubborn facts. Compare pre-Euclidean with post-Euclidean surveying and construction to see the practical power of the general principles of geometry. Thus, we continue to seek more general principles initially for theoretical reasons but ultimately for practical reasons. We seek fewer principles

---

information. That conjecture was a *priori* with a smattering of anecdotal evidence. In an attempt to be clear on my meaning I used the analogy of a conditioned response in psychology and phrased the conjecture in terms of users being conditioned to respond to our reports. As subsequent events proved, that was unfortunate phraseology because it set off a firestorm of protest. Regardless of what it is called, however, it is clear that the combined test results are not a falsification of the second conjecture. In my mind at least, the combined results support the second conjecture and this causes me to worry about us being in a vicious circle in which supplying historical costs strengthens the demand for historical costs and the measurement of the demand strengthens our resolve to supply historical costs. Perhaps a reader can convert this vague conjecture into a testable hypothesis which will shed some light on the issues.

with broader ranges of application. To put it negatively, we would like to avoid inconsistencies due to the confusion stemming from too many special principles or from incompleteness in principles which require additional *ad hoc* principles. It is my contention that the very nature of the cost principle severely limits its range of application. To illustrate that the limitations are fundamental and pervasive, let us consider a few simple cases.

*3.11 Exchanges*    A basic element of accounting is an exchange which, in general form, is symbolically represented by the following entry:

| Time t | Account i | Dr |
|--------|-----------|-----|
|        | Account j | Cr |

The entries that we deal with are of two basic types:

**a.**  Measure the debit and set the credit equal.
**b.**  Measure the credit and set the debit equal.

An example of a type (b) entry is a purchase in which we measure the cash sacrificed, set the debit to the asset equal and call it a cost. An example of a type (a) entry is borrowing funds in which we measure the cash received, set the credit to the payable equal and do *not* call it a cost. The cost principle is silent in regard to type (a) entries. Its range of application has been exceeded because neither the cash nor the payable is a cost. When we sell inventory we normally break the compound entry down into a type (b) entry for cost of goods sold and a type (a) entry for revenue. All compound entries can be decomposed in that fashion so that if we look to the elementary or simple (not compound) entries we can say that the cost principle does not apply to type (a) entries. Sometimes it does not apply to type (b) entries. For example, if we lend money, we measure the cash credit and set the receivable equal but seldom if ever do we speak of the receivable as a cost; instead we call it a loan or investment.

The point is that whether or not we apply the cost principle depends upon the *type of exchange*. Sometimes the cost principle applies and sometimes it does not. In order to know how to account we must know how to classify exchanges by type and then either apply the cost principle or apply some other special principle. If we are looking for a hierarchy of principles, we must seek the more general principle which allows us to classify exchanges because the type of exchange determines which special principle applies. In so far as I am aware, no such general principle exists.[9] We can distinguish the types of entries with ease in the majority of cases but in the absence of a general principle which classifies exchanges we will encounter difficulties as illustrated by barters.

*3.12 Barters*    Recall that the cost principle requires that the purchased share be set equal to the cash paid and no gain or loss is recognized at the event of purchase. At sale the cash received is matched with the cost, either historical or current, and a gain

---

[9] In Sterling and Flaherty [1971] the hypothesis was offered that the general principle was the relative liquidity of the exchanged assets. The test in Sterling, Tollefson and Flaherty [1979] revealed that the classification of barters by type (a) or (b) was more complicated since both conservatism and acquisition influenced the classification. Thus, the general principle, if it exists, eluded that test.

or loss is recognized. The concepts are clear and easily applied when the exchanges are for cash but they provide no guidance when the share is exchanged for a non-cash asset. The first question that arises is whether the exchange is a purchase or a sale, a type (a) or type (b) entry. The question is important because different concepts are utilized. In terms of realization, historical cost prohibits the recognition of a gain until sale so that the sale is sometimes referred to as the "crucial event." The event of a sale is also crucial in current costing since it utilizes the same concept of matching costs and revenues at the event of sale.

Suppose that the cash maximizer acquired a share with a price of $1,000 by sacrificing land that had a historical cost of $500. This simple exchange is a quandary for historical costs since one cannot determine whether it is a purchase or sale because cash was not exchanged. If it is considered a sale, then the value of the share must be determined and the difference recorded as a gain. But that means that a gain is recognized upon acquisition of the share whereas previously a gain was prohibited upon acquisition of the share. If it is considered a purchase, then the value of the share is set equal to the sacrifice. That sacrifice could be taken to be the $500 historical cost but in a purchase the sacrifice is usually independently valued and the $500 is a previous sacrifice, not a current sacrifice. Setting the value of the share equal to $500 is utilizing the sacrifice of the cash for land instead of the current sacrifice for the share. But if we want to set the share equal to the current sacrifice it would require writing up the land to the current cost or exit value and such write-ups are prohibited by historical costs. That it is a quandary, that the cost principle does not extend to barters, is evidenced by two factors. First, it has required the issuance of a special principle based on the relative case of determination of the acquisition or the sacrifice. Second, an empirical test of how practitioners would record this simple exchange revealed that there were considerable differences of interpretation. (See Sterling, Tollefson and Flaherty [1979].)

In this simple case the share can be recorded at any one of the following amounts:

1.  Current cost of the share.
2.  Exit value of the share.
3.  Current cost of the land.
4.  Exit value of the land.
5.  Historical cost of the land.

That the cost principle does not extend to this case (or that the practitioners were confused by too many special principles) is evidenced by the fact that each of the five values was selected by some practitioners. That the cost principle does not aid in distinguishing purchases from sales is evidenced by the fact that some practitioners recorded the difference as a realized gain and some as an unrealized gain.

Current costing results in less variation but it also requires that purchases be distinguished from sales because a different value is recorded at sale. Edwards [1975], one of the pioneers of current costing, states the question clearly and succinctly: "The point at issue, of course, is not *whether* to value by current entry or exit prices, but *when* to shift from entry to exit values" (p. 240). After stating the alternative points at which one can shift, he says: "The realization principle normally rests on the sale event to signal the displacement of entry values by exit values" (p. 240). Unfortunately, that answer does not extend to barters where the very question is whether it is a purchase or a sale.

To illustrate the problem, assume that the current cost of the land is $800. If this is a purchase we would set the share equal to the sacrifice.

| | | | |
|---|---|---|---|
| 1 Jan. | Marketable Securities | $800 | |
| | Land | | $800 |

If this is a sale, that would be the event at which we displace current costs with exit values.

| | | | |
|---|---|---|---|
| 1 Jan. | Marketable Securities | $900 | |
| | Land | | $800 |
| | Gain on Sale | | $100 |

Apparently current cost concepts do not extend to this case because we do not know which of the entries is appropriate, we do not know whether the exchange is a purchase or a sale. There is another issue involved because when an identical share was purchased in Section 2 it was recorded at $1,100 rather than either the $800 or $900 in the above entries. Thus, we must report different amounts for identical assets if we adopt either of the above entries. Of course, we can record the exchange either way and then write the share up to the $1,100 current cost. But if we do that we have made the determination on the type of asset, not on the type of exchange.

3.13 *Assets*    Although it is often said that *all* assets are valued at cost, in fact only *some* assets are valued at cost. The exit value of an account receivable is measured at the time of sale and it continues to be reported at its exit value until collection. We do not write up accounts receivable to current cost as was a possibility when we acquired a share in the barter. But the acquisition of an account receivable and the sacrifice of land is, in fact, a barter since cash was not exchanged.

The point is that some types of assets are reported at their exit value and others at their cost. In the phylum of assets there are two classes:

**α.**    those at exit value such as cash and accounts receivable;
**β.**    those at cost such as inventory and equipment.

It seems to me that the argument of cost versus exit value reflects a significant difference in assets so that in classifying them we should take the first cut there. It is a much more significant difference than the current versus fixed classification that we now use. In addition, it is this classification that permits us to distinguish a purchase from a sale. A purchase is a type (b) exchange *because* the acquired asset is in class ($\beta$) and the sacrifice comes from class ($\alpha$). The confusion about barters is *because* both the acquired share and the sacrificed land are in class ($\beta$). As a consequence it is neither a purchase nor a sale: one can look at it as purchasing a share as easily as selling land. For this reason, *ad hoc* principles are required and have in fact been used but the principle of ease of determination still does not resolve the question of whether the exchange should be treated like a type (a) or type (b) or some other special type.

As indicated by its name, the cost principle applies to those assets in class ($\beta$) but is silent in regard to those assets in class ($\alpha$). The problem in regard to the barter then, is whether the share belongs in class ($\beta$) and should be reported at cost regardless of how acquired or whether its method of acquisition makes it a type (a) entry and therefore should be reported at exit value regardless of its class. I fear that the two concepts will be in perpetual opposition.

*3.14 Summary*    Classification of assets and exchanges by type is a prerequisite to applying the cost principle. The range of application of the cost principle is limited to those assets that are stated at their sacrifice value and those exchanges that are classified as purchases. For all other types of assets and exchanges, other special principles are required.

Many recent controversies stem from the limited range of application of the cost principle. Purchase-pooling, for example, is in essence a barter question and the argument was over what type of exchange occurred. If it was a purchase, we got one kind of answer and if it was not a purchase, we got another. Front-end loading is, in essence, a barter question and the argument was about what type of exchange occurred. If it was a sale, we could realize income but if it was not a sale, we should not realize income. $R + D$, for example, is an asset classification question. If we try to measure its present benefits we get one type of answer but if we set it equal to its sacrifice value on the basis of expected future benefits, we get another answer. $R + D$ is the same type of question as whether the acquired share should be treated like a receivable and valued at its exit value or treated like inventory and valued at its cost.

This indicates that the cost principle is a special principle and that a prerequisite is the provision of a general principle that will permit unambiguous classification of exchanges by type and assets by class. Exit values are fundamentally different. The concept is that all assets are, in essence, the same in regard to the measured attribute. The objective is to measure the benefit value of all assets. The exchange is a relatively unimportant event since it is conceived of as merely changing the form of benefit values, not a signal for switching from one kind of value to another. It is for these reasons that I believe that exit values have the potential of providing a much more general principle of valuation.

### 3.2 Restatement

Prior to extending the analysis to other special cases, I will restate the marketable security case in a more general and compact form. The elements of all three accounting methods are displayed in Exhibit 4. Column A is the future cash receipts from the terminal exit value. The future and past dividends, if any, are not displayed since they affect all accounting methods, decisions and income in exactly the same way. Since the terminal exit value lies in the future, I have entered a U for unknown in the pertinent cells. Columns B and C refer to the present, the date of the financial report, but B refers to the benefit of the cash receivable if sold while C refers to the sacrifice of the cash payable if purchased. Since the present price and

---

**EXHIBIT 4**

| Attribute | | A | B | C | D |
|---|---|---|---|---|---|
| | | Exit Value | | Cost | |
| Accounting Method | | Terminal | Current | Current | Historical |
| 1 | Historical Cost | U | | | K |
| 2 | Current Cost | U | | K | K |
| 3 | Exit Value | U | K | | K |

commission are known I have entered a K in the pertinent cells. Column D is the sacrifice of the past cash paid at purchase and it is also known.

Historical cost, row one, can be stated in terms of the ultimate gain, G.

$$A - D = G \tag{1}$$

Since A is unknown, G cannot be reported on the income statement nor can A be reported on the present balance sheet. It is often said that the principal problem of accounting is that the future is unknown. In my view that is a misstatement of the problem. I would state the problem as the need to divide the total gain into the future expected gain versus the past gain, which requires the measurement of the present. To make the same point in different words, the present needs to be measured in order to make forward-looking decisions *and* to make backward-looking measurements of past gains.

That statement of the problem deserves emphasis. I used "ultimate gain" because "ultimate income" has been used by Canning [1929] and others to refer to the net cash receipts after liquidation of the firm. The ultimate income is what was reported in venture accounting and it referred to the cash receipts of the venture at liquidation minus the cash paid at formation. The switch to periodic reporting was undertaken because there was need for interim information between formation and liquidation of the firm. The same concept can be applied to individual assets. The ultimate gain from an asset is venture accounting and it refers to the cash received at sale minus the cash paid at purchase. We need to switch to periodic reporting because there is a need for interim information between purchase and sale of the asset. Thus, current price accounting is simply an extension of the idea of periodic reporting.

Historical cost accounting does not address the problem of periodic reporting of assets. It does not attempt to measure the present. Instead, it reports D on the present balance sheet, which is not relevant to present exchange decisions, and it reports a zero gain on the present income statement, which is a failure to attempt the measurement of past gains.

Both current cost and exit value address the problem of periodic reporting for assets, of measuring the present, but they measure different attributes. Current costs, row 2, divides the future from the past on the basis of the sacrifice from a present purchase.

$$(A - C) + (C - D) = G \tag{2}$$

The first term, A − C, is the expected future gain and the second term, C − D, is the past holding gain. The first term is relevant to the purchase versus not-purchase decisions since, in the absence of expected future dividends, a cash maximizer would not purchase the asset if A < C. However, since the asset is owned, the purchase versus not-purchase decision has already been made and therefore, the current cost of owned assets is irrelevant to exchange decisions regarding owned assets. The past holding gain depends upon the cause of the current cost increase as to whether its benefit is conjectural, dubious or detrimental and therefore, it is not a reliable measure.

Exit values, row 3, divide the future from the present on the basis of an immediate sale.

$$(A - B) + (B - D) = G \tag{3}$$

The first term, A − B, is the expected future gain and the second term, B − D, is the past value gain. The first term is relevant to the sell versus not-sell decision since, in the absence of expected future dividends, a cash maximizer would sell the asset if A < B. The second term, B − D, indicates the amount of the increase in the cash balance there would be if the asset were sold. Hence, it is a measurement of the incremental equivalent cash balance.

Therefore, I conclude that exit values should be reported on the present balance sheet since they are necessary, but not sufficient, for exchange decisions regarding owned assets; and that they be used to measure past gains since they are measures of incremental equivalent cash balances. I will leave open the question of the reporting of forecasts of A, the terminal exit value, since A is undeniably relevant but the forecast of A presents other problems.

### 3.3  Extension to Other Assets

Using Exhibit 4 and the three equations as the basis let us explore the measurement and reporting problems of three other types of assets. In effect, these are different types of firms. The marketable security case is what I have previously called a "trading firm" which buys and sells in the same market. The inventory case is concerned with a "merchandising firm" which buys in one market, e.g. wholesale, and sells in another market, e.g. retail. The firm does not change the form of the goods but merely holds them for sale, i.e., it adds time and place utility. The depreciables case is a "producing firm" which is characterized by buying in the factor market and producing a product which it sells in a different market. In this case the firm produces a service, i.e., a perishable product. Receivables is a special case.

*3.31 Inventory*    To separate the issues, consider a firm that holds no depreciables so that we can concentrate on inventory. The only activity of this firm is to purchase in one market for the wholesale price and sell at a later time in another market for the retail price. To hold the practical problem of determining the current cost or exit value in abeyance, let us consider goods where the wholesale market is fairly active and therefore the prices are fairly easy to observe. A real-world example is a retail coin dealer. In such a company there is no analogue for dividends. The inventory is analogous to the growth share with zero dividends.

Column A is the unknown future retail price. Of course the firm can mark up the cost and thereby *offer* the unit at any retail price that it chooses but whether it can sell for the offering retail price is problematical. It may be forced to mark down the retail price in order to sell. Another way to state the problem is that there is a delay, sometimes lengthy, between purchase and sale so that even if the firm is adamant about the retail price, the time period between purchase and sale is problematical. Viewing the future and the present as the same is the cause of the confusion about exit values recognizing a gain on purchase. Retail prices are exit values in the sense that they are selling prices but they are future exit values, not current exit values. For the same reason that we cannot report the terminal exit value of a marketable security, we cannot report the terminal exit value—retail price when sold—of a unit of inventory. The best we could do would be to report the forecasted retail price.

The current exit value, column B, is the wholesaler's purchase price less ancillary costs such as freight. The wholesaler also attempts to buy cheap and sell dear so that the wholesale purchase price is less than the wholesale selling price. The current cost, column C, is the wholesaler's selling price plus ancillary costs. Thus, the current cost of the retailer is greater than the exit value by the amount of wholesaler's margin plus twice the ancillary costs. The historical cost, column D, is the wholesaler's selling price plus ancillary costs at the event of purchase.

Given that interpretation, A − D is the total gain, G, or in more familiar terminology A is the revenue. D is the historical cost of goods sold and G is the gross margin. The historical cost method would wait until the sale is consummated before recording a gain. Current cost and exit value would record interim gains as shown in equations (2) and (3).

The relevance of the exit value can be demonstrated in the same fashion as in Section 3.2. The expected future gain is A − B and a cash maximizer will sell now for B if A < B. Alternatively, if the firm sets the price at A, then the time period until sale is the variable to be forecasted. The interest on B is forgone from holding the inventory until it can be sold for A and if that interest is greater than A − B, then a cash maximizer will sell now for B. For the same reasons, B is a measure of the present equivalent cash balance and therefore B − D is a measure of the incremental equivalent cash balance.

One reason I selected a retail coin dealer as the prototype firm is that the wholesale price, and the wholesaler's margin, is fairly well known and therefore there is not much of a problem in determining the retailer's current cost or exit value. Another reason is that in recent years it has often been the case that A < B and the retailer has, in fact, sold for the exit value. The sharp price increases of gold and silver resulted in sharp price increases in the wholesale price for common gold and silver coins because they had passed the melt-down point. The retail price was less responsive to the price of gold and silver resulting in many retailers deciding to sell their common coins to the wholesalers for the exit value. That is, deciding to sell for B because A < B was not a rare occurrence. Those who did not sell expected A > B. Some expected the retail price to become more responsive while others expected the price of gold and silver to continue to increase and therefore the wholesaler's purchase price would continue to increase. Thus, the terminal exit value was either the future retail price or the future wholesale price and we do not know which it was for any given retailer but we do know that they forecasted an A such that A > B. The point is that B was relevant to the decision regardless of whether their expected future gains were from retail sales or from, in effect, speculating in gold and silver. Their past gain, B − D, was the incremental equivalent cash balance at the time of the decision.[10]

---

[10] Subsequent events, particularly silver prices, have shown that those who expected A > B were wrong. The retail price never did move up to parallel the earlier higher current cost and the wholesale price of silver coins declined precipitously. Exit values would report that subsequent decline as a loss in subsequent periods. Some would say that the subsequent loss proved that the previous reported gain was "wrong" and "misleading." The search is for irrevocable profits which subsequent events cannot erase. I fear that the search is doomed to fail because the realized gains that were in fact reported by coin dealers were in fact erased by subsequent events when they reported realized losses. Thus, the criterion of irrevocable gains does not discriminate. The same is true for the criterion of "yo yo profits." Value gains would in fact yo yo in this case as would holding gains. Those dealers who did not sell would report a zero realized gain which did not yo yo. But the difference then is concerned with the *report* of the phenomena, not the phenomena. I could measure my past weight and continue to report that magnitude so that the result would be a *reported* zero weight gain. If my weight did yo yo then we have a choice of the report faithfully representing that yo yo gain or reporting a zero gain. The notion of yo yo profits is a definition of a different method of reporting, not a criterion. In addition, the realized profits did in fact yo yo so that the notion does not discriminate.

The expected gain from purchase is A − C because a retailer would not purchase if A < C but since the inventory is owned, the current cost is irrelevant to exchange decisions. The past holding gain, C − D, depends upon future events. The fact that retail prices were not responsive to wholesale prices in this case is another example of the same kind of problem discussed in Section 2 regarding price increases and commission increases. Thus, C − D is at best conjectural, it may be dubious and perhaps it is detrimental.

Historical cost, D, was relevant to the purchase decision but since the purchase has been made it is no longer relevant. Reporting D or G = O is irrelevant to present exchange decisions, both purchase versus not purchase and sell versus not sell. If the inventory has been allocated by LIFO, FIFO, moving average or whatever then it is not relevant to any decision—past, present or future—that I have been able to identify.

For the same reasons as given in Section 2.4, I cannot prove the irrelevance of current costs or historical costs. I can only rephrase Conjecture 1 by substituting 'inventory' for 'share' and offer the same challenge. One caveat is that extending the time period beyond the sale of the inventory now on hand requires the forecast of the future cost so that even if one assumes continued replacement of identical units, it is the future cost, not the current cost, that is relevant to the decision. The long-run decisions require the forecast of the long-run net cash flows which in this case consist of the inflows from future retail prices and outflows for future wholesale prices plus ancillaries as well as the quantities purchased and sold and the dates of purchase and sale. Once all those forecasts have been made, then we can discount the net cash flows to make long-run decisions. In the meantime we must remember the ancient economic axiom that the long run consists of a series of short runs.

*3.32 Depreciables* To separate the issues, let us consider a firm that holds no inventory so that we can concentrate on depreciables. To hold the practical problems of determining current cost or exit value in abeyance, let us consider the depreciation of an automobile since the active market for used automobiles will allow us to concentrate on the concept rather than the magnitude. A real-world counterpart is a taxi company. In such a company the analogue for dividends is the cash inflows from fares less the cash outflows for fuel, repairs, etc. Since these net cash flows, both past and future, are the same for all three accounting methods, they are omitted from Exhibit 4.

Column A is the unknown future salvage value. The magnitudes for columns B and C would be obtained from the current listings of used car prices, with B obtained from the "wholesale price" column and C from the "retail price" column. That is, if the automobile were to be purchased, one would have to pay the retail price to the automobile dealer and hence that is its current cost while if it were sold, one would receive the wholesale price and hence that is its exit value.

Given that interpretation, A − D is the ultimate gain, G, which is expected to be negative in this case and therefore it is an expected ultimate loss. In more familiar terminology, it is the expected total depreciation. The historical cost method would amortize or allocate that amount to each time period. Current cost and exit values would record interim losses (depreciation expense) as shown in equations (2) and (3).

The relevance of the exit value can be demonstrated in the same fashion as in Section 3.2. The expected future value loss is A − B and a cash maximizer would sell now for B if the future net cash flow from fares is less than the forecasted value loss. If the opposite is true, then we can only say that the cash maximizer would tend to not sell. In addition, since the terminal exit value is likely to be far in the future and relatively insignificant, it will be more convenient to include it as one of the future cash inflows. Then all future cash flows would be discounted and compared to B in order to decide to sell or not sell. Similarly B − D is the decline in the equivalent cash balance and therefore B − D is a measure of decremental cash to date.

Current cost would be relevant if one were deciding to purchase or not purchase an identical automobile but it is not relevant if the automobile is already owned. If the time horizon goes to or beyond replacing, then the future replacement cost, not the current cost, is relevant because it is one component of the forecasted future cash outflows. In regard to the holding loss, C − D, we face similar problems to those discussed above. If Detroit-built taxis increase in price and Japanese-built taxis decrease in price with concomitant increases and decreases in current costs, will the owners of Detroit taxis be better off and the owners of Japanese taxis be worse off? The effect on the future cash flows from fares due to such current cost changes is at best conjectural. The analogue for a commission increase is a sales tax increase or the imposition of a transaction tax which would increase the current cost and decrease the exit value of the automobile. The effect of such a tax on the future cash flows from the terminal exit value is detrimental. Therefore, C − D is not a reliable measure of past gains.

Historical cost depreciation is defined as an allocation and $(A − D)/L$ is a straight line where L is the life, $2[(A − D)/L]$ is first year double declining balance, and so forth. Some have proposed that "current cost depreciation" be defined as the cost of a *new identical* asset which is then allocated in the same fashion as historical cost. Others have proposed "replacement cost depreciation" which is an allocation of the cost of a *new non-identical* asset. The characteristic common to all such proposals is that they are allocations, not measurements, and such allocations are not relevant to any decisions that I have been able to identify. Current cost is relevant to the present purchase decision and historical cost—past cash paid—was relevant to the past purchase decision but I have never found one instance of decision relevance for an allocated cost, neither current, historical nor replacement.

For the same reasons as given in Section 2.4, I cannot prove the irrelevance of current costs, historical costs or allocated costs. I can only rephrase Conjecture 1 and offer the same challenge. The same caveat applies regarding the future costs versus the current costs.

*3.31 Receivables*    It is rare to find mention of receivables in the context of costs, either historical or current. I include this discussion for precisely that reason. Consider a firm that holds an interest bearing note receivable. The interest is the analogue for dividends and is excluded from Exhibit 4. Since notes are traded we could determine the amount of cash that would be paid if purchased or received if sold (factored or discounted without recourse) and we could enter these amounts in columns B and C.

It would appear that under GAAP notes receivable are in class (α)—stated at exit value—having been acquired in a sale or type (a) exchange. But the provision for doubtful accounts makes it appear that we are forecasting a terminal exit value instead of measuring a current exit value. Thus, there is a question of whether GAAP would place notes in column A, the terminal exit value, or in column B, the current exit value. The literature is of little help. First, it is exceptionally sparse. Second, it is exceptionally terse and far from explicit. It seems that the tight focus on costs, on type (b) exchanges and class ($\beta$) assets, has resulted in a benign neglect of type (a) exchanges and class ($\alpha$) assets. Since the cost principle does not extend to notes and since the literature is sparse and terse, I cannot determine exactly what it is that we have been trying to measure in this case.

I think that others share my confusion. The problem is exemplified by the following entries:

| Type (a) | Notes Receivable | Face |
|---|---|---|
|  | Revenue | Face |
| Type (b) | Cost of Land Sold | Cost |
|  | Land | Cost |

That the cost principle does not extend to the type (a) entry and the class ($\alpha$) notes is evidenced by two factors.

First, accountants were rocked by the bad press resulting from disclosures about land dealings, especially "front end loading." The problem was that the notes issued in payment for development land were very long term, with interest rates much below the market, with miniscule down payments and, as subsequent events proved, they had an enormous default rate. Why did the auditors issue a clean opinion on the financial reports of land development companies and their financiers? One hypothesis that was advanced in the press is that they were immoral or grossly negligent. My hypothesis is that they did not have an adequate theory to guide them, that the theory they applied was based on costs so that they focused on the second entry almost to the exclusion of the first entry.

Second, consider our reaction to the bad press. In its surprise and dismay, the AICPA issued some very specific principles regarding when a sale is a sale, that is, when we should apply accrual methods as opposed to cost recovery or instalment methods. Many of the tests for the distinction are based on future events. My hypothesis is that the reason the AICPA had to issue such specific and complex rules is that there was no general concept that could be used as guidance, that the concepts at hand were so focused on costs that the standard setters could not do much other than what they did. Consider their words: "*Implicit* in the realization principle is the assumption that consideration received in the exchanges can be valued with reasonable certainty" (AICPA [1973], p. 4, emphasis added). Whether or not my hypothesis is correct, the principles issued are (1) so specific that they are not likely to be applicable to the next, unknown problem which will result in a bad press; (2) so detailed that they almost invite compliance with the letter instead of the spirit; (3) so complex that they are difficult to apply; and (4) require that the auditor forecast the future.

That description is too brief to cover such an important topic but it provides a broad outline. My proposed solution is to insert the notes receivable in column B. That is, to ask what is the amount that they would fetch in an immediate sale, i.e., factored or discounted without recourse. Column A is the unknown amount of cash that will be collected in the future just as the terminal exit value of a share is unknown. Columns C and D are not applicable since receivables are not costs.

The relevance analysis is the same. A cash maximizer would sell the notes for B if A < B. If A > B the maximizer would tend to keep them for collection and A − B is the expected future gain. Note that (A − B)/B *is* the market rate of interest for notes of *this* risk class. That is, in the same way that the market rate of interest for a bond is determined by observing its current price, the market rate for the notes is determined by observing their current exit values. Thus, B is relevant to exchange decisions for notes in the same way as it was relevant for marketable securities.

The use of B to determine the revenues is consistent with the idea of using cash to determine the revenues when the sale is for cash. That is, B is an attempt to determine how much cash would be received if the notes were sold. Note, incidentally, B would be much less than the face value of the notes and would be much closer to, perhaps even less than, the cost of the land which would prohibit front-end loading.

No one can deny that it will be difficult to determine the amount that the notes would fetch in an immediate sale. But is it reasonable to think that it is easier to forecast the future collections via forecasting the uncollectables? I think not. Is it more practical to apply the specific, complex rules which require determining such things as whether the property will be useful for residential purposes at the end of the payment period, i.e., what the developer will do in the future? I think not. In short, I think that determining the exit value is more practical and less difficult than the application of the specific rules. In considering that issue we should distinguish the difficulty of determination from the determination of a zero amount. Sometimes we say that it is impossible to factor the notes without recourse and therefore they have *no* exit value. If that statement refers to the fact that there is an inactive market, it is an expression of a difficult measurement problem. If it refers to the fact that no one would purchase the notes, it is an expression of a zero exit value. If the latter, then we should record the notes at zero, recognizing a loss, and wait for future collections before recording a gain. That is not an application of a specific instalment-sales-method-of-realization rule but rather the application of the general concept of measuring the amount that would be received from an immediate sale of *any* asset.

### 3.4 Extension to Multiple Assets

The previous cases may be characterized as single asset firms. The question is whether we can extend the analysis and conclusions to firms with multiple assets. My answer is: I am not sure. To illustrate the nature of the problem, I will return to considering marketable securities since their simplicity aids in understanding as well as exposition. The question is whether the analysis and conclusions regarding a single share can be extended to a block of several shares. If the decision context is to purchase or sell the block, it is clear that it can be extended. But a problem arises if we do not know the decision context because the sum of the exit value of each share is likely to be different from the exit value of the block.

This has become known as the "additivity" or the "aggregation" problem and has received considerable attention. The problem can easily be explained in this simple case. An extra commission, called an "odd lot differential" is charged for sales of single shares. For shares traded in blocks of 100, called "round lots," no odd lot differential is charged. If the odd lot differential is $0.25, then the exit value of a round lot is $25 greater than the exit value of 100 single shares. To use the same figures as in the journal entries, if there were 100 shares at a price of $10 each, instead of one share at a price of $1,000, the exit value of the round lot is $900 but it is $875 for the single shares. The question is whether we should report the $900 or the $875 as the exit value.

Examination of the various proposed solutions to the problem would lead us too far afield. Suffice it to say that many think that the problem is intractable (see Vickrey

[1970]) and it has often been used as a criterion in criticizing exit values. I, too, am not completely satisfied that the problem in all its ramifications has been solved. Notice, however, that the problem is symmetrical. It affects current costs in exactly the same way. Since current cost is the amount of cash paid if purchased, then the amount paid for 100 single shares would be $1,125 instead of $1,100 for the round lot. Thus, the criterion of additivity fails to discriminate.

In regard to historical costs, it is the same problem but it is called aggregation or disaggregation. If we have 100 shares at a price of $10 each, we multiply 100 times $11.25 (or $8.75) and call the product of $1,125 (or $875) the current cost (or exit value) of the 100 shares when the current cost (or exit value) of a round lot of $1,100 (or $900). If we have $1,100 historical cost of the round lot, we divide $1,100 by 100 shares and call the quotient of $11 the historical cost per unit when the cost per unit is $11.25. Any questions raised about the multiplication must also be raised about the division. If there is a problem of aggregation there will be a problem of disaggregation stemming from the same cause. Thus, the criterion of aggregation fails to discriminate.

The problem can be divided. First, is the question of whether cash receivable or payable can be added. There is general agreement that it can. (See Vickrey's [1970] discussion of "numerosity.") Second, is the question of the category we should use to measure the cash receivable or payable. For example, one category is the single share and another is the round lot. Given a categorization, additivity can be demonstrated. (See Trowell [1978] for a rigorous mathematical demonstration, or Sterling [1979], Section 10.3 for a verbal demonstration.) But that leaves open the question of what categories should be used. Should we use the category of single shares, of round lots, of all shares of the same kind (e.g., all GM in one category and all GE in another) or all shares in the portfolio? The problem has me stumped. I had hoped that separating additivity from categorization would make it more tractable but it has not. Perhaps the reader can provide a solution. In the meantime, note that the problem is applicable to both current costs and exit values. Thus, categorization does not discriminate current costs from exit values.

The problem also extends to historical costs. We must decide on account categories when we make the entry for purchases. When prices have fluctuated we set up sub-categories by time of purchase. Then at sale we must decide which of these sub-categories should be used to make the entry. In more familiar terminology, we must choose between FIFO and LIFO. Thomas [1974] has demonstrated that the selection of the category—LIFO versus FIFO—is arbitrary. But the same can be said for the choice of categories in current costs or exit values. They are equally arbitrary and therefore the criterion of arbitrary categories does not discriminate.

However, the criterion of relevance does discriminate. The current cost of any given category is relevant to decisions regarding purchases of *that* category. The exit value of any given category is relevant to decisions regarding sales of *that* category. By contrast, the historical cost categories are not relevant to any decision model that I have been able to identify.

To put it another way, the historical cost categories do not have an empirical referent. To add different past costs of shares does not result in a sum that refers to anything in the real world that I have been able to identify. Until that empirical referent has been identified, we must say that allocated historical costs are not additive and therefore the additivity criterion discriminates allocated historical costs from current prices. For the same reason, they are not empirically testable. In previous works I have proposed a sub-criterion of empirical testability because that is a necessary, but not a sufficient, condition for relevance.[11]

The above analysis can be extended to other assets with the same results. For example, the additivity of GM plus GE shares is the same type of problem of adding inventory and a depreciable asset. Choosing the category of the entire portfolio versus the categories of GM plus GE is the same type of problem as deciding to value the firm as a whole versus summing the assets. However, there is no analogue for adding class ($\alpha$) and ($\beta$) assets. In adding the shares we were always adding either costs or exit values but in adding the assets of the firm the cost principle requires that we add costs to exit values. That concerns me since it is the summation of different attributes. Exit valuation does not face that problem since all assets are measured by the same attribute. For that reason I would give exit valuation the edge in determining total assets by summing various asset categories.

### 3.5 Summary and Conclusions

Application of the cost principle requires that assets be divided into classes ($\alpha$) and ($\beta$). When the exchange is interclass it permits the distinction between type (a) and (b) entries but when the exchange is intraclass we cannot make the distinction. A requirement of application of the cost principle is a separate principle for all intraclass exchanges. To date we have not identified a general principle for intraclass exchanges so that each new exchange requires a principle specific to that exchange. For this reason, we have witnessed controversies as new exchanges are invented and it has required the issuance of *ad hoc* principles to resolve each controversy. We can expect new exchanges to continue to be invented and each to bring a new controversy.

The criterion of relevance can be extended to other types of assets. Each type of asset is similar to the simple marketable security case and there is an analogue for dividends, either zero as in inventory or positive as in depreciables, and an analogue for the various values. Therefore, the conclusions drawn in Section 2 are applicable to each type of asset by simply substituting different names of assets. The conjecture and challenge is also applicable with the same substitution of names.

The criterion of relevance can also be extended to multiple assets but with less definitive conclusions. The problems of additivity and categorization plague all three accounting methods and therefore we cannot use those problems as criteria for choosing a method. Since exit values do not have two classes of assets based on measuring different attributes, they suffer less from this problem than does cost. For the same reason, exit value is a more general principle and therefore should require fewer *ad hoc* principles.

---

[11] In addition, in a fundamental sense it is a necessary, but not a sufficient, condition for auditability. Except in the sense of recalculation, historical cost categories are not auditable because they are not additive, not empirically testable. Contrast the method of auditing the quantity of the inventory to the book value of the inventory. That quantities are additive, empirically testable, is evidenced by separate physical count which confirms the sum of the quantity numerals in the accounts. That historical costs are not additive is evidenced by the fact that there is no way to measure separately the book value which would either confirm or deny the sum of cost numerals in the accounts.

## 4. GENERALIZATION

The ways in which assets vary are almost infinite. One general variation is that some assets produce a dividend or analogue which we call by various names such as interest, rent, net proceeds from sale of the outputs less the cost of purchasing the inputs. Other assets do not produce a dividend; the only future cash inflow comes from the terminal exit value or analogue. Examples are growth (zero dividend) shares, non-interest-bearing notes, unrented land, and inventory.

Asset commonalities are few but significant. Exhibit 5 displays the commonalities that have been discussed in this essay.

**EXHIBIT 5**

| Price \ Temporal Location | Past | Present | Future |
|---|---|---|---|
| Purchase | Historical Cost | Current Cost | Replacement Cost |
| Sale | Historical Exit Value | Current Exit Value | Terminal Exit Value |

There are two prices—purchase and sale—for any given asset at any given moment in time. Except for rare and temporary conditions, such as arbitraging, the cost of purchasing any asset is greater than the exit value from the sale of that asset at all moments in time. We have a choice of prices, of reporting the cost or the exit value. In addition, we have a choice of temporal locations, of reporting a past, present, or forecasted future price. Thus, we have a choice of six values to report. Of course, there are many other variations. Past prices could be allocated, for example, and forecasted future prices could be discounted but, at base, the six values displayed in Exhibit 5 are the choices that we face.

Since six values are undoubtedly too many to report, we must select which one(s) to report. The criterion for selection proposed in this essay is relevance to specific decision models as opposed to unspecific usefulness or as opposed to criteria that do not discriminate. I believe that the decision model examined in this essay is applicable to all assets. That is, one must decide to own or not to own any given asset, to purchase or not purchase if unowned or to sell or not to sell if owned. That decision model specifies the current exit value and terminal exit value, as well as the future dividends or analogue if any, of all owned assets. That decision model does not specify the cost, neither historical nor current, of owned assets.

Since the terminal exit value and future dividend is unknown, the only relevant value that we can report, as opposed to reporting somebody's forecast of a future value, is the current exit value. Therefore, I conclude that at a minimum we should report the current exit value of all owned assets.

There are many problems in reporting exit values. One is additivity or categorization but since all valuation methods are equally vexed by that problem, it fails to discriminate.

Another is measurement when markets are incomplete or thin but that problem also effects all valuation methods equally and therefore does not discriminate. Such problems have been sufficient to cause many accountants to reject the conclusion that we report exit values. I agree that exit valuation presents problems but I think that it presents fewer problems than the alternatives that have been tried or proposed.

It often seems to me that those who reject reporting exit values because of additivity, incomplete markets, social welfare effects and similar reasons are looking for perfection, for a valuation method that will be problem free. Until such a perfect method is discovered, until the millennium arrives, we must report something even if imperfect. Therefore, it seems clear that we must compare the alternatives, apply the criteria with equal force to all alternatives, and then select the alternative that best meets the criteria, to choose the one that is least imperfect. When I follow that procedure in seeking a generalized method of reporting, I reach the same conclusion as Churchill in regard to democracy: exit valuation is the worst form of reporting except for all those other forms that have been tried or proposed from time to time.

## REFERENCES

American Institute of Certified Public Accountants, *Accounting for Retail Land Sales* (An AICPA Accounting Guide), AICPA, 1973.

Bedford, N. M. and J. C. McKeown, "Comparative Analysis of Net Realizable Value and Replacement Costing," *The Accounting Review*, April 1972.

Benston, G. J. and M. A. Krasney, "DAAM: The Demand for Alternative Accounting Measurements," *Journal of Accounting Research*, Supplement, 1978.

Canning, J. B., *The Economics of Accountancy*, Roland Press, 1929.

Edwards, E. O., "The State of Current Value Accounting," *The Accounting Review*, April 1975.

Edwards, E. O. and P. W. Bell, *The Theory and Measurement of Business Income*, University of California Press, Berkeley 1964.

Financial Accounting Standards Board, Statement of Financial Accounting Standards No. 33, *Financial Reporting and Changing Prices*, FASB, September 1979.

Ijiri, Y. and R. K. Jaedicke, "Reliability and Objectivity of Accounting Measurements," *The Accounting Review*, July 1966.

McDonald, D. L., "A Test Application of the Feasibility of Market Based Measures of Accounting," *Journal of Accounting Research*, Spring 1968.

Revsine, L., *Replacement Cost Accounting*, Prentice-Hall, Englewood Cliffs, N.J. 1973.

Rosenfield, P., "Reporting Subjunctive Gains and Losses," *The Accounting Review*, October 1969.

Samuelson, R. A., "Should Replacement-Cost Changes be Included in Income?" *The Accounting Review*, April 1980.

Staubus, G. J., *Making Accounting Decisions*, Scholars Book Co., Houston 1977.

Sterling, R. R., *Theory of the Measurement of Enterprise Income*, The University Press of Kansas, 1970.

————, *Toward a Science of Accounting*, Scholars Book Co., Houston 1979.

Sterling, R. R. and R. E. Flaherty, "The Role of Liquidity in Exchange Valuation," *The Accounting Review*, July 1971.

Sterling, R. R., J. O. Tollefson and R. E. Flaherty, "Exchange Valuation: An Empirical Test," *The Accounting Review*, October 1979.

Thomas, A. L., Studies in Accounting Research No. 9, *The Allocation Problem: Part Two*, American Accounting Association, 1974.

Trowell, J., "A Study of the Additivity of CCE with Respect to Assets," unpublished Master's thesis, University of New England, Armidale, N.S.W. 1978.

Tweedie, D. P., "Cash Flows and Realisable Values: the Intuitive Accounting Concepts? An Empirical Test," *Accounting and Business Research*, Winter 1977.

Vancil, R. F. and R. L. Weil, *Replacement Cost Accounting: Readings on Concepts, Users & Methods*, Thomas Horton & Daughters, 1976.

Vickrey, D. W., "Is Accounting a Measurement Discipline?" *The Accounting Review*, October 1970.

# III-A 3 *Accounting for Inflation*

R. J. CHAMBERS

Conventional (historical cost based) accounting is almost universally recognized to be defective under inflationary conditions. Experience under these conditions has prompted the search for a dependable alternative.

There have been under consideration two major alternatives or supplements to conventional accounting: (1) current purchasing power (C.P.P.) accounting, and (2) replacement price accounting (R.P.A.) of which current cost accounting is a variety.

The first method deals with ways of taking account of some of the effects of changes in the purchasing power of money, but disregards the effects of changes in the prices of particular assets. The second proposes the use of the replacement prices of assets in financial statements, but disregards the general effects of changes in the purchasing power of money. As both types of change occur concurrently during inflationary periods, both of the above methods are partial or incomplete, and therefore potentially misleading.

This Exposure Draft deals with a method of accounting—continuously contemporary accounting—which takes into account both changes in particular prices and changes in the general level of prices. It is thus more comprehensive than the two methods previously mentioned. And the financial statements it yields are up-to-date, more realistic and more readily comprehensible.

## PART I—ACCOUNTING GENERALLY

**1. The discussion and conclusions to be presented will have reference to business firms generally.**

Any method of business accounting should be expected to be serviceable in shareholders, creditors and others. For this reason much of the discussion will relate which accounts relate. However, the most extensive array of uses of accounting information is exemplified by the relationships between companies and their shareholders, creditors and others. For this reason much of the discussion will relate to companies and company accounting. But, because the principles or rules which emerge are equally pertinent to companies and other types of business ownership, the

R. J. Chambers, "Accounting for Inflation," Exposure Draft, University of Sydney, Australia, September 1975. Reprinted by permission of the author.

general term "business firm" or simply "firm" will be commonly used. Also the terms "net profit" and "net income" will be used interchangeably, as synonyms.

### 2. Financial statements are expected to represent fairly and in up-to-date terms the financial characteristics of firms.

The products of the accounting process are dated balance sheets and income (profit and loss) statements. These are expected, by the laws relating to companies, to give a true and fair view of the financial positions and of the results of companies as at the dates and for the periods to which they relate. They are put to use by a variety of parties; by actual and potential investors and creditors; by investment advisers and underwriters and trustees for creditors; by tribunals concerned with wages and prices; and by governmental authorities for fiscal and other regulatory purposes. The decisions and actions of all of these parties are taken in the light of what they know, at the time, of the past results and present financial positions of companies (or of firms generally). Unless the financial statements of companies correspond fairly well with their actual positions and results, actions based upon them may affect adversely, and quite unexpectedly, the interests of companies or of other parties related to them.

### 3. The survival and growth of firms depends on their command of money and money's worth.

The actions of all the above mentioned parties are directly related to money receipts and payments of a company—receipts by way of sales income, loans or credits, subsidies or bounties, and the proceeds of new share issues; payments by way of purchases, wages, taxes, interest, and loan repayments. The capacity of a company to grow or to change its operations, on a small or large scale, as new opportunities arise and present operations become less attractive, depends on its command of money or money's worth. In the ordinary course of events, companies are expected to pay their debts to others when they fall due. In some circumstances they may find it worth while, or be forced, to repay debts before they fall due. Generally, then, the ability to meet debts owed is a condition of survival. For all these reasons, it is a matter of importance that the managers of companies, and that other parties having financial interests in companies, shall know from time to time the money and money's worth at the command of companies and their outstanding financial obligations.

### 4. Financial position is a dated relationship between assets and equities.

The money and money's worth at the command of a company at a point of time is given by the sum of its holdings of cash and receivables and the market (resale) prices of its other (non-monetary) assets. The resale price of an asset at a given date is its money equivalent at that date. Possession of the asset is financially equal to possession of the sum of money representing its resale price. It is therefore possible to add amounts of cash and receivables and the money equivalents of other assets to obtain a financially significant aggregate. The total amount of liabilities to short and long term creditors represents money claims against the aggregate money's worth of assets. The difference between total assets and total liabilities is a genuine money amount, since the amounts of total assets and total liabilities are genuine money amounts. This difference represents the residual interest of shareholders or owners in the total assets, or the total investment at risk in the business of the company. It also represents the amount of net assets, or assets financed otherwise than by credit.

### 5. The amount of income is deduced from changes in dated financial positions.

A balance sheet in which assets are represented at their money equivalents gives to all users of it an up-to-date indication of the total wealth of a company at a point of time and total claims against or interests in that wealth. Given two such balance sheets, in the absence of inflation, the increment in the amount of net assets represents the retained profit of the intervening period (provided there has been no new share issue). The sum of retained profit and the dividends paid in the period is the net profit or net income of the period. Net income may be calculated by setting out the several classes of gain or loss of a company in a period. But the amount so obtained is necessarily equal to the difference between the opening and closing money amounts of net assets. It is a genuine increment in money's worth, since the net assets figures are genuine money amounts (para. 4).

### 6. Financial positions and results are aggregative; their elements must satisfy the rules of addition and relation.

Total wealth, total liabilities, the amount of net assets, the calculation of net profits, all entail addition and subtraction. Other calculations made by investors and creditors, such as rates of return and debt to equity ratios, are relations between aggregates. All particular elements of financial statements must therefore be capable of proper addition and relation. The money amounts and money equivalents referred to in the two previous paragraphs satisfy this condition. By contrast, no logical or financial significance can be assigned to the sum of an amount of money and the purchase price, past, present or future (including replacement price) of any good. No such sum can properly be related to any debt outstanding, or to any plan to purchase goods or services, or to pay taxes and dividends.

### 7. Financial positions and results are both the consequences of past actions and the cases of future actions.

The financial position of a firm is a consequence of past (historical) events up to the date for which it is ascertained. No future event or expectation of a future event has any bearing on it. But given an ascertained financial position (and other information and expectations), choices may be made among the courses of action available to the firm. If at a given date the liquidity of a firm is strained, action to restore its liquidity is necessary. If at a given date a firm is heavily in debt, liquidity cannot readily be restored by further borrowing. If the results of the immediately past period are unsatisfactory in any sense, action must be taken to improve the result in the following period. All deliberate actions having financial consequences must be considered in the light of the aggregative financial characteristics of the firm at the time of choice. And all estimations of the probable financial consequences of future actions must be based on the position of the firm at the time of choice of future courses of action. Financial position as described is the one common element in all calculations relating to choices of future actions.

### 8. The money equivalents of assets, the purchase prices (replacement prices) of assets and the user-values of assets are used in conjunction; none is a substitute for the other.

If a prospective course of action entails the "replacement" of an asset, it is necessary to know the money equivalent of the present asset and the purchase price of the new asset. If a prospective action entails the purchase of additional assets, their purchase prices must be known. Whether or not any such course is financially "feasible" can only be ascertained by comparison of those purchase prices with the money equivalents of present assets, or some selection of present assets. Which is to be preferred of the feasible courses of action is indicated, inter alia, by comparisons of the expected net proceeds of the alternative projects or investments in assets. Expected net proceeds, or present (discounted) values, are user-values. They are personal estimates based on expectations of the future; they are therefore subjective. They represent the expected outcomes of specific possible future actions. They cannot therefore be used in balance sheets as indicative of the financial feasibility of *any* course of action, even of those courses to which they relate. In short, the money equivalents of assets, the purchase prices of goods not presently held, and user-values of assets or projects are used when considering specific possible courses of action. But each is used for its own purpose and in its own way. None is a substitute for the other. None of them may properly be added together. Only the money equivalent of assets are properly useable for the representation of financial position at a given date.

## PART II—THE EFFECTS OF INFLATION

### 9. Changes in the structure and in the general level of prices occur concurrently but not equally.

In an inflationary period two things occur which affect the positions and results of companies. The prices of particular goods change relatively to one another. There is a change in the *structure* of prices. Such changes may occur at any time as the wants of consumers change, technology changes or the policies and outputs of companies change (collectively, supply and demand conditions). There is also a change in the general *level* of prices. "Inflation" is descriptive of a rise in the general level of prices, or of its counterpart, a fall in the general purchasing power of money. When inflation occurs all prices do not rise to the same extent or at the same time. Some may fall as rises in others force business firms and consumers to change their spending habits. Inflation may thus cause changes in the structure of prices, to the benefit of some firms and to the detriment of others. The beneficial or detrimental effects may arise from changes in the money equivalents of assets held, or from changes in the profit margins obtainable for goods and services sold.

### 10. The effects on a firm of changes in the structure and level of prices can only be ascertained in the aggregate.

When changes in the structure of prices and changes in the general level of prices occur in the same period, it is not possible to say that any particular price change is caused by inflation, or by the shift in the relation between the supply and demand conditions, or partly by the one and partly by the other. All that is known is that prices and the level of prices are different from those of an earlier date. Nevertheless, it is possible to calculate the aggregate effects of changes in prices and the general level of prices on the positions and results of firms. Because changes in particular prices and changes in the general level of prices influence one another, the effects of both should be brought into account. One cannot be considered as isolated from the other. Whatever the outcome, it cannot be said whether any part of the result is due solely to managerial judgements or solely to accidental or unforeseeable factors. Managers may be expected to use their best judgements at all times. Only the results in aggregate will indicate with what effect firms have been able to meet the conditions through which they have passed.

**11. The conventional money unit, in terms of which financial positions are represented, is equally serviceable for that purpose in inflation.**

Financial position has been described as the dated relationship between amounts of assets and equities (para. 4). The dating of a financial statement represents both (a) that the money unit used in it has reference to that date and (b) that the number of money units appearing beside any item is the appropriate money equivalent of that item at that date. To suppose otherwise would be anachronistic, and confusing. The money unit is by its nature the unit of general purchasing power and debt-paying power at any specified date whatever, and the unit in which the money equivalents (resale prices) of assets are expressed. That the same nominal money unit may have a different general purchasing power at some other date is of no consequence when determining a dated financial position.

**12. The increment in the nominal amount of net assets during a year is not serviceable as indicating net income in an inflationary period.**

Calculation of net income in the manner described in para 5 brings into account the effects of all changes in the money equivalents of assets, in the absence of inflation. If particular assets have risen or fallen in price during a year, for whatever reason, these changes in the structure of prices will be captured by taking the resale prices of assets at the opening and closing dates of the year. Since, in the absence of inflation, there is no change in the general purchasing power of money, the net income so calculated will represent a genuine increment in the general purchasing power or debt-paying power of the net assets of a firm. Part of it will be the resultant of trading costs and revenues, and part the resultant of rises and falls in the money equivalents of assets since the beginning of the period or since (the subsequent) date of purchase. The rises and falls during the year in the money equivalents of assets held at the end of a year may be described as *price variation adjustments*. But if the purchasing power of the money unit has changed during the year, the difference between the opening and closing amounts of net assets will not represent a genuine increment in general purchasing or debt-paying power.

**13. Provision must be made for the loss of purchasing power in an inflationary period of the amount of net assets (or capital employed) at the beginning of the accounting period.**

Money holdings and claims to fixed amounts of money may be described as monetary assets. Their money equivalents at any date may be discovered directly. All other assets are non-monetary assets. Their money equivalents at any date must be discovered by reference to market resale prices at or near that date. Monetary assets held during an inflationary period lose general purchasing power. Likewise every dollar representing the money equivalent of non-monetary assets at the beginning of a period loses general purchasing power. And likewise every dollar owed during an inflationary period loses general purchasing power; borrowings thus constitute a "hedge" against losses in the purchasing power of money. By subtraction, the amount at risk of loss in general purchasing power during inflation is the amount of net assets (total assets less liabilities) at the beginning of the accounting period. The amount of the loss thus sustained must be made good out of other surpluses before it can be said that a surplus in the nature of net income has arisen. This amount may be described as a *capital maintenance adjustment*, since its object is to secure that, in calculating net income, provision is made for the maintenance of the general purchasing power of the opening amount of net assets (or capital employed).

It may be noted that, across a whole community, the aggregate amount of price variation adjustments might be expected to correspond with the aggregate amount of capital maintenance adjustments, since the general price index is indicative of the average of changes in specific prices. But particular firms are affected differentially by changes in prices and in the price level. Rises in the prices of particular goods do not correspond with or offset falls in the general purchasing power of money. That is why the aggregates of both should be taken separately in the accounts of firms.

### 14.  Net income is the algebraic sum of trading surpluses, price variation adjustments and the capital maintenance adjustment.

The amount of the capital maintenance adjustment is the opening amount of net assets multiplied by the proportionate change in the general level of prices. Thus, if a firm begins a period with net assets of $1,000 and an index of changes in the general level of prices rises from 130 to 143 in the period, the amount of the capital maintenance adjustment is $1,000 × 13/130, or $100. A general price index is used because the amount of net assets is a genuine dated money sum, irrespective of the composition of assets, and because the firm is considered to be free to lay out any part of its assets or the increment in its assets in any way it pleases. The index to be used would be chosen on the basis of competent statistical advice. From the two preceding paragraphs, net income will be the algebraic sum of trading surpluses, price variation adjustments and the capital maintenance adjustment. The amount charged as capital maintenance adjustment will be credited to a capital maintenance reserve. If any part of this reserve were appropriated as a dividend, it would impair the general purchasing power of the opening amount of net assets. (See also para 34).

## PART III—GENERAL PRINCIPLES OF CONTINUOUSLY CONTEMPORARY ACCOUNTING

### 15.  The method of accounting described is called continuously contemporary accounting (CoCoA).[1]

Asset valuations are brought up-to-date, at least at the end of each accounting period, by reference to independent sources of information. Those valuations are in terms of the purchasing power unit at the time. That the balance sheet is a dated statement implies that the amounts stated in it relate to that date and that the dollars in which those amounts are expressed are dollars of dated purchasing power (see para

---

[1] The text of the original publication (1975) used "CCA" with reference to continuously contemporary accounting, an abbreviation used by the author since 1967. That abbreviation has since been widely used with reference to "current cost accounting." To avoid confusion, in this reprint "CoCoA" is used as an abbreviation for continuously contemporary accounting. Some minor changes have also been made in the prefatory note and the introductory material of Appendix B.

11). CoCoA satisfies this requirement. Shareholders' equity amounts are augmented by the capital maintenance adjustment periodically and the balance of net income is a sum also expressed in dollars of the same dated purchasing power as other items in the balance sheet. All reported balances of a given date are therefore contemporary with that date. There are no prices of different dates nor purchasing power units of different dates in the balance sheet of any date. Hence the description "continuously contemporary accounting."

### 16. Accounts may be brought up to date periodically or more frequently.

The price changes affecting a firm may be occasional or frequent, and individually large or small. As up-to-date information on a firm's assets and liabilities is the only dependable basis for managerial action, the accounts may be continually adjusted for changes in the prices of assets. In principle this is the most desirable mode of accounting. But for external reporting it is sufficient to bring the account balances to their money equivalents at the end of each reporting period. Accounts could be kept just as they are presently kept during the accounting period. But at the end of the period all account balances are adjusted to their current money equivalents. The variations of money equivalents from book balances are summarized and charged or credited, as price variation adjustments, in the income account. And of course the capital maintenance adjustment is computed and charged. The method may be called "continuously contemporary" because, in principle, accounts can be kept continuously up-to-date, even though in practice adjustments may be made less frequently than price changes occur. Under either process the results will be exactly the same.

### 17. CoCoA conforms with the established principle of periodical, independent verification of account balances (the objectivity principle).

To verify the physical existence of, and legal title to, assets at balance date is a well established principle. Independent checking of cash balances and receivables balances has long been regarded as a necessary safeguard against misrepresentation. But the same process of verification is not applied, under traditional historical cost accounting, to the money amounts assigned to other assets. The mere checking of physical existence and legal title is inconsistent with the fact that financial statements relate to the *financial* characteristics of firms, not to physical or purely legal characteristics. The financial characteristics of assets should be independently verified, no less than other characteristics. CoCoA applies this principle uniformly to all assets.

### 18. CoCoA conforms with the well-established accrual principle.

The accrual principle entails accounting for changes in the financial characteristics of a firm independently of the conversion of assets and obligations to cash. Revenue is brought into account when customers are billed; earlier, that is, than cash is received from customers. Depreciation is brought into account periodically; that is, long before the diminution in value of an asset is discovered on its resale. Applications of the principle pervade current practice. Yet there are also numerous cases in traditional practice where the principle is not applied. Changes in the prices of assets are not accrued usually, unless they are downward changes. And quite generally the effects of advantageous changes are not accrued but the effects of disadvantageous changes are accrued; thus depreciation is charged, but appreciation is not brought into account. These inconsistencies cannot yield realistic and up-to-date statements of financial position and results. CoCoA avoids inconsistency by applying the accrual principle uniformly to all assets and liabilities, and hence also to shareholders' equity.

### 19. CoCoA conforms with the well-established going concern principle.

The going concern principle entails that the financial position as represented in a balance sheet shall be indicative of the position of a firm as a going concern. The significant financial characteristics of a going concern are its ability to pay its debts when due, to pay for its supplies of goods and labour service, to change the composition of its assets, liabilities and operations if the present composition hinders its survival or growth, and the ability to earn a rate of profit consistent with the risks of the business. The ability of a firm to pay its debts, to pay for its necessary inputs, to borrow on the security of its assets, and to change the composition of its assets and operations, is indicated only if assets are shown at their money equivalents, since all the matters mentioned entail receipts and payments of money. The ability of a firm to earn an adequate rate of profit may be judged only if the profit earned is a genuine increment in purchasing power and the amount of net assets (or shareholders' equity) to which it is related is a genuine money sum. The use of market (resale) prices in CoCoA has nothing to do with liquidation of a business; it is simply the only way to find the present money equivalents of non-monetary assets from time to time.

### 20. CoCoA satisfies the requirements of stewardship accounts.

As financial statements indicate in general terms the disposition of assets and increments in assets from time to time they are regarded as the basis upon which the performance of a company and its management may be judged. Such judgements must be supposed to be made periodically in respect of the year recently past; their formal expression lies in the resolutions of annual general meetings. It is necessary, therefore, to know the amount of assets available for use and disposition by the management at the beginning of each year, if a satisfactory account is to be given of the use, disposition and increase of assets in that year. If the amounts of assets from time to time were stated on any basis other than their money equivalents, there would be no firm and satisfactory basis for determining the use and disposition of assets. Since all uses and dispositions in a period entail movements of money or money equivalents, financial statements based on the money equivalents of assets provide information on which periodical performance may fairly be judged.

### 21. CoCoA adheres closely to the principle of periodical accounting.

Financial statements generally purport to represent dated positions and the results of defined periods. But the effects of events in one period are frequently allowed to influence what is reported of another. This occurs whenever some future event or outcome is anticipated (as in the usual calculation of depreciation charges), or whenever some actual effect on results or position is "deferred" for recognition in a later period. CoCoA makes no such concessions, on the ground that reports which do not represent the effects of events in a defined period cannot properly be interpreted, singly or in series, by reference to that dated context of business events and circumstances. It may be objected that to base accounts on a dated selling price could be misleading if the price were anomalous. But exactly the same can be said of dated purchase prices which are used in other forms of accounting. In any case the anomaly might be expected to be explained rather than concealed.

## PART IV—THE DETERMINATION OF MONEY EQUIVALENTS

### 22. Any asset for which there is not a present resale price cannot be considered to have a present financial significance.

A company may have assets for which there is no present resale price. They may have a high user-value (see para 8), but they cannot be considered to have financial significance in the sense of purchasing or debt-paying power or as security for loans. Investors, creditors, suppliers and others would be misinformed of the financial capacity for action by balance sheets in which money amounts were assigned to assets having no current money equivalents. The assets to which this rule applies include some work in progress, and specialized plant and equipment for which there is no market in the ordinary course of business. The same rule applies to expenditures on exploratory or developmental work which has yielded no vendible product or asset. The notion of conservatism in traditional accounting would tend to have the same effect as the treatment suggested. But that notion is vague and loosely applied, whereas the principle here stated is definite and it yields information which is relevant to the judgements and decisions of parties financially interested in companies. If it is desired, on any ground, to indicate that a company has assets, or has incurred costs and outlays, having no present money equivalent, parenthetical or footnote information may be given.

### 23. The determination of the money equivalents of assets at a stated date is necessarily approximate.

Prices may vary from place to place for the same goods on any given day. What is required is a fair approximation to the current money equivalent of each asset. This may require the exercise of judgement, but abuse of judgement is constrained by the necessity of approximating a definite characteristic of the asset and by the prices discovered at or about the balance date. In any case, no form of accounting escapes the use of dated prices; even historical cost accounting uses dated prices which may or may not have been the only prices, or representative prices, at dates of purchase. Any attempt to distort results and positions by the choice of prices which are not fair approximations to money equivalents is constrained by the independent inspection and judgement of auditors. It is also constrained by the fact that the whole of the asset balances of one year determine the amounts of the price variation adjustments, and hence the income, of the following year. There are no alternative permissible rules by resort to which this constraint may be avoided.

### 24. Resale prices are accessible to most firms for most assets.

All proposals considered in anticipation of purchases and the settlement of debts include at some point sums of money which are presently available, or which could shortly become available by the sale of assets (inventory or other assets), or which could be borrowed on the security of assets. In the latter two cases some approximation to the money equivalent or resale price of non-monetary assets is required. Changes in the prices of goods and services used and in the markets for a firm's products may at any time force its management to reconsider the costs of its present mode of operations. And if it is assumed that one of the functions of management is the pursuit of efficiency or economies, the possibility of changes in its operations and assets will be under examination from time to time. It follows that some person or persons will be acquainted with the approximate market prices of the assets the firm presently holds, and with changes in those prices from time to time. It is possible for any firm to draw on its purchasing officers, salesmen, engineers and project evaluation officers for information on the prices of assets; and to have recourse to prices published in trade journals and the general press as well as direct inquiry. A great deal of information of this kind is readily available without recourse to specialist valuers. But valuations by specialists on an asset resale basis may also be obtained, where necessary of themselves, or as a check on the information available otherwise.

### 25. Receivables: The amount to be reported will be the amount deemed, on the evidence available, to be recoverable from debtors in the ordinary course of business.

Generally this will be the face value or book value of debtors' accounts, for that is the amount of the claims against debtors at balance date. There is no need to speculate about the possibility that some debtors may take advantage of discounts offered for prompt settlement. Whether they do so or not, the consequence will lie in the following period and will be then reported. Where there is evidence that the full amount of a debt will not be recovered, the amount of the debt may be reduced or written off according to the evidence then available. The amount of receivables yielded by these rules will be the best approximation to the money equivalent of receivables in the light of the information then available, without speculative allowances for what may subsequently occur.

### 26. Inventories will be valued consistently on the basis of their present market selling prices in the parcels or quantities in which they are customarily sold by the firm.

In the ordinary course of events, raw materials will have a somewhat lower money equivalent than their recent purchase prices, since the user is not a trader in those materials. Work in progress inventories may have a substantially lower money equivalent than their costs, for such work in progress may not be salable in its then state and condition. Finished goods inventories will generally have higher money equivalents (current selling prices) than their costs.

To report inventories at market resale prices is not novel. Nor is it novel that work in progress may appear at a low or zero value; for the traditional rule, "lower of cost and market", should produce the same result. By comparison with the recorded costs, the higher money equivalents of finished goods will to some extent "offset" the lower money equivalents of raw materials and work in progress. But whether the resulting aggregate differs much or little from a cost-based aggregate is less important than the fact that a uniform rule—market price—is used throughout, and that the aggregate has a definite, dated money significance which "cost" and the "lower of cost and market" do not have.

**27. Plant and equipment will be valued at market resale prices, in the units or combinations in which, in the ordinary course of business, they are bought, sold, or put out of use.**

The object of the traditional method of accounting for plant is to record its cost and to provide out of periodical revenues sufficient to reduce that cost to its market resale price, or scrap value, by the time it is put out of service. The method of CoCoA has exactly the same object; but it is attained by direct reference to market prices year by year, rather than by relying on an arithmetical formula and disregarding the actual changes, up or down, in market prices from time to time. Market resale prices may be estimated from information obtained by the methods mentioned in para 24. The prices sought are not prices obtainable on liquidation or under duress. They are to be the best approximations to the money equivalents of assets in the ordinary course of business. To determine the best approximation entails skill and judgement; but judgement is to be applied to the information obtainable on prices, not to construct imaginative valuations. Checks on the possibility of manipulation are (i) that auditors must be satisfied that the assigned market values are based on current price information, (ii) that excessive understatement reduces the profit of the year and the asset backing of shares and debt at the end of the year, and (iii) that excessive overstatement reduces the profit of a subsequent year and improperly boosts the asset backing of shares and debt. The use of market resale prices may entail heavy charges, due to the sharp drop from cost to money equivalent of some plant, in the early years of use. Some assets may have virtually no resale price, but high user-value. Such occurrences necessarily reduce the adaptive capacity of firms, their command of money and money's worth. The reduction is made explicit in the amounts by charges against revenues, or against other shareholders' equity accounts if the amounts are extraordinary. (See also para 22 above).

**28. Land and buildings will be valued at market resale prices, or approximations based on official valuations, prices of similar property and expert valuations.**

The same considerations apply to land and buildings as to plant and equipment. Local government valuations (for taxing or rating purposes) provide evidence additional to that from other sources. No single valuation or price need necessarily be taken as a proper approximation to money equivalent; but the chosen valuation must be justifiable in the circumstances. The checks mentioned in para 27 tend to limit arbitrary or unusual valuations.

**29. Investments in the shares of other companies will be valued at net market prices where the shares are publicly traded; otherwise at the proportionate interest in the net assets of the investee company.**

Holdings of listed shares are readily priced by reference to stock exchange quotations (i.e. "buyer"). Allowance may be made for commissions payable on sale, to obtain the net money equivalent of the investment. There is no readily available and dependable price for non-listed shares. An alternative is required which yields the best approximation to the money equivalent of the investment. If CoCoA is used uniformly, the proportionate interest in the net assets of the investee will provide an approximation; for the accounts of the investee will represent assets at money equivalents. Strictly the amount so calculated will not be the same as a share price; but it is a better approximation than the original cost, or a valuation related to user-value (e.g. based on capitalized prospective earnings).

### 30. Liabilities will be represented by the amounts owed and payable to creditors in the ordinary course of business.

No amount shall be shown as a liability unless it represents an amount owed to and legally recoverable by a creditor. Whether the due date is near or distant is immaterial. Long-dated obligations may become due and payable if any circumstance threatens the security of creditors.

## PART V—OWNERS' EQUITY ACCOUNTS

### 31. All transactions of a period will be recorded at their actual effective prices, and so charged or credited in the income (profit and loss) account.

All transactions have determinate effects on balances of cash or receivables and payables. The general purchasing power of the cash receipts and payments during an inflationary period will change from time to time. But the aggregate effect of changes in the purchasing power of the money unit is brought into account by way of the capital maintenance adjustment at the end of the accounting period. By showing the actual amounts of receipts and payments, all such amounts are traceable, and identical with their counterparts elsewhere in the accounts.

### 32. Price variation accounts will be credited with all increases in the book values of assets, and debited with all decreases, during the period.

The book balances of accounts, other than monetary item accounts, may be adjusted for changes in asset prices during the year. The valuation of all assets at the end of the year at their resale prices gives effect to all variations in prices which have not previously been brought into account. The amounts by which the book values of assets are increased (decreased) during the year to correspond with market resale prices will be debited (credited) to the asset accounts and credited (debited) to the price variation accounts. There may be price variation accounts for as many separate asset classes as is deemed necessary. Under CoCoA, the depreciation account, representing a fall in the market resale price of an asset or class of assets, is a price variation account. The price variation accounts are closed by transfer of their balances to the income account.

### 33. The capital maintenance adjustment will be calculated by applying to the opening amount of net assets the proportionate change in the index of changes in the general level of prices.

The net amount of price variations will tend to be (but will not necessarily be) positive during inflation. But these are gross increments, and the resulting asset balances are in units of year-end purchasing power. The full effect of the change in the purchasing power of money on the results of the year is given by the calculation of the capital maintenance adjustment. The calculation is a mathematically proper calculation, since under CoCoA the opening amount of net assets is a genuine, dated money sum to which a change in the index may legitimately be applied. The capital maintenance adjustment is debited in the income account (in inflationary years).

34. **The amount of the capital maintenance adjustment will be credited proportionately to the opening balance of undistributed profits and to other opening balances of owners' equity accounts.**

The amount of net assets at the beginning of a year is equal to the sum of the balances of the owners' equity accounts. The object of crediting the amount of the capital maintenance adjustment to owners' equity accounts is to restate the aggregate of the opening balances in units of purchasing power at the end of the year. Part of the capital maintenance adjustment may therefore be credited directly to the retained profits account, a part equal to the opening balance of retained profits multiplied by the proportionate change in the index of changes in the general level of prices. The remainder of the adjustment will be the appropriate amount to credit to a capital maintenance reserve. Where the amount subscribed by shareholders is required to be shown in balance sheets, this money amount may be carried indefinitely in the accounts. Following the above rules, the sum of the amount described and the balance of the capital maintenance reserve at the end of any year will be the purchasing power equivalent at that time of all sums deemed to have been subscribed by shareholders.

35. **Where there are outstanding issues of preference shares, these shall be treated as equivalent to outstanding debt, for the purpose of calculating the capital maintenance adjustment.**

Preference shares are, like debts, redeemable at fixed, contractual money amounts. Therefore, like debts, they provide a hedge against the effects of changes in the general purchasing power of money. The amount of outstanding preference shares will therefore be deducted (together with all other liabilities) from total assets to obtain the amount of net assets to be used in the calculation of the capital maintenance adjustment.

36. **Net income of a year will be the algebraic sum of transaction surpluses (para 31), price variation adjustments (para 32), and the capital maintenance adjustment (para 33).**

The balance of the income account after incorporating the consequences of transactions and the price variation and capital maintenance adjustments will be the net income in units of year-end purchasing power. The whole of it may be paid out without impairing the purchasing power of the opening amount of net assets. Or if it or any part of it is transferred to a retained profits account, the whole of the balance of that account could be paid out (as dividends) without impairing the purchasing power of the amounts subscribed or deemed to have been subscribed by ordinary shareholders.

# PART VI—SOME FEATURES OF THE SYSTEM

### 37. All original entries relate to the amounts of transactions; all adjustments are based on information from sources external to the firm.

These features ensure that all amounts represent actually experienced or accrued effects on a firm's position and results. Doubts about the magnitudes of accrued effects are resolved by recourse to external information, not to internal formulae. There are no arbitrary apportionments, no questionable assumptions about future events or uniformities, and no arbitrary demarcations between outcomes which are and which are not controllable, in some sense, by firms and their managements. The accounts and financial statements may be audited, therefore, with reference to independent sources of information; and the representations they make will be pertinent to the financial relations of the firm with the rest of the world.

### 38. CoCoA applies a single valuation rule throughout, avoiding the addition of different kinds of magnitudes in balance sheets.

There are no optional rules for asset valuation, as there are in all other systems. There is no possibility, therefore, that the significance of aggregates will be distorted by the addition of magnitudes of different kinds. Although the transactions figures and price variation adjustments are magnitudes expressed in money units of different purchasing powers, the combined effect of them and the capital maintenance adjustment is a net income in units of the same purchasing power as other items in a closing balance sheet.

### 39. CoCoA entails uniform valuation rules for all companies, making possible comparison of the financial features of companies.

Under accounting systems which allow optional valuation rules, the financial significance of the resulting figures is always open to doubt, and strictly to direct comparison of financial magnitudes, rates and ratios is possible. Financial statements based on market resale prices, on the other hand, yield technically proper and practically significant indications of the composition of assets, of current ratios, debt to equity ratios, and rates of return—all of which may be directly compared with corresponding features of other companies and with corresponding features of the same company in prior years.

### 40. Some of the figures yielded by CoCoA may seem unusual by contrast with traditional accounting; they should be considered, not separately, but as parts of the whole system.

To value finished goods inventory at market price, when higher than cost, may seem unusual; and to value raw materials and work in progress at current market price, when lower than cost, may also seem unusual. It may appear that to calculate net income on such a footing is to "anticipate profits." But in the first place, the use of one valuation rule yields a comprehensible aggregate. Second, the "unusual" effects are to some extent offsetting. And third, the overriding charge for the capital maintenance adjustment is built-in protection against the overstatement of period-ical net income. The same reasoning applies to the bringing to account of changes in the market prices of other non-monetary assets.

### 41.  No right or advantage which arises only on disposal of the company as a whole is brought into the accounts.

CoCoA is strictly concerned with a company as a going concern. No value is assigned to such things as developmental costs, goodwill and specialized plant having no resale value, which are realizable only on liquidation or disposal of part or whole of the company. Insofar as any amount has been paid out in respect of these items, it constitutes a sunk cost, and is not available as such for any financial purpose in the ordinary course of business. Such amounts may be charged against shareholders' equity directly, or treated in the manner of the "double account" system, above the balance sheet proper. This treatment is in accordance with the practice of financial analysis, and avoids the impression that the company has assets which are convertible to cash in the ordinary course of business. The mixing of subjective user-values with objective financial values has led, in many cases, to serious misdirection of investors and other financial supporters (see also para 8).

### 42.  The information given by CoCoA is consistent with that demanded by lenders and analysts of business affairs, and with the sense of the legislation relating to financial disclosure.

Lenders on the security of property are concerned with the up-to-date market values of assets; they alone constitute effective cover for debt. Press discussion of company affairs has drawn attention repeatedly to the differences between "account-ing values" and market values—both when specific prices have been rising and when they have been falling. The statutory requirements relating to financial disclosure have increasingly stipulated the publication (by footnote or otherwise) of market values, or have indicated that realizable value is important information to users of financial statements. Examples are the disclosure of the market values of listed securities, general provisions relating to the valuation of current assets, provisions relating to the valuation of property charged as security by borrowing companies, and the U.K. provision requiring directors to comment on differences between market values and book values of interests in property. CoCoA does systematically what all these practices, in piecemeal fashion, imply.

### 43.  The financial statements yielded by CoCoA constitute, in series, a continuous history of the financial affairs of a company.

Because the method of CoCoA embraces the consequences of actual transactions and of external changes which affect the wealth and results of companies, the statements for any period and at any date are all-inclusive. Taken in series, they represent a continuous record of shifts in wealth, solvency, gearing or leverage and achieved results. They are historical, avoiding the defects of dated speculation about the future; they are fully historical, avoiding the defects of partial representation of what has occurred up to any date or between any two dates.

## PART VII—SUMMARY

### 44. The rules of continuously contemporary accounting are:

1. All the assets should be stated at the best approximation to their money equivalents, in their then state and condition, at the date of the balance sheet.
2. All transactions shall be accounted for in the amounts at which they occurred.
3. All variations from the costs or book values of assets, which are not already brought into account by the sale of assets in the period, shall be brought into the income account at the end of the period as price variation adjustments.
4. There shall be charged against total revenues, in calculating net income, the amount of a capital maintenance adjustment, so that the amount of net income is a surplus by reference to the maintenance of the general purchasing power of the opening amount of net assets.
5. Net income is the algebraic sum of the outcomes of transactions, price variation adjustments and the capital maintenance adjustment.

# III-A 4 *Some Thoughts on "Inflation Accounting" in Great Britain and the United States*

PHILIP W. BELL

The importance of relevant and reliable accounting data on business perfor-mance to aid in effective decision-making, so essential for the efficient per-formance of a market economy, can hardly be over-emphasised. Many business managers as well as outside evaluators do, however, greatly underestimate the role that accounting can at least play in decision-making. I doubt that the real reason is that the subject of accounting is too much a mystery and "hocus-pocus" for managers to master, as was once suggested by Geoffrey Bardsley, International Banking and Investment Manager of Xerox:

> "I once studied a little accounting because the Bank of England insisted that one take certain examinations at the London Institute of Bankers. I absorbed with reasonable ease the premise that for every debit there must be a credit, which seemed logical and reasonable. But when I found that I was supposed to identify the credit that corresponds with a particular debit and, having identified it, decide into which general ledger account it had to go, I gave up. Ever since then I have pictured accountants as a kindly group of experts on whom, hopefully, I could rely if need be." ("Managing Interna-tional Transactions," *International Journal of Accounting*, Fall 1972, p. 67.)

Rather, the significance of accounting has been underplayed over the years because most accounting data that have been accumulated have in fact been largely irrelevant for purposes of planning and for evaluating performance—an exercise necessary in part to aid in future planning. I have asked many chief executive officers

Philip W. Bell, "Some Thoughts on 'Inflation Accounting' in Great Britain and the United States," *The Accountant's Magazine*, October 1982, pp. 356–373. Reprinted with the permission of the author.

of American corporations over the years what role accounting information plays in their decision-making. They invariably answer, often expressing some surprise that I should ask such a silly question, that accounting information plays no role at all in their most time-consuming activity—planning and budgeting. Accounting data are formulated for tax authorities and to meet "stewardship" responsibilities of company managers in satisfying shareholders and creditors that their contributions have been used properly and have not ended up in someone's pocket, *ie*, that there has been no fraud or theft. Accounting practitioners have readily acquiesced in this line of thinking as well; indeed, most have tended to promote it.

Such a narrow stewardship view of accounting was prevalent in 1924, when Henry Hatfield wrote his famous "An Historical Defense of Bookkeeping," although even then Hatfield, known—certainly later—for his conservatism, envisaged a somewhat broader and more interesting role for accounting to play in society, concluding his spirited piece (reprinted from *The Journal of Accountancy* in Baxter and Davidson, *Studies in Accounting Theory*) as follows:

> "I have tried to remove the stigma attached to accounting by showing that in its origin it is respectable, nay, even academic; that despite its present disrepute it has from time to time attracted the attention of men of unquestioned intellectual attainment; that it justifies itself in that it has arisen to meet a social need. Its functions are to locate responsibility, to prevent fraud, to guide industry, to determine equities, to solve the all-essential conundrum of business: 'What are my profits?'; to facilitate the government in its fiscal operations, to guide the business manager in the attempt to secure efficiency. Are not these efforts worthy of any man's attention?"

The critical importance of "profits," which were to be earned by using accounting data to perform "efficiently," was recognized, although the case surrounding the rationale for this was not really developed. But Hatfield had earlier in his piece put his finger very clearly on why measurement of "profit" was a conundrum for accountants:

> "And so accountants are asked to perform the hopeless task of taking this economic continuum, of chopping it up into arbitrary and meaningless lengths called a year, and apportioning to each such year a proper part of the cost of a building which will last fifty years, of a machine which will be used for twenty years, of a blast furnace which will last ten, and of a stock of coal bought in December which will all be consumed before spring again appears."

If the Period Convention in accounting did not exist and one simply had to keep track of cash contributed and earned during a firm's life and cash paid out for inputs and distributed during a firm's life, with a single report made at the end of, say, its 100-year existence, all the difficult (hence interesting) problems in accounting would evaporate. Accountants *would* then indeed be simply the plodding bookkeepers that they are often pictured to be. The Period Convention is essential for purposes of comparability. Performance data for a firm (based primarily on a "bottom line" figure for "profits") are not very useful if they cannot be compared in a meaningful way with data measuring the firm's performance in other like periods and with data measuring the performances of other business firms in analogous periods.

It was not until 1940 that Paton and Littleton, in their classic *Introduction to Corporate Accounting Standards*—a work that has had an influence on worldwide accounting as it is practised today, probably second only to Pacioli's 1494 treatise on double-entry accounting—"solved" the periodic profit determination problem with their famous "matching" concept of revenue realized with the related historical cost of inputs used in earning that revenue. As a young, very bright instructor of accounting at the University of Michigan in 1918, Paton had visualized, in a brilliant piece, accounting as it was to become in the 1980s (see the reprint of his article in Stephen A Zeff: *Asset Appreciation, Business Income and Price-Level Accounting: 1918–1935*). Like so many of us, Paton moved a bit further to the right with each advancing year. His very conservative 1940 solution employed the Realization Convention (to input as well as output values) and the Money Convention (the value of the monetary unit may change with inflation, but it is not up to the accountant to do anything about it) to solve the Period Convention problem. This "solution," to my mind, kept accounting from advancing into the still largely uncharted waters of "decision-usefulness" which Paton himself had sketched so tantalizingly in 1918.

## THE BEGINNINGS OF CHANGE

In the 1920s and 1930s there had been undercurrents of rebellion as to what had to be done—in both Europe and the United States. (I have not yet heard a claim from the Soviet Union in this matter.) When prices change, accounting data based on the Realization Convention were not concerned with "current values"; hence, they did not serve the replacement needs of a "going concern" (Schmidt in Germany and Limperg in the Netherlands). In the face of inflation, traditional accounting did not present a "true and fair" picture in real terms because of the changing value of the unit of currency used in measurement: that is to say, traditional accounting did not take care of the defect in the Money Convention (Schmalenbach in Germany and Sweeney in the United States, the latter also worrying, but only peripherally, about "current values"). In either case traditional accounting did not fit into an economic concept of income which economists said was appropriate for measuring "better-offness" and for making decisions (Canning in the United States, Lindahl in Sweden and Ronald Edwards in Great Britain)—this concern drifting into involvement with "Hicksian income" considerations, stemming from Irving Fisher. In the 1940s and 1950s these undercurrents of rebellion gradually began to be taken seriously by practitioner bodies overseeing the work of the profession, particularly by the American Institute of Certified Public Accountants, which published, among other works, *The Search for Accounting Principles* (a perceptive little 1964 book by Reed Storey, which explained the growth of the Institute's concerns, and those of others, and consequent research).

It was not really until the beginning of the 1960s, however, that the twin concerns suggesting that accounting data should be "useful" for decision-making purposes on the one hand and that price change effects should be incorporated into accounting information on the other began to merge in some people's minds. And as inflation became severe in the later 1960s in the United States, spreading to Europe with the formation of OPEC in the early 1970s, with consequent greater volatility in relative prices and hence current values of different individual assets held by different businesses, professional accounting bodies and governments began to do something about it. First there was a move all around the world, in 1972–1974, to do something about the inadequacies of the Money Convention. The myth that the dollar or pound was an unchanging unit of measurement, like degrees on a thermometer or distance in kilometres on a highway, was recognized for the fiction that it was, and there was a move to adjust historical cost values so as to reflect the real decline in the value of the currency unit over time, *ie*, historical costs were to be adjusted to reflect changes in the general price level. But enough was enough! Do not also tamper with the Realization Convention, thus getting into the confusing bailiwick of specific price changes and current values as opposed to historical costs. Historical costs were, after all, based on actual transactions, it was argued, not on some ephemeral "market value" that one might or might not be able to find a quotation for, and which, if found, might or might not apply to the price which a particular firm might have to pay if, in theory, if were to replace the asset today, or receive perhaps if it were to sell the asset today. (Besides, was it "entry" or "exit" value that was relevant? Even accounting theorists seemed to differ on that one.)

## SANDILANDS, THE SEC AND FASB

But governments, at least in Great Britain and in the United States, would not let accounting bodies ignore "current costs" or "current values." (The term "value" when used in "current value accounting" sometimes seems to be, to an accountant, what a red flag is to a bull. But "cost" is, after all, an "entry value." And for reasons suggested below [associated with the reporting of "cost savings" or "holding gains"], in comparing the present American and British systems for correcting accounts for changes in prices, "current value accounting" may be a more appropriate term than "current cost accounting.") In 1975 the British Government-appointed Sandilands Committee, and the American regulatory body, the Securities and Exchange Commission (SEC), both made a step in the right direction by developing separate frameworks for correcting, in part, for specific price changes in the accounts and in effect overthrowing the Realization Convention, at least in its holding dimension, so that some recognition could given current values of at least assets (but not liabilities) in a company's books.

Unfortunately for Great Britain the Sandilands approach was the better of the two. I say "unfortunately for Great Britain" because *both* 1975 approaches were badly flawed. The SEC approach was so obviously and admittedly limited, however, that the Financial Accounting Standards Board (FASB) in the United States recognized the limitations and did something very positive and substantive about them, in an exposure draft on *Financial Reporting and Changing Prices*, in December 1978, and then, after some revision, in Statement of Financial Accounting Standards No. 33 with that title, in September 1979. Seemingly much more comprehensive than the SEC effort, the Sandilands version of "what ought to be," on the other hand, has been kept basically in place in Great Britain in SSAP 16 "Current Cost Accounting" (March 1980) with amendments to the Sandilands notion of a CCA profit figure involving "working capital" and "gearing" adjustments.

The 1975 efforts, and particularly the Sandilands approach, were badly flawed essentially because they adopted a notion of "income" that was tied to the physical maintenance of capital or, more loosely and fuzzily, to "operating capability" of an enterprise rather than a notion based on associating "income" with increases in real financial wealth. One particular possible concern of a company, involving the replacement of inventory and plant and equipment in the fact of rising prices, was allowed to dominate the accounting figure that was to measure "better-offness." In this respect Sandilands followed the 1920s writings of Schmidt in Germany and Limperg in the Netherlands—in part. (The SEC followed Schmidt and Limperg also, although the American agency made no effort in 1975–76 to require any total "current income" figure, but simply required footnoted current values (*a*) for assets in the balance sheet and (*b*) for cost of goods sold and depreciation expenses on the income statement.) The Sandilands Committee also adopted the notion of "deprival value," which is essentially a British re-interpretation of the 1930s work of an American (Bonbright) which in turn, unknown to English-speaking accountants, was evidently tucked away in the 1920s Dutch-language work of Limperg. Sandilands, however, improved on Schmidt and Limperg in that the Committee stressed the "current operating profit" component of total "real business profit," as enunciated by Edwards and Bell in 1961. That component, now known in Britain and the Commonwealth as "CCA profit," tends to stress changing current replacement needs *period-by-period* (to the extent replacement was at issue—a matter *not* stressed by Edwards and Bell), rather than, as in Schmidt and Limperg, stressing continual *cumulative* replacement needs from a starting point zero. With Schmidt and Limperg, the resultant "income" figure is bound up inevitably with "backlog" depreciation and thus has little to do with "current operating profit," *ie*, simply the *current* (present-period) profitability of the enterprise based on subtracting current costs at current prices from current revenues at current prices (this being the rationale for reporting this component of total "real business profit" stressed by Edwards and Bell).

The basic flaws in the Sandilands approach (which have been substantively remedied in FASB Statement No 33 but are still embedded in SSAP 16) are: (1) certain gains or "cost savings," which result from early purchase of an asset when its price was below that prevailing currently, are ignored in the computation of income period-by-period; (2) no attention is paid to the changing value of the pound as a result of general inflation (in spite of the title of the Sandilands Report—"Inflation Accounting"). Only partial recognition is thus given to the defects of the Realization Convention, and no recognition is given to the defects of the Money Convention. Nor do the monetary working capital and gearing adjustments serve to remedy these defects. These amendments are both orientated toward the single-minded notion of replacement, and funds needed to replace assets being currently used up—possible concerns if a company in fact plans to replace such assets with like assets. But these concerns have no bearing on the measurement of whether or not a company and its shareholders are, or are not, "better off" in terms of real financial wealth, which is what the concept "income" is supposed to measure.

In contrast, the Financial Accounting Standards Board in its approach to current value accounting, albeit not fashioning an ideal format for accounting, does meet head-on, and basically conquers, both defects of the CCA approach. The FASB was clearer on these matters in the exposure draft for FAS No. 33 than in the final document. Recognizing the still-existing pressures within the accounting profession for price-level-adjusted historical costs (called CPP in Britain), the FASB ostensibly offered a choice in paragraph 21 of the exposure draft between that and the full current value accounting system (termed a "current cost/constant dollar" framework), which it espoused. In fact, it stipulated in that draft that the CPP choice could be made if, and only if, it could be shown that CPP offered a "better" depiction of events of a period than that based on correcting for both specific prices and the general price level. The presumption (see para 25 of the exposure draft) was that CPP could never in fact be "better," but might be "sufficient" if: "(1) cost of goods sold and depreciation expense are not significant or (2) cost of goods sold and depreciation expense are significant but price changes in those categories of expense have been approximately the same as the change in the general price level." Inevitably, as seems to happen in all accounting standard-setting, political pressures in the form of strongly-voiced arguments from seven of the Big Eight firms forced the FASB to amend the wise approach taken in the exposure draft, and in the final standard (Statement 33) companies are actually required to field two sets of data: historical cost/constant dollar accounts and current cost/constant dollar accounts. As it deserves to be, the former seems destined to become the political aberration of relevance perhaps to accounting historians. The latter framework, albeit often misunderstood, is in my view the soundest theoretical approach to accounting for changing prices extant and one which US companies (a) are not finding hard to put into practice, and (b) are finding useful in the internal decision-making process as well as in explaining to outsiders what is really happening to the enterprise in meaningful and interpretable fashion. Unlike CCA in Britain, it is rapidly gaining widespread acceptance because, I suggest, it is a valid and comprehensive system rather than a partial system based primarily on one particular concern of a business enterprise, replacement of assets.

## CURRENT COST/CONSTANT DOLLAR FRAMEWORK

First, let us consider what the "current cost/constant dollar" framework of the FASB is *not*. As its title suggests, it is not the simple current cost or CCA framework as it is often described. Nor, however, in contrast to what Geoffrey Whittington suggests in his "Inflation Accounting: All the Answers" (Deloitte Haskins & Sells Lecture, University of Cardiff Press, 1981), is it a combination of CCA and CPP. CCA puts accounts into nominal current value terms on a comparative balance sheet and on an income statement, ignoring in the latter, however, the gains resulting from early purchase. Further, it makes no adjustment for the fact that the current pound value on the beginning and ending balance sheets are expressed in currency units that have different values because inflation has occurred over the year; ie, it makes no adjustment for changes in the general price level. CPP adjusts historical cost values for changes in the general price level but gives no recognition to changing specific prices, hence no recognition to current values. The FASB current cost/constant dollar framework in effect: (1) adjusts historical cost asset values to their nominal current value amounts; (2) adjusts these nominal current asset values along with historical cost liability values for changes in the value of the dollar; and (3) thereby yields a current real income figure which is *in toto* consistent with the change in real net worth as would be given by a comparative balance sheet formulated in these terms were the FASB to require this. This total current real income figure is further dichotomized into CCA profit ("income from continuing operations") on the one hand, and "real realizable cost savings or holding gains" on the other. Unfortunately the FASB does not require a specific price- and price-level-adjusted comparative balance sheet nor a full income statement. Had it done so, both the *procedures* and *results* embodied in the current cost/constant dollar framework would have been clearer. Further, until November 1981, when the FASB came down firmly on the side of income as a comprehensive measure of the total change in real financial capital or wealth, the Board could not make up its mind between the physical and real financial approaches to capital maintenance income concepts. Hence it required companies to formulate all the relevant data for both, but not necessarily to add them up so as to yield the real financial income concept. A reader can easily add the three or four figures provided, and some firms like Exxon do this work for him. Presumably such addition will now become part of normal practice. Let's hope that a comparative current real balance sheet, which is consistent with the required current real income statement, will also soon be regularly provided. (The FASB has actually withdrawn the November 1981 exposure draft on *Reporting income, cash flows and financial position of business enterprises*; but this may well be for reasons other than the fact that the document resolves finally the financial versus physical capital maintenance issue.)

The FASB current value accounting framework thus has not one, but two significant differences which distinguish it from its British SSAP 16 counterpart, *before* the fundamental British figure is further amended by monetary working capital and gearing adjustments. The FASB in effect adds a price-level adjustment for the nominal current asset values on beginning and ending balance sheet figures so as to reflect the effects of inflation over the year. At least the total income figure is consistent with these price-level-adjusted current value figures that would appear on a comparative current real value balance sheet. Income thus includes not only current revenues less current costs at current prices ("income from continuing operations" or basic CCA profit) but also real realizable cost savings (*ie*, nominal cost savings adjusted for general price-level changes). These real realizable cost savings usually more than *offset* the higher *hypothetical* current costs which entered the CCA calculation, because assets were in fact held at the beginning of the period when prices were lower than the period-average used in the CCA calculation. As the American data show, real realizable cost savings (more often termed "holding gains") can be substantial. It is very wrong to ignore them and thus provide only part of the picture. And the information prevents firms from getting into what they can justifiably regard as a "Catch-22" situation: "the CCA approach, at least so far, has not improved my tax situation but has perhaps worsened my share market situation by making me look in worse shape than I really am." The dichotomized total change in real financial wealth stressed by the FASB gives a basis for tax relief (by showing the CCA figure) yet tells shareholders that there are offsetting cost savings or capital gains from early purchases to lighten the bleak CCA picture. The "gearing" adjustment, especially one based on *realized* cost savings or holding gains as it is in Great Britain (but not in New Zealand, where it is based on *realizable* cost savings), does not do this. Obviously the "gearing" adjustment does nothing for the non-leveraged firm, and its twisted meaning for the leveraged firm has more kinship to the general price-level adjustment for liabilities in the American standard than with price adjustments for assets in that standard. (For a detailed, algebraic comparison of the two systems, see Philip W. Bell, *CVA, CCA and CoCoA: How Fundamental Are the Differences?* Australian Accounting Research Foundation, 1982; for a simpler arithmetical illustration of some of the differences, see Bell, "Current Value Accounting: what it is and why we need it," *Bedrifts Økonomen* (Norway), August 1982.)

## THE PROBLEM OF DETERMINING CURRENT VALUES

And what of current value accounting and "practice"? What of the poor practitioner who must determine the "current value," not only of a car or machine which may be regularly traded in used form in the market place, but of perhaps a highly specialized North Sea oil rig? Determining values by "arbitrary allocations" as we do by following a FIFO or LIFO rule or a particular depreciation method applied to historical costs is, admittedly, easier on the individual accountant. No judgment is required; he or she can follow an accepted rule. But does that make the calculation "objective"? The rule itself is subjective! And the resultant "value" has little to do with reality. Current values can be measured, at least in theory, without making any of the arbitrary allocations as among periods which properly worried conservative Henry Hatfield so much way back in the 1920s. Such values can normally be found for inventory stocks directly in the market place. (We sometimes forget that under historical cost accounting even the beginning inventory figure is not a "hard," objective acquisition price but in fact is the result of an arbitrary allocation of the previous period's cost of goods available for sale into cost of goods sold and ending inventory.) Where viable used asset markets do not exist, as with many fixed assets, one may have to find a way of "approximating" what the market value might likely be. If the practitioner objects to being put in the position of having to pass on that, I can only say better to be approximate, with information relevant for user needs, than to be "exact"—following an arbitrary, subjective rule—with information of little or no relevance for user needs.

# III-B  Capital Maintenance

## III-B 1  *Financial Versus Physical Capital Maintenance: A Review of the Arguments*

KENNETH W. LEMKE

## 1. INTRODUCTION

### 1.1 Overview

An old saw claims that the fellow who keeps on saying "and no two ways about it," is a bachelor. Bachelor or no, he probably is not an accountant. Interminable and inconclusive debates on alternative solutions to controversial issues seem to be a hallmark of the accounting discipline, reflecting, perhaps, a resolute optimism that ultimate consensus can and will be achieved. The Edmonton capital maintenance Symposium might have been expected to contribute just another forgettable chapter in this tradition. On the contrary, the papers and discussion focussed attention on what I perceive to be some critical but new or neglected issues related to the choice of a capital maintenance concept—issues that have implications for the potential viability of *FAS 33* and like proposals. In addition, the opportunity was provided for a comparative review of some recent efforts of the standard setters in four countries. The purpose of the Symposium was to debate the relative merits of financial and physical capital maintenance concepts. Perhaps the participants were a biased sample, but it seemed to me that the result was a runaway for financial capital

Kenneth W. Lemke, "Financial versus Physical Capital Maintenance: A Review of the Arguments," in *Maintenance of Capital: Financial Versus Physical* ed. R. Sterling and K. Lemke, Scholars Book Co., 1982. Reprinted with the permission of the Scholars Book Co.

maintenance, though the battle took the form of an assault on physical capital rather than a defence of financial capital. One consequence of this preoccupation with physical capital is that no clear consensus emerged (or was sought) as to a preferred concept of financial capital maintenance.

My task is to provide a synthesis of the papers presented at the Symposium. I have interpreted that task rather liberally in order to provide something that is hopefully useful to the reader who wants a review of the main issues discussed and the range of views expressed. The result is part synthesis, part summary, part exposition and part critique.

The papers presented at the Symposium form a complementary (if not an integrated) group. This is largely because a number of major issues raised by Sterling in relation to *FAS 33* and current cost accounting (CCA) models in general are taken up by other authors. Specifically, Sterling argues that physical capital maintenance is an untenable concept in the face of non-identical asset replacement, decreasing input cost levels, "trading" situations and surplus cash positions. Additionally, he challenges any alleged superiority of current costs and current cost income concepts as predictors of future cash flows. Three authors discuss these (and other) issues in relation to CCA standards or proposed standards in their own countries—Lee for the U.K., Ma for Australia and Skinner for Canada. Revsine's paper includes a discussion of most of the same issues, though it purports to be restricted in scope to a national policy decision perspective. Carsberg is largely concerned with the predictive ability issue and does some complementary theorizing. The Livingstone and Weil paper is the only one that does not comment on the issues raised by Sterling. Instead, it focuses on an analysis and critique of *FAS 33's* disclosure requirements along with some related conceptual and measurement issues.

Among the discussants, Butterworth, with his agency theory perspective, moves outside the orbit traversed by the other authors. He believes that a different income paradigm and a different methodological approach are necessary to solve the central problems addressed by the Symposium. Scott lends some related comment, if not support, to this viewpoint. Milburn's discussion paper, in my opinion, makes an important contribution in articulating the issue as to whether the cost of replacing an item sold is a cost (expense) of the sale (as implied by physical capital maintenance) or a new investment made in expectation of a future return. Hanna presents a couple of controversial "counter-examples" to Sterling's decreasing cost case. Taking up a suggestion of Livingstone-Weil, he also argues for an expanded funds-flow statement rather than the income statement as the place to report the financial impact of maintaining (and expanding) productive capability.

If one had to categorize the Symposium authors and discussants, Sterling, Lee, Carsberg and probably Milburn would have to be described as unequivocal proponents of financial capital maintenance. Skinner and Ma come down more cautiously on the side of financial capital maintenance (the final version of Ma's paper being much more restrained than the original in its criticism of physical capital mainte-nance). For Skinner, financial capital maintenance is a pragmatic choice. In terms of an "ideal," he is more in sympathy with Livingstone-Weil, Revsine and Scott, who take a catholic type of stance—a "different concepts for different purposes" approach. Revsine, however, is unequivocal in his advocacy of physical capital maintenance for macro-economic decisions. Hanna and Butterworth might best be described as neutrals—they want to see more research done before a choice is made. However, Hanna does favour financial capital maintenance in conjunction with his expanded funds-flow statement, and, as we shall see, Butterworth's agency theory approach also seems to point in the direction of financial capital maintenance.

Bob Sterling's marathon essay, the "Limitations of Physical Capital" is unquestionably the keystone paper of the Symposium. It has been taken as a point of reference by several of the other authors. Moreover, it is a comprehensive statement of a number of issues which other authors address with little or no preliminary exposition. Therefore, it seems appropriate for a synthesis to include a review of the main arguments put forward in Sterling's paper, and, after a few preliminaries, I shall proceed on that basis with extensive reference to other authors and discussants. In so doing, most of the major controversial issues debated at the Symposium will be explored. Some remaining issues will then be reviewed. (It should be noted that, hereafter, author and section number references are to *this volume* unless otherwise stated.)

## 1.2 A New Trend Among The Standard Setters

A concept of capital maintenance provides a benchmark that can be used to determine whether or not income has been earned. Corporate income then is the maximum amount that can be distributed by way of dividends without an erosion of capital. Different concepts of capital maintenance yield different measures of reported and distributable income. The choice of a capital maintenance concept is therefore a matter of fundamental importance to accountants and to those who use the financial statements prepared by accountants.

The tradition of financial capital maintenance (in nominal dollars) is currently threatened by a trend towards adoption of a physical capital maintenance concept by standard setters in a number of English-speaking countries. The essential difference between the two concepts is in the treatment of holding gains and losses (i.e., differences between historical costs of assets and their current input prices). *Financial* capital maintenance concepts include holding gains/losses in income on either a realized or a realizable basis, depending on the accounting model—e.g., the generally accepted accounting principles (GAAP) model includes them on a realized basis. Physical capital maintenance concepts exclude holding gains/losses from income—"on the grounds that, if positive, they do not enable an enterprise to increase its operating capability or, if negative, they do not force a reduction" (Carsberg, Section 1.2).

Standards in the U.S. and the U.K., a Provisional Standard (and related Exposure Drafts) in Australia and an Exposure Draft in Canada came under discussion at the Symposium (FASB, 1979; ASC, 1980a and 1980b; AARF 1979 and 1980; ICAA/ASA, 1978a and 1978b; CICA, 1979). The avant garde member of this quartet is the U.K.'s *SSAP 16*, which permits financial statements prepared on a CCA basis to be designated as the "main accounts." According to Lee (oral presentation), the ultimate aim of the professional bodies in the U.K. is to have CCA as the main system of accounting as quickly as possible. CCA can, of course, incorporate either a financial or a physical capital maintenance concept—depending on whether holding gains/losses are included or not in current cost income. In all four countries under discussion, the physical capital maintenance version of CCA has been adopted or proposed.

The concept of physical capital favoured by the standard setters is not a given bundle of productive assets of fixed type and description, but a constant "operating capability." This is defined in similar terms in all four countries as the fixed quantity of goods and services that can be supplied currently with existing resources (FASB, 1979, paras 124 and 94 [b]; ASC, 1980a, para. 39; ICAA/ASA, 1978b, para. 11.01 [a]; CICA, 1979, para. .09 [d]). The defined concept of physical capital is thus an output rather than an input quantity, but nonetheless a specified physical quantity. Some have argued (e.g., Lee and Ma) that this concept is more ambiguous and imprecise than the idea of maintaining a particular collection of productive physical assets. The reason is that operating capability can be quantified in different ways in the not uncommon case where different product ranges or different product mixes can be obtained from given facilities.

### 1.3 Why Physical Capital Maintenance?

The basic arguments for physical capital maintenance are essentially expressions or elaborations of the plausible normative proposition that a given quantity of real (i.e., physical) goods rather than a given amount of money wealth should be the benchmark for determining whether income has been earned. Replacement of an asset with one that is identical or has equivalent service potential does not make the owner(s) any better-off or worse-off in real (physical) terms. Therefore, income cannot arise until provision has been made for replacement. Also, repeated failure to maintain physical capacity can be inimical to the survival of the firm, each failure being a step on the road to extinction. Since assets have to be replaced at current cost, holding gains/losses cannot be viewed as income—they represent the change in investment level needed to maintain well-offness in real (physical) terms. Thus, as expressed in "Proposition 3" of Sterling's explication of the physical capital model (Section 2.3): "Income is the change in physical capital and is determined by deducting current costs from revenues."

A corollary of this line of argument is said to be that historical cost/nominal dollar accounting produces "false profits." Sterling argues to the contrary. The distinction between nominal dollar and physical unit measures of capital is not that one is true and the other false, but that they measure different attributes of capital (Sterling, Section 2.2). When these measures are represented by net assets at historical cost and current cost respectively, the same is true—i.e., they reflect different attributes of the referents of accounting measurement. Skinner's view of historical cost is less tolerant. In his illustration of the "steady state firm," a number of performance indexes computed from historical cost financial statements record improvement during a period of rising prices when no improvement in real terms has occurred. The conclusion—historical cost accounting is at least "misleading" under conditions of changing prices (Section 1). The reason—historical cost is a "fact," but not a dimension of current "economic reality" (Section 2.1).

Whatever the view of historical cost, advocacy of a capital maintenance concept is based on normative propositions with respect to the objectives of accounting and on related claims concerning the alleged advantages of a particular capital maintenance concept as a means to attainment of some chosen objective(s). In this context, Sterling divides the proponents of physical capital maintenance into two camps. Firstly, there are those who take physical capital maintenance as the objective—perhaps with an eye to survival of the firm. Secondly, there are those who take the maintenance of future cash flows as the objective and see physical capital maintenance as a means to this end (Section 1.2). In light of these objectives, physical capital measures are claimed by their proponents to offer advantages with respect to the formulation of dividend and pricing policies within the firm and tax policies at the macro level, assessment of managerial performance, prediction of future cash operating flows and dividend payments, and provision of a surrogate for the unmeasurable ideal—"economic income" (Sterling, Section 2.4).

## 2. STERLING'S FOUR "CONDITIONS"

Sterling is a stern critic of the physical capital maintenance concept. Broadly stated, his criticism is that the concept is incapable of general application to all or many firms because it tacitly assumes compliance with four conditions that cannot all be met by many firms. The four conditions are that the firm—

1. continually replaces with identical units;
2. faces continuously increasing costs;
3. does not buy and sell in the same market; and
4. is fully invested in physical units (Section 3.1).

These conditions—especially the first two—were the subject of considerable discussion at the Symposium, and they will be addressed separately in what follows.

### 2.1 Replacement With Non-Identical Units

*2.11 Merchandise Inventories*   What is the measure of physical capital, and how is such a measure to be meaningfully employed, in the not unusual case where a firm responds to changing circumstances and opportunities by changing the kinds of product units it makes or trades? Such changes might occur because of changing fashions (e.g., maxi-skirts in place of mini-skirts), changing seasons (e.g., skates instead of cleats), changing technology (e.g., electronic calculators instead of slide rules) or changing directions of the firm (e.g., plastics instead of glass). Should the current replacement price of the old (discontinued) unit, the current purchase price of the new (and different) unit, or some other measure, be used as the basis of accounting? How does the financial reporter compare one set of physical units at the beginning of a period with a different set at the end and obtain a meaningful capital maintenance and income answer? These are the kinds of questions prompted by Sterling's illustrative case in which mini-skirts are replaced by maxis. The recommendations of the standard setters are virtually silent on this issue (except for the treatment of seasonal items as a "special situation" in the U.K.'s *Guidance Notes on SSAP 16*).

Ma has one possible answer from the economist A. C. Pigou who proposed that "heterogeneous physical units in use can be reduced to a common dimension by their exchange ratios at the end-period date." In a non-barter system, the dollar would become the standard unit of measurement ("common dimension") and the end-of-period values would be the exchange ratios (Ma, Section 1.2). Lee argues to a similar conclusion. The financial reporter is almost forced to "standardize" the opening and closing physical units in terms of a surrogate unit. "The monetary unit is the most immediate surrogate to hand but, paradoxically, to regard it as the primary capital attribute would cause the capital maintenance approach to revert to the traditional financial one" (Lee, Section 5.1). In fact, the *Guidance Notes on SSAP 16* permit a reversion to financial capital maintenance in their recommended treatment of certain seasonal items of inventory where replacement with similar products is not intended. Para. 76 suggests that such inventory be treated as monetary working capital. Para. 102 permits a "general index" to be used in computing the related "monetary working capital adjustment." "In this way, it is presumed that the physical attribute inherent in such [inventory] is too difficult to identify and account for, and that it should be regarded more as part of the reporting entity's specific pool of purchasing power. This recommendation is more akin to financial rather than physical capital maintenance" (Lee, Section 5.1). This leads to what I consider to be one of the most significant observations to be found in the Symposium papers—namely, that financial capital maintenance offers "a more flexible approach to accounting in which we are not bound by the existing asset structure ... In other words, the financial approach can assume a changing asset structure without abandoning the assumption of the entity as a going concern" (Lee, Section 6).

The foregoing addresses the question of how to measure current cost when inventory is replaced with non-identical units. A more basic question is whether it is even meaningful to speak of physical capital maintenance or maintenance of operating capability when the nature of the physical unit changes. The answer probably is "no." In the case of firms that often reposition or restructure their asset holdings (e.g., real estate firms or dealers in fashion goods), the standard of operating capability becomes kaleidoscopic at best. Skinner observes (Section 4.3) that when replacement is uneconomic and recoverable amount has to be substituted for current cost, the standard of operating capability (i.e., the physical good) is abandoned altogether, and we are reduced to saying that the operating capability of $x cash is $x. Similarly, Sterling notes that, under these circumstances, the reported numbers cannot be interpreted in terms of physical units, even though the objective is to measure physical units (Section 3.11, fn 8). Skinner argues further that when recoverable amount has to be substituted for current cost, the significance of the current operating profit figure shifts from portraying the viability of a going concern (maintenance of operating capability test) to portraying the potential for return from some alternative use of cash to be derived from sale or use of existing assets (maintenance of earning power test) (Sections 4.3 and 5). He concludes that theoretical justification for the maintenance of operating capability concept is too closely tied to a view of the business population as generally comprised of enterprises locked into their present lines of business indefinitely (Section 4.2). Thus the operating capability concept of capital maintenance is of restricted application and does not hold promise of development into a comprehensive theory. It therefore fails as a comprehensive response to the problems of price change and inflation (Skinner, Section 5).

Other participants in the Symposium gave equally harsh judgments. Ma, for example, in the original version of his paper, says the operating capability concept "can be readily understood and implemented for those businesses not subject to large changes (whether of technology or fashion) in their operations." Outside of these situations the concept is "ill-defined and ambiguous." This "limitation" is a "fundamental problem since it is inherent in the physical capital concept itself."

In sum, Sterling received strong support for his contention that physical capital measures are not applicable to firms that replace with different units. It is a contention with sweeping implications: "In time all firms must either adapt to changing tastes and changing technology by replacing with different units or fail to adapt and die. Thus physical capital measures eventually become inapplicable to all living firms, to all going concerns" (Sterling, end of Section 3.11).

*2.12 Fixed Assets and Technological Change*   Thus far, the discussion of replacement with non-identical units has been directed mainly to inventory items. Obviously, physical capital measures are equally inapplicable to the case where fixed assets are replaced by totally different items following a revolutionary change in the nature of the business. None of the standard setters' proposals for physical capital maintenance provide any guidance for this situation. True, revolutionary changes of direction are somewhat rare, but a comprehensive theory of accounting must be able to accommodate them.

However, evolutionary changes in fixed assets due to technological advances are commonplace and result in replacement with non-identical units. Replacement with new improved models and types or with completely different assets designed to do the same or a similar job, is explicitly dealt with in the recommendations of all four countries represented at the Symposium. Australia's *PAS 1.2* (ICAA/ASA, 1978b) opts for the lower of reproduction cost and replacement cost in such cases (paras. 13.06 and 13.07). *FAS 33* (para. 180), the *Guidance Notes on SSAP 16* (Appendix 1) and the Canadian *Exposure Draft* (para C.21) in effect define current cost in such cases as the cost of the new asset adjusted for the estimated value of differences in service potential (e.g., differences in operating costs) between the old and new assets. It seems to me that current cost, after making this service potential adjustment, can result in a depreciation expense charge that is inconsistent with the physical capital mainte- nance objective. For example, say a machine will be replaced in a few years' time by a technologically superior model which has the same output capacity. Current replacement cost is $100,000. "Current cost" of the new machine after a service potential adjustment for operating cost savings of, say, $40,000, is $60,000; but (in the absence of further price changes) the firm will have to pay out $100,000, not $60,000, to maintain its operating capability (since both machines have the same output capacity). Therefore, even if backlog depreciation is ignored, the annual depreciation charge must be based on replacement cost of $100,000, not on current cost of $60,000 (nor on reproduction cost), in order to arrive at the income that can be distributed without an erosion of operating capability (physical capital) in this case.[1]

A counter-argument is that the outlay of $100,000 buys anticipated operating cost savings of $40,000; so the net cost of replacement is really $60,000. (More correctly, the operating cost savings should be expressed in present value terms.) There are some problems with this counter-argument. First, a logical extension of it is that the outlay of $100,000 buys expected future net revenues which have a present value of $100,000 or more, so replacement has a zero cost. It might be objected that the $40,000 is excluded from the current cost of replacing *existing* productive capacity because it represents a *difference* in service potential between the old and new machines. True, but a major objective of the physical capital maintenance model is to provide for

---

[1] There is an additional problem. When replacement prices are continually increasing from year to year, the cash which depreciation charges cause to be withheld from distribution may not be enough to pay the cost of new equipment unless backlog depreciation is provided. "May not" rather than "will not" because staggered regular replacement of multiple units can overcome the problem. (E.g., see *FAS 33*, para. 127.) The standards or proposed standards of all four countries represented at the Symposium discuss backlog depreciation, but none of them *require* that provision be made for it as a charge against income or retained earnings.

maintenance of operating capability (e.g., *FAS 33*, paras 3 [c], 94 [b] and 124–130; Canadian *Exposure Draft*, paras B.12 [i] and B.29–B.36). The cost of doing so is $100,000, not $60,000.

The $40,000 of operating cost savings cannot be attributed to a change in operating capability (thereby making $60,000 rather than $100,000 the cost of maintaining the existing level of operating capability). The old and new machines in our example have the *same* output capacity and operating capability is defined as a fixed quantity of output (e.g., *FAS 33*, para. 121). The level of input costs (e.g., operating costs) does not enter into the definition. Perhaps the standard setters want CCA to maintain *service potential* rather than *operating capability*. Paras 58, 126 and 180 of *FAS 33* seem to imply as much, but, if so, these paragraphs are in conflict with the explicitly stated objective of maintaining operating capability.

There is a second problem with the counter-argument. The $40,000 of operating cost savings will be reflected in post-replacement income statements. To also anticipate these savings in computing current cost depreciation prior to replacement is surely double counting. There might be a temptation to argue that double counting will be negated by the fact that (in the absence of further price changes) the depreciation base will be $100,000, not $60,000, after replacement has occurred. Post-replacement depreciation based on $100,000 rather than $60,000 will offset the post-replacement realization of operating cost savings, thus eliminating any double counting. The problem with this argument is that under a CCA system the function of depreciation charges is to reduce distributable income by a current cost estimate of the *next* replacement, not to offset the realization of operating cost savings anticipated by a *prior* replacement. In fact, the CCA model certainly does *not* assume that part of post-replacement depreciation is an offset to realized operating cost savings. In our example, the net income effect of such an offset would be equivalent to using a depreciation base of $60,000 *after* replacement. (Call this replacement the n'th replacement.) In order to provide for the (n + 1)'th replacement, it would therefore be necessary to restore the effective depreciation base to $100,000 (or more, if replacement costs have risen further) and to increase the effective depreciation expense in accordance with this base. As the CCA model does not provide for such restoration adjustments, it apparently does not make the offset assumption.

In sum, the anticipation of operating cost savings in computing CCA depreciation does seem to be a form of double counting which, in my view, fails the objective of maintaining operating capability. Current cost depreciation (plus backlog depreciation) withholds $60,000 for the n'th replacement, whereas $100,000 is needed to maintain operating capability. The remaining $40,000 is never charged to income on account of the n'th replacement.

Thus, it would appear that Revsine concludes too readily "that the absence of replacement-in-kind is not a particularly troublesome issue" (Section 4.2). His dismissal of the problem of technological change rests on the argument that, in a frictionless market, the market mechanism should adjust the prices of the old technology such that risk-adjusted ex ante rates of return on the old and new technologies are the same.[2] "Of course the greater are the frictions, the more coarse is the correspondence" (Revsine, this volume, Chapter 3, Section 4.2). There are at least

[2] In Revsine, 1979 (pp. 308–9, 310, 313), a "complete and frictionless market" is the stated condition for this market adjustment. In Revsine's Symposium paper (this volume, Chapter 3, Section 4.2), "the absence of extreme frictions" is the stated condition.

two reasons why this argument does not permit the conclusion that replacement with non-identical assets (due to technological change) is not a troublesome issue. Firstly, the argument relates only to the potential usefulness of physical capital measures in forecasting future cash operating flows (Revsine, 1979, p. 307), and not at all to the objective of maintaining operating capability. As illustrated above, where maintenance of operating capability is the objective, we cannot be indifferent between current cost, replacement cost and reproduction cost. The equivalence of ex ante rates of return does not change this. Secondly, the correspondence of ex ante rates of return on old and new technologies is perfect only in a frictionless market, and the extent and seriousness of market frictions are matters to be empirically determined. It is easy to postulate plausible situations where frictions would be substantial. For example, prices of multiple-use assets are affected by their value-in-use in industries or functions other than a particular one with which we may be concerned, whereas this is not a factor in the pricing of special-purpose items. Thus, in the case of a replacement decision which means switching from special-purpose to multiple-use equipment or vice versa, ex ante rates of return on old and new technologies will not necessarily be the same. Also, technological change can result in new multiple-use equipment which has a different range of capabilities than existing multiple-use equipment or is superior to it in some but not all uses. In such cases the old and new technologies will not necessarily have the same *relative* values in different industries and functions.

## 2.2 Decreasing Current Costs

*2.21 Analysis of the Problem*   In the physical capital maintenance version of CCA, holding gains/losses are (with some few exceptions discussed below) equity adjustments, not income. Hence, in periods of falling asset prices it is entirely possible for a firm to report "profits" (and to pay dividends out of and taxes on those profits) while financial capital (stockholders' equity) is eroded in both money and general purchasing power terms because of the effects of holding losses taken to equity. At the same time, physical capital is, of course, maintained intact (Sterling, Section 3.12).

Sterling, and several other Symposium authors, object to the firm reporting a distributable profit when the owners have suffered a loss. The implication is that only a perverse kind of accounting would report as distributable profit an amount whose distribution would (*ceteris paribus*) preclude the maintenance of current dividend and share price levels and erode stockholder wealth in nominal dollar terms (and probably in constant dollar terms as well). However, it seems equally perverse to condemn an accounting model for failure to maintain financial capital when that is not its purpose. (Scott, Section 1.2, and Hanna, Section 2.54, also comment to this effect).

The real issue here is: What should be the objective(s) of accounting? This is a matter to which we shall return later. In the meantime, it can be said that rejection of a model is legitimate if it does not serve the chosen objective. Skinner, for one, believes that maintenance of operating capability is not an objective that will have wide appeal when the accounting implications under conditions of falling prices are considered (Section 4.5). The qualms of the Australian standard setters lend some credence to this belief. When a decrease in the current cost of an asset "marks impairment of the financial viability of the entity," the decrease is charged to the profit and loss account (AARF, 1980, paras 15 and 17). As Ma points out, this treatment is "asymmetrical and therefore difficult to justify theoretically" (Section 3.2). Current cost increases are not income, while *some* decreases in current cost are charged to the income statement and some are not. It seems that the doctrine of conservatism would lead a schizophrenic life under current cost accounting. In both the U.K. and Australia, write-downs of assets from depreciated current cost to recoverable amount (net realizable value or economic value) are charged to income (*SSAP 16*, para. 54; *PAS 1.1*, para. 3.07). In *FAS 33* (para. 126) and the Canadian *Exposure Draft* (para. B.32), even these values losses bypass the income statement and are taken directly to stockholders' equity. Hence:

> "... if the NRV and EV constraints on current cost values are observed, current operating results *must*, over the longer run, be a profit."
> (Skinner, Section 4.3. Emphasis in original.)

This is a startling implication of the U.S. and Canadian versions of physical capital maintenance. One participant in the Symposium commented from the floor that he thought CCA would be popular in North America because firms would find it much more difficult to report a loss under CCA than under the present generally accepted accounting principles (GAAP) model.

*2.22 Hanna's Decreasing Cost Counter-Examples*    Hanna questions Sterling's arguments on the decreasing cost case by posing "counter-examples" to Sterling's Radio Shack pocket calculator case. According to Hanna, the first counter-example produces "the opposite of Sterling's results" (Section 1.5), while the second points to a "shortcoming in Sterling's analysis" (Section 1.6). However, it seems to me that Hanna's counter-examples illustrate a different point than Sterling's decreasing cost case. Sterling shows that, in periods of falling prices, it is *possible* for a firm to maintain physical capital and report current cost profits while financial capital is being eroded. Hanna shows that, in periods of falling prices, income under physical capital maintenance is sometimes a better estimate of "economic income" (i.e., income under a present value model of asset valuation and income determination) than is income under financial capital maintenance. Thus, Sterling and Hanna illustrate different rather than contradictory conclusions. In fact, by assuming an average-of-year replacement cost less than $9,000, Case (b) of Hanna's first counter-example could be used to confirm Sterling's point as well as Hanna's. (Also, it should be noted that if Hanna's first counter-example is extended to year 1, income under physical capital maintenance in Case (b) does not equal economic income as in year 0. Moreover, equality of these two incomes in year 0 occurs for a replacement cost of $9,000 only.)

In Hanna's second counter-example, (an extension of Sterling's pocket calculator case), financial capital declines from $100 to $50 under the "productive capacity" maintenance approach, thus illustrating rather than contradicting Sterling's contention. It is true that Sterling is concerned to maintain financial capital in order to keep up the level of dividend payments to stockholders. However, in Hanna's example, the physical capital model seems to have no advantage over financial capital in this respect. Under physical capital, Hanna in effect refunds $50 of financial capital as part of the January dividend of $90 and anticipates $90 net income per month thereafter. Under financial capital maintenance, the January dividend is only $40, but net income per month thereafter will exceed $90 by a return on the additional $50 capital which is retained by limiting the January dividend to $40.

## 2.3 Trading Firms—i.e., Firms That Buy And Sell In The Same Market

Sterling notes that: "Arguments for current costing are invariably couched in terms of merchandising or manufacturing firms" (Section 3.13). If transaction costs are ignored, share traders, commodity traders and other so-called "trading" firms would always report virtually zero operating profits/losses under a strict application of the physical capital maintenance concept. This is because replacement costs and selling prices are equal for identical units. As Sterling says: "The consequent of a zero profit for *all trading firms*, for *all exchanges* for *all price changes* is absurd. There is no point in measuring profit if one knows a priori that its magnitude will always be zero" (Section 3.13). Several Symposium authors seem to agree that this is a sizable chink in the armour of physical capital. On the contrary, Revsine has, in my opinion, an eminently sensible remedy for this problem. Holding gains/losses are integral to and result from the *operating* activities of trading firms. In fact, holding gains/losses *are* operating income to such firms and should be treated as such (Revsine, Section 4.52). I venture that the treatment of holding gains/losses as operating income in such cases would be no more inconsistent than the treatment of a Mack truck as inventory by a vehicle distributor and as plant by a civil engineering contractor.

Whereas Revsine sees the case of the trading firm as an exception to the rule of operating capability maintenance, the Australian standard setters found an ingenious turn of phrase to avoid the appearance of making an exception. "The operating capability of an entity buying and selling on the same market is its reinvestment ability" (AARF, 1980, para 6). "Reinvestment ability" is measured by the current cost of assets held. It is maintained when end-of-period current cost equals or exceeds beginning-of-period current cost adjusted by a general price index (specifically, the consumer price index). Real changes in current cost (i.e., differences between movements in the specific prices of assets held and changes in the general price level) represent changes in reinvestment ability (operating capability) and are recognized as gains and losses. Ma correctly sees the recommended treatment as "inconsistent with the treatment of current costs generally" (Section 3.3). In effect, it amounts to application of a financial capital maintenance concept in conjunction with a current market price basis of asset valuation.

Even if we accept that holding gains/losses are operating income in trading firms, a problem remains as to how merchandising and manufacturing firms should account (under a physical capital maintenance model) for marketable securities and other assets that they buy and sell in the same market. Such transactions can hardly be described as "operating" transactions, and perhaps for this reason could be designated as "exceptions" to the rule of operating capability maintenance. Revsine argues (Section 4.51) that since many of the assets in question are essentially non-physical assets, a physical capital maintenance concept ceases to be relevant. On the other hand, it is noteworthy that a sale of plant and equipment does not qualify as an "exception" to the rule of operating capability maintenance under the Canadian *Exposure Draft*. Sterling cites this as evidence that "reporting a zero profit for such exchanges is precisely the objective of physical capital proponents" (Section 3.13, fn. 12).

No doubt, the standard setters could devise a logical set of rules for determining the "exceptions." However, merchandising and manufacturing firms would then be required to apply different capital maintenance concepts to different groups of assets—financial capital maintenance to the "exceptions," and physical capital maintenance to other items. Also, some would argue that the Revsine proposal for treating holding gains/losses of trading firms as operating income is a reversion to financial capital maintenance for the trading assets of those firms. A move from single to multiple capital maintenance concepts within firms and to different capital maintenance concepts for different firms surely conflicts with the accounting profession's aim to narrow the range of alternative practices.

The standard setters have dealt with the trader rather unevenly. The Australian treatment has been outlined above. In the U.K. and Canada, the trading inventory is to be treated as a monetary asset (entering into the monetary working capital adjustment) and transaction profits/losses are to be reported on an historical cost basis (by direction in the U.K., and by implication in Canada). (See *Guidance Notes on SSAP 16*, paras. 79, 102; Canadian *Exposure Draft*, para. C.35.) *FAS 33* does not address the issue.

### 2.4 Partial Investment In The Physical Unit

Sterling finds fault with the physical capital maintenance model because it does not take account of the opportunity cost of holding cash. Cash could have been invested in physical assets that would yield holding gains/losses. Since the gain or loss from not investing cash in other assets is not taken into account, the procedure of deducting current costs from revenues does not, in Sterling's opinion, achieve the objective of reporting distributable income (and maintaining physical capital) (Sterling, Section 3.14).

It seems to me that two factors ameliorate the force of this criticism. Firstly, there appears to be a presumption, with no citation of supporting empirical evidence, that firms hold significant amounts of *idle* cash. It is only cash in excess of working capital needs that is available for alternative uses. Cash comprising needed working capital includes both the "transactions" and the "precautionary" cash of economic theory and forms part of the investment required to maintain operating capability. With respect to this cash, Sterling's question as to "which price index should be used to adjust the cash" has an answer in the U.K's monetary working capital adjustment and a similar recommendation in the Canadian *Exposure Draft*.

Secondly, the physical capital model claims to maintain actual, not potential physical capital. Idle cash is not essential to maintenance of existing operating capability but offers the potential to increase that operating capability. Alternatively, one can say that the physical form of cash is cash, and it takes $x to maintain x physical units of cash. Under this interpretation, physical and financial capital maintenance coincide in the case of cash. However, this is admittedly a controversial interpretation. It is probably overstretching the definition of operating capability to include units of money among the physical goods and services to be maintained.

In the context of physical capital maintenance, there is another problem related to certain cash resources. Skinner points out that current cost depreciation charges cause cash to be withheld from distribution and so provide for future replacement of operating capability. However, if prices are continually rising, such withholdings will not be sufficient for their purpose. He therefore criticizes CCA because it "makes no provision for maintenance of the operating capability of cash withheld from distribution for *future* replacement of physical operating capability *already consumed*." (Section 4.2. Emphasis in original.) The problem can be solved by making provision for backlog depreciation a requirement rather than the option it is in the standards or proposals of all four countries under discussion (Skinner, incidentally, does not like this solution.) Another plausible answer to Skinner's complaint can be found in the *Guidance Notes on SSAP 16*: "... depreciation charges create retained funds which are normally reinvested in other assets, fixed or current. These assets are then subject to adjustments to allow for price changes. In this way allowance for price changes is made on the funds retained in the entity as a result of past depreciation charges" (para. 52).

### 2.5 Summary

Of the four circumstances that, according to Sterling, invalidate or make impossible the application of physical capital measures, one—replacement with non-identical units—appears to be intractable (the only feasible solution being a virtual reversion to financial capital maintenance). Another—decreasing current costs— begs the question as to what capital maintenance objective should be adopted by accountants. The other two circumstances pose difficult problems—how to account for assets bought and sold in the same market, and how to interpret the physical capital maintenance implications of (idle) cash balances. In my view, the latter two problems are capable of satisfactory resolution, though some readers might find the solutions suggested above somewhat strained.

Even if we take the optimistic view that a changing asset structure and technological change present implementation and measurement problems to which time will bring satisfactory solutions, we are still left with the fundamental question of objectives. Why should maintenance of the firm's physical capital be a primary objective of accounting? This question is addressed below.

### 3. A QUESTION OF OBJECTIVES

It is true, as Sterling observes, that the business entity per se, being inanimate, has no objectives. It pursues the goals that humans set for it (Sterling, Section 3.22). Which group of human participants in the affairs and fortunes of the firm should then be dominant—i.e., whose interests should we account for, and what capital maintenance concept best serves those interests?

I want to avoid becoming mired in the related question as to whether the interests of different groups of participants can be satisfied by a single accounting. Although the reporting of current cost and historical cost/constant dollar measures as supplementary data is an example of data expansion already in operation, I would also prefer to eschew the question of multiple reports and assume that a single set of so-called general-purpose or multiple-purpose reports (with limited supplementary data) is the most practicable form of external reporting for the immediate future.

However, on these matters, Skinner has some pertinent comments that are worth attending. He observes that stockholders and debt-holders may place emphasis on different measures (e.g., operating profit, liquidity), but sees that as a problem of providing enough information for both rather than choosing between them. Moreover, all stakeholders in the firm must be interested in such key measures as profitability (however measured) and solvency, because the interests of all are affected by the entity's ability to survive. Skinner therefore believes that even under a decision-usefulness approach to accounting, accountants should report key dimensions of a multi-faceted "economic reality of an entity's position and past performance as one input into user decision processes" (Sections 2.1 and 2.2). This economic reality "does not change dependent on the user." (However, Section 6 of Skinner's paper implies that the key dimensions of economic reality and their bases of measurement can be different for different broad categories of business.) Many accountants talk glibly about some nebulous concept of "economic reality," and Scott (Section 2.1) questions what Skinner means by the term. The answer, as far as can be gleaned from Skinner's paper, is that "economic reality" refers to economic *facts* that are observable or verifiable by reference to real-world phenomena or can be deduced logically from such phenomena. Examples are cost prices and selling prices. In contrast, "income" is an "artificial construct."

In portraying "economic reality," disaggregative multi-dimensional reporting is necessary to illuminate the principal factors affecting enterprise performance. For example, since holding gains/losses and operating income are affected by different economic forces, reporting them separately has what Skinner aptly terms "analytical value" in assessing future prospects (and in evaluating historical results) (Sections 4.2 and 5). In the context of disaggregative multi-dimensional reporting, a single bottom line "Net Income" figure is not only unnecessary, says Skinner, but gives unwarranted pre-eminence to a particular measurement methodology and a particular combination of economic components (Sections 2.1 and 2.2). Thus, like Hanna (Section 1.7), he commends the FASB's decision in *FAS 33* to present information on alternative measurement bases and thereby avoid any preferred definition of net income (Skinner, end of Section 2.2). To Sterling, the same decision confirms his view that the FASB sees its function as one of achieving compromise among its constituents. Instead of offering a "smorgasbord of data" (in the words of a dissenting member of the FASB), the FASB must, in Sterling's view, "select one of its positions" to avoid muddled confusion and attendant dissatisfaction among users (Section 1.1). In the end, practical considerations also bring Skinner closer to this view. Along with some other Symposium participants, he concludes that a single-valued "income" is so firmly fixed in the public mind as the principal output of the accounting process, that it will be necessary to humour users' expectations of a bottom line and adopt a definition of income for at least the immediate future (end of Section 2.2, and end of Section 6).[3] Thus we have come full circle to the question of whose interests we should account for.

In North America, the position of the stockholders (and potential stockholders) as the dominant interest group for external financial reporting purposes is unchallenged. The stockholder generally wishes to buy a wide range of consumer goods and services, whereas the firm's interests tend to be more specialized. It is therefore plausible to argue that, whereas the well-offness of the firm can be maintained by keeping up its physical capital, the well-offness of the stockholder depends on his buying power as a consumer. Thus, protection of the stockholder's interests demands

---

[3] Also, in critiquing *FAS 33's* three-column income statement/(para. 70, Schedule B), Livingstone and Weil argue that the credibility of accounting statements requires "a single story not three" (Section 2.3). This criticism is directed at the reporting format rather than at the inclusion of the three income concepts. However, disapproval of the latter seems to be implied by a later comment that "a more logical conclusion ... is that the required disclosures ... are too complex" (end of Section 2.3).

a financial capital maintenance concept with general purchasing power as the measuring unit. (E.g., see Sterling, Section 3.21, and Skinner, Section 2.2)

It seems to me that the conclusion derived here for the stockholder can be extended to the firm. If flexibility and adaptability in directions taken and product range manufactured or traded are important to the firm, maintenance of purchasing power over a broad range of goods would seem to be appropriate to the firm as well as to the stockholder. Skinner, for one, argues that the use of an index (which reflects a changing basket of items) is a "sufficient" answer to the problem of replacement with non-identical goods in many cases (e.g., retailers could use a "chained index" of the goods in which they deal) (Section 4.3). The broader the range of goods, the broader the index, moving in the extreme to a general index (Skinner, Section 4.3), and therefore, I surmise, to financial capital maintenance.

Also, in our earlier discussion of replacement with non-identical units, we castigated the physical capital maintenance concept because its assumption of a static asset structure makes it inapplicable to many firms. It would be inconsistent to now approve it as a suitable capital maintenance concept for the firm in contrast to a financial capital maintenance concept for the owners. While a given firm may be interested in a narrow range of goods at a given time, the nature of its activities and the types of assets it buys and sells will in many cases change over time. True, a broadening of the firm's activities into *new* fields calls for an *addition* to physical capital rather than a *change* in the composition of existing physical capital. However, a *change* in the firm's activities calls for a change in the structure of physical capital, and a different set of prices becomes relevant to maintenance of operating capability. The concept of physical capacity cannot handle the dynamics of changing directions and changing technology of the firm.

Lee tells us that "in the U.K. the reporting entity is more and more being viewed by accountants as a collection of different stakeholders, only some of which will be its owners." In this context, physical capital maintenance can be viewed as a means of achieving a common objective—survival of the reporting entity (Lee, Section 5.5). Presumably, a decline in physical capital is deemed to be a step towards oblivion. Revsine too, finds merit in physical capital measures by focussing his analysis on "an examination of what capital maintenance concept appears to be most appropriate for aggregate national policy decisions" (Section 1). It is the firm—and not its stockholders—that is regulated, taxed or controlled as the focus of attention in national policy decisions. Add the assumption that tax or regulatory policy should not confiscate capital, and define capital in "real" terms as the economist does. It follows that physical capital measures and not financial capital measures are appropriate for national policy decisions (Revsine, Section 2.1).

The failure of physical capital maintenance to cope with the dynamics of change remains. However, putting this problem aside for a moment, it is interesting to speculate about the appropriate form of accounting if survival of the firm (calling for physical capital maintenance) and maintenance of general purchasing power are dual objectives of the stockholder as the dominant party for whom we account. Stockholder well-offness (in general purchasing power terms) will be amply protected by maintenance of physical capital when the general price level is rising more slowly or falling faster than the prices of assets held by the firm. But physical capital maintenance will not give this protection when the general price level rises faster or falls more slowly than prices of the firm's assets. This is somewhat different from Lee's opinion that "The maintenance of physical capital may be sensible when prices are rising, but maintenance of financial capital ... may be more sensible when they are falling" (Section 5.2).[4]

However, it is also clear that maintenance of the general purchasing power of stockholders' equity would not maintain physical capital when the general price level is increasing more slowly or falling faster than prices of the firm's assets. I somehow doubt that advocates of financial capital maintenance would be content to regard net income as fully distributable if 100% distribution would reduce the operating capability of the firm. In the jungle of business competition, maintenance (or even growth) of the physical size of the firm might well be a condition of long-run survival, and survival is necessary to long-run maintenance of stockholder wealth measured in any terms.

Thus, in order to achieve the stockholders' dual objectives (and in order to meet the legitimate interests of other stakeholders in survival of the firm), the capital to be maintained would have to be the higher of physical and financial capital. (Thus, incidentally, Scott probably meant to say "higher" rather than "lower" in suggesting a "lower of physical or financial rule" (Scott, Section 1.2), unless he was referring to distributable income rather than capital to be maintained.) Both general price level adjustments and the specific prices of the firm's assets would then have to be incorporated into the accounts. I shall, of course, avoid further exploration of the ramifications of such an accounting system by pleading that I have already strayed too far from the legitimate task of a synthesizer. In any case, we have arrived at this system only by putting aside the inability of physical capital measures to cope with the dynamics of change.

## 4. CURRENT COST INCREASES—CURRENT EXPENSE OR INCREMENTAL INVESTMENT?

As we have seen, the essential difference between financial and physical capital maintenance concepts is the treatment of holding gains/losses. Under financial capital maintenance, holding gains/losses are included in income; under physical capital maintenance, they are not. Milburn takes up this distinction to expound with crystal clarity a point that I have always thought to be especially critical in evaluating and choosing between the two capital maintenance approaches. Given its importance (in my opinion), I will state the matter at some length.

It is plausible to argue that if an item was bought for $10, the buyer is better-off in some sense than if he had to pay the current cost of $12. This is the financial capital maintenance point of view. On the other hand, the physical capital maintenance perspective sees no benefit to the owner from the cost saving as replacement requires $12 if the item is sold. Even when the $2 saving is realized by sale of the item, it is excluded from income under physical capital maintenance because it represents no change in physical operating capacity.

Leaving aside the possibility of non-identical replacement, physical capital logic holds that when an item is sold, its current replacement cost rather than its original

---

[4] It also differs in some respects from Sterling's analysis in Section 3.12. Both Lee and Sterling seem implicitly to assume no change in the general price level.

(historical) cost is an expense of making the sale. An implication is that the selling price should be sufficient to cover current cost, and perhaps that profit margins should be geared to current cost rather than to historical cost. Milburn suggests that the validity of this implied cause and effect (or input-output) relationship between costs and revenues is open to serious challenge. There is a fundamental question here as to whether current cost is a legitimate cost of the item sold or a new investment made in expectation of a future return. The operations of an entity can be looked upon as a series of ventures, each one comprising a cycle running from cash outlay (investment) to recovery of investment (plus a profit margin) through collection of sales revenues—i.e., back to cash. Upon completion of one cycle. rising input prices might mean that entry to a new cycle at the same level of operating capacity calls for an increased dollar investment outlay—such as the increase from \$10 to \$12 in our example. The investment should, of course, be made if the expected return on investment is satisfactory. But the expected return is evaluated in relation to the actual investment outlay, not in relation to some future and as yet unincurred level of replacement cost that will constitute the investment required to enter the next cycle. (See Milburn, Section 2.)

Milburn uses the case of replacement with a non-identical item (Sterling's mini-skirt maxi-skirt example) to exemplify the confounding effects of incorporating next period's input costs into this period's income computation. Say a company sells mini-skirts this period (or cycle) and replaces with maxi-skirts that will be sold next period (cycle). "It seems entirely inappropriate to use the current cost of maxis as the basis for measuring income from minis.... [T]here are clearly two 'ventures'—the miniskirt venture in period 1 and the maxiskirt venture in period 2." Also: "The results of the mini venture may not be repeatable—they may be a lousy indicator of the future—but that is the venture the company was in during the period. I suggest that repeatability of results should *not* be a condition for the recognition of income ..." (Milburn, Section 3. Emphasis in original.)

Milburn's analysis points up the fact that the assumed cycle of business activity is from cash to cash under financial capital maintenance and from physical units to physical units under the physical capital maintenance approach—a difference also noted by Sterling (Section 4.23). Where should the cycle of activity be deemed to commence—with cash or physical assets? Perhaps an answer to this question takes us into the domain of subjective preference, but I believe there is a fundamental social issue here. Should firms be permitted to charge higher current selling prices because it will cost more to buy replacement items for sale in the future? Certainly, examples of public rejection of this idea can be cited. Skinner reports that oil and gas companies in some jurisdictions are forbidden by government to raise selling prices to reflect purchase price increases, until inventories bought at the old prices are deemed to be exhausted (Section 2.2). Also, the newspapers report from time to time that instances of raising the retail prices of goods already in stock when replacement costs increase are condemned by consumers and consumer organizations as "profiteering." On the other hand, the practice of selling real estate, works of art and certain other kinds of assets at market value without reference to historical cost is universally accepted. In adopting physical capital maintenance, society would be sanctioning a general repudiation of any necessary connection between historical costs and selling prices. Of course, competitive forces may sever this connection too, but historical costs do currently play a significant role in economic price theory.

## 5. PREDICTIVE ABILITY

An issue addressed by many participants in the Symposium is the alleged usefulness of the physical capital maintenance model in pursuing the objectives of forecasting and maintaining or maximizing future cash flows. As noted in *FAS 33* (para. 2), provision of information that will assist prediction of future cash flows was taken as a fundamental objective of accounting in the FASB's *Statement of Financial Accounting Concepts No. 1* (FASB, 1978). Also, the maintenance (or, rather, maximization of the present value) of future cash flows coincides with the objectives of owners. Therefore, any model possessing predictive power with respect to such flows has much to commend it. The issue is, of course, an empirical one and conclusive evidence favouring any particular model is still lacking.[5] The jury must therefore remain out on this issue.

However, the prospects for vindication of the current cost model's alleged predictive prowess are by no means promising. Revsine (1973, pp. 108–114 and 121–22) and Carsberg (Section 2.1) give plausible reasons why changes in current costs (holding gains/losses) and changes in cash operating flows sometimes will and sometimes will not covary in the same direction. Thus, with respect to either the inclusion of holding gains/losses in income (financial capital maintenance) or their exclusion from income (physical capital maintenance), one cannot generalize that the trustworthiness of income as a predictor of future cash operating flows will be improved thereby. Nor can one generalize that current cost in the balance sheet will be reliable in a predictive role. In fact, it is only under very stringent and unrealistic conditions that a priori argument can justify current cost as a reliable surrogate for the discounted present value of future cash flows or concede any kind of predictive accuracy to either the physical or financial capital versions of current cost income. (See Revsine, 1973, Chapter 4.)

Butterworth points out that the ability of a firm to generate future cash flows depends on numerous factors (such as management skills, research capability and labour relations) that are reflected in neither the financial statements nor the market prices of capital assets. It is therefore "a source of wonder" to Butterworth that accounting writers give any attention to capital asset prices as a basis for the valuation of future cash flows (Section 1). In any case, as Carsberg observes: "The predictive ability approach ... is agnostic as far as capital maintenance is concerned" (Section 2.3). Predictions of cash flows might be improved by reporting holding gains/losses separately from the results of operating activities, but the predictions will be the same whether holding gains/losses are labelled as income or not. Skinner exemplifies this agnosticism by declaring that he does not care whether changes in current cost are reported as income or not, as long as they are reported somewhere (Section 4.5).

One cannot deny Sterling's conclusion that "the ability of physical capital measures to forecast themselves or to forecast cash flows has not been demonstrated" (Section 5). In fact, none of the Symposium authors expressed much faith in the predictive power of any kind of income measure. However, Sterling, I think,

---

[5] The findings of a couple of relevant empirical studies are summarized in Revsine (1973, pp. 134–38), and Revsine (this volume, Chapter 3, end of Section 4.4).

unnecessarily overstates the case against the predictive ability of current cost measures. For example, the claim that more rapid inventory turnover can increase sales volume without any increase in inventory investment depends (as Revsine notes, Section 4.1) on an implicit assumption that inventory control is inefficient. In fact, if the quantity sold is "independent" of the quantity on hand (as Sterling claims, Section 4.11), it follows that firms would not need to carry inventory at all. Moreover, I think few participants in the Symposium would agree with Sterling's view that exit values (or "cash equivalents" of assets) provide a "generalized surrogate for management's expectations"[6] (Section 4.16, and end of Section 4.14). Certainly, exit values of specialized or immobile assets can be insignificant by comparison with expectations of their cash flow generating potential and will therefore be poor surrogates for the latter. Carsberg exemplifies the typical view in seeing the normal business situation as one where use of the asset represents a better option than sale, both before and after a change in its price[7] (end of Section 2.1). In that case, current cost should often be a better representation than exit value of management's expectations. However, we have also seen that neither a priori logic nor the sparse empirical evidence gives us any reason to have faith in the ability of current cost to accurately reflect future cash flows. Moreover, the predictive ability of a measure is an empirically testable hypothesis, and, until the evidence is in, there is little to be gained from armchair speculation.

Nevertheless, Revsine turns the lack of evidence about the predictive ability of current cost into an argument for physical capital maintenance. He complains (end of Section 3.1) that:

> "The primary deficiency of the current input cost financial capital mainte-
> nance approach is that it monitors changes in only one element—input
> costs—to reflect changes in well-offness ... It is the relationship between
> changes in input costs and changes in output selling prices which determines
> whether a firm's relative position has improved, deteriorated, or remained
> constant."

This criticism is directed at the recognition of holding gains/losses as an element of income without full knowledge of what will be the revenue effects (if any) of the cost changes comprising holding gains/losses, and without knowing the lag between cost changes and revenue effects. "By denying any income statement impact to these holding gains/losses until they do show up in operating profit, the physical capital approach avoids reporting ex ante profit signals which, in the face of uncertainty, may subsequently not come to fruition" (Revsine, Section 3.3).

Revsine's argument seems to be: Saving $1 of costs today might (or might not) result in $1 loss of revenue tomorrow (or might be related to the same source as such a loss), so today's saving should not be recognized as income (even if realized). Carsberg

---

[6] In conversation, Sterling has indicated that "floor of management's expectations" would better express his meaning than "surrogate for management's expectations."

[7] In similar vein, Skinner argues (end of Section 4.3) that when recoverable amount has to be substituted for current cost, the significance of the current operating profit figure shifts from portraying the viability of a going concern to portraying the potential for return from alternative uses of cash to be derived from sale or use of existing assets.

articulates an alternative point of view (Section 2.1, emphasis added):

> "Price changes are relatively unreliable predictors of changes in cash flows and that is a strong argument for reporting their effects as *separate components of income*. Users can then assess their significance in the light of their background knowledge of the economy and of market conditions in the industry concerned."

The financial capital maintenance version of CCA which recognizes *unrealized* holding gains/losses as income is certainly vulnerable to Revsine's criticism. However, neither the standard setters nor the proponents of financial capital maintenance attending the Symposium (with the possible exception of Carsberg) appear to be advocating that kind of financial capital maintenance model. The financial capital maintenance models sanctioned by *FAS 33* are "historical cost in nominal dollars" and "historical cost in constant dollars." The only holding gains/losses included in income under both of these models are *realized* holding gains/losses. Any unrealized future revenue effects are, as Revsine would agree, hypothetical. However, even a conservative "bird in the hand" principle of accounting would recognize *realized* cost savings as income.

## 6. PURCHASING POWER GAINS/LOSSES AND POLITICS

Little reference has been made so far to the Livingstone-Weil paper. This is because it addresses different concerns than those which tend to integrate the other papers. What distinguishes the Livingstone-Weil paper is that it focuses intensively on an analysis and critique of *FAS 33*'s disclosure requirements, and deals with some related conceptual issues and implementation problems. There is even a critique of *FAS 33*'s illustrative disclosure *formats*, along with proposals for improvements in format—e.g., to eliminate or minimize the potential confusion inherent in adding and subtracting incommensurate units.

Livingstone-Weil identify seven different income measures that are either reported under *FAS 33* or derivable from the reported numbers. We have already noted Sterling's view of this *embarras de richesse* as the politics of compromise in action—yielding a smorgasbord of data which has something for everyone. Livingstone-Weil find that two of the seven income measures even lack an interpretable concept of capital maintenance. Both of these are *constant dollar* measures of "Income from Continuing Operations," but both exclude the "Purchasing Power Gain/Loss on Monetary Items." (See Section 2.25.) Livingstone-Weil point out that *any* constant dollar income measure must include this gain/loss in order to have an interpretable concept of capital maintenance. Moreover, they assume as axiomatic that "without some concept of capital to be maintained by a measure, that measure cannot be an income measure" (Section 3).

One of the two measures at issue is "Historical Cost/Constant Dollar Income from Continuing Operations," a prime reporting requirement of *FAS 33*. *FAS 33 requires* that this number be reported separately from (and exclusive of) purchasing power gains and losses on monetary items. Rationalizations offered by Livingstone-Weil for reluctance to admit purchasing power gains/losses to income are that they are not cash flows and that the timing of realization is controversial in the case of gains/losses on noncurrent items. However, Weil, in his presentation at the Symposium, speculated (rather shrewdly, according to one well-informed member of the audience) that the risk of attracting income tax on purchasing power gains (if reported as income) was a major reason for the separate reporting requirement. Consequently, one of *FAS 33*'s principal income measures not only lacks theoretical merit but is readily explicable in terms of political expediency.

Livingstone-Weil see the unresolved problem of what to do with purchasing power gains/losses on monetary items as a major weakness (or gap) in the theoretical underpinnings of *FAS 33*. They suggest two possible solutions. Both are controversial. Current cost accounting for debt is one solution. The other, which they seem to prefer, is based on the "theorem" that, over the life of a firm, constant dollar income differs from nominal dollar income by an amount equal to the purchasing power gain/loss on the cash investment by the owners (Section 3.3). Thus, it is suggested that periodic increments in the purchasing power gain/loss on cash invested by owners be added to/subtracted from nominal dollar income (Section 3.3). Under this mode of accounting, purchasing power gains on net debt never have to be reported. Also, net income will always be lower in years of inflation than under the conventional GAAP (nominal dollar) model. Livingstone-Weil argue that these results "match the intuition of both the unsophisticated reader and the experienced analyst" (Section 3.3). Clearly such results also have strong political appeal, and some will be tempted to view the proposed method of accounting as a rationalized escape route from a political dilemma. Livingstone-Weil would certainly argue for theoretical merit against political expediency as a standard-setting criterion. Nevertheless, one needs to be mindful of the warning sounded by Watts and Zimmerman (1979) that rationalizations or "excuses" can be found for any one of numerous alternative accounting treatments. As a result, perceptions of relative theoretical merit can sometimes become a matter of political bias. Moreover, the temptation for standard setters to camouflage political compromise with plausible arguments must be strong.

In the same context, Scott observes (perhaps on a teasing note) that the central problem addressed by the Symposium—the choice of a capital maintenance concept (along with its accompanying rationalizations)—has an obvious solution if the goal is to minimize reported income in periods of rising prices (Section 3). Lee, however, is very serious about *SSAP 16* being a political expedient (though most of his comments to this effect came in the oral presentation). According to Lee, the U.K. accounting profession was reluctant to do away with historical cost accounting but felt under pressure to do something. The result is a document which is lacking even in plausible rationalizations, concentrating on the "how" rather than the "why." The politics of standard-setting in Canada and Australia received scant discussion. Perhaps, as Scott says, the political dimension of the standard-setting process deserved more attention in the Symposium papers than it was given.

## 7. SOME SPECIAL FEATURES OF THE STANDARDS

Two novel features of *SSAP 16* are the "gearing adjustment" and the "monetary working capital adjustment" (MWCA). Identical adjustments incorporated into the Canadian *Exposure Draft* are called the "financing adjustment" and the "net productive monetary items adjustment" (NPMIA), respectively. Different, but comparable, adjustments with similar objectives are proposed in Australia. Neither adjustment is required by *FAS 33*. (See *FAS 33* paras. 128-9). Opinions differed among

Symposium participants on the merits of these adjustments, which we will discuss below under their *SSAP 16* names.

### 7.1 The Gearing Adjustment

The U.K., Canadian and Australian versions of a CCA Income Statement feature two income numbers. Terminology differs between the three countries, but "Current Cost Income of the Enterprise" is one name for the surplus after maintaining operating capability in full (but before interest and taxes in the U.K. and Canada). The second income number—"Current Cost Income Attributable to Shareholders"—makes incomplete provision for maintenance of operating capability. It assumes that positive or negative increments in current cost of the debt-financed portion of operating capability will be matched by increments in debt finance and can therefore be taken to income. Thus a difference between the two income numbers is the "Gearing Adjustment," which (in the U.K. and Canada) recognizes a portion of realized holding gains/losses as a component of "Current cost Income Attributable to the Shareholders." The proportion recognized is basically equal to the percentage of long-term debt in the total capital structure. (The Australian gearing adjustment is simply the purchasing power gain/loss on long-term debt.) The rationale for the gearing adjustment is quite straightforward. It assumes that a firm's debt-equity ratio will remain fairly stable and that a portion of current cost increases can therefore be financed by debt (without changing the risk characteristics of the firm).

Lee objects to this assumption as "dangerous" (Section 3). Ma's final position seems to be one of approval (Section 2.21). Presumably because the gearing adjustment assumes certain funding arrangements, Livingstone-Weil see the funds flow statement rather than the income statement as the proper place for it (Section 4). In fact, they join Hanna in proposing that the funds flow statement rather than the income statement is the appropriate place to reflect the financial impact of maintaining (and expanding) productive capacity (Hanna, Section 2.2; Livingstone-Weil, Section 4). Skinner's reservations about the gearing adjustment culminate in a recommendation that it be eliminated by uncoupling the accounting for holding gains/losses from the provision for maintenance of equity capital and maintaining the latter in general purchasing power terms.

Like Scott (Section 1.3) and Hanna (Section 2.53), I was surprised at the negative reactions to the gearing adjustment. The assumption of a fairly stable debt-equity ratio seems to accord with common financial practice. Failure to make the gearing adjustment would seem to imply that cost increases are to be 100% equity financed. Also, as Scott says, the adjustment fills a gap in CCA systems. A major impact of changing prices on the firm is the monetary gain/loss on long-term debt, and this is precisely what the Australian gearing adjustment is. The gearing adjustment in the U.K. and Canada is a similar such gain/loss computed according to a firm-specific (and therefore firm-relevant) index of current capacity cost. However, in interpreting the U.K. or Canadian gearing adjustment, one must not forget that it comprises a portion of *realized* holding gains/losses only. As Skinner observes: "Possibly, therefore, a substantial part of the outcome of the debt financing is omitted from the reckoning (even though interest ... is shown in full as a reduction of income for the residual equity)." While there are probably good practical reasons for excluding unrealized holding gains/losses, the omission does reduce the explanatory power of the gearing adjustment (Skinner, Section 4.5).

## 7.2 The Monetary Working Capital Adjustment

When prices change, accounts receivable and accounts payable balances and the amount of cash required to support operating activities—i.e, monetary working capital requirements—will also change. The MWCA gives explicit recognition to this fact in a charge/credit to income for an estimate of the change in monetary working capital needs due to price changes. The adjustment therefore recognizes monetary working capital as part of the operating capability of the business.

The MWCA attracted little negative comment from Symposium authors and discussants. Livingstone-Weil would put it in the funds statement along with the gearing adjustment. Skinner points out that it can yield anomalous results in some cases of short-run fluctuations in working capital requirements. He concludes "somewhat uneasily" that a clear case for the MWCA as a charge against income has not been made (Section 4.2). I find this curious because elsewhere in his paper Skinner takes the position that even nonproductive monetary assets should be included in the capital to be maintained under CCA. On the technical side, he faults the method of calculating part of the adjustment and notes a lack of consensus on what items to include in it (Section 4.4).

On the positive side, Scott defends the MWCA on the same grounds that he supports the gearing adjustment—it is in effect a loss/gain on net short-term monetary assets calculated by means of a firm-specific (and therefore firm-relevant) index (Section 1.4).

*7.3 Incomplete Measurement Of Physical Capital*    Skinner (Section 4.2) and Lee (Section 2.2) criticize the omission of certain assets from the capital to be maintained at current cost under CCA proposals. Although directed to proposals in their own countries, the comments of both authors have general application.

Skinner points out that, with the exception of the so-called "trading inventories," non-productive non-monetary assets (such as portfolio investment) are left to be accounted for at historical cost (Section 4.2). *FAS 33* does not even make an exception for "trading inventories." Thus total capital is not maintained at current cost. The reason lies in the choice of operating capability as the capital to be maintained. It would hardly be feasible to prescribe maintenance of the "operating capability" of non-operating assets. Skinner also complains that capital invested in non-productive monetary assets—e.g., cash in excess of current operating needs—is maintained indirectly by the back-door method of treating it as negative borrowing in computing the gearing adjustment (Section 4.2). This treatment is open to the criticism that it achieves maintenance of the relevant capital in arriving at "Current Cost Income Attributable to Shareholders" but not in computing "Enterprise Income," yet the assets are assets of the enterprise.

Physical capital is operationally defined in *FAS 33* as comprising inventories and property, plant and equipment (e.g., see para. 104(b)). In the U.K., Canadian and Australian versions of CCA, physical capital also includes monetary working capital as part of the investment needed to maintain operating capability. Lee points out that a company's physical capital includes much more than these items. Human resources, research capability, leased assets, patents and other intangibles may be key elements of a company's operating capability. (Butterworth makes the same point.) Maintenance of operating capability should therefore provide for replacement of these items at current cost, says Lee (Section 2.2), but none of the CCA proposals do so. Of course, neither do many of these items appear in the GAAP model balance sheet, or they do so at nominal amounts. However, this does not invalidate Lee's criticism. The concept of operating capability is not defined in relation to the balance sheet. Lee also holds that a complete CCA system should account in current cost terms for such period cost charges as rents, city taxes, heat and light, and even selling and administrative costs (Section 2.2).

Finally, it should be noted that none of the CCA proposals under consideration require that backlog depreciation be provided (though the concept is discussed in all of them). Failure to make this provision can prevent maintenance of operating capability in some cases.

In short, the extant CCA proposals represent only a *partial* application of the physical capital maintenance standard.

## 8. EXCURSIONS INTO ECONOMICS

### 8.1 Income And "Well-Offness"

Ma and Skinner both remark on the tendency of accountants to look to the discipline of economics for concepts of income that will prove viable in the construction of accounting theory.

To Ma, this is reason enough to conduct a tour through selected aspects of the theories of Pigou, Hayek, "early" Hicks, Lindahl and "late" Hicks, categorizing the authors as "fundists" and "materialists" along the way. The outcome is interesting, but unfruitful, notwithstanding the fact that a theoretical base for CCA can be forged (not in the pejorative sense) from Lindahl-Hicks. "Economists' definitions are often too subjective to be of use to accountants . . . Further, on this [i.e., concepts of income] as on most other matters, economists hold widely divergent and seemingly irreconcilable views" (Ma, Section 4).

Skinner's exploration of the concept of well-offness was similarly unfruitful. Many would agree that "income" is an "artificial construct." However, Skinner sees the potential for turning it into an operational concept by linking it with a definition of well-offness that can be "demonstrated empirically" (Section 2.2). Unfortunately, "well-offness" is not a single-valued concept, as Skinner, Revsine, Ma, Butterworth and others all note. Even the oft-quoted J. R. Hicks, who is credited (or blamed?) for originating the concept, saw it as ambiguous, ill-defined, lacking in operational meaning, a poor tool for economic analysis and too subjective to be usable in practice. (See Ma, Section 1.1, reporting on Hicks.) It is therefore not surprising that the outcome of this and Skinner's further excursions into conceptual issues is to conclude that neither capital maintenance, "true income," nor entity concepts are likely to lead us to consensus on methods of accounting in the face of price changes. Therefore, our aim should be to portray the multi-faceted "economic reality of an entity's financial position and past performance" (Skinner, Section 2.3).

There is nothing here to guide us in the choice of a capital maintenance concept, or even to suggest that a choice should be made in preference to following a "smorgasboard approach" to financial reporting.

### 8.2 An Agency Theory Perspective

Agency theory is a younger, more ambitious (and perhaps more promising) offspring of economic theory than is the concept of well-offness. At the Symposium,

Butterworth was chief spokesman for this new oracle of accounting rationale, with Scott adding some neutral comment. According to Butterworth, the central issue addressed by the Symposium calls for a radical change in both the accounting income paradigm and the conventional analytical methodology used in the papers presented. The new paradigm might be termed (in Scott's words) an agency theory perspective on the role of accounting. For the uninitiated reader, the following précis (based on Butterworth, et. al., 1981) of some key aspects of agency theory might be helpful.

The theory of risk sharing is concerned with the problem of dividing a risky return among two or more participants in an optimal manner. The optimum depends critically on the risk attitudes of the participants. The scope of the theory of risk sharing includes the problem of risk sharing among the stockholders, bondholders and other constituents of a corporation. An optimal sharing of risks and rewards is attainable only in a situation of complete mutual trust—i.e., in the absence of "moral hazard." The problem of "moral hazard" arises when an economic outcome can be influenced by the unilateral action of one party to a contract (e.g., an insured person setting fire to his house). Managers, as economic agents of investors, are subject to moral hazard with respect to the way they operate a company and report on its operations. In the presence of moral hazard, the rules for sharing economic benefits must be modified so as to provide appropriate incentives for a manager to take agreed actions and report the consequences using an agreed measurement and reporting system. Hence, an optimal contract between a manager and those who finance the entity managed must represent a trade-off between efficient sharing of economic consequences and efficient motivation of contractual performance. Agency theory is concerned with the changes needed in the form of efficient sharing rules when an economic agent must be provided with an incentive designed to counter the moral hazard present in pure risk sharing contracts. Ex post monitoring of managerial performance and of the computations that give effect to contractual arrangements is necessary to protect the interests of the contracting parties. However, monitoring is a costly process, and the aim should be to strike some optimum balance or trade-off between the costs of monitoring and constraining a manager's activities and the likely costs to holders of financial interests if poor monitoring permits free rein to self-interested managerial behaviour.

Butterworth's comments at the Symposium have to be interpreted in an agency theory context. Thus, he asserts that it is not the primary purpose of accounting to forecast cash flows or to facilitate capital maintenance. Rather it is to supply the information base and the set of rules needed to compute, in accordance with contractual sharing rights, the various financial interests in the firm, and to monitor the performance of managers as agents of these interests. In this context, the primary role of the income calculation turns out to be an incentive role. "Net Income" defined by an agreed set of measurement rules specifies the monetary amount accruing to certain key financial interests as a result of operations during a given period. It is therefore a suitable basis for evaluating, monitoring and compensating management. In this way, managers can be stimulated to pursue the interests of investors, and, in particular, the interests of the residual equityholders as reflected in the residual income number. In the process, an efficient utilization of resources within the economy should result. However, this is at the expense of "efficient risk sharing" among different categories of financial claimants, since the need to motivate and monitor management is not without cost to the optimal sharing of risks and rewards.

Unfortunately, Butterworth cannot tell us what form accounting should take in its incentive role. Resolution of this matter must await development of "an analytic approach which is completely different from that which has been conventionally followed ... " (This Volume, Chapter 5, Section 2). (See also Butterworth et. al., 1981, p. 62.) Scott, however is willing to speculate on the outcome. Ex post monitoring calls for an income number that is highly correlated with the quality and effort level of management and depends on objective data. In a cursory application of these criteria, Scott conjectures (on rather precarious grounds) that financial capital maintenance with realized holding gains/losses included in income is likely to be better than physical capital maintenance for the ex post monitoring role (Section 1.5).

Elsewhere, Butterworth, et. al., (1981, pp. 46–47) have argued in an agency theory context that objectivity, additivity and irrevocability are desirable properties of accounting information. These criteria, they say, together suggest the use of the money amount of actual transactions as the basis for aggregation in accounting, and "virtually preclude the use of any current value technique which is not based on some objective device such as an agreed time series." Moreover, they claim (p. 43) that any form of economic data other than transactions data as a basis for accounting "raises moral hazard difficulties since market exchanges which are not consummated cannot be verified, and therefore do not meet the objectivity criterion." On the other hand "the use of financial reports based on historical cost is a natural consequence of the incentive contract point of view" (p. 33). These appear to be strong pointers in the direction of historical cost, (in either nominal or constant dollars), which, of course, implies a financial capital maintenance concept.

## 9. CONCLUSION

What conclusions can be drawn with respect to a choice between physical and financial capital maintenance concepts for external reporting purposes?

Economic concepts of income and well-offness provide no answers; nor do they promise to repay further study of the matter. Agency theory has to postpone its answer, pending development and application of an analytic approach derived from the agency theory paradigm. The prognosis, however, strongly favours financial capital maintenance. A choice of capital maintenance concept cannot yet be made on the basis of ability to predict future cash flows, as the needed empirical evidence is lacking. Moreover, a priori logic does not support an expectation of consistently superior cash flow prediction on the part of any particular capital maintenance approach. Predictive ability and agency theory are potentially powerful avenues of inquiry, but they offer no immediate guide to the selection of a capital maintenance concept.

Our consideration of accounting objectives found some potential utility in both physical and financial capital maintenance, but we ran into the problem that the concept of physical capital maintenance cannot cope with the dynamics of a changing economic and technological environment. This problem emerged from our analysis of non-identical replacement. Inability to deal with non-identical asset replacement restricts the applicability of physical capital maintenance to firms with a static asset structure. To me, this is a critical limitation—a decisive reason for rejection of physical capital maintenance. Firms do change direction; they do change the composition of their product ranges, and there are associated changes in the nature and composition of physical plant and facilities. A resort to the monetary unit as the common dimension in which to express heterogeneous physical units is a reversion to financial capital maintenance. So too is the alternative of using a general price index to update the money "equivalent" of physical capital.

Also, in a world of rapidly changing technology, old plant and equipment is rarely replaced with an exact duplicate. To calculate the current cost depreciation base, replacement cost has to be adjusted for differences in operating costs and other differences in service potential. An editorial in *Business Week* (August 9, 1976, p. 80) aptly suggests that when accountants have done this, "they wind up in a curious dream world where *companies subtract savings they did not realize from costs they did not incur to derive earnings they did not make*" (emphasis added). Others have alluded to the same process as "what if?" accounting.

Of course, a financial capital maintenance version of CCA is also subject to the vagaries of "what if?" accounting and the shortcomings of contrived ad hoc responses to non-identical replacement. These are limitations of CCA, not of physical capital maintenance alone. However, the loss of objectivity occasioned by these limitations would at least be neutralized in the income statement by a financial capital maintenance version of CCA which included holding gains/losses in income on a realized basis only. Total net income would then be the same as under the GAAP model, with a breakdown between "Operating Income" (on a current cost basis) and "Realized Holding Gains/Losses." (See cell 3 (a) in Livingstone-Weil's Exhibit 1, and column (4) in their Exhibit 2). The information "advantages" of such a model by comparison with GAAP would be the disaggregation of income into components (albeit with some degree of subjectivity) and the reporting of current values in the balance sheet.

In any case, financial capital maintenance does not depend on CCA. Other models, perhaps with more tractable problems, are available—though, of course, each model adopts a different concept of financial capital. The Symposium did not directly address the matter of choosing among alternative financial capital maintenance models. However, several authors and participants made approving reference to the idea of using a one-line adjustment in the income statement to maintain common equity in constant dollars. (e.g., Skinner, Section 6; Hanna, Sections 2.2 and 3; Livingstone-Weil, Section 3.3.) Presumably, a one-line income statement adjustment would avoid the misleading asset values given by a general price level adjusted historical cost balance sheet when movements in specific and general price levels are significantly different. Subsequent to the date of the Symposium, the FASB Exposure Draft "Reporting Income, Cash Flows, and Financial Position of Business Enterprises" (November 16, 1981) recommended that "comprehensive income, which measures the overall performance of the enterprise, should be based on the financial concept of capital" (para. 14). A constant dollar measuring unit is also favoured in para. 14, but the choice of both measuring unit and attribute to be measured (e.g., historical cost, current cost) is postponed by paras 15 and 16 to later phases of the conceptual framework project.

Some Symposium authors concluded, in effect, that different concepts of capital maintenance are pertinent to different objectives or different sets of circumstances (e.g., Livingstone-Weil, Section 7). Thus, a niche was preserved for physical capital maintenance by designating it as appropriate for certain purposes (e.g., Revsine's national policy decisions) or for certain types of firms (e.g., Skinner's firms locked into their present lines of business indefinitely). I believe the limitations of the concept of physical capital maintenance go deeper than this. When accountants choose between FIFO and LIFO, they are choosing between two methods, both of which are capable of application to any inventory situation. A choice between the "full cost" and "successful efforts" approaches to accounting for oil and gas producing companies is a choice between two concepts both of which are capable of implementation in principle, even if the numerous tiers of subjective or arbitrary allocations cast doubt on the credibility of the results in practice. Physical capital maintenance, however, is not even applicable *in principle* to situations of non-identical replacement. The very idea of "maintaining" a kaleidoscopic physical capital is self-contradictory. When the firm is in the process of *changing* the nature or composition of its physical capital (operating capability), it is nonsensical to talk about *maintaining* it. To me, this is the critical flaw in the concept of physical capital maintenance. While no concept of capital maintenance forbids *growth* of capital in new directions, it does attribute certain continuing characteristics to the capital that is to be maintained. Thus, maintenance of physical capital (as defined by the standard setters) implies continuation of the existing physical characteristics of the fixed quantity of goods and services comprising operating capability. In this sense, the concept of physical capital maintenance is a static one which its proponents and the standard setters are compelling to serve in a dynamic setting, and it simply is not qualified to do the job. Hence it is found necessary to shore up its limitations with ad hoc adjustments. A concept of capital maintenance which is pledged to a fixed structure of capital (operating capability) as far as existing capital is concerned, lacks the flexibility necessary for adaptation to a dynamic real-world environment of changing products and changing production facilities.

Several of the Symposium authors (e.g., Sterling, Skinner, Milburn, Ma) observe that if the physical capital model does not work for certain types of firms or under certain circumstances, then the theory fails the test of general applicability. At best then, it can only be part of a more fundamental theory which tells us when different capital maintenance concepts are appropriate and how to interrelate or combine them (for example, in the case of a firm with both operating and trading type assets). Physical capital maintenance therefore fails to provide a comprehensive response to the problems of price change and inflation. Thus, it is difficult to disagree with Sterling's conclusion that "... measuring physical capital is, at best, a special case" (Section 3.15).

Financial capital maintenance, on the other hand, can handle changes in the nature and direction of operations without any change in the nature of the unit of capital, and without introducing estimates of differences in service potential. There are no heterogeneous units to express in a common dimension—except for dollars of different vintage, and these can be converted to constant dollars by means of a general price level index. In other words, financial capital maintenance has the flexibility needed to cope with a dynamic environment. Physical capital maintenance is best fitted for a static economic and technological environment. Thus, physical capital is under a severe handicap when the question is raised as to whether different capital maintenance concepts best serve different purposes. We saw that when survival of the firm or national policy-making are the objectives, there seems to be a case for physical capital maintenance, but only if we ignore its inability to cope with the dynamics of change.

There is another major reason to challenge the concept of physical capital maintenance. From a societal perspective, it implies a questionable philosophy of cost recovery. It implies that the selling price of an item should cover the item's replacement cost (adjusted for service potential differences) rather than its actual cost. Given that replacement follows sale, it is implied that unexpended future outlays (at current cost levels) rather than past expended costs are to be covered by current revenues. This implies a radical change in both the traditional view of the investment recovery cycle and the traditional method of computing return on investment. It is not clear that society either does or should approve such changes.

## 10. REFERENCES

Accounting Standards Committee (ASC), "Current Cost accounting," Statement of Standard Accounting Practice 16 (SSAP 16) (1980a).

———, "Guidance Notes on SSAP 16: Current Cost Accounting" (1980b).

Australian Accounting Research Foundation (AARF), "The Recognition of Gains and Losses on Holding Monetary Items in the Context of Current Cost Accounting," Revised Exposure Draft (August 1979).

———, "Current Cost Accounting—Omnibus Exposure Draft," Exposure Draft (March, 1980).

Butterworth, J. E., M. Gibbins and R. D. King, "The Structure of Accounting Theory: Some Basic Conceptual and Methodological Issues" (Clarkson Gordon Foundation Research Symposium, "The Nature and Role of Research to Support Standard Setting in Financial Accounting in Canada," Halifax, May 20–21, 1981).

CICA Accounting Research Committee, "Current Cost Accounting," Exposure Draft (December, 1979).

Financial Accounting Standards Board (FASB), "Financial Reporting and Changing Prices," Statement of Financial Accounting Standards No. 33 (FAS 33) (September, 1979).

———, "Objectives of Financial Reporting by Business Enterprises," Statement of Financial Accounting Concepts No. 1 (SFAC 1) (November, 1978).

———, "Reporting Income, Cost Flows, and Financial Position of Business Enterprises," Exposure Draft (November 16, 1981).

Institute of Chartered Accountants in Australia and Australian Society of Accountants (ICAA/ASA), "Current Cost Accounting," Statement of Provisional Accounting Standards (PAS 1.1) (August, 1978a).

———, Explanatory Statement, "The Basis of Current Cost Accounting" (PAS 1.2) (August, 1978 b).

Revsine, L., "Technological Changes and Replacement Costs: A Beginning," *The Accounting Review* (April, 1979), pp. 306–322.

———, *Replacement Cost Accounting* (Prentice-Hall, 1973).

Watts, Ross L., and Jerold L. Zimmerman, "The Demand for and Supply of Accounting Theories: The Market for Excuses," *The Accounting Review* (April, 1979), pp. 273–305.

# III-C   Monetary Gains and Losses

## III-C 1   *Inflation Gains and Losses from Holding Monetary Assets and Liabilities 1918 to 1936: A Study of the Development of Accounting Thought in the United States*

DALE BUCKMASTER

## INTRODUCTION

The current state of the art of accounting for holding gains and losses on monetary items in the United States stimulated this study. Authoritative accounting groups, such as the Accounting Principles Board, the Financial Account-

Dale Buckmaster, "Inflation Gains and Losses from Holding Monetary Assets and Liabilities 1918 to 1936: A Study of the Development of Accounting Thought in the United States," *International Journal of Accounting Education and Research*, Spring 1982, pp. 1–22. Reprinted with the permission of the *International Journal of Accounting Education and Research*.

ing Standards Board, and the Securities and Exchange Commission, have abrogated their responsibility by specifying nothing more than measurement technique and reporting placement for monetary gains and losses. There is some, but not much, recent academic literature concerning the nature of holding gains and losses on monetary items and their role in financial statements, but none of the work is well known. Most U.S. accountants appear to be totally indifferent to questions related to these items. The project described here was begun to determine whether some reason(s) for this primitive state of accounting thought could be identified.

The result of the examination of early literature relating to holding gains and losses on monetary items may be partially successful. This paper will ultimately suggest some factors that have retarded the development of theory on the subject. There are other benefits as well. Reviewing the development of concepts of monetary gains and losses reveals much concerning objectives of accounting and the criteria for the selection of accounting methods during the period of the study.

The related literature is introduced chronologically in this paper. However, the development of ideas relating to monetary gains and losses may also be divided into three categories: (1) specification of monetary assets and liabilities, (2) measurement techniques, and (3) financial statement treatment. We examine the development of concepts of holding gains and losses on monetary items within the context of these classifications.

## THE LITERATURE, 1918–1936

### Middleditch's "Should Accounts Reflect the Changing Value of the Dollar?"

Contrary to common opinion, Sweeney was not the first to write concerning the idea of price-level adjusted accounts and monetary gains and losses in the United States. Sweeney's first published work on the subject was preceded by nine years by an article by Middleditch[1] which must be considered within the thought of the period. Not only was the idea of index-adjusted accounts and the resulting "monetary fluctuation" adjustment new, but the balance sheet was considered the primary statement with income measurement of secondary importance. The primacy of the balance sheet is reflected throughout the article, but is also given specific emphasis with the statements:

> Altogether to disregard the changing dollar in accounts does not permit the true condition of affairs to be set forth. When the inaccuracy attains to a considerable magnitude is surely worthy of correction.... Adjustments would be made at balance-sheet dates with a view to expressing all the items of the balance-sheet in terms of the same unit and to apportioning whatever advantages or burden these might be to the period in which it belongs. Individual yearly variations may be relatively unimportant, but the cumulative effect may be great.[2]

[1] Livingston Middleditch, Jr., "Should Accounts Reflect the Changing Value of the Dollar?" *Journal of Accountancy* (February 1918): 114–20.
[2] Ibid., p. 115.

Balance sheet emphasis surely affected the overall model described by Middle-ditch. He divided assets for adjustment purposes into "current" and "fixed" rather than "monetary" and "nonmonetary," but the overall approach is basically the same as today. Current assets and liabilities were analogous to monetary assets and liabilities. It is not clear exactly how he intended long-term debt to be considered (treated). He stated, "Fixed liabilities would be treated in an analogous way (to current liabilities), but opposite in effect, to fixed assets."

The Middleditch model reflects the assumption that nonmonetary current assets turn over rapidly enough not to be affected by general price changes. The adjustment for current assets and liabilities, including inventory, is similar to the current adjustment for monetary assets and liabilities. That is, beginning balances are converted to end-of-year balances with the adjustment being an income statement item. Apparently, Middleditch did not intend changes in the holdings of current assets and liabilities during the period to be considered in the adjustment. One might hypothesize that his disregard of these changes and the inclusion of nonmonetary assets and liabilities in the adjustment may be the result of a combination of an embryonic understanding of the concept of price-level accounting and the secondary importance of the income statement.

Measurement technique for monetary gains and losses is basically the same for all model variations. That is, the relevant asset and/or liability balances are multiplied by the appropriate index numbers. Each model can vary in three ways: (1) definition of the appropriate assets and liabilities to be adjusted, (2) the technique for considering changes in the balances during the period, and (3) the selection of the type of index to be used for the adjustment. Technique is of little importance in this paper since it generally reflects a concern for precision rather than being affected by any variation of concept. In the case of Middleditch's article, as with most other writers on this subject, selection of appropriate index is important since index selection reflects the concept of capital to be maintained. His selection of the Bradstreet's "business barometer" is dictated by the ideas that accounts should reflect general (as opposed to specific) price movements for businesses (as opposed to stockholders).

Net gain or loss from holding current assets and liabilities would appear in the income statement under the caption, "Monetary Fluctuation," with the offsetting debit or credit appearing in the "Net Worth" (Stockholders' Equity) section of the balance sheet. Middleditch was very explicit in indicating that "Monetary Fluc-tuation" should be labeled as not being from business operation.

If we interpret literally Middleditch's statement that fixed liabilities are opposite in effect to fixed assets, then the gain (in an inflationary period) from holding long-term debt would be in a balance sheet account called "Monetary Fluctuation of Fixed Liabilities (Long-Term Debt)" and the offsetting debit would be to a stockholders' equity account. Again, Middleditch indicated that the debit is not to be considered a part of retained earnings. Presumably, this debit would go into the same equity account as the current items and noncurrent asset adjustments.

There is little in Middleditch's article that indicates the origin of the model he proposed. The only reference in the article to a source other than the price-change index is to Fisher's *The Purchasing Power of Money*.[3] Presumably, the methodology

---

[3] Irving Fisher, *The Purchasing Power of Money* (New York: Macmillan, 1911).

was developed by Middleditch with the underlying concepts being influenced by the work of Irving Fisher.

### Sweeney's "Correspondence—German Inflation Accounting"[4]

Sweeney's first published work on accounting for price change was his "Effects of Inflation on German Accounting."[5] He described inflation in Germany from 1914 through 1923 and German accountants' reaction to the hyperinflation of the 1921–23 period. From this description, he moved into an explanation of the superiority of depreciation of fixed assets adjusted for general price-level change over depreciation based on replacement costs for determining capital maintenance. This discussion is totally in terms of nonmonetary assets, and there is no mention (or hint) of recognition of holding gains or losses on monetary items.

### "German Inflation Accounting"

This is the sequel to his 1927 article on German inflation, and he described the German "stabilization" method. It is clear from this second article why no mention was made of monetary items in the first article. The reason is simply that the German method did not make the monetary/nonmonetary dichotomization necessary. All balance sheet accounts were converted to their equivalent in gold marks. That is, the ending balance for each balance sheet account was converted to its gold price equivalent on the statement date. Then the conversion method of, for example, cash and plant assets is identical. The amount of cash reported in the balance sheet changes just as the amount of a nonmonetary asset changes.

The debit or credit required to convert the paper mark balances to gold mark balances for each account is illustrated in the sample income statement in the article. There is a section of the income statement called "Money value loss on" under which each of the balance sheet accounts requiring a debit adjustment is listed with the required debit. There is a corresponding section called "Money value gain on" under which the balance sheet accounts requiring credit adjustments and the adjustments are listed. No distinction is made among the types of adjustment other than that of gain or loss. Asset, liability, and equity adjustments all appear together in the two sections.

Two things concerning monetary gains and losses are obvious from the article. First, Sweeney had yet to develop any concept of the nature of holding gains and losses on monetary items. Secondly, the relative unimportance of income measurement during this period retarded serious consideration of the nature of any type of holding gains or losses.

Although Sweeney's concepts were rather primitive at this time, there are some interesting statements that are indicative of his ultimate position. He recognized that altering the balance sheet amounts of monetary assets is not satisfactory. Sweeney stated:

> Assets and liabilities representing contractual amounts expressed in the depreciating currency should have their paper-mark balances shown, as well

---

[4] Henry W. Sweeney, "Correspondence—German Inflation Accounting," *Journal of Accountancy* (April 1928): 310–11.

[5] Henry W. Sweeney, "Effects of Inflation on German Accounting," *Journal of Accountancy* (March 1927): 180–87.

as the gold mark balances.... The gold-mark equivalent of the final balance represents the gold value of such balance, but the paper-mark balance shows the amount that is actually receivable and thus the amount that will be the source of varying gold values in the future.[6]

Another comment indicative of his subsequent position is this:

Perhaps they [holding gains and losses] should be designated as adjustments inasmuch as they are not in every case true gains or losses...as no profit from monetary depreciation could have occurred as yet.[7]

This statement signals his later position that monetary gains and losses should be reported as "realized" and "unrealized."

Sweeney closed this article with a statement that indicates both his original motivation for reviewing the German literature and the overall concept that determines the nature of his development of his system of "stabilized accounting." He stated:

But the method that Germany developed of necessity to express values in terms of a unit more stable than the current money is still strongly applicable, not only in Germany but also in the United States. For although the monetary unit of a strong nation no longer fluctuates in terms of *gold*, it still fluctuates in terms of *value*, which, as economists have long been demonstrating, is measured in the last analysis by purchasing power over goods and services.[8]

### Allen's "Correspondence"

An interesting letter from Mr. J. H. Allen appeared in the "Correspondence"[9] section of the *Journal of Accountancy* a few months after "German Inflation Accounting" was published. Mr. Allen felt that "stabilized balance sheets" were appropriate, but he also felt that the unrealized gains from holding debt should not be run through the "profit-and-loss account." The dominance of the conservatism and realization concepts is reflected in his statement, "We should adhere to accounting principles, which require that provision be made for all possible losses and that no unrealized gains be taken up as profits."[10]

It is tempting to suggest that Allen's letter was provoked by concern for income measurement, but that inference may not be justified. Allen suggests that unrealized gains and losses on monetary items should be recognized in a currency adjustment account, a credit balance being reported

as a reserve against subsequent fluctuations, or, if a debit, should be offset by an equivalent appropriation from surplus.... If the money-value differences

[6] Henry W. Sweeney, "German Inflation Accounting," *Journal of Accountancy* (February 1928): 113.
[7] Ibid., p. 114.
[8] Ibid., p. 118.
[9] J. H. Allen, "Correspondence—German Inflation Accounting," *Journal of Accounting* (April 1928): 310.
[10] Ibid.

are carried to an account such as the one suggested, then it will be necessary to change the depreciation in paper marks, so that the profit and loss does not contain both gold and paper marks.[11]

These comments taken within the context of accounting thought of that period suggest that Allen might have been as much or even more concerned with balance sheet classification as with income measurement.

### Sweeney's "Response to Allen"

Sweeney's response[12] is both enlightening and somewhat surprising. It is enlightening in that there is no indication that he had started to develop the ideas of the treatment of monetary gains and losses he suggested in this later work. His comments on the merit of Allen's suggestion are limited to the statement:

> Mr. Allen's suggestion seems quite sound, . . . with regard to present orthodox accounting theory, and would have to be considered very carefully if any adaptation of German methods were to be attempted in this country.[13]

Sweeney offered an explanation of the German methods. (He mentions Mahlberg and Schmalenback specifically.) The nature of this explanation is surprising in that it is totally in terms of practicality rather than his more typical rationale based in economic theory. Sweeney suggested that Allen's method was not used by the Germans because (1) it is too difficult to segregate gains and losses from price-change and operations, (2) "the final losses would have seemed unbearable if all price-variation profits and losses resulting from application of balance-sheet stabilization had been excluded,"[14] and (3) toward the end of the hyperinflationary period, prices did not seem likely to drop so that a "reserve" would not be necessary.

### Sweeney's "Maintenance of Capital"

Like his first article on German inflation, Sweeney's "Maintenance of Capital"[15] did not mention holding gains or losses on monetary items. But this article has important implications for the development of his ideas in subsequent articles and his book.[16] In "Maintenance of Capital," Sweeney developed his arguments for the appropriate concept of capital maintenance which determines his index selection for obtaining "stabilized accounts."

Sweeney began with the proposition that "the fundamental purpose of accounting should consist of an attempt to distinguish clearly between the capital and income."[17] He proceeded to examine several capital maintenance concepts. And, like all good economists, he concluded that maintenance of *real* capital is the only appropriate concept, more specifically, "maintenance of absolute capital measured in

---

[11] Ibid.

[12] Sweeney, "Correspondence—German Inflation Accounting," pp. 310–11.

[13] Ibid., p. 311.

[14] Ibid.

[15] Henry W. Sweeney, "Maintenance of Capital," *Accounting Review* (December 1930): 277–87.

[16] Henry W. Sweeney, *Stabilized Accounting* (1936; reprint ed., New York: Holt, Rinehart, and Winston, Inc., 1964).

[17] Sweeney, "Maintenance of Capital," p. 277, attributes this idea to J. M. Clark, "Valuation for the Balance-Sheet and Profits," *II et International Accountants-congres* (Amsterdam, 1926).

terms of general purchasing power."[18] The substance of the reasoning that led him to select this particular concept of capital maintenance and, consequently, the most comprehensive general index available as appropriate for "stabilizing" accounts is contained in the following paragraph.

> Most men who invest capital do not, however, definitely plan to use it or its income, if any, to acquire eventually any particular combination thereof, and even if they do, they are quite likely to change their minds, under the rapidly moving conditions of modern life, before the eventual date for such use of the purchasing power arrives. Unless, therefore, there is quite definite intention to employ an investment for eventual acquisition of a specific commodity or group of commodities—and not merely the intermediate current acquisition of business goods and services necessary for attainment of the ultimate goal—the most practical assumption in the light of experience is that greater general economic command, which will be available for later expenditure in any direction, is the actual object of business endeavor and that, therefore, maintenance of capital should be based upon the general price index.[19]

Subsequently, Sweeney stated, "Real capital should, of course, be ascertained on the basis of the national general index."[20]

The preceding statements summarize Sweeney's ideas of capital maintenance in terms of the investor, not the business, and indicate that the investor may either reinvest or consume capital returned from the business. This frame of reference is crucial as support for adjustment using an economy-wide index. Two other facets of Sweeney's thinking are in evidence although not explicitly stated: (1) he was working within the context of the "proprietary theory," and (2) he based his arguments on the assumption that the balance sheet and the income statement may be used as long-run models of the firm.

It is apparent from Sweeney's first two articles[21] and his frequent references to post-World War I inflation in France and Germany and to the accounting literature of those countries that he was influenced by the French and German experiences to investigate the problem of accounting for changing prices. But English-speaking economists seem to have provided the dominant ideas upon which the capital maintenance portion of his theory is based. The key references supporting his ideas of capital maintenance are to Marshall[22] and Van Strum.[23]

### Wasserman's "Accounting Practice in France during the Period of Monetary Inflation (1919–1927)"

By 1931 *Accounting Review* standards, Wasserman's article[24] was extremely long. In a time when *Accounting Review* articles were normally from six to ten pages, he used thirty-two pages to review the reaction of French accounting theorists to post-

---

[18] Ibid., p. 284.
[19] Ibid., p. 285.
[20] Ibid.
[21] Sweeney , "Effects of Inflation," and "Correspondence—German Inflation Accounting."
[22] Alfred Marshall, *Principles of Economics*, 8th ed. (London: Macmillan, 1920).
[23] K. S. Van Strum, *Investing in Purchasing Power* (New York: Barrons, 1925).
[24] Max J. Wasserman, "Accounting Practice in France during the Period of Monetary Inflation (1919–1927)," *Accounting Review* (March 1931): 1–32.

World War I inflation. Wasserman begins with a description of the French inflation and the problems it posed for businesses. The remainder of the article is devoted to describing five different variations of inflation accounting proposed by French theorists.[25] Several points that the current author believes to be new in American accounting literature are made in both Wasserman's introduction to and review of French methods.

The French theorists, like the Germans, were concerned with the relationship of the paper franc to the price of gold. That is, the conversion methods were designed to stabilize the franc in terms of gold. Wasserman, presumably following the lead of the French theorists, implied that the paper franc/gold index was representative of a general purchasing-power index.

A most interesting aspect of Wasserman's analysis is his emphasis on problems of maintaining real working capital in a period of inflation. American accounting theorists were concerned with capital maintenance and replacement of physical assets; if Wasserman was not the first to identify working capital maintenance as an accounting problem, he certainly was the first to discuss it extensively. His introduction contains a discussion of French companies' problems with eroding real working capital,[26] and he frequently re-emphasizes the importance of the problem in the article.

Wasserman recognized the working capital problem as (1) arising because of inventory profits, and (2) the increased absolute amounts of monetary working capital required to maintain real monetary working capital. He described the problem of erosion of real monetary working capital as follows:

> Whenever credit was extended on open account to the customers during a period of rising prices, the firm was repaid in depreciated francs, that is, in francs having a lower purchasing power. The longer the period of credit, the lower the purchasing power of the francs received finally from the sale of goods. This practice did much to reduce the effective working capital of some firms during inflation. While the nominal value of working capital was maintained, and in most cases increased, its purchasing power or its gold value declined very steadily. Of course, if the company received equal credit terms from its creditors that it extended its clients, then the working capital showed no depletion, and if shorter terms and amounts were extended than it received, then the working capital increased. It was only those firms who extended larger credit terms and amounts than they received who suffered.[27]

Wasserman's concern with maintaining effective monetary working capital was probably the result of Leger's work.[28] Leger, according to Wasserman, classified "loss on the excess of the incorporeal (monetary) working capital assets over the incor-

---

[25] P. C. Raffegeau and A. Lacout, *Etalissement des Bilans en Francs-or* (Paris: Payot, 1926); Gabriel Faure, *Bilans et Comptes en Francs-or*, 2nd ed. (Paris: Nouvelle Librosie Nationale, 1926); Fernand Leger, *Le Redressement des Bilans en Francs-pepier* (Paris: Editions Experta, 1926); Gail Fain, *Comment se Defendre Contre L'inflation* (Paris: Compagnie des Chefs de Comptabilite de la Region Parisienne, n.d.); and Lucian Thomas, *La Tenue des Comptabilites en Periode D'instabilite monetaire* (Paris: Editions Experta, 1927).

[26] Wasserman, "Accounting Practice," p. 5.

[27] Ibid., p. 4.

[28] Leger, "Le Redressement."

poreal working capital liabilities." [29] Leger suggested, says Wasserman, that "for that part of working capital which cannot be so invested (in nonmonetary assets) . . . a reserve be constituted by a debit to profit and loss sufficient to compensate for the decline in the gold value of this element of the working capital." [30] Leger's treatment of monetary items was apparently vague as were those of the other French theorists who suggested adjustments for monetary items.

Of the systems reviewed by Wasserman, Thomas' method seems to be exceptionally complete. From Wasserman's description, it appears that Thomas would have a control account for all offsetting debits and credits including monetary items required to adjust paper franc amounts to gold franc equivalents. It also appears that for the non-monetary assets, the conversion is not simply an index conversion, but a restatement to replacement cost in terms of gold. This is of some consequence if the present author's interpretation is proper, since it provides evidence of an early replacement cost model that also recognized the replacement cost of monetary stocks.

Wasserman indicated that long-term debt would also be adjusted through Thomas' control account. Also, in the introductory section, the following point is made:

> The account for bonds is also always exact since it expresses a legal relation. The corporation can only be obliged to pay back the bonds in terms of nominal francs. However, the depreciation of the purchasing power of the bonds constitutes an element of profit for the business which classical inflation theorists have long stressed. Unfortunately the books do not show this gain and it would be wise to install an accounting method which would bring out this element of profit. [31]

It is not clear from Wasserman's description of Thomas' method if the control account was to be run through the income statement. In fact, income measurement is treated in a very cavalier manner. Again, it appears that the relative unimportance of that statement during the first part of this century was a very important factor in determining the attention given holding gains and losses on monetary items. Perhaps had the income statement been given the prominence that it is today, progress in developing specific treatments of holding gains and losses would have been accelerated. Certainly, the essential ideas necessary for the development of methods similar to contemporary methods were imbedded in the French literature and only lacked refinement.

### Sweeney's "Income" [32]

Although Sweeney's obsession with realization was evident in his 1928 article and the related correspondence, [33] he used this article to introduce a position that subsequently resulted in his realized/unrealized dichotomization of monetary holding gains and losses. He argued that the "realization" principle is useful, but both realized and unrealized value increments are income. Therefore, both should be

---

[29] Wasserman, "Accounting Practice," p. 21.
[30] Ibid., p. 23.
[31] Ibid., p. 5.
[32] Henry W. Sweeney, "Income," *Accounting Review* (December 1933): 323–35.
[33] Sweeney, "Correspondence—German Inflation Accounting."

reported, but the unrealized portion must be identified. His caution is reflected in the following statement:

> For an apparent opportunity; e.g., to sell goods at a profit, on an apparent increase in the value of capital asset, may turn out to be a mere illusion,— the result of deceptive appearances or a faulty reasoning or of more unwarranted optimism; and so any action that may have been based upon a belief in the existence of such income can very easily prove disastrous.[34]

### Wasserman's "French Enterprise under Inflation: A Balance Sheet Analysis"[35]

Wasserman examined the financial statements of forty French firms during the period 1919 through 1925 in this article. He was attempting to determine if "business profits by inflation due to the rise in prices which it engenders," or if "inflation is a grave danger to business, gutting enterprises of their working capital."[36]

The approach was to (1) obtain averages of certain financial statement items for the forty companies, (2) deflate the averages with an overall wholesale price index, and (3) identify the apparent trends. Since average real capital was maintained and 30 percent of new plant and equipment was financed with internally generated funds, Wasserman was convinced that business benefited from inflation and that, on average, inflation does not cause serious working capital problems.

Within the context of a balance sheet analysis, Wasserman's study may have provided convincing evidence concerning the impact of inflation on the monetary position of the firm. But the modern theorist, with his concern for capital maintenance income models, will find no answers in a study such as Wasserman's. His findings are as we would expect. On average, real working capital would be maintained (particularly when there is an obvious survivor bias and there is no adjustment for growth or decline). Rather, our question would be "What are the costs of maintaining working capital and what is the impact of inflation on these costs?" In no sense is this question answered.

### Paton's "Aspects of Asset Valuation"[37]

No new concepts or methods are introduced in this article, yet it does contain two considerations of interest: (1) the position of the leading U.S. accounting theorist of the time toward accounting for holding gains and losses is explicitly stated; and (2) there is an explicit statement of an attitude prevailing throughout the period of the study that, with the unimportance relegated to income measurement, explains why more attention was not given holding gains and losses on monetary items.

Paton was very explicit in stating his position toward including monetary gains and losses in financial statements. He stated, "Such accounting [measuring holding gains and losses] would be quite incorrect, as a substitute for our present procedures, in connection with all entries in account [sic] involving cash, receivables, and

---

[34] Sweeney, "Income," p. 333.
[35] Max J. Wasserman, "French Enterprise under Inflation: A Balance Sheet Analysis," *Accounting Review* (June 1934): 130–39.
[36] Ibid., p. 130.
[37] William A. Paton, "Aspects of Asset Valuations," *Accounting Review* (June 1934): 122–29.

liabilities."[38] Rather, as a better means of providing information useful for coping with price changes, Paton suggested:

> What is needed, it seems to me, is the development of supplementary statistical procedures, quite outside the ledger technique, which will attempt to answer special questions in which the owners and managers are or should be interested.[39]

From these statements, it is obvious that Paton felt that including monetary holding gains and losses in financial statements is inappropriate.

The other interesting aspect of this section of the article concerns the role that reporting monetary holding gains and losses might fulfill. As Paton continued this passage, he indicated that a study might be made of the impact of changing prices on monetary working capital requirements over a period of years so that policies might be formulated for handling funds and incurring liabilities.[40] Even though Paton included owners as statement users early in the passage when he recognized specific information needs, they are the needs of management, and there is no consideration of the type of ownership we find in the large publicly held corporation. This is typical of the literature. This attitude surely affected the importance generally attributed to measuring holding gains and losses on monetary items. Management needs much more decision-specific information than is provided by measurement of monetary holding gains and losses. Explicit measurement of monetary holding gains or losses does not replace any of the other conventionally required information (for example, cash forecasts and capital budgets) and may not have any incremental value at all. If measurement of holding gains and losses on monetary items has any value at all, that value is probably derived from the information provided statement users external to the firm, and then value may exist only when the measurement is an integral element of some form of capital-maintenance income model.

### Sweeney's "How Inflation Affects Balance Sheets"

The sole incremental contribution of this article is Sweeney's identification of Carl Snyder's revised general index prepared for the Federal Reserve Bank of New York as the best general price-level index for the United States.[41]

### Sweeney's "How Inflation Would Affect Balance Sheet of a Business"

Two additional elements of Sweeney's final system appear in this article.[42] The more general element is reflected in his discussion of monetary items in a "stabilized" balance sheet at their nominal (legal) value. As a result, Sweeney discussed the

---

[38] Ibid., p. 128.

[39] Ibid.

[40] William Paton, Jr., did conduct just such a study twenty-four years later; see *A Study in Liquidity: The Impact of Inflation Monetary Accounts* (Ann Arbor: Bureau of Business Research, University of Michigan, 1958).

[41] Henry W. Sweeney, "How Inflation Affects Balance Sheets," *Accounting Review* (December 1934), p. 275.

[42] Henry W. Sweeney, "How Inflation Would Affect Balance Sheet of a Business," *Controller* (June 1935), pp. 106–10.

monetary/nonmonetary (money-value/real value) distinction in his published work for the first time.

The more specific aspect of accounting for monetary items that appears for the first time in the literature is his identification of redeemable and/or callable preferred stock as a monetary item. He listed the monetary items as cash, "accounts and notes receivable, accounts and notes payable, mortgages and bonds owned, mortgages and bonds owed, and outstanding preferred stock that is voluntarily or involuntarily redeemable."[43]

### Sweeney's "The Technique of Stabilised Accounting"

The publication of this article[44] marked the completion of the development of Sweeney's "stabilized" accounting model. Sweeney is, of course, best known for his 1936 book, *Stabilized Accounting*, but no substantive ideas or model modifications are added by the book. This article illustrates the model just as completely as the book does.

Sweeney's earlier articles are of three types. First, he described European techniques for coping with inflation and/or how the application of these techniques affected balance sheets of the countries being discussed. Second, he used the article to develop an important idea that supports his model. Finally, in the later articles, he related some element of the model to the U.S. environment and provided an example of the impact of that element. This last article of the series illustrates with a comprehensive example the ideas that Sweeney had been developing in all the earlier articles of the series.

Much of Sweeney's earlier work had implied the necessity of conversion of each transaction to end-of-period dollars. The major element introduced in this article is the application of the "stabilized balance sheet" method to the example. Of course, this method is the European method adapted to the Sweeney model, but any attempt to apply the Sweeney model would be impractical without some similar methodology. Thus, the "stabilized balance sheet" technique is matched with the Sweeney model in order to make the model a practical possibility.

One interesting position indicated in the article reflects a compromise of an earlier position. Sweeney argued that general purchasing power is the appropriate measure rather than specific purchasing power in his conceptual articles of the early thirties. He did not necessarily abandon his earlier position; rather, he stated, as a secondary argument, that his general purchasing-power adjustments might be considered surrogates for replacement costs.

Sweeney was not so naive as to believe that general purchasing power adjustments were good estimates of replacement costs. He makes this clear in an earlier article[45] in which he examines possible methods of obtaining replacement costs. Rather, the inclusion of this position most likely reflects an attempt to obtain broader-based support for his model.

Sweeney's concern for the distinction between realized and unrealized income appeared frequently and consistently in his articles. In this last article, the fruition of

---

[43] Ibid., p. 108.

[44] Henry W. Sweeney, "The Technique of Stabilized Accounting," *Accounting Review* (June 1935): 185–205.

[45] Henry W. Sweeney, "Approximation of Appraisal Values by Index Numbers," *Harvard Business Review* (October 1934): 108–15.

this concern is illustrated. As we would expect, he divided his income statement into realized and unrealized sections, and holding gains and losses are to be identified and reported in this manner. Sweeney also confirmed that he had not started to develop his specific treatment of monetary gains and losses prior to J. H. Allen's comment[46] on his article that appeared early in 1928. Sweeney stated:

> For the stimulation that led to the eventual development of ways to compute accurately the realized and unrealized profits and losses on changes in the value of money the author desires to acknowledge indebtedness to J. H. Allen's criticism ... of the author's "German Inflation Accounting...."[47]

### Jones' "Financial Statements and the Uncertain Dollar"

This article and the Sweeney article just discussed are the first two articles dealing with historical cost/constant dollar accounting in which income measurement considerations are treated as important. Also, this is the first article on the subject to make the argument for general price-change accounting in order to induce tax authorities to recognize the impact of inflation on real income. Jones stated:

> The chances of the adoption [by tax authorities] of such a rule [exempting that portion of revenue required to maintain capital because of price changes] would be materially improved if it should become the accepted accounting practice rigorously to exclude all such fictitious gains and losses from the income account.[48]

Jones' attitude toward holding gains and losses on monetary items is somewhat puzzling. He considered the net gain or loss real, yet excluded it from the income statement.[49] His position can be compared to those theorists who have recently supported a replacement cost model as a capital maintenance model, yet fail to provide for maintenance of monetary stocks.

### Sweeney's Stabilized Accounting[50]

Stabilized accounting is the culmination of Sweeney's serious efforts to develop a price-change accounting model. In his "Editor's Forward to the Reissue," Stephen Zeff states, "Ideally, one should begin with Sweeney's first article [1927] and proceed through the succeeding 14 (1928–1935) prior to digging into the book."[51] But the reader's objective determines the appropriateness of this advice. If the reader is interested only in practical aspects—application methods, cost of application, and the potential impact on reported numbers—then the book is adequate and previously published materials will add little to the achievement of the reader's objective. If, on

[46] Allen, "Inflation Accounting."
[47] Sweeney, "Technique of Stabilized Accounting," p. 188.
[48] Ralph Caughenour Jones, "Financial Statements and the Uncertain Dollar," *Journal of Accountancy* (September 1935): 177.
[49] Ibid., p. 183.
[50] Sweeney, *Stabilized Accounting*.
[51] Stephen Zeff, "Editor's Forward to the Reissue," in *Stabilized Accounting* by Henry W. Sweeney, p. X.

the other hand, the reader is interested in Sweeney's development of the model, the conceptual rationale for the model, and the criteria applied to evaluate choices, then it is imperative that the reader at least examine the *Accounting Review* articles.

Sweeney did six things in the book. First, he provided a general statement of rationale for historical cost/constant dollar accounting and referred the reader to his articles for support for his statements. Second, he illustrated the model and the methodology of adjustment with a simple example. Next, he discussed the causes of the absolute dollar differences between historical cost/constant dollar numbers obtained in his example. He then demonstrated his model in a replacement cost context; and then he demonstrated the practicability of his model by applying it to the accounting data for three firms and estimating the cost and time required for application. Finally, he attempted to answer the objections to historical cost/constant dollar accounting that had been brought to his attention.

The well-constructed conceptual arguments of Sweeney's middle period articles[52] are not included in *Stabilized Accounting*, so the reader interested in the conceptual basis of Sweeney's position must seek out the articles. A more commanding reason for a reader interested in Sweeney's rationale to read the articles is that in *Stabilized Accounting*, Sweeney was either abandoning an earlier position or being intentionally misleading.

A rather serious and important contradiction of his position as stated in his conceptual articles appears early in *Stabilized Accounting*. Remember that Sweeney had consistently argued that the appropriate capital maintenance concept is maintenance of "real" capital, which he interpreted to apply to all goods in the economy—both consumption and production goods. From this, he deduced that a general price-level index is the appropriate conversion index. Yet in *Stabilized Accounting*, he appeared to argue for a consumer index as the appropriate index. He stated:

> It may be argued, the things that men buy with money are not always consumption goods. Much of the time they are "production goods," such as factory machinery and buildings. When men buy production goods, however, they do so only because in most cases they hope thereby to obtain eventually more of the consumption goods that they want than they could obtain by buying them in the first place.
>
> In consequence of the foregoing, accounting data should ideally be measured with reference to the progress made in obtaining either more consumption goods or greater power over them. These consumption goods are those represented in the cost of living.[53]

It is rather difficult to believe that Sweeney had changed his position on such an important element of his model. More likely, he was playing the same game that he did in "The Technique of Stabilized Accounting" with his argument for general price-level adjustments as a surrogate for replacement costs. That is, he may have been

---

[52] Henry W. Sweeney, "Maintenance of Capital"; "Capital," *Accounting Review* (September 1933): 185–97; "Stabilized Depreciation," *Accounting Review* (September 1931): 165–78; "Stabilized Appreciation," *Accounting Review* (June 1932): 115–21; "Income."
[53] Sweeney, "Stabilized Accounting," p. 4.

introducing the consumer idea in order to gain support for his model. Immediately after making his consumer index argument, he dismissed it:

> There is a decisive practical objection, though, to using the cost-of-living index in this manner. It is simply that no *comprehensive* cost-of-living index has been compiled, at least in the United States, for periods as short as months prior to 1920—and without, at least, monthly indexes, accurate enough results cannot be obtained in the many cases where figures for dates prior to 1920 are still prominent in the figures on the accounting statements.... Fortunately, however, there is an index series that is related to the cost-of-living index in both its content and in its actual index numbers and that does exist in monthly form back to a sufficiently distant point in the past. This index is the index of the general price level ... compiled by Carl Snyder....[54]

Nothing more was written of a consumer price index.

The illustration of his model requires no comment in this paper. It is brief, easy to follow, and complete. The bulk of the incremental contribution of the book is contained in his case studies and cost of application estimates. The case studies are easy to follow and complete. He convincingly demonstrated that application of the model is practical. However, nothing of conceptual interest was discussed in these sections.

The most interesting section of the book if one has read the series of articles is contained in a section describing Sweeney's differences with Professor Schmidt, a German scholar.[55] It becomes obvious early in the series of articles that Sweeney was working within the context of the proprietary concept and the theory that financial statements were amenable to long-run assumptions. In this section, Sweeney admitted to the latter of the two characteristics: "The writer pleads guilty to this accusation of trying to make the ultimate attainment of a long-time aim."[56] That he is working within a proprietary concept is obvious from his frequent and consistent concern, even in his later work, with the balance sheet as the primary statement and with his treatment of noncash firm assets at a consumption price.

It seems to this author that Sweeney's arguments are particularly susceptible to attacks upon his use of statements as long-run devices. Professor Schmidt must have been exercising considerable constraint when he refrained from noting that the firm would either (1) continue for some time into the future, or (2) cease operations and distribute assets to investors. If the firm is to continue operation for at least one or two more periods, then consumption indices have no relevance now and intervening variables between the current reporting date and future liquidation will most likely destroy any predictive value of current application of consumer price indices. Specifically, application of consumer price indices is totally irrelevant to future cash flows of the firm through operations or liquidation. If, on the other hand, the firm is to liquidate, then liquidation value provides a better measure of ultimate cash flow and purchasing power to the consumer than historical cost adjusted for general price change.

[54] Sweeney, "Technique of Stabilized Accounting," p. 5.
[55] Ibid., pp. 40–41.
[56] Ibid., p. 41.

## SUMMARY AND CONCLUSION

When Henry Sweeney wrote "Forty Years After: Or Stabilized Accounting Revisited" for the reissue of *Stabilized Accounting*, he made the following statement concerning the then recently issued *Accounting Research Study No. 6*[57]:

> The main flaw in the Study is its indecisive and unrealistic handling of an inescapable and substantial element in nearly all practical stabilization procedure [*sic*], to wit, money-value gain and loss.... The Study's treatment of money-value gain and loss is, first, indecisive because it fails to furnish a clear understanding of whether that common and substantial form of profit and loss ought to be treated as income in nature or as capital in nature.[58]

This same indecisive, unsatisfactory situation still exists in the United States. The Financial Accounting Standards Board's *Statement of Financial Accounting Standards No. 33*[59] is equally vague in indicating what the board intended holding gains and losses on monetary items to represent. The present author wished to know why authoritative accounting groups in the United States were so vague in supporting their position and describing the nature of holding gains and losses on monetary items. Thus, this study was begun. By tracing the history of ideas related to monetary holdings gains and losses, it was hoped that the key to current failures could be found. Even though the literature examined represents only the formative period of thinking regarding holding gains and losses on monetary items, the review of this literature provides some rather interesting insight into contemporary accounting policy.

Henry Sweeney's work still dominates American ideas of holding gains and losses on monetary items just as it did during the thirties. Accounting policy makers in the United States seem to be mentally incapable of separating holding gains and losses from Sweeney's stabilized accounting model. The decision makers seem to recognize that monetary gains and losses are real and should be recognized, but the general price-level adjustment model within which the gains and losses were first recognized does not seem to mesh with contemporary thought. Sweeney's model, the only model that recognizes holding gains and losses on monetary items that was familiar to any substantial number of accountants during the period studied, was as much the product of the economic environment and accounting thought of the time as it was of Sweeney's original ideas. Some of the concepts underlying the work on monetary holding gains and losses during the study period are still applicable, but many of the constraints and ideas are only of historical interest. As has been intimated, policy makers in the United States seem to fail to recognize these antiquated ideas. Consequently, accounting policy makers in the United States are tentative and indecisive in attacking the problem of holding gains and losses on monetary items.

---

[57] Staff of the Accounting Research Division, American Institute of Certified Public Accountants, *Accounting Research Study #6: Reporting the Financial Effects of Price Level Changes* (New York: AICPA, 1963).

[58] Sweeney, *Stabilized Accounting*, p. xxxiii.

[59] Financial Accounting Standards Board, *Statement of Financial Accounting Standards No. 33: Financial Reporting and Changing Prices* (Stamford, Conn.: FASB, 1979).

The result in *Statement of Financial Accounting Standards No. 33* is recognition of net holding gains and losses but failure to integrate them into the financial statements.

An attitude that had considerable impact on the development of concepts of monetary holding gains and losses was the dominance of balance sheet considerations. Since the income statement was of little consequence, there was little stimulus to examine the role of holding gains and losses in income measurement.

The question of realized and unrealized income was brought to Sweeney's attention in 1928, and he subsequently devoted much attention to dichotomizing monetary holding gains and losses into "realized" and "unrealized."[60] The realization concept may also have resulted in influencing Jones' recommendations to omit monetary holding items from the income statement.

Another factor that may have resulted in diminishing the attention given monetary items was that financial statements were viewed as primarily tools for management decisions. In the absence of an emphasis on investor information, reporting the effects of holding monetary items is of much less consequence. In the context of management decision making, the primary benefit from recognition of such holding gains and losses is in planning for the balances of monetary items necessary for operation. Measurement of holding gains might facilitate the budgeting process but certainly will not replace it.

An environmental factor existing then, as now, that tended to divert attention from accounting for the impact of price changes on monetary items was the presumed much greater impact of changing prices on nonmonetary items. Changing prices have a much more obvious impact on nonmonetary items and, where there is an allocation of research effort and published space, problems of accounting for nonmonetary items will invariably dominate both allocations.

Environmental factors operated during the period of the study to minimize research effort devoted to the subject of holding gains and losses on monetary items. Yet Henry Sweeney and R. C. Jones, to a much less degree and toward the end of the period, had the foresight to recognize the potential importance of these economic elements in the reporting process. The form of the Sweeney model, however, reflected the accounting criteria and conventions of his time. He felt that the objective of the financial statements was to measure stockholder wealth. His own interpretation of the objective was his insistence that the measure should reflect the long-run use of firm resources. By joining these two ideas, the natural consequence is his selection of a measure that represents general purchasing power. This result of his logic has carried into a time when most of us would define the objectives of financial reporting as something other than the measure of owners' wealth. Policy makers should consider whether they are willing to support an accounting model that has not been justified outside the proprietary concept and contains mixed elements of long- and short-run analysis.

This author suggests that the impact of Sweeney's work is still evident in the accounting policy making process in the United States, and his continued influence is not totally beneficial. If we are to use Sweeney's ideas, they must be adapted to contemporary thought.

---

[60] This dichotomization is, of course, an important element of his model that is illustrated in his "Technique of Stabilized Accounting" which also was published in June 1935.

## APPENDIX. CHRONOLOGICAL LISTING OF CHANGES IN CONCEPTS OR TREATMENTS

Financial Statement Treatment

**Source:** Middleditch, "Should Accounts Reflect the Changing Value of the Dollar?" *Journal of Accountancy* (February 1918)

**Treatment of Concept Introduced:** Current asset adjustment presented in the income statement as an expense with the offsetting credit (in an inflationary period) going to a "reserve" account or to "net worth." Separate treatment is also recommended for current liabilities and long-term debt. In an inflationary period, the debit would be to "reserve for monetary fluctuation" or "net worth." The credit is an income item, but not an operating income item.

**Source:** Sweeney, "Effects of Inflation on German Accounting," *Journal of Accountancy* (March 1927)

**Treatment of Concept Introduced:** *All* measured holding gains and losses are included in the income statement. A section "Money value loss" is illustrated and includes the measured holding loss on each of the balance sheet accounts. There is also a section, "Money value gain," which contains a list of the measured holding gain for each of the balance sheet accounts.

**Source:** Sweeney, "Income," *Accounting Review* (December 1933): 323–35

**Treatment of Concept Introduced:** Argues that both realized and unrealized income should be reported, but that the unrealized portion should be identified.

**Source:** Sweeney, "How Inflation Would Affect Balance Sheet of a Business," *Controller* (June 1935)

**Treatment of Concept Introduced:** Discusses holding gains and losses on monetary items in terms of general price-level adjustment. Since nominal value is the reported amount, Sweeney writes of the monetary/nonmonetary dichotomization for the first time.

**Source:** Sweeney, "The Technique of Stabilized Accounting," *Accounting Review* (June 1935)

**Treatment of Concept Introduced:** Provides a complete illustration of financial statements that would be obtained from his model. The income statements contain two primary sub-classifications: realized and unrealized. Holding gains and losses are classified accordingly.

**Source:** Jones, "Financial Statements and the Uncertain Dollar," *Journal of Accountancy* (September 1935)

**Treatment of Concept Introduced:** Holding gains and losses on monetary items are treated as adjustments of retained earnings even though the income statement is treated as an important element of the reporting process. The rationale for his treatment is not discussed.

Specification of Monetary Assets and Liabilities

**Source:** Middleditch, "Should Accounts Reflect the Changing Value of the Dollar?" *Accounting Review* (February 1918)

**Treatment (Concept) Introduced:** Does not have a monetary/nonmonetary dichotomy. Considers four classes of "adjustment for monetary fluctuation": (1) current assets, (2) current liabilities, (3) fixed assets, and (4) fixed liabilities. He considers current assets and current liabilities "similar, but opposite in effect." Likewise for fixed assets and fixed liabilities.

**Source:** Sweeney, "Effects of Inflation on German Accounting," *Journal of Accountancy* (March 1927)

**Treatment (Concept) Introduced:** Does not have a monetary/nonmonetary dichotomization. All holding gains and losses are treated in the same manner.

**Source:** Wasserman, "Accounting Practice in France during the Period of Monetary Inflation (1919–1927)," *Accounting Review* (March 1931)

**Treatment (Concept) Introduced:** Uses the term "incorporeal" assets and liabilities. These items are identified as cash, accounts receivable, other fixed monetary amounts owed to the firm, accounts payable, and bonds payable.

**Source:** Sweeney, "How Inflation Would Affect Balance Sheet of a Business," *Controller* (June 1935)

**Treatment (Concept) Introduced:** Lists monetary items as "cash, accounts and notes receivable, accounts and notes payable, mortgages and bonds owned, mortgages and bonds owed, and outstanding preferred stock that is voluntarily or involuntarily redeemable." (p. 108)

# IV International Accounting

This part of the book is concerned with the international harmonization of accounting standards, accounting for multinational enterprises, Soviet uniform accounting, and the concept of an accounting court in the Netherlands.

Section A considers the internationalization of accounting standards for both developed and underdeveloped countries. Thomas (1983) describes various developments underway aimed at harmonizing accounting methods world-wide. In Thomas's view, harmonization will take a long time to come to fruition, but progress could be hastened by providing greater support to the International Accounting Standards Committee (IASC) in the development of accounting standards, stimulating other international organizations involved in harmonization to openly endorse the IASC, and encouraging the European Economic Community to participate in broader international groups. Samuels and Oliga (1982) question the purpose and desirability of applying international accounting standards to the Third World. The basic themes of this paper are that accounting systems evolve to fit the specific environmental conditions in which they operate, and that there are conceptual and practical problems relating to world-wide uniformity of accounting standards.

Section B consists of one piece on the "functional currency" choice set forth in FASB *Statement No. 52*, "Foreign Currency Translation" (1981). In his article, Revsine (1984) explains the purpose of the functional currency concept and the factors underlying the functional currency choice. Statement 52 was issued with the intent of reflecting the economic substance of foreign exchange translation "gains" or "losses."

With regard to accounting in the Soviet Union, the subject of Section C, Gorelick (1973) delineates the evolution of its uniform accounting system and discusses several problems inherent in Soviet accounting. Marxist theory, in Gorelick's judgment, has had a detrimental impact on Soviet accounting. Management accounting—e.g., differential costing, standard costing, opportunity costing—is not highly developed, even to this day. Soviet accounting is essentially based on uniform standards, which constitute laws. While Soviet accounting has been a catalyst in effectuating the transformation from an agrarian nation to an industrial one, this accounting framework has been largely stewardship rather than decision-oriented at the enterprise level. It should be emphasized, however, that accounting information is used by the central planners for decision-making purposes. According to Gorelick, Soviet accounting has been retarded by the absense of objectively determined market prices. Since this article appeared in the Fall 1973 issue of the *International Journal of Accounting*, there have been few changes of substance in Soviet accounting apart from greater experimentation in standard costing and bonus and profit incentive plans, as well as computerization of accounting information.

Section D contains an article by Klaassen (1980) on the role of an accounting court in the Netherlands. The impact of this court on financial reporting and accounting standards is examined. In Klaassen's judgment, the court does not constitute an appropriate forum for establishing accounting standards since the court adjudicates only specific cases affecting plaintiffs and particular companies, and such decisions are binding only upon the companies in question.

# IV-A  International Harmonization

## IV-A 1  *International Harmonization— Recent Developments in the Pursuit of Comparability in General Purpose Reports of Multi- national Enterprises*

BARBARA S. THOMAS

### INTRODUCTION

The internationalization of capital markets and the dramatic increase in the foreign direct investments of multinational enterprises have increased the need for relevant, timely and comparable information about the activities of business enterprises having operations in more than one nation. This article describes some of the current developments that are tending toward a degree of commonality in accounting and reporting standards at national, regional, and international levels, speaks to the need for comparable information in general purpose reports of multinational enterprises, and summarizes the activities of regional and international organizations that are involved in work that is expected to result in greater uniformity in financial information disclosures. The article also summarizes recent changes in the requirements of the SEC which are applicable to the filings of foreign private issuers under the Securities Act of 1933 and the Securities Exchange Act of 1934. Finally, several suggestions are made regarding additional measures which should be taken to achieve further improvements in the quality of information included in general purpose reports of multinational enterprises.

## WHY HARMONIZED STANDARDS ARE NEEDED

In Statement of Financial Accounting Concepts No. 2, *Qualitative Characteristics of Accounting Information*, the Financial Accounting Standards Board[1] stated:

> Information about a particular enterprise gains greatly in usefulness if it can be compared with similar information about other enterprises and with similar information about the same enterprise for some other period or some other point in time. Comparability between enterprises and consistency in the application of methods over time increases the informational value of comparisons of relevant economic opportunities or performance. The significance of information, especially quantitative information, depends to a great extent on the user's ability to relate it to some benchmark.[2]

That statement is as valid in regard to the multinational enterprises of various nations as it is to the domestic enterprises of a particular nation. Investors, creditors, and other users of the financial information in general purpose reports need information that is comparable across national boundaries.

Rapid technological advances have made the world smaller in terms of the time required to communicate and transact commercial and other transactions internationally. Such advances have also increased the interdependency of nations, not only in terms of commercial trading markets but also in the context of financial and capital markets. Foreign private issuers raise capital in the United States for both domestic and foreign use, and American companies raise capital in other parts of the world for deployment within and outside the United States.[3] Therefore, managers

---

[1] The Financial Accounting Standards Board (FASB) was created in 1973 as the designated organization in the private sector for establishing standards of financial accounting and reporting. The FASB is in the process of establishing a conceptual framework that will set forth fundamentals on which financial accounting and reporting standards will be based. To date, four statements have been issued in the concepts series. *See* Financial Accounting Standards Board, *Rules of Procedure* (Jan. 1978), and Statements of Financial Concepts Nos. 1–4.

[2] Statements of Financial Concepts No. 2, *Qualitative Characteristics of Accounting Information*, Financial Accounting Standards Board, at xii (May 1980).

[3] For example, the internationalization of securities markets has resulted in a dramatic increase in the trading by American investors in the securities of foreign issuers. Americans held

often make their capital formation and investment/disinvestment decisions in the light of international considerations rather than solely on the basis of the domestic environment of the decision maker.[4]

The expansion made in direct investments in other countries that establish operations outside the country of domicile has increased enormously since World War II. For example, at the end of 1981 the United States direct investment abroad totaled $227.3 billion.[5] Consequently, developing countries have experienced dramatic increases in the amounts of foreign capital invested in their countries. The host developing countries contended that there was insufficient available information to effectively monitor the activities of foreign investors,[6] and they sought the help of the United Nations (U.N.) and other organizations.[7]

Developing country governments are not alone in the search for comparable, relevant information about business enterprises that operate across national borders. For example, the European Economic Community (EEC or Community) is engaged in a considerable effort expected to result in the establishment of a common disclosure system in the ten-member Community. The Organisation for Economic Cooperation and Development (OECD) is also working to improve the quality and quantity of the disclosures made by multinational enterprises. The efforts of these organizations are further described below.

There is a degree of universal usefulness that attaches to any financial information about the financial condition, results of operations, and changes in financial position of a business enterprise. However, to be most useful such information, in addition to being relevant and reliable, must also be comparable— within industries and, to a lesser extent, across industry lines and national boundaries. Some minimum set of relevant, reliable, and comparable information appears essential to an informed investment or similar decision regardless of the nationality or the geographic location of the decision maker. If that is true, a consensus about kinds of data necessary to form such a nucleus should be attainable, and it should be possible to reach an acceptable degree of uniformity in the methodology used to quantify those data.

The nonfinancial information typically included in general purpose reports may not be susceptible to the same degree of universality as financial information.

---

investments in foreign stocks and bonds of about $21.7 billion in 1971. By 1981, the total of such investments was almost three times that, totalling about $63 billion. *See* Scholl, *The International Investment Position of the United States: Developments in 1981*, 62 Survey of Current Business, at 42, 45 (Table 3) (Aug. 1982); Scholl, *The International Investment Position of the United States Developments in 1972*, 53 Survey of Current Business, at 18, 21 (Table 3) (Aug. 1973).

[4] For example, Dow Chemical issued $100 million of yen-denominated debt securities in the Japanese Samurai market in January 1982. Also, the Eurocurrency market is used extensively as an international money market; McKinnon, *The Eurocurrency Market*, Essays on International Finance, No. 125, Princeton University (December 1977).

[5] *See* Whichard, *U.S. Direct Investment Abroad in 1981*, 62 Summary of Current Business, at 11, 20 (Table 12) (Aug. 1982).

[6] Although governments have an interest in the general purpose reports of multinational enterprises, governments usually need more particularized data, and such needs are better served by special purpose reports tailored by the user governmental body to elicit the desired information.

[7] *See Report of the Commission on Transnational Corporations on its Sixth Session*, U.N. Official Records of the Economic and Social Council 1980, Supp. No. 8 (E/1980/40/Rev. 1).

Because nonfinancial information is often user specific, it must be tailored to the particular needs of different user groups. For example, the informational needs of employee organizations may focus on wages and hours, health and safety, and the like, while governments may need information on such subjects as transfer pricing and currency movements.[8] Therefore, the nonfinancial information included in general purpose reports of multinational enterprises may be less susceptible to standardization and subject to different cost/benefit assessments.

Looking to the quantity and quality of the financial information disclosed in general purpose reports of business enterprises, we find important differences because the various national governments approach accounting measurement and financial disclosure matters differently. The following major items typify the differences which adversely affect the comparability of financial information in general purpose reports.

First, consolidation practices vary widely, even among the developed countries of the world. For example, in some countries it is not customary to present consolidated financial statements; parent company financial statements are of primary interest.[9] In other countries, only domestic subsidiaries are consolidated.[10] A further problem is that the accounting for less-than-majority-owned entities continues to be widely based on the acquisition cost of such investments.[11]

Second, in some countries there is either actual or practical linkage between income tax and financial reporting.[12] Where this happens, the fair presentation of financial information may be frustrated by the different perspectives and objectives of fiscal authorities as opposed to other users of financial statements. Governments should consider seriously the necessity to continue any such linkage between fiscal and financial reporting.

Third, accounting for postemployment benefits varies widely, from no prescribed accounting (where the pay-as-you-go method may be used) to required disclosure (but not recording) of the actuarial present value of accumulated benefits and related net assets.[13]

Fourth, all leases are treated as operating leases in many countries. Therefore, the economic substance of a financing lease is ignored in those countries, and no asset or liability is recognized in the accounts.[14]

---

[8] For example, the report of the U.N.'s Ad Hoc Intergovernmental Working Group of Experts on International Standards of Accounting and Reporting (E/C. 10/1982/8, 24 May 1982) sets forth a number of nonfinancial information items to be provided by individual enterprises. Such items include information on labor and employment, production, investment programs, organizational structure, net contribution to the balance of payments in the host country, observance of legal requirements, transfer of technology, environmental measures, and value added information. For the most part, such items were sought by representatives from developing countries, and the developed countries noted that such information is better suited to special purpose reports.

[9] See Organisation for Economic Cooperation and Development, Paris, *Accounting Practices in OECD Member Countries*, at 47 (May 1980) (ISBN 92-64-12076-9).

[10] *Id*. at 68 and 69, for example.

[11] *Id*.

[12] *Id*. at 64 and 81, for example.

[13] See Fitzgerald, Stickler & Watts, *International Survey of Accounting Principles and Reporting Practices*, at 169–75, Price Waterhouse, Ontario, Canada (1979).

[14] Indeed, in some countries it may be illegal to include leased properties as assets. Thus, a lease is accounted for in accordance with its legal form, and not its economic substance. Those that

Fifth, in an age of multinational enterprises engaged in diverse business activities, comprehensive information by line of business and geographic area is not required in many countries.[15]

Sixth, foreign currency translations are measured and reported in a variety of ways.[16] In some cases, users of general purpose reports cannot determine the method used for translation or the effect that foreign currency translations had on the reported results of operations and financial condition. In an environment of volatile currencies, there may be significant effects resulting from transactions denominated in a particular foreign currency, even where there are no foreign operations to be translated in connection with the preparation of consolidated financial statements.[17]

Seventh, in many parts of the world financial statements are required only annually, and they are often not required to be published sooner than six months after the balance sheet date.[18] Delays of this sort can render even the most relevant financial data virtually useless.

Eighth, a statement of source and application of funds or similar statement is not required as part of the financial statements in some jurisdictions.[19]

Ninth, the standards governing the qualification of independent auditors and audit examinations of financial statements vary widely, and users are not necessarily justified in ascribing a further degree of credibility to financial information because of auditor involvement.[20]

---

favor accounting for all leases as operating leases argue that over the lease term the result will be the same irrespective of which accounting method is used. But that argument is not persuasive because there often are dramatic differences that occur in the intervening periods if a financing lease is treated as an operating lease and thus is not capitalized. If such an argument were valid, the same case could be made for the cash basis of accounting, since in the long run it will be identical to accrual accounting.

[15] This condition is changing rapidly, however. There has been a requirement in the United States for some segment information since 1969. *See* SEC Securities Act Release No. 4988, 34 Fed. Reg. 12, 176–77 (1969), and Statement of Financial Accounting Standard No. 14, *Financial Reporting for Segments of a Business Enterprise*, Financial Accounting Standards Board (Dec. 1976). The EEC's Fourth Directive, *see infra* note 42, and the OECD Guidelines, *infra* note 29, require segment information on a geographic basis, and the International Accounting Standards Committee (IASC) has issued a standard covering segment data for years beginning on or after January 1, 1983. *See* International Accounting Standard IAS 14, *Reporting Information by Segment*, International Accounting Standards Committee (Aug. 1981). The principal reason that segment reported is mentioned as an important difference is that it is only in the United States, Canada and in those countries of the EEC that have implemented the Fourth Directive and there is an actual compulsion to disclose—the other "requirements" depend on voluntary compliance by preparers of financial statements.

[16] *See supra* note 13, at 29.

[17] For example, Statement of Financial Accounting Standards No. 52, *Foreign Currency Translation*, requires translation of loans denominated in a foreign currency to be translated at the current exchange rate and any difference resulting from the translation to be included in the results of operations.

[18] *See* Ernst & Whinney, *Ernst & Whinney International Series*, Cleveland, Ohio (1980 and 1981).

[19] *See, e.g.*, Article 2, EEC Fourth Directive, *infra* note 42.

[20] There are developments in this area, however. For example, the International Federation of Accountants is actively involved in establishing professional standards internationally. *See* American Institute of Certified Public Accountants (AICPA) *AICPA Professional Standards*, AU § 8000.01, and *infra* note 23. The Union Europeene des Experts Comptables Economiques et Financiers (UEC) is also involved in a similar and complementary way. *See* U.E.C., Annual Report 1981, Munich, Germany.

The foregoing items by no means constitute an exhaustive list of the troublesome differences that exist in the context of international accounting and reporting. There are many others—some subtle, such as differences between extraordinary and unusual items in operating statements, and some more fundamental, such as differences in revenue recognition methods or the methods used to account for business combinations. The above list does demonstrate, however, that fundamental differences exist among national standards for measuring and reporting financial data. As the world's capital markets become more internationally oriented, these annoying differences will prove even greater problems in the context of comparable financial information.

## ORGANIZATIONS INVOLVED IN THE STANDARDIZATION OF REQUIREMENTS

In the last ten years, a number of regional and international bodies have responded to expressions of need for a better quality of comparable information in general purpose reports of business enterprises. These organizations which include the International Accounting Standards Committee (IASC), the OECD, the U.N., and the EEC, have been working toward the standardization of accounting and reporting requirements. Each of these organizations has made a positive contribution to the trend toward the standardization of financial and, to a lesser extent, nonfinancial information requirements. The relevant activities of these organizations are summarized in this section.

### International Accounting Standards Committee

Since its founding in 1973,[21] the IASC has issued twenty international accounting standards and at March 31, 1983, had four exposure drafts outstanding and four additional projects under study. To say at this point that the IASC has developed a comprehensive body of accounting principles would be an overstatement, but IASC standards do treat many complex measurement and reporting issues. Indeed, the IASC has issued standards in some areas which have not been addressed by the national standard-setting bodies in some of the founding member countries.[22]

At the time of the XII International Congress of Accountants in October 1982, the IASC and the International Federation of Accountants (IFAC)[23] acknowledged that both organizations were operating within the common framework of the inter-

---

[21] The founding members of the IASC were the accountancy bodies in Australia, Canada, France, Federal Republic of Germany, Japan, Mexico, the Netherlands, the United Kingdom and Ireland, and the United States. Currently, the professional accountancy bodies in about 50 countries are IASC members. The role of IASC is to contribute to the development and adoption of accounting principles that are relevant, balanced and comparable internationally and to encourage their observance in the presentation of financial statements. *See* International Accounting Standards Committee, *Objectives and Procedures*, (Jan. 1983).

[22] For example, the IASC has issued standards on leases, segment reporting, the effects of changing prices, and accounting for retirement benefits (IAS Nos. 17, 14, 15 and 19, respectively), but not all IASC member countries have standards in all of these areas.

[23] The International Federation of Accountants, like the IASC, is an organization of professional accountancy bodies. *See* IFAC, *Agreement and Constitution* (1977). Effective January 1, 1984, the membership of the IASC and the IFAC will be identical. The IFAC's focus is the development and enhancement of a coordinated, worldwide accountancy profession.

nationally organized accountancy profession and were sponsored by and reported to the same professional bodies. Accordingly, the two organizations entered into a mutual commitments agreement under which they will have identical memberships, the IFAC Council will nominate the thirteen members of the IASC Board, and the IFAC will promote the worldwide acceptance and observance of IASC standards.[24]

A consultative group of nonmember organizations was created by the IASC in 1981 in order to widen the input to the standard-setting process by providing a forum for discussion between the nonmember organizations and IASC Board.[25] Additionally, provision has been made in the revised constitution for representation of up to four nonaccounting organizations on the IASC Board.[26]

### The Organisation for Economic Cooperation and Development

The OECD's membership comprises twenty-four developed countries, including the ten nations that are members of the EEC.[27] The objectives of the OECD are to (1) seek long-term economic growth within the member countries, (2) support the expansion of world trade, and (3) assist the economic growth of the developing countries of the world.[28] By declaration in June 1976, the governments of the OECD member countries issued a set of guidelines related to the activities of and the disclosure of information by multinational enterprises.[29] Through the issuance of the guidelines, the OECD formally recognized the need for a better quality of information.[30] The guidelines encourage multinational enterprises to consider certain factors in the course of conducting business in host countries, and a chapter on the disclosure of information calls on multinational enterprises to regularly publish financial statements and other pertinent information at least annually.

The information that multinational enterprises are invited to publish as a supplement to information disclosed under national law of the individual countries in

---

[24] *See supra* note 21, Appendix 3.

[25] The Consultative Group consists of participants nominated by the following organizations:
Federation Internationale des Bourses de Valeurs (the international federation of stock exchanges);
International Association of Financial Executives Institutes;
International Chamber of Commerce;
International Confederation of Free Trade Unions;
International Co-ordinating Committee of Financial Analysts' Associations;
The World Bank.
In addition, a member of the OECD Secretariat and a member of the U.N. Centre on Transnationals are invited to attend as observers.

[26] *See supra* note 21, Appendix 2.

[27] The members of the OECD are Australia, Austria, Belgium, Canada, Denmark, Finland, France, the Federal Republic of Germany, Greece, Iceland, Ireland, Italy, Japan, Luxembourg, the Netherlands, New Zealand, Norway, Portugal, Spain, Sweden, Switzerland, Turkey, the United Kingdom, and the United States. *See* OECD, International Investment and Multinational Enterprises, at 2, *Review of the 1976 Declaration and Decisions* (Paris, 1979) (ISBN 92-64-11970-1).

[28] *See* USA-BIAC Committee on International Investment and Multinational Enterprises, *A Review of the Declaration on International Investment and Multinational Enterprises* (Nov. 1976).

[29] *See* Organisation for Economic Cooperation and Development, *Declaration on International Investment and Multinational Enterprises* (Paris, June 21, 1976).

[30] *Id.* at 7.

which they operate includes, among other items:

1. operating results and sales by geographical area and sales in the major lines of business;
2. significant new capital investment by geographical area and, if practicable, major line of business for the enterprise as a whole;
3. a statement of source and use of funds;
4. research and development expenditure; and
5. the accounting policies used, including the consolidation policies used in compiling the published information.[31]

In order to facilitate compliance with the disclosure items in the guidelines, the OECD created an ad hoc working group on accounting standards in 1978 and a permanent working group in 1979. The permanent group meets biannually to develop guidance and elaboration on guideline disclosure items, and to encourage the harmonization of international standards of accounting and reporting through an exchange of views with and among standard-setting bodies.[32] There is unanimous agreement among the member states that the working group will not function as a standard-setting body.

The working group found it expedient to form a limited number of subgroups to consider some of the underlying technical issues associated with OECD guideline disclosures. The activities of the subgroups are restricted to the identification of differing accounting and reporting practices and making recommendations to the working group regarding possible approaches to encourage national and regional standard-setting bodies to harmonize requirements in the area studied. So far, subgroups have been formed to consider the relationships between fiscal and financial reporting requirements and the accounting methodology employed in the translation of foreign currencies.

### United Nations

In 1973, the Secretary-General of the U.N. appointed the Group of Eminent Persons to study the impact of multinational corporations on development and international relations. Their report noted a serious lack of both usable financial and nonfinancial information on the activities of transnational corporations, as well as the limited comparability of corporate reports.[33] The recommended remedy was the development of an international system of accounting and reporting, and in that connection, it was recommended that an expert group be convened under the auspices of the newly established Commission on Transnational Corporations. The Secretary-General acted on that recommendation and appointed an International Group of Experts on International Accounting and Reporting. In July 1977, that group issued a report that included a comprehensive list of minimum disclosures of financial and

---

[31] *Id.* at 14.

[32] The working group is exploring the feasibility of holding a convocation of accounting standard-setting bodies in 1984 or 1985 to discuss the problems associated with the harmonization of accounting and reporting standards.

[33] United Nations, *The Impact of Multinational Corporations on Developments and on International Relations* (1974) (U.N. Doc. E.4.II.A.5).

nonfinancial information for inclusion in general purpose reports.[34] The report of the group, however, was not endorsed by all members of the Commission on Transnational Corporations, and at its fourth meeting in May 1978, the Commission recommended the establishment of an ad hoc international governmental group of experts. The U.N.'s Economic and Social Council subsequently established the Ad Hoc Intergovernmental Working Group of Experts on International Standards of Accounting and Reporting consisting of representatives from thirty-four nations. This group met in six two-week sessions, the last of which was in April 1982. Although the ad hoc group's report closely follows the format used in the report of the earlier expert group, the report of this later group contains numerous items on which the developed and developing countries were unable to find agreement.[35]

In late 1982, the Social and Economic Council established a permanent Intergovernmental Working Group of Experts on International Standards of Accounting and Reporting with a mandate very much like that of its predecessor group.[36] The new group will meet yearly in two-week sessions. The first meeting was held in late February 1983, at which time the group outlined a general work program for the next three sessions and agreed on several items which were not resolved by the ad hoc group.[37] The work program contains many of the disclosure items that were left unagreed by the ad hoc group.[38] The new group will report annually to the Social and Economic Council, and in 1985 the Council will review the mandate, terms of reference, and achievements of the new group with a view to deciding on the advisability of its continuation.[39]

### The European Economic Community

The ten-nation EEC[40] is actively involved in a number of diverse areas which affect business enterprises. The EEC members comprise nearly one-half of the OECD membership and represent most of the industrialized nations of Western Europe, representing almost one-quarter of total world trade. Bound by the provisions of the 1957 Treaties of Rome, member countries are required to conform their national laws to the directives of the Council of Ministries.[41]

The Fourth Directive, approved by the Council of Ministries in 1978, sets forth requirements governing the form and content of financial statements for limited liability companies and is the most important directive dealing with financial

---

[34] *See* United Nations, *International Standards of Accounting and Reporting for Transnational Corporations* (Oct. 18, 1977) (U.N. Doc. E/C. 10/33).

[35] *See supra* note 8.

[36] *See* United Nations, *Economic and Social Council, Official Records, 1982*, at 1, U.N. Doc. E/1982/18, E/C. 10/1982/19.

[37] For example, it was agreed that financial statements should contain adequate information to give a true and fair view, and agreement was reached regarding the disclosure of contingent assets and liabilities.

[38] For example, the new group agreed to consider movements in certain assets, subsidies, transfer pricing, value added, and a number of other items during the second session next year.

[39] *See supra* note 36, at 2.

[40] The ten nations that comprise the Community are Belgium, Denmark, France, Greece, Ireland, Italy, Luxembourg, the Netherlands, the United Kingdom, and the Federal Republic of Germany.

[41] *See* United States Council for International Business, *Corporate Handbook to the European Community* (1981).

statements issued to date.[42] Each EEC directive specifies the period of time within which member countries must conform their national laws to the requirements of the directive. Thus far, only Denmark and the United Kingdom have enacted legislation to implement the Fourth Directive, even though the implementation period expired over two years ago.

The EEC issued its Proposed Seventh Directive in 1976.[43] Subject to the usual derogations allowed national governments, the proposed directive, when issued and implemented,[44] generally will require every company governed by the national laws of member states to draw up consolidated accounts and a consolidated annual report if that company has "subsidiary undertakings." Further, the non-EEC parents having operations within the Community will be required to publish consolidated information in conformity with, or equivalent to, the directive, whether or not that entity otherwise has a reporting requirement in its domicile country. The proposed directive provides detailed guidance on the preparation of such consolidated accounts.

The Community also has issued a Draft Eighth Directive dealing with the professional qualifications of statutory auditors.[45] In addition, directives have been issued covering the conditions governing stock exchange listings; the listing particulars to be published in connection with a stock exchange listing; and interim reporting requirements for listed companies.[46]

### Implementation Considerations

The EEC has a significant direct influence on the standard-setting processes within the Community and an indirect effect outside the Community. The influence of the EEC reaches the international level by virtue of its impact on multinational enterprises operating within its area and through the active participation of EEC representatives in the U.N. and OECD working groups on accounting and reporting standards. The EEC's directives will cause many of the differing standards among the member states to be harmonized, and the effect will reach beyond the Community to the EEC operations of multinational enterprises domiciled in other countries. But the EEC must be viewed with some ambivalence. Since EEC requirements become statutory law in each of the member states, there may be an inability to respond quickly to needed changes in standards.

The existing IASC standards evidence significant progress toward the development of a comprehensive set of international accounting standards. The most serious problem regarding the efforts of the IASC is that there is no effective way to assure implementation of the standards once they are issued—IASC standards are not enforceable. Although IASC members make a commitment to support the standards and use their best efforts to ensure that published financial statements are prepared in conformity with them, auditors generally are not bound to qualify their opinions if the standards are not followed, and the standards do not otherwise have the force of law.

---

[42] See Official Journal of the European Communities L222, Vol. 21, at 14 (Aug. 14, 1978).
[43] See Bulletin of the European Communities, Supp. 7108–S/9 (Sept. 1976).
[44] Id. Article 26 of the Proposed Directive directs member states to amend their laws, etc., to comply with the directive within 18 months of notification.
[45] See Bulletin of the European Communities, Supp. ISBN 92–825–0401–8 (Apr. 1978).
[46] Council Directives of Mar. 3, 1979, Mar. 17, 1980, and Feb. 15, 1982, respectively.

Like the IASC's accounting standards, the ultimate success of the OECD's guidelines depends on a responsive constituency for effective implementation. OECD member countries have undertaken to support the guidelines by encouraging home-country multinational companies to apply them. However, companies can make meaningful responses to the guideline items only if a common understanding of the intent and meaning of guideline terms exists. Therefore, the clarifications and elaborations being developed currently by the OECD Accounting Working Group should make a meaningful contribution to the effort to improve the relevance and comparability of information disclosed by multinational enterprises in OECD member countries.

Because of the differences that exist in environments, philosophies, perspectives and objectives, it is unlikely that a total convergence of standards will ever be achieved. That is not to say, however, that the participants in these efforts should not continue to work diligently to narrow differences. But patience must be exercised because the process is slow and involves the development of an awareness about the needs and methods of others. In addition, the process must accommodate the variety of ways in which standards are established and recognize that flexibility and respon-siveness are generally lessened in jurisdictions where requirements are statutory. In the interim, consideration should be given to the recognition of a body of standards to be used as a benchmark for gauging the effect of the other standards.

## SEC REQUIREMENTS IN FILINGS BY FOREIGN PRIVATE ISSUERS

The increase in transnational capital flows has influenced the SEC's rules and regulations applicable to foreign private issuers. Prior to 1967, the financial statements included in the periodic reports filed by foreign private issuers under the Securities Exchange Act of 1934 (the Exchange Act) were not required to conform with, or be reconciled to, accounting principles generally accepted in the United States (U.S. GAAP) or with the Commission's regulation S-X.[47] Further, the Commission's rules did not require such issuers to identify differences between the principles used to prepare the financial statements and U.S. GAAP requirements, and the financial statements were not required to be audited. In 1967, the form 20-K annual report requirements for foreign private issuers were amended to conform the financial statement requirements to those specified under the Exchange Act for domestic issuers. Although compliance with U.S. GAAP still was not required, material variations between the accounting principles or practices used in the financial statements and the form and content requirements of the Commission's regulation S-X (but not variations from U.S. GAAP) were required to be disclosed and, to the extent practicable, quantified.

In November 1979, the Commission rescinded form 20-K and adopted new form 20-F as a combination registration and reporting form for foreign private issuers filing under the Exchange Act.[48] Although registration statements filed under the Securities Act of 1933 (the Securities Act) continued to require a reconciliation of any material differences between the financial statements included in such filings and the requirements of U.S. GAAP and the Commission's regulation S-X, form 20-F expanded

---

[47] 17 C.F.R. §§ 210.1–01 to 210.12–29 (1982).
[48] See 17 C.F.R. §§ 240.3a12–3, 240.15d–16, 249.220f, 249.306 (1982).

the form 20-K provisions by requiring issuers to disclose and quantify, where practicable, any material variations from U.S. GAAP and regulation S-X.

Form 20-F is used primarily by foreign issuers that have registered securities for sale in the United States or listed securities on a stock exchange in the United States.[49] The 1979 revisions substantially upgraded the previous disclosure requirements for foreign issuers reporting under the Exchange Act,[50] but certain expressed concerns of foreign issuers were accommodated by modifying several reporting requirements that remain applicable to domestic companies. For example, form 20-F permits foreign issuers to: provide disclosures about remuneration of management as a group rather than individually; report revenues, but not profits, by industry and geographic segments, with a narrative discussion if the relative revenue and profit contributions from the respective segments differ materially; and use their foreign financial statements, adding footnote disclosures about material differences between foreign accounting principles and U.S. GAAP.[51]

In a subsequent rule-making proceeding in November 1982,[52] the Commission adopted an integrated disclosure system for non-Canadian foreign issuers which parallels to a large extent the integrated disclosure scheme recently adopted for domestic issuers.[53] The new rules permit foreign issuers meeting certain criteria to use abbreviated disclosure documents under the Securities Act for registration of newly offered securities. Certain "world class issuers"[54] may incorporate by reference information from the form 20-F into a Securities Act prospectus, and foreign issuers who file periodic reports with the Commission for three years may attach their

[49] Foreign issuers must report under the Exchange Act using form 20-F if they distribute their securities in the United States, list their securities on a U.S. stock exchange, or have at least $3 million in assets and 500 shareholders, 300 of whom are residents of the United States. Foreign issuers in the last category, however, need not report on form 20-F if they furnish all of the information to the Commission that is made public about them pursuant to foreign law. *See* rule 12g3–2(b) under the Exchange Act, 17 C.F.R. § 240.12g3–2(b) (1982). On October 28, 1982, the Commission issued a proposal to amend rule 12g3–2(b) to limit its application to securities traded in the over-the-counter market, other than securities which are quoted in the NASDAQ system. *See* 47 Fed. Reg. 48,988–89 (1982).

[50] Foreign issuers previously registered under the Exchange Act on form 20, 17 C.F.R. § 249.220, and reported on form 20-K, 17 C.F.R. § 249.320 (rescinded 1979). Most of the upgraded requirements entail narrative disclosures pertaining to items in the form, such as description of the issuer's business, description of property, beneficial ownership of voting securities, pending legal proceedings, description of the registrant's principal trading market outside the United States, and description of securities and taxes applicable to American securities holders. *See* 17 C.F.R. §§ 240.3a12–3, 240.15d–16, 249.220f, 249.306 (1982).

[51] Release No. 16,371, *supra* note 48 at 70,135. The Commission made these accommodations in response to arguments that equivalent disclosure requirements would put foreign issuers at a competitive disadvantage with respect to other foreign corporations and that some proposed requirements were inconsistent with the commercial practices, privacy concepts, and accounting principles of other countries. The Commission also found that these disclosure accommodations were consistent with the rules and guidelines of the Organization for Economic Cooperation and Development, the European Economic Community, and other international organizations. *Id*. at 70,133–34.

[52] SEC Securities Act Release No. 6437, 47 Fed. Reg. 54,764 (1982).

[53] For the new rules applicable to domestic issuers, see SEC Securities Act Release No. 6383, 47 Fed. Reg. 11,380 (1981).

[54] A world class issuer is described as a foreign private issuer that has voting stock, held by nonaffiliates, with an aggregate market value worldwide of no less than $300 million, or that is registering "investment grade debt securities." Release No. 6437, *supra* note 52, at 54,778. Investment grade debt securities are those that at least one nationally recognized statistical rating organization has rated in one of the four highest categories. *Supra* note 52, at 54,774.

form 20-F to a Securities Act prospectus instead of including certain information directly in the prospectus.[55] To effectuate this integrated disclosure system, the new rules for foreign issuers permit the incorporation of information by reference to form 20-F if the issuer has elected to include the additional financial information specified in optional item 18 of form 20-F. This upgrading is designed to ensure that the information disclosed in form 20-F approximates more closely the information required in registration statements under the Securities Act.[56] Except for offerings of investment grade debt by issuers that have been subject to the Exchange Act reporting system for at least three years and certain offerings to existing shareholders, the form 20-F financial statements incorporated by reference are required to be reconciled to U.S. GAAP and include all other information required by U.S. GAAP and regulation S-X. The Commission again has accommodated foreign issuers by requiring less disclosure in form 20-F for issuers that do not contemplate using the form 20-F report in connection with a new securities offering.[57] Consequently, some of the financial information included in the annual report of such issuers will not be fully comparable to the information which U.S. issuers publish and with which U.S. investors are familiar.

These revisions in some respects are counter to the developments in other forums mentioned above. However, one should remember that the pronouncements of IASC, OECD, and the U.N. are not compulsory, and it is not suggested here that they should be. But in the absence of a compulsion to implement international standards, the national requirements of many countries lag behind the progress being made at the international level. The SEC proposals simply recognize that fact and evidence a

---

[55] The rules allow a world class issuer, *supra* note 54, who has reported with the Commission for three years to use abbreviated form F-3 and to incorporate by reference information from form 20-F. If the issuer either is world class or reports for three years with the Commission, it may attach form 20-F to form F-2, another abbreviated prospectus. In both cases, however, the financial statements included in form 20-F must be in compliance with the requirements of item 18, which requires financial statements to be reconciled to U.S. GAAP and include all disclosures required by U.S. GAAP and regulation S-X. If the registrant is a world class issuer registering investment grade debt or certain offerings to existing shareholders, only the requirements of item 17 must be met. Item 17 permits the omission of certain disclosures required by U.S. GAAP and regulation S-X. Other issuers must use form F-1, which requires the inclusion of form 20-F information and other information in the prospectus. *See* Release No. 6360, 46 Fed. Reg. 58,517 (1981).

[56] The concept of integrated disclosure is based upon the premise that disclosures made in forms under the Exchange Act are substantially equivalent to the disclosures made in forms under the Securities Act. *See* Release No. 6360, *supra* note 55, at 58,519. To reduce duplicative disclosure, information from Exchange Act forms can be used in the Securities Act offering prospectus. Accordingly, the rules provide an election to upgrade the disclosures in form 20-F so that the Exchange Act information incorporated by reference into the Securities Act prospectus is substantially equivalent to the information requirements under the Securities Act. *See generally* Release No. 6383, *supra* note 36, Release No. 6360, *supra* note 55.

[57] *See* Release No. 6437, *supra* note 52, at 54,787. Although the new rules do not require foreign issuers to prepare financial statements in accordance with U.S. GAAP, such issuers are required to reconcile the financial statements included in form 20-F filings with U.S. GAAP measurement principles. Further, the financial statements included in Securities Act registration statements (except certain debt and other offerings referred to above) must be reconciled or otherwise conformed to the measurement and disclosure requirements of U.S. GAAP and the Commission's regulation S-X. This entails recomputing the amounts contained in the foreign financial statements as if the statements were prepared under U.S. GAAP and regulation S-X. The inclusion of complete segment disclosures and certain information about employee benefit plans are examples of other items which are also required. *Id.* at 54,788.

willingness to consider some accommodation to the existing environment on a short-term basis. Looking further ahead, foreign private issuers should expect that the SEC's requirements generally will be symmetrical for domestic and foreign private issuers.

## FUTURE STEPS

It is apparent from the foregoing that a sizable number of organizations are involved in setting standards at the regional and international levels. In addition, there are numerous other bodies that significantly influence both standard setting and the implementation process.[58] The activities of regional and international organizations in these areas has heightened the awareness of national and other standard-setting bodies to the importance of developments in other forums. Meaningful progress is being made toward the development of a set of accounting measurement and financial disclosure requirements that are expected to result in the disclosure of financial and certain nonfinancial information which is relevant and reasonably comparable across national boundaries. Some standard-setting bodies are consciously seeking to avoid the development of requirements that conflict with standards in other jurisdictions, and some are consulting with their counterparts in other parts of the world in regard to controversial or complex issues.[59]

The harmonization of accounting and reporting standards internationally is an enormous undertaking, and we should not expect satisfactory progress to come swiftly. In order to make significant progress toward the objective of more meaningful financial information, the following steps should be given serious consideration:

1. Providing support to the IASC in developing a comprehensive body of accounting principles. Such principles could serve as the recognized international benchmark mentioned above. Variant national standards could be compared with IASC standards, and the effects of differences could be quantified and disclosed.

2. Encouraging the U.N. and the OECD to openly endorse IASC standards and to encourage preparers of financial statements to comply with them as minimum or baseline standards of accounting and reporting.

3. Monitoring developments in the EEC and encouraging its representatives to continue active participation in the international groups in order to foster greater understanding about the possible impact of EEC pronouncements within and outside the Community.

Notwithstanding the substantial dependence or voluntary acceptance inherent in the process of establishing international norms, the process is worthwhile. There is a salutary effect that comes from having concerned people meet and discuss issues. Progress on the harmonization of standards will come slowly. It is an evolutionary process, but progress is being made.

[58] For example, professional accounting organizations, such as the AICPA, not only suggest topics and comment on proposals but effect implementation through the promulgation and enforcement of audit reporting standards. *See* AICPA, *Professional Standards*, General and Technical Standards, rules 202 and 203 (1982).

[59] For example, the FASB's task force on foreign currency translation included representatives from other standard-setting bodies. *Supra* note 17, at 73.

# IV-A 2  *Accounting Standards in Developing Countries*

J. M. SAMUELS AND J. C. OLIGA

## INTRODUCTION

In contemporary accounting thought and practice, the problem of harmonization of accounting standards has progressively become more politically intricate, theoretically complex, and operationally uncertain, yet the drive for uniformity seems to continue unabated. This appears to be true at both the domestic and international levels of concern, but in the latter case, the drive for harmonization of accounting principles and practices in developing countries with those in the rest of the world seems to present conceptual and practical problems of far wider dimensions. In this paper, the authors question the rationale and the desirability of "broadening" the so-called international accounting standards to encompass the Third World.

The paper argues that where economic, sociopolitical, cultural, and contextual differences between countries, nations, or societies exist, the problem of appropriate accounting standards will assume a different conceptual meaning as well as contextual significance. The paper further argues, in the case of developing countries where such differences tend to be not only highly pronounced, but also in a highly dynamic and fluid state, the relevance of international accounting standards becomes even more questionable. The paper illustrates these arguments with a brief historical case study of one developing country (Egypt) in terms of dramatic politicoeconomic changes spanning the 100 years between 1882 and 1981.

Thus, this paper is concerned with two aspects of international accounting, namely the comparative research and the attempts at harmonization of accounting standards. The comparative international accounting literature suggests that it is possible to group countries together on the basis of their accounting practices.[1]

J. M. Samuels and J. C. Oliga, "Accounting Standards in Developing Countries," *International Journal of Accounting Education and Research*, Fall 1982, pp. 69–88. Reprinted with the permission of *International Journal of Accounting Education and Research*.

[1] R. C. Da Costa, J. C. Bourgeois, and W. M. Lawson, "A Classification of International Financial Accounting Practices," *International Journal of Accounting* (Spring 1978): 73–85; W. G. Frank, "An Empirical Analysis of International Accounting Principles," *Journal of Accounting Research* (Autumn 1979): 593–605; and R. D. Nair and W. G. Frank, "The Impact of Disclosure and Measurement Practices on International Accounting Classification," *Accounting Review* (July 1980): 426–50.

Countries can thus be grouped into clusters, and within each cluster, it is assumed that there is much in common in the accounting system. In the future, the number of groupings would be expected to fall, thereby further facilitating harmonization.

There are now more than forty countries which are members of the International Accounting Standards Committee (IASC) and which supposely work together toward the international harmonization of accounting standards. The International Federation of Accountants (IFAC), which also wishes to harmonize standards, works closely with IASC, and there are proposals that beginning in 1982, the two bodies are to formalize their working relationship. This means that from 1984, the membership of the bodies would be identical, comprising professional accounting associations in over sixty countries.[2] If the proposals are accepted, IFAC will undertake to support the adoption of international accounting standards, with each of its members bringing pressure to bear on their respective governments and business communities to adopt such standards.

In the next section, the paper briefly examines the motives underlying the quest for international harmonization. Extension and international legitimation of certain accounting practices and standards rather than harmonization would seem to be the essence of the exercise. In the next section, the authors will introduce an analytical framework for discussing issues of harmonization. In the next section, the problems of harmonization at the theoretical level will be discussed, while similar problems at the contextual level are the subject of the next section. The final section refers both to the arguments in the paper and the illustrative insights for the Egyptian case study.

## HARMONIZATION OR INTERNATIONAL LEGITIMATION AND EXTENSION OF CURRENTLY DOMINANT PRACTICES?

Although all the parties striving for a greater degree of international harmonization of accounting standards implicitly hold the same assumption that such an objective is globally desirable, they may do so for very different reasons. Those organizations, national or international, which are active in setting accounting standards see worldwide harmonization as essentially a means to achieve compatibility in the financial reporting of international companies.[3] Professional accounting bodies seem to be motivated more by the need to maintain standards of professional ethics and credibility, with issues of consistency and reliability especially significant. The international business community sees harmonization as a means to facilitate international trade and business, especially in the areas of capital flows,[4] and reliability of information as a basis for foreign investment decision making.[5] Others see harmonization as an integrative device for bringing about a unified business environment (for example, the European Economic Community). The United Nations has been interested in harmonization, partly for evaluative purposes with regard to the impact of multinational companies' operations on developing countries. Individuals and certain interest groups, including those in developing countries, have perhaps supported the international harmonization efforts for reasons not excluding

[2] "Arms Linked for Mexico '82," *Accountancy* (August 1981).
[3] Ernst & Whinney, International Accounting Standards, 1981.
[4] S. M. Farag, "The Problem of Performance Evaluation in International Accounting," *International Journal of Accounting* (Fall 1974): 45–53.
[5] Belverd E. Needles, Jr., "Implementing a Framework for the International Transfer of Accounting Technology," *International Journal of Accounting* (Fall 1976): 47–62.

enhancement of personal or group interests and status. However, whatever the real motives underlying support for harmonization, such support is usually rationalized in terms of greater international understanding and better economic efficiency in the allocation of scarce resources, including avoidance of duplication in the cost of producing accounting reports.

Although the present authors believe that these efforts at international harmonization are for the most part well intentioned, they nonetheless see them as misguided insofar as developing countries are concerned. An examination of the sources of existing accounting systems in most developing countries reveals that those systems were for the most part either imposed by powerful foreign investors or extended from the home to the host countries through the influence of multinational companies, foreign aid, and education. As Wilkinson[6] argues,

> The accounting principles of one country have never been "sold" to another country on the basis of convincing arguments in support of those principles. Accounting principles of one country have moved to another country when two conditions have existed:
> 1. The second country had no organized body of accounting principles in the first place and
> 2. Large amounts of capital from the first country were invested in business in the second country, with the consequent ability on the part of those investors to impose their own accounting requirements on the businesses.

Briston[7] has similarly noted that in Indonesia, as a result of the influence of multinational companies, international firms of accountants, and U.S. aid, university accounting courses became strongly biased toward American texts. He also noted that the Indonesian Institute of Accountants adopted a set of accounting and auditing standards which were virtually identical to those of the American Institute of Certified Public Accountants. No doubt more examples could be cited, but the point is that most developing countries had little chance to evolve accounting systems which truly reflected the needs and circumstances of their own societies. Their existing systems are largely extensions of those in developed countries. In this light, the benefits of their being more deeply integrated into systems that predominantly suit developed countries becomes questionable. For the Third World, international harmonization may do more harm than good if it preempts the possibility of changing the old, inappropriate systems and evolving new ones which are better suited to their development needs. Furthermore, given that Anglo-American accounting principles and practices currently dominate the attempts at harmonization,[8] the attempt becomes largely a one-sided exercise, and "international" standards essentially represent internationalization of domestic standards of dominant members of the

---

[6] T. L. Wilkinson, "United States Accounts as Viewed by Accountants of Other Countries," *International Journal of Accounting* (Fall 1965): 11–12.

[7] R. J. Briston, "The Evolution of Accounting in Developing Countries," *International Journal of Accounting* (Fall 1978): 105–20.

[8] Gerhard G. Mueller, "Accounting Principles Generally Accepted in the United States versus Those Generally Accepted Elsewhere," *International Journal of Accounting* (Spring 1968): 91–103; R. C. Laughlin and A. G. Puxty, "On the Construction of International and Domestic Accounting Principles: A Cross-Cultural Research Model" (University of Sheffield Discussion Paper No. 81.2, 1981); and Desmond McComb, "International Harmonization: Myth or Ideal?" (Paper presented at the Fourth Annual Conference of the European Accounting Association, Barcelona, April 1981).

standard-setting bodies.[9] This paper will not pursue the question of Anglo-Saxon dominance in accounting thought even in the Western world itself; rather, the authors see it as evidence of the more severe imbalance of power between developing countries and such dominance, in the process of negotiating for "international harmonization." International standard-setting process thus becomes a means of legitimating worldwide certain values, accounting principles, and practices which may or may not be appropriate to other countries or societies. This problem is essentially entailed in one's view of the nature of accounting and its relationship to its environment. It is this problem to which we now turn.

## PURPOSE OF ACCOUNTING AND THE NATURE OF ITS SUBJECT MATTER: METATHEORETICAL ISSUES

Using a system approach, we can represent accounting as a system (with inputs, throughput, and outputs) interacting with its environment. The system takes its inputs from the environment and transforms them into outputs which go back to the environment.[10] The most immediate environment of an accounting system is, of course, the organization of which it is part. If viewed as essentially embedded in the organization, however, the accounting system's relevant environment becomes the same as that of the organization itself, the latter now becoming the focal system interacting with its environment. Exhibit 1 represents these ideas.

Exhibit 1 is a model of a typical accounting system, where part of the output goes to the external environment (I) as external financial reports and therefore concerns issues of disclosure requirements. The second part of the output is internal to the organization and is mainly intended for management (VI). Evaluation of the degree of organizational effectiveness being achieved is feedback to the system (VIII), while a similar position within the system is shown as representing feedwithin inputs (VII). The purpose of the outputs (at I and VI) dictates the type of inputs that are necessary to achieve those outputs (that is, feedforward inputs at II, feedwithin inputs at VII, and feedback inputs at VIII). The transformation process at IV and the resultant outputs (V) are a consequence of the given purpose of the outputs and the type of inputs selected from the environment.

Exhibit 1 thus illustrates that for any purposive system, the question of *why* the system is in existence (or came to being) is logically prior to *what* the system should be doing; the latter is logically prior to *how* the system should be conducting its activities within a given context. Put differently, the *purpose* (or objectives) of the system logically implies the *problems* to be addressed and hence the *solutions* that are deemed appropriate within a given *context*. This logical hierarchy can be represented in terms of *metatheory*, concerned with fundamental issues of purpose; *theory*, concerned with issues of problems and their solutions; and *reality*, defining the contextual setting.[11] Exhibit 2 represents the essential isomorphisms between these

[9] Laughlin and Puxty, "Accounting Principles," and McComb, "International Harmonization."

[10] Van Court Hare, *Systems Analysis: A Diagnostic Approach* (New York: Harcourt, Brace & World, 1967); and G. Klir, *An Approach to General Systems Theory* (New York: Van Nostrand Reinhold, 1969).

[11] E. A. Lowe and A. M. Tinker, "An Educational Design for 'Shifting' Degenerate Social Science Paradigms: An Application of General Systems Theory," *International Journal of General Systems*, vol. 2 (1976): 231–37.

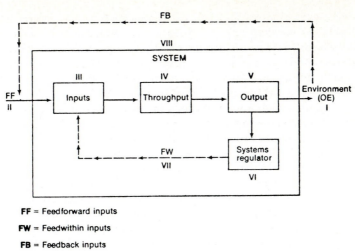

FF = Feedforward inputs

FW = Feedwithin inputs

FB = Feedback inputs

OE = Organizational effectiveness

   I = Represents the "Why?" issues in accounting

II, III, VII,
and VIII = Represent  the "What?" issues in accounting measurement

IV and V = Represent  the "How?" issues in accounting measurement

   VI = Represents the dynamic management of the relationship
between "Why?" "What?" and "How?"

## EXHIBIT 1

**Accounting as a System and Its Environment**

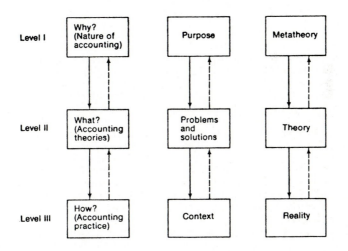

## EXHIBIT 2

**The Accounting Problem: An Analytical Framework**

logical hierarchies, including the feedback (represented by dashed arrows) between the three levels. As we shall argue in subsequent sections, it is this kind of base analytical framework that should underscore discussions concerning the accounting problem: the search for an "agreed" conceptual framework for accounting standards setting[12] capable of encompassing all issues relating to the three levels of (logical) hierarchy is, as we shall argue, highly misdirected.[13]

We now turn to an elaboration of the issues at the metatheoretical level; issues relating to the theoretical and empirical levels of analysis will be briefly examined later. Accounting, in common with all scientific inquiry, is concerned essentially with the search for and generation of knowledge or claims to knowledge about the world. Not every inquiry, however, can claim to produce valid knowledge. To evaluate the validity of inquiry activities and the status of the resultant knowledge claims, one should examine the underlying theories and presuppositions concerning the nature of proper inquiry. This evaluative task defines the essence of epistemological and ontological disciplines. Epistemology addresses the question of the nature and possibility of knowledge, truth, and reason. Ontology relates to a conception of the nature of the subject matter under inquiry and the fundamental views concerning the capacities of human beings as knowing subjects. Epistemological and ontological theories can therefore be considered as fundamental presuppositions (or philosophical doctrines) from which empirical sciences (or theories) derive their justification.[14] Relating this to the analytical framework in exhibit 2, it can be seen that epistemology and ontology correspond to the level of metatheories. At that level of analysis, we would be concerned with questions regarding the epistemic status of accounting knowledge and the ontological nature of the subject matter for accounting thought and inquiry. The very issues of knowledge and the objective conditions for that knowledge, however, entail questions of the knower's (subject's) set of values and beliefs since it can be argued that ultimately the aim of all empirical science is the improvement of the control by man and society over their physical and social environment.[15] There is thus a dialectical relationship between metatheory and theory in that metatheory presupposes theory or objective conditions in which control can be realized, and theory presupposes metatheory as the source of its

---

[12] Financial Accounting Standards Board, Statement of Financial Accounting Concepts No. 1, *Objectives of Financial Reporting by Business Enterprises* (Stamford, Conn.: FASB, 1978); R. MacVe, *The Possibilities for Developing an Agreed Conceptual Framework for Setting Accounting Standards: Preliminary Report* (London: Institute of Chartered Accountants in England and Wales, 1979); McComb, "International Harmonization," pp. 4–5; and Laughlin and Puxty, "Accounting Principles," p. 16.

[13] A. M. Tinker, "Towards a Political Economy of Accounting: An Empirical Illustration of the Cambridge Controversies," *Accounting, Organisations and Society*, vol. 5, no. 1 (1980); and J. Habermas, *Communication and the Evolution of Society* (London: Heinemann, 1979). The present authors believe that the only way in which an "agreed" conceptual framework for standards setting could be reached would be via Habermas' theory of "communicative competence" which postulates that moral judgments can be made on the basis of a rational consensus predicated on critical argumentation by "free" parties seeking to satisfy their emancipatory interests.

[14] For this view of epistemology and ontology, see D. Beyleveld, "Epistemological Foundations of Sociological Theory: An Examination of Recent Critiques of 'Positivism'" (Ph.D. Dissertation, University of East Anglia, 1975).

[15] N. Weiner, *The Human Use of Human Beings* (Boston: Houghton Mifflin, 1950); and Lowe and Tinker, "General Systems Theory."

justification in terms of basic, subjective values, and beliefs,[16] even if one is logically prior to the other.

Relating this discussion to the accounting problem, two related issues immediately arise: first, there is the question of what the epistemic nature of accounting knowledge is, and second, there is the question of what the ontological nature of the subject matter of accounting is. A full discussion of these issues is beyond the scope of this paper; it is not necessary for our argument against the uncritical approach to international harmonization of accounting standards. The purpose of raising the two questions is rather to point to the variety of epistemological and ontological positions that are possible and thereby demonstrate that harmonization of standards at the levels of theory and practice, based as it is on an implicit assumption of a consensus at the metatheory level, is misguided right from its most fundamental level. Two polar cases and a "middle-of-the-road" position can be used to illustrate the potential variety both in epistemologies[17] and ontologies.[18] Positivism as a polar case illustrates objectivist epistemologies, which assume that the sense of an object is inherent in that object and hence independent of any relation to a knowing subject. Under this position, the nature of accounting reduces to a mere "technology" or "technical" issues. Such a position would emphasize, *inter alia*, objectivity, verifiability, reliability, and neutrality in accounting knowledge (or information). Idealism as a polar case illustrates subjectivist epistemologies, which assume that reality is whatever mental concepts the mind calls forth. Under this position, accounting knowledge would be conceived more in terms of subjective judgment (with emphasis being generally on relevance of information for decision making). Realism has been used to describe the middle-of-the-road position,[19] which recognizes the unity of subject and object, the unity of thought, and experience. Under this position, the importance of both subjective and objective aspects of accounting knowledge is recognized.

The variety of ontological positions can be illustrated by reference to individualism and holism as polar cases, with systemism as the middle-of-the-road position. In accounting terms, individualism would represent the position where the subject matter of accounting is seen solely in terms of individual users or user-groups (for example, shareholders, lenders, creditors, and so on). Holism would represent the position where the identity of individual users or user groups is entirely lost, with only the organization being recognized; it is an extreme reification of the organization. Systemism would represent recognition of the systemic nature of the relationship between the organization and its participants, the reality of the organization together with its emergent properties being as well recognized as the reality of its participants.

---

[16] For this line of argument based on dialectical phenomenology, see R. W. Bologh, *Dialectical Phenomenology* (London: Routledge & Kegan Paul, 1979); see also E. A. Lowe and J. C. Oliga, "Perceived Uncertainty and Organizational Control: A Pluralist Dialectical Approach to the Modeling of Human Systems" (Proceedings of the International Conference on Systems Methodology and the 26th Annual Meeting of the Society for General Systems Research, Washington, D.C., January 1982), pp. 987–94.

[17] Bologh, *Dialectical Phenomenology.*

[18] M. Bunge, "A Systems Concept of Society: Beyond Individualism and Holism," *General Systems* (24): 27–44.

[19] Bologh, *Dialectical Phenomenology.*

Some important implications derive from the discussions in this section. First, the definition of the nature of accounting as well as that of its subject matter derives from the epistemological and ontological positions one takes. The purpose of accounting is only meaningful in terms of those definitions. Because of the variety of conceptions, values, and beliefs possible at the metatheoretical level, international harmonization of accounting standards (at the levels of theory and practice) is fundamentally misguided by making an implicit assumption that consensus obtains regarding the nature of accounting and that of its subject matter. Second, because values and beliefs are entailed essentially in any attempt to define or conceive of accounting, accounting cannot be value free. That accounting, as a social science, cannot be value free is being increasingly recognized in the literature.[20] Accounting information or knowledge cannot but be value laden since by being humanly determined as an empirical belief, it presupposes and entails the inquirer's value systems.[21]

It is also being increasingly recognized in the literature that accounting is necessarily grounded in societal need and that in fulfilling such need, it acts as a mechanism for social control.[22] At a general level, the function of accounting can therefore be defined in terms of social control. Even if all were agreed on such a definition, however, it would not follow that an "agreed" conceptual framework would emerge since such a definition would still leave open issues, such as control for what and by whom, how, and in whose interest? These are fundamental and formidable questions relating back to epistemologies and ontologies that one adopts. It is in this context that we argue that attempts at worldwide harmonization face politically intractable problems at the metatheoretical level. In the next section, attention is focused on the theoretical implications of this quandry to the case of developing countries.

## INTERNATIONAL HARMONIZATION IN DEVELOPING COUNTRIES: A CRITIQUE AT THE THEORETICAL LEVEL

In presenting alternative epistemological and ontological positions in the preceding section, we did not imply a relativistic basis of choice among them.[23] Rather, we wished to emphasize that a particular position is presupposed in the very act of engaging in any normative, theoretical discourse. Thus, our critique in this section necessarily entails a particular value stance.

In December 1980, Egypt, a developing country, considered adopting international accounting standards. The Syndicate of Commerce Professions held an international accounting conference under the auspices of President Anwar Sadat,

---

[20] E. A. Lowe, A. G. Puxty, and A. M. Tinker, "Improving the Accounting Function for Society: Proposals for GST-Based Newcomer to Social Science," in *Proceedings of the Fifth European Meeting on Cybernetics and Systems Research*, ed. R. Trappl (Hemisphere, 1979).

[21] A. Kaplan, *The Conduct of Inquiry* (Intertext Books, 1973); and W. F. Soo, J. C. Oliga, and A. G. Puxty, *The Population Ecology Model and Managerial Action, A Review Study of Organizations and Environments, J. Enterprise Management*, vol. 2 no. 3 (1980): 317–25.

[22] American Accounting Association, *Accounting Review*, supplement to vol. 52 (1977); E. A. Lowe and A. M. Tinker, "Siting the Accounting Problematic," *Journal of Business Finance and Accounting* (Autumn 1977): 263–76; and A. G. Puxty, J. C. Oliga, and W. F. Chua, "Accounting and Western Imperialism in the Third World" (Paper presented to the Fourth Annual Conference of the European Accounting Association, Barcelona, 1981).

[23] Habermas, *Communication*.

which led to a recommendation that Egypt adopt international standards.[24] This is what many people in the West would like to see, since it would help to harmonize accounting standards. However, is it in Egypt's best interests?

One of the objects of the formation of IASC was to harmonize, as far as possible, the diverse accounting standards and accounting policies presently in use in different countries. The main reason for this was said to be due to the demands of international trade and business which require the application of an acceptable uniform code of accounting standards. Undoubtedly this is true; international trade and business does benefit if information, such as accounting information, is clearly understood by all users. But what is the situation within a developing country? One of the main objectives of corporate reports is to assist users to make economic decisions. International standards assist those making decisions at an international level, but within a developing country, it is not clear what information should be used as a basis for economic decision making. The information required might not be just that relating to financial costs and returns. The whole of the cost benefit literature emphasizes that economic decisions in a developing country should be based on a knowledge of shadow prices and shadow costs, on a knowledge of foreign currency flows, and on a knowledge of opportunity costs, based on world prices rather than domestic prices. This cost-benefit literature is not subversive literature designed to destroy the private sector of an economy. The most widely used manuals on the subject are those produced by the World Bank and the United Nations, both very much supporters of the private enterprise system.

As accountants, we do say that "the basic objective of financial statements is to provide information useful for making economic decisions."[25] When accountants speak of economic decisions, however, they are defining economic decisions very narrowly. The harmonization of standards may be helpful to those groups in society who base economic decisions on just the financial analysis. The objectives of IAS state, "The accounting profession cannot normally impose its views except upon its own members and the task therefore is to persuade by example, leadership, and exhortation, the classes of persons referred to ... to support the standards,"[26] the persons referred to being "governments, the authorities controlling securities markets and the industrial and business community that published accounts." According to the guidance being given by the World Bank and the United Nations, governments should base their economic decisions on more information than that which would be provided by accounts conforming to international standards.

It might be argued that this paper is confusing decision making at the public and private levels, but this is not the case. In most developing countries, the public sector is very large and dominates the economy. Accountants cannot, therefore, ignore the requirements for economic decision making within that sector. The accounting profession in the United Kingdom has been criticized for not sufficiently concerning itself with the accountability of the public sector. Perhaps the differences in this respect between the developed and the developing countries are not so great. In the developing countries, the private sector must justify its existence; it must satisfy the

---

[24] R. J. Briston and A. A. El-Ashker, "The Egyptian Accounting System—A Case Study in Western Influence" (Copies available from the University of East Anglia, England).

[25] American Institute of Certified Public Accountants, *Objectives of Financial Statements* (New York: AICPA, 1973).

[26] International Accounting Standards Committee, *The Work and Purpose of the International Accounting Standards Committee* (IASC, 1975).

government that it is contributing to economic development. The accounting reports required, therefore, from both the public and private sectors are not necessarily those that would just satisfy shareholders and bankers. The point here is that accounting professions in developing countries should try to assist in designing reporting systems that are the most useful for economic decision making within the country, rather than trying to persuade the country to adopt systems which are needed for international trade and business. It is possible the two can be developed simultaneously, but the latter should not be seen as a substitute for the former.

As Chetkovich has noted, accounting in each country should develop in a manner relevant to the society in which it exists.[27] He argues that an accounting objective study group is necessary for different countries. One country might benefit from the work of another, but this does not mean that the results of such studies in other countries will necessarily be similar to results reached in the United States, for example. The other countries will benefit from the experiences of the leading groups and hopefully avoid some of the problems. We must recognize that different environments will lead to different accounting objectives and, therefore, different standards. Chetkovich also mentions the strong influence of nationalism which limits effective communication and rejects the experience of others for the preferences of going it alone. He also notes the difficulty in developing countries where there is a lack of qualified accountants.

Accountants cannot argue that they are not interested in the impact that financial reports may have on governments or on the public at large; they cannot argue that they are reporting only to shareholders; they cannot argue that accounting standards are politically neutral. Horngren commented that "the setting of accounting standards is as much a product of political action as of flawless logic or empirical findings."[28] According to Solomons, "The setting of standards is a social decision."[29]

Unfortunately, therefore, accounting standards and accounting reports are not politically neutral. According to the American Accounting Association, "in practice as well as in theory, the social welfare impact of accounting reports apparently is recognized. Therefore it is no surprise that the Financial Accounting Standards Board is a political body."[30] The International Accounting Standards Committee is a political body; its standards are those appropriate for industrial countries with a large private sector and a well-developed capital market. The main users of accounting reports in such countries are the shareholders, analysts, bankers, and other businesses. Accounting reporting practices and standards are quite rightly designed to provide these users with the information they require.

There is no agreed theory of accounting, no commonly accepted conceptual framework. Accounting is not a neutral technology, recording all information required for the purposes of stewardship and the measurement of performance. The data that it is decided to record, and the way in which this is disclosed in accounting

---

[27] Michael N. Chetkovich, "Unit in Establishing Accounting Standards," *International Journal of Accounting* (Fall 1972).

[28] Charles T. Horngren, "The Marketing of Accounting Standards," *Journal of Accountancy* (October 1973): 61–66.

[29] D. Solomons, "The Politicization of Accounting," *Journal of Accountancy* (November 1978).

[30] Robert G. May and Gary Sundem, "Research for Accounting Policy: An Overview," *Accounting Review* (October 1976): 747–63.

statements are based on what a society, or certain groups within that society, consider to be relevant to users' needs.

It can be argued that in a developing country, different information from that required in a developed country should be disclosed. The problems are different; what are considered to be the important issues differ. International accounting standards are based on the needs of users in developed countries; therefore, they are not particularly relevant to the needs of Egypt and other less developed countries. In Egypt, it is necessary to be able to ascertain how the development strategies are working; how the regional policy is working; whether funds are flowing into or out of Egypt. Where accounts prepared according to international standards will serve the needs of the small number of private and foreign investors, these investors constitute only a very small part of the capital market in the country. In reporting its performance in Egypt, a company should provide information appropriate to the major issues of that society. The accounting numbers disclosed and the standards should result in data that are useful for economic decision making, and data that are needed for the social and political debates taking place within a country.

Accounting information is not politically neutral, and there is a danger that in encouraging developing countries to adopt international standards which are ideal for a set of social, religious, political, and economic circumstances different from their own, we may be doing more harm than good. We may be helping to destroy within the country the very economic system we are attempting to encourage. As accountants, we should be more interested in designing accounting systems that best suit the needs of a country than in designing systems to suit world trade. We should not let the tail wag the dog.

As Enthoven stated in 1973, if accounting "is to play a useful and effective role in society, [it] must not pursue independent goals. It must continue to serve the objectives of its economic environment."[31] He adds that we must not assume that what might be good accounting for the developed countries "will automatically be economically relevant and good for the emerging nations and the process of development." This should be borne in mind by the International Accounting Standards Committee who have as an objective "to promote the worldwide acceptance and observance" of its standards. It should also be remembered by those pressure groups in developing countries who would benefit from the adoption in their country of the international standards.

## ACCOUNTING IN EGYPT: AN EMPIRICAL ILLUSTRATION OF THE HARMONIZATION UNCERTAINTIES IN DEVELOPING COUNTRIES

### Accounting in Egypt

It has been claimed that bookkeeping existed in Egypt in 3000 B.C. The claim relates to bookkeeping, not the double-entry version. The Egyptian pharaohs had a form of internal control operating within their treasury.[32] The techniques could well

---

[31] Adolph J. H. Enthoven, *Accountancy and Economic Development Policy* (Amsterdam: North Holland, 1973).

[32] Labib Aly El-Gammal claimed in a paper placed on the table at the International Accounting Conference held in Cairo in December 1980 that "the ancient Egyptians did bookkeeping. In particular it was claimed Amin Houtok was the first bookkeeper, ... five thousand years ago."

have been taken to Egypt sometime between 5000 and 3000 B.C. by Indian traders. Sodhbans has claimed that bookkeeping existed in India at this earlier date.[33] India was then the center of a great trading empire that certainly embraced Egypt. The traders had a system of keeping records which could claim to be bookkeeping.

It is interesting, but perhaps no more than a coincidence, that double-entry bookkeeping did not appear in Italy until the Crusaders opened the Middle East to trade with the Italians, and "the latter began an acquaintance with the achievements of the Byzantine and Arab civilisations."[34] Islam moved into Egypt in 641 A.D., and Alexandria became the cultural and business center of a vast empire. From 1882 to 1956, the central political and business influence in the country came from the United Kingdom. The main social and cultural influence continued, however, to be Islam.

The U.K.'s political influence until 1956 meant that the organization of the accounting profession and the financial reporting practices in Egypt closely followed those of the United Kingdom.[35] The public sector was very small, with private ownership being the most important form of business activity. A stock exchange existed, having been formed in Alexandria in 1883, and in Cairo in 1890. The training of accountants, the law regulating companies, and disclosures standards were all based on those in the United Kingdom.

In 1956, following the invasion of Suez, the politics of the country completely changed. The new economic system required a different set of information from accountants. The changes required were so dramatic that the organization of the profession had to change. The Egyptians developed an accounting system of their own. A number of accounting control boards were created, each responsible for a different sector of the economy. Initially, each board tried to design an accounting system which it was hoped would best be able to measure the financial activities of that sector. However, this could have resulted in numerous different systems, and so in 1966, the Central Auditing Agency introduced a "uniform accounting system" which was to be followed by all publicly owned companies.[36]

During the 1970s, the position again changed dramatically. The Russians were asked to leave the country; slowly the influence of the private sector increased in importance. An open-door policy was introduced with foreign companies encouraged to invest in Egypt. New pressure groups developed. The professional accounting organizations grew in importance and stature. International accounting links were redeveloped. In the late 1970s and early 1980s, new political influences were felt in Egypt. In 1981, President Sadat was assassinated. Suddenly the move to a capitalist system based on Western ideas seemed threatened. Islamic ideas regarding banking and money had increased in importance in the Middle East. Attitudes toward Western ideas were changing. The future path of the Egyptian economy and consequently that of the accounting profession and accounting requirements in Egypt became uncertain again, proving that accountants do not control their environment; they respond to it.

---

[33] P. S. Sodhbans, "Regulations Affecting Accounting in India" (Proceedings of the Fifth International Congress of Accountants, Berlin, 1938).

[34] D. T. Bailey, "European Accounting History," in *International Accounting*, ed. H. Peter Holzer (in press).

[35] Committee on International Accounting, "Accounting Education and the Third World" (American Accounting Association, 1978).

[36] B. Metwalli Amer, "Impact of Public Ownership on the UAR Accounting Profession," *International Journal of Accounting* (Spring 1969).

### Comparative Research

Of what use is the type of comparative international accounting research that attempts to classify countries on the basis of factor analysis? It is generally agreed that to understand any accounting system, one must consider the cultural, social, economic, legal, and religious systems of a country.

In the case of developed countries, these factors may be sufficiently stable to enable classifications to be made that are reasonably consistent over time, but, unfortunately, in the case of developing countries, changes in the environment can be frequent and dramatic and so reduce the significance of any attempt to categorize. Factor analysis looks at the situation at only one point of time; yet by definition, developing countries are changing and so should not be expected to remain for long within one grouping. In Egypt's situation, there could well be four different economic systems in twenty-five years, each economic change being accompanied by social change. This illustrates the difficulty of using a classification of accounting systems to predict changes.

Mueller concluded in one of his pioneering papers on the subject that ten distinct sets of business environment existed.[37] One of the sets was "the developing nations of the Near and Far East." Egypt clearly comes within this set. Mueller describes the characteristics of this set:

> Modern concepts and ethics of business have predominantly Western origins. The concepts and ethics often clash with the basic oriental cultures.... Political scenes and currencies are most shaky. Major economic advances are probably impossible without substantial assistance from the industrialized countries.

Mueller draws attention to the instabilities within this set. It is because of such propensities to frequent and rapid changes over time that it is suggested that the recent interest in using cluster analysis in the international accounting area is highly misguided. Cluster analysis is a technique in search of an area of application: it is not a method for studying a problem and deciding what can usefully be said or done about it.

### Accounting Standards

There are three stages in the standard-setting process in any country: political, production of the standards, and marketing of the standards. These stages will be briefly explained before the process at work in Egypt is described in detail.

First there is the political stage. The word *politics* is used here to mean "the relationship of men in society, especially relationships involving authority or power."[38] For instance, a pressure group within a country becomes active. It may be in the interests of this group to publish and have accepted generally accepted accounting principles. This pressure group may be responding to outside criticism of

---

[37] Gerhard G. Mueller, "Accounting Principles Generally Accepted in the United States versus Those Generally Accepted Elsewhere," *International Journal of Accounting* (Spring 1968): 91–103.

[38] Collins, *English Dictionary* (1979).

existing reporting methods, and they are therefore concerned to put their own house in order. They may be responding to changing economic and social conditions which result in new opportunities for members of the group.

With a group which would like to see the existence of standards having emerged, the next stage in the process is the production of the standards. This can be an expensive and time-consuming process. The next stage is marketing, which involves the attempt by the accounting standard-setting body to ensure that its standards are acceptable to the more powerful groups in the society. These other groups would be interested in the standards, either as users or by being involved in their preparation in some way. Users would include politicans and different organs of the government.

As the reported information can and does affect human behavior, the items to be disclosed must meet with the approval of the most powerful groups in the society. The standards must therefore be acceptable to this group.

We will now trace the development of accounting standards in Egypt through these three stages. In regard to the political stage, as explained earlier in the paper, in 1956 Egypt began to move in the direction of being a centrally planned economy. Central planning has need for standardized data, and so a "uniform accounting system" was introduced affecting both public and private companies. With the "opening up" of the economy in the 1970s, international trade and international business assigned increasing importance. The accounting profession, responding to changing circumstances benefiting them, wished to improve reporting practices and saw the advantages in adopting international standards. A new stock exchange was to be introduced in Egypt, and accepted standards for external reporting would improve the allocation of resources through the exchange. The increasing collaboration with international audit firms and multinational business would be much easier if accounting reports could be based on the same principles and practices.

At a National Conference in Accounting and Auditing held in June 1980, the Syndicate of Commerce Professions, together with the Egyptian Society of Accountants and Auditors, proposed the formation of a committee, one of the purposes of which was to set accounting principles to be applied in Egypt in line with generally accepted international principles. At a subsequent international conference organized by the syndicate in December 1980, the conference confirmed the necessity for formulating accounting standards to be adopted in Egypt in the preparation of financial statements for external reporting. One recommendation was that

> the accounting standards should take into consideration the economic and accounting environment and needs in Egypt and should conform whenever possible with the accounting standards published by the International Federation of Accountants which has admitted Egypt to its membership.[39]

This, then, shows the standard-setting process at work. A pressure group consisting of the syndicate, the Egyptian accounting professional body, and the Central Auditing Agency, among others, created a committee to formulate and publish accounting and auditing standards. The fact that they intended to adopt international standards meant that the production stage would not be time consum-

[39] Recommendations of International Conference on Accounting and Auditing, held in Cairo December 13–15, 1980. For a report on the conference, see M. Renshall, *World Accounting Report* (February 1981): 19–20.

ing. Unfortunately, in Egypt, 1981 turned out to be a year of upheaval which could be expected to interfere with the marketing stage.

In this section, the position of reporting practices and accounting standards in one country has been considered. This country case study illustrates two points: that it is dangerous to attempt to place countries into categories on the basis of the accounting system, and that the adoption of international accounting standards by developing countries may not only be irrelevant to the problems of the countries but may be harmful.

## CONCLUSION

The drive for harmonization of accounting standards, both at domestic and international levels, is now a major preoccupation of bodies organized by governments (for example, United Nations, Organization for Economic Cooperation and Development, European Economic Community, and so on) and by independent professional accounting bodies (IFAC, IASC, and such). The unquestioned assumption underlying all these harmonization efforts is that uniformity of standards is both desirable and feasible. The present paper argues that there are both conceptual and practical problems that expose the futility of such an exercise, especially insofar as developing countries are concerned. At the metatheoretical level, there are intractable problems of differing values and beliefs as well as epistemological and ontological positions. This makes for little congruence in the definition of the nature of the subject matter of accounting as well as the nature and purpose of accounting itself. This is the very denial of the assumption of consensus at the metatheoretical level by the "harmonization school."

As Fantl has argued, "One of the chief and least recognized misconceptions which occurs in international accounting is the assumption that accounting objectives are uniform."[40] He makes the point that if we are going to achieve harmonization, we can do so when all countries have the same objectives from the accounting systems.

Theoretical discussion regarding the inappropriateness of "internationally imposed" (or pseudoagreed) standards upon developing countries and the empirical illustration provided by the Egyptian case study would appear to show that, as regards developing countries, their "membership" in the "international harmonization club" seems misguided, if not harmful.

As is noted in the report of the AAA International Accounting and Auditing Standards Committee, "We observe that the task of setting international accounting standards is fraught with economic and political questions which have escaped the serious attention of scholars in accounting."[41] Unfortunately, much research is concerned with international accounting only as it applies to multinational companies. The international accounting standards are, however, meant to apply to companies within a country whether or not they are multinational. The paper has argued that we need to consider the accounting needs within a country, particularly the developing countries, not just the needs of the international business community.

---

[40] Irving L. Fantl, "The Case against International Uniformity," *Management Accounting* (May 1971).

[41] International Accounting and Auditing Standards Committee, American Accounting Association, *Report* (1981).

# IV-B "Functional Currency" in FASB Statement No. 52

## IV-B 1 *The Rationale Underlying the Functional Currency Choice*

LAWRENCE REVSINE

F ASB Statement Number 52 on Foreign Currency Translation was issued in December 1981. This Statement superseded the highly controversial Statement 8. Statement 8 was attacked because of the widespread belief that firms were compelled to report foreign currency gains and losses that bore little correspondence to the economic effects that they were actually experiencing. Under Statement 8, firms might report foreign exchange *gains* when their underlying real foreign exchange position was *deteriorating*, and vice versa. By contrast, Statement 52 is intended to achieve compatibility between firms' reported exchange gains and losses and these firms' underlying real economic changes.

Statement 52 tries to achieve compatibility between the accounting numbers and the underlying economic effects by allowing firms discretion in selecting a foreign subsidiary's *functional currency*. The FASB describes the subsidiary's functional

The author gratefully acknowledges the helpful comments of Arthur R. Wyatt of Arthur Andersen & Co. and Professor Robert P. Magee of Northwestern University.

Lawrence Revsine, "The Rationale Underlying the Functional Currency Choice," *The Accounting Review*, July 1984, pp. 505–51. Reprinted with the permission of *The Accounting Review*.

currency as "the currency of the primary economic environment in which the entity operates..." To illustrate, if a U.S. parent has a Dutch subsidiary that conducts business in both Holland and France, the functional currency might be the parent's currency (the dollar), or the subsidiary's currency (the guilder), or even the French franc. Individual circumstances must be used to determine which currency should be selected as the functional currency.

Understanding the factors that govern the functional currency choice is crucial for achieving the primary objective of Statement 52—i.e., compatibility between financial numbers and underlying economics. Unfortunately, the underlying goals and objectives for selecting among the possible functional currencies of a subsidiary are complicated. The concepts underlying the procedures are often particularly difficult for students to grasp. To overcome the problem, this paper explains the rationale behind the functional currency choice by using three illustrative case settings.

Case I presents a series of foreign currency transactions and shows their financial statement effects. Case II is identical to Case I in an economic sense except that the foreign transactions are undertaken through a subsidiary that acts as a conduit for transforming foreign currency flows into dollars. The example demonstrates that applying the FASB's functional currency guidelines in Case II leads to financial statements identical to those derived in Case I. This equivalence is not accidental; instead, the FASB guidelines are designed to generate consolidated results for a conduit subsidiary that are identical to the statement results that arise when the foreign transactions are undertaken directly by the parent. Finally, Case III introduces a modification of the Case II assumptions that alters the underlying economics. The example shows how the FASB guidelines lead to the selection of a different functional currency in Case III and why the chosen functional currency captures the altered economic circumstances.

Thus, the objective of this paper is to clarify the rationale underlying the functional currency choice. A thorough understanding of the rationale should enable students (who will soon become managers, auditors, and external statement users) to apply and interpret Statement 52 in an informed manner and thereby achieve the compatibility benefits sought by the FASB.

## FOREIGN CURRENCY TRANSACTIONS: CASE I

The need to select a functional currency exists only when the financial statements of a foreign subsidiary are consolidated with those of the parent or when the equity method is used. While the functional currency choice arises only as a prelude to combining intercorporate interests, it is easier to understand the rationale behind the Statement 52 rules if we first consider a simple non-consolidation setting which will be called Case I.

Assume in Case 1 that the Wildcat Corporation, a U.S. company, desires to sell its product in Britain. On January 1, 19x5, when the exchange rate was 1£ = 1.50$, Wildcat purchased a warehouse building in London to facilitate product distribution. The building cost £200,000, which is equivalent to $300,000 at the date of purchase. It also deposited £5,000 (equivalent to $7,500) in a London bank. On July 1, 19x5, it makes credit sales totalling £100,000 when the exchange rate is still 1£ = 1.50$. Wildcat produced these goods in the U.S. at a total cost of $110,000. The receivables are collected on August 1, 19x5, when the exchange rate is 1£ = 1.40$. The proceeds are converted into dollars and remitted to Wildcat's U.S. headquarters. (For simplicity, we ignore all other costs which might be incurred.) Further assume that the exchange rate was 1£ = 1.39$ on December 31, 19x5.

In Case I, there is no foreign subsidiary. The facts simply describe a series of foreign currency transactions encompassing purchase of a foreign nonmonetary asset (a building), a monetary asset (the £ deposit), and the credit sale.

The accounting for these transactions is straightforward and noncontroversial under the assumed conditions. The transactions that would be recorded on Wildcat's books are described below.

### Purchase of a Foreign Nonmonetary Asset (London Building)

At the time of purchase, the dollar equivalent cost of the building would be recorded. The entry would be:

DR    Building                                    $300,000
     CR    Cash                                        $300,000
(To record purchase of building for £200,000 when the exchange rate was 1£ = 1.50$.)

No adjustment to the gross book value is needed at the end of 19x5, despite the fact that the exchange rate is then 1£ = 1.39$. This is a direct consequence of historical cost accounting; original transaction amounts (in this case, the dollar equivalent cost) are entered and not subsequently adjusted. (For simplicity, we ignore depreciation.)

### Purchase of a Monetary Asset (Sterling Deposit)

When the pound sterling account is opened, the following entry is made:

DR    Cash ($ equivalent of £
     deposit)                                    $7,500
     CR    Cash                                        $7,500
(To record deposit of £5,000 when the exchange rate was 1£ = 1.50$.)

Again for simplicity, we assume that the account balance was maintained intact throughout the year. Since the year-end exchange rate has fallen to 1£ = 1.39$, the dollar equivalent of the sterling deposit is only $6,950; thus, a loss has arisen as a consequence of the foreign currency transaction. In accordance with existing U.S. accounting practice, monetary assets are shown at net expected realizable value and therefore the loss to date must be recognized in the accounts of Wildcat. The entry is:

DR    Foreign exchange loss                        $550
     CR    Cash                                        $550
(To reflect the decline in the dollar equivalent of the foreign currency deposit balance; $7,500 − $6,950.)

### Foreign Currency Sales Transaction

Wildcat Corporation's British sales were denominated in pounds sterling; these are clearly foreign currency transactions. Exchange rate changes between the time of the original transaction and the time of eventual conversion into dollars result in foreign exchange gains or losses. The accounting entries are:

| | | | |
|---|---|---|---|
| DR | Accounts receivable | $150,000 | |
| | CR    Sales revenue | | $150,000 |
| DR | Cost of goods sold | $110,000 | |
| | CR    Inventory | | $110,000 |

(To record sterling denominated sales of £100,000 at their dollar equivalent in terms of the then prevailing exchange rate of 1£ = 1.50$ and to record associated cost of goods sold.)

Upon collection, the foreign currency receivables are immediately converted to dollars at the exchange rate of 1£ = 1.40$. The entry on Wildcat's books would be:

| | | | |
|---|---|---|---|
| DR | Cash | $140,000 | |
| DR | Foreign exchange loss | $ 10,000 | |
| | CR    Accounts receivable | | $150,000 |

(To record collection of £100,000 receivables and conversion to dollars at a rate of 1£ = 1.40$.)

To help the reader visualize the overall effect of this accounting treatment, a partial balance sheet and income statement for Wildcat Corporation are presented in Figure 1. These statements include only the foreign assets and results of the foreign operations that are included in the example.

---

**FIGURE 1**

**Wildcat Corporation Partial Balance Sheet
(as of December 31, 19x5) and Income Statement
(for the Year Ended December 31, 19x5)**

*Balance Sheet*

| | | | |
|---|---|---|---|
| Cash | | | |
| Dollar deposits | $140,000 | | |
| Sterling deposit— dollar equivalent | 6,950 | | |
| | | Retained earnings | |
| Building | 300,000 | ($150,000 − 110,000 − 10,000 − 550) | |
| | | | $29,450 |

*Income Statement*

| | |
|---|---|
| Sales revenues | $150,000 |
| Cost of goods sold | (110,000) |
| Foreign exchange loss (10,000 + 550) | (10,550) |
| Net Income | $ 29,450 |

---

It will be useful to summarize the accounting treatment incorporated in the example. First, foreign currency transactions, whether completed (i.e., the dollar proceeds from sales) or uncompleted (i.e., the sterling deposit), have an immediate or potentially immediate impact on future dollar cash flows. Because of this dollar flow impact, foreign currency gains or losses are recorded as they occur and are included in income. Second, nonmonetary asset acquisitions follow the historical cost convention; therefore, the original dollar cash equivalent of the nonmonetary asset cost is carried forward in the accounts, despite subsequent exchange rate changes.

With this background, we are now able to turn to the central issue—an explanation of the rationale underlying the choice of functional currency.

## THE DOLLAR AS THE FUNCTIONAL CURRENCY: CASE II

The theory underlying the selection of a functional currency will be illustrated using a slightly altered version of the Wildcat Corporation example, called Case II. All assumptions in Case I are retained except that we now further assume that Wildcat forms a wholly owned British subsidiary, Proper Kitty, Ltd., which handles British sales. As before, however, all goods are shipped from the U.S., and British sales receipts are converted into dollars and remitted back to the U.S.

When Proper Kitty, Ltd. is formed, Wildcat Corporation would make the following entry:

| DR | Investment in subsidiary | $307,500 | |
|----|--------------------------|----------|----------|
|    | CR    Cash               |          | $307,500 |

(To record formation of subsidiary which purchases a building for £200,000 and deposits £5,000 in a London bank. The exchange rate at the time of formation is 1£ = 1.50$.)

Immediately after formation, Proper Kitty, Ltd.'s balance sheet would appear as follows:

Proper Kitty Ltd.
Balance Sheet as of January 1, 19x5

| Cash | £   5,000 | | |
|------|-----------|--------|----------|
| Building | 200,000 | Equity | £205,000 |
| | £205,000 | | £205,000 |

Notice that Proper Kitty's equity (£205,000) when translated at the exchange rate of 1£ = 1.50$ is precisely equal to the $307,500 investment in subsidiary account on Wildcat's books.

When Wildcat ships goods to Proper Kitty, we assume that the following entry is made on Wildcat's books:

| DR | Receivable due from subsidiary | $150,000 | |
|----|--------------------------------|----------|----------|
| DR | Cost of goods sold | 110,000 | |
|    | CR    Inventory    |          | $110,000 |
|    | CR    Sales revenue |         | 150,000 |

(To reflect shipment of goods to subsidiary, accounted for at eventual sales value.)

Assuming that Wildcat bills Proper Kitty Ltd. in sterling, when the dollar proceeds from the £100,000 sales are remitted to Wildcat on August 1, 19x5, the following entry would be made on Wildcat's books:

| | | | |
|---|---|---|---|
| DR | Cash | | $140,000 |
| DR | Foreign exchange loss | | 10,000 |
| | CR | Receivable due from | |
| | | subsidiary | $150,000 |

(To reflect receipt of proceeds from £100,000 sales when the exchange rate was 1£ = 1.40$.)

After remitting the cash back to Wildcat, Proper Kitty's balance sheet will be identical to that shown above for January 1, 19x5. Since no further entries take place during 19x5, these balances also reflect balance sheet carrying amounts at December 31, 19x5. The income statement would show:

Property Kitty, Ltd.
Income Statement for the Year Ended
December 31, 19x5

| | |
|---|---|
| Sales revenues | £100,000 |
| Cost of goods sold | 100,000 |
| Net Profit | 0 |

Obviously, forming a subsidiary has complicated Wildcat's accounting entries considerably. Intercompany accounts must now be kept and consolidation adjustments and eliminations must be made. However, the reader should verify that the underlying transactions and basic economic effects in Case II are absolutely identical to those in Case I. Whereas Wildcat itself undertook the transactions in the earlier example, here these same transactions are performed through a subsidiary. But the organizational form does not alter the ultimate economic effects. *The two cases are completely equivalent in an economic sense.*

If the two cases are equivalent, logic suggests that the consolidated numbers that result from a subsidiary's foreign transactions should be identical to those that would have resulted if the parent had undertaken the transactions directly. This is precisely what the FASB's functional currency guidelines accomplish. Let's see how.

Prior to consolidation, Statement 52 requires a company to identify the functional currency of its foreign subsidiaries. In Case II, the question is whether Proper Kitty's functional currency is the pound or the dollar. It is important to understand two characteristics of this choice:

1. The functional currency will not *always* be the currency in which the subsidiary's statements are expressed; and
2. The functional currency choice is intended to trigger a set of accounting mechanisms which result in reported foreign exchange numbers that correspond to the underlying economics.

The FASB presents guidelines for choosing the functional currency. These guidelines are reproduced in Table 1.

---

**TABLE 1**

**Statement 52 Guidelines for Functional Currency Choice***

---

A. Cash Flow Indicators
  (1) Foreign Currency—Cash flows related to the foreign entity's individual assets and liabilities are primarily in the foreign currency and do not directly affect the parent company's cash flows.
  (2) Parent's Currency—Cash flows related to the foreign entity's individual assets and liabilities directly affect the parent's cash flows on a current basis and are readily available for remittance to the parent company.

B. Sales Price Indicators
  (1) Foreign Currency—Sales prices for the foreign entity's products are not primarily responsive on a short-term basis to changes in exchange rates but are determined more by local competition or local government regulation.
  (2) Parent's Currency—Sales prices for the foreign entity's products are primarily responsive on a short-term basis to changes in exchange rates; for example, sales prices are determined more by worldwide competition or by international prices.

C. Sales Market Indicators
  (1) Foreign Currency—There is an active local sales market for the foreign entity's products, although there also might be significant amounts of exports.
  (2) Parent's Currency—The sales market is mostly in the parent's country or sales contracts are denominated in the parent's currency.

D. Expense Indicators
  (1) Foreign Currency—Labor, materials, and other costs for the foreign entity's products or services are primarily local costs, even though there also might be imports from other countries.
  (2) Parent's Currency—Labor, materials, and other costs for the foreign entity's products or services, on a continuing basis, are primarily costs for components obtained from the country in which the parent company is located.

E. Financing Indicators
  (1) Foreign Currency—Financing is primarily denominated in foreign currency, and funds generated by the foreign entity's operations are sufficient to service existing and normally expected debt obligations.
  (2) Parent's Currency—Financing is primarily from the parent or other dollar-denominated obligations, or funds generated by the foreign entity's operations are not sufficient to service existing and normally expected debt obligations without the infusion of additional funds from the parent company. Infusion of additional funds from the parent company for expansion is not a factor, provided funds generated by the foreign entity's expanded operations are expected to be sufficient to service that additional financing.

F. Intercompany Transactions and Arrangements Indicators
  (1) Foreign Currency—There is a low volume of intercompany transactions and there is not an extensive interrelationship between the operations of the foreign entity and the parent

company. However, the foreign entity's operations may rely on the parent's or affiliates' competitive advantages, such as patents and trademarks.

(2) Parent's Currency—There is a high volume of intercompany transactions and there is an extensive interrelationship between the operations of the foreign entity and the parent company. Additionally, the parent's currency generally would be the functional currency if the foreign entity is a device or shell corporation for holding investments, obligations, intangible assets, etc., that could readily be carried on the parent's or an affiliate's books.

* Note: Table 1 is taken directly from FASB [1981], pp. 26–27.

The FASB guidelines help determine whether the subsidiary is a free-standing unit or simply an intermediary that exists only as a conduit for transforming foreign currency transactions into dollar cash flows. When the subsidiary is simply a conduit, the consolidation approach treats the foreign currency statements of the subsidiary as artifacts which must be remeasured into dollars.

In Case II, FASB indicators A(2), D(2), and F(2) identify Proper Kitty as simply a conduit for foreign transaction cash flows back into dollars. In other words, the subsidiary is artificial; it is as if Wildcat had engaged in the foreign transactions directly. In such situations, the functional currency is the dollar, not the pound. The reporting goal is to end up with financial statements equivalent to those that would have resulted had Wildcat entered into the foreign transactions directly (i.e., as in Case I), rather than through Proper Kitty. This result is accomplished by using the temporal method [FASB, 1975, Appendix D] to remeasure pounds into dollars and by treating any remeasurement gains or losses as an element of Wildcat's income.

In the temporal method, monetary assets are translated at the current rate of exchange, nonmonetary assets at the historical rate of exchange, and income statement items at the rate that was in effect at the time of the transaction.[1] After using these rates to remeasure Proper Kitty's accounts, the result yields a dollar measure for each account that would have resulted had the original transactions been recorded initially in dollars. This is illustrated in Figure 2, where the temporal method is applied to Proper Kitty Limited and the resulting dollar measures are consolidated with Wildcat Corporation.

Notice that the consolidated dollar numbers in the right-hand column of Figure 2 are identical to the numbers shown in Figure 1 where Wildcat undertook the foreign transactions directly, rather than through a subsidiary. This equivalence is no accident. Since the economics of the two cases are identical, the FASB has selected an accounting method for the foreign subsidiary which leads to the same dollar result that would have existed had the transactions been undertaken directly by Wildcat.

---

[1] An exception exists for nonmonetary asset expirations. These expenses on the income statement are usually translated at the historic rate that existed at the time of original asset acquisition. Since our example does not encompass such items, we ignore this issue.

## FIGURE 2

**Partial Consolidated Financial Statements**
**(Includes Only Foreign Assets and Results of Foreign Operations)**
**Case II**

| Account Title | Property Kitty, Ltd. £'s | Exchange Rate (Temporal Method) | Remeasured In $'s | Wildcat Corporation | Consolidation Eliminations (DR) CR | Consolidated $'s |
|---|---|---|---|---|---|---|
| Dollar deposit | | | | $140,000 | | $140,000 |
| Sterling deposit | £ 5,000 | 1.39 | $ 6,950 | | | 6,950 |
| Investment in subsidiary | | | | $307,500 | (1)  307,500 | |
| Building | 200,000 | 1.50 | 300,000 | | | 300,000 |
| | £205,000 | | $306,950 | $447,500 | | $446,950 |
| Original Equity | 205,000 | 1.50 | 307,500 | | (1)  (307,500) | |
| Retained Earnings | | | (550) | 40,000 →(10,000) | | 29,450 |
| | £205,000 | | $306,950 | $ 30,000 | | $ 29,450 |
| Sales | £100,000 | 1.50 | $150,000 | $150,000 | (2)  (150,000) | $150,000 |
| Cost of Goods Sold | 100,000 | 1.50 | 150,000 | 110,000 | (2)  150,000 | 110,000 |
| | | | | 40,000 | | |
| Foreign Exchange Loss | | | (550) | →(10,000) | | (10,550)* |
| Net Income | | | (550) | $ 30,000 | | $ 29,450 |

* Note:  This total is comprised of:

| | |
|---|---|
| Foreign exchange loss on sale proceeds | $10,000 |
| Foreign exchange loss on sterling deposit | 550 |
| | $10,550 |

To summarize, when the Statement 52 guidelines identify the parent's currency as the functional currency:

1. The subsidiary is treated for accounting purposes as a mere conduit.
2. One implication is that foreign transactions are deemed to have an immediate (or potentially immediate) impact on dollar cash flows of the parent. For this reason, all foreign exchange gains and losses are taken through income.
3. Since the subsidiary is an artifact, all balance sheet numbers are reflected at amounts that would have existed had the subsidiary's account initially been recorded in the functional currency. The temporal method is designed to achieve this result.

## THE FOREIGN CURRENCY AS THE FUNCTIONAL CURRENCY: CASE III

We have seen that when the foreign subsidiary is merely a conduit for dollar cash flows, the functional currency is the dollar. By contrast, when the foreign subsidiary's operations "are relatively self-contained and integrated within a particular country or economic environment" [FASB, 1981, para. 80], then the functional currency is the currency of that foreign country.

To illustrate the rationale behind this rule, we introduce a Case III variation on the Wildcat Corporation setting. Consistent with Case II, we assume in Case III that Wildcat Corporation forms a U.K. subsidiary, Proper Kitty, Ltd., by investing $307,500 when the exchange rate was 1£ = 1.50$. Again, as in Case II, the investment proceeds are used to buy a building for £200,000 and to open a £5,000 account in a London bank. Sales totalling £100,000 are again made on July 1, 19x5, and collected on August 1. In contrast to the previous cases, however, we now assume that these goods were not shipped from the U.S.; instead, they were acquired by Proper Kitty from an unaffiliated U.K. supplier at a cost of £73,333 (which is equivalent to $110,000 at the then prevailing exchange rate). The sales proceeds are used to pay the supplier and the remaining cash (£26,667) is retained in the London account to finance Proper Kitty's future operations, expansion, and growth.

Notice that the economics of this case are quite different from the previous ones. In Case III, Proper Kitty does not engage in transactions merely to influence near-term dollar cash flows. Thus, the effect of an exchange rate change on future dollar cash flows is unclear.

In its Conceptual Framework, the FASB [1978] argues that the goal of financial reporting is to provide a forecast base for assessing "the amounts, timing, and uncertainty of prospective net cash inflows." Applying this logic to the circumstances of Case III (where the cash-flow impact of exchange rate changes is unclear), these exchange rate changes are not included in income under FAS 52. Specifically, in Cases I and II the decline in the pound from $1.50 to $1.40 between the time of sale and the time of collection resulted in an unequivocal $10,000 foreign exchange loss, which is deducted from income. No such loss is included in the Case III income number since Proper Kitty is an on-going, self-contained entity that will redeploy the sales proceeds in the U.K. In other words, it is not at all clear that a loss has occurred in Case III. Under such circumstances, the functional currency is designated as the foreign currency, and the decline in the dollar equivalent of the sales proceeds is taken directly to a special owners' equity account, rather than deducted from income. Similar treatment is accorded to the change in the dollar equivalent of the £5000 deposit in the London bank.

Furthermore, when the foreign entity is a self-contained unit, as in Case III, the FASB contends that the balance sheet translation process "should retain the financial results and relationships that were created in the economic environment of the foreign operations" [FASB, 1981, para. 74]. In other words, after translation, the foreign subsidiary's financial statement items should bear the same proportionate relationship to one another in dollars as they did in the foreign currency. This can be accomplished only if all items are translated using the same exchange rate. For this purpose, the FASB mandates the use of the current rate as of the balance sheet date. Using the current rate method on the income statement, all items are translated at the rate of exchange as of the transaction date.

Considering Proper Kitty's functional currency to be the pound and using the current rate method leads to the consolidated result shown in Figure 3. Notice carefully that the consolidated result in Figure 3 is quite different from the Case I result that was derived in Figure 1. This difference reflects the fact that Case III and Case I are not identical. In Case III, it is not at all clear that the impact of the exchange rate changes on the initial cash balance and subsequent cash collections will necessarily affect future *dollar* flows. Since Proper Kitty is a self-contained entity, these pound balances will be redeployed within the U.K., and the eventual dollar impact of these reinvestment activities may not materialize for years. For this reason, the FASB concludes that the effect of these rate changes should be excluded from the income computation.[2]

Also notice that the dollar equivalent carrying balance for the nonmonetary asset differs from Case I. In Case I, the building was translated at the historic rate of exchange, in accordance with historical cost accounting principles. But in Case III, Proper Kitty is a self-contained entity. The FASB contends that in such circumstances, financial statements are more informative if they maintain proportionate relationships that exist in the functional currency. Thus, the building is also translated at the current rate of exchange and most ratio relationships for Proper Kitty's dollar statements are equal to those contained in the pound statements (i.e., compare ratios based on column 3 data versus column 1 data in Figure 3).

To summarize, when a foreign entity is a self-contained unit:

1.  The functional currency is the currency of the foreign economic environment.

2.  The impact of rate changes on future dollar flows is uncertain. Thus, translation gains and losses are not run through income; instead, they are accumulated in a separately designated owners' equity account.

3.  Subsidiary balance sheets should preserve the proportionate relationships that existed in the functional currency. Therefore, all assets and liabilities

---

[2] The FASB's decision to exclude from income uncompleted foreign transactions with uncertain dollar flow effects is arguable. Although consistent with the dominant treatment of uncompleted transactions in existing practice, the FASB approach ignores the fact that existing rates in foreign exchange markets may be a least biased indicator of dollar flows that will ultimately be realized. In this view, changes in exchange rates signal changes in expected future flows. Since the FASB views income as a potential cash flow predictor, such exchange rate changes might (consistent with FASB [1978]) be includable in income.

## FIGURE 3

### Partial Consolidated Financial Statements
### (Includes Only Foreign Assets and Results of Foreign Operations)
### Case III

| Account Title | Property Kitty, Ltd. £'s | Exchange Rate | Translated In $'s | Wildcat Corporation | Consolidation Eliminations (DR) CR | Consolidated $'s |
|---|---|---|---|---|---|---|
| Cash | £ 31,667 | 1.39 | $ 44,017 | | | $ 44,017 |
| Investment in subsidiary | | | | 307,500 | (1) 307,500 | |
| Building | 200,000 | 1.39 | 278,000 | | | 278,000 |
| | £231,667 | | $322,017 | | | $322,017 |
| Original equity | 205,000 | 1.50 | 307,500 | | (1) (307,500) | |
| Retained earnings | 26,667 | 1.50 | 40,000 | | | 40,000 |
| Cumulative translation adjustment | | To balance (25,483)* | (25,483)* | | | (25,483) |
| | £231,667 | | £322,017 | | | $ 14,517 |
| Sales | £100,000 | 1.50 | $150,000 | | | $150,000 |
| Cost of goods sold | 73,333 | 1.50 | 110,000 | | | 110,000 |
| | £ 26,667 | | $ 40,000 | | | $ 40,000 |

* Note:
The cumulative translation adjustment in this simplified example is determined by multiplying the decline in the value of the £(1.50 − 1.39) by the net asset balance of £231,667 just prior to the decline.

are translated at the current rate of exchange. Any gain or loss on translation is put into a special owners' equity account rather than through income.

## WILL STATEMENT 52 LEAD TO COMPATIBILITY?

The previous analysis demonstrates how the functional currency choice required by Statement 52 is crucial for achieving compatibility between accounting signals and underlying economic consequences. But since choice injects potential for error, it is legitimate to question whether Statement 52 will lead to its intended result.

To some accountants, the latitude inherent in the functional currency choice may be troublesome, since the existence of latitude raises the specter of statement manipulation. However, statement manipulation via the functional currency choice does not appear to be a major threat since firms have a built-in motive to make the "correct" choice. For example, firms would be ill-advised to select the dollar as the functional currency in order to gain some near-term income enhancement (i.e., from foreign exchange gains that are included in income under the temporal method). The reason is that this short-run benefit may backfire if and when the foreign exchange effect reverses in subsequent years. That is, today's income enhancement may lead to tomorrow's income decrement. Thus, the likelihood of statement manipulation arising from the functional currency choice appears slight.

A much more real danger is that firms, their auditors, and outside analysts may not understand the subtle philosophy that underlies the functional currency choice. As a consequence, innocent but incorrect choices and assessments may be made, and compatibility may not be achieved. Unfortunately, the FASB's guidelines for the functional currency choice, reproduced in Table 1, may increase the likelihood of this possibility. That is, unless the theory underlying the selection mechanism is understood, some firms may be tempted to merely count-up the indicators in each direction; the choice would simply depend on which currency (the dollar or the foreign currency) garners more indicators. This simplistic application of Statement 52 is unsatisfactory since, for example, five indicators may point to the foreign currency as the functional currency and only one may point to the dollar. Despite this, the one criterion which points to the dollar may clearly dominate. Unless those making the selection clearly understand the theory underlying the choice, an incorrect selection is very likely using a straightforward tally of the indicators in each direction. It is to forestall precisely this possibility that this paper was written.

## REFERENCES

Financial Accounting Standards Board, *Statement of Financial Accounting Standards No. 8*, "Accounting for the Translation of Foreign Currency Transactions and Foreign Currency Financial Statements" (October 1975).

———, *Statement of Financial Accounting Concepts No. 1*, "Objectives of Financial Reporting by Business Enterprises" (November 1978).

———, *Statement of Financial Accounting Standards No. 52*, "Foreign Currency Translation" (December 1981).

# IV-C  Soviet Accounting

## IV-C 1  *Notes on the Development and Problems of Soviet Uniform Accounting*

GEORGE GORELIK

A s in all modern industrial societies, the paramount goal of the Soviet Union is steady and rapid growth in its gross national product (GNP). To achieve this goal the Soviets have adopted a system of state ownership of almost all nonhuman factors of production, state-determined prices, and comprehensive central planning and control. Accounting plays a crucial role in this system. Its function is to provide information for economic decision making to various managers within the huge Soviet administrative pyramid. This information is generally prepared on the basis of uniform standards and measurement rules.

The purpose of this paper is two-fold:

1. To outline the historical development of Soviet uniform accounting; and
2. To consider briefly some of the major problems that Soviet accounting is currently facing.

### THE HISTORICAL DEVELOPMENT OF SOVIET UNIFORM ACCOUNTING

At the base of Soviet accounting lies the accumulated experience of both prerevolutionary Russia and Western Europe.

The development of Russian accounting dates from the ninth century. According

George Gorelik, "Notes on the Development and Problems of Soviet Uniform Accounting," *International Journal of Accounting Education and Research*, Fall 1973, pp. 135–148. Reprinted with the permission of *International Journal of Accounting Education and Research*.

to Sumtsov,[1] accounting records were first used in the states of Novgorod and Kiev by princes and boyars who conducted trade in bread, honey, and wax with Greece and other nations. Later, in the sixteenth and seventeenth centuries recordkeeping spread to the estates of churches and monasteries.

One of the oldest accounting records in existence in Russia today is the expenditures book of a Pskov church for the year 1531. Other relics of the past include the receipts and disbursements book of the Volkonski monastery for the year 1594 and the receipts and disbursements books of Prince Galitzine for the years 1685 and 1686.

In the eighteenth century, recordkeeping spread to government departments and estates of landowners. The records of the time consisted of the receipts and disbursements books in which narrative entries were made in chronological order of the changes in monetary and nonmonetary resources of the particular entity. In order to validate the records, an inventory of actual resources on hand was taken periodically.

The double-entry bookkeeping model appeared in Russia sometime during the eighteenth century. The terms *debit, credit*, and *balance*, as well as instructions on the method of calculation and accounts, appeared for the first time in "The Regulations of the Admiralty" approved by Peter I. The double-entry model of bookkeeping was first applied in central and local government departments and spread from there to trade, industry, and estates of landowners. In 1844 the Russian government enacted a law requiring enterprises to keep accounting records. Between 1844 and 1917 a number of textbooks were published setting forth the principles of double-entry as they applied to the fast-growing trade and industry. Some of the noted accounting writers of the period were Prokofiev, Klinge, Reinbot, and Galagan. Beginning in 1888 the first Russian accounting periodical appeared in St. Petersburg, and in 1909 the first congress of accountants met in Moscow to discuss questions of accounting theory and practice. In both these areas diversity prevailed.

By 1917 the double-entry bookkeeping model was firmly established in Russian trade and industry. It was characterized by the equation: Assets − Liabilities = Proprietorship. Similar to the practice in the United States at that time, the accounting concepts of assets, liabilities, revenues, and expenses, and classifications thereof, were conceived by the Russians from the point of view of the proprietor.

Since the October Revolution the tasks of accounting in the Soviet Union have changed although the accounting methodology has remained largely the same. Instead of serving narrow, private business interests, the double-entry capitalist accounting of the prerevolutionary days was called upon to assist the new leaders in the development of the Soviet state capitalism.

The adoption of the double-entry framework for the development of Soviet accounting has enabled the Soviets to introduce most of the conventional accounting concepts of the prerevolutionary capitalist era into the Soviet accounting vocabulary and use. The words *balans* for balance, *debet* for debit, *kredit* for credit, *aktiv* for assets, and *passiv* for equities, have the same meaning in Soviet as they have in American accounting terminology. The transfer of capitalist accounting concepts to serve the Soviet planned economy was also greatly assisted by the Soviet administrative concept of *khozraschet*—an administrative unit within the giant Soviet

---

[1] A. Sumtsov, *Kurs Teorii Bukhgalterskogo Ucheta (Course on Accounting Theory)* (Moscow: Gosfinzdat, 1958), pp. 19–20.

"corporation." Under the khozraschet concept the enterprise is given the status of a semiindependent activity unit with limited powers of utilizing the resources allocated to it, of entering into contracts, and of carrying on other necessary activities in the course of its plan fulfillment.[2] Enterprise transactions with other activity units and households are settled through the use of money, and in general enterprise operations must be self-sustaining, that is, profitable. In its internal productive operations, the Soviet enterprise is very similar to a division of an American industrial corporation with similar information needs for cost and revenue data for each important activity or product.

Marxist economic theory appears to have had a largely negative influence on the development of Soviet accounting. Its chief role appears to have been that of excluding from accounting, especially accounting for management, contributions to the accounting thought and practice made by Western economic theory. Such concepts as opportunity costs, differential costs, and marginal analysis in general have until recently been alien to Soviet economic thought. So far, Soviet accounting has not been affected by these concepts.

Positive influences of Marxist economics on Soviet accounting have been slight. For the most part they amounted to only minor changes in accounting terminology such as the use of the words *basic means* to designate the notion of fixed assets, or the words *charter fund* instead of charter capital. There are two main reasons for the relative absence of Marxist economic influence in Soviet accounting. First, the essential structure of Soviet accounting was developed in the 1920s by accountants with prerevolutionary education. In the words of the noted Soviet economist Strumilin, these men were "... accountants of the old school, excellent practical men, but for the most part far removed from any kind of influence of the theory of Marx in the field of their special activity."[3] Second, the Soviet central planning and control model which in the main determines the nature of accounting measurements, has only slightly been influenced by Marxian economics.[4]

The centralized direction of the Soviet economy created the need for consistent and comparable data—for a uniform system of recordkeeping (*edinaya sistema ucheta*). The result was a gradual development of three interrelated systems of recordkeeping which rely generally on the same primary data:[5]

1. Operational-technical recordkeeping (*operativno-tekhnicheskii uchet*), dealing with narrow processes and operations and serving the purposes of current operational management. It usually employs physical measurements.

2. Statistical recordkeeping (*statisticheskii uchet*), dealing with aggregate economic data used for central planning and control.

3. Accounting (*bukhgalterskii uchet*), dealing with assets, equities, revenues, and expenses in financial terms. Bukhgalterskii uchet corresponds closely to what is known as conventional accounting in the United States.

[2] Robert W. Campbell, *Accounting in Soviet Planning and Control* (Cambridge: Harvard University Press, 1963), pp. 12–13.

[3] S. G. Strumilin, *Izbrannye Proizvedeniya v Piati Tomakh, Tom I, Statistikal Ekonomika (Selected Works in Five Volumes, Vol. 1, Statistics and Economics)* (Moscow: Izdatelstvo Akademii Nauk SSSR, 1963), p. 4.

[4] Campbell, *Accounting in Soviet Planning*, pp. 255–56.

[5] I. I. Poklad, *Kurs Bukhgalterskogo Ucheta (Course on Accounting)* (Moscow: "Finansy," 1967), pp. 8–11.

The standardization of the Soviet system of recordkeeping essentially involved determining "...(1) standard definitions, (2) mutually consistent definitions for such different items as might be brought together in the course of economic analysis and planning, and (3) uniform and standardized methods of collecting, reporting, and classifying data."[6]

The standard classification of accounts, which was adopted by all Khozraschet enterprises in 1960, is a good example of uniformity in Soviet accounting.[7] This classification is used to aggregate accounting data at two levels: primary and secondary. At the primary level sixty-nine summary or control accounts are prescribed for the recording of transactions according to the main classes of assets, equities, revenues, and expenditures, such as fixed assets, depreciation, raw materials, and supplies. Transactions are recorded in summary accounts in value terms only. At the secondary level a number of subaccounts are presented for each summary account which explain in value terms the transactions accumulated in summary accounts in greater detail. Thus, for example, the summary account Raw Materials and Supplies is composed of the following five subaccounts:[8] (1) raw materials, basic materials, and purchased semifabricated products; (2) auxiliary materials; (3) agricultural stocks and products; (4) packaging and packing materials; and (5) materials subcontracted to outside organizations.

In addition to standard summary accounts and subaccounts, detailed accounts are usually introduced into the enterprise accounting system on instructions from either the Central Statistical Agency (CSA) or the Ministry of Finance. The nature of these accounts varies from one enterprise to another. Their purpose is to provide comprehensive data in value and physical terms on such items as inventories, individual assets, and costs.

The quest for uniformity in accounting standards, classifications, and measurements, which began in 1919 when the Council of Recordkeeping was formed within the Department of Finance to develop uniform documentation and uniform standards for accounting in state industrial enterprises, has continued until the present under the joint direction of the CSA and the Ministry of Finance.[9] The continuation of a unified policy with respect to accounting is stressed by Kosygin in connection with the 1965 economic reforms which led to some decentralization of decision making but not of information systems in the Soviet Union.[10]

Although considerable debate on accounting matters is allowed in the Soviet Union, once accounting instructions and standards have been promulgated by the CSA and the Ministry of Finance they have the power of law. Professor Tatur, a noted

[6] Gregory Grossman, *Soviet Statistics of Physical Output of Industrial Commodities, Their Compilation, and Quality* (Princeton, N.J.: Princeton University Press, 1960), p. 27.

[7] P. Bezrukikh and G. Granovskii, "The Uniform Classification of Bookkeeping Accounts and Instructions on Its Use," *Bukhgalterskii Uchet* 2 (1960): 63–71.

[8] V. A. Goloshchapov, *Spravochnik Po Bukhgalterskomu Uchetu (Handbook on Accounting)* (Moscow: Izdatelstvo "Finansy," 1965), pp. 26–27.

[9] *Sumtsov, Kurs Teorii*, pp. 21–25; and G. Gofman and S. Kapelush, *Ocherki Rasvitiya Form Bukhgalterskogo Ucheta (Essays on the Development of Accounting)* (Moscow: "Finansy," 1966), pp. 43–121.

[10] Joint Economic Committee, *New Directions in the Soviet Economy* (Washington, D.C.: U.S. Government Printing Office, 1966), p. 1044.

Soviet writer on accounting states:

> All basic bookkeeping questions—such as what is to go into accounting reports and how they are to be drawn up, and also by whom they are to be approved—are defined by law....
> The statutes, which are binding on all Union Republics, ensure a uniform system of bookkeeping at all enterprises of the Soviet Union, and as a result accounting data can be compiled for the individual branches of the national economy and for the national economy as a whole. These consolidated data on the results of fulfillment of the national–economic plans make it possible to use the resources of the socialist economy most expediently.[11]

The existence of a uniform system of bookkeeping is a necessary but not sufficient condition for the production of useful information. For information to be useful it must also be reliable and relevant to a given decision maker. The Soviet accounting system is presently experiencing significant difficulties in the production of reliable and relevant information. We turn now to the discussion of some of these difficulties.

## PROBLEMS OF SOVIET UNIFORM ACCOUNTING

On the whole Soviet uniform accounting has served its masters well in that it has succeeded in facilitating the achievement of the main Soviet objective, namely, conversion of the Soviet Union from a predominantly agrarian nation to an industrial world power. Even by conservative estimates of Western observers, Soviet industrial growth has been spectacular. Campbell for example estimates that Soviet industrial growth has averaged at between 7 and 8 percent per annum during the thirty-three year period from 1928 to 1961.[12] Bornstein maintains that the Soviet GNP has grown during 1950-58 "... at an average annual rate of 6 percent as compared with a rate of over 3 percent for the United States."[13] Although these impressive rates of growth are attributed primarily to such factors as the organizational structure of the Soviet command economy, the Soviet late industrial takeoff, and an abundance of natural resources, due credit must also be given to the Soviet accounting system which is the main source of information for economic decision making. In fact, if the notion of capitalism is interpreted broadly to include state capitalism then the history of the success of double-entry bookkeeping in the service of the Soviet state provides some support to the now famous hypothesis posited by Sombart on the relationship between the rise of capitalism and double-entry bookkeeping, namely that:

> One can scarcely conceive of capitalism without double-entry bookkeeping: they are related as are form and content. It is difficult to decide, however,

---

[11] S. Tatur, "The Organization of Accounting in the Soviet Union," *Accountants Magazine* (Scotland, May 1959): 379–80.

[12] R. W. Campbell, *Soviet Economic Power: Its Organization Growth and Challenge* (Boston: Houghton Mifflin Co., 1966), p. 124.

[13] M. Bornstein, "A Comparison of Soviet and United States National Product," in *The Soviet Economy: A Book of Readings*, ed. M. Bornstein and D. R. Furfeld (Homewood, Ill.: R. D. Irwin, Inc., 1966), p. 288.

> whether in double-entry bookkeeping capitalism provided itself with a tool to make it more effective or whether capitalism derives from the "spirit" of double-entry bookkeeping.[14]

The Soviets have definitely found in the double-entry bookkeeping model a tool to make the functioning of the Soviet economy more effective. The model has greatly facilitated the processing of an enormous volume of economic information which is necessary for the management of the giant Soviet economy.

The effectiveness of Soviet accounting in generating relevant information has by no means been uniform as far as different decision makers, economic subgoals, and time periods are concerned. In particular this effectiveness has considerably decreased in recent years.

During the Stalinist era when the goal of a rapid industrial growth was well defined, Soviet accounting was generally successful in providing the necessary information to central planners on the state of the country's resources and accomplishments. Since 1958, however, the commitments of the new leadership have proliferated beyond the goal of rapid industrial growth

> . . . to include consumer welfare, growth based on new technology and parity with United States in sophisticated weaponry. In contrast, the wherewithal to sustain this expanded array of priorities has worsened, both in terms of basic resource availability and of the efficiency with which these resources have been employed.[15]

The demands for relevant accounting information have increased with the multiplication of Soviet economic goals. The effectiveness, however, of Soviet accounting to deliver this information appears to have been greatly constrained by the Soviet price system, the structure of the accounting system, and the process by which accounting rules and procedures are implemented.

One of the most important environmental factors affecting the usefulness of accounting data has been and continues to be the absence of an objectively determined price system. Soviet prices are generally determined centrally. As a rule, they do not respond to the prevailing conditions of supply and demand. Once fixed, they continue to be in effect for long periods of time. This affects the validity of all economic calculation and particularly the determination of accounting profits and profitability which have recently become the chief indicators of enterprise efficiency. Accounting profits and profitability can be used as measures of enterprise efficiency only if prices are a measure of economic efficiency. Since Soviet prices do not reflect economic efficiency, Soviet accounting profits also fail to measure the economic efficiency of enterprise operations.

In an attempt to make their prices more meaningful the Soviets undertook the monumental task of price revisions which culminated in a new set of industrial prices which were put into effect in 1967. The new prices represent the results of the first comprehensive revision of industrial prices since 1955.

---

[14] Werner Sombart, *Der Moderne Kapitalismus* (München and Leipzig: Dunker und Humbolt, 1924) vol. 2, part 1, p. 118, trans. B. S. Yamey; "Introduction," in *Studies in the History of Accounting*, ed. A. C. Littleton and B. S. Yamey Homewood, Ill.: R. D. Irwin, Inc., 1956), p. 9.

[15] U.S. Congress Joint Economic Committee, "Trends in Soviet Gross National Product," in Bornstein and Fusfeld, *The Soviet Economy*, p. 292.

The results of the price reform so far indicate that only some of the initial objectives of the Soviet price-setters have been achieved. The revision of prices has succeeded in making all the major branches of industry "profitable" and in reducing the spread in profitability rates among different branches of industry. This is necessary for the implementation of profit and profitability measures as new indicators of enterprise efficiency and related incentive schemes. Other objectives of price-setters are still far from being achieved. Schroeder, for example, reports that:

> ... the new prices have not solved the problem of stimulating the output of higher quality of products; the new prices have not solved the problem of the larger dispersion of profit rates among enterprises in a given branch or of the great differences in profitability of the various items in the product mix of individual enterprises; the problem of how to combine price-flexibility with price stability has not been solved.[16]

The reasons for this failure are deeply rooted in the system of the command economy with its centralization of all major economic decisions, absence of free markets, and the imposition of the leaders' will on the Soviet economy.

The constraining influences of the structure of Soviet accounting are revealed in:

1. The adoption of a centralist point of view in the design of the accounting system; and
2. The lack of built-in sensitivity in the accounting structure to cope with the rising complexity in the Soviet economic environment.

The methodological unity of Soviet accounting has been conceived primarily from the point of view of central organs. The information needs of central agencies for planning and control of enterprise operations take precedence over the information needs of subordinate agencies and particularly the information needs of enterprise management.

The uniform Soviet accounting system generally satisfies the information needs of Gosplan (the State Planning Commission) and the Ministry of Finance. It is not comprehensive enough, however, to meet at the same time the diverse information needs of the middle managerial hierarchy in the Soviet administrative pyramid and the finer information needs of the Soviet enterprise management in particular.

The failure to satisfy fully the information needs of industrial ministries, *glavks* (chief subdivisions of ministries), and other intermediate administrative agencies is evidenced by the persistence of requests by these agencies for unsanctioned or "wild" reports. These reports persist despite specific instructions forbidding superior units from requiring, and the reporting units from submitting, statistical and accounting reports whose forms and destinations have not been established by CSA or the Ministry of Finance.[17]

---

[16] G. E. Schroeder, "The 1966–67 Soviet Industrial Price Reform: A Study in Complications," *Soviet Studies*, vol. 10, no. 4 (April 1969): 473.
[17] D. Gallik, C. Jesina, and S. Rapawy, *The Soviet Financial System: Structure, Operation, and Statistics* (U.S. Department of Commerce, Bureau of the Census, Series P-90, no. 23, 1968), p. 197.

Decision making at the enterprise level requires that relevant information be provided on alternative choices considered. Marginal costs, opportunity costs, fixed and variable costs, departmental costs, and other relevant cost information is needed. Such information is generally not available to Soviet enterprise managers simply because:

1. It is not currently a part of the process which generates accounting information;
2. In the accountant's order of priorities, the provision of information services to enterprise management stands second to the preparation of numerous accounting reports for superior administrative agencies; and
3. The Soviet accountant cannot possibly do both jobs at present; that is, he cannot serve equally well both top and enterprise management because of inadequate computational and data processing facilities.

Generally, the sensitivity of Soviet accounting to reflect differences among cases of the same class is very low. The rules for overhead allocation and depreciation are good examples of this built-in insensitivity.

Almost all the overhead expenses are allocated in Soviet accounting practice in proportion to the wages of production workers. Thus, according to Sibiriakov:

> At the present time the proportion of overhead costs (departmental and general factory overhead expenses, etc.) in the total cost of a product has a tendency to grow, while the proportion of wages of production workers has a tendency to decrease. Inclusion of overhead expenses in the product costs in proportion to the wages of production workers (as it is presently practised in the engineering industry) more and more distorts the actual product costs.[18]

Although the Soviets are aware of more exact methods of distributing overhead expenses, they have retained the method of allocation in proportion to wages because of its simplicity.

In the case of depreciation of assets, only the straight-line method is permitted. The depreciation rate is determined in accordance with the following formula:[19]

$$\text{Rate} = \frac{\text{(Original cost + Estimated capital repairs − Salvage)}}{\text{Economic life of the asset} \cdot \text{Original cost}} \cdot 100$$

The resulting rate is then applied to the replacement cost, and, if not available, to the original cost of fixed assets, in order to compute the periodic depreciation charge. Uniform depreciation rates, differentiated according to the type of fixed assets, have been in force in the Soviet Union since 1963. For example, the rate on factory buildings with steel structures is 2.5 percent per annum applied to their balance sheet value; the rate on metal cutting machines ranges from 12.1 to 16.4 percent, depending on the weight of machines; machines and equipment in the textile industry are depreciated at the rate of 9.4 percent per annum; and wooden houses at the rate of 4.3 percent per annum.[20]

---

[18] L. E. Sibiriakov, "Perfection of Enterprise Accounting," *Bukhgalterskii Uchet*, 12 (1972): 62.
[19] Poklad, *Kurs Bukhgalterskago*, p. 125.
[20] Ibid., p. 124.

The preference for the straight-line depreciation method is justified on the grounds of cost stability which is necessary for Soviet pricing and interperiod cost comparisons.[21] Application of the same accounting measurement rule, however, to different situations is most likely to produce wrong signals about the real states of nature, and thus lead to wrong economic decisions. As a result, losses from wrong decisions may far outweigh any benefits that are expected from the uniform application of accounting rules.

The need for adaptation of Soviet accounting to changes in the economic environment is recognized by a number of Soviet writers on accounting. Professor Dodonov, for example, expresses his frustration at the lack of progress in this respect in the following way:

> We cannot any longer tolerate the absence of a scientific center which would coordinate and direct the creative efforts of scientists and practitioners in the realm of accounting and its mechanization.
>
> It is wrong to assume that 10–15 practitioners in charge of the administration of accounting and reporting in the Ministry of Finance USSR are capable of taking on the complex task involved in further improvement and simplification of accounting of the whole economy.[22]

The allocation of slight resources to the direction and development of Soviet accounting indicates that extensive changes in this area are not at present contemplated by the Ministry of Finance.

Finally, Soviet accounting, as accounting in capitalist countries, faces problems of implementation. The mere issuance of directives by central organs on accounting matters is apparently not a sufficient condition for the effective implementation of accounting rules and procedures even in the Soviet Union. The main reason for this lies in the fact that while accounting rules and procedures are established centrally, their implementation rests primarily with subordinate administrative units. Often, however, it is not in the interest of subordinates to comply fully with the prescribed accounting procedures.

Falsification of accounting records concerning industrial output is a glaring example of the willful noncompliance by Soviet administrative units with the centrally established procedures. This falsification occurs because:

> The output reports submitted by the enterprises and their administrative superiors simultaneously constitute the factual basis for national production statistics, provide the information for planning and the issuance of production orders, and determine the rewards or punishments meted out to the management and the rest of production personnel. The rewards for plan fulfillment and overfulfillment by the enterprise are great; the punishment for failure may be severe.... Thus, disinterestedness in the reporting of output by the worker to his superiors, or by the enterprise to its administrative superiors..., is virtually ruled out.[23]

[21] B. N. Horwitz, "Depreciation and Cost Stability in Soviet Accounting," *Accounting Review* (July 1966): 819–26.

[22] A. Dodonov, *Problemy Bukhgalterskogo Ucheta v Promyshlennosti SSSR (Problems of Accounting in Industry of the USSR)* (Moscow: "Ekonomika," 1961), pp. 324–25.

[23] Grossman, *Soviet Statistics*, p. 128.

Manipulations of accounting measurements which have been a common occurrence throughout Soviet history apparently go on in the Soviet Union today.[24] These manipulations are a consequence of the use of accounting measurements in the evaluation of managerial performance. They are possible despite the existence of an elaborate internal control system because of collusion of the parties concerned.

The chief enterprise accountant, the party secretary, the enterprise manager, and controlling officials are all united in a common interest to fulfill and overfulfill the production plan by any means possible, including, for example, fictitious write-ups of output.[25] Consequently, any falsification of accounting reports is concealed jointly.

Another example of implementation difficulties is the Soviet attempt to introduce a standard cost system into enterprise accounting. Despite the fact that the basic principles of standard costing were established by central authorities some time ago, only 15 percent of industrial enterprises were using some elements of the standard costing system as of July 1, 1972. According to Dementsev, deputy minister of finance, USSR:

> U.S.S.R. and Republican ministries and departments, and, in the first place, their chief accountants are responsible for taking the necessary steps to ensure that in the near future standard costing becomes the prevalent method of costing in industrial and construction enterprises. All the necessary conditions for this already exist. The basic principles concerning planning, accounting and calculation of cost of production in industrial enterprises have been approved long ago. On the basis of these principles ministries and departments are developing branch instructions which anticipate the wide application of the standard cost system. Unfortunately, a number of U.S.S.R. and Republican ministries and departments have not yet completed the prescribed task which greatly impede the perfection of industrial cost calculation.[26]

It is apparently not easy to establish and maintain an acceptable set of cost standards for the Soviet industrial branches now producing a wide assortment of products. One of the reasons for this difficulty lies in the fact that the establishment of such standards requires knowledge of the local conditions and, therefore, cooperation of enterprise managers. Such cooperation is usually not forthcoming since Soviet managers tend to view cost standards as additional constraints on the limited freedom of action that they now enjoy.

To remedy some of the deficiencies of accounting, the Soviets have embarked on an extensive centralization and mechanization. Numerous "independent" accounting units within large enterprises have been consolidated into single accounting departments and placed under the direction of the enterprises' chief accountants. A number of accounting data centers have also been set up to service the needs of small enterprises. In 1972 there were in the Soviet Union 5,100 such data centers serving 66,500 small enterprises. In addition, in 1972 there were 55,000 data centers serving the needs of the state budgetary departments.[27]

[24] A. SH. Margulis, "Development of Accounting and Its Perspectives," *Bukhgalterskii Uchet* 12 (1972): 21.

[25] Grossman, *Soviet Statistics*, pp. 85–99.

[26] V. V. Dementsev, "Accounting in Service of USSR National Economy," *Bukhgalterskii Uchet* 12 (1972): 9.

[27] Dementsev, "Accounting in Service," p. 10.

According to Dementsev, there were more than one million calculating machines in use in the Soviet economy in 1972.[28] The breakdown of these machines as to types, however, is not given. Judging by the persistent references by the Soviets themselves to sharp inadequacies in their country's computational capability, there appear to be still relatively few electronic computers in use in the Soviet economic administration today.

The present efforts to streamline the Soviet accounting system are directed primarily at aspects of information processing. In their preoccupation with centralization and mechanization of the accounting system, Soviet methodological councils have so far almost completely neglected to consider the all-important questions of reliability and relevance of accounting information in contemporary economic decision making. As a result, mere mechanization of the old manual accounting procedures is likely to perpetuate the present inadequacies of the Soviet accounting system.

## SUMMARY AND CONCLUSIONS

In this paper the development of Soviet accounting was outlined and some of the major problems facing Soviet accounting today were discussed.

In response to the needs of central managements, the Soviets over the years have developed an accounting system that is now characterized by a high degree of uniformity in concepts, classifications, measurement rules, and reporting procedures. The need for uniformity in Soviet accounting stems from the basic requirement of all economic decision making, namely, that comparisons of interrelated economic events in the process of economic analysis, planning, and control be done on the same basis.

The development of standard and mutually consistent definitions of accounting concepts, classifications, and measurement rules has great merit in that such standardizations generally save cerebration and enhance communication among individuals. Without a uniform system of recordkeeping, management of the Soviet command economy from the center (Moscow) would have been very difficult. However, the rigidity of Soviet prices, implementation difficulties, a singular absence of adaptability of Soviet accounting to the changing economic environment in general, and the indiscriminate application of accounting rules to dissimilar cases in particular, and *not* the existence of uniformity in Soviet accounting as such, have greatly diminished the potential of Soviet accounting as a management information system.

Current inadequacies of Soviet accounting have, among other things, strengthened the hand of protagonists of decentralized decision making. This group appears to have succeeded in bringing about some decentralization of decision making with the introduction of 1965 economic reforms. The supporters of centralized decision making, however, hope to win their battle in the long run with the help of computers and mathematical methods. Although the outcome of the present Soviet struggle on the issue of centralization versus decentralization of economic decision making is hard to predict, one thing is certain. The Soviets must develop a better economic information system than the one they use at present if they want to succeed in combating the growing administrative complexity of their economy.

---

[28] Ibid., p. 11.

# IV-D  An Accounting Court

## IV-D 1  *An Accounting Court: The Impact of the Enterprise Chamber on Financial Reporting in the Netherlands*

JAN KLAASSEN

A s in other countries, there have been many changes in financial reporting in the Netherlands during the last few years.[1] One of these has been the introduction of a court, called the Enterprise Chamber, to settle disputes between companies and parties interested in their financial statements. To understand the Chamber and its impact, it is useful to review the important elements of the institutional framework of Dutch financial reporting, including the operation of the court.

The author is grateful for the useful suggestions of Professors G. G. M. Bak, J. W. Schoonderbeek, L. J. Seidler, L. Traas, Dr. J. Boersema, and Dr. J. van Helleman.

Jan Klaassen, "An Accounting Court: The Impact of the Enterprise Chamber on Financial Reporting in the Netherlands," *The Accouning Review*, April 1980, pp. 327–341. Reprinted with the permission of *The Accountancy Review*.

[1] The current status of Dutch company law is described in English by Sanders [1977]. In addition, the Dutch, British, and American accounting institutes have published works in English about the institutional framework for financial reporting in the Netherlands. See *Act* [1972], Beeny and Chastney [1978], and AICPA [1975].

# THE INSTITUTIONAL FRAMEWORK FOR FINANCIAL REPORTING IN THE NETHERLANDS

## The Act on Annual Accounts

The Act on Annual Accounts, effective since 1971, contains most of the legal framework for financial reporting by business enterprises in the Netherlands. In 1976, the Act became part of the Civil Code.[2] All corporation (of which two types are distinguished, namely the public company (*naamloze vennootschap*, NV) and the private company (*besloten vennootschap*, BV)) are subject to the provisions of the Act, whether or not they are obliged to publish their financial statements. For all NVs and larger BVs, publication of the financial statements is mandatory. Publication takes place by filing the financial statements with a regional trade registrar, where they are available for public inspection. In addition, these firms must make copies of the financial statements available to anyone upon request.

The Act can be divided into three parts:

- general requirements.
- disclosure requirements, and
- rules concerning the Enterprise Chamber.

The *general requirements* of the law state the objectives of financial reporting according to the law and the general criteria to which companies should adhere in applying valuation and measurement rules:

- Section 307 defines the annual accounts, as consisting of a balance sheet, profit and loss account, and the explanatory notes.
- Section 308 requires the annual accounts to provide sufficient information to permit a sound judgment to be formed on the financial position and results of the enterprise and, as far as the financial statements permit, on its solvency and liquidity.
- Section 309 requires the financial statements together with the notes to reflect fairly and systematically the amount and composition of the enterprise's net worth and net income for the fiscal years.
- Section 310 requires that the disclosure and classification of data in the annual accounts be aimed at the objectives defined in Section 308.
- Section 311 prescribes that bases underlying the valuation of the assets and liabilities and the determination of the financial results comply with the standards that are *acceptable* in the business environment.

No strict valuation rules are given. On the contrary, the law is consciously designed to provide a general framework for valuation and measurement, in order to give flexibility. Much depends upon what is meant by "standards that are acceptable in the business environment" (section 311).

This approach is in accordance with practices of financial reporting which prevailed in the Netherlands before the passage of the Act on Annual Accounts. The

---

[2] As far as the author knows, there is no complete English translation of the Civil Code. However, Act [1972] contains the complete text of the Act on Annual Accounts in English.

Minister and Parliament decided that a flexible law would permit an easier introduction of new developments. It would also enable the business community to take an inventory of the accounting and reporting practices within the contraints of the Act. To do this job, the Tripartite Accounting Standards Committee was formed.

In most cases, the published annual reports of Dutch companies contain, in addition to the financial statements, other reports such as:

- a general report of the Board of Managers,
- a report of the Supervisory Board,
- an auditor's report, and
- a ten-year survey of financial data and ratios.

The Act does not consider these reports, however, to be part of the financial statements. Since information disclosed according to the law is to be included in the financial statements, the disclosure of such information in one of the above-mentioned sections of the annual report, outside the financial statements, is not in accordance with the law.

The *disclosure requirements* of the Act refer to:

- the accounting principles used, including disclosure of accounting changes and their effects upon net worth and net income,
- the remuneration of members of the Supervisory Board,
- the appropriation of net income, and
- the disclosure of the corresponding figures for the previous year.

Sections 315 through 336 contain specific disclosure requirements referring to items appearing in the balance sheet and the profit and loss statement. The information concerning these items (assets, liabilities, revenues, and expenses) can either be shown in the balance sheet and profit and loss statement or in the explanatory notes. Among the most important disclosure requirements is section 319, which prescribes that a company should disclose the information relating to its subsidiary's financial statements. However, this obligation can be met by providing as part of the notes a set of consolidated financial statements which are in accordance with the provisions of the law, or by providing separate or combined financial statements of the subsidiaries. Therefore, under Dutch company law "the" balance sheet of a company is a balance sheet in which subsidiaries are carried mainly on the equity method, the consolidated balance sheet being "only" part of the notes. Consolidation is not mandatory, but most enterprises include consolidated figures in their financial statements, since it is the most efficient method for disclosing infor-mation on subsidiaries. Finally, a very important requirement is the disclosure of all changes in reserves. In the Netherlands, the "all-inclusive concept of income" is not followed by many companies, so that changes in net worth not resulting from re-ported net income can be of considerable magnitude.

The recently adopted 4th Directive of the European Economic Community will replace some of these requirements. In addition, it will reduce flexibility by introducing uniformity in the format of the financial statements.

Since the passage of the Act on Annual Accounts, statutory audits have been required for NVs and the larger BVs. If financial statements do not comply with the requirements of the Act, the auditor's report should, according to section 314, mention such a departure. If there is no departure, the auditors do not refer to the Act and generally state that the financial statements present fairly the size and composition of the capital and the results for the year.

The *rules concerning the Enterprise Chamber* (also referred to hereinafter as "the court") are contained in sections 337 through 341 of the Civil Code. This Chamber, which is a special section of the Court of Justice at Amsterdam, is comprised of three judges and two experts. No jury is involved.

Individuals or institutions who have a direct interest in the financial statements of a company subject to the Act on Annual Accounts can bring a charge of failure to comply with the Act against the company within two months after the date of publication or after the date of approval of the financial statements. The Public Prosecutor can also bring proceedings if he considers it to be in the public interest. Auditors cannot be charged under this Act. The procedure is not aimed at compensation for damages due to false or insufficient information, but at the improvement of financial reporting. Of course, the disposition of such a proceeding may affect the outcome of a separate case aimed at compensation for damages.

The plaintiff's charge should indicate to what extent the financial statements should be corrected. The task of the court is to decide on the charge of the plaintiff. Both parties retain lawyers to handle their case and give written arguments to support their positions. The court hears both parties as well as the auditor in a session which is *not* open to the public. The auditor is not a party in the case, but acts as a witness to provide the court with information. The court states in its verdict whether and, if so, how the company should correct its financial statements for the year in question and/or whether accounting and reporting changes should be made in the future. The verdict is a public document and contains a great deal of information about the case. The Supreme Court, in the Hague, is a Court of Appeal for verdicts of the Enterprise Chamber. If the prescriptions of the court are not followed by the company, its officers can be punished. Strictly speaking, the verdicts of the Chamber are applicable only to the financial statements of the defendant company. However, the court can indicate grounds for its decisions which may influence reporting practices of other companies.

### The Auditing Profession

The members of the auditing profession in the Netherlands are known as *registeraccountants*. Their professional status is based on a law of 1967, which includes rules concerning the Nederlands Instituut van Registeraccountants (NIVRA), the Disciplinary Court, the Register, and Accountants Examinations. Based on this law, NIVRA developed its Rules of Conduct and Professional Practice (1977), which are mainly rules on professional ethics and standards of reporting. NIVRA has only recently started issuing standards of field work. However, all students must pass a uniform examination before they can be enrolled as a *registeraccountant*. The uniform examination is prepared by NIVRA in close cooperation with the universities. Audits were not required until 1971, nor did NIVRA engage in setting accounting standards. There were neither lawsuits against auditors nor against firms concerning financial statements. The auditors did their job without much public attention or criticism.

If auditors do not follow the Rules of Conduct, they can be brought before the Disciplinary Board and eventually before the Board of Appeal. In very serious cases, they can be expelled from the profession. This disciplinary function of NIVRA has a long history and has been much more important in the past than lawsuits based on the Civil Code.


## THE TRIPARTITE ACCOUNTING STANDARDS COMMITTEE

This Committee was formed at the request of the Government after the enactment of the Act on Annual Accounts, and is comprised of representatives of Dutch employers organizations, the Dutch trade unions, and NIVRA. It reviews the accounting principles adopted by companies, and decides on the acceptability of these practices within the framework of the Act on Annual Accounts.

The pronouncements of the Committee are intended to have an impact upon practice, but it is neither mandatory for companies to follow these pronouncements, nor is it obligatory for auditors to qualify their reports if the pronouncements are not followed. The pronouncements of the Committee can best be described as authoritative opinions of an influential private group. As such, the pronouncements are also used by the Enterprise Chamber, but it need not, and sometimes does not, follow them. Thus far, the Committee has issued several pronouncements after public comment was solicited on exposure drafts. The number of comments submitted by companies is increasing steadily. The pronouncements of the Committee are, so far, compromises between the opinions of the participating groups. NIVRA usually prepares proposals for new pronouncements and is, therefore, quite influential within the Committee. The topics covered generally relate to the valuation of assets and liabilities, the allocation of costs and revenues, and disclosure requirements.

The pronouncements are not intended to achieve uniformity between companies, but to allow for the circumstances and distinctive characteristics of individual companies. The emphasis is on the stewardship function as related to the individual entity. The shareholders are not well organized enough to express their information needs and are not even represented on the Tripartite Standards Committee. A majority of the larger companies follow most of the pronouncements, but in important cases some of them did not. However, some influence is exerted by auditors recommending that the pronouncements be followed [NIVRA, 1979, pp. 13–15].

The pronouncements issued to date include those regarding:

- the allocation of revenues and costs, in which the application of the realization and matching principles are required, and
- the valuation of fixed assets and inventories. Net operating income must be shown both on a current replacment cost and on an historical cost basis, one as supplementary information to the other.

This latter pronouncement has just been issued. In the past, the Committee recommended the disclosure of certain replacement cost data only if they would represent a material departure from historical cost.

In my opinion, the main role of the Committee's pronouncements is to help companies and auditors follow the vague rules of the Act on Annual Accounts, in the absence of other authoritative regulations. However, auditors cannot require companies to follow these pronouncements, nor do they need to mention noncompliance with the statements of the Tripartite Standards Committee.

## Some Court Cases

Although the Act on Annual Accounts has been effective since 1971, the first verdict in a case was handed down by the court in January 1977. In 1977 and 1978, ten cases were adjudicated, and at the end of 1978, eight cases were still in process.

In the first case, Douwe Egberts BV [1977], a company whose products include tobacco, coffee, and tea, was taken to court by some of its shareholders. The company has a net worth of approximately Dfl 370,000,000 (1 Dfl = $0.40), and is very well known for its special brands. It is not quoted on the Amsterdam Stock Exchange. The case concerned the company's 1974 financial statements.

The first point at issue was whether the funds statement is part of the financial statements. The defendant company stated that it is not, since the Act on Annual Accounts does not mention the funds statement. The plaintiff, however, maintained that, since the funds statement was presented in a section of the annual report under the heading of the financial statements, it was part of them. Therefore, the funds statement should be accompanied by some explanatory notes, since certain data could not be reconciled with information from other parts of the financial statements without such an explanation.

The court decided that the plaintiff was right and, therefore, ordered the company to provide the required additional information. This decision clearly has significance for other companies. If the funds statement is presented as part of the financial statements, the funds statement should be interpretable. If, however, the funds statement is not presented as part of the financial statements, but is placed in a different section of the annual report, it is not subject to the provisions of the Act on Annual Accounts. Note the similarity to the current U.S. debate about supplementary financial information, its location, and the auditors' responsibilities.

A second issue related to inventories. Generally, the *physical* inventories are included in the balance sheet. However, firms engaged in trading raw materials often have economic positions in commodities. The shareholders contended that the futures contracts for coffee and tea should have been mentioned in the notes. They complained that it was not clear from the financial statements how price decreases on current purchase contracts had been dealt with. In addition, the liabilities for these contracts were not shown. The defendant denied having sales contracts in the futures markets and contended that the disclosure of current purchase contracts would not be useful information. Douwe Egberts also stated that no losses on such contracts were to be expected; therefore, such disclosure would not be necessary. However, the court decided that *for a company like Douwe Egberts* the disclosure of only inventories on hand (including the valuation of this stock) provided insufficient information to form a judgment on the firm's net worth, its solvency, and its liquidity. Since the prices of raw materials are an important part of the total costs of its finished products and are an important determinant of net income, information concerning the firm's economic position in commodities is very relevant, regardless of its magnitude. The Enterprise Chamber required a disclosure of the current purchase and sales contracts, an indication of the valuation bases applied to these contracts, and the effects on net income, if any. This requirement probably will affect only those companies which can take economic positions in futures and which are comparable to Douwe Egberts with respect to the significance of their raw materials in relation to the total cost of their products. The court also concluded that on a number of other disputes concerning the company's financial statements the information provided was insufficient. However, these defects were not so important that Douwe Egberts was required to produce new financial statements for 1974. Instead, the required additional information was to be included in the financial statements for 1975 and future years. Douwe Egberts appealed to the Supreme Court. That court, however, only changed the verdict on one minor point [Douwe Egberts BV., 1979].

In a second case, two workers' unions brought proceedings against a company called Homburg BV, a producer of meat products [Homburg BV., 1977]. The main complaint of the plaintiffs was that profit was paid to the (British) holding company by means of interest on a loan provided by the holding company. The holding company had replaced part of its investment in the share capital of Homburg with a loan to Homburg at a yearly rate of 11.5 percent. Homburg had also repaid a 9.5 percent loan and replaced it by a 11.5 percent loan. The unions contended that the interest rate of 11.5 percent was above the market rate of about 9 percent, the difference being, in an economic sense, a profit distribution which should be accounted for accordingly. The defendant, however, pointed to the underlying contracts between the holding company and the subsidiary, containing an interest rate of 11.5 percent, and stated that the calculation of the cost of interest was based on this agreement. Further, the defendant contended that the real point at issue was that the workers' unions were dissatisfied with the decision of the firm to engage in loan agreements at such (in their opinion, unfavorable) terms. The company asserted that the unions should not use a case concerning the financial statements to bring this issue to court. In case of mismanagement, they could require the court to bring an investigation. The court concluded, against the unions, that the terms of the loans should be followed in calculating profit. Since the holding company and its subsidiary had agreed on two 11.5 percent loans, the interest was to be calculated according to this percentage.

A second point at issue in this case was whether the workers' union were entitled to bring a charge against the company. According to section 337 of the Act, the plaintiff must have a direct interest in the financial statements. The defendant stated that the unions had no direct interest, since the defendant had agreed with the unions that the loan transaction mentioned above would not have any impact on the profit on which employees' profit-sharing was based. In addition, the defendant stated that the works council of the company should represent the workers in such a question instead of the unions. The works council is a consultative body representing all employees, which has the right to advise management on certain decisions. The unions represent the employees in wage negotiations. The court, however, used the arguments of the plaintiffs to conclude that the unions had a direct interest, since

- the unions are supposed to represent workers and have the right to ask for an investigation,
- they play, according to the collective employment contract, a consulting role in certain important decisions of management, and
- the workers have profit-sharing rights.

In the next two cases, the court decided that the defendant companies should correct their financial statements. In both cases, the plaintiff was a pressure group of shareholders interested in the improvement of financial reporting. This group is not primarily concerned with making investments in firms, but in order to be recognized by the court as an interested party, it buys some shares. This group, called *SOBI* (*S*tichting *O*nderzoek *B*edrijfs *I*nformatie—literally, Foundation to Study Company

Reporting) has been the plaintiff in most of the cases concerning financial reporting brought before the Enterprise Chamber.

In both cases, the defendant companies challenged SOBI as not being an interested party, since it had not yet bought a share in the defendant companies when it brought proceedings. However, the court recognized SOBI as an interested party. Since SOBI had considered buying a share at that time, and actually bought a share later on, the court stated in the first case [Vulcaansoord, 1977] that SOBI had a direct interest in the financial statements of the preceding year. In the second case, the defendant company KSH contended that SOBI had bought a share only to be able to take KSH to court. By this action, SOBI acted as a private prosecutor. Instead, the plaintiff should have asked the Public Prosecutor to institute proceedings in the public interest. The court, however, agreed with the plaintiff and ruled that SOBI's *being* a shareholder was decisive; its *motivation* for becoming a shareholder did not matter.

The first case concerned the financial statements of Vulcaansoord NV for the year June 1, 1974—May 31, 1975. Vulcaansoord is a metal company showing a net worth of about Dfl 6 million and a net income of about Dfl 1,400,000. The plaintiff alleged that correction of the financial statements was needed for eight different items. I will discuss only two. First, the financial statements, as approved by the general meeting of shareholders, did not contain a set of financial statements of the holding company alone, but consisted only of the consolidated financial statements. The court stated that the financial statements were incomplete and should be corrected. According to the Act, consolidated financial statements, according to the law, are part of the notes to the financial statements. In the balance sheet of official financial statements, the participations[3] are disclosed as assets and accordingly are valued by either the equity method or the cost method.

The second point in this case involved the disclosure of liabilities for the pension rights of employees. The law contains no provisions concerning the measurement of such liabilities. In the company's pension scheme, benefits are funded via a separate trust for metal-industry employees. Because of inflation, additional payments for past service had to be made. However, additional past service liabilities were not paid immediately. They were to be paid in the future by each company in the industry, according to a certain scheme related to the number of employees. The auditor stated, during a hearing of the court, that the company had made a provision in its balance sheet for the past service cost of pensions in the previous year. Since other companies in the industry, however, did not have such a provision, the company during the current year had changed its system, and had included the previous year's provision of about Dfl 415,000 in its net income. The auditor stated that the obligation to pay past service would arise only if the company kept its employees. In case of liquidation, past service would not have to be paid by the company. The auditor recognized that it would be useful to disclose in the explanatory notes the amount of past service cost to be paid in the future. The defendant company gave arguments similar to those of the auditor. The plaintiff suggested, among other things, that the present value of the past service should be included as a liability in the balance sheet, and, therefore, the company should not have changed its system, and should not have included the

[3] Participations are long-term investments of at least 25 percent of the investee company's outstanding shares.

gain of Dfl 415,000 in its net income. The fact that the firm need not pay this liability in case of liquidation is not a valid basis for not including the amount in question in its balance sheet, since it should be assumed that Vulcaansoord is a going concern.

The court agreed with the plaintiff. Without presenting a thorough analysis in its verdict, the court ordered that Vulcaansoord should not have changed its accounting system. The court stated that since this liability is substantial and since it can increase rapidly under inflationary conditions it is necessary that the firm include the present value of its past service cost in its financial statements to enable the user to form a sound judgment, according to section 308 of the Act on Annual Accounts. The court ordered Vulcaansoord to correct its financial statements and to have these corrected financial statements approved at its general meeting of shareholders.

The above-mentioned points are relevant for other firms and to current accounting disputes in the United States. The presentation of past service cost as ordered by the court is, however, disputed, and it is not clear whether the opinion of the court will be applicable outside the metal industry. Even if applicable, the wording of the verdict does not rule out the possibility that it is sufficient to disclose the amount in the explanatory notes.

In the second case, SOBI sued KSH, a producer of food with net worth amounting to Dfl 382 million and revenues amounting to Dfl 321 million [KSH NV, 1978]. The plaintiff's objection to KSH's financial statements of 1974/1975 concerned 14 points, the most important of which related to the presentation of fixed assets and inventories (and related costs) in the balance sheet. Concerning fixed assets, the court agreed with SOBI that KSH should clearly describe the valuation basis applied. KSH had mentioned in the notes that the fixed assets were valued at estimated replacement cost. The plaintiff required a description of *how* the replacement cost was estimated. The court emphasized the importance of a proper explanation of the valuation basis in the notes and ruled that the description given was insufficient.

Secondly, concerning the fixed assets, the plaintiff contended that KSH, in applying the replacement cost system, should have continued to make a provision for deferred taxes of 48 percent of the revaluation surplus, in order to recognize in the balance sheet that replacement cost depreciation is not tax-deductible. KSH had made an accounting change and had transferred the respective provision for deferred taxes to the revaluation surplus. KSH defended its position by stating that in a going concern such a provision for deferred taxes in cases of revaluation is not necessary and is not required by law. Only in case the assets are sold would tax be paid. According to the court, this accounting change was not acceptable, since the new method, in which there is no provision for deferred taxation with respect to assets valued at replacement cost, is not common practice.

A second accounting change was disputed: in the past, the firm had used the base stock method for valuing its inventories. In 1974, a change was made to historical cost (FIFO). This change increased its net income by approximately Dfl 8 million. The plaintiff contended that historical cost valuation was not in accordance with section 311 of the Act on Annual Accounts, which contention was denied by the defendant company and the court. However, according to the court, KSH should have given a clear argument for the accounting change. In addition, it should have disclosed the effect of the accounting change on its net assets and net income for the year. Finally, it should not have included an amount of Dfl 15.9 million in its net income. This amount was the excess of the valuation of inventories at FIFO prices over the valuation at prices used in the base stock method. It consisted actually of *realized* holding gains which were credited in the past directly to a reserve account (which is part of the shareholders' equity) under the base stock method. These *realized* holding gains were included in net income for 1974/1975 when the firm no longer applied this method. The court agreed with the plaintiff since "it is not acceptable with respect to the information that the financial statements should provide, to include in net income an amount which has previously been part of shareholders' equity." The court ordered correction of the financial statements. The company decided to appeal to the Supreme Court, which annulled the verdict of the Enterprise Chamber, since it had not properly asked the auditor's opinion on all the issues which supposedly needed correction. Therefore, the Enterprise Chamber will decide this case again (see KSH NV. [1979]).

In the above case, some of the opinions expressed by the court could have significance for a large group of companies. The requirement concerning the description of the valuation method may lead to more detailed descriptions in the notes. The position of the court with respect to the presentation of deferred taxes resulting from a revaluation of assets is in accordance with the practice of most enterprises and will create some uniformity. The general statement that an amount previously included in shareholders' equity should not be included in net income probably will restrict certain accounting practices of other firms.

Finally, I will discuss some points at issue in a very recent case: SOBI versus Pakhoed Holding NV, a company specializing in warehousing and transportation, concerning Pakhoed's 1977 financial statements [Pakhoed, 1979]. The first point brought out by SOBI concerned the valuation of an investment of 177,600 shares in a competing company called Van Ommeren. The shares were non-voting and were listed on the Amsterdam Stock Exchange. Pakhoed presented this asset in its balance sheet as a non-consolidated participation. In the notes, it explained that this so-called "strategic" participation was valued at the lower of cost or the book value of the shares, according to the balance sheet of Van Ommeren. Of this package:

- the cost was Dfl 44 million.
- the book value was Dfl 95 million, and
- the market value of the shares was Dfl 23 million.

Pakhoed had valued this asset at cost (Dfl 44 million). SOBI contended that Pakhoed should have valued this package at market price (Dfl 23 million), since it should not be classified as a participation but as a temporary investment. Pakhoed emphasized that the shareholding was a strategic long-term participation. It could use its power in case of a take-over bid, which would be very important because Van Ommeren was second in the market of oil storage in tanks, in which Pakhoed was first. The court judged that these arguments of Pakhoed justified classification as a participation, because this investment could contribute to the success of Pakhoed's own activities. It also ruled that the valuation basis used for this participation is in accordance with section 311 of the Civil Code. Further, the court decided that it is not necessary to value such a participation at the market price of the shares. However, the market value of the shares should be disclosed in the notes in order to comply with section 308 of the Civil Code.

A second issue referred to income tax allocation. Pakhoed had deducted the tax benefit from a loss on the liquidation of a participation (which will be taken into account in the determination of taxable income in the year in which the liquidation is completed) from its provision for deferred taxation. According to SOBI, the tax benefit should have been taken into account in the year in which the tax benefit would be receivable. Allocation of this tax benefit would be inconsistent with the principles of conservatism and realization. Pakhoed, however, maintained that, according to its public accountant, the amount of deferred tax credits was such that the negative taxable income arising from the liquidation of the participation will be offset by positive taxable income arising from the deferred tax credits. So Pakhoed has rightly deducted the tax benefit resulting from the loss carried forward of Dfl 10,000,000 from its deferred tax account.

The court, however, agreed with SOBI. The tax benefit can be realized only if there will be a net positive taxable income in the year in which the loss carried forward will be taken into account. Even though Pakhoed may be able to influence the magnitude of its taxable income, it is not yet certain that there will be such taxable income. The method used by Pakhoed is not consistent with the concept of prudence, which should be applied in the valuation of future gains. Pakhoed's contention that this gain was being offset by deferred taxes is irrelevant, according to the court. The Enterprise Chamber ruled that Pakhoed need not correct its 1977 financial statements, but that it should take the orders of the court into account for its financial statements for future years.

This court case in particular illustrates the role of the court. Regarding the issue of the participation, it ruled that valuation at cost was in accordance with section 311 of the Civil Code, but it did not answer the question of whether such a valuation would also be acceptable if the market value of the shares would have been much higher. This clearly demonstrates the position of the court: it acts as a referee between two parties. Only the issues put forward by the plaintiff are judged by the court. It does not take a position on other issues. It makes its judgments only on the specific circumstances of each case. This makes the Enterprise Chamber an inadequate vehicle for the development of accounting standards. Its main function is to decide on questions disputed by interested parties. In addition, the Public Prosecutor could take the initiative to bring proceedings concerning accounting and reporting practices if it is in the interest of the public. So far, however, he has never used this power.

## SOME EFFECTS OF THE COURT CASES

It is difficult to estimate the effect of the court cases on the financial reporting practices of companies subject to the Act on Annual Accounts. Such an assessment would require a speculation on the state of financial reporting were there to have been no cases at all. So far, no empirical research has been done to estimate these effects. As a direct effect, companies being ordered by the court to make corrections in their financial statements must comply, since if they do not, the members of the Board of Managers would be guilty of a criminal offense. Due to the small number of court cases, the direct effects are of minor importance. However, the cases can have a much more indirect impact. This impact could occur through:

- the influence of court orders on the accounting and reporting policies of other firms subject to the Act on Annual Accounts, and
- the influence of court cases on the position of public accountants *vis-à-vis* the management.

Strictly speaking, a court order pertains only to the defendant company. Other companies need not comply with its provisions unless the directions and rulings of the court are of a general character, and are not confined to the special circumstances of the case. Even the general directions and rulings of the court, based on considerations not specific to the case, probably have a limited impact, unless companies comply with them, fearing that otherwise they would risk a court case. Finally, some directions refer to the specific circumstances of the defendant company, and, therefore, these will have no impact at all on other companies. So, assuming that companies do not fear court cases, the impact of the orders of the court on other companies will be very limited. However, it could be asked: What factors would influence a company's attitude towards the risk of being sued in a case concerning its financial statements? One might expect that negative publicity could be an important determinant. So far, the verdicts of the Enterprise Chamber have attracted a greal deal of publicity. When companies have been sued, the court case has produced negative publicity, since the allegations have been published in many newspapers. In addition, the leading newspapers and financial news magazines have published major portions of the verdicts. Most companies do not like to be sued, and, therefore, the orders of the court will have some indirect impact on them.

Furthermore, special articles concerning these cases have been written in the financial press, in which the position of the auditors has been subject to criticism (*e.g.,* van der Beek [1978]). The negative publicity concerning the role of the auditor has referred mainly to the unqualified auditors' opinions accompanying financial statements which had been found to be defective by the court. Since auditors are obliged to state in their opinions to what extent the financial statements do not comply with the law, it had been believed that unqualified opinions would guarantee compliance of financial statements. Therefore, the auditors of companies losing their cases were accused of negligence. This reaction has induced the public accounting firms involved in these cases to apply for an examination by the Disciplinary Board of NIVRA in order to have their reputations cleared. In addition, the Board of NIVRA decided to require an examination of the auditor's performance by the Disciplinary Board in all cases in which the Enterprise Chamber ordered financial statements to be corrected [Burggraaff, 1978].

The Board of NIVRA takes the public position that since auditors cannot anticipate the orders of the Enterprise Chamber, an unqualified audit report does not guarantee that the financial statements will not be corrected by order of the court. An unqualified auditor's report implies only that, in the opinion of the auditor, the annual accounts are in compliance with the law. However, there is room for a difference of opinion here, because many aspects of financial statements are not even mentioned in the law. Therefore, these aspects are subject only to its general provisions (sections 307–314). It is obviously difficult for the auditor to anticipate the opinion of the court based on such general provisions.

In publications, the president of the Board of NIVRA has emphasized that the auditors are not a party in the cases being heard by the Enterprise Chamber, but that such a court proceeding is primarily a dispute between the firm and the plaintiff [Burggraaff, 1978]. Nonetheless, a publicly observable effect of the court cases is that the auditing profession has been put in a defensive position. This position might generate some activities to improve accounting standards. Since the global nature of the provisions of the Act on Annual Accounts leaves many questions unanswered, some guidance for auditors in the area of accounting standards was badly needed. The

Tripartite Accounting Standards Committee might provide such guidance. Accountants did hope that its pronouncements would be supported by the verdicts of the Enterprise Chamber [Burggraaff, 1977, p. 275]. However, since this Committee is only a private group, there is no reason why the court must render its decisions in conformity with the Committee's accounting standards. The court must only apply the law, and accounting standards clearly have a lower status than the law.

This lack of status of the accounting standards, however, need not imply that auditors should not, or do not, urge management to comply with the pronouncements of the Tripartite Accounting Standards Committee. In fact, they do. Also, many public accounting firms are active in submitting their views concerning exposure drafts of Accounting Standards. In addition, the Board of NIVRA has expressed its opinion that accounting standards should become stricter and more binding on the interested parties [NIVRA, 1978, p. 151].

As long as the pronouncements have no official status, compliance will be voluntary. Still, there may be good reasons for voluntary compliance. First, the accounting standards could play an important role, by giving companies which apply these standards a means of defense in court cases. In such cases, the defendant company could state that it applied an accounting standard accepted by the representatives of the interested parties. Such a defense could be helpful only if the point at issue were not very specific, since the standards are written at a general level. So far, the pronouncements of the Tripartite Committee have only rarely been used by defendant companies.

Second, so far the court's arguments in support of its rulings as they might apply to future cases are less strict than the respective accounting standards, so that companies complying with these standards probably run only a very low risk of being forced in a court case to correct their financial statements. In addition to the reaction of NIVRA, the attitude of the public accounting firms is most important. Some firms are strengthening their own internal controls to avoid attracting bad publicity from new court cases. Auditors are keenly aware of the increased public attention due to the publicity resulting from the recent court cases. They have reacted by emphasizing the need for standard setting.

Finally, a very important limitation on the effect of court cases on financial reporting is the nature of the court's activities. The court and the Public Prosecutor have so far been passive in the sense that they have not taken the initiative to sue companies for non-compliance with the Act. It is left to the interested parties to complain. Only if someone is willing to run the risk of a court case, will the court address the accounting and reporting practices in question. If the number of court cases is low, many practices will not be judged by the court. But even if there were many court cases, these could not be considered a good substitute for setting accounting standards by some institutional body, since the court only decides on cases, and does not give a comprehensive and general treatment of accounting and reporting problems.

## CONCLUSION

Court cases can, at best, induce companies to comply with the Act. However, since the Act on Annual Accounts is very general on certain points, it is not always clear whether certain practices are acceptable under the Act. Since the role of the court is to settle disputes, it cannot act as a standard-setting body. The Tripartite Accounting Standards Committee produces accounting standards, but these have no statutory basis. Under these conditions, it is hard for an individual auditor to judge if certain accounting and reporting practices comply with the Act. It is, therefore, understandable that, so far, hardly any auditor's report attached to the larger corporations' financial statements mentions noncompliance with the Act. Auditors can clearly consider the requirements of the Act only with respect to the limited number of issues in which the court has taken a general position.

### Some Concluding Remarks

From the preceding review, it is clear that the regulation of financial reporting is not very strict in the Netherlands. This conclusion has two bases:

- the Act on Annual Accounts, which has only a very limited number of detailed provisions for the disclosure of certain information, but which does not give any strict rules concerning valuation, measurement, or classification of data; and
- the absence of any standard-setting body with a statutory basis.

Although the rules laid down so far could be called a form of public regulation, the Act on Annual Accounts is mainly a codification of existing practice. The lack of detailed regulation allows companies to follow their own accounting and reporting policies to a large extent. Some parties interested in financial reporting have so far not been very active in the discussion of accounting and reporting matters. For instance, the Stock Exchange, commercial banks, and financial analysts are not actively engaged in work of the Tripartite Accounting Standards Committee, nor have they published their requirements in this area. Apart from the lawsuits before the Enterprise Chamber, it looks as if most interested parties are satisfied with this low level of regulation. The system enables companies to make some progress, in the sense of increased disclosure of financial information, on a voluntary basis.

To some extent, however, this atmosphere has changed during the past few years. Accountants, especially, plead for more accounting standards via the Tripartite Accounting Standards Committee. They hope that the status of its pronouncements will be accorded standing by the Enterprise Chamber, but so far the court has not explicit cited these standards, and in a few cases it has reached conclusions different from the pronouncements of the Tripartite Accounting Standards Committee. Thus, the relationship between pronouncements of the Tripartite Accounting Standards Committee and the orders of the Enterprise Chamber remains to some extent unclear. However, the court cases demonstrate that a company court is not a proper institution to produce accounting standards.

In the current situation, a fundamental weakness remains: the lack of a means for enforcing compliance with pronouncements of the Tripartite Accounting Standards Committee. Therefore, much depends on the voluntary compliance of companies with these accounting standards. Current investigations by NIVRA suggest that, in practice, compliance is less than complete. Many accountants, however, believe in voluntary compliance with the accounting standards, which leaves room for departures if circumstances justify them. Under such a system, the auditor's responsibility is considerable; most auditors seem to be prepared to take this responsibility, and most other interested parties seem to share their view. There is, at least, very little demand for stricter public regulation of accounting and reporting practices.

## REFERENCES

*Literature*

*Act on Annual Accounts of Enterprises* (NIVRA, Amsterdam, 1972).

AICPA, *Professional Accounting in 30 Countries* (American Institute of Certified Public Accountants, 1975).

Beek, van der, J. M., (1978), "Accountant niet veroordeeld maar wel beoordeeld door uitspraak Ondernemingskamer," *Het Financiële Dagblad* (October 25, 1978).

Beeny, J. H. and J. G. Chastney (1978), *European Financial Reporting: 4 The Netherlands* (Institute of Chartered Accountants in England and Wales, 1978).

Burggraaff, J. A. (1977), "Een eersteling: met gejuich begroet?" *Maandblad voor Accountancy en bedrijfshuishoudkunde* (juni 1977), pp. 274–281.

———, (1978), "Arrest Ondernemingskamer houdt niet in, dat accountant in beroepsuitoefening is tekortgeschoten," *Het Financiële Dagblad* (October 13, 1978).

Commissies jaarverslaggeving van de Raad van Nederlandse Werkgeversbonden, FNV, CNV en het Nederlands Instituut van Registeraccountants, TO (1976), *Beschouwingen naar aanleiding van de Wet ep de Jaarrekening van ondernemingen* (Deventer, 1976).

Nederlands Instituut van Registeraccountants (NIVRA) (1979), *Onderzoek jaarverslagen 1977* (Deventer, 1979).

Nederlands Instituut van Registeraccountants (NIVRA) (1977), Rules of Conduct and Professional Practice of Registeraccountants (NIVRA, Amsterdam, 1977).

Nederlands Instituut van Registeraccountants (NIVRA) (1978), "Logboek van het Bestuur," *De Accountant* (October 1978), p. 151.

Sanders, P., (1977), *Dutch Company Law* (London, 1977).

*Cases*

Cases of the Enterprise Chamber as published in *Jaarrekening van ondernemingen*, deel 2, afd. IV onder redactie van P. Sanders en R. Burgert, Samsom Alphen a/d Rijn:

| | |
|---|---|
| Douwe Egberts BV. | 1977, pp. 1–29 |
| Homburg BV. | 1977, pp. 39–53 |
| KSH NV. | 1978, pp. 113–143 |
| Vulcaansoord NV. | 1977, pp. 53–91 |
| Pakhoed Holding NV. | 1979 (not yet published; a photocopy of the verdict was used as my source). |

Supreme Court Cases (photocopies of verdicts used as source material):

| | |
|---|---|
| Douwe Egberts BV. | (1979), verdict in cases 4973 and 4974, dated January 17, 1979. |
| KSH NV. | (1979), verdict in case 5127, dated June 20, 1979. |

# V Expansion in the Contents of Financial Reports

In this part of the book, several issues are considered, including: (1) pension accounting, with emphasis on the nature of assets and liabilities; (2) deferred income taxes, the arguments for and against, including the issue of discounting deferred taxes; (3) solvency and liquidity disclosures in financial reporting, including working capital and cash flow; and (4) other controversies such as the value added statement and accounting for executory contracts, human assets, and the social performance of the firm.

Section A is devoted to the issues underlying pension accounting, and consists of two articles. The first, by Lucas and Hollowell (1981) presents the case for recognition of pension liabilities, which the authors maintain do exist and should be reported as such with a view to increasing the usefulness of financial reporting. Nonetheless, various questions have to be resolved, including how to measure the liability, what the nature of the offsetting debit should be, and how the assets held by the plan should be shown on the employer's balance sheet. In the second piece, Brownlee and Young (1985) examine the historical development of American pronouncements on pension accounting with an accent on the perennial issues such as the recognition on the balance sheet of a liability or an asset stemming from under- or overfunded pension plans, the periodic recognition of both prior and normal service cost, and the choice of actuarial cost methods as well as the underlying actuarial assumptions. Pension accounting has been a thorny, controversial problem area for some 40 years, attempting to reflect the short-run impact of long-run actions.

Section B captures the debate over deferred income taxes, including the controversy on discounting deferred taxes. Rosenfield and Dent (1983) are opposed to the reporting of deferred taxes, basically, on the grounds that such taxes are not receivables or payables in the normal sense. The authors contend that income taxes should be accounted for without allocation among periods. Defliese (1983), in response to Rosenfield and Dent, takes the opposite point of view, favoring deferred income taxation. Defliese argues that Rosenfield and Dent's approach to accounting for income taxes constitutes a cash framework, and adoption of this approach would be a step backward in financial reporting. In Defliese's view, deferred taxation is the best approach for periodic income measurement, not balance sheet presentation. According to Defliese, deferred taxation emphasizes the importance of properly matching costs against revenues. Rosenfield and Dent (R&D, 1983) reply by saying that while they support the FASB definition of a "liability," indicating that an obligation stems only from past events, Defliese has a countervailing view, which includes obligations arising from past and future events. R&D maintain that it is incongruous to reflect a liability in this year for next year's income taxes, and that footnote disclosure would be more appropriate. R&D do not treat the balance sheet as secondary to the income statement as Defliese apparently does in regard to accounting for income taxes. R&D assert that they are not calling for a cash-basis approach to accounting for income taxes, but recommending an accrual approach without interperiod allocations. Additionally, they say that the matching principle is concerned with comparing costs incurred to revenues generated in the period in question, not future, unincurred taxes to current revenues. R&D also criticize deferred taxation as a means of income smoothing. The foregoing debate provoked a number of letters to the editor of *The Journal of Accountancy*, which published all the articles in this section, and these letters represent the third piece in Part V-B of this book. One respondent points out that deferred taxes often become indefinite deferrals, more like contingencies than liabilities, and that deferred taxes have a distortive impact on financial statement ratios. Other respondents emphasize that the issue does not involve liabilities, but rather economics with respect to the appropriate interperiod allocation of costs. Another respondent asserts that deferred taxation, which is incompatible with FASB Concepts Statement No. 1 (1978), requires an accounting for events that might have occurred, but did not actually occur. Still another respondent accuses R&D of ignoring the going-concern assumption of expected future cash flow from the firm.

In the fourth and last piece in this section, Stepp (1985) considers whether deferred taxes should be discounted, given that the FASB has been emphasizing the comprehensive liability approach to deferred taxes. Those who support discounting say that it is a more appropriate measure of the deferred tax liability. Such a liability is not, however, an account payable at a fixed time. Reversals of timing differences between accounting and tax-return incomes will occur in the future. Deferred taxes stem from the tax law, and are not affected by changes in market interest rates. The economic incentive in deferred taxation is an interest-free loan granted by the government. There are other problems associated with discounting, including which discount rate(s) to use and what the discount period should be. Stepp concludes that deferred income taxes should not be discounted.

In Section C, entitled "Solvency and Liquidity," Heath and Rosenfield (1979) recommend that greater emphasis be placed on conveying solvency information in the financial statements. In the long run, solvency and profitability are compatible. Accordingly, users of financial reports ought to be concerned about solvency. The authors contend that the balance sheet structure for assets and liabilities is based on an outdated notion of solvency assessment and that the funds statement has failed to reflect solvency. In another selection, Heath (1980) criticizes the concept of working capital as a measure of solvency and calls for its retirement. Heath recommends disclosure of supplemental information about the attributes of specific assets and liabilities, classification of liabilities in terms of the different credit sources, and arrangement of the assets in the conventional way without using the *current-noncurrent* classification. In the third piece in this section, "Working Capital as a Tool" (1981), several individuals comment on the usefulness of working capital, in response to the preceding article. One respondent suggests that the definitions of *current* and *noncurrent* be tightened to enhance the relevance of working capital. Another respondent agrees to Heath's recommendation for improving the balance sheet and recommends in particular an emphasis on the following equation: fixed assets + working capital = owners' equity + loan capital. A third respondent believes that the balance sheet classification can be improved upon, but finds Heath's proposal for an unclassified balance sheet "cumbersome." In his rejoinder to the foregoing responses, Heath argues that users can calculate their own ratios irrespective of accounting classifications.

Section D consists of four articles. In the first, Morley (1979) illuminates the pros and cons of a value added statement, emphasizing that a number of the claims for this statement are difficult to validate. Morley asserts that if particular changes were to be made, including standardization of the statement, the usefulness of a value added statement would be augmented. In a short piece on "executory contracts," Henderson and Peirson (1983) make the point that accountants use that term in an unclear manner. The authors recommend that the term be used by accountants only in its legal sense—i.e. a contract is executory if something remains to be carried out by either party involved. Henderson and Peirson suggest that, where necessary, accountants ought to use the phrases "contracts the two sides of which are equally proportionately unperformed" or "contracts where rights and duties are exactly offset." In an article on human asset accounting, Lev and Schwartz (1971) argue that human capital is on a par with nonhuman forms of earning assets, and attempt to provide a practical measurement procedure as a first step toward incorporating human resources in financial statements. The article outlines ways in which human resource information might be used to improve investor decisions and explores a variety of conceptual issues. Ramanathan (1976), in a piece on social accounting, notes that traditional performance criteria may be in conflict with social priorities, and provides an approach to incorporating social effects into the firm's formal performance measurement system. Ramanathan accepts the notion of a "social contract," which implies that a set of social performance dimensions can be developed. A definition of socially responsible performance may then lead to methods of performance measurement and evaluation.

# V-A   Pensions

## V-A 1   *Pension Accounting: The Liability Question*

TIMOTHY S. LUCAS AND BETSY ANN HOLLOWELL

F inancial reports are not telling the whole story about pensions. But how should that story be told? Should some part of the pension obligation not currently recognized as a liability be included on the balance sheet of the employer? Is there an unrecorded liability for pensions under existing generally accepted accounting principles?

We want to discuss this aspect of pension accounting for three reasons. First, the many questions in the pension accounting area are so complex that they all cannot be effectively discussed at once, and the answer to the liability question does not appear to depend on answers to other questions. Second, and more important, the question is one of the most significant in terms of the changes from current accounting that could result from the Financial Accounting Standards Board's pension accounting project. That significance can help us to achieve our primary objective—to stimulate thinking about and discussion of the issues involved in the board's project. Third, a majority of the speakers at the FASB's July 13–15 public hearings in New York on its discussion memorandum (DM), *Employers' Accounting for Pensions and Other Postemployment Benefits*,[1] took positions against including pension obligations on employers' balance sheets and provided a variety of supporting arguments. We

Timothy S. Lucas and Betsy Ann Hollowell, "Pension Accounting: The Liability Question," *Journal of Accountancy*, October 1981, pp. 57–66. Copyright © 1981 by the American Institute of Certified Public Accountants, Inc. Opinions expressed in the *Journal of Accountancy* are those of editors and contributors. Publication in the Journal of Accountancy does not constitute endorsement by the AICPA or its committees.

Ed. note: Expressions of individual views by members of the Financial Accounting Standards Board staff are encouraged. The views expressed herein are those of the authors. Official positions of the FASB on accounting matters are determined only after extensive due process and deliberation.

[1] Financial Accounting Standards Board Discussion Memorandum, *Employers' Accounting for Pensions and Other Postemployment Benefits* (Stamford, Conn.: FASB, 1981).

believe an interesting case can be made *for* recognizing pension liabilities, and that case should be considered and debated by those who are interested in pension accounting questions.[2]

To understand better how the weight of pension liabilities can affect major decisions of management, consider the following report in the press: "Esmark announced recently that it was putting its meat-packing subsidiary, Swift Fresh Meats Division, on the market—and funding the subsidiary's 'sizable' unfunded pension liabilities.

"'They had to do that to make it saleable,' one Esmark analyst commented."

The same article also included a description of another situation: "One instance where pension liabilities were not adequately covered in the original deal—and later came back to haunt a firm—involved the spin-off in 1976 of Facet Enterprises from The Bendix Corp. The divestiture was ordered by the Federal Trade Commission, and Bendix formed Facet as a subsidiary, transferred certain business units to Facet and in 1976 distributed all of the stock of Facet to the common stockholders of Bendix. Included in the transfer to Facet were large unfunded pension liabilities.

"Facet eventually filed suit against Bendix, charging the company was unaware of 'highly detrimental financial consequences' the transfer of the obligation would have on Facet."[3]

Facet Enterprises subsequently notified the Pension Benefit Guaranty Corp. that it was terminating the pension plan, which covered some twenty-two hundred employees and retirees. Facet said that terminating the pension plan was necessary to rescue its financially troubled automotive parts divisions and that the plan's unfunded liabilities of about $31 million exceeded the net worth of the three units it covered.

At about the same time, *Fortune* reported

"When Kaiser Steel was considering liquidation last September ... some people saw an opportunity for a quick profit in the stock. They believed the sell-off of Kaiser's various properties would fetch considerably more than the $44 per share its stock was going for. This reasoning, however, overlooked the company's unfunded vested pension liability of about $9 per share *and* the even larger amount Kaiser says it would have had to fork over to provide health insurance and other benefits to retirees. When Kaiser's directors eventually voted not to liquidate, they gave as one

---

[2] The liability question is one of eight issues addressed in the DM. This article does not attempt to cover other closely related questions, including how to measure the liability if it is to be recorded and the nature of the offsetting debit that arises if a liability is recorded. Measuring or determining the amount of the liability is complex and involves two problems. First, any measure of the pension obligation involves estimating future events, such as how long retirees will live and how many employees will leave before vesting or die before retiring. Second, even after all the estimates are made, there are different attributes of the obligation that may be measured, including vested benefits, accumulated benefits and prior service cost determined under one or more actuarial cost methods. Determining the amount that might be recorded as a liability is beyond the scope of this article, but it involves understanding events related to the growth of the pension obligation as an employee's career progresses from hiring to retirement. The possible choices with regard to the nature of the offsetting debit that arises if a liability is recorded discussed in the DM include recording the debit as an intangible asset or as some kind of charge on the income statement.

[3] Maria Crawford Scott, "Pension Liabilities May Hurt Merger," *Pensions and Investments*, October 13, 1980, p. 4.

reason the size of these burdens. The board concluded the liquidation value could actually be *below* the $44 market price."[4]

In these situations, which unfortunately are not unique, a pension obligation had an unexpected and newsworthy effect on the economic potential and well-being of the company. The pension obligation was not suddenly created in any of these situations. It existed all along, but it was not reported as a liability. Although each company had prepared financial statements in accordance with GAAP, the pension situation was not fully understood, even by knowledgeable readers of those statements.

## CURRENT PENSION GAAP

Employer accounting for pensions is based, at present, on Accounting Principles Board Opinion no. 8, *Accounting for the Cost of Pension Plans*,[5] as amended by FASB Statement no. 36, *Disclosure of Pension Information*.[6] Opinion no. 8 allows pension cost to be determined under any of a number of acceptable actuarial cost methods. Typically, the method used to determine funding of a pension plan (the annual contribution to the pension fund or trust) is also used for accounting.

Under current GAAP, most balance sheets do not include a line item labeled "pension liability." Nevertheless, under Opinion no. 8 part of the pension obligation is recorded as a liability. The amount of liability recorded (debit expense, credit liability) typically is equal to the amount of liability discharged by the contribution (debit liability, credit cash). This is because contributions to the pension plan are recorded as discharges of the pension liability and because most companies fund pension cost accrued. The resulting net liability—the amount appearing on the balance sheet—is zero. But the amount expensed and contributed to the plan cannot be called an unrecorded liability in the usual sense. It does not appear on the balance sheet only because the transfer of assets to the pension fund is regarded as payment of the liability. If, instead, we view the transfer as a segregation or setting aside of assets, it would be logical to add the accumulated amounts expensed (the liability) and the assets held by the plan to the balance sheet.

But for most employers and most plans another part of the pension obligation has not yet been expensed, recorded as a liability or "discharged" by contributions to the plan. The pension obligation that is not recorded as a liability under current GAAP results, primarily, from plan amendments. Parts of that obligation also may result from establishment of new plans and from cumulative experience gains and losses, but for simplicity we will focus on plan amendments. When a pension plan is amended to increase benefits, the increased benefits usually are granted based on service, including service rendered before the date of the change. In some cases benefits also are increased for former employees who are already retired. After such an amendment, the employer's pension obligation is larger than it was before. It is this incremental obligation that some believe should be recorded as a liability. This view is based on the idea that the employer has an obligation for benefits already earned by employees. The amount of benefits earned (however measured) will not necessarily

---

[4] Mary Greenebaum, "The Market Has Spotted Those Pension Problems," *Fortune*, December 1, 1980, p. 146.

[5] Accounting Principles Board Opinion no. 8, *Accounting for the Cost of Pension Plans* (New York: AICPA, 1966).

[6] FASB Statement no. 36, *Disclosure of Pension Information* (Stamford, Conn.: FASB, 1980).

coincide with the accumulation of prior years' normal costs and amortization of prior service costs recorded under Opinion no. 8.

For convenience, let's assume that we are dealing with a typical company that sponsors a single-employer, defined-benefit pension plan. The plan provides a retirement income benefit of, say, $50 per month for each year of an employee's service. In the current year, the company amends the plan to increase the benefits to $60 per month per year of service for all active employees and for retirees who are receiving pensions. The amendment provides for increased benefits based on all of an employee's years of service, past as well as future. Actuaries will review the change and compute the new, increased amount of contribution the company will pay over a period of years to fund the increased benefits. The accounting question is, When the plan is amended, does a recordable liability arise for that part of the increased benefits attributed to past years of service?

Opinion no. 8 accounting reflects such an amendment prospectively, usually based on the way the cost of the amendment will be funded. No increase in liability is recorded immediately as a result of the event that occurred when the plan was amended. Instead, it is provided for and recorded as expense and a liability a little bit at a time.

Whether a recordable liability arises when the plan is amended depends on what kinds of things belong on balance sheets. Accountants and users of financial statements generally understand the nature of items on balance sheets, including liabilities. That knowledge makes the balance sheet useful. Liabilities such as accounts payable, notes payable and bonds payable all have something in common. And, most important, all accounts, notes and bonds payable are included. If each company had the flexibility to omit some of these items in preparing its balance sheet, disclosing the omitted items in the footnotes, the usefulness of the balance sheet would be reduced. Analysts would doubtless add the "footnote liabilities" to those on the statement and construct their own adjusted balance sheets (as some do today with pension disclosures), but the convenience of having a complete balance sheet would be lost and some users might be misled because they expect all liabilities to be included.

The FASB has begun the process of describing the kinds of things that belong on the right-hand side of a balance sheet by providing a definition of liabilities. Financial Accounting Concepts Statement no. 3, *Elements of Financial Statements of Business Enterprises*, defines liabilities as "probable future sacrifices of economic benefits arising from present obligations of a particular entity to transfer assets or provide services to other entities in the future as a result of past transactions or events."[7]

The concepts statement also identifies three essential characteristics of a liability inherent in the definition: ". . . (a) it embodies a present duty or responsibility to one or more other entities that entails settlement by probable future transfer or use of assets at a specified or determinable date, on occurrence of a specified event, or on demand, (b) the duty or responsibility obligates a particular enterprise, leaving it little or no discretion to avoid the future sacrifice, and (c) the transaction or other event obligating the enterprise has already happened."[8]

---

[7] Financial Accounting Concepts Statement no. 3, *Elements of Financial Statements of Business Enterprises* (Stamford, Conn.: FASB, 1980), par. 28.

[8] Ibid., par. 29.

In addition, it discusses other features often found in liabilities: "Liabilities commonly have other features that help identify them—for example, most liabilities require the obligated enterprise to pay cash to one or more identified other entities and are legally enforceable. However, those features are not essential characteristics of liabilities. Their absence, by itself, is not sufficient to preclude an item's qualifying as a liability. That is, liabilities may not require an enterprise to pay cash but to convey other assets, to provide or stand ready to provide services, or to use assets. And as long as payment or other transfer of assets to settle an existing obligation is probable, the identity of the recipient need not be known to the obligated enterprise before the time of settlement. Similarly, although most liabilities rest generally on a foundation of legal rights and duties, existence of a legally enforceable claim is not a prerequisite for an obligation to qualify as a liability if the future payment of cash or other transfer of assets to settle the obligation is otherwise probable."[9]

A careful reading of the above excerpts reveals that the definition of liabilities is primarily a description of current practice; it is not a radical change but a formal description of the kinds of things that we already think of as liabilities. Accountants are likely to agree, for example, that accrued salaries payable is a liability because the company has a responsibility or obligation to employees who have performed services for which they have not yet been paid. The obligation probably will be satisfied by paying the accrued amounts (transferring assets) at a future date, and the event that obligated the company (the performance of the services) has already occurred.

On the other hand, a budgeted expenditure to replace a machine is not a liability, even though the transfer of assets may be virtually certain and the need to replace the machine acute. The budgeted expenditure does not entail the essential obligation— the duty or responsibility to another entity. That obligation will be created by a future event.

The same understanding of a liability (as formalized by Concepts Statement no. 3) can be used in considering the pension liability question. In the example described earlier, when the plan is amended is there an obligation to make a probable future payment? Has the event that obligated the company already happened? It seems clear to us that a case can be made for an affirmative answer to those questions. If so, the pension obligation is similar to other obligations that are recorded as liabilities, and the balance sheet would be incomplete—its usefulness diminished—if the pension liability was excluded, just as it would be incomplete without bank loans or accounts payable.

The news excerpts quoted earlier suggest that economic decisions sometimes are affected by the failure of decision makers to fully understand or consider pension obligations. As noted, the pension obligations that are not recorded and may therefore be overlooked result primarily from plan amendments. The incremental pension obligations that result from a plan amendment are now recorded as liabilities only over future periods. If those obligations were included on the balance sheet as liabilities when incurred, it seems to us, they would be less likely to be overlooked, and the balance sheet would provide a more complete picture of the financial position of the company. We also noted that some analysts adjust present balance sheets to consider some measure of pension obligations. If, as we have

---

[9] Ibid., par. 29.

suggested, the unrecorded pension obligation looks like other obligations afforded balance sheet status, why do some people still want to exclude pension obligations from balance sheets?

## ARGUMENTS FOR AND AGAINST DEFERRED RECOGNITION OF PENSION LIABILITIES

The remainder of this article explores some of the reasons advanced for continuing the present practice of deferred recognition of pension liabilities resulting from plan amendments. Our opinions as to why those reasons have not been convincing also are discussed. The arguments for and against recognition generally apply equally to the obligation resulting from plan amendments and to that resulting from other factors such as experience gains and losses.

1) *The company's obligation is only to make contributions.* Some people suggest that the company does not have an obligation directly to the employees but only an obligation to make scheduled contributions to the plan. They conclude that there is no liability if contributions called for (by the actuary) have been made.

We believe this confuses the existence of a liability with its maturity date. If there is an obligation to the plan—an obligation to make future contributions—resulting from past events such as plan amendments and past service, that obligation may qualify as a liability. The fact that the contributions are scheduled for payment in future years does not mean that the obligation should remain unrecorded; most liabilities have scheduled future payment dates. The obligation to the plan and the obligation to the employees are two different ways to describe the same thing. The crucial question is whether there is a present obligation as a result of past transactions or events, not the identification of the obligee.

In addition, the idea that the existence of the pension plan or trust as a separate legal entity somehow avoids what would otherwise be the company's liability leads to other questions. Suppose a company set up a similar trust to be funded over a period of years to pay off a major lawsuit settlement. Should the full amount of the agreed on settlement be recorded as a liability or is it only an obligation of the trust?

2) *It is not a legal liability.* Some argue that the pension liability should be excluded from the balance sheet because it is not a "legal" liability. As the excerpt we quoted from Concepts Statement no. 3 notes, legal status is not required for an obligation to be recorded as a liability. In addition, the meaning of the term *legal liability* in this context is unclear. Pension obligations have been held to be legally enforceable in various circumstances.

3) *It will never have to be paid.* If a pension plan is assumed to continue in effect, the liability will never be fully paid since there will always be active employees whose pensions are not yet payable. Some people suggest that the pension obligation need not be recorded on this basis.

The same thing may be said, however, of many other liabilities. For example, if a company continues in business, it is unlikely ever to reduce the balance of accounts payable to zero, but it is still considered useful to record and report the total amount of the obligation at the end of each period. This argument seems to be more relevant to funding decisions than to accounting questions.

4) *The amount of the obligation can't be measured.* Some argue that the pension obligation should be excluded from the balance sheet because it is too uncertain or too

hard to measure. They note that several future events must be estimated to calculate the amount of the obligation and that it is expected that these estimates will have to be adjusted as experience unfolds. The need to estimate and project future events is not unique to pensions. Accounting unavoidably involves many estimates and must be able to deal with changes in those estimates. The best current estimate of the amount of the pension obligation, based on the experience and knowledge of the professional actuary, is useful information. Pension accounting is already based on the same estimates; the only difference is that the amounts are spread over a number of future periods.

Spreading the effect of a plan amendment over a number of future periods tends to obscure, rather than report, the effect of the change. The obligation for future pension payments or contributions clearly is greater after a plan amendment than it was before the amendment. Financial Accounting Concepts Statement no. 1, *Objectives of Financial Reporting by Business Enterprises*, states

"Financial reporting should provide information about the economic resources of an enterprise, the claims to those resources (obligations of the enterprise to transfer resources to other entities and owners' equity), and the effects of transactions, events, and circumstances that change its resources and claims to those resources."[10]

Since the plan amendment is an event that changes the employer's obligation— an event that increases employees' claims to the company's resources—financial statements should reflect that event.

5) *The increased benefits are granted in exchange for future service.* Some suggest that increases in pension benefits are granted in anticipation of future employee services, even though the amount of increase may be computed based on the number of years of prior service. In this view, the employer would be unlikely to increase benefits unless he expected to receive something of value in return. Since the value of past services cannot be enhanced retroactively, the employer must expect to receive benefits in the form of future services. The suggested conclusion is that the liability arises only as the future service is rendered.

The use of this line of reasoning for benefit increases granted to those already retired is based on the idea that current employees will provide services in exchange for benefits paid to other individuals already retired because they expect to receive similar increases after they retire.

The problem with that argument is it does not address whether the employer has a liability—a present obligation to transfer assets as a result of past transactions or events. After a plan amendment becomes effective, that obligation exists. What the employer receives in return for incurring the liability is another issue. An asset can exist as a result of the amendment, for example, if employees are motivated to work harder. Concepts Statement no. 3 has defined assets as "probable future economic benefits obtained or controlled by a particular entity as a result of past transactions or events."[11] Whether an intangible asset exists after a plan amendment is beyond the scope of this article.

6) *Liability recognition would have economic consequences.* Some suggest that

---

[10] Financial Accounting Concepts Statement no. 1, *Objectives of Financial Reporting by Business Enterprises* (Stamford, Conn.: FASB, 1978), par. 40.
[11] Concepts Statement no. 3, par. 19.

recognizing the unrecorded pension liability would cause some employers to go bankrupt, to be denied access to credit markets or to be unwilling to improve pension plans. These and other predicted economic consequences are perceived as undesirable. They are said to be costs that exceed any possible benefit that might result from changes in pension accounting.

The FASB addressed the relationship between economic consequences and accounting standards in Financial Accounting Concepts Statement no. 2, *Qualitative Characteristics of Accounting Information*:

"While rejecting the view that financial accounting standards should be slanted for political reasons or to favor one economic interest or another, the Board recognizes that a standard-setting authority must be alert to the economic impact of the standards that it promulgates. The consequences of those standards will usually not be easy to isolate from the effects of other economic happenings, and they will be even harder to predict with confidence when a new standard is under consideration but before it has gone into effect. Nevertheless, the Board will consider the probable economic impact of its standards as best it can and will monitor that impact as best it can after a standard goes into effect. For one thing, a markedly unexpected effect on business behavior may point to an unforeseen deficiency in a standard in the sense that it does not result in the faithful representation of economic phenomena that was intended. It would then be necessary for the standard to be revised.

"Neutrality in accounting is an important criterion by which to judge accounting policies, for information that is not neutral loses credibility. If information can be verified and can be relied on faithfully to represent what it purports to represent— *and if there is no bias in the selection of what is reported* — it cannot be slanted to favor one set of interests over another. It may in fact favor certain interests, but only because the information points that way, much as a good examination grade favors a good student who has honestly earned it.

"The italicized words deserve comment. It was noted earlier in this Statement that reliability implies completeness of information, at least within the bounds of what is material and feasible, considering the cost. An omission can rob information of its claim to neutrality if the omission is material and is intended to induce or inhibit some particular mode of behavior."[12]

The board also has recognized its responsibility to limit changes in existing practice to situations in which the perceived benefits exceed the perceived costs of the change.

Economic consequences, however, can work both ways. There also may be economic consequences of failing to change accounting rules that do not reflect economic reality or that are not neutral and unbiased. The costs of not improving accounting are probably as hard to measure as the costs of changes, but they may be significant.

The economic consequences argument against recognizing the pension liability presumes that markets and decision makers will not become aware of the liability if it is not recorded. It also assumes that situation to be desirable. That assumption conflicts with the basic objective of reporting neutral and unbiased information that is relevant to decision makers.

---

[12] Financial Accounting Concepts Statement no. 2, *Qualitative Characteristics of Accounting Information* (Stamford, Conn.: FASB, 1980), pars. 106, 107, 108.

Consider, for example, the suggestion that recording the pension liability will deny some companies access to credit. Decisions to grant or deny credit to a particular company are not made by the FASB; they are made by people, such as bankers, who are concerned with the ability of the company to repay. Credit decisions are based, in part, on accounting information, and those who must decide to grant or deny credit rely on having unbiased information, including information about a company's liabilities. It is inappropriate for the FASB to refuse to recognize a liability that exists just because knowledge of that liability might cause the banker to deny credit to a particular company. Indeed, that may be a persuasive reason to require recognition of the liability.

## CONCLUSION

Based on our work to date, we are not convinced by the arguments against recording a liability when a pension plan is established or amended. We believe that an accounting liability does exist and that including it with other liabilities in the balance sheet will significantly improve the usefulness of financial statements.

CPAs may or may not agree with out conclusion. However, even if they, and the members of the FASB, ultimately do agree, a number of important related questions must be resolved before any change in pension accounting can be implemented, including

- What is the appropriate measure of the liability? Is it vested benefits, accumulated benefits, prior service cost or something else?
- If a liability is recorded, what is the nature of the offsetting debit? Is it expense, an extraordinary charge, an intangible asset or something else?
- How should the assets held by the plan be reflected on the employer's balance sheet? Depending on the measure of the liability, plan assets might exceed the liability for many companies.

These and other related issues are now being considered as part of the FASB's project on employers' accounting for pensions and other postemployment benefits. The answers to the issues may have a significant effect on how financial statements reflect pension activities. We encourage accountants to help in finding answers that improve financial reporting by participating in the board's process.

# V-A 2 *Pension Accounting: A New Proposal*

## E. RICHARD BROWNLEE II AND S. DAVID YOUNG

For nearly 40 years the accounting profession has sought an acceptable solution to the pension accounting puzzle. Progress has been slow, but acceptable alternatives have been narrowed and disclosure requirements improved. For the most part, however, the key accounting issues have remained unchanged and unresolved. The FASB's current pension accounting project comprises many of the issues previously addressed by the Board's predecessors: the Committee on Accounting Procedure, and the APB.

The complexities of corporate pension plans and the diversity of opinion regarding both their underlying nature and appropriate cost attribution have suggested to some that a satisfactory solution to pension accounting may not be possible. This perspective was reinforced when the FASB, having begun its pension project in 1974, presented its tentative conclusions and recommendations in November 1982. The response to the Board's *Preliminary Views on Employers' Accounting for Pensions and Other Postemployment Benefits* was so overwhelmingly negative that there was cause for concern about the project's future.

To the Board's credit, however, it held fast to the belief that pension accounting standards need to be reexamined and some fundamental issues resolved. After listening to comments concerning the *Preliminary Views*, the FASB went back to the drawing board and produced an *Exposure Draft* (ED) intended to improve pension accounting and reporting. Issued in March 1985, the Proposed Statement of Financial Accounting Standards titled *Employers' Accounting for Pensions* contains recommendations that are, for the most part, substantially different from both the *Preliminary Views* and currently accepted accounting standards.

This article traces the development of pension accounting and reporting standards through the recent ED. It gives particular attention to the issues that have been the most controversial and difficult to resolve, examines the principal provisions of the ED, and compares them with existing pension standards and with the *Preliminary Views*.

## THE EVOLUTION OF PENSION ACCOUNTING STANDARDS

Corporate pension plans represent one of accounting's most vivid examples of an ever-present financial reporting conundrum: presenting the short-term financial consequences of long-term economic activities. In addition to the accounting dimensions, pensions present other important considerations in the areas of law, tax, finance, and actuarial science. The interrelationships among these factors have made it difficult to achieve agreement on the presentation of pension information in corporate financial statements and related footnotes.

## Committee on Accounting Procedure Pronouncements

The first authoritative pronouncement on employer's accounting for pensions did not appear until the late 1940s. ARB No. 36, *Pension Plans: Accounting for Annuity Costs Based on Past Services*, was issued by the Committee on Accounting Procedure (CAP) in November 1948.

It dealt solely with the treatment of pension costs arising from past service incurred under pension plans involving payments to outside agencies. CAP concluded that "(a) Costs of annuities based on past service should be allocated to current and future periods, and (b) costs of annuities based on past service should not be charged to surplus." Funding of past service costs, actuarial methods to be used to determine past service costs, and calculation of current service costs were not considered.

The first authoritative pronouncement to address pension accounting comprehensively was ARB 47, *Accounting for Costs of Pension Plans*. Issued by the CAP in September 1956, it reaffirmed the Committee's prior views regarding the nature and purpose of corporate pension plans and the appropriate treatment of past service costs. It gave consideration to opposing pension accounting philosophies and ultimately recommended the full accrual of pension costs, including those pertaining to past service. ARB 47 was the first accounting pronouncement to distinguish between funding and expensing, to provide guidance on the determination of current service cost, and to require pension-related footnote disclosure.

ARB 47 also contained a discussion of the divergent viewpoints surrounding the accrual of pension costs. While the CAP acknowledged that, in the view of many, pension costs accruals should not necessarily be governed by a strict legal interpretation of pension obligations, it nevertheless concluded that "as a minimum, the accounts and financial statements should reflect accruals which equal the present worth, actuarially calculated, of pension commitments to employees to the extent that pension rights have vested in the employees, reduced, in the case of the balance sheet, by any accumulated trusteed funds or annuity contracts purchased."

## Accounting Principles Board Pronouncements

Despite the provisions of ARB 47, pension accounting practices continued to vary among companies, often resulting in large year-to-year fluctuations in annual pension costs. Shortly after APB superseded CAP in 1959, pension accounting was placed on the APB's agenda for reconsideration. In 1966, APB issued Opinion No. 8, *Accounting for the Cost of Pension Plans*. It is still the authoritative pronouncement for pension accounting and reporting, except for amendments by FASB in disclosure requirements in SFAS No. 36, *Disclosure of Pension Information*.

APB Opinion No. 8 was issued because the Board felt the need to clarify certain existing pension accounting principles and to narrow the practices used in determining annual corporate pension costs. Its principal objective was to establish acceptable limits for the amount of annual pension cost to be charged to expense. It drew a clear distinction between pension expense (an accounting concern) and pension funding (a managerial cash-flow concern) and emphasized that the two need not be the same. The APB viewed the determination of the amount funded as a financial matter outside the purview of accounting principles.

The diverse philosophies toward pension accounting first articulated in ARB 47 were acknowledged but not resolved by Opinion No. 8. While there was a concensus that pension cost should be accounted for on the accrual basis, general agreement on the nature of pension cost was not reached. The Board concluded in APB No. 8 that the annual provision for pension cost should be based on an accounting method utilizing an acceptable actuarial cost method resulting in an amount within a specified minimum and maximum. The principal difference between the minimum and maximum provisions centered on the treatment of past and prior service cost and represented a compromise between the divergent pension philosophies discussed in ARB 47.

In accordance with the requirements of Opinion No. 8, there are several instances when a company's balance sheet will contain a pension-related asset or liability. The first is when a company funds an amount different from that which it expenses. Excess funding gives rise to a prepaid pension asset; excess expensing results in a pension liability. The second instance occurs when a company has a legal pension obligation in excess of the amounts funded and accrued. In these circumstances, the excess should be shown in the balance sheet both as an asset (deferred charge) and a liability. A third instance that can give rise to pension balance sheet recognition occurs, under APB Opinion No. 16, *Business Combinations*, when a business combination accounted for as a purchase requires the acquiring company to record a pension liability even if none exists in the balance sheet of the acquired company.

Opinion No. 8 concluded that a variety of actuarial cost methods were acceptable for use in determining annual pension expense. It expressed no preference as to methods and stated only that "to be acceptable for accounting purposes, an actuarial cost method should be rational and systematic and should be consistently applied so that it results in a reasonable measure of pension cost from year to year."

Other major provisions of Opinion No. 8 dealt with the treatment of actuarial gains and losses and the disclosure of pension information in financial statement footnotes. It did not address the basis upon which the total assets in the pension fund should be determined: cash or accrual, historical cost or market value. Despite the controversial nature and complexity of the issues involved, Opinion No. 8 was adopted unanimously by the APB.

### Financial Accounting Standards Board Pronouncements

The passage of the Employee Retirement Income Security Act of 1974 (ERISA) led the FASB to issue in December 1974 Interpretation No. 3, *Accounting for the Cost of Pension Plans Subject to the Employee Retirement Income Security Act of 1974*, in order to modify the requirements of Opinion No. 8 for the effects of ERISA. The Interpretation stated that the provisions of Opinion No. 8 continued to be applicable and provided guidance concerning the accounting for and disclosure of the effects of pension plan amendments (e.g., vesting and funding) brought about by ERISA.

In May 1980, FASB issued SFAS No. 36, *Disclosure of Pension Information*, as an interim measure pending completion of its major project on accounting by employers for pensions and other postemployment benefits. SFAS No. 36 pertained solely to the disclosure of pension information and was based, in part, on certain conclusions contained in SFAS No. 35, *Accounting and Reporting by Defined Benefit Pension Plans*. It did not affect either the amount of annual pension expense or the determination of any pension-related asset or liability to be included in balance sheets. The pension requirements affecting financial statements continued to be those prescribed by APB Opinion No. 8.

SFAS No. 36 accomplished the Board's objectives of increasing pension plan disclosures and unifying the basis upon which plan assets and plan benefits were determined. However, it created considerable confusion among users and was criticized for understating pension obligations. Much of the confusion was due to the failure of many users to realize that the actuarial methods and assumptions used to arrive at the amounts presented in the pension footnote were often not the same as those used in determining both the annual pension expense and any balance sheet liability. Because companies could use present salary levels and current interest rates in calculating the present value of accumulated plan benefits presented in the footnotes, many corporations drastically reduced or eliminated their footnote pension obligations. This brought severe criticism from those who believed that corporate pension plans were already seriously underfunded and that the new disclosure requirements might serve to worsen the situation.

## THE FASB'S PENSION ACCOUNTING PROJECT

In response to the passage of ERISA and concern expressed over perceived deficiencies with generally accepted pension accounting standards, the FASB added the pension topic to its agenda in 1974. This project has probably generated the greatest display of controversy and dissent of any FASB project to date. In opening the Board's five-day public hearing on pensions in January 1984, Chairman Donald J. Kirk remarked: "From the responses we have received it would be difficult to argue that opinion has crystallized or that accounting has completed its transitional stage. There is no readily apparent answer that would satisfy all of the Board's constituents."

Although there are numerous controversial issues associated with contemporary pension accounting and reporting, two are dominant:

- The major controversy centers around the recognition in balance sheets of a liability or asset arising from an underfunded or overfunded pension plan.
- The second key issue pertains to the periodic recognition of both prior and normal service cost. The crux of this dilemma centers on the selection of the actuarial cost method (or methods) and the underlying actuarial assumptions used to calculate annual pension expense, including assumptions about salary increases and rates of return on pension assets.

The pension accounting and reporting standards recommended by the FASB in its March 1985 ED represent significant changes from those currently accepted. Some of the Board's proposals are identical to those contained in its *Preliminary Views*, others are modifications of the *Preliminary Views'* proposals, and still others represent substantial departures from both existing standards and those proposed in the *Preliminary Views*. Exhibit 1 contains a comparison of the major provisions of APB Opinion No. 8 (as amended), the *Preliminary Views*, and the recent ED.

### FASB Preliminary Views

The *Preliminary Views* called for the recognition in corporate balance sheets of two new pension-related items. The first was either a net pension asset or a net pension liability calculated as follows:

**The pension benefit obligation**
**Less**
**The fair value of the plan's net assets**
**Plus or Minus**
**A measurement valuation allowance**

The pension benefit obligation represented the actuarial present value of the accumulated benefits attributed to employee service. It included normal and prior service costs, vested and nonvested benefits, and was measured based on estimates of future compensation levels. The *Preliminary Views* also called for the use of a single actuarial cost method for reporting purposes. Referred to as the "projected unit credit" method, it was similar in all but one important respect to the approach required by SFAS No. 36 for footnote disclosure purposes. The difference was that the projected unit credit method used expected future rather than current compensation levels in the determination of annual pension expense and the pension obligation. If adopted, these provisions would have resulted in pension obligations far greater than those shown in pension footnotes and would have placed them in balance sheets as liabilities.

In an attempt to avoid potential undesirable fluctuations in reported net pension liabilities brought about by inevitable inaccuracies or changes in actuarial assumptions, the *Preliminary Views* recommended the establishment of a "measurement valuation allowance" as a component of the net pension liability. As actuarial gains and losses occurred, they would be recognized in the pension benefit obligation (or in the pension assets if investment related), but an equal offsetting change would be made in the measurement valuation allowance. The balance in the measurement valuation allowance would be amortized as a charge or credit to pension expense over the average remaining service period of the active plan participants.

The second new balance sheet item proposed by the *Preliminary Views* was an intangible asset representing the expected economic benefits to be realized by an employer as a result of the initiation or amendment of a plan. As employers generally grant credit to their employees for prior services, this retroactive credit would increase the net pension obligation and, thus, the net pension liability. Presumably, however, employers would not incur such an obligation without some expectation that they will realize future economic benefits in return. The intangible asset was an attempt to give these benefits balance sheet recognition. It would be equal in amount to the increase in the employer's pension benefit obligation, amortized over the average remaining service period of plan participants, and reported as a separate asset in balance sheets.

### FASB Exposure Draft

In the ED, the FASB significantly reduced the balance sheet effects from those proposed in the *Preliminary Views*. For balance sheet purposes only, the Board dropped its proposed use of the projected unit credit method and recommended that

**EXHIBIT 1**

**A Comparison of the Major Provisions of APB Opinion No. 8 (as Amended), the Preliminary Views, and the Exposure Draft**

| Issue | APB Opinion No. 8 (as Amended) | Preliminary Views | Exposure Draft |
|---|---|---|---|
| 1. Assets & liabilities | | | |
| (a) Recognition of asset for funding more than accrued net periodic pension cost | Required | Required | Required |
| (b) Recognition of liability for funding less than accrued net periodic pension cost | Required | Required | Required |
| (c) Recognition of additional pension liability | When an employer has a legal obligation in excess of amounts funded and accrued | When an employer has a net pension liability | When an employer has an unfunded accumulated benefit (vested and nonvested) obligation |
| (d) Recognition of asset when additional liability is recognized | Deferred charge | Intangible asset | Intangible asset (In certain instances, also a reduction of equity) |
| (e) Recognition of additional pension asset | No provision | When an employer has a net pension asset | No provision |

| | | | |
|---|---|---|---|
| 2. Net periodic pension cost | | | |
| (a) Attribution method | Any "acceptable" actuarial cost method | Based on terms of plan. Generally equivalent to projected unit credit method | Based on terms of plan. Generally equivalent to projected unit credit method |
| (b) Recognition of prior service cost | Not required. Affected by actuarial cost method used. If amortized, should be rational and systematic. Minimum and maximum provisions apply. | Percentage method applied to net unrecognized balance. Rate equal to 1 divided by average remaining service. | Generally assignment of equal amounts to each future period of service of active employees. So, period relates to remaining service of closed group. |
| (c) Actuarial gains and losses | Delayed through the use of asset valuation methods and then by amortization. | Delayed through the use of a measurement valuation allowance. | Delayed through the use of a "corridor" approach. |
| (1) Recognition | Not required | Required | Required |
| (2) Disclosure | | | |
| (3) Amortization | Variety of methods allowed. Suggested period 10 to 20 years. | Percentage method applied to net unrecognized balance. Rate equal to 1 divided by average remaining service. | Only the amount in excess of the "corridor" is amortized. Any systematic method is allowed. Minimum rate equal to 1 divided by the average remaining service. |
| (d) Actuarial assumptions | Not addressed | Explicitly addressed | Explicitly addressed |

entities show as a balance sheet liability the excess of their accumulated benefit obligation over the fair value of pension assets. The accumulated benefit obligation would include vested and nonvested benefits but, except for automatic benefit increases specified by the plan, would include no assumption about future compensation levels. In essence, the Board decided to retain the approach currently required by SFAS No. 36 for disclosure purposes but to move any resulting obligation from the footnotes to the balance sheet. It is important to understand that the ED contains no provision for the recognition of an asset in those instances, of which there are many, where the fair value of pension assets exceeds the accumulated benefit obligation.

The Board retained its proposal for recognizing an intangible asset as the offset to its new pension liability. The ED provides, however, that the intangible asset cannot exceed the amount of unrecognized prior service cost. Any excess would be reported as a separate component of (and reduction in) stockholder's equity. The intangible asset would be amortized in decreasing amounts over the expected future years of service of active participants at the date of recognition.

The determination of the amount of the proposed pension liability, if any, would be made annually as of the balance sheet date. Thus, both its existence and amount would likely be subject to considerable fluctuation. Annual adjustments to the liability would be offset by equal adjustments to the intangible asset or equity component. For companies with more than one plan, the ED requires that each plan be treated separately; that is, overfunded plans cannot be used to reduce the pension obligation to be reported in the balance sheet resulting from underfunded plans.

In what appears to be an unprecedented move, the FASB has recommended a different approach for determining annual pension expense than that for the pension liability. For income statement purposes, the ED calls for net periodic pension cost (the Board's new term for pension expense) to be calculated in accordance with the projected unit credit method. In other words, annual pension cost would be based on an actuarial cost method that includes assumptions about future compensation levels. Total net periodic pension cost could thus include one component that recognizes anticipated future compensation levels and another component—amortization of the intangible pension asset—that ignores future compensation levels.

The Board also discarded its proposed measurement valuation allowance approach to smoothing the recognition of actuarial gains and losses in favor of what it calls the "corridor" approach. This approach would recognize only actuarial gains and losses that exceed a predetermined limit (the corridor). The limit proposed is ten percent of the greater of the projected benefit obligation (i.e., the obligation determined with future compensation levels) or the fair value of the plan's assets, both of which would be calculated as of the beginning of the year. Although a minimum amortization method is stipulated, any systematic amortization method consistently applied that would result in an amount equal to or greater than the minimum would be acceptable.

Finally, the ED proposes disclosure of a considerable amount of pension information not currently required by SFAS No. 36. New disclosures would include the individual components of net periodic pension cost, the actual return on pension assets, the projected benefit obligation and its components, the weighted average assumed discount rate and rate of compensation increase assumed, and the effect on the projected benefit obligation and net periodic pension cost of a one percentage point change in the assumed discount and compensation rates.

## SUMMARY AND CONCLUSION

If adopted, the *Proposed Statement of Financial Accounting Standards* would supersede all existing standards for employers' accounting for pensions. Although additional disclosures would be required for employers participating in multi-employer plans and those sponsoring defined contribution plans, the most significant changes to current practice would affect the accounting for single-employer defined benefit pension plans.

On balance, the ED would require less radical changes than those proposed in the *Preliminary Views*. Of particular significance would be the use of the accumulated benefit obligation instead of the projected benefit obligation to measure the pension liability shown in the balance sheet. As a result, the FASB estimates that only about 20 percent of major American corporations would show the new pension liability in their balance sheets. On the other hand, no pension asset would be permitted for companies whose pension assets exceed their accumulated benefit obligations. Thus, the only new pension-related asset would be the intangible asset recorded as an offset to the pension liability.

The use of the projected unit credit method for attributing pension benefits to periods of employee service would result in a different approach for income statement purposes than for balance sheet purposes. The recognition of actuarial gains and losses would be smoothed or indefinitely postponed through the use of a "corridor" approach rather than through a measurement valuation allowance. Considerably more disclosure would also be required so as to make pension data more complete, understandable, and comparable.

We believe that the Board has issued an ED that represents a reasonable compromise between what accounting theory suggests and accounting practice will currently allow. The Board itself acknowledged the need to make some major theoretical concessions in order to achieve constituent support when it discussed the rationale for recommending use of the accumulated benefit obligation (minimum liability approach) for balance sheet purposes.

Major controversies are likely to occur over the use of different approaches for balance sheet and income statement purposes, over the width of the "corridor" for purposes of recognizing actuarial gains and losses, and over a proposed amendment to APB Opinion No. 16. Although the inconsistency between the two financial statements may take some getting used to, the desirability of using different methods has previously been considered for inventory and deferred tax accounting. In addition, the use of the projected unit credit method for determining annual net periodic pension cost will result in the gradual recognition of projected benefit obligations in balance sheets. Entities are likely to continue opposing the addition of any new pension liability, particularly when no pension asset is allowed for overfunded plans. However, having seen the approach taken in the Board's *Preliminary Views*, many may be inclined to accept the less onerous pension liability provisions of the ED.

The FASB has asked for comments regarding the width of the "corridor." Previously set at 20 percent during the Board's deliberations, it was changed to ten percent in the ED. Thus, a change in either the rate or the benchmark to which the percentage is applied seems likely. We also expect to see some opposition to the proposal that, for business combinations accounted for by the purchase method, the assignment of the purchase price to individual acquired assets and liabilities assumed shall include (1) for single-employer defined benefit plans, the recognition of a pension liability if the projected benefit obligation exceeds pension assets, or the recognition of a pension asset if pension assets exceed the projected benefit obligation; and (2) for multi-employer plans, the recognition of a liability for the estimated amount that would be due upon plan withdrawal.

According to the FASB, the broad objectives of the ED are: (1) to provide a measure of a net periodic pension cost that is more representationally faithful, understandable, and comparable and is, therefore, more useful than those used in current practice; (2) to improve pension balance sheet reporting; and (3) to provide disclosures that will allow users to understand better the extent and effect of an employer's undertaking to provide employee pensions. In view of the realities of the standard-setting environment, we commend the Board for producing a document that reflects these objectives.

In the Introduction to the ED, the FASB stated:

> This Statement continues the evolutionary search for more meaningful and more useful pension accounting. The FASB believes that the conclusions it has reached are a worthwhile and significant step in that direction, but it also believes that those conclusions are not likely to be the final step in that evolution. Pension accounting in 1985 is still in a transitional stage. It has not yet fully crystallized, but the Board believes this Statement represents significant progress, especially in the measurement of net periodic pension cost.

We agree that the proposed changes would be a significant step forward in pension accounting and reporting. The "pension liability" issue has been debated for almost forty years. At this point, achieving adequate disclosure of useful pension data is preferable to maintaining the status quo while continuing to seek a consensus. While the expanded footnote disclosure is not a perfect substitute for balance sheet recognition, in view of the evolutionary nature of pension accounting, it seems to be a timely alternative. We urge the FASB's many constituents to work with the Board so that new pension accounting standards may be forthcoming soon.

# V-B   Deferred Income Taxes

## V-B 1   *No More Deferred Taxes*

PAUL ROSENFIELD AND WILLIAM C. DENT

Just before Accounting Principles Board Opinion no. 11, *Accounting for Income Taxes*,[1] was issued in 1967, requiring deferred taxes (interperiod income tax allocation), the American Institute of CPAs director of accounting research said that "whether taxes should be allocated or whether the taxes currently payable should be the income tax expense for a period has never been adequately studied."[2] However, the profession has hardly considered that question since then.[3] The Financial Accounting Standards Board is currently studying accounting for income taxes.[4] It should consider seriously whether deferred taxes should or shouldn't be part of accounting for income taxes.

Deferred taxes began with an idea, put forth almost 40 years ago, that accounting periods should each be allocated an amount of income tax expense that bears a "normal relationship to the income shown in the income statement."[5] To let reported

Authors' note: We are grateful to a number of persons who gave us counsel during the preparation of this article, especially Thomas W. McRae, CPA, American Institute of CPAs assistant to the president–technical; Robert T. Sprouse, vice-chairman of the Financial Accounting Standards Board; Reed K. Storey, CPA, assistant director of research and technical activities at the FASB; Arthur R. Wyatt, CPA, a partner of Arthur Andersen & Co.; and the staff of the AICPA accounting standards division. The views expressed are, of course, solely our responsibility.

*Ed. note: Mr. Rosenfield is an employee of the American Institute of CPAs, and his views, as expressed in this article, do not necessarily reflect the views of the AICPA. Official positions of the AICPA are determined through certain specific committee procedures, due process and deliberation.

[1] Accounting Principles Board Opinion no. 11, *Accounting for Income Taxes* (New York: AICPA, 1967).

[2] Reed K. Storey, "Director's Statement," in Accounting Research Study no. 9, *Interperiod Allocation of Corporate Income Taxes*, Homer A. Black (New York: AICPA, 1966), p. vii.

[3] Pages 4 and 5 of the report of the technical issues committee of the private companies practice section of the AICPA division for CPA firms entitled *Sunset Review of Accounting Principles* (New York: AICPA, 1982) suggested that private companies should be exempt from deferred taxes.

[4] Financial Accounting Standards Board, *Action Alert*, February 3, 1982.

income taxes follow reported income has been the objective of accounting for income taxes ever since. Other voices were raised during those years but weren't heard. Their cry was, "*Let reported taxes follow the tax return!*"[6] We agree and believe there should be no more deferred taxes.

## A WORLD WITHOUT DEFERRED TAXES

Instead of applying deferred taxes, we recommend that financial statements

- Present income tax expense for a year equal to the amount of income taxes in the income tax return for the year.
- Accrue a receivable for income tax refunds due from taxing authorities or a payable for unpaid current or past income taxes.[7]
- Disclose in the notes to the financial statements differences between the income tax bases of assets and liabilities and the amounts at which they appear in the balance sheet.

With the information on differences disclosed in the notes and with other information, such as on changes in income tax laws and regulations, users of the financial statements could consider what effects they think the differences and changes may have on future income taxes to be paid by the enterprise. Users commonly give similar consideration to many other imponderables concerning the amount, timing and uncertainty of future cash receipts and payments of all enterprises.[8]

The recommended accounting should be adopted because it provides users of the financial statements with all the information available about

- Income taxes incurred period by period up to the balance sheet date.
- Factors that may cause changes in the incidence or rate of incidence of income taxes the enterprise will incur in the future.

In addition, it provides that information without the defects of accounting based on the three theories of deferred taxes—the deferred theory, the liability theory and the net-of-tax theory.

---

[5] Accounting Research Bulletin no. 23, *Accounting for Income Taxes* (New York: AIA, 1944), p. 185.

[6] John W. Coughlan, "Tax Reductions and Tax Deferrals," *Journal of Business*, April 1958, p. 131.

[7] Some contend that accounting without deferred taxes is a cash basis, not an accrual basis, of accounting for income taxes. For example, paragraph 11 of International Accounting Standard no. 12, *Accounting for Taxes on Income* (London: International Accounting Standards Committee, 1979), says that "...the taxes payable method...is not in accordance with the accrual assumption...." However, all that is required for a type of accounting to be an accrual basis is that revenue is recognized when it is earned, not merely when cash is received, and that costs are recognized when they are incurred, not merely when cash is paid. ("*Accrual.* Determination of periodic income and financial position depends on measurement of economic resources and obligations and changes in them as the changes occur rather than simply on recording receipts and payments of money." [APB Statement no. 4, *Basic Concepts and Accounting Principles Underlying Financial Statements of Business Enterprises* (New York: AICPA, 1970), par. 121.]) Accounting can be on an accrual basis without allocating recognized income or costs among periods. The recommended accounting without deferred taxes therefore is an accrual basis of accounting for income taxes.

[8] FASB Concepts Statement no. 1, *Objectives of Financial Reporting by Business Enterprises* (Stamford: FASB, 1978), Pars. 37 and 39.

## THE DEFERRED THEORY—NUMBERED DAYS?

The deferred theory of deferred taxes is the basis of APB Opinion no. 11 and, thus, of most deferred taxes in the U.S. today. It involves accounting for the "tax effects of transactions which reduce [or increase] taxes currently payable."[9] In that context, saying that income taxes were reduced doesn't mean they are lower this year than they were last year. It means they are saved: "This concept of interperiod income tax allocation revolves around the notion of current tax saving...."[10] Income taxes are lower than they would have been had there been no timing difference, that is, had accounting in the current income tax return been the same as accounting in the current income statement. What happened is better than what didn't happen, which is the definition of an income tax saving and all other kinds of cost savings, for example, savings obtained by replacing an old machine with a new, labor-saving machine. Under the deferred theory, the difference[11]—the saving—is accounted for.

Accounting for such savings leads to unacceptable financial statement items. An income statement would present items that are differences between what happened and what didn't happen to the enterprise. For example, an income statement would present the difference between the labor expense that was incurred this year by using the new machine and the labor expense that would have been incurred this year, had the old machine been used. Under the deferred theory of deferred taxes, an income statement presents the difference between the income taxes in the current income tax return and the income taxes that would have been in the current income tax return, had accounting in the current income tax return been the same as accounting in the current income statement. When an equal but opposite difference emerges in the future (the timing difference reverses), the income statement under the deferred theory again presents a difference between what happened and what didn't happen to the enterprise.

Differences between what happened and what didn't happen to the enterprise shouldn't be presented in its income statements, which should simply present what happened to the enterprise.

Presenting items in income statements that don't represent what happened to the enterprise leads to presenting balance sheet items that don't represent assets or liabilities. The APB said as much: deferred taxes "do not represent receivables or payables in the usual sense."[12] The FASB agrees. It said that the balance sheet items presented under the deferred theory don't fit its definitions of balance sheet items.[13]

Items that don't represent assets or liabilities of the enterprise shouldn't be presented in its balance sheets.

---

[9] APB Opinion no. 11, par. 19.

[10] Black, ARS no. 9, p. 22.

[11] A general discussion of such differences is presented in Paul Rosenfield, "Reporting Subjunctive Gains and Losses," *Accounting Review*, October 1969, pp. 788–797.

[12] APB Opinion no. 11, par. 57.

[13] FASB Concepts Statement no. 3, *Elements of Financial Statements of Business Enterprises* (Stamford: FASB, 1980), par. 164. In paragraph 163, the FASB states that the liability and net-of-tax theories are compatible with the definitions in Concepts Statement no. 3. We interpret that to mean simply that the definitions cover the balance sheet items in which the debits and credits would appear if the liability or net-of-tax theory is demonstrated to be sound. Because Concepts Statement no. 3 doesn't analyze the liability or net-of-tax theory, we conclude that the statement doesn't mean that the FASB believes that the balance sheet amounts resulting from those theories would, when analyzed, necessarily conform with those definitions or that either or both of the theories are necessarily sound.

The deferred theory should be rejected, because it results in unacceptable financial statement items. Because the FASB has said the items don't fit its definitions of the elements of financial statements, its days appear numbered.

## THE LIABILITY THEORY—A "PRESENT OBLIGATION" FOR FUTURE INCOME TAXES?

Under the liability theory of deferred taxes, a liability is presented in the current balance sheet for income taxes on income that has been reported in current or prior income statements and is expected to be reflected in taxable income in future income tax returns. Whether the liability theory should be adopted depends on whether the amount it treats as a liability should be treated as a liability.

The FASB defines liabilities as "probable future sacrifices of economic benefits arising from present obligations of a particular entity to transfer assets or provide services to other entities in the future as a result of past transactions or events."[14]

That definition requires all these three criteria to be met for an amount to be a liability:[15]

1. A probable future sacrifice. An enterprise probably will have a sacrifice, such as a cash payment; after the balance sheet date.
2. An obligation to another entity. The future sacrifice would discharge an obligation of the enterprise to another entity.
3. The obligation has already been incurred. The enterprise has incurred the obligation by the balance sheet date.

*Probable future sacrifice.* Most enterprises probably will have to pay income taxes that will appear in their future income tax returns. The amount that would be reported as a liability based on the liability theory would therefore meet the first criterion, that the enterprise probably will have a sacrifice after the balance sheet date.

*Obligation to another entity.* The second criterion requires that the sacrifice discharge an obligation to another entity. Such obligations may be "imposed legally or socially; [they may be] that which one is bound to do by contract, promise, moral responsibility, etc. . . . [They] include equitable and constructive obligations as well as legal obligations."[16] And the obligations needn't be due and payable when incurred.

All payments of income taxes discharge obligations to income tax authorities, so the second criterion is met.

*Obligation already incurred.* The third criterion requires the enterprise to have incurred the obligation by the balance sheet date. It must have a "present obligation" that is "a result of past . . . events." That requires the obligation to be a result solely of past events and not to be a result of future events, alone or in conjunction with past events.

To illustrate: A payment of 12 months' interest on June 30, 1983, discharges an obligation that was a result solely of events to December 31, 1982, that is, an obligation for one-half of the payment, and the enterprise has an obligation at December 31, 1982, for that amount.

---

[14] FASB Concepts Statement no. 3, par. 28.
[15] In Concepts Statement no. 3, paragraph 29, the FASB lists three characteristics of liabilities, which contain the three criteria stated here but in a different arrangement.
[16] Concepts Statement no. 3, n. 14.

In contrast, a plaintiff engages the services of an attorney and agrees that, if the plaintiff receives a settlement or a judgment from the defendant, the plaintiff will pay the attorney one-third of the amount received. The attorney works on the case for six months before the balance sheet date and six months after the balance sheet date. The plaintiff receives a settlement and pays one-third of it to the attorney. No part of the obligation to pay the attorney is a result solely of efforts of the attorney before the balance sheet date. All of the obligation is a result of efforts of the attorney after the balance sheet date, in conjunction with his efforts before the balance sheet date, and the plaintiff has no obligation at the balance sheet date for the payment to the attorney.

Some of the types of events associated with an obligation are ancillary to the obligation, that is, the obligation isn't a result of those types of events, as the term *a result of* is used in the FASB's definition of liabilities. The expectation that such ancillary events will occur between the balance sheet date and the time the obligation is expected to be discharged wouldn't prevent the third criterion from being met. Some of those ancillary types of events are

- The passage of time.[17]
- Discovery by the enterprise that it will have a future sacrifice.
- Discovery by the enterprise of which entity will be the beneficiary of the future sacrifice.
- Enforcement of the right to receive the benefits of the future sacrifice by the entity that will be the beneficiary of the future sacrifice.
- Events defined under paragraph 8 of FASB Statement no. 5, *Accounting for Contingencies*,[18] that confirm that the enterprise will have a future sacrifice.

To illustrate: An enterprise discovers after the balance sheet date that it will have to pay for repairs to products sold under warranty before the balance sheet date. The warranties are for defects existing at the time the products were sold. Discovery after the balance sheet date of the necessity to make future payments to repair preexisting defects is an ancillary event that doesn't result in the obligation to make the payments, which is a result solely of selling defective products before the balance sheet date and not of any subsequent event. The discovery merely brings to light a preexisting obligation.

To implement the third criterion, therefore, the events that are expected to occur after the balance sheet date that would be associated with a future sacrifice must be evaluated to determine whether the obligation to make the sacrifice would be a result of those future events, alone or in conjunction with past events. If the obligation wouldn't be a result of those future events, that is, if those future events would be merely ancillary to the obligation, the obligation would be a result solely of past events, and the third criterion would be met. If the obligation would be a result of those future events, the criterion wouldn't be met.

Two types of differences between income tax accounting and financial accounting can be used to illustrate the application to accounting for income taxes of the criterion that, for a liability to be present at the balance sheet date, the obligation to

---

[17] The passage of time may or may not be ancillary for items such as interest and rent that, by law, contract or otherwise, accrue based on the passage of time, and further analysis is required for those items.

[18] FASB Statement no. 5, *Accounting for Contingencies* (Stamford: FASB, 1975).

make the future sacrifice must be a result solely of past events and not a result of future events, alone or in conjunction with past events:

- Early deductions—expenses deducted in income tax returns before they are reported in income statements.
- Late revenue inclusion—revenue included in taxable income after it is reported in income statements.

To illustrate an early deduction: At the beginning of the first year of an enterprise, it buys a machine with a three-year life for $3,000. It receives $2,000 revenue during the first year. It uses straight-line depreciation for financial reporting and double-declining-balance depreciation for income tax reporting. The following amounts appear on its income statement and income tax return for the first year:

|  | *Income statement* | *Income tax return* |
| --- | --- | --- |
| Revenue | $2,000 | $2,000 |
| Depreciation | (1,000) | (2,000) |
| Taxable income | | $ -0- |
| Income before income taxes | $1,000 | |

The $1,000 of income reported in the income statement will probably be reflected in taxable income and income taxes in the enterprise's future income tax returns. If so, the obligation for some of the future income taxes expected to be paid by the enterprise would be a result at least of past events, the earning of the $1,000 of income reported in the first-year income statement. But all of the revenue earned in the first year was reported in the first year's income tax return. Taxable revenue would have to be earned in the future for the enterprise to have an obligation for income taxes that would appear in its future income tax returns. Earning the future revenue wouldn't be merely ancillary to the obligation. The obligation for all of the future income taxes would be a result of earning the taxable revenue in the future, in conjunction with the past events. The third criterion, that the obligation for future income taxes must not be a result of future events, alone or in conjunction with past events, wouldn't be met.

The third criterion is independent of the first criterion, that there will probably be future sacrifices. Earning revenue in the future may be probable or even certain, for example, if it is earned after the balance sheet date but before the financial statements for the period ending on that date are prepared. Also, it may be contended that presenting amounts for assets in the financial statements is based on the assumption that revenue will be earned. But that pertains to how probable the future income taxes are—the first criterion—not to what the obligation for those future income taxes would be a result of—the third criterion—and their probability or certainty wouldn't affect the conclusion that the obligation would be a result of earning revenue in the future, in conjunction with past events, and that the third criterion therefore wouldn't be met.

To illustrate late revenue inclusion: In 1982, an enterprise sold for $2,000 an asset whose book value and income tax basis were both $1,000. The proceeds of the sale were to be received in four $500 installments, one due at the end of each year starting with 1983. The enterprise reported a gain of $1,000 on the sale in its income statement for 1982. It treated the sale as an installment sale for income tax purposes and thus reported no income in its 1982 income tax return for the sale.

The $1,000 gain on the sale reported in the current income statement will probably be reflected in taxable income and income taxes in the enterprise's future income tax returns. If so, the obligation for some of the future income taxes expected to be paid by the enterprise would be a result at least of a past event, the sale. But the installments would have to be received in the future for the enterprise to have an obligation for income taxes related to the sale in its future income tax returns. Receiving the installments wouldn't be merely ancillary to the obligation for future income taxes related to the sale. The obligation for future income taxes would be a result of receiving those installments in the future, in conjunction with a past event, the sale, and the third criterion wouldn't be met.

Like earning future revenue in the previous illustration, receiving the future installments may be probable or even certain. Also, it may be contended that presenting the receivable is based on the assumption that the installments will be received. But, again, that pertains to the first criterion—how probable the future income taxes are—not to the third criterion—what the obligation for the future income taxes would be a result of. Even if the future receipts of the installments are certain, the obligation for future income taxes nevertheless would be a result of them, in conjunction with a past event, and the third criterion wouldn't be met.[19]

To generalize: An obligation for income taxes is a result of events that occur during the period covered by the income tax return in which they are reported, alone or in conjunction with events of prior periods. No enterprise has a present obligation for income taxes that may appear in its future income tax returns.

Because advocates of the deferred theory and the net-of-tax theory support systems that result in balance sheets that report no such present obligation, we conclude that they agree that there is no present obligation.

To summarize:

- An enterprise will probably have to pay income taxes that will appear in its future income tax returns.
- The payments would discharge obligations of the enterprise to income tax authorities.
- But the enterprise hasn't incurred the obligations by the balance sheet date.

---

[19] Some contend that an asset and a liability related to an event, for example, an installment sale, should be treated alike, because assets are defined as being the result of past events (FASB Concepts Statement no. 3, paragraph 19) just as liabilities are. The view is that, if an installment sale doesn't result in a liability for income taxes in the period of the sale, it also doesn't result in a receivable in the period of the sale. Not reporting the income tax liability while reporting the receivable currently would violate that requirement. Accounting without deferred taxes would therefore produce unacceptable results under that view. However, the receivable and the liability should each be reported when it comes into existence, that is, when the events it is a result of occur. The receivable comes into existence at the time of the sale and is a result of the sale. Nothing else has to happen besides the passage of time before the benefits are to be received. In contrast, the income tax liability doesn't come into existence until the installments are collected. It is a result of the collections, together with the sale. The receivable and the liability are results of events that occur in different periods, and accounting without deferred taxes properly presents that.

The liability theory of deferred taxes should be rejected, because it would result in reporting liabilities before they are incurred.

Those who support the objective of having reported income taxes follow reported income and who therefore believe that presenting income in one income statement and income tax on that income in another income statement is unsatisfactory shouldn't support presenting unacceptable financial statement items, as under the deferred theory, or liabilities not yet incurred, as under the liability theory. They should consider modifications of amounts at which acceptable financial statement items are presented, such as under the net-of-tax theory, in an attempt to achieve that objective.

## THE NET-OF-TAX THEORY—BETTER INCOME REPORTING?

Based on the net-of-tax theory, the amounts called income taxes in the income statement and the balance sheet would be the same as they would be without deferred taxes. Instead of affecting items called income taxes, the net-of-tax theory affects allocation to income statements of increases or decreases in other assets or liabilities, such as decreases of assets due to using up assets or increases of assets due to sales. The objective is to allocate such a decrease or increase net of its income tax effects, not simply the decrease or increase, to income statements in a pattern considered desirable.

To illustrate application of the net-of-tax theory to an asset decrease: Depreciation accounting is one type of accounting intended to recognize asset decreases in both income statements and income tax returns. These are two of the depreciation methods that have been accepted for both income statement and income tax purposes:

- Method 1: Straight line—allocate the cost of the asset in equal amounts in the years of the asset's expected useful life.
- Method 2: Double declining balance—allocate the cost of the asset by charging each year an amount equal to the difference between the cost of the asset and depreciation previously charged, divided by one-half of the asset's original expected useful life; charge the remaining net book value in the last year.

    The net-of-tax-theory leads to a third method to allocate the decrease, to income statements only:

- Method 3: Net of tax—allocate the cost of the asset so that the allocations less the income tax reductions year by year have the pattern that allocations of the cost have under method 1. The effect is to allocate the portion of the cost incurred to obtain the income tax benefit of depreciation deductions to the income statements in the patterns in which the deductions are taken and to allocate the remainder of the cost by the straight-line method.

The illustration of depreciation given above can be extended to demonstrate the three methods of allocation:

| | |
|---|---|
| Cost | $1,000 |
| Expected useful life | Three years |
| Income tax allocation method | Method 2 (double declining balance) |
| Income tax rate | 50 percent |

Exhibit 1, page 54, presents accounting for depreciation and the related income tax items in the income statements under income statement methods 1, 2 and 3.

To illustrate application of the net-of-tax theory to an asset increase: Assets are increased when inventory is sold for more than it costs and the proceeds are received. Two methods are accepted to allocate the increase in both income statements and income tax returns:

1. Method 1: Immediate recognition—allocate the excess of the proceeds over the cost all to the year of the sale.
2. Method 2: Installment basis—allocate the excess of the proceeds over the cost ratably in the years in which the proceeds are collected.[20]

    The net-of-tax theory leads to a third method to allocate the increase, to income statements only:

3. Method 3: Net of tax—allocate the excess of the proceeds over the cost minus the income taxes expected to be paid because of the sale, that is, the excess net of tax, to the income statement in the year of sale and allocate the remainder of the excess of the proceeds over the cost in the years and in the pattern in which income taxes are expected to be paid because of the sale.

The illustration given above of an installment sale can be extended to demonstrate the three methods of allocation:

| | |
|---|---|
| Sales price | $2,000 |
| Cost | $1,000 |
| Collections | $500 in each of the four years following the sale |
| Income tax allocation method | Method 2 (installment basis) |
| Income tax rate | 50 percent |

Exhibit 2 presents accounting for the gain on sale and the related income tax items in the income statements under income statement methods 1, 2 and 3.

Advocates of the net-of-tax theory consider it to be a refined method of allocating charges or credits to income statements. They support it as improving income reporting.

Allocations in accounting don't correspond, nor are they intended to correspond, year by year, with effects of events that happen to the reporting enterprise.[21] Whether one method of allocating amounts to income statements is better than

---

[20] Felix P. Kollaritsch and Ray G. Stephens, "Sales and Receivables," in *Accountants' Handbook*, 6th ed., ed. Lee J. Seidler and D. R. Carmichael (New York: John Wiley & Sons, 1981), pp. 17.67 and 17.68.

[21] APB Statement no. 4, *Basic Concepts and Accounting Principles Underlying Financial Statements of Business Enterprises* (New York: AICPA, 1970), par. 159, states that allocation is used "in the absence of a direct means of associating cause and effect...." That characteristic is discussed in Arthur L. Thomas, *The Allocation Problem in Financial Accounting Theory*, Studies in Accounting Research no. 3 (Sarasota: American Accounting Association, 1969), and *The Allocation Problem: Part Two*, Studies in Accounting Research no. 9 (Sarasota: AAA, 1974). That research is summarized in Arthur L. Thomas, "The FASB and the Allocation Fallacy," JofA, Nov. 75, pp. 65–68.

## EXHIBIT 1

**Net-of-tax Accounting Applied to Depreciation**

| | Income Statement Effects | | | |
| | Year 1 | Year 2 | Year 3 | Total |
|---|---|---|---|---|
| Income statement | | | | |
| Method 1 (timing difference, | | | | |
| no deferred taxes): | | | | |
| Depreciation expense | $1,000 | $1,000 | $1,000 | $3,000 |
| Income tax reductions | (1,000) | (333) | (167) | (1,500) |
| Allocation of | | | | |
| decrease net of tax | $ –0– | $ 667 | $ 833 | $1,500 |
| | | | | |
| Income statement | | | | |
| Method 2 (no timing difference, | | | | |
| no deferred taxes): | | | | |
| Depreciation expense | $2,000 | $ 667 | $ 333 | $3,000 |
| Income tax reductions | (1,000) | (333) | (167) | (1,500) |
| Allocation of | | | | |
| decrease net of tax | $1,000 | $ 334 | $ 166 | $1,500 |
| | | | | |
| Income statement | | | | |
| Method 3 (timing difference, | | | | |
| deferred taxes under | | | | |
| the net-of-tax theory): | | | | |
| Depreciation expense | $1,500 | $ 833 | $ 667 | $3,000 |
| Income tax reductions | (1,000) | (333) | (167) | (1,500) |
| Allocation of | | | | |
| decrease net of tax | $ 500 | $ 500 | $ 500 | $1,500 |

another is, therefore, unavoidably a matter of opinion that can be finally settled only the way standard-setting bodies finally settle issues—by vote.

To the necessity, for example, of determining the depreciable life of an asset, the net-of-tax theory adds further complexities such as determining in advance whether income tax benefits or detriments will occur related to the asset, when they will occur and what their total will be. Because of the added complexities and because, in any event, allocations don't correspond, year by year, with effects of events that happen to the enterprise, we believe the added refinement of basing allocation to income statements of increases or decreases in assets partly on income tax benefits or detriments fits into the APB's category of activities that are "considered to serve no useful purpose."[22]

Advocates of the net-of-tax theory also consider it to be an improved way to report assets stated in the balance sheet at current market value or net realizable

[22] APB Statement no. 4, par. 160.

**EXHIBIT 2**

**Net-of-tax Accounting Applied to an Installment Sale**

| | *Income Statement Effects* | | | | |
|---|---|---|---|---|---|
| | | Years of Collection | | | |
| | Year of sale | 1 | 2 | 3 | 4 | Total |
| Income statement Method 1 (timing difference, no deferred taxes): | | | | | | |
| Allocation of profit on sale | $1,000 | $ –0– | $ –0– | $ –0– | $ –0– | $1,000 |
| Income tax expense | –0– | (125) | (125) | (125) | (125) | (500) |
| Allocation of profit net of tax | $1,000 | $(125) | $(125) | $(125) | $(125) | $ 500 |
| | | | | | | |
| Income statement Method 2 (no timing difference, no deferred taxes): | | | | | | |
| Allocation of profit on sale | $ –0– | $ 250 | $ 250 | $ 250 | $ 250 | $1,000 |
| Income tax expense | –0– | (125) | (125) | (125) | (125) | (500) |
| Allocation of profit net of tax | $ –0– | $ 125 | $ 125 | $ 125 | $ 125 | $ 500 |
| | | | | | | |
| Income statement Method 3 (timing difference, deferred taxes under the net-of-tax theory): | | | | | | |
| Allocation of profit on sale | $ 500 | $ 125 | $ 125 | $ 125 | $ 125 | $1,000 |
| Income tax expense | –0– | (125) | (125) | (125) | (125) | (500) |
| Allocation of profit net of tax | $ 500 | $ –0– | $ –0– | $ –0– | $ –0– | $ 500 |

value, for example, installment receivables. Under the net-of-tax theory, assets are stated at what the assets would bring on realization less the income taxes that would be expected to be paid because of the realization.

Whether assets stated at current market value or at net realizable value should be stated gross or net of tax is also unavoidably a matter of opinion to be settled by vote. We believe they should be stated gross, for reasons akin to those concerning the income statement effects of the net-of-tax theory.

Our vote would be that the net-of-tax theory should be rejected.

### Sufficient Unto the Day Are the Income Taxes Thereof

We believe the case against deferred taxes is convincing and urge that deferred taxes be cast out of the house of GAAP.

# V-B 2 *Deferred Taxes— Forever*

A re deferred taxes a necessary part of periodic income determination? In this article, Philip L. Defliese, *CPA*, says that interperiod income tax allocation is the most suitable approach. Defliese offers his rebuttal to the article "No More Deferred Taxes," which appeared in the February 1983 issue of the Journal (pages 44–55). The reply by the authors, Paul Rosenfield, *CPA*, and William C. Dent, *CPA*, follows. In their article, Rosenfield and Dent advocate accounting for income taxes without allocating them among periods.

There is only one point in the Rosenfield-Dent article on which everyone can agree: the controversy over interperiod income tax allocation can be settled only by vote.

That vote was taken in 1967 (when a two-thirds vote was needed) by the Accounting Principles Board, composed of 20 prestigious and practical-minded accountants who were keenly interested in giving investors a meaningful measure of the annual earning power of U.S. companies. That objective, as well as the attendant espousal of accrual accounting and matching of costs and revenues in the determination of periodic income, has since been reaffirmed by the Financial Accounting Standards Board in FASB Concepts Statement no. 1, *Objectives of Financial Reporting by Business Enterprises*.[1]

## BACKGROUND OF OPINION NO. 11

The article's implication that APB Opinion no. 11, *Accounting for Income Taxes*,[2] was issued without adequate study is a biased viewpoint at best. A careful reading of the opinion and a knowledge of subsequent events reveal that all the pros and cons were then well considered and that no new ideas or opinions on the subject have surfaced since. Considering that corporate management generally dislikes anything that diminishes reported income, either temporarily or permanently, I believe that it was a courageous act by a board largely comprising practitioners. After considerable debate, the APB ultimately espoused the deferred method of income tax allocation. Rosenfield and Dent refer to it as a theory. I believe it is a practical solution. The board carefully weighed the "various concepts of accounting for income taxes" before

Philip Defliese, "Deferred Taxes—Forever," *Journal of Accountancy*, August 1983, pp. 94–103. Copyright © 1983 by the American Institute of Certified Public Accountants, Inc. Opinions expressed in the *Journal of Accountancy* are those of editors and contributors. Publication in the *Journal of Accountancy* does not constitute endorsement by the AICPA or its committees.

[1] Financial Accounting Standards Board Concepts Statement no. 1, *Objectives of Financial Reporting by Business Enterprises* (Stamford: FASB, 1978).

[2] Accounting Principles Board Opinion no. 11, *Accounting for Income Taxes* (New York: AICPA, 1967).

requiring "comprehensive interperiod allocation."[3] The APB concluded that the deferred method was the "most useful and practical approach"[4] to implement the concept. Board members agreed conceptually with the liability and net-of-tax methods but opted for the deferred method to avoid the problems of changing income tax rates and of awkward presentations.

Accountants get bogged down on the issue of which tax rate to apply—especially with fluctuating effective income tax rates (largely the influence of many permanent differences rather than timing differences). The practical approach devised by the APB in selecting the deferred method was to compute each year's income tax provision by the use of that year's effective rate—on an accrual basis. The required use in the balance sheet of deferred debits and credits—which are mixtures of asset and liability effects—was a practical solution to a presentation problem. The opinion, I believe, carefully explained why they "as such do not represent receivables or payables in the usual sense."[5] Balance sheet purity was a lesser concern.

## THE RECONSIDERATION OF DEFERRED TAXES

Since then, the corporate world has lived with, understood and mostly embraced deferred taxes. The U.S. income tax code, whose increased complexity has been brought about by the proliferation of incentives creating timing differences, has now made deferred taxes an essential ingredient of periodic income determination. Nevertheless, the issue has once again been raised—this time by the FASB.

The deferred credit figure, an item much misunderstood by the unsophisticated, has accumulated to substantial amounts in many growing companies as the divergencies between tax and accounting income have increased. Those amounts are a cause for alarm by those who never fully accepted the 1967 decision and by balance sheet purists with narrow views of its elements. The FASB's new conceptual framework project has offered an opportunity for this reexamination, and the FASB has decided to press forward with this reexamination despite the fact that the crucial and controversial segments of recognition and measurement are yet to be agreed on and issued.

## THE ROSENFIELD-DENT POSITION

The Rosenfield-Dent approach to taxes is essentially a cash-basis one, with additional disclosures presumably sufficient to allow users to calculate periodic income. The APB overcame the dichotomy between cash- and accrual-basis accounting by requiring a statement of changes in financial position as an integral part of the reporting process to enable users to compare accrual income with cash or working capital flow. Analysts have little difficulty understanding deferred taxes in this environment. To revert to cash-basis accounting would be a retrogression and a complete abdication of financial reporting objectives by the profession. FASB Concepts Statement no. 1 states: "Information about enterprise [periodic] earnings and its components measured by accrual accounting generally provides a better indication of ... performance than information about current cash receipts and

[3] Ibid., par. 34.
[4] Ibid., par. 35.
[5] Ibid., par. 57.

payments."[6] Over the years, economists and accountants have disagreed among themselves, and with each other, on the meaning of periodic income. Nevertheless, accountants shouldn't give up the attempt to make what they consider their best determinations. Truth, in accounting, requires more than solely devotion to truthful principles.

Some devotees of the efficient market hypothesis take the extreme position that, as long as all relevant facts are fully disclosed, the accounting principles used aren't important. The "market," they believe, will reach the correct conclusions and stock prices will adjust accordingly. Rosenfield and Dent would have us provide explanations in the notes of the tax effects not recognized in determining periodic income and let the efficient market sort it out. However, the efficiency of the market in absorbing disclosures depends on the emphasis given them in press releases and how the information is interpreted by the media. The abbreviated earnings reports published in most newspapers will be inadequate for that purpose, and it may take weeks (as it sometimes does now) for sophisticated analysts to reach conclusions and affect the market.

## ANOTHER VIEW OF THE ROSENFIELD-DENT POSITION

Rosenfield and Dent base their conclusions on their interpretation of selected quotes from FASB Concepts Statement no. 3, *Elements of Financial Statements of Business Enterprises*, particularly the definition of liabilities as "probable future sacrifices of economic benefits arising from present obligations of a particular entity to transfer assets or provide services to other entities in the future as a result of past transactions or events."[7] They overlook the definition of *assets*, whose "future economic benefits"[8] may be impaired by a lack of tax deductibility and ignore the net aspect of the "future sacrifices" of liabilities that have a future tax recovery aspect—all based on past transactions. To paraphrase their thrust, they say that, because there is no liability for future taxes until taxable revenue is generated in the future, no tax accrual is needed.

The incongruity of that position can be illustrated by a simple transaction in which a $100 million gain is reported in year one without a tax provision, because the tax is paid in year two when the receivable is collected. Of course, Rosenfield and Dent would recommend disclosure of the income tax aspects of the transaction in the notes, but what about the floor traders who see only what the broad tape chooses to print?

To say that a tax obligation can arise only when taxable revenue is earned in the future is to ignore the going-concern assumption on which all financial reporting rests, a concept also reaffirmed by the FASB. Only two assumptions are available

1.   A company will be profitable in the future, particularly if it already is. (If it is profitable one year and has a loss in the succeeding year, the tax carry-back recovery will be reduced by the timing difference.)

---

[6] FASB Concepts Statement no. 1, par. 44.
[7] FASB Concepts Statement no. 3, *Elements of Financial Statements of Business Enterprises* (Stamford: FASB, 1980), par. 28.
[8] Ibid., par. 19.

2. A company currently isn't profitable and won't be profitable in the future—in which case we must question it as a going concern. (Since no tax benefit has been derived, no deferred taxes are recognized.)

Consequently, probable future benefits or sacrifices (obligations)—tax effects—based on past events must be recognized. Whether those benefits and sacrifices are presented as liabilities or as reductions of assets (net of tax) isn't pertinent to the conceptual issue. In the previous illustration, it isn't relevant whether the deferred tax is shown as a liability or as a reduction of the realizable value of the receivable. Does anyone really believe that, in a profitable environment, the tax won't be paid?

Ordinarily, the debate over deferred taxes gravitates to the "rollover" issue—whether tax benefits of anticipated future investments should be considered. Adherents of that view say that deferred taxes will never be paid because, over the long term, new items—asset purchases—arise that replace the reversal of the old, leading to perpetual deferment. According to Rosenfield and Dent, however, rollover isn't an issue. They would never recognize deferred taxes, even if the reversal was within one year. (The rollover issue isn't debated here.)

## DEFERRED TAXES AND THE CONCEPTUAL FRAMEWORK

If another vote is to be taken on deferred taxes, I hope that it will be delayed until all the pieces of the new conceptual framework are in place and well accepted. I also hope that another vote would be based on logic and reasoning, although in accounting, unfortunately, they are always in the eyes of the beholder.

No amount of study—empirical or conceptual—can definitely prove whether deferred taxes are necessary. The issue rests entirely on differing opinions regarding concepts of periodic income and how the objectives of financial reporting can be achieved. I believe that the concepts statements produced so far are so general that any viewpoint can be considered compatible. Although the framework is still incomplete, the FASB has created a "comprehensive income"[9] concept as a catchall for all changes in equity and has deferred the definition of *earnings*. It has implied, but avoided direct consideration of the issue, that the asset–liability approach to income determination (comprehensive or otherwise) should prevail over the revenue–expense approach. That approach emphasizes that the beholder is viewing the balance sheet's year-end position at the "split-second of midnight." Our book-keeping origins tell us that a "balance sheet" is a list of account balances after the year's profit or loss is determined. Are we moving in a completely new direction?

Rosenfield and Dent point out that deferred taxes began with the idea that accounting periods should each be allocated an amount of income tax expense that bears a "normal relationship to the income shown in the income statement."[10] Subsequent refinements of that idea limited deferred taxes to timing differences that were expected to reverse. Accrual accounting, matching and allocation were the underlying principles relied on, and so far the FASB hasn't abandoned them. The

---

[9] Ibid., par. 14.

[10] Accounting Research Bulletin no. 23, *Accounting for Income Taxes* (New York: AIA, 1944), p. 185.

reference to deferred taxes as an interest-free loan from the government has become prevalent, and all knowledgeable users now understand it. Whether, because of rollover, the resultant deferred debits and credits will continue to increase depends on circumstances. Recently, with the shrinking of some capital-intensive enterprises, we have seen some reductions—proof that the concept works.

Opponents of deferred taxes, particularly academics, are sometimes influenced by their own philosophies. For example, those who believe that current value accounting should replace historical cost accounting often oppose deferred taxes for somewhat the same reasons as do Rosenfield and Dent. However, some would acknowledge that value determinations should recognize the degree to which an asset has or hasn't tax deductibility. After a struggle with the current value issue, the FASB finally recognized that for now historical cost accounting must continue as the basis for our primary financial statements.

## TAXES WITHIN THE HISTORICAL COST FRAMEWORK

Because of this, emphasis must be given to historical cost, uninfluenced by any extraneous issues. Conceptually, the carrying amount of an asset in a historical cost framework should be what was paid for it less what has been depreciated (allocated to income determination) and less any excess tax benefit recovered. When, as with accelerated depreciation, the government has advanced money (through reduced taxes), it becomes a temporary reduction of invested cost (that is, net of tax). Even the government has recently renamed depreciation accelerated cost recovery, and public utility regulators, after much confusion and congressional prodding, now almost uniformly deduct deferred taxes from plant assets in the rate-making process. When an installment receivable will in all likelihood be taxed on collection, the tax represents a reduction of the amount receivable by the enterprise (net realizable value)—or a liability to be paid on collection. It doesn't matter how it is presented on the balance sheet, except to balance sheet purists, as long as the concepts that make up the historical cost framework are recognized.

The recognition and measurement concepts of assets and liabilities—even in a historical cost framework—have yet to be settled by the FASB. In doing so, it will no doubt be influenced by the definitions promulgated in FASB Concepts Statement no. 3. There the board states that an asset "embodies a probable future benefit ... to contribute ... to future net cash inflows."[11] Hence, recognition would have to be given to the extent to which cost has been recovered in advance by accelerated tax depreciation, a sure impairment of the future benefit an asset could contribute.[12]

Although it has proclaimed its neutrality on the interperiod tax allocation issue, the FASB has ruled the deferred method as incompatible with its "elements"—no doubt at the prodding of some people long opposed to deferred items in the balance sheet. It did, however, acknowledge the relevance of the liability and net-of-tax methods and indicated a "possible compatible rationale for the results of the [deferred] method."[13] I hope that, after concluding consideration of the recognition and measurement concepts, the FASB may find that interperiod tax allocation is

[11] FASB Concepts Statement no. 3, par. 20(a).
[12] The net-of-tax aspect of asset valuation has been accepted practice since the promulgation of APB Opinion no. 16, *Business Combinations* (New York: AICPA, 1970); see par. 89.
[13] FASB Concepts Statement no. 3, par. 165.

conceptually sound and that the deferred presentation is the most practical approach to implement the concept.

## CONCLUSION

Much is to be said on behalf of sound interperiod allocation of costs and revenues, even though some may claim the effect is to smooth periodic income. Interperiod tax allocation isn't a smoothing device. It is an attempt to produce a conceptually sound approach to periodic income. Investors need to have a good understanding of a company's annual earning power. Years ago, George O. May is said to have stated, "The determination of periodic income would be indefensible if it were not indispensable." Let us not throw out the baby with the wash water.

### Rosenfield-Dent Reply

In his note, Professor Defliese presents a number of arguments against our conclusion that there should be no more deferred taxes. We discuss those arguments in this reply.

## WHEN IS THERE A LIABILITY?

The note states that if "a company will be profitable in the future," a liability for future income taxes has been incurred and should therefore be presented now. Because we say that such a liability hasn't been incurred and therefore shouldn't be presented now, the note says the accounting for income taxes we recommend is unsatisfactory.

That is a difference of opinion on the key issue of when a liability has been incurred.

In our article, we used the Financial Accounting Standards Board's definition of a liability to help determine when a liability has been incurred. The definition states in part that, for a liability to have been incurred, there must be an obligation that is "a result of past transactions or events."[14]

That part of the definition requires interpretation, because it doesn't state explicitly whether the obligation must be a result of only past transactions or events or may be a result of both past and future transactions or events.

We interpreted it to mean that the obligation must be a result of only past transactions or events, that is, that all the events the obligation is a result of must have occurred before the liability has been incurred. That interpretation doesn't distinguish the relative importance of the various events the obligation is a result of. Some of those events may seem more important than others. But, an obligation isn't simply a concept, a number in a financial statement. It is a relationship between the reporting entity and another entity. The obligation is incurred—comes into existence—when the last, not the most important, event it is a result of has occurred. Regardless of how likely or certain it is that it will later become an obligation, the obligation hasn't been incurred until all the events it is a result of have occurred.

The other interpretation, that the obligation may be a result of both past and future transactions or events, means that a liability has been incurred when some but not all events the obligation is a result of have occurred. In our opinion, that is an

---

[14] Financial Accounting Standards Board Concepts Statement no. 3, *Elements of Financial Statements of Business Enterprises* (Stamford: FASB, 1980), par. 28.

unreasonable interpretation of the definition, and applying that interpretation gives unsatisfactory results.

For example, an enterprise incurs a liability to repair or replace defective goods sold to customers. The liability is based on an obligation that is a result of at least two events: manufacturing defective goods and selling them. The liability hasn't been incurred when some but not all the events the obligation is a result of have occurred, namely, when defective goods have been manufactured but haven't been sold. Presenting the liability then would be unsatisfactory. The liability has been incurred when the defective goods have been both manufactured defectively and sold and should be presented then.

For the enterprise to have to pay to repair or replace the goods, the customer would have to discover the defect and put in a claim. But, the obligation wouldn't be a result of those events, although they may confirm the prior existence of the obligation. Payment would be a result of those events. Determining when an obligation has been incurred requires distinguishing the events an obligation is a result of from additional events payment is a result of, as we said in our article.

Like the obligation for defective goods sold, an obligation for income taxes can be a result of more than one event.

Taxable revenue appears in an income tax return in which income taxes appear. The income taxes in the return are a result of the event or events in which the taxable revenue was obtained. All taxable revenue is obtained in events that occur in the year covered by the income tax return in which the taxable revenue is reported, so the obligation is a result of an event or events that occurred in the year covered by the tax return, as we said in our article.

The obligation may also be a result of events that occurred before the year covered by the tax return, some of which may seem like important or even key events the obligation is a result of. But, because at least one of the events an obligation for income taxes is a result of occurred in the year covered by the tax return in which the income taxes appear, the liability has been incurred and should be first presented in that year.

That conclusion could be avoided to achieve a desired income statement result by abandoning the idea of determining when to report a liability based on when the events the obligation is a result of have occurred. If the idea is abandoned, however, the discipline over the income reporting process provided by the FASB's definition of a liability or by any other sensible definition of a liability would be lost, along with the chance of improving the balance sheet.

### Babies and wash water

The note says "balance sheet purity was a lesser concern." But the quality of the balance sheet should be of concern, because a sound balance sheet provides, among other things, needed discipline for income reporting. Without a requirement that income statements report only the results of changes in assets and liabilities, soundly defined and soundly measured, income statements could equally present fact or fiction.

In pleading not to "throw out the baby with the wash water," the note implies that deferred taxes is the baby and impurities in the balance sheet are the wash water. But it is the balance sheet that is the baby, not deferred taxes. Dismissing the balance sheet to dismiss the questions it raises concerning deferred taxes is the real way to throw out the baby with the wash water.

### Incongruous result

The note illustrates results it describes as incongruous that would be caused by not reporting liabilities currently for income taxes that may appear in future income tax returns and says that such reporting is therefore unsatisfactory. In the illustration, a $100 million gain is reported in the income statement for the first year without reporting income tax expense related to the gain because there is no taxable revenue in the illustration until the receivable is collected. In the second year, the gain isn't reported but income tax expense related to the gain is reported.

In our opinion, that makes sense. The gain was obtained in the first year, and it should therefore be reported in that year. By excluding elements from the balance sheet that aren't assets, liabilities or equity, FASB Concepts Statement no. 3, *Elements of Financial Statements of Business Enterprises*, has in effect decided that costs are incurred only when assets decrease or liabilities increase. Because no liability for income taxes related to the gain was incurred in the first year, no income tax cost, and therefore no income tax expense related to the gain, was incurred that year.

The note disclosure we recommended would inform the users of the financial statements covering the first year that the enterprise has the prospect that it might in the future incur an income tax liability related to the gain. Income tax cost is incurred in the second year by incurring a liability to pay income taxes related to the gain, and the cost should be reported as an expense that year.

We believe that, rather than the results of accounting without deferred taxes being incongruous, it is the idea that an entity can have a liability this year for next year's income taxes that really is incongruous.

Other income statement results can be obtained that might seem satisfactory to those to whom the income statement results in the illustration seem incongruous, without reporting a liability before it is incurred. Under the net-of-tax theory of deferred taxes, the receivable obtained in the transaction would be stated net of the income taxes anticipated to become payable and thought to be related to the gain. It would in effect report the gain net of such anticipated income taxes in the first year and no income statement result due to the transaction in the second year.

Though we oppose that treatment because the receivable would be stated at less than its amount and income taxes not yet incurred would be anticipated, that treatment is less objectionable than the treatment proposed in the note of presenting a liability before it is incurred. The net-of-tax theory reports satisfactory items at unsatisfactory amounts. The liability theory, we believe, is even more objection-able—it reports unsatisfactory items.

### Accrual yes—allocation no

The note states that accounting for income taxes without allocating them among periods is cash-basis accounting and unsatisfactory for that reason. However, as we said in footnote 7 of our article, accrual accounting and allocation are not synonymous, and accounting for income taxes can be on the accrual basis without allocating them among periods.

The accrual basis differs from the cash basis in several ways. One difference is that accrual accounting but not cash-basis accounting requires reporting liabilities when they are incurred and before they are paid. Accounting for income taxes without deferred taxes is on the accrual basis: it reports liabilities for income taxes when they are incurred and before they are paid.

But, the accrual basis doesn't require or even permit reporting liabilities before they are incurred. Because it reports liabilities before they are incurred, the kind of accounting proposed in the note isn't on the accrual basis.

### A mismatch

The note implies that accounting for income taxes without allocating them among periods is bad matching and that that kind of accounting is therefore unsatisfactory.

The term *matching* means that costs that have been incurred should be matched with related revenue that has been realized and that the costs should be treated as expenses of the periods in which the related revenue is recognized.

Income tax costs are incurred in the years in which liabilities for such income taxes are incurred, the years they appear in income tax returns. As the FASB stated in its Statement no. 5, *Accounting for Contingencies*, "the accounting concept of matching...does not apply to costs that have not been incurred."[15] By matching income taxes anticipated to appear in future income tax returns, and therefore not yet incurred, with revenue already realized, deferred taxes—not the accounting for income taxes we recommend—mismatches costs and revenue.

### Income taxes of a going concern

The note implies that the going-concern concept requires deferred taxes. The note asks whether anyone believes "the taxes won't be paid" in a profitable environment, assuming the concern keeps going. But, as we pointed out in our article and above, whether taxes (or salaries or utility bills or a myriad of other kinds of amounts) will be paid isn't the issue. The issue is, when did the going concern incur the liability to pay them? That issue is discussed above.

### Historical cost and deferred taxes

The note says that those who favor current value concepts often oppose deferred taxes but that, for now, accounting for income taxes should be based solely on historical cost concepts and, based on those concepts, deferred taxes are required.

Under neither the historical cost basis nor any other basis should balance sheets report items that don't represent resources, obligations or equity, as required under Accounting Principles Board Opinion no. 11, *Accounting for Income Taxes*,[16] or liabilities before they are incurred, as proposed in the note. Further, although allocations are made under the historical cost basis, that basis itself neither requires allocation in particular areas nor specifies the kinds of allocations that should be made if they are made.

### "Interest-free loans"

The note refers to the common expression that certain income tax provisions provide taxpayers with "interest-free" loans "through reduced taxes" and implies

---

[15] FASB Statement no. 5, *Accounting for Contingencies* (Stamford: FASB, 1975), par. 98.

[16] Accounting Principles Board Opinion no. 11, *Accounting for Income Taxes* (New York: AICPA, 1967).

that such loans make deferred taxes necessary. But, as a taxing agency, the government makes no loans to taxpayers, interest free or otherwise. Taxpayers are entitled to apply the income tax laws and regulations to incur as little income tax as allowed and to incur it as late as allowed. The reduction of income taxes said to be such a loan is the difference between the income taxes the taxpayer incurred and the income taxes it would have incurred had it applied the laws and regulations less prudently or had the laws or regulations been different from what they were.

Such differences between what happened and what didn't happen aren't loans, and, as we said in our article, don't belong in financial statements.

### Information outside the number columns

The note implies that all essential information should be presented in the number columns of financial statements, and it says that, because we recommend note disclosure of the differences between income tax and book bases of assets and liabilities rather than recognition of potential income tax effects of the differences in the number columns, the accounting for income taxes we recommend is unsatisfactory.

The current requirements for disclosure outside the number columns of financial statements are based on the sound view that some of the information needed by users of financial statements can't be meaningfully reported in the number columns. Information on possible future expenses is an example of such information, and the potential income tax effects of differences between income tax and book bases of assets and liabilities are such possible future expenses.

Users should consider possible future expenses and make what they will of them. That is how we recommend the information on the differences be used, not the way suggested in the note, simply "to allow users to calculate periodic income."

### Pro forma presentations

The note apparently would have financial statements report the "earning power" of the reporting enterprise, which sounds like a report on what the enterprise would ordinarily earn, not what it did earn. That, in effect, is a recommendation for pro forma presentations rather than a recommendation to have the financial statements report the earnings of the enterprise and leave to the users of the financial statements the task of forming opinions on the earning power of the enterprise. The note's recommendation is apt, because deferred taxes, by reporting based on what didn't happen or what hasn't yet happened, results in pro forma presentations rather than history.

### Smoothing

Though the purpose of deferred taxes may not be to smooth the trend of reported net income, as the note states, its effect is to smooth that trend, and it will likely be strongly supported because of that.

Accounting for income taxes, like accounting for all other matters, should be judged based on whether it presents information that corresponds with the events that have occurred and with their effects on the reporting enterprise. If the effects of income taxes are variable period by period and if recognizing the effects leads to a variable rather than a smooth trend of reported net income, as it may under the accounting for income taxes we recommend, that result should be accepted.

## ON TO SOUND ACCOUNTING

The note starts with what it calls the "concept" of comprehensive interperiod income tax allocation, apparently based on the view that reported income taxes should follow reported income, and treats selection of the "method" of such allocation as implementation. It apparently reflects a preference for the liability or net-of-tax approach but suggests selection of the deferred approach on practical grounds. We could start with another concept, that reported income taxes should follow income tax returns, and see how to implement that.

The issue couldn't be settled that way, however. That is why we analyzed and discussed the financial statement results of the various theories or approaches or methods or what have you of deferred taxes. The note dismisses the unsatisfactory financial statement results of deferred taxes as unimportant. We ask those who agree with the conclusion in the note to consider those unsatisfactory financial statement results.

Those who promulgated APB Opinion no. 11 obviously studied the issue of how to allocate income taxes a great deal. But, as we pointed out in our article, the AICPA director of accounting research said shortly before Opinion no. 11 was issued that whether income taxes should be allocated at all "has never been adequately studied,"[17] and the opinion itself dismisses accounting for income taxes without interperiod allocation with the comment that "this concept has not been used widely in practice and is not supported presently to any significant extent."[18]

We urge the FASB to give a fair hearing to the idea that there should be no more deferred taxes, along with all other ideas on accounting for income taxes. And we hope that, rather than start with an idea of what may seem to be desirable income statement results concerning income taxes, the FASB will start by considering the events that affect the obligations of enterprises for income taxes and then let its understanding of those events lead it to prescribe sound accounting for income taxes.

---

[17] Reed K. Storey, "Director's Statement," in Accounting Research Study no. 9, *Interperiod Allocation of Corporate Income Taxes,* Homer A. Black (New York: AICPA, 1966), p. vii.
[18] APB Opinion no. 11, par. 24.

# V-B 3 *Letters to the Editor*

## DEFERRED TAXES

Congratulations on the article in the February *Journal of Accountancy* (pages 44–55) by Paul Rosenfield and William C. Dent entitled "No More Deferred Taxes." It's about time that someone pointed out that the "emperor's new clothes" aren't really clothes at all. Many deferred taxes in this day of deferral to never-never land have become contingencies much more than liabilities.

While the article deals forcefully with the overall concept, it doesn't deal with the distorted effect current deferred taxes have on working capital calculations, ratio calculations and expected cash flows. Many of these deferred taxes will clearly not be paid within the 12-month cycle usually associated with current liabilities. However, because of their association with current assets, they have been classified as current. Readers of financial statements and financial analysts are certainly not well served by what has become an accounting fiction rather than a financial reality.
*Edward A. Weinstein, CPA*

We were shocked by the Rosenfield—Dent article—shocked because the straw men raised had nothing to do with the case for deferred taxes and because the *Journal* chose to consult only those with one point of view.

We believe that the case for deferred taxes is economic rather than legal because there is no "liability" question involved. Instead, the question is that of proper interperiod allocation of costs.

Those who argue against deferred tax accounting need to accept the premise that a purchase discount on acquisition or installation of capital assets is current income. This clearly suggests overstating the future costs of long-lived assets, thus ensuring our continued inability to compete in the world markets for autos, steel, aluminum, fertilizer or anything else.

It is time that we recognize—as economists if not as accountants—that benefits which arise from decisions to make massive capital investments can't result in current profits to be distributed through cash dividends and then somehow collected from future customers. Those customers will likely turn to Japanese or Third World suppliers rather than buy U.S. goods whose prices have been artificially inflated by short-sighted bookkeeping.

The financial health of U.S. industry won't be enhanced by crediting the early lives of a long-lived capital investment with the tax benefits associated with it while

apportioning related financial charges to later periods. That is what the deferred tax controversy is all about.
*Gordon R. Corey, CPA*

*Leonard Spacek, CPA*

Messrs. Rosenfield and Dent deserve a Halleluyah Chorus for their fine article. For more than 15 years, "deferred tax accounting," coupled with one of the "spreading methods" of accounting for the investment credit, has undermined the integrity of financial statements by (1) mandating that we account for what might have happened but didn't, (2) introducing confusing accounting terminology and (3) adulterating the basic accounting equation.

*Deferred* used to refer to past cash flows that hadn't been charged to expense or credited to revenue. Future cash flows were the province of accruals. The basic accounting equation used to be: assets = liabilities + owners' equity or, stated another way: assets − liabilities = owners' equity. Since the advent of deferred tax accounting, no necessary relationship has existed between deferrals and cash flows. The accounting equation is now: assets and other things = liabilities and other things + owners' equity (or assets and other things − liabilities and other things = owners' equity). Deferred taxes have a direct effect on reported income, as does at least one of the methods for spreading the investment credit under APB Opinion no. 2, *Accounting for the Investment Credit.* They don't affect the amount of assets or liabilities because they produce "balance sheet accounts" that are neither true assets nor true liabilities but that are excluded from owners' equity. In addition, non-U.S. deferred taxes can produce wild fluctuations in reported income under FASB Statement no. 52, *Foreign Currency Translation,* without any cash flow effects.

Statement no. 52 requires remeasurement of all foreign deferred taxes at the current rate. Many foreign subsidiaries with U.S. dollar functional currencies were able to report millions of dollars of foreign exchange transaction gains on foreign deferred taxes for 1982 because the dollar strengthened against most host country currencies. These so-called gains were unrelated to cash flows—past, present or future. When the dollar weakens against those currencies, millions of dollars of foreign exchange transaction losses will be reported that are equally unrelated to cash flows—past, present or future.

The abolition of deferred tax accounting would remove a formidable barrier to financial statements that are compatible with the objectives cited in FASB Concepts Statement no. 1, *Objectives of Financial Reporting by Business Enterprises.* It would also restore the accounting equation to its unadulterated form. I hope that the FASB will give adequate consideration to the arguments presented by Messrs. Rosenfield and Dent and that the cover of the February *Journal* is prophetic.
*Cecilia V. Tierney, CPA*

Congratulations on the article on deferred income taxes. I am glad the *Journal* published it because we now have a current article in the literature regarding the "no allocation" position.

The article, which attempts to tie the case against deferred taxes to the definition of a liability, as espoused in FASB Concepts Statement no. 3, *Elements of Financial Statements of Business Enterprises,* is a good one. I hope we can find out whether the authors' disagreement with deferred tax accounting is a substantive one. Perhaps, through continued analysis of the major attributes of a liability, we can pinpoint where the real disagreement lies. Otherwise, the arguments degenerate into an emotional issue (which no one can ever resolve).

I still maintain that an obligation exists that should be recognized for deferred income taxes in most situations. Where the authors and I seem to differ is best illustrated by the article's example on warranties. In the example, the warranty expense recognized is a function of the revenue earned in that period for financial reporting purposes. In other words, there would be no warranty expense if there were no sales. Thus, there is a defect in the sale that should be recognized in the current period.

The same can be said for income tax expense. If there is no revenue, there is no income tax expense. However, if there is revenue, there is income tax expense even if it isn't paid until a future period. In short, in a system where revenue is earned, a very real expense is income tax. It may turn out that you won't have to pay the income taxes because you have no income. Nevertheless, that result will occur because of some set of transactions other than the original sale. Assuming all other factors are equal, the company will have to pay these taxes for that transaction. Thus, since income tax expense is a result of a past transaction (the earning of the revenue), I believe it should be recognized at that point.

At what amount is a debatable point. If, for example, as a result of a certain future event, the company won't have to pay these taxes, then the amount to report would be zero. The same could be said for the warranties. Consequently, we should recognize the warranties, but perhaps the individuals who received defective merchandise won't return the goods (cost—benefit considerations might suggest this if the defects are minor or if only a small number who have defective goods demand satisfaction). In this case, the liability should be reduced. In short, the reason for the warranty expense is that goods were sold; the reason for income taxes is that goods were sold. In both situations, these expenses should be recognized. If it can be shown that these amounts aren't going to be paid, then no amount should be recorded.
*Jerry J. Weygandt, CPA*

I strongly disagree with the article, and I am disappointed that the authors would seriously take such a myopic view of a very important matter. I can only hope that their article was designed to encourage discussion of deferred taxes rather than purport to be a supportable basis for changing our existing rules.

Their rejection of deferred tax accounting is based solely on a narrow interpretation of the definition of a liability. That is, an obligation must "be a result solely of past events and not to be a result of future events, alone or in conjunction with past events." Since a company must have income in future years to generate a tax liability, all future taxes depend in part on future events. Therefore, the authors state, no deferred taxes should be provided on timing differences.

I don't believe deferred tax accounting issues can be narrowed down to this single definitional problem. The authors casually brush aside or ignore more important concepts such as the going-concern presumptions of future cash flow and the basic income—expense matching concept.

The article's exhibit, which shows alternate accounting methods for an installment sale, only serves to point out how the proposed accounting (no deferred taxes) could significantly distort reported earnings. It shows how a company would report a large gain in the year an installment sale is made and then report losses for each of the next four years. Does this provide for better reporting of the transaction than the current deferred tax method? Definitely not.

Although I agree the issues surrounding deferred taxes should be reexamined (and I personally would embrace discounting deferred tax amounts), I believe articles like the one by Rosenfield and Dent are counterproductive.
*James S. Cox, CPA*

The Rosenfield—Dent article is the best piece of technical writing that has appeared in the *Journal* since I became a member of the AICPA in 1967.

This sort of enlightened analysis of the deferred tax morass has been too long in coming. The authors' proposal for a cure is clear, rational and understandable. Most important, it takes a position on income taxes that can be understood by readers of financial statements who aren't highly trained accountants knowledgeable in the area of deferred taxes as laid out in APB Opinion no. 11, *Accounting for Income Taxes*, and later pronouncements. The article reasonably sets forth the position that was taken by a number of the accounting faculty at the Graduate School of Business of the University of Chicago when I was there in the mid-1960s. As I recall, their position was, "Taxes are what you pay."

I would hope that the FASB takes quick action to implement the proposals of Messrs. Rosenfield and Dent.
*David B. Sarver, CPA*

Speaking as a sole practitioner, I find that deferred tax calculations, reconciliations and the drafting of related footnotes aren't cost-effective or relevant services for the majority of my clients. Consequently, performing work that is neither cost-effective nor relevant jeopardizes client relationships. Therefore, I agree with the conclusions of Messrs. Rosenfield and Dent that accounting for deferred taxes shouldn't be required by generally accepted accounting principles. My reasoning is based on the fact that tax planning is a cost-effective client service that enhances client relationships. It probably is the major client service of most smaller practice units. Its focus is normally on minimizing the liability of the next fiscal year anticipated to be subject to taxation. This is the main reason for differences between pretax accounting income and taxable income or the differences in net tax liability. Deferred tax timing differences usually reverse or turn around in later periods. However, it is this same tax planning service that usually results in the turnaround tax effect in the later period being offset by the tax effects of other differences originating in that later period.

Nevertheless, I am also aware of the concerns expressed by Joseph E. Connor, chairman of Price Waterhouse, in the Statement in Quotes section of the December 1982 *Journal of Accountancy* (pages 98–106), regarding the hardship which would occur to certain types of regulated industries and others if deferred tax accounting disappears.

Given these contending viewpoints, I believe that deferred taxes are, in essence, just another type of contingent liability. It also seems that deferred taxes could more appropriately and more flexibly be accounted for under FASB Statement no. 5, *Accounting for Contingencies*, and related interpretations.

I hope the FASB will give consideration to this compromise viewpoint. I believe it offers a reasonable solution to concerns regarding relevancy and cost-effective client service and also provides for the concerns and needs expressed by Mr. Connor.
*Michael J. Daillak, CPA*

*Authors' reply.* The thrust of Professor Weygandt's argument concerns a reporting entity that makes a sale and incurs an obligation for income taxes. He says that, if the entity wouldn't have incurred the obligation in the absence of the sale, the obligation is a result of the sale. Accordingly, he believes the obligation should be reflected as a liability in the year of the sale. In contrast, we recommend no more deferred taxes and would have the obligation first reflected as a liability in the year the income taxes appear in the income tax return rather than in the year of the sale.

His argument doesn't distinguish conditions necessary and conditions sufficient.

An obligation is a relationship between the reporting entity and another entity, not merely an accounting entry. An obligation should be recorded when the relationship comes into existence, not merely to achieve financial statement results that are perceived as desirable.

An obligation may be a result of two or more events. The relationship of an obligation comes into existence when the last event from which it results has occurred rather then when any earlier event occurs, regardless of how much that earlier event contributed to the formation of the obligation.

Earning revenue from a sale is an event an obligation for income taxes may be a result of. Therefore, it may be a condition necessary to the incurrence of the obligation. Nevertheless, it wouldn't be the only event from which the obligation results, so it wouldn't be a condition sufficient to incur the obligation. At least one event that results in the obligation occurs in the year covered by the income tax return in which the income taxes appear, as discussed in our article and in our reply to Professor Philip L. Defliese's Professional Note in the August 1983 *Journal* (pages 98–103).

Therefore, no liability for income taxes is incurred before the year covered by the income tax return in which they appear, and none should be reported before then—no taxpayer has a liability this year for next year's income taxes.

Messrs. Corey and Spacek state that the method we recommend for accounting for income taxes would improperly burden future income statements with costs that should be recognized in earlier income statements, much as accounting for purchase discounts on depreciable assets as current income would improperly burden future income statements with higher depreciation expense. Further, they argue that the reasoning behind our recommendation for no more deferred taxes would lead to an unsatisfactory recommendation to report purchase discounts as current income.

A purchase discount on the acquisition of an asset is simply part of one way of stating its price. The price may be stated gross, less the discount—for example, $100 less 10 percent, or $90. The same price may also be stated in any number of other ways—for example, $120 less 25 percent, or $90. Another way to state its price is simply to state it as $90.

A purchase discount shouldn't be reported in financial statements; only the price paid for an asset, regardless of how it is stated, should be recorded.

The acquisition of depreciable assets may lead to income tax benefits. However, the benefits depend on the incurrence by the reporting entity of income tax obligations, not merely on the acquisition of assets. By following the income tax laws and regulations, amounts related to the acquisition of the assets enter into the calculation of income tax obligations. As stated previously, those obligations are incurred in the years covered by the income tax returns in which the income taxes appear and should be first reported then. It is the incurrence of the income tax obligations, rather than items such as income tax benefits that enter into the calculation of their amounts, that should be accounted for.

The concern of Messrs. Corey and Spacek for proper interperiod allocation of costs could be accommodated without accounting for income tax benefits (which shouldn't be accounted for) by modifying the interperiod allocation of amounts that should be accounted for, such as the acquisition costs of assets. The allocation of acquisition costs could be changed to the net-of-tax approach. Though we oppose that approach for reasons stated in our article and in our reply to Professor Defliese, it does at least have the virtue of accounting for items, such as acquisition costs, that should be accounted for.

Mr. Cox contends that our interpretation of the FASB's definition of a liability is too narrow.

By definition, a definition defines. It sets limits. It provides discipline. Damage can be done by discarding a definition simply because applying it in particular circumstances leads to results perceived as undesirable.

We stated our belief in our article, in our reply to Professor Defliese and above that the part of the definition calling for an obligation that is a result of past transactions or events should be interpreted as calling for an obligation that is a result of only past transactions or events. The only other possible interpretation— that it calls for an obligation that may be a result of both past and future transactions or events—turns a definition that is basically sound and is helpful into one that is unsound and fruitless.

Mr. Cox says we didn't deal with the going-concern concept and the matching principle. He implies that either or both of them require deferred taxes to avoid distorting reported earnings.

We did ignore those matters in our article, because we believed the argument in the article was complete without them. Because Professor Defliese raised those matters in his note, we addressed them in our reply to his note. We indicated reasons that neither of those matters requires deferred taxes and that accounting without deferred taxes can conform with both.

Mr. Daillak says that deferred taxes should conform to the guidance provided by FASB Statement no. 5, *Accounting for Contingencies*, and implies that the guidance would sometimes require reporting liabilities this year for next year's income taxes.

The guidance in Statement no. 5 wouldn't require or even permit reporting such liabilities. It discusses events that confirm that "a liability had been incurred at the date of the financial statements." No such confirming events could occur, because, as already discussed, no liability for income taxes has been incurred until the year covered by the income tax return in which they appear.

Mr Daillak refers to the concerns expressed by Joseph E. Connor in the December 1982 *Journal* regarding hardship that might occur to certain types of regulated industries if deferred taxes is eliminated from financial reporting. Mr. Connor said that "some regulated industries would suffer severe economic consequences if deferred tax accounting disappeared without at least a comparable substitute in their rate structures to compensate for the ravages of inflation. Supported by the method's status as a generally accepted accounting principle, industry leaders, through years of concerted effort, have succeeded in obtaining wide acceptance of the deferred tax provision as a component of the cost of service.... An FASB decision to remove the platform on which their position rests would have severely adverse consequences."

The FASB is mindful of economic consequences. Nevertheless, it stated in paragraph 98 of Statement no. 5 that "the Board ... does not believe that pricing considerations should dictate ... accrual ... for financial accounting purposes." Furthermore, FASB chairman Donald J. Kirk recently said that "the FASB['s] ... mission, simply stated, is to establish standards that improve the relevance and reliability of accounting information and thereby enhance the ability of those who use that information to make economic decisions.... the Board's primary concern must be the relevance and reliability of the information that results, not the effect that the new rule might have on a particular interest."

It is those who use that information who would benefit from adoption of our recommendation for no more deferred taxes.

*Paul Rosenfield, CPA*

*William C. Dent, CPA*

# V-B 4   *Deferred Taxes: The Discounting Controversy*

JAMES O. STEPP

S hould deferred taxes be discounted? Although much attention has been directed to this question, the proscription against discounting has been in place since Accounting Principles Board Opinion no. 10, *Omnibus Opinion—1966.*

The Financial Accounting Standards Board has been reconsidering the accounting for income taxes, and its timetable indicates that an exposure draft is imminent. Discounting was a principal concern of the August 29, 1983, discussion memorandum, but the subject won't be addressed in the exposure draft. The board may consider discounting of deferred taxes in the future, but it isn't currently on the agenda. The American Institute of CPAs accounting standards executive committee (AcSEC) has established a task force to study the broad issue of discounting, including its potential application to deferred taxes, and initial discussion by AcSEC is expected in the near future.

An examination of the conceptual difficulties and implementation problems in discounting deferred taxes offers strong arguments against a change in policy. First, though, a look at the conceptual basis of deferred taxes expected in the exposure draft seems in order.

## THE COMPREHENSIVE LIABILITY FRAMEWORK

Deferred taxes are provided to reflect timing differences between financial accounting and taxable income originating in the current or prior periods and not yet reversed at the balance sheet date.

One of the major issues the FASB had to consider in its income taxes project was the conceptual basis for providing deferred taxes. Three different approaches were proposed—liability, deferred and net of tax—as well as combinations of these methods. The FASB settled on the liability method, under which the deferred tax credit represents a liability for taxes payable on realization of the carrying value of assets (liabilities) because of their lower (higher) tax bases.

Another significant issue was whether allocation should be partial or compre-hensive. Under the form of partial allocation most widely understood, deferred taxes wouldn't be provided for reversals of timing differences expected to be replaced by new, originating differences from similar transactions. Although partial allocation generally is considered a subset of the liability method, the FASB has decided that comprehensive allocation should be followed.

Given the FASB's tentative conclusion that deferred taxes should be provided under the comprehensive liability approach, it is now much easier to focus on the discounting issue. Indeed, it seems that the strongest arguments for discounting can be made under this approach.

The deferred method merely defers the past tax effects of timing differences, focusing on past cash flows, whereas the liability method attempts to measure future tax cash flows. Although the net-of-tax method can look to either past or future tax cash flows, it is usually proposed in the context of past tax cash flows.

Similarly, partial allocation dissipates, if not the arguments for discounting, the fervor with which they are advanced. Partial allocation generally would serve to reduce the deferred tax liability considerably, and further reductions for discounting would entail computational complexity with little effect.

## CONCEPTUAL DIFFICULTIES

Increasingly, the time value of money is reflected both in structuring transactions and in the accounting for them. The high interest rates of recent years have underscored the fact that a dollar today is worth more than a dollar several years in the future. Following the adoption in 1971 of APB Opinion no. 21, *Interest on Receivables and Payables*, the prevailing presumption has been that liabilities should be measured and recorded at present values. If deferred taxes represent amounts payable in future periods, why shouldn't such amounts be recorded at their present values?

Advocates of discounting argue that present value is clearly a more meaningful measure of the deferred tax liability. In addition, they assert, deferred taxes and taxes currently payable should be reflected differently—that is, the amount of deferred taxes should be smaller as the length of the discount period increases, and the charge to income for $1 of tax currently payable should be higher than the charge to income for $1 of tax payable in the future.

It should be noted, however, that frequently there is a considerable difference between deferred taxes and liabilities on which interest imputation is required by Opinion no. 21. Timing differences can be distinguished between (1) those reflected first in financial reporting income and subsequently in taxable income and (2) those reflected first in taxable income. Indeed, many respondents to the discussion memorandum found this distinction compelling and recommended the liability method for the former timing differences and the deferred or net-of-tax method for the latter.

For timing differences first reflected in financial reporting income—for example, gross profit on installment sales—there is a future tax cash flow that can be predicted to occur on reversal when the timing difference is reflected in taxable income. When the timing difference is first reflected in taxable income, however, the tax cash flow has already occurred, and the future reversal of the timing difference is accomplished by its reflection in financial reporting income. Included in this group of timing differences is accelerated tax depreciation, which, in a macroeconomic sense, is clearly the most important source of timing differences.

For depreciation, actual tax cash flows follow the allocation method prescribed or elected for tax purposes, but a different allocation, deemed better to reflect the benefit of the capital asset's use in operations, is used for financial reporting. Deferred taxes, in this case, are provided to reflect the absence of an actual tax deduction in the future periods when the cost of the capital asset is "recovered" by financial reporting depreciation.

Reversal entails an actual tax cash flow only in the sense that taxable income derived from use of the asset won't be reduced by tax depreciation equal to financial reporting depreciation. The timing of reversal of the deferred tax liability will change if the depreciation methods or lives used for financial reporting depreciation are changed.

Clearly, the deferred tax liability represents a future tax cash flow only in a limited sense.

Moreover, unlike the Opinion no. 21 liabilities, deferred tax liabilities aren't fixed sums payable at fixed dates, and arguments for discounting are weaker as a result. As for payment dates, reversals of certain timing differences may depend on future events, and for certain timing differences the occurrence of reversals can be determined only by arbitrary ordering. The amount and timing of the tax payable on reversal of timing differences will depend on the tax rates enacted for future periods and the taxpayer's tax position, including taxable income or loss, carry-back availability, and available credits and carry-forwards.

Another distinction is that the transactions covered by the opinion are negotiated between buyer and seller or borrower and lender, and the interest rate used to impute interest is that presumably implicit in the negotiation, that is, the market rate at that time. By contrast, the ability to generate timing differences that defer income taxes by entering into specified types of transactions isn't a result of negotiation but of availability of provisions of the tax law. Such provisions aren't directly affected by changes in the market interest rate and are available on the same basis to all taxpayers regardless of their creditworthiness.

The most important timing differences represent economic incentives—the temporary deferral of tax payments—that the government provides for specific transactions. The "discount" on the deferred taxes (the difference between the gross amount of the deferred tax liability for reversing timing differences and the present value of that gross tax) arguably measures the amount of the economic incentives. Proponents of discounting believe that it would provide useful information by reflecting directly the availability and use of these incentives.

But the economic incentive that timing differences provide is an interest-free loan from the government, and not discounting reflects this. When deferred taxes are recorded gross in the balance sheet, the benefit of timing differences is reflected as it is realized as the absence of interest on deferred tax balances. This is the measure of the subsidy that the government has provided, and it shouldn't be anticipated by discounting.

The most important timing difference incentive is accelerated tax depreciation. For recording depreciation in financial statements such interest methods as sinking fund and annuity, methods that credit early operating periods with an interest equivalent for funds invested in the capital asset, are precluded by generally accepted accounting principles. The depreciation assigned to periods of use doesn't reflect the fact that funds may have been invested in the asset for many years before "recovery" by depreciation.

In these circumstances there is no compelling reason to adopt an accounting technique (discounting) to reflect the fact that the tax depreciation from the same asset acquisition may serve to defer cash outflow for taxes.

The dichotomy between financial statement depreciation and discounting deferred taxes arising from tax depreciation is perhaps sharpest when the question raised by discounting the deferred taxes is considered: Should the benefit provided by the government's economic incentive be reflected in income immediately or, rather, be spread over the life of the asset as a type of subsidy or cost reduction? This is the same question that has made the accounting for the investment tax credit controversial since its enactment in 1962. The Revenue Act of 1971 effectively precludes those who set accounting standards from prescribing either the flow-through or the deferral method of accounting for the investment tax credit, and the FASB has elected not to deal with the issue.

Because the "discount" on the deferred taxes measures the benefit that the government's economic incentive has made available, its treatment as a subsidy would result in its amortization over the life of the property. Under this approach, deferred taxes would be reduced by the "discount," and the "discount," representing the subsidy, would also be reflected separately as a deferred credit. The aggregate "discount" would be accreted by charge to income on an interest method over the period to payment of the deferred taxes and would be credited to income over the life of the fixed asset as an adjustment of depreciation. This approach would complicate the accounting, and the resulting effect on income would only be the difference between two spreading patterns.

The sidebar on pages 104–105 compares the effects of not discounting and discounting, and the two approaches to the "discount" arising from accelerated tax depreciation are illustrated.

## IMPLEMENTATION PROBLEMS

In addition to its conceptual shortcomings, discounting would create serious implementation problems. One of the FASB's primary objectives in reconsidering income taxes was simplification, and it is probably the complexity and increased computations required by discounting, more than conceptual considerations, that caused the FASB to defer indefinitely its consideration of discounting. Among other considerations, implementation of discounting would require largely arbitrary rules for choosing the rate and the period.

### Discount Rate

A number of questions would arise in any attempt to select the discount rate:

1.  Should an investment or a borrowing rate be used?
    In most discounting applications in accounting, a borrowing rate is used. In recording a specific debt instrument, for example, interest imputation ascribes to the debt the current market interest rate applicable to the debtor's credit rating, the maturity of the debt, its priority and the collateral securing it. This is the typical approach to discounting other types of liabilities.

By contrast, the discounting concept used in accounting for pension obligations under APB Opinion no. 8, *Accounting for the Cost of Pension Plans*, is an investment rate, which embodies a funding and growth or accumulation concept.

It can be argued that an investment rate is more relevant than a borrowing rate in discounting deferred taxes because the "borrowing" from the government doesn't arise through direct negotiations and, therefore, the creditworthiness of the debtor isn't relevant. On the other hand, use of a borrowing rate could be based on the premise that, absent the deferred taxes, additional borrowing would have been required.

2.  Should a pretax or an aftertax rate be used?

Presumably, the discount rate should be an aftertax rate. Accretion of a discounted deferred tax liability would have to accumulate aftertax dollars.

3.  Should a company-specific or an external rate be used?

Valid conceptual arguments can be made for using a company's specific rate in discounting deferred taxes. But if a borrowing rate is used, an anomalous result of using a company's specific rate is that the benefit of discounting deferred taxes would be greater for less established, less profitable, higher risk companies. The lower the taxpayer's credit rating, the lower the recorded deferred tax liability.

If an investment rate is used, the investment possibilities attributable to such funds would include

- Investment in capital assets.
- Research and development activities.
- Investment in equity or interest-bearing securities.

Use of a company's specific investment rate would entail practical difficulties in measurement and verification (for example, in determining the use and related return for incremental funds). Use of an external rate would avoid the subjectivity inherent in a company-specific rate.

4.  Should a single rate or multiple rates be used?

Because yields available or demanded in interest markets depend on maturities, rates should vary for different discount periods. Although a certain amount of grouping and imprecision would be acceptable, a number of discount rates could be required to reflect adequately the different "maturities" of the deferred taxes.

It is likely that the FASB would require the use of external, aftertax, risk-free investment rates.

### Discount Period

Determining the discount period would involve considerable mechanics. The cumulative timing differences at the balance sheet date would have to be scheduled by the expected year of reversal. This requirement would go well beyond the information about the period of reversal of timing differences required by the liability method.

In applying the liability method, information about specific reversal periods will be important only when (1) rate changes have been enacted to take effect in some future period, therefore applying to some but not all reversals, or (2) carryforwards exist and it must be determined whether reversals will occur within or beyond the carryforward periods.

In an article in the September 1984 *Journal of Accountancy*, "Accounting for Income Taxes: Predicting Timing Difference Reversals," Barry Robbins and Steven Swyers discuss three categories of timing differences:

1.  Reversal isn't dependent on future events (or the occurrence and timing of the future event is highly predictable), and either origination or reversal takes place within a single, discrete period. Examples are gross profit on installment sales and deferred gain on sale-leasebacks.

2.  Reversal isn't dependent on future events, but both origination and reversal take place over several periods. Although the reversals follow a predetermined schedule, the association of specific originations with specific reversals requires the selection of an arbitrary ordering, such as Fifo, Lifo or average. The primary example is depreciation, for example, the straight-line method for financial reporting and accelerated methods and shorter recovery periods for tax.

3.  Reversal depends on future events, and predicting the period of reversal may be difficult and estimates may be subject to change over time. Examples include depreciation or amortization related to operating levels (for example, intangible drilling costs in the oil and gas industry), revenue recognition on long-term construction contracts, and warranty reserves.

Obviously, when timing differences fall into the third category, imprecision, subjective judgments and frequent revision of the reversal period used in the discounting computation are likely. Calculating the reversal periods for the second category of timing differences would entail substantial computations.

In considering the discount period for reversal of cumulative timing differences at the balance sheet date, there is a conceptual position similar to the form of partial allocation already described. Under this approach, the discount period would be extended by future originations scheduled or predicted to occur to offset the reversals. Prediction of continuing rollover of deferred taxes by future originations could extend the discount period indefinitely and, accordingly, minimize the discounted amount of deferred taxes.

### Other Problems

Adoption of any discounting methodology would raise another question: Should there be a comprehensive recalculation at each balance sheet date using the discount rate determined by conditions at that date, or should "discount" on deferred taxes be established separately for each period of origination and worked forward using the discount rate assigned in the period of origination? The latter approach is the typical accounting for liabilities in the historical cost framework: The original interest rate is used regardless of subsequent changes in market interest rates.

Tracking discounted deferred taxes by year of origination probably would be impractical, however, and recalculation is more consistent with the liability method, in which the deferred tax amount is revalued to reflect tax rate changes. Given the frequency and magnitude of interest rate changes, a comprehensive recalculation at each balance sheet date could give rise to considerable volatility in reported numbers and therefore in reported income.

Assuming comprehensive recalculation, a number of factors would change the amount of "discount" applied to reduce deferred tax balances in a given period:

- New tax rates that would change the "principal," the gross amount of deferred taxes payable.
- The "discount" on new, originating differences (and possibly the "discount" applicable to scheduled or predicted future originations).
- Changes in the discount rate(s) applied.
- Accretion of "discount" on deferred taxes previously provided (there would be a question whether this amount should be shown in the tax provision or in interest expense, possibly eligible for capitalization under FASB Statement no. 34, *Capitalization of Interest Cost*).
- Changes in estimated periods of reversals (for example, changes resulting from changed amortization methods or lives for capital assets or by reserve estimate changes or additions to the full-cost pool for intangible drilling costs).

Several of these changes could interact to affect the change in the amount of "discount" in a given year, and it is unlikely that any specific effect could be isolated.

Special consideration would have to be given to timing differences arising from transactions in which discounting is integral to pretax accounting. Examples are pensions, direct financing leases and capital leases. The accounting literature for these transactions establishes the interest rate used in pretax accounting. Across-the-board application of discounting to all deferred tax balances would apply a different interest rate to the tax effects.

Separate discounting calculations would have to be made for each taxing jurisdiction, and a different discount rate (or a series of rates) would have to be selected for each foreign jurisdiction.

The effects of discounting would have to be reflected in interim periods as well as in the annual computation. Short-cut methods possibly could be devised for interim calculations. For example, the change in the amount of "discount" for the year could be estimated and considered part of the annual effective tax rate. But this would entail predictions of the interest rate to be used in the year-end computation. More important, it would be conceptually at odds with the basic discounting technique that charges annual periods for the benefit of having the use of funds interest free, such charges varying with the amount of funds available, the time period of their availability and the applicable rate.

The alternative—a discrete approach to discounting in interim periods—isn't attractive either. The discrete assignment of the effects of timing differences to interim periods would be arbitrary at best. For example, should the excess tax over financial reporting depreciation for the year be assumed to occur one-fourth in each quarter? Should that related to the current year's additions be reflected as the additions are placed in service? Or should originations be deemed to occur when they affect taxes payable (for example, on quarterly prepayment dates)?

It is important to note that if changes, especially discount rate changes, are reflected by catch-up adjustments for comprehensive recalculations, at interim dates, of the amount of "discount," interim provisions could be subjected to severe volatility.

## THE QUESTION IN CONTEXT

Should deferred taxes be discounted? It would at first appear, given the time value of money in an environment of high interest rates, that the obvious answer is yes. But a consideration of the nature of deferred tax liabilities produces compelling arguments for not discounting.

Regardless of conceptual appeal, discounting would add considerably to the complexity of tax computation. The routine bookkeeping made possible by the advent of computers might indicate that discounting deferred taxes is an idea whose time has come. But in recent years increasing concern about standards overload has been expressed, and there is a demand, especially from small businesses and small CPA firms, for simpler standards. Consideration of the arbitrary rules and mechanical problems involved makes it clear that deferred taxes should not be discounted.

## WITH AND WITHOUT DISCOUNTING: A COMPARISON OF EFFECTS

A comparison of the effects of not discounting and discounting is illustrated in the accompanying table by a hypothetical transaction in which a fixed asset is purchased for $1,000 in cash in year 1 and depreciated straight line over 10 years for financial reporting.

The following additional assumptions are made:
- The entire cost of the asset is deductible in the year of acquisition (an unrealistic assumption for a U.S. taxpayer but one made for the sake of simplicity).
- A tax rate of 50 percent is effective in the year of acquisition and doesn't change over the 10-year period.
- The tax effects for a specific year are deemed to occur at the fiscal year-end date.
- An aftertax discount rate of 6 percent is appropriate throughout the 10-year period.

Absent discounting, deferred taxes of $450 are provided at the end of year 1 because $100 of depreciation will be recorded for the purpose of financial reporting in each of the nine years 2 through 10 without any actual tax deductions available in these years. Beginning in year 2, the deferred tax balance is reduced annually by the $50 tax effect of reversing depreciation differences. Without discounting, the benefit of the accelerated tax depreciation is reflected simply as the absence of an interest charge on the deferred tax liability.

In discounting, the present value of the reversing deferred taxes of $50 in each of the years 2 through 10 is computed to be $340 at the end of year 1. The difference between gross deferred taxes and present value is $110 at the end of year 1; this is the measurement of the benefit of the accelerated tax depreciation. Starting in year 2, the deferred tax balance is reduced by the annual $50 reversal but is also increased by the interest shown in column G at the assumed 6 percent rate.

In this hypothetical example, all the cash flows (ignoring those that will be generated by use of the asset in operations) appear in columns A and C. The taxpayer expends $1,000 and obtains a related $500 tax reduction in year 1. Columns B and F illustrate that, without discounting, depreciation and its tax effects are spread in the same pattern over the 10-year period. Discounting deferred taxes would recognize that the tax reduction is actually availed of before its reflection in income; yet no recognition is given to the fact that the cash disbursement for the fixed asset is made in advance of its charge to income as depreciation.

Columns K and L illustrate the effects on income if discounting is adopted and should be compared with column F. Column K reflects the effects of discounting if the entire benefit of accelerated tax depreciation is reflected in the year it is deducted on the tax return. The net tax benefit in year 1 comprises the $50 tax effect of financial reporting depreciation and the $110 "discount" on the deferred tax liability; in subsequent years the net tax benefit comprises the $50 tax effect of financial reporting depreciation reduced by interest on the deferred tax balance.

Column L reflects the effects of discounting if the $110 benefit of accelerated tax depreciation is considered a type of subsidy—a reduction in the cost of the fixed asset—and is spread in the same pattern (straight line over 10 years) as financial reporting depreciation. The net tax benefit comprises the $50 tax effect of financial reporting depreciation, increased by the $11 annual amortization of the subsidy, reduced (beginning in year 2) by interest on the deferred tax balance.

| | A | B | C | D | E | F |
|---|---|---|---|---|---|---|
| | | | | **WITHOUT DISCOUNTING** | | |
| | | | | *Deferred Taxes* | | |
| Year | *Expenditure for Asset* | *Depreciation* | *Taxes Payable* | *Provision* | *Balance* | *Net Tax (Benefit)* |
| 1 | $1,000 | $ 100 | $(500) | $450 | $450 | $ (50) |
| 2 | | 100 | | (50) | 400 | (50) |
| 3 | | 100 | | (50) | 350 | (50) |
| 4 | | 100 | | (50) | 300 | (50) |
| 5 | | 100 | | (50) | 250 | (50) |
| 6 | | 100 | | (50) | 200 | (50) |
| 7 | | 100 | | (50) | 150 | (50) |
| 8 | | 100 | | (50) | 100 | (50) |
| 9 | | 100 | | (50) | 50 | (50) |
| 10 | | 100 | | (50) | 0 | (50) |
| | $1,000 | $1,000 | $(500) | $ 0 | | $(500) |

| G | H | J | K | L |
|---|---|---|---|---|
| WITH DISCOUNTING | | | | |
| | Deferred Taxes | | Net Tax (Benefit) | |
| Discount and Accretion | Provision | Balance | Immediate Recognition | Subsidy Treatment |
| $(110) | $340 | $340 | $(160) | $  (61) |
| 20 | (30) | 310 | (30) | (41) |
| 19 | (31) | 279 | (31) | (42) |
| 17 | (33) | 246 | (33) | (44) |
| 15 | (35) | 211 | (35) | (46) |
| 13 | (37) | 174 | (37) | (48) |
| 10 | (40) | 134 | (40) | (51) |
| 8 | (42) | 92 | (42) | (53) |
| 5 | (45) | 47 | (45) | (56) |
| 3 | (47) | 0 | (47) | (58) |
| $    0 | $   0 | | $(500) | $(500) |

# V-C  Solvency and Liquidity

## V-C 1  *Solvency: The Forgotten Half of Financial Reporting*

LOYD C. HEATH AND PAUL ROSENFIELD

The management of a business enterprise is concerned with two broad objectives: to operate the business profitably and to maintain its solvency. Profitability refers to a company's ability to increase its wealth. Solvency refers to its ability to pay its debts when due.

During the first three decades of this century, issues of solvency evaluation clearly dominated financial reporting. Income statements were not in common use, the balance sheet was referred to as *the* financial statement and short-term creditors, particularly bankers, were assumed to be the primary users of that statement. In 1927, Paul-Joseph Esquerré observed:

"It is undeniable that today almost every business balance sheet proceeds on the assumption that it is going to be used to obtain bank loans; and as the banker is presumed to loan only on the security of liquid assets, all the efforts of the statement of financial status are directed towards the proof of that liquidity."[1]

The authors would like to thank Thomas W. McRae, CPA, a manager in the accounting standards division of the American Institute of CPAs, for his invaluable comments and suggestions during the preparation of this article.

[1] Paul-Joseph Esquerré, *Accounting* (New York: Ronald Press Company, 1927), p. 41. See also Hector R. Anton, *Accounting for the Flow of Funds* (New York: Houghton Mifflin Co., 1962), p. 5; A. C. Littleton and V. K. Zimmerman, *Accounting Theory: Continuity and Change* (Englewood Cliffs, N.J.: Prentice-Hall, Inc., 1962), pp. 113–117; and Eldon S. Hendriksen, *Accounting Theory*, 3rd ed. (Homewood, Ill.: Richard D. Irwin, 1977), pp. 56–59.

Beginning around 1930, accountants began to shift their attention from issues of solvency evaluation to those of profitability. By 1952 the pendulum had swung completely:

"... the determination of periodical profit or loss from enterprise operations constitutes the crux of the accounting problem, the central issue around which all other considerations revolve and to which they are unavoidably related."[2]

Since 1952, the focus of financial reporting has remained on profitability. Accounting theorists, accounting educators, groups responsible for promulgating accounting standards, practicing accountants and auditors have been concerned with profitability reporting almost exclusively. With few exceptions, reporting information useful in evaluating the solvency of a company has either been ignored or given a role that is clearly secondary to that of reporting profitability. Financial reporting for solvency evaluation is the forgotten half of finanical reporting.[3]

## THE RELATIONSHIP BETWEEN SOLVENCY AND PROFITABILITY

Solvency and profitability are clearly related. Long-run solvency depends on long-run profitability. No method of obtaining money to pay debts will be available in the long run to an enterprise that is not profitable. In the short run, however, solvency and profitability do not necessarily go together. An unprofitable enterprise may remain solvent for years because its cash collections continue to exceed its required cash payments. On the other hand, a profitable enterprise in need of cash to finance increasing receivables, inventory and plant may tie itself to an unrealistic debt repayment schedule that could eventually result in its insolvency:

Though my bottom line is black, I am flat upon my back,
My cash flows out and customers pay slow.
The growth of my receivables is almost unbelievable;
The result is certain—unremitting woe!
And I hear the banker utter an ominous low mutter, "Watch cash flow."[4]

## THE IMPORTANCE OF SOLVENCY

Investors and creditors, the primary users of general purpose financial statements, need to evaluate the solvency as well as the profitability of companies in which they have interest. Creditors are obviously concerned with solvency. In fact, evaluation of solvency is often referred to as credit analysis, although that term should not be taken to mean that creditors are the only parties interested in a company's solvency or even that creditors are more interested in solvency than other financial statement users. If a company becomes insolvent, equity investors are likely to lose even more than creditors because creditors' rights are senior to those of stockholders in bankruptcy and reorganization proceedings.

[2] Maurice Moonitz and Charles C. Staehling, *Accounting: An Analysis of Its Problems*, vol. 1 (Brooklyn, N.Y.: Foundation Press, Inc., 1952), p. 107.
[3] Some of the material for this article was developed in connection with the preparation of Accounting Research Monograph no. 3, *Financial Reporting and the Evaluation of Solvency*, by Loyd C. Heath (New York: AICPA, 1978).
[4] Herbert S. Bailey, Jr., "Quoth the Banker, 'Watch Cash Flow,'" *Publishers Weekly*, Jan. 13, 1975, p. 34.

Even if a company never reaches the point of insolvency, the mere threat or suspicion of insolvency is likely to result in losses to stockholders. The more obvious consequences are that the market value of their shares is likely to decline and that increased credit costs will tend to reduce profits. But less obvious consequences may be just as serious. Even if there is no imminent threat of insolvency, a company that is short of cash will have to pass up profitable investment opportunities and restrict cash payments in ways that are likely to affect long-run profitability.

Other financial statement users are also concerned with a company's solvency. Employees, suppliers and customers are concerned because loss of solvency usually means loss of jobs, loss of customers, and disruption of sources of supply. The U.S. government's guarantees of loans to Lockheed Aircraft Corp. several years ago illustrate society's concern over the solvency of at least one major corporation.

## EVALUATING SOLVENCY

Solvency is a money or cash phenomenon. A solvent company is one with adequate cash to pay its debts; an insolvent company is one with inadequate cash.[5] Evaluating solvency is basically a problem of evaluating the risk that a company will not be able to raise enough cash before its debts must be paid.

Solvency analysis is not simply a matter of evaluating a company's so-called current assets and liabilities to determine the adequacy of its working capital "cushion." During the last 25 years the emphasis in solvency analysis by sophisticated users of financial statements has shifted from static analysis of working capital position (or "proof of . . . liquidity" as Esquerré called it) to dynamic analysis of cash receipts and payments in much the same way that the emphasis in security analysis shifted from static analysis of balance sheet values to dynamic analysis of net income during the 1930s and 1940s. Today, it is recognized that most of the cash a company will receive within the next years is not represented by assets classified as current (or any other assets now on the balance sheet, for that matter); and most of the obligations it will have to pay during that time are not represented by liabilities classified as current.

Any information that provides insight into the amounts, timing and certainty of a company's future cash receipts and payments is useful in evaluating solvency. Statements of past cash receipts and payments are useful for the same basic reason that income statements are useful in evaluating profitability: both provide a basis for predicting future performance.[6] Information about the due dates of receivables and payables is also useful in predicting future cash receipts and payments and, therefore, in evaluating solvency.

Since cash receipts and payments can never be predicted with certainty, solvency evaluation also involves evaluating a company's capacity to control or adjust cash receipts and payments to survive a period of financial adversity, a concept that has

---

[5] Liquidity is closely related to solvency but it is a narrower concept. The term "liquidity" is usually used to refer to a company's asset characteristics or to its asset and liability structure. As discussed later in this article, a company's ability to remain solvent depends on more than its present financial position as reflected in its balance sheet.

[6] For a specific proposal that enterprises publish statements of past cash receipts and payments, see Loyd C. Heath, "Let's Scrap the 'Funds' Statement," *The Journal of Accountancy* Oct. 78. pp. 94–103, and the monograph referred to in footnote 3.

been called financial flexibility.[7] Some of the things included under the concept of financial flexibility are a company's unused borrowing capacity and its ability to liquidate assets without adversely affecting the profitability of its remaining assets.

Information about a company's cash receipts and payments is also relevant in evaluating a company's profitability but in a different way. The timing of a company's receipts and payments is irrelevant in the measurement of income except insofar as timing affects the amounts at which assets and liabilities are recorded. The sale of an item for $10,000 cash and the sale of that item for a $10,000 note receivable due in five years with interest at 10 percent are regarded as equivalent transactions in evaluating profitability. They are not equivalent, however, in evaluating solvency because the timing of the cash receipts differs greatly in the two cases. The timing of future cash receipts and payments is the sine qua non of solvency evaluation and the heart of the distinction between issues of solvency reporting and profitability reporting.

## EVIDENCE OF NEGLECT

We have neglected solvency. Evidence of that neglect and bias toward the income measurement or profitability point of view can be found in both accounting practice and discussions of accounting problems.

### Misleading Balance Sheet Classification

One of the principal methods now used to report information for use in solvency evaluation is to classify assets and liabilities as current or noncurrent. That practice began shortly after the turn of the century in response to the needs, or at least the perceived needs, of commercial bankers. The bulletin that governs current-noncurrent classification today, chapter 3A of Accounting Research Bulletin no. 43, *Restatement and Revision of Accounting Research Bulletins*, first appeared in 1947 as ARB no. 30 and has remained virtually unchanged since that time. That bulletin is defective in many ways. It is based on an outmoded, simplistic, static model of solvency evaluation; it contains incomprehensible definitions of current assets and current liabilities together with lists of assets and liabilities that appear to contradict those definitions; it ignores basic principles of classification; and it not only fails to provide information useful in evaluating solvency but it also provides misleading information.[8] The fact that a bulletin that provides guidance on the major device in financial statements intended for solvency evaluation is so defective and has been allowed to remain in effect for over thirty years with no serious effort to change it is a prime example of how little attention has been given to solvency issues by accounting policymakers.

### Misdirected "Funds" Statements

"Where got—where gone" statements, the forerunners of statements of changes in financial position (funds statements), were viewed as tools for use in solvency analysis. William Morse Cole, credited with being the father of funds statements, observed in 1915:

---

[7] The concept of financial flexibility is discussed more fully in chapter 2 of the monograph referred to in footnote 3.

[8] For a discussion of these points, see chapter 4 of the monograph referred to in footnote 3.

"It is obvious that an important result of constructing such a table ... is the possibility of seeing from it at a glance the changes in solvency."[9]

During the 1920s when H. A. Finney popularized funds statements that explained changes in working capital, providing information for use in solvency evaluation was still the principal objective of those statements. Working capital was considered to be *the* measure of a company's debt-paying ability, and the funds statement was viewed as a way of explaining changes in that measure.

In spite of the fact that financial statement users have shifted their emphasis from working capital analysis to analysis of a company's cash receipts and payments, nearly all funds statements found in practice today are still based on the outmoded and useless concept of working capital.

To make matters even worse, beginning with APB Opinion no 3, *The Statement of Source and Application of Funds*, in 1964, companies were required to report "significant" financing and investing activities that did not affect working capital as if they did, so that even changes in working capital are not now reported in an understandable way. Duff and Phelps, Inc., an investment research firm, describes the current form of funds statement as "not much more than a miscellaneous collection of plus and minus changes in balance sheet items" and observes that "the predominant emphasis on working capital serves little purpose since working capital is not an important analytical figure."[10] Earl A. Spiller and Robert L. Virgil note that, under APB Opinion no. 19, *Reporting Changes in Financial Position*, "as long as certain types of transactions are disclosed in the required way, apparently any, all, or no underlying concept of funds is appropriate."[11]

The important point is that the original objective of funds statements—that of providing information for solvency analysis by explaining changes in some measure of debt-paying ability—has been lost. Funds statements are now viewed as the residual or "third" financial statement whose function is to report any "significant" information not reported elsewhere.[12]

### Rejection of Users' Demands

Some of the strongest evidence of pro-income measurement, anti-solvency bias appears in the accounting profession's response to suggestions by financial statement users that statements of cash receipts and payments would be useful in solvency evaluation because income statements based on accrual accounting conceal the timing of cash movements. Those suggestions have often been interpreted as challenges to the supremacy of the income statement and contemptuously (perhaps fearfully) dismissed. For example, in 1961 J. S. Seidman, a prominent practitioner who was both president of the AICPA and a member of the Accounting Principles Board, stated:

---

[9] William Morse Cole, *Accounts: Their Construction and Interpretation*, rev. and enl. ed. (Boston, Mass.: Houghton Mifflin Co., 1915), p. 102.

[10] Duff and Phelps, Inc., *A Management Guide to Better Financial Reporting* (New York: Arthur Andersen & Co., 1976), pp. 81–82.

[11] Earl A. Spiller and Robert L. Virgil. "Effectiveness of APB Opinion No. 19 in Improving Funds Reporting," *Journal of Accounting Research*, Spring 1974, p. 115.

[12] For suggestions on how to improve disclosure of some of the information now reported in funds statements, see the Heath article referred to in footnote 6.

"... instead of studying various ways and terminology for presenting cash flow statements, I think the profession is called upon to report to companies, to analysts, to stockholders, and the exchanges that cash flow figures are dangerous and misleading and the profession will have no part of them."[13]

More recently, statements of cash receipts and payments were rejected by the Financial Accounting Standards Board in its exposure draft *Objectives of Financial Reporting and Elements of Financial Statements of Business Enterprises*. The board explained in paragraphs 33 and 34:

"Financial statements that show only cash receipts and payments during a short period, such as a year, [cannot] adequately indicate whether or not an enterprise's performance is successful.

"Information about enterprise earnings (often called net income or net profit) and its components measured by accrual accounting generally provides a better measure of enterprise performance than information about current cash receipts and payments. That is, financial information provided by accounting that recognizes the financial effects of transactions and other events when they occur rather than only when cash is received or paid is usually considered a better basis than cash receipts and payments for estimating an enterprise's present and continuing ability to bring in the cash it needs."[14]

Ruling out statements of cash receipts and payments on the grounds that they cannot "adequately indicate whether or not an enterprise's performance is successful" indicates the board considered only one aspect of a company's performance to be relevant in measuring success, that is, its earnings performance. Apparently the board did not consider a company's success in generating cash and paying off its liabilities to be part of its "performance." Obtaining cash needed to survive and obtaining increased wealth are both necessary parts of an enterprise's performance. Assuring survival and prospering require different kinds of achievement, not simply different amounts of achievement.[15]

The board's argument that enterprise earnings are a "better" indicator of cash-generating ability casts income statements and statements of cash receipts and payments as competing methods of disclosure although they are not. Income statements report the effects of a company's operations on its long-run cash-generating ability; the question of when cash has been or will be received or paid is ignored except as it affects amounts at which receivables and payables are recorded. Statements of cash receipts and payments, on the other hand, report the effects of operations on cash movements during the year; when those movements have affected or will affect income is ignored. Thus, income statements and statements of cash received and payments are complementary, not competing forms of disclosure. They report different things for different purposes. The board's rejection of statements of receipts and payments at the objectives level based on the argument that income statements are "better" indicators of cash-generating ability than cash flow statements indicates an insensitivity to the timing of cash movements and, therefore, an insensitivity to solvency issues.

---

[13] J. S. Seidman, *Journal of Accountancy*, June 61, p. 31.

[14] FASB, *Objectives of Financial Reporting and Elements of Financial Statements of Business Enterprises* (Stamford, Conn.: FASB, 1977).

[15] For a discussion of this point, see Paul Rosenfield, "Current Replacement Value Accounting—A Dead End," *Journal of Accountancy*, Sept. 75, p. 72.

### Confusion Between Income Effects and
### Cash Effects of Operations

Undoubtedly one of the reasons that users' demands for statements of cash receipts and payments have not received more serious consideration is that income measurement so dominates the thinking of many accountants that they do not even distinguish between a company's income and the cash it has generated through operations; they speak of income as if it were synonymous with cash. Thus, they often refer to the retirement of debt and the purchase of plant and equipment "out of profits" when they really mean out of cash generated by operations, and they refer to the income statement as *the* statement of operations even though it shows only one effect of operations. Other effects of operations such as those on cash, on plant and equipment or on capital structure are not, of course, reported in that statement. In fact, before APB Opinion no. 19 became effective in 1971, CPAs routinely stated in their standard reports that a company's financial statements "present fairly ... the results of its operations" even though only the income effects of operations were reported; no statement was required that even purported to report the effects of operations other than the income effects.

Further evidence of the confusion between the income effects and other effects of operating activities can be found in the common yet confusing and misleading practice of showing income as a "source" of working capital or "funds" on statements of changes in financial position even though this "attempt to tie in these statements with profit and loss misses the major point that these statements are neither segments nor elaborations of income-measuring data, but instead are reports on changes that have occurred in other directions."[16] If accountants are going to provide information useful in solvency evaluation, they must first recognize that net income is not the only effect of operations and that other effects, particularly the cash effect, may be as important as net income.

### Effects of Inflation on Solvency

A period of rising prices creates a cash problem and therefore a solvency problem for many companies, because increased amounts of cash are needed to replace higher priced assets. To meet that need, either cash receipts and payments from operations have to be adjusted or additional outside financing must be obtained. Information useful in evaluating the magnitude of a company's need for additional cash to replace higher priced assets is relevant for evaluating solvency under those conditions. Statements of cash receipts and payments, particularly if they are available for several years in which there have been different rates of inflation, and disclosure of the replacement costs of assets held are two types of information that would be useful in estimating a company's need for additional cash to replace assets.

The problem of financial reporting during a period of rising prices has usually been considered only from the perspective of income measurement rather than from the perspective of solvency. The use of replacement prices has been supported on the grounds that it provides a superior measure of income, not that it provides information for estimating a company's future cash requirements. Even when the solvency dimension of the problem has been recognized, the solution often suggested

---

[16] Maurice Moonitz and Louis H. Jordan, *Accounting: An Analysis of Its Problems*, rev. ed.,
vol. 1 (New York: Holt, Rinehart and Winston, Inc. 1963), p. 103

has been to exclude the excess of the replacement value of an asset over its cost from income to obtain a measure known as "distributable" income—a solution that combines and confuses the income measurement and the solvency dimensions of the problem.[17]

## Economic v. Legal Entities

The distinctions between separate legal entities are ignored when consolidated financial statements are prepared; companies within the consolidated group are treated as one economic entity. Legal distinctions between entities, however, are often necessary to evaluate solvency because creditors' rights attach to the separate entities, not to the consolidated entity. From the solvency perspective, a consolidated balance sheet may be misleading because "the pressing liabilities may be in the parent company, but the liquid assets which give promise of meeting these liabilities may be in a subsidiary ... [where they are] unavailable to the parent...."[18]

Similarly, one subsidiary may have adequate cash available, but the "pressing liabilities" may be those of another subsidiary and legal restrictions may prevent transfer of assets from one subsidiary to another.

Recently the Advisory Committee on Corporate Disclosure to the Securities and Exchange Commission noted this point and made the following suggestion:

"Where there are material blockages to free movements of cash within a consolidated entity (e.g., caused by loan indentures, foreign currency restriction, or other legal constraints which limit a parent's or a subsidiary's movement of cash to another entity within the consolidated group), separate funds statements might be required for the entity in which the blockage had occurred in order to disclose adequately the significance of this blockage to the ability of the consolidated entity as a whole to meet its dividend, debt service, and other commitments from internally-generated cash."[19]

While separate statements of cash receipts and payments for some or all the companies comprising a consolidated entity probably would be useful in the situation described, they are not a complete solution to the problem described because balance sheets, too, can be misleading under those conditions. The point in raising this issue, however, is not to recommend a solution but to point out that consolidated financial statements raise an important issue in the evaluation of solvency that has received little or no attention from accountants.

Consolidated financial statements are usually justified with the argument that they are intended to portray the economic substance of parent-subsidiary relationships rather than their legal form. That argument is specious because a financial statement user concerned with solvency considerations often finds that the legal form

---

[17] For discussion of this point, see FASB discussion memorandum, *An Analysis of Issues Related to Conceptual Framework for Financial Accounting and Reporting: Elements of Financial Statements and Their Measurement* (Stamford, Conn.: FASB, 1976), ch. 6. See also Rosenfield, pp. 72–73.

[18] Ted J. Fiflis and Homer Kripke, *Accounting for Business Lawyers: Teaching Materials*, 2d ed. (St. Paul, Minn.: West Publishing Co., 1977), p. 604. For discussion of a recent example in which this issue is raised, see Abraham J. Briloff, "Whose 'Deep Pocket?'" *Barron's*, July 19, 1976, p. 5.

[19] *Report of the Advisory Committee on Corporate Disclosure to the Securities and Exchange Commission*, printed for the use of the House Committee on Interstate and Foreign Commerce, 95th Congress, 1st sess., Committee Print 95–29. November 3, 1977. p. 505n.

of a relationship *determines* its economic substance, and legal form therefore cannot be ignored. The use of consolidated financial statements, like the problem of financial reporting during periods of changing prices, needs to be looked at from the solvency point of view as well as from the income measurement point of view.

### Information on Funding Pension Obligations

A company's obligation to make periodic payments to fund its pension plan often represents a significant cash drain and may be an important consideration in evaluating its solvency. The amount of that obligation cannot be determined by the amount of pension expense reported on its income statement because funding requirements may differ from pension expense reporting requirements.

Current generally accepted accounting principles do not require a company to provide any information about its obligation to provide funding for its pension plan over the next several years. They do not even require it to disclose the amount of its contribution to its pension fund for past periods. APB Opinion no. 8, *Accounting for the Cost of Pension Plans*, is, as its title suggests, concerned almost exclusively with the *cost*, that is, the income effect, of pension plans. It ignores their impact on a company's solvency.

## LET'S NOT FORGET SOLVENCY

The solvency perspective that dominated U. S. financial reporting for the first three decades of this century was lost when accountants turned their attention to problems of income measurement during the 1930s. For the past 40 or 50 years nearly all financial reporting issues have been considered almost exclusively from the standpoint of income measurement. Reporting practices that have as their objective providing information useful in evaluating solvency, such as classification of assets and liabilities as current and noncurrent and providing a funds statement, are based on an old model of solvency evaluation that has since been rejected by financial statement users as naive or simplistic.

The solution to the problems discussed here does not lie simply in searching for a new basis of balance sheet classification, in replacing funds statements with statements of cash receipts and payments, in disclosing due dates of receivables and payables, in disclosing replacement costs of assets held, in presenting separate statements of companies comprising a consolidated entity or in disclosing more information about pension obligations—although all those steps would probably help. Those solutions deal only with the current symptoms.

The basic problem is that accountants have forgotten the solvency point of view—not just accounting policymakers but all accountants including management accountants, auditors and accounting educators. The only solution to that basic problem is for them to understand how today's users of financial statements look at solvency issues and to adopt that viewpoint when considering all matters of financial reporting. This does not, of course, mean neglecting the profitability point of view. But unless increased attention is given to providing information useful in solvency evaluation, the accounting profession is likely to find itself subject to increased criticism for failing to provide early warning signals of business failures, of which the Penn Central and W. T. Grant debacles are only two famous examples among thousands that occur every year.

# V-C 2  *Is Working Capital Really Working?*

LOYD C. HEATH

Accounting practices that have developed under conditions existing at one point in time may become so firmly embedded in our thought processes that they will come to be regarded as natural or inevitable. As a result, these practices may not be reexamined and reevaluated in the light of changed circumstances and conditions. The practice of classifying assets and liabilities as current or noncurrent to determine the difference between them—an amount commonly known as working capital—is one such practice. It began early in this century in response to the perceived needs of commercial bankers and today is a vestige of a bygone era. I believe this practice is misleading and should be abandoned.[1]

My reasons are set forth in this article, which explains why the present practice is not useful in evaluating a company's solvency and recommends an alternative that would be neither a radical departure from present disclosure practices nor costly to implement.

## MISCONCEPTIONS OF CLASSIFICATION

Many accountants view the practice of classifying assets and liabilities as current or noncurrent as one of identifying the "actual" or the "true" amount of a company's working capital. For example, Anson Herrick, who was a member of the committee on accounting procedure of a predecessor organization of the American Institute of CPAs at the time the current bulletin on working capital[2] was issued and who claimed

Author's note: I would like to thank Thomas W. McRae, CPA, and Paul Rosenfield, CPA, manager and director of the American Institute of CPAs accounting standards division, respectively, for their invaluable comments and suggestions during the preparation of this article.

[1] The analysis and recommendations that follow are based on my monograph, *Financial Reporting and the Evaluation of Solvency*, Accounting Research Monograph no. 3 (New York: AICPA, 1978).

[2] Chapter 3A, "Current Assets and Current Liabilities," Accounting Research Bulletin no. 43, *Restatement and Revision of Accounting Research Bulletins* (New York: American Institute of Accountants, 1953).

to be the person responsible for developing the bulletin's definitions of current assets and current liabilities,[3] later described the work of that committee as follows:

"As the bulletin . . . indicates, it was believed that the existing procedures for the determination of working capital were arbitrary, inconsistent, and frequently did not result in the development of a *true* amount of working capital and, accordingly, it would be desirable for procedures to be provided which would do so. There was no thought that the committee was doing anything other than developing a more logical concept of working capital which, because *more accurate*, would be more useful." [Emphasis added.][4]

Contrary to Herrick's assumption, current-noncurrent classification, like all classification, is not a search for the truth; it is a purposive human activity. How we classify things or whether we classify them at all depends on the objectives we wish to achieve by classification:

"What we call things and where we draw the line between one class of things and another depend upon the interests we have and the purposes of the classification.

"Classification is not a matter of identifying 'essences' as is widely believed. It is simply a reflection of social convenience and necessity — and different necessities are always producing different classifications."[5]

The terms current assets and current liabilities have no "true" meaning independent of the purposes to be served in defining them. They can be defined for financial reporting in many different ways. A search for the "true" definitions of current assets and current liabilities or definitions that identify the "essence," the "substance" or the "fundamental characteristic" of current assets, current liabilities or working capital can only result in confusion and, ultimately, in failure.

## PRESENT PRACTICE NOT USEFUL

The primary objective of classifying assets and liabilities as current or noncurrent is to provide information useful in evaluating a company's solvency. Chapter 3A, "Current Assets and Current Liabilities," of Accounting Research Bulletin no. 43, *Restatement and Revision of Accounting Research Bulletins*, begins with the statement "The working capital of a borrower has always been of prime interest to grantors of credit," and Leopold A. Bernstein noted that "the popularity of working capital as a measure of liquidity and of short-term financial health is so widespread that it hardly needs documentation."[6]

There are at least three ways in which the current-noncurrent classification might be useful in evaluating a company's solvency:

1.   As a means of disclosing important attributes of assets and liabilities.
2.   As a tool in predicting financial failure.
3.   As a convenience to users who wish to calculate ratios.

---

[3] Anson Herrick, "A Review of the Work of the Accounting Procedure Committee," JofA, Nov. 54, p. 627.

[4] Anson Herrick, "Comments by Anson Herrick," JofA, Nov. 60, p. 52.

[5] S. I. Hayakawa, *Language in Thought and Action*, 2d ed. (New York: Harcourt Brace Jovanovich, 1964), pp. 215 and 217.

[6] Leopold A. Bernstein, *Financial Statement Analysis Theory, Application and Interpretation*, rev. ed. (Homewood, Ill.: Richard D. Irwin, Inc., 1978), p. 447.

• *Failure to disclose attributes.* A prerequisite to the effective communication of attributes through classification is that all items classified the same way have some attribute in common. That attribute is the criterion used to partition the items into classes. A user of classified data then knows that, if an item is classified in a certain way, it possesses a certain attribute. Communication of attributes is one of the principal functions of nearly all forms of classification.

Present balance sheet classification has been described in accounting literature as "inconsistent," "illogical" and "irrational" because the items classified as current have no meaningful attribute in common. There is no identifiable attribute that all assets classified as current have that all assets classified as noncurrent do not have.

For example, Philip E. Fess said it was inconsistent to classify a three-year prepaid insurance premium as current while machinery with a three-year life is classified as noncurrent,[7] Arthur Andersen & Co. questioned the "logic" of classifying crude oil inventories in tanks as current while similar underground reserves are classified as noncurrent;[8] and Huizingh labeled "irrational" and "inconsistent" the practice of classifying as current the materials and supplies that will be used to maintain fixed assets while the fixed assets themselves are classified as noncurrent.[9] In all three cases the basic problem is that the assets classified as current and other assets classified as current have no common attribute that distinguishes them from assets—classified as noncurrent.

Because of these questionable asset classifications, describing an asset as current or as noncurrent communicates no useful information about it. Assets classified as current cannot be described as "those that will normally be converted into cash within a year" because many that will not be so converted are classified as current while others that will are classified as noncurrent; they cannot be described as assets "reasonably expected to be realized in cash or sold or consumed during the normal operating cycle" because many that will be so realized during the next operating cycle (whatever its length)—such as a portion of plant and equipment and wasting assets—are excluded; they cannot be described as those resources that will be used to pay liabilities classified as current because cash generated from the use of all assets is used to pay liabilities (both current and noncurrent).

The only attribute that all assets classified as current have in common is that they are the assets that, under present accepted practice, are classified as current—an attribute that has no informational content whatever to a user of financial statements concerned with evaluating the solvency of a business enterprise. This same criticism also applies to present practice in classifying liabilities; a current liability can only be described as a liability that is classified as current.

• *Misleading disclosure of attributes.* Many classification rules followed in practice not only fail to communicate information but they also mislead the user who believes that accountants classify assets and liabilities on the basis of one attribute when they actually use an entirely different criterion. For example, the user who believes that current assets are "cash and other assets that are reasonably expected to be realized

---

[7] Philip E. Fess, "The Working Capital Concept," *Accounting Review*, April 1966, p. 267.

[8] Arthur Andersen & Co., *Accounting and Reporting Problems of the Accounting Profession.* 4th ed. (Chicago, Ill.: Arthur Andersen & Co., 1973), pp. 169 and 173–74.

[9] William Huizingh, *Working Capital Classification* (Ann Arbor, Mich.: University of Michigan, 1967), p. 107.

in cash or sold or consumed during the normal operating cycle of the business or within one year if the operating cycle is shorter than one year"[10] is misled by the common practice of classifying a three-year prepaid insurance premium as a current asset even though the operating cycle of the insured is less than one year. The user is also misled by the classification of underground oil reserves that are "reasonably expected to be ... sold ... within one year" as noncurrent assets.

• *Poor prediction of financial failure.* One approach to evaluating the usefulness of financial information is to measure its ability to predict the outcome of future events.[11] This approach has been used by several researchers in recent years to evaluate the usefulness of financial ratios in predicting financial failure.[12] One of William H. Beaver's studies is of particular interest here because it was concerned with the relative predictive power of different types of ratios[13] rather than with the more general question of the predictive power of a group of ratios.

Beaver found ratios based on current-noncurrent classification to be mediocre predictors of financial failure. None of them predicted nearly as well in any of the five years before failure as the ratios of cash flow to total debt, net income to total assets or total debt to total assets. In four of the five years before failure, the current ratio did not even predict as well as the ratio of just plain cash to total assets.

• *Calculation convenience—a disservice to users.* It might be argued that accountants should continue to classify assets and liabilities as a convenience to users who wish to examine the current and other working capital ratios to spare them the need to do their own classification. That argument is not convincing, however, because many users ignore the accountant's classification and classify in their own ways. For example, after pointing out that the definition of current assets in chapter 3A of ARB no. 43 begins with the phrase "for accounting purposes," Roy A. Foulke comments: "This definition as indicated by its first three words is not for credit purposes, management purposes, or analysis purpose; it is solely 'for accounting purposes.'"[14]

He then lists those assets that he believes should be classified as current and adds: "In this volume, operating supplies and ordinary maintenance material and parts, receivables from officers and employees, no matter how they arose, and prepaid expenses are excluded from current assets."[15]

[10] Accounting Principles Board Statement no. 4, *Basic Concepts and Accounting Principles Underlying Financial Statements of Business Enterprises* (New York: AICPA, 1970), par. 198.

[11] For a discussion of this approach, see William H. Beaver, John W. Kennelly and William H. Voss, "Predictive Ability as a Criterion for the Evaluation of Accounting Data," *Accounting Review*, October 1968, pp. 675–83.

[12] For discussion and citations of these studies, see Baruch Lev, *Financial Statement Analysis: A New Approach* (Englewood Cliffs, N.J.: Prentice-Hall, Inc., 1974), ch. 9.

[13] William H. Beaver, "Alternative Accounting Measures as Predictors of Failure," *Accounting Review*, January 1968, pp. 113–22.

[14] Roy A. Foulke, *Practical Financial Statement Analysis*, 6th ed. (New York: McGraw-Hill, Inc. 1968), p. 71n. See also Morton Backer, *Financial Reporting for Security Investment and Credit Decisions*, NAA Research Studies in Management Reporting no. 3 (New York: National Association of Accountants, 1970, pp. 47–48.) Graham, Dodd and Cottle note: "From the analyst's viewpoint it is best to include in the current assets all cash items that are within the company's control, including those which it does not show as current but *could show* if it so elected." (Benjamin Graham, David L. Dodd and Sidney Cottle, *Security Analysis: Principles and Technique*, 4th ed. [New York: McGraw-Hill, Inc., 1962], p. 203.)

[15] Foulke, p. 72n.

## MODERN SOLVENCY EVALUATION

A simplistic solution to the problems of current-noncurrent classification, such as adopting a one-year classification rule, will not work because it deals with the symptoms and not with the cause of the problem. Current-noncurrent classification was originally adopted in the belief that it would provide information helpful to users who wanted to see how much protection they would have if the enterprise should become insolvent and be forced to liquidate. A two-to-one current ratio supposedly meant that, if current assets fell by 50 percent, current creditors would still come out whole. But the entire approach by financial statement users to the evaluation of solvency has changed since then.[16] Today, users of financial statements realize that they virtually never come out whole or anywhere near it after a bankruptcy. Their primary need is for information that helps them evaluate whether the enterprise will remain solvent. The current-noncurrent distinction is of little use for that. Modern solvency evaluation is based on users' estimates of the company's prospective cash receipts and payments and evaluation of its financial flexibility.[17]

There are two basic reasons why a simple current-noncurrent classification system is an ineffective way to communicate the information users need to estimate prospective cash receipts and payments and to evaluate financial flexibility. First, two classes are inadequate to disclose all the information that needs to be disclosed about some assets and liabilities. Receivables and payables, for example, must be broken down by maturity dates into more than two classes for users to be able to estimate a company's cash receipts and required payments. Second, the same classification criteria cannot be applied to all assets and liabilities. Inventories, for example, cannot be broken down on the same basis as receivables because it is not known when they will be sold. Classifying them as either current or noncurrent may provide a misleading indicator of prospective cash movements. An increasing current ratio may conceal slow collections and slow-moving inventories.

## RECOMMENDED ALTERNATIVE TO PRESENT PRACTICE

What is needed is a new approach to providing balance sheet information that is useful in modern solvency evaluation. I recommend the following alternative to the current-noncurrent classification:

1. Disclosure of supplemental information about the attributes of specific assets and liabilities.
2. Classification of liabilities on the basis of the different types of credit sources available to business enterprises.
3. Arranging assets in the conventional order now used but discontinuing the practice of classifying them as current or noncurrent.

• *Disclose supplemental information.* In addition to the information now disclosed in the notes to the financial statements, users concerned about evaluating a

---

[16] See chapter 2 of the monograph described in footnote 1.
[17] The term "financial flexibility" refers to a company's capacity to control its cash receipts and payments to survive a period of financial adversity. The concept is discussed more fully in the monograph described in footnote 1.

company's solvency should have information about the amounts and timing of cash receipts and payments from receivables and payables. Such information would help them estimate a company's cash receipts and required cash payments. A lengthening of the age of a company's receivables, for example, may portend reduced cash receipts in the following period.

Disclosing the amounts and timing of receivables and payables cannot be accomplished by simply showing when the balance sheet amounts of those accounts are due. Many receivables and payables are carried at their present values rather than at the amounts of cash to be received or paid in future periods.[18] A company that issues $1 million of 10-year 10 percent bonds at par, for example, would show a $1 million liability on its balance sheet even though it is obligated to pay a total of $2 million—$100,000 per year for 10 years plus an additional $1 million at the end of the tenth year. The amounts and timing of cash flows from receivables and payables should be disclosed in a separate schedule rather than in the balance sheet itself.

• *Classify liabilities based on sources of credit.* Hunt, Williams and Donaldson distinguished between two basic sources of credit available to a company: spontaneous and negotiated.[19] They described spontaneous or self-generating sources as those that "grow out of normal patterns of profitable operation without especial effort or conscious decision on the part of owners or managers,"[20] such as normal trade credit, accrued expenses and accrued taxes. Negotiated sources are those requiring conscious effort or specific negotiation by owners or managers such as bank loans, sales of commercial paper, sales of bonds, installment purchases and financing leases.

The distinction between spontaneous and negotiated sources of credit is relevant to the evaluation of both a company's financial flexibility and its future case requirements. It is relevant to evaluating financial flexibility because different underlying considerations determine the amount of credit available from each of them. The amount available from spontaneous sources depends on considerations such as the volume of purchases of inventories and supplies, normal credit terms of a company's suppliers and conventional practices such as the frequency of salary and wage payments. Credit available from spontaneous sources tends to increase as sales rise and to fall as sales decline.

Credit available from negotiated sources, on the other hand, depends more on lenders' evaluations of a company's ability to repay a loan when it is due. The total amount of credit available to a company through spontaneous sources tends to be limited to a rather narrow range. It is inexpensive or even cost free up to a certain point; beyond that, it becomes very costly as cash discounts are lost, suppliers refuse to ship goods and so forth. The amount of credit available from negotiated sources

---

[18] See APB Opinion no. 21, *Interest on Receivables and Payables* (New York: AICPA, 1971).

[19] Pearson Hunt, Charles M. Williams and Gordon Donaldson, *Basic Business Finance*, rev. ed. (Homewood, Ill.: Richard D. Irwin, Inc., 1961), pp. 116 and 169. R. K. Mautz made a similar distinction in sources of financing. Referring to "primary financing interests" and "incidental financing interests," he argued that incidental financing interests including, for example, trade creditors and employees, "provide financing, but this is neither the primary intent of the particular interest nor the basic reason for the transaction." (R. K. Mautz, *An Accounting Technique for Reporting Financial Transactions*, Special Bulletin no. 7[Urbana, Ill.: University of Illinois Bureau of Economic and Business Research, 1951], pp. 21–22.)

[20] Hunt, Williams and Donaldson, p. 116.

varies widely, depending on creditors' evaluations of the overall credit worthiness of a company.

The distinction between spontaneous and negotiated sources of credit is also relevant in estimating a company's future cash requirements. Liabilities that arise from spontaneous sources tend to "roll over" more or less automatically; debts that are paid are more or less constantly being replaced by new debts. Consequently, it is not necessary to consider a company's spontaneous liabilities when estimating its forthcoming need for cash unless there is reason to expect that, because of a decline in sales or a change in business practices, the amount of those liabilities will change. Negotiated liabilities on the other hand, whether short term or long term, are expected to be paid off, and they must therefore be considered in estimating a company's cash needs. Some of them may be rolled over or refinanced, but that is different from the rolling over of spontaneous liabilities. It does not occur automatically in the normal course of purchasing goods and paying wages and taxes but requires arm's-length negotiation with a creditor who will once again evaluate the company's overall credit worthiness.

• *Keep asset order without classification.* For most industries other than regulated utilities, assets are presented in the order of cash, marketable securities, trade receivables, inventories and so forth. That order has no particular significance,[21] but both accountants and financial statement users are familiar with it. Assets should continue to be arranged in the conventional order because changing it would confuse users in much the same way that changing the order of the keys on a typewriter would confuse typists.

## ILLUSTRATION AND DISCUSSION OF RECOMMENDED CHANGES

The balance sheet in exhibit 1, page 60, and the supporting schedule of receivables and financing liabilities in exhibit 2, this page, for Example, Inc., illustrate the recommended balance sheet format and the recommended types of additional disclosures. Liabilities are classified as operating, tax and financing. Operating and tax liabilities are provided from spontaneous sources of credit; financing liabilities are provided from negotiated sources. The term "financing liabilities" is used rather than negotiated liabilities because it is more likely to be readily understood.

Information on when receivables and payables are due is included in the maturity schedule (exhibit 2). The total amounts to be received or paid differ from the related balance sheet figures by amounts that represent interest. The amount of overdue receivables is identified because it provides an objective indication of the quality of a company's receivables.

For many years there has been a clear trend toward disclosing more information about the attributes of specific assets and liabilities in the notes to the financial

[21] Trying to list assets in order of liquidity is a waste of time because the term "liquidity" has no agreed-upon meaning. Some accountants view it in terms of the number of steps an asset must pass through before it is converted into cash (receivables are more liquid than inventory because inventory must be converted into receivables before being converted into cash); some view it in terms of the amount of time that will normally pass before an asset is converted into cash (some inventory will be converted into cash before some receivables): and still others view it in terms of how quickly an asset can be converted into cash (some plant and equipment *can* be converted into cash faster than some inventory).

# EXHIBIT 1

## Example, Inc., Balance Sheet

|  | 12/31/79 | 12/31/78 |
|---|---|---|
| *Assets* | | |
| Cash | $ 21,968 | $ 15,666 |
| Marketable securities (current market value $23,608 and $29,198) | 18,459 | 21,521 |
| Trade accounts and notes receivable | 70,143 | 66,276 |
| Allowance for uncollectibles | (973) | (906) |
| Net receivables | 69,170 | 65,370 |
| Inventories | | |
| Finished goods | 73,610 | 62,102 |
| Goods in process | 22,109 | 16,998 |
| Raw materials and supplies | 13,167 | 10,605 |
| Total inventories | 108,886 | 89,705 |
| Prepayments | 8,164 | 5,222 |
| Properties | | |
| Land, buildings and equipment at cost | 349,615 | 319,101 |
| Accumulated depreciation | (136,171) | (125,591) |
| Net properties | 213,444 | 193,510 |
| Other assets | 1,609 | 3,873 |
| Total assets | $441,700 | $394,867 |
| *Liabilities and Stockholders' Equity* | | |
| Operating liabilities (due within one year) | | |
| Trade accounts and notes payable | $ 47,662 | $ 49,518 |
| Accrued expenses | 29,601 | 26,401 |
| Total | 77,263 | 75,919 |
| Tax liabilities | | |
| On reported taxable income | 13,061 | 11,996 |
| Withheld from employees and miscellaneous | 3,906 | 4,111 |
| Deferred as a result of timing differences in depreciation | 39,664 | 37,605 |
| Total tax liabilities | 56,631 | 53,712 |
| Financing liabilities | | |
| Notes payable to banks | 48,605 | 15,513 |
| Mortgage payable | 26,000 | 28,000 |
| 7% debentures payable, due December 31, 1995 | 25,000 | 25,000 |
| Total financing liabilities | 99,605 | 68,513 |
| Total liabilities | 233,499 | 198,144 |
| Stockholders' equity | | |
| 5% convertible preferred stock $100 par value | 40,000 | 70,000 |
| Common stock $10 par value | 90,000 | 70,000 |
| Capital in excess of par | 41,609 | 24,114 |
| Retained earnings | 36,592 | 32,609 |
| Total stockholders' equity | 208,201 | 196,723 |
| Total liabilities and stockholders' equity | $441,700 | $394,867 |

---

**EXHIBIT 2**

**Example, Inc., Maturity Schedule of Receivables and Financing Liabilities**

|  | *12/31/79* | *12/31/78* |
|---|---|---|
| *Trade Accounts and Notes Receivable* | | |
| Overdue | $ 1,398 | $ 1,206 |
| Due within one year | 37,111 | 36,692 |
| Due one-two years | 24,906 | 21,605 |
| Due two-three years | 9,205 | 10,331 |
| Due after three years | 4,915 | 4,034 |
| Total | 77,535 | 73,868 |
| Less: amount representing interest | 7,392 | 7,592 |
| Per balance sheet | $ 70,143 | $ 66,276 |
| *Financing Liabilities* | | |
| Due within one year | $ 28,435 | $ 23,054 |
| Due one-two years | 15,670 | 5,830 |
| Due two-three years | 15,510 | 5,670 |
| Due three-four years | 15,350 | 5,510 |
| Due four-five years | 15,190 | 5,350 |
| Due five-ten years | 23,550 | 24,350 |
| Due ten-fifteen years | 17,710 | 20,350 |
| Due after fifteen years | 33,750 | 35,500 |
| Total | 165,165 | 125,614 |
| Less: amount representing interest | 65,560 | 57,101 |
| Per balance sheet | $ 99,605 | $ 68,513 |

---

statements. Much of that information is clearly relevant in evaluating a company's financial flexibility and in estimating its future cash receipts and payments. Disclosure of credit commitments, compensating balance requirements and minimum amounts due under long-term leases are examples. Other disclosures will undoubtedly be proposed in the future. When they are, the guiding consideration should be whether the proposed disclosure can reasonably be expected to be useful in evaluating a company's financial flexibility and in estimating its future cash receipts and payments.

## A MODEST PROPOSAL

This is a proposal that additional information about the attributes of individual assets and liabilities be disclosed as an alternative to classifying assets and liabilities as current or noncurrent. It is a modest proposal. It would not require a radical departure from present disclosure practices nor be costly to implement. The rationale underlying it is that the recommended approach would provide more useful information for evaluating a company's solvency than present practice based on current-noncurrent classification. That practice is directed toward the calculation of the current ratio and other measures based on the concept of working capital as a measure of solvency; the recommended alternative emphasizes the disclosure of additional data that can be combined and used in various ways related to the solvency dimension of financial statement analysis.

# V-C 3 *Working Capital as a Tool*

LEOPOLD A. BERNSTEIN, KENNETH S. MOST, *and* MAX BLOCK *comment on the article, "Is Working Capital Really Working?" The reply by author* Loyd C. Heath, *follows.*

## BERNSTEIN'S COMMENTS

In his article, Professor Heath argues for the abolition of the practice of classifying assets and liabilities as current and noncurrent and for substituting additional disclosure about the attributes of certain assets and liabilities for it. I believe that the working capital concept is useful and that recognition of the fact that the concept is subject to many weaknesses as an analytical tool for the evaluation of short-term solvency does not validly lead to the conclusion that it should be abolished.

The widespread popularity of working capital measures as analytical tools in the evaluation of short-term liquidity is unquestionably due more to ease and simplicity of use than to the validity of conclusions that can be drawn from their simple application. My own analysis[1] of the analytical usefulness of these tools has led to the conclusion that if we define liquidity as the ability to balance required cash outflows with adequate inflows, including an allowance for the unexpected interruptions of inflows or increases in outflows, then these working capital tools are not fully up to the task. This is so particularly because there is nothing in the relative size of current assets to current liabilities (i.e., the current ratio) that measures and predicts future fund flows and measures the adequacy of future inflows in relation to outflows.

Such measures are critical to an assessment of short-term liquidity. However, the current ratio is not fully up to this task because it is a static or "stock" concept of what resources are available at a given moment to meet the obligations at that moment. Moreover, working capital, i.e., the existing net reservoir of funds (as defined), does not have a logical or causative relationship to the future funds which will flow through it. These future flows are, of course, the focus of our greatest interest in the assessment of short-term liquidity. And yet, these flows depend importantly on elements not included in the current ratio, such as sales, profits and changes in business conditions.

Leopold A. Bernstein, S. Most, and Max Block, "Working Capital as a Tool," *Journal of Accountancy*, December 1981, pp. 82–94. Copyright © 1981 by the American Institute of Certified Public Accountants, Inc. Opinions expressed in the *Journal of Accountancy* are those of editors and contributors. Publication in the *Journal of Accountancy* does not constitute endorsement by the AICPA or its committees.

[1] Leopold A. Bernstein, *Financial Statement Analysis: Theory, Application and Interpretation*, rev. ed. (Homewood, Ill.: Richard J. Irwin, Inc., 1978), pp. 442–470.

It is those shortcomings that I view as the primary limitations of the working capital concept, rather than such technical deficiencies noted by Heath as the fact that prepaid insurance (which is mostly not of a material amount) is misclassified as current because it includes three years of premiums or that the components of some noncurrent assets could logically or definitionally be shifted to the current section.

Sophisticated analyses of solvency do, in fact, focus on cash flows. Indeed, in training seminars for bank loan officers, I put relatively minor emphasis on the static current ratio measure because we have developed and can use more relevant and powerful tools of analysis. Thus, the analysis of cash flow from operations and of other sources of cash as a means of predicting future flows is accorded much greater importance and emphasis.

Heath's proposals for supplementary disclosures, such as maturity schedules of receivables and liabilities, are significant and welcome because they would help sophisticated analysts compile more accurate cash flow projections. But these proposals cannot, as can be seen from the following discussion, represent substitute information for those who, for whatever reasons, rely on such measures of solvency as working capital or the current ratio.

## THE "CURRENT RATIO" TOOL

The major usefulness of the current ratio lies in its use as a rough and ready tool by those who cannot or will not perform the more rigorous and more demanding types of analyses mentioned above.

Thus, the popularity of this measure is significantly due to the fact that it serves many as a rough index or indicator of liquidity. The demand for readily available and easily usable and understandable indexes of conditions or performance has always been great. Witness, for example, the demand for and the widespread use of the earnings per share (EPS) statistic. Most sophisticated analysts know that the EPS number for any given year is not a valid index of an enterprise's earning power and that only a complete analysis of a series of income statements covering a number of years can yield a valid approximation of such a measure. And yet the accounting profession would not now suggest that we deny the public the EPS statistic simply because its uninformed use may lead to invalid conclusions and bad decisions. The competent use of any financial measure or decision tool is ultimately the responsibility of the user.

For the same reasons, the users of financial statements should not be denied the accountant's informed and disciplined classification of current assets and current liabilities. What can be said about the misuse of this classification can generally be said about the interpretation of any other parts of the financial statements, i.e., that careless or uninformed use may be dangerous to the user's decision-making process and financial health.

While not useful in predicting cash inflows and outflows, the working capital concept and its derivative, the current ratio, have some valid uses:

1.   It measures the degree to which current liabilities are covered by current assets at a given time. The higher the amount of current assets in relation to current liabilities, the more assurance exists that such liabilities can be paid out of such assets. Supplementary measures will help here. Thus, turnover

ratios of receivables and inventories will shed light on the quality (realizability) and the liquidity of these important components of working capital. For we know that not all inventories are created equal nor are booked receivables all of equal collectibility.

    One could argue that in a going concern, current assets (other than cash) are of a revolving nature, that is, for example, collected receivables can be replaced with newly created ones and, thus, not be available for payment of current obligations. But bankers and other creditors have the right to view loan collection as a condition of last resort and, thus, think in terms of liquidation rather than going concern. There seems little doubt that the original users of this ratio, many decades ago, had a salvaging of assets in mind as a last resort.

2.    The excess of current assets over current liabilities can be viewed as a buffer against losses which may have to be incurred in the forced liquidation of current assets other than cash. The more substantial such a buffer, the more secure the short-term creditors are justified in feeling. Thus, the current ratio is also a measure of the margin of safety available to cover any possible shrinkage in the value of current assets.

3.    Working capital provides a measure of the reserve of liquid funds (as defined) in excess of current obligations which stands available as a margin of safety against uncertainty and the random shocks to which the flow of funds in an enterprise is subject. Random shocks, such as strikes, extraordinary losses and other uncertainties, can unexpectedly and temporarily stop or reduce the inflow of funds. Under such emergency conditions, receivables and inventories can be used as collateral for loans, or the collection of receivables and the realization of inventories can be speeded up and the payment of trade payables deferred.

4.    There is even value to a behavioral assessment of working capital presentation. The astute analyst who perceives management's desire to stretch the current-noncurrent distinction to the limit in order to present a more favorable financial position than is really warranted will be alerted to the fact that all may not be well with the enterprise's short-term financial condition.

    The working capital figure, which is based on the accountant's balance sheet classification of current assets and current liabilities, and its derivative ratios have uses beyond those mentioned above; a few more examples should suffice. Working capital can be related to sales in order to measure the net investment an enterprise is making in receivables and inventories (net of trade credit) in the pursuit of its profit-directed activities. Such relationships are especially meaningful if they are compared to those prevailing in similar enterprises in the same industry. Working capital or current ratio maintenance requirements in loan agreements or bond indentures represent a convenient and shorthand way of specifying the fiscal discipline which the lender expects the borrower to adhere to.

    Interested governmental agencies not only compile aggregate working capital figures for industries as a way of tracing changes in liquidity over time but they also analyze the significance of these changes with a variety of objectives in mind, including their use as aids to making economic policy decisions. Admittedly, the accuracy of these measures cannot rise above that of the working capital concept itself. But such measures, limited as they are, are far better than none.

Last, but certainly not least, in judging the usefulness of the working capital concept, we have only to observe how widespread the use of the working capital measures is in actual practice. Almost all credit reporting, credit rating, financial reporting and evaluation services use and report them in one way or another. Sophisticated cash flow analysis? Certainly not. But it is a rough substitute where otherwise there would be none. The use of this measure has spawned improvements as well—through the analytical use of related ratios such as the acid test or quick ratio, the ratio of cash flow to current and long-term debt and various turnover measures that enhance its meaning and aid in interpretation.

This widespread use by such a wide variety of reporting services and decision makers seems inconsistent with the assumption that the market has been fooled and has for decades clung to a worthless concept by sheer adherence to tradition. Let us not so quickly assume that the Robert Morris Associates, the Dunn & Bradstreets, the Moodys, the Standard and Poors or the Value Lines have, by their use of the working capital concept, engaged in a meaningless ritual.

## KEEP THE WORKING CAPITAL CONCEPT

Numerous writers, including this one, have pointed out the weaknesses of classification as well as the conceptual limitations to which the published working capital figures are subject. There is great scope to a reexamination of the definition of current assets and current liabilities on which so many rely. After 27 years of use, many established assumptions and definitions deserve reexamination, and current efforts in this direction are welcome. Should certain "current portions" of fixed assets be considered in the same way that the current portion of liabilities is now considered? Or, for example, is it right for a very slow turnover tobacco inventory to be considered current while the debt incurred to finance it is considered long term?

The continued usefulness of the working capital concept suggests that the accounting profession has an obligation to users to improve it and tighten up the definition of what is current and what is not. But, by all means, let us not abandon it.

## *MOST'S COMMENTS*

Heath claims that the working capital concept began early in this century in response to the perceived needs of commercial bankers. The concept is older than that. It was well known to nineteenth century economists under the name "circulating capital." Capital is invested in two distinct forms—fixed assets and working capital. That distinction is important.

Contrary to Heath's assertion, the prime objective of classifying assets and liabilities as current and noncurrent is to determine working capital—that is, that part of a company's capital that is invested in materials, customer credit and operating costs. It is not primarily to measure liquidity and short-term financial health.

The maintenance of working capital is of great social importance. For, if industry cannot maintain its working capital, employment will decline. This has been happening in the U.K. for the past two decades and could easily happen in the U.S. if inflation continues to increase the real burden of taxation on business. It is not a valid criticism of the working capital concept to point to the problems of classifying assets and liabilities as current or noncurrent. Many of the concepts on which we base our lives are incapable of precise definition. We mostly approximate.

The conventional rule that current assets are those reasonably expected to be realized in cash or sold or consumed during the normal operating cycle of the business is only indicative and not conclusive. Heath is incorrect when he states that the only attribute current assets and liabilities have is that they are classified as such. Accountants, after all, are subject to the dictates of the market and would soon be out of work if they produced nonsense regularly. The characteristic feature of a current asset is that it is an investment in activity, not capacity. It is money used for operations, not for equipment. Similarly, the characteristic feature of a current liability is that its payment is a necessary condition of continuing operation. Thus, the current portion of a long-term liability is properly classified as a negative component of working capital, whereas no part of the investment in equipment (such as next year's depreciation) is properly classified as a current asset.

As for the objective of improving balance sheet classification, I agree that it is desirable. My aim is to sharpen the current-noncurrent dichotomy, not to abolish it. I would like to see the basic equation stated as fixed assets + working capital = owner's equity + loan capital.

I prefer all long-term (capacity) assets included in fixed assets, intangibles and investments being important subcategories. Some European accountants are already moving in this direction. I would like to see any assets not required for operations, no matter how liquid, excluded from current assets. And I look forward to the day when the cash balance will cease to be the most prominently displayed balance sheet item.

I would like to see proposals for improving financial statements meet the test of better disclosure of the facts about business finance, investment and operations. They are what accounting is about.

## BLOCK'S COMMENTS

Heath refers to the working capital ratio as a response to the perceived needs of commercial bankers early in the century, which is today only a vestige of a bygone era. Has the author consulted bankers who make short-term seasonal loans year in and year out to regular clients? Have they stopped using the ratio? With whatever deficiencies it may have, I believe it is still widely used. Credit grantors know the problems in using the ratio and they make their own recomputations, as they do with all items in the balance sheets they review.

The details in the article's second exhibit are no innovative contribution. Well-prepared annual reports contain such supporting data. The unclassified balance is offered as a solution, yet short-term credit grantors are concerned mainly with a company's ability to repay its loan. And to make this determination they concentrate on those segments of the balance sheet that are directly relevant to the short term.

The unclassified balance sheet imposes on the user the task of estimating "the company's prospective receipts and payments and evaluations of its financial flexibility." Many readers might have welcomed an added exhibit demonstrating how the recommended information could be developed from exhibits 1 and 2.

Why should users have to make this determination? The statement preparer should do this, as he has far more information about what lies ahead for the company than does the user. Some companies are already providing earnings forecasts with their financial statements.

Statement analysts evaluate a company's solvency not only with a working capital ratio but also with a "quickie" (or other term) ratio which excludes inventory. The ratio is a convenient rule of thumb for many users. Consistency gives to working capital, with its frailties, a solvency trend which is a valuable tool. Perhaps the present classifications of current assets and liabilities can be improved.

### HEATH'S REPLY

To restate and summarize my position, I believe we should disclose additional information about assets and liabilities, but stop classifying them as current or noncurrent for two reasons:

1.  Present classification practice communicates no useful information about assets and liabilities. Classifying a trade receivable as current does not tell users when it is due, and that is what they need to know. Classifying inventory as current tells users nothing because all inventory is classified as current and so forth.
2.  Current-noncurrent classification is misleading. If, for example, materials and supplies used to maintain plant and equipment are classified as current, some users believe those supplies will result in cash inflows in the near future, and that is not true. Similarly, if deferred taxes that result from use of the installment method are classified as current, that leads some users to believe those taxes will have to be paid within a year, and that is also not true.

### USED VS. USEFUL

One of the principal arguments used by all three respondents is that working capital figures are widely reported and widely used. That should not be determinative in deciding whether accountants should continue to label certain assets and liabilities as current. People use what is given to them, and that use does not prove that no changes are needed.

The question that needs to be addressed is whether there is a better way of disclosing information that is useful in assessing a company's future cash flows, not whether working capital measures are now used. I believe the alternative I proposed would provide all the information now disclosed, it would provide additional useful information and it would report that information clearly. Furthermore, it does not contain the misleading inferences now found in practice. If readers disagree with my proposal, they should address my assumptions and arguments. The simple assertion that working capital figures are now used does not address the question—unless, of course, one believes that every accounting practice, once begun, should be retained as long as it is used by someone.

### IRRELEVANT ARGUMENTS

Many of the arguments used by all three respondents are not relevant to my recommendations. For example, Block's comment that short-term creditors "concentrate on those segments of the balance sheet that are directly relevant to the short term" is irrelevant because they could also do that if my proposal was adopted. In fact, their task would be easier. They would have all the information they now have and more. His comment that some analysts supplement the current ratio with the quick ratio only serves to strengthen my argument that we should discontinue current-noncurrent classification. If users can calculate quick ratios when accountants do not designate which assets they believe are quick, they could also calculate current ratios if accountants were to stop designating which assets they believe are current.

Bernstein's argument that "creditors have the right to ... think in terms of liquidation rather than going concern" is obviously true, but my approach would not deprive them of that right or even make it more difficult for them to think in those terms. If, however, they do, they need to know the liquidating values of assets, not whether they are classified as current. His argument that the "excess of current assets over current liabilities [is] a buffer against [possible] losses ... in ... forced liquidation" is irrelevant for the same reason. In liquidation all liabilities must be paid with the proceeds of all assets; whether they are labeled current or noncurrent doesn't matter.

Bernstein is correct when he points out that, during a period of financial adversity, a company can reduce its investment in receivables and inventories or use them as collateral. That argument, however, is irrelevant because a company can also use its noncurrent assets that way. It can sell and lease back its plant and equipment or liquidate its noncurrent investment in an affiliate. More important, however, is that even if it were true that only current assets could be used in the way he suggests, Bernstein's argument is still not relevant because I have not proposed that the amounts of those assets not be disclosed. The question is whether they should be labeled as current, and labeling them that way reveals nothing about whether they could be sold or used as collateral.

Bernstein's argument that "working capital can be related to sales ... to measure the net investment an enterprise is making in receivables and inventories" is also irrelevant. If one wants to know how much has been invested in receivables and inventories during the year, changes in those accounts would provide that information. If one wants to relate receivables and inventories to sales, that, too, can be done without attaching a current label to those assets.

Undoubtedly, one of the most irrelevant arguments is Most's point that "the maintenance of working capital is of great social importance [because] if industry cannot maintain its working capital, employment will decline." That same dire result, however, would also issue from failure to maintain factories. The dire result, in other words, has nothing to do with the practice of identifying certain assets and liabilities as current. Most's further point that this "could easily happen in the U.S. if inflation continues to increase the real burden of taxation" indicates that his real concern is with taxes, not balance sheet classification.

## FURTHER COMMENTS ON MOST

Contrary to Most's claim, I did not say that the working capital concept "began early in this century"; it was the accounting practice of designating certain balance sheet items as current that began early in this century. As he indicates, the concept of working capital has its historical roots in the writings of Adam Smith, John Stuart Mill and other eighteenth and nineteenth century economists who distinguished between what they called fixed and circulating capital. The important point, however, is that Most accepts their distinction as appropriate for use in accounting today and I do not because their objectives were different; they were not concerned with providing information useful for investment and credit decisions. Most claims that determining working capital is itself an objective of classification but I do not accept that assertion.

## FURTHER COMMENTS ON BERNSTEIN

My article began with the observation that accounting practices that have developed under conditions existing at one point in time may become so firmly embedded in our thought processes that they will come to be regarded as natural or inevitable and will not be reexamined and reevaluated in the light of changed circumstances and conditions. I believe Bernstein regards working capital classification as natural or inevitable. He says he is willing to reexamine the definitions of current assets and liabilities, but he is not willing to consider the more fundamental question of whether the whole practice itself should be abandoned, even though that is where his reasoning leads. Thus, he acknowledges that "working capital tools are not fully up to the task [of short-term liquidity or solvency analysis]"—not because the definitions need to be refined but because "the focus of ... short-term liquidity" is future cash flows and future flows "depend importantly on elements not included in the current ratio." Also, when he trains bank loan officers, he puts primary emphasis on the analysis of future cash flows, undoubtedly because he considers that information rather than working capital measures relevant to the decisions those officers will have to make. Nevertheless, he still feels compelled to defend the practice of classifying certain assets and liabilities as current. Let us examine his arguments.

The argument that working capital and the current ratio measure the degree to which current liabilities are covered by current assets is based on an assumed but nonexistent relationship between sources and uses of cash. A company generates cash from the joint use of all of its assets, not just its current ones. It is as meaningless to ask whether a company's cash came from the use of its current or its noncurrent assets as it is to ask whether the output of a person was due to his heart, his liver or his lungs.

I doubt that Bernstein is serious when he argues that companies should be required to designate certain assets and liabilities as current so that analysts can catch them if they "stretch" the definitions. There must be a better argument for even as worthless a practice as current-noncurrent classification.

I agree with Bernstein that working capital measures are often used in the restrictive covenants of loan agreements for the reason he states—that is, because they are a "convenient and short-hand way" of dealing with the problem. But "convenient" ways of dealing with a problem are not necessarily effective. It is "convenient" to look for a lost set of keys in the light under a lamppost even though it is known they were lost in the dark far from the lamppost, but that approach is not likely to solve the problem. It is not effective. If accountants were to discontinue the practice of designating certain assets and liabilities as current, I am sure creditors would develop relevant and effective measures to use in specifying what Bernstein refers to as the fiscal discipline expected of borrowers.

Bernstein's final argument that working capital measures have "spawned improvements" such as "the ratio of cash flow to ... long-term debt" convinces me that he views working capital as natural or inevitable. Ratios of cash flow to various measures of debt would obviously be useful in solvency analysis but that is no argument for current-noncurrent classification. I have proposed a method of reporting that would focus attention on that type of information, but Bernstein rejects it, apparently because it does not have the current-noncurrent labels he is familiar with.

# V-D  Other Issues

## V-D 1  *The Value Added Statement in Britain*

MICHAEL F. MORLEY

Since 1975, a new form of accounting statement has been appearing in the corporate reports of some of the larger British companies. It is the Value Added (*VA*) Statement. Already approximately one quarter of the 100 largest companies are voluntarily including a VA Statement in their annual reports, and this proportion is still growing. Further growth seems inevitable, as the government has indicated that it intends to make all substantial British companies include a VA Statement in their annual reports [Department of Trade, 1977].

This development of the VA Statement is especially interesting, as it represents a new direction in which financial reporting, in theory and practice, can go. The main thrust of financial accounting development in recent decades has been in the area of *how* we measure income, especially in the face of changing prices. The question of *whose income we measure* has been largely ignored, though Hendriksen's text [1977] is an exception. We accountants ignore the question because we are aware of only one answer. When asked, "whose income?" many accountants reply that net income or profit is the reward of the proprietors, *i.e.*, the shareholders in the case of a company. Proponents of Value Added reply that there are advantages in defining "income" in such a way as to include the rewards of a much wider group than just the shareholders. One can include shareholders and all suppliers of long- and short-term loan capital, together with employees and the government. The "income" of this team is called Value Added, and equals net profit with tax, interest, and wages costs all added back.

The structure of double-entry means that there is another way of arriving at Value Added, which is by deducting from sales revenue the cost of all materials and services which were bought-in from outside suppliers. This will give the same figure for VA, because the reward of our wider team must equal gross team revenues (*i.e.*,

Michael F. Morley, "The Value Added Statement in Britain," *The Accounting Review*, July 1979, pp. 618–629. Reprinted with the permission of *The Accounting Review*.

sales) less amounts payable to persons outside the team (*i.e.*, bought-in costs). The relationship between VA and profit can be expressed algebraically. We start by defining the retained profit for a given fiscal year as what is left after all costs, dividends, and taxes have been deducted from sales revenue, thus:

$$R = S - B - Dep - W - I - Div - T \tag{1}$$

where $R$ is retained profit, $S$ is sales revenue, $B$ is the total of bought-in materials and services, $Dep$ is the annual depreciation charge, $W$ is the year's wage cost, $I$ is the interest payable for the year, $Div$ is the total of dividends payable for the year, and $T$ represents corporate taxes.

Re-arranging (1) we have:

$$S - B - Dep = W + I + Div + T + R \tag{2}$$

Each side of Equation (2) equals Value Added. As will be seen, there is controversy in theory and divergent practice regarding depreciation in VA Statements, so we call the above *Net* VA, to make clear that it refers to VA after deducting depreciation.

Many accountants would prefer to rearrange Equation (1) thus:

$$S - B = W + I + Div + T + Dep + R \tag{3}$$

Each side of Equation (3) then equals *Gross* Value Added, or Value Added before deducting depreciation.

Equations (2) and (3) follow the format of VA Statements prepared in practice. The left-hand side of each equation relates to the upper part of the VA Statement, where bought-in costs are deducted from sales revenue. Having arrived at the figure for the year's VA, the lower part of the VA Statement shows its division among team members, which is symbolically represented in the right-hand sides of Equations (2) and (3).

Table 1 shows the Value Added Statement included in the annual report of BOC International Ltd., (formerly British Oxygen) for 1977. BOC has chosen the Net VA form of presentation rather than Gross VA, and so its VA Statement illustrates Equation (2). It can be seen how the company deducts bought-in costs and depreciation from sales to arrive at VA for the year of £259.5 million. The investment income is then added (a complication which has been ignored in Equation 2), and the total available for sharing among team members is £263.7 million. The division of this among the various sub-groups in the team then follows. The heading "to partners in companies not wholly owned by the group" refers to dividends payable by BOC subsidiaries to minority shareholders in subsidiaries not wholly owned by the group. The amounts payable to each, team member sum to £238.9 million, leaving £24.8 million as the group's retentions.

It is interesting to consider why so many British companies are, like BOC, deciding to present a VA report. Although the VA Statement is a very recent development, the concept of VA is considerably older. It originated in the U.S. Treasury in the eighteenth century [Cox, 1978], and periodically accountants have discussed whether the concept should be incorporated into financial accounting practice (see Suojanen [1954], for example). However, the VA Statement has taken

**TABLE 1**

**BOC International Ltd. and Subsidiaries Value Added Statement Year to September 30, 1977**

|  | £ million |
|---|---|
| Sales | 670.6 |
| *Less* | |
| Bought in materials, services and depreciation | 411.1 |
| Value added | 259.5 |
| | |
| *Add* | |
| Investment income | 4.2 |
| Available for application | 263.7 |
| | |
| *Applied as follows:* | |
| To employees as pay and Group companies' contributions to pensions and state welfare schemes | 180.8 |
| To banks and other lenders as interest | 19.6 |
| To government as taxes on profits | 25.6 |
| To partners in companies not wholly owned by Group | 3.6 |
| To shareholders of BOC International | 9.3 |
| | 238.9 |
| | |
| Profits retained by ourselves and our partners for expansion | 24.8 |
| | 263.7 |

root only in Britain,[1] and that very recently, and two immediate factors can be suggested as causes. First, Britain introduced a Value Added Tax (VAT) in April, 1973. The administration of this point-of-sale tax does not require production of a VA Statement, and the Statement cannot be used for tax verification due to complicated rules on goods and services which are exempted or zero-rated. However, the tax has led to increased awareness in the business world of the meaning of VA. Second, the British Accounting Standards Committee, sponsored by the principal U.K. and Irish accounting bodies, published *The Corporate Report* [ASC, 1975], a discussion paper on the purposes of annual reports, and in it the authors suggested that such reports should include a VA Statement.

---

[1] A few companies in the Netherlands include VA information in their annual reports, but the disclosures often fall short of being a full VA Statement, and the method of arriving at VA is grossly non-standardized. The annual reports of the Dutch companies Akzo N.V. Internatio-Müller, N. V., and SHV Holding N. V. are especially interesting, giving an idea of the variety of VA reporting practice.

It is worth mentioning that a frequent synonym for VA is "wealth creation," and this may have encouraged many industrialists to link VA reports on wealth creation with remedial action to halt Britain's relative industrial decline.

## ADVANTAGES

The advantages claimed for the VA Statement are considerable. First, it is said that it improves the attitudes of employees toward their employing companies. This effect is alleged to occur because the VA Statement reflects a broader view of the company's objectives and responsibilities. Few workers are said to be enthusiastic about maximizing profit, which is somebody else's reward, and, therefore, a profit statement has little interest or motivational value for employees. However, a company's VA represents the wealth creation available for the company team, in which employees are seen as responsible participants. When fully informed about VA, they should be better motivated to work, be more cooperative and more identified with their company. This hoped-for behavioral change links with ideas on industrial democracy which are popular in some British political circles. (See, for example, the Bullock Report [1977].) Many companies include VA reports in their employee newspapers or other vehicles of communication with their staff, and so the inclusion of a VA Statement in the annual report is said to add credibility to the use of VA elsewhere.

This type of behavioral hypothesis is notoriously difficult to test, as it depends on the sincerity of management, who might merely be producing a VA Statement to follow the herd, with no intention of evolving a more "team-centered" approach to the work force.

A second advantage claimed for the VA Statement is that it makes it easier for the company to introduce a productivity bonus scheme for employees based on VA. A number of British companies, of which Imperial Chemical Industries Ltd. is the best known, have introduced such schemes to enhance productivity. The employees receive bonus payments and/or shares in the company according to a formula based on demonstrated improvements over time in the VA/payroll ratio. If a company wishes to install such a scheme, or wishes to keep open its options to do so, then including a VA Statement in its annual report will be advantageous because it will spread knowledge of and trust in VA. Suspicion of VA should be lessened if VA is reported to shareholders in the annual report as well as forming the basis for productivity schemes.

A third advantage claimed is that VA-based ratios (like the VA/payroll ratio mentioned above) are a useful diagnostic and predictive tool. In many British companies, employees receive 70 percent or thereabouts of VA. Trends in this ratio, comparisons with other companies, and international comparisons may all be useful. This is esepecially so if the ratio is based on inflation-adjusted VA data. To date, three British companies have presented VA Statements adjusted for inflation: one (Colt International Ltd.) used the single-index, or current purchasing power method, while two (Alcan Aluminium (U.K.) Ltd. and Bowater Corporation Ltd.) used the replacement cost or current cost method. The figures produced by Alcan were especially interesting. Table 2 shows how the payroll costs absorbed 66 percent of VA when measured according to historical cost conventions. However, when the costs of bought-in materials and services and also depreciation were adjusted to current costs, the ratio rose to 110 percent. Naturally, no business could long sustain a figure of over 100 percent for long. The jump from 66 percent to 110 percent is unusually large, but

**TABLE 2**

**Alcan Aluminium (U.K.) Ltd. and Subsidiaries Value Added Information Year to December 31, 1976***

|  | Current Cost £ millions | Historic Cost £ millions |
|---|---|---|
| Sales | 227.3 | 227.3 |
| Less bought-in costs | 175.1 | 162.0 |
| Gross Value Added | 52.2 | 65.3 |
| Depreciation | 17.3 | 6.7 |
| Net Value Added | 34.9 | 58.6 |
| Payroll costs | 38.7 | 38.7 |
| Payroll/VA ratio | 110% | 66% |

* Extracted from p. 16 of Annual Report, December 31, 1976.

one can see how this ratio draws attention to trends in labor costs and may be helpful in wage bargaining as a means of informing labor representatives. For example, the relationship between this ratio and the level of retained profit (hence investment and longer-term job security) is made clear in the VA Statement.

Another VA-based ratio which is popular is that of taxation to VA. The difficulty with this ratio is that there is a great lack of standardization in the classification of taxes in VA Statements. The recent annual reports of Esso Petroleum Company Ltd. illustrate this. In the 1976 annual report, the company's VA was £729 million, and central and local government took 74 percent of this in taxes. In the 1977 annual report, VA was down to £301 million, and the government took only 23 percent. This drastic change is surprising, until one reads the detail and sees that the company has changed its accounting policy for treating excise duty and Value Added Tax. In 1976, these were included in VA and in the government's share, but in 1977 they were excluded from both. In brief, Esso has partly fallen into line with prevailing practice in Britain, for most companies report only corporation tax under the government's share. Esso still shows taxes paid to local government and royalties paid to governments under the government's share, neither of which practices is widespread.

Provided taxes are classified consistently and uniformly, this ratio and trends therein are useful for inter-industry and international comparisons.

One other popular ratio is VA/Sales, which measures the degree of vertical integration of a group of companies, and also can be interpreted as an index of vulnerability to disruptive action affecting supplies of materials and services.

Before leaving the topic of VA-based ratios, it is worth mentioning how relevant they are to the testing of rival theories of Britain's relative industrial decline since the end of World War II. Such theories abound, and the VA Statement throws light on most of them. Is the root cause of the problem a disinclination to hard work? The ratios of VA per employee and VA to wages cost are relevant, especially when international comparisons are made. Has the government over-taxed British industry? Ratios of taxes to VA would throw light on this, especially if the ratios for different industries were compared with their growth rates. Is under-investment to blame, or insufficient research and development? Again, the proportions of VA being allocated to these activities will help assess the rival hypotheses.

A fourth advantage of the new Statement is that VA provides a very good measure of the size and importance of a company. To use sales figures as a basis for company rankings can cause distortion, because sales may be inflated by large bought-in expenses which are passed straight on to customers. Capital employed, which is also sometimes used for rankings, can likewise be misleading. For example, a capital-intensive company with few employees may appear to be more important than a labor-intensive company. In a key industry, VA does not have these disadvantages and is, therefore, superior to sales and to capital employed as a ranking basis.

A fifth advantage of the VA Statement is that it links a company's financial accounts to national income. With a number of qualifications, which will be listed later, it is true that a company's VA indicates the company's contribution to national income. Furthermore, the sum of the Values Added by each company will equal national income. VA reports, therefore, start off with an inheritance of credibility, for most users of accounting statements have at least a broad comprehension of, and trust in national income figures. Hence VA, by providing a link between financial statements and the economists' macroeconomic data, will assist the inter-professional exchanges of data and expertise. For example, the VA Statement is closely related to the economists' input/output analysis of inter-industry relationships. The Statement should, therefore, increase the possibility of companies using input/output methods to improve their internal decision making. Also there are possibilities for the national income data to be verified and eventually, perhaps, derived from the underlying VA Statements of individual companies, thereby enhancing the accuracy of macro-economic statistics. This would improve economic forecasts and hence make possible the more timely and accurate use of the instruments of economic policy.

The principal qualifications to the general rule that the sum of the Values Added by all companies equals the economist's national income figure are:

1. National income includes Value Added by government and by other public bodies. For example, the Value Added by defense expenditure is assumed to be equal to its cost.

2. The VA of a company may arise partly in foreign territories. Similarly, Value may be Added in the domestic country by a foreign concern.

3. Economic measures of national income concentrate on production rather than on sales. Differences arise, therefore, in the valuation of increases/decreases in inventories.

4. National income conventions involve several major simplifying assumptions which are not used by financial accountants. For example, the output of durable consumer goods is assumed to have been consumed in the year of manufacture. In effect, the economist depreciates a car by 100 percent in the first year, while the accountant would write off his company's fleet of vehicles at, say, 25 percent of cost in each year.

A final advantage claimed for the VA Statement is that it is built on the basic conceptual foundations which are currently accepted in balance sheets and earnings statements. Concepts such as going concern, matching, consistency, objectivity, and substance-over-form are all just as applicable to the VA Statement as to the earnings statement. Also, the alternative theories of income measurement (based on historical cost, replacement cost, realizable values, deprival values, *etc.*) can all be translated into terms of VA measurement. This point may be expressed in a different form by saying that the VA Statement is identical with a conventional earnings statement except for the matter of whose earnings are included: "earnings" refers to the return accruing to shareholders while VA refers to the return accruing to the whole team of providers of labor and of capital, plus the government.

Having reviewed the advantages which are claimed for the VA Statement, it is natural to consider whether there are any disadvantages in its inclusion in annual reports.

## DISADVANTAGES

The first disadvantage of the new Statement is that it implicitly treats a company as a team of cooperating groups, and this attitude may be grossly at variance with the facts. VA is said to be the reward which is earned by the joint and interdependent efforts of employees (who provide labor services), shareholders and lenders (who provide capital), and the government (which provides law and order, defense services, infrastructure, a legal framework for contract-enforcement, *etc.*) It is the government which is the least natural member of the alleged team. The government was not invited to join the team, it plays no part in team decision making, and its share of VA (*i.e.*, corporation tax) is proportional to profits rather than to VA. Another case where team membership seems to be strangely defined is where a supplier of bought-in materials is a specialist supplier to a sole customer. This supplier would be excluded from the team even though he had no other outlet for his production. We have already mentioned the British company BOC, which has a near-monopoly of the supply of industrial gases. Suppose BOC bought all its steel gas cylinders from XYZ Ltd., which makes no other product and has no other market for its cylinders. Under the VA conventions, XYZ would be *excluded* from the BOC team even though its entire commercial future were tied up with BOC. However, a bank which extended temporary credit to BOC would be *included* in the BOC team (as a capital provider) even though it was not committed to or knowledgeable about the industrial gas industry. Common sense here would suggest the exact opposite, *i.e.*, that XYZ Ltd. was part of the team while the bank was not.

The best that can be said to defend the VA Statement from this attack is that for most companies there is already some validity in drawing a line around workers, capital-providers, and government and declaring those included to be a team. And indeed the objection discussed has a certain circularity, for one of the advantages claimed for the VA Statement is that it will lead team-members to regard themselves as part of a team. In short the objector is saying, "I do not find your team-definition to be natural," while the VA proponent is replying, "You will find it natural when all companies adopt it and, moreover, the definition suggested will improve teamwork."

A second disadvantage of the VA Statement is that its inclusion in an annual report can cause confusion with the earnings statement. What would a non-accountant reading the annual report infer if he saw that VA was rising while earnings were falling? Or, indeed, what would he make of the annual report if he saw VA was positive but earnings were negative? This last case would not be all that unusual and can be illustrated by a simple example. Suppose a company's sales for the year were £100, bought-in costs were nil, and it paid £150 in wages. In these circumstances VA for the year would be £100, for that would be the Value placed on the company's efforts by its customers. However, a loss of £50 has been made. What has happened here is that the team has earned £100 of VA but has overdistributed to team members. In effect, shareholders have lost £50 of the company's reserves, as this is the excess of wages over VA. The shareholders can rightly say they have lost Value to the extent of £50, but the VA Statement is not a report on shareholders' welfare. It is a report on the welfare of a more broadly defined team, and that team taken as a whole has benefited by Value Added of £100.

A third disadvantage of the VA Statement is that it raises a new danger of inefficient management, since managers may wrongly seek to maximize their company's VA. One book has already been published which exhorts managers to accept this improper objective [Gilchrist, 1971]. This unsound advice could lead to grossly wasteful decisions in which shareholders' capital would be dissipated in subsidizing uneconomic output. Consider, for example, a company which currently buys a component from a supplier for £100. A manager investigates the possibilities of making the component within the company and finds that to do so would cost £80 in direct materials and £70 in direct labor (overheads are assumed to be nil for simplicity). The foolish VA-maximizer would now decide on internal manufacture, as his bought-in costs would then fall from £100 to £80 and so the VA would rise by £20 for each component. However, this £20 of additional VA would involve an extra £70 of wages, and so shareholders' earnings would fall by £50 per component. The VA-maximizer would, therefore, be dissipating shareholders' capital by manufacturing instead of buying in.

A fourth argument against the VA Statement is that its inclusion in the annual report would involve extra work, therefore extra costs and delay and also a slight loss of confidentiality in view of the additional disclosure involved. In practice the extra work, cost, and delay have proved to be negligible. The only extra disclosure involved for British companies has been their overseas wage cost. This arises because current disclosure requirements cover *U.K.* wage costs, and, therefore, the inclusion of *total* wage cost in the VA Statement implicitly reveals overseas wages. This could be an embarrassing or damaging disclosure if all overseas wage costs arose in one country, *e.g.*, because of considerations of competitiveness with overseas rivals or political sensitivity as in southern Africa.

The final objection to the VA Statement is a very serious one: VA Statements are flagrantly unstandardized. Indeed, an unscrupulous accountant could manipulate the choice of methods of VA calculation to produce almost any VA figure desired. To illustrate the variety and massive effect of VA reporting practices, one can refer back to the accounts of Esso already mentioned. Another example comes from the 1975 and 1976 annual reports of Allied Breweries Ltd. In the former year Allied's VA was £379 million and the government's share was 50 percent. In the latter year VA was £247 million and the government took only 13 percent. Had the beer drinkers *and* the government both become abstemious? In fact, the company had merely decided to re-classify the special excise tax on alcohol as a bought-in cost rather than as part of the government's share of VA.

All the companies mentioned in this article have made clear how they have arrived at the figures used in their VA Statements and so no readers of the Statements should have been misled. However, it is clear that the VA Statement will not long retain the public's confidence unless it is standardized. The Accounting Standards

Committee is already studying the questions of classification and definition in the VA Statement. Depreciation and taxes are the main problems.

It has already been seen that a VA Statement can be framed as a report on Net VA, after deducting depreciation, and Table 1 which showed the Net VA of BOC illustrated this. However, the majority of British companies prefer to set forth their VA Statement as a report on Gross VA, so that depreciation is an application of VA rather than a cost to be deducted in calculating VA. Table 3 shows an example of a report on Gross VA, that of Imperial Chemical Industries Ltd. The VA Statement of ICI shows how depreciation can be added to the retained profit for the year, thereby giving a total which ICI has described as "re-investment in the business." The Gross VA for the year was £1,874 million, and the depreciation charge was £221 million. Had ICI chosen to present a report on Net VA, its VA would have been £1,653 million (*i.e.*, £1,874 million less £221 million). In this case, the choice of Gross or Net VA makes a difference of 13 percent of the Net VA. One can see how the treatment of depreciation has a material effect, especially on the ratios referred to earlier. For example, the reported share of VA going in wages will be higher if we adopt the Net VA definition than if we decide in favor of Gross VA.

The reasons for reporting Gross VA are three. First, Gross VA is a more objective figure than Net VA. This is because depreciation is more prone to subjective judgment than are bought-in costs. Depreciation involves opinions as to likely asset lives, scrap values, straight-line versus percentage of declining balance, and so on. Bought-in costs will involve some subjectivity, for example, regarding closing stock values, but the general run of bought-in costs such as repairs, fuel, telephone costs, and electric power, will be fairly objective. This point has special force if VA is to be used as a basis for some sort of productivity bonus to employees. Workers may suspect the management of manipulating VA to produce lower bonuses if a subjective cost like depreciation is deducted in arriving at VA.

Second, the Gross VA format involves reporting depreciation alongside retained profit. The resultant subtotal usefully shows the portion of the year's VA which has become available for reinvestment. This ratio is less readily calculable from a Net VA Statement where depreciation is separated from retentions.

Third, the practice of reporting Gross VA would lead to a closer correspondence between VA and national income figures, for economists generally prefer gross measures of national income to net ones.

The present writer sees some merit in these arguments but believes that the principal reason why most British companies have reported Gross VA is that they have unthinkingly followed the advice given in *The Corporate Report* [ASC, 1975]. That document did not even mention the possibility of the alternative Net VA format. The following reasons for preferring Net VA are substantial and, in the present writer's opinion, outweigh the earlier points.

## ARGUMENTS FOR NET VA

First, it has been explained how "wealth creation" is often used as a synonym for VA. Wealth creation is overstated if no allowance is made for the wearing out or loss of value of fixed assets which occurs as new assets are created. Another way of putting this is to say that a company theoretically could distribute 100 percent of its *Net* VA in the form of wages, taxes, interest, and dividends. But it could not long continue to distribute 100 percent of *Gross* VA, since the company would be consuming its seed

**TABLE 3**

**Imperial Chemical Industries Ltd., and Subsidiaries Value Added Statement Year to December 31, 1977**

| Sources of income | | £ million |
|---|---|---|
| Sales | | 4,663 |
| Royalties and other trading income | | 39 |
| Less: Materials and services used | | (2,866) |
| Value added by manufacturing and trading | | 1,836 |
| | | |
| Share of profits of principal associated companies and investment income | | 96 |
| Exchange loss on net current assets of overseas subsidiaries | | (29) |
| Extraordinary items | | (29) |
| Total value added | | 1,874 |
| | | |
| Disposal of total value added | | |
| Employees | | |
| —pay, plus pension and national insurance contributions | 1,063 | |
| —profit-sharing bonus | 29 | 1,092 |
| | | |
| Governments—corporate taxes, less grants | | 202 |
| Providers of capital | | |
| —interest paid on borrowings | 107 | |
| —dividends to shareholders | 93 | |
| —minority shareholders in subsidiaries | 26 | 226 |
| | | |
| Re-investment in the business | | |
| —depreciation set aside | 221 | |
| —profit retained | 133 | 354 |
| | | 1,874 |

corn, and its operations would grind to a halt when the fixed assets were exhausted. If, therefore, Net VA is distributable while Gross VA is not, then Net VA is a better denominator for distribution ratios such as payroll/VA.

Second, Net VA is a fairer base for calculating productivity bonuses than is Gross VA. Several British companies have introduced schemes which pay productivity bonuses based on achieved increases in VA. If these schemes are based on Gross VA, then they make no allowance for capital changes. A company's VA might rise after new capital had been invested in a major plant modernization, and employees might be given "their share" of this increase as a bonus. But if that share is based on VA before depreciation, then no recognition is given to the need for an increased depreciation charge. In short, the wrong people benefit, since the providers of capital deserve the credit for the VA increase. Net VA does not entirely do away with this unfairness, but it lessens it.

Third, the concepts of consistency and matching demand that depreciation be deducted along with bought-in costs to derive Net VA. Bought-in materials are assets bought from outside suppliers, and the cost thereof is matched against sales revenue in the upper part of the VA Statement. Depreciable fixed assets will also have been bought from outside suppliers,[2] and the cost of these should, therefore, also be matched against sales revenue over the assets useful lives. Net VA treats materials and fixed assets consistently, as both will appear as deductions from VA in accordance with their becoming used up. Gross VA is inconsistent, for costs would be charged under the bought-in heading if the item has a life of under one year. But if the item has a longer life it would be treated as a depreciable fixed asset and its cost would *never* appear as a charge against VA.

Fourth, Net VA involves no double-counting, while Gross VA does involve some double-counting and is misleading. The double counting arises from the non-deduction of depreciation. Where one company buys a product from another company, the seller's VA will be augmented and the buyer's diminished by the amount of the sale. This elimination of the intermediate transaction reflects the idea that national income arises when a final consumer buys the product but no national income arises merely from inter-company transactions. If company A sells £100 worth of fuel to company B, then no Value is Added, or no wealth is created just by this transaction. The VA will arise when B uses the fuel to generate saleable output which will end up as a consumer product. If B did not deduct the £100 as bought-in cost, then the £100 of VA would be double-counted by A and by B. The VA Statement deals with these transactions satisfactorily so far as materials are concerned. But if the asset which A sold to B had been a depreciable fixed asset, then (a) Net VA would eliminate the double-counting as B would, over the years, deduct the £100 in the form of depreciation alongside other bought-in costs, while (b) Gross VA would not eliminate the double-counting.

Fifth, the team concept behind VA fits Net VA better than Gross VA. If one looks at the Net VA Statement in Table 1, one sees that the team consists of workers, government, and capital providers. The surplus VA which remains after the share-out among team members is retained, and this retained profit is a deferred application of VA to shareholders, who are team members, and may thereby benefit by higher quoted share values and eventually higher dividends. The team concept works. However, if one looks at a Gross VA Statement, as in Table 3, one may justifiably ask how depreciation relates to the team concept. One of the ways in which VA has been "disposed" in Table 3 is "depreciation set aside." But depreciation is not an employee, or a capital provider, or the government. In fact the disposal reported as depreciation is a part of wealth which was in the past "distributed" or paid to the company which originally supplied the depreciable fixed asset. In short, suppliers of fixed assets are honorary team-members. This distorts the concept of the company team and introduces inconsistency between classes of supplier.

---

[2] Some fixed assets may have been made by the company, as where a building contractor builds his own offices. In these cases, the capitalized value of the home-built fixed asset should be added to sales in the VA Statement, the costs (bought-in material, labor, *etc.*) being reported elsewhere. In subsequent years the depreciation on the home-built fixed assets should be merged with depreciation on all other fixed assets in the VA Statement.

Accordingly the present writer considers that the VA Statement should be standardized as a report on *Net* VA.

## TAXATION

The second major area of non-standardization in current VA practice is taxation. Some companies report only tax levied on profits (which in Britain is corporation tax) under the heading of "VA applied to governments." Other companies report an extensive range of taxes, including withholding taxes deducted at the source from workers' wages, local government charges for sanitation and roads, and taxes levied on the company's outputs. The two examples already referred to (Esso and Allied Breweries) show how large an effect the choice of accounting treatment can have, but these examples are abnormal as they come from industries which attract especially high rates of excise tax (petroleum and alcohol).

Most companies have chosen to include only corporation tax under the government's share of VA. This practice has many advantages. It avoids the need to make subjective judgments as to where to draw the line, for there is a long list of government imposts which could be regarded as part of the government's share. Examples of difficult items include road vehicle taxes, oil royalties, training levies to government-run training schemes for employees, and fines paid. Further, subjectivity arises over how widely "government" is defined—one could include government-sponsored bodies which regulate aviation and broadcasting, or utilities. Related to this danger of a subjective decision on which taxes to include is the simplicity and cheapness of the alternative. Taxes can be left in the accounts into which they have already been analyzed, and the VA Statement will then not require costly additional analysis work. This point is especially applicable where a group of companies with many subsidiaries, some overseas, is preparing a VA Statement. A further advantage of the suggested practice is that the VA Statement is easy to reconcile with the earnings statement if only corporate taxes on profit are included under the government's share of VA. This ease of reconciliation is lost if a wide range of taxes is included.

There are a number of additional minor areas of non-standardization in VA Statements. These include the classification of rents payable (under bought-in costs or under interest payable?) and the way in which the results of associated companies are handled (see Morley [1978]). But it is broadly true that the Accounting Standards Committee could achieve substantial standardization of the VA Statement, thereby defusing the main argument against the Statement, if it prescribed (a) that depreciation should be deducted with bought-in costs, thereby reporting Net VA, and (b) that the government's share of VA should contain only corporation tax.

## CONCLUSION

In many ways, the VA Statement is an unsatisfactory innovation to encounter. It is easy enough to understand and to prepare. Much is claimed for it, but the claims are hard to pin down and to verify. The benefits claimed are principally improvement in attitude, motivation, and behavior, and these are remarkably difficult to research. The present status of the VA Statement is that it has achieved sudden popularity in Britain and will probably soon appear in the corporate reports of all major British companies. It is likely that the dangers inherent in the wide selection of accounting treatments will lead the Accounting Standards Committee to issue a standard definition for each major heading in the VA Statement. Standard-setting committees have in the past often operated by discovering the most widespread practice, pronouncing it good, and making it compulsory. This will work well enough for the VA Statement except for the question of depreciation, where, for the reasons given earlier, the prevailing practice should be changed.

## REFERENCES

Accounting Standards Committee, *The Corporate Report* (London, 1975).

Alcan Aluminium (U.K.) Ltd., Annual Report (December 31, 1976).

Allied Breweries Ltd., Annual Reports (September 30, 1975 and September 30, 1976).

BOC International Ltd., Annual Report (September 30, 1977).

Bowater Corporation Ltd., Annual Report (December 31, 1977).

Bullock, Lord, *Report of the Committee of Inquiry on Industrial Democracy* (Department of Trade, Cmnd. 6706, H.M.S.O., 1977).

Cox, B., *Value Added—an Appreciation for the Accountant Concerned with Industry* (Institute of Cost and Management Accountants, 1978).

Department of Trade, *The Future of Company Reports* (Cmnd. 6888, H.M.S.O., 1977).

Esso Petroleum Company Ltd., Annual Reports (December 31, 1976 and December 31, 1977).

Gilchrist, R. R., *Managing for Profit: The Added Value Concept* (Allen and Unwin, 1971).

Hendriksen, E. S., *Accounting Theory* (Richard D. Irwin, 1977).

Imperial Chemical Industries Ltd., Annual Report (December 31, 1977).

Morley, M. F., *The Value Added Statement* (published for the Institute of Chartered Accountants of Scotland by Gee & Co., 1978).

Suojanen, W. W., "Accounting Theory and the Large Corporation" THE ACCOUNTING REVIEW (July 1954), pp. 391–398.

# V-D 2  *A Note on Accounting and Executory Contracts*

SCOTT HENDERSON AND GRAHAM PEIRSON

There is general agreement that an asset cannot exist if the right to receive services is exactly offset by an equal duty to render services. It is also agreed that a liability cannot exist if the duty to render services is exactly offset by a right to receive equal services.

This situation was first made explicit by Canning in 1929 in his well known definitions of an asset and a liability

> An asset is any future service in money of any future service convertible into money (*except those services arising from contracts the two sides of which are proportionately unperformed*) the beneficial interest in which is legally or equitably secured to some person or set of persons. Such a service is an asset only to that person or set of persons to whom it runs. (p. 22)[1]

> A liability is a service, valuable in money, which a proprietor is under an existing legal/or equitable duty to render to a second person (or set of persons) and *which is not unconditionally an agreed set-off to its full amount against specific services of equal or greater money value due from this second person to the proprietor.* (p. 55–6, emphasis added)

In his discussion of the nature of assets and liabilities, Canning introduced the term 'executory contract' which in accounting is generally regarded as a contract which does not result in assets and liabilities. For example, The American Institute of

Scott Henderson and Graham Peirson "A Note on Accounting and Executory Contracts," *Abacus* Vol. 20 No. 1, 1983. Reprinted with the permission of *Abacus*.

[1] There are two aspects of this definition which warrant comment. First, the definition would probably be clearer if "equally" was inserted before "proportionately unperformed." Second, Canning followed his definition with a statement that "If the matter in parenthesis were removed the definition would be more useful to the economist and probably to all concerned." This has been interpreted as meaning that the definition would be improved without the parenthetical material. See, for example, Hendriksen (1982, p. 251). However, Canning is not saying that his *definition* is defective but that the *concept of assets* should probably be expanded to include rights arising from contracts "the two sides of which are (equally) proportionately unperformed."

Certified Public Accountants in *Opinion No. 5*, wrote:

> The rights and obligations related to unperformed portions of executory
> contracts are not recognized as assets and liabilities in financial statements
> under generally accepted accounting principles as presently understood.
> (A.P.B., 1965, p. 30)

The use of the term "executory contract" is so widespread in the accounting
literature that it is seldom defined. It appears to be assumed that the meaning of the
term "executory contract" is either obvious or well understood. However, where
definitions are offered, there are often significant differences between them. In
Henderson and Peirson (1983), for example, we follow Canning and define an
executory contract as a contract "the two sides of which are proportionately
unperformed" (p. 93). Carpenter and Wojdak (1971) define an executory contract as a
contract under which performance by one or more of the contracting parties is not
complete" (p. 40). Birnberg (1965) defines an executory contract as "an agreement
between two or more parties in which no party has yet performed any of the acts
required of him by the agreement" (p. 814).

The differences between these definitions can be illustrated with a simple
example. Suppose, for example, that A contracts to employ B for six months with a
salary payment at the end of each month. At the date of the agreement, the contract
would be classed as an executory contract under all three definitions. After six weeks,
the Henderson and Peirson definition would not class the contract as executory
because it is not equally proportionately unperformed. A has still to perform
approximately 5/6 of the obligations under the contract while B has still to perform
approximately 3/4 of the obligations under the contract. The contract would be
executory under the Carpenter and Wojdak definition because both A and B "still
have obligations to perform under it", but Birnberg's definition would not class the
contract as executory because both A and B have performed some of the acts required
by the agreement. At the time the salary is paid at the end of two months, Henderson
and Peirson and Carpenter and Wojdak would classify the contract as executory, but
Birnberg would not.

It appears, therefore, that while the accounting literature implicitly assumes that
the nature of executory contracts is well understood, in fact, there are significant
differences in interpretation.

This apparent confusion over the nature of executory contracts is, however,
much deeper than a simple inability to frame an acceptable definition for accounting
purposes. From a legal viewpoint, "a contract is said to be executory so long as
anything remains to be done under it by any party" (Halsbury, 1974, p. 82). This is a
much broader interpretation of an executory contract than is found in the accounting
literature. Many contracts which are executory from a legal viewpoint result in assets
and liabilities. For example, credit sales and purchases are executory until payment is
made. All prepayments are executory until the service is performed. All borrowing is
executory until the interest and principal are repaid. In all of these cases, an
executory contract has resulted in assets and liabilities.

This apparent divergence between the legal and the accounting interpretations
of an executory contract probably arose from a misunderstanding of Canning by
accountants. Although he wrote of "contracts, the two sides of which are proportionately unperformed" and "executory contracts," nowhere did he imply that
these terms were synonymous.

A careful reading of Canning shows that he used the term "executory contract" in its legal sense. For example, he wrote that: "unequal part performance of executory contracts does result in the recognition of assets and liabilities by accountants" (p. 19). He also explained that "executory contracts wholly unperformed" (p. 18) would not result in assets and liabilities, and that "if the services to be received under contracts executory on both sides were always completely offset," then no asset or liability would result. It is apparent, therefore, that Canning used the term "executory contract" to describe any contract which had not been completely performed by either party. According to Canning, only those executory contracts which are equally proportionately unperformed by both parties do not result in assets and liabilities. All other executory contracts do result in assets and liabilities.

Accountants, it seems, have interpreted Canning's explanation that *some* executory contracts do not result in assets and liabilities as meaning that *all* executory contracts do not result in assets and liabilities.

A lawyer who reads in the accounting literature that rights and obligations arising from executory contracts result in no assets and liabilities would be justifiably confused. The implication is that only contracts which are not executory can result in assets and liabilities. From a lawyer's viewpoint, a contract which is not executory must be executed or wholly performed by all parties. An executed contract, however, has no rights or obligations attaching to it. It would appear to the lawyer, therefore, that assets and liabilities cannot arise from any contract!

We thus have a situation where accountants are using a term the exact meaning of which seems to be unclear to them. Furthermore, whatever they mean by the term, it is different from the legal meaning. If accountants continue to use the term "executory contract" in this way they are risking confusion amongst themselves and misunderstanding and possible conflict with the legal profession.

In our opinion, accountants should cease using the term "executory contract" except in its legal sense. This would mean substituting the phrase "contracts the two sides of which are equally proportionately unperformed" or "contracts where rights and duties are exactly offset" for "executory contract." For example, the generally accepted accounting principle of the APB would become: "the rights and obligations relating to contracts the two sides of which are equally proportionately unperformed are not recognized as assets and liabilities in financial statements under generally accepted accounting principles as presently understood."

## REFERENCES

Accounting Principles Board (APB), "Reporting of Leases in Financial Statements of Leases," *Opinion No. 5*, AICPA, New York 1965.

Birnberg, J. G. "The Reporting of Executory Contracts," *The Accounting Review*, October 1965.

Canning, J. B., *The Economics of Accountancy*, Ronald Press, New York 1965.

Carpenter, C. G. and J. F. Wojdak, "Capitalizing Executory Contracts: A Perspective," *The New York Certified Accountant*, January 1971.

*Halsbury's Laws of England*, 4th edn, 1974.

Henderson, S. and G. Peirson, *Financial Accounting Theory: Its Nature and Development*, Longman Cheshire, Melbourne 1983.

Hendriksen, E. S., *Accounting Theory*, 4th edn, Irwin, Illinois 1982.

# V-D 3 *On the Use of the Economic Concept of Human Capital in Financial Statements*

BARUCH LEV AND ABA SCHWARTZ

*"The most valuable of all capital is that invested in human beings." Alfred Marshall,* Principles of Economics.

## INTRODUCTION

The dichotomy in accounting between human and nonhuman capital is funda-mental; the latter is recognized as an asset and therefore is recorded in the books and reported in the financial statements, whereas the former is totally ignored by accountants. Most economists, on the other hand, have a different view on this issue. Milton Friedman, for example, states:

> From the broadest and most general point of view, total wealth includes all sources of "income" of consumable services. One such source is the productive capacity of human beings, and accordingly this is one form in which wealth can be held. [8, p. 4]

The definition of wealth as a source of income inevitably leads to the recognition of human capital as one of several forms of holding wealth, such as money, securities, and physical (nonhuman) capital. This attitude toward human capital has a broad range of applications in economics. For example, the value of human capital appears in some demand functions for money (of business enterprises as well as households) as an argument along with other forms of nonhuman wealth [8, pp. 9, 13], human capital is recognized as an important factor in explaining and predicting economic growth

The authors are deeply indebted to Professor Sidney Davidson, Dean of the Graduate School of Business, University of Chicago, for helpful comments.

Baruch Lev and Aba Schwartz, "On the Use of the Economic Concept of Human Capital in Financial Statements," *The Accounting Review*, January 1971, pp. 103–112. Reprinted with the permission of *The Accounting Review*.

[2], etc. Human capital is thus treated in modern economic theory on a par with other forms of earning assets.

On the other hand, the different attitude of accountants toward human capital was succinctly expressed as follows:

> A favorite cliché for the president's letter in corporate reports is "our employees are our most important—our most valuable—asset." Turning from the president's letter and looking to the remainder of the report, one might ask, "where is this human asset on these statements which serve as reports of the firm's resources and earnings? What is the value of this most important or most valuable asset? Is it increasing, decreasing, or remaining unchanged?" [4, p. 217]

The objective of this article is to provide a practical measurement procedure by which some of the questions raised in the preceding quotation can be answered. Specifically, the possibility of using the economic concept and measurement of human capital in financial statements is explored. It is shown that the suggested method provides decision makers with information about organizational matters hitherto not reported by accountants. The order of discussion is as follows: Section II provides a discussion of the concept of human capital and its measurement. Section III extends this concept to the firm's level. Section IV elaborates on implications for decision makers from human capital reporting. Section V discusses some conceptual accounting problems involved in incorporating human capital values in the financial statements. Finally, Section VI provides some concluding remarks. The Appendix presents a hypothetical example demonstrating the measurement of a firm's human capital.

## THE CONCEPT OF HUMAN CAPITAL

Irving Fisher, one of the originators of human capital theory, notes:

> Capital in the sense of capital value is simply future income discounted, in other words, capitalized.... But the basic problem of time valuation which nature sets us is that of translating the future into the present, that is, the problem of ascertaining the capital value of future income. *The value of capital must be computed from the value of its estimated future net income, not vice versa.* [7, pp. 12–14, emphasis supplied.]

Capital is thus defined as a source of income stream and its worth is the present value of future income discounted by a rate specific to the owner of the source (or to the potential buyer).

Fisher's definition does not distinguish between human capital, which is a source of income embodied in a person (in the form of his brute force and his natural and acquired skills), and nonhuman capital. There is, however, an important distinction: the ownership of human capital is nontransferable (in a nonslave society) while nonhuman capital can be traded in the market. In a world of certainty this distinction is of no consequence for the determination of capital values since certainty implies a perfect knowledge of future income streams associated with the source and of future discount rates. Given this knowledge, the present value (i.e., worth) of human as well as nonhuman capital can be uniquely determined. In a world of uncertainty, however, future income streams and discount rates are not perfectly known and consequently the present value of the source cannot be uniquely (objectively) determined. Nevertheless, in the case of nonhuman capital we can still infer its value from observed market prices which reflect the present value of future earnings to the traders. Such a derivation of value from market prices cannot be made in the case of human capital since it is not traded. Thus, in a world of uncertainty an important distinction exists between human and nonhuman capital.

The difficulty in determining the value of human capital under uncertainty is responsible for the initial lack of systematic treatment of the subject in economics. However, during the last two decades economists have become aware of the grave consequences of this omission, as Gary Becker notes:

> Recent years have witnessed intensive concern with and research on investment in human capital, much of it contributed or stimulated by T. W. Schultz. The main motivating factor has probably been a realization that the growth of physical capital, at least as conventionally measured, explained a relatively small part of the growth of income in most countries. The search for better explanation has led to improved measures of physical and to an interest in less tangible entities, such as technological change and human capital. [2, p. 1.]

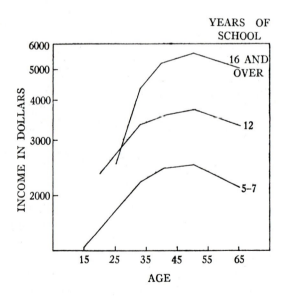

**FIGURE 1**
**Earnings Profiles of U.S. Males, 1949**

SOURCE: U.S. CENSUS OF POPULATION (1950), SER. P-E, NO. 5-B: EDUCATION, TABLES 12, 13

Consequently, a theory of human capital measurement has been developed and its impact on macroeconomic problems investigated [2, 3, 9, 11, 12, 14, 15, 16, 17, 18]. An extension of this approach to the firm's level, as advanced in this paper, seems natural.

### The Earnings Profile

An earnings profile is a graphic or mathematical presentation of the income stream generated by a person (i.e., by his human capital), see Fig. 1. A typical earnings profile first increases with age, reflecting the capability of human beings to learn (on the job or elsewhere) and thus increase their productivity. As the person ages, productivity declines because of technological obsolescence and health deterioration, a fact expressed by a decrease in the annual earnings. Since the profile reflects only earnings from employment and not from capital assets it terminates at retirement or on death if that occurs earlier.

### Measurement of Human Capital

The value of human capital embodied in a person of age $\pi$ is the present value of his remaining future earnings from employment. This value for a discrete income stream is:

$$V_\pi = \sum_{t=\pi}^{T} \frac{I(t)}{(1 + r)^{t - \pi}} \tag{1}$$

where:

$V_\pi$ = the human capital value of a person $\pi$ years old.
$I(t)$ = the person's annual earnings up to retirement. This series is graphically represented by the earnings profile.
$r$ = a discount rate specific to the person.
$T$ = retirement age.

Strictly speaking, expression (1) is an *ex post* computation of human capital value at any age of the person, since only after retirement is the series $I(t)$ known. This is of little use in our case where we need the *ex ante* values of human capital. Hence, the observed values of $I(t)$ in (1) should be replaced by estimates $I^*(t)$ of future annual earnings. The best source of information for these estimates is current data on earnings distribution classified by age, education, skill, etc. Consider, for example, the problem of estimating the future earnings series of an industrial engineer, 25 years of age. We have current data (from the census and other sources) on average earnings of industrial engineers 25 years of age, 26 years of age, and so on up to retirement. We can, therefore, estimate next year's earnings of our 25 year old engineer on the basis of current earnings of an equivalent engineer 26 years of age, the estimate of earnings two years hence will be based on current average earnings of 27 year old engineers, and so on. Generally, the observed *across persons* earnings profile $I°(t)$ can be transformed to *over-time* earnings profile, providing the required estimates of future earnings $I^*(t)$:

$$I^*(t) = f[I°(t)], \qquad t = r, \dots, T. \tag{2}$$

The function $f$ in (2) is a transformation of current to future earnings reflecting expectations of future technological changes, changes in demand for the specific skills of the person, government intervention, and most important—the person's subjective evaluation of his capabilities relative to others in the professional group. Since information on such future events is difficult to obtain, it is customary in human capital studies to assume that the function $f$ is the identity transformation, i.e.,

$$I^*(t) = I^\circ(t), \qquad t = \pi, \dots, T \tag{3}$$

Thus, the prediction of next year's earnings of the 25 year old engineer will be equal to (not just based on) current earnings of a 26 year old equivalent engineer.[1] The estimated human capital value of a person $\pi$ years old is thus:

$$V_\pi^* = \sum_{t=\pi}^{T} \frac{I^*(t)}{(1+r)^{t-\pi}} \tag{4}$$

where $I^*(t)$ is determined by (3).

Expression (4) ignores the possibility of death occurring prior to retirement age. This can be incorporated into the model by the use of mortality tables which provide the death probabilities. Specifically, the probability of a person dying at age $t$ is presented by the long-run mortality rates of persons with the same characteristics (race, sex, education, etc.). When this probability is $P_T(t)$, the *expected value* of the person's human capital is:[2]

$$E(V_\pi^*) = \sum_{t=\pi}^{T} P_\tau(t+1) \sum_{i=\pi}^{t} \frac{I_i^*}{(1+r)^{t-\pi}} \tag{5}$$

### Statistical Sources

Since our main purpose is to advance a *practical* application of human capital concepts in accounting we briefly discuss some sources of data.

Practically all empirical studies concerned with human capital measurements in the U.S. are based on the 1960 census data published by the Bureau of the Census [19]. This census provides cross-sectional data on earnings classified by age, race, sex, education, geographic area of employment, etc., and most useful for our application— by profession or skill. Average earnings profiles of professional groups of employees (e.g., unskilled employees in the meat packing industry) can be determined from these data. The earnings profiles can be refined by keeping constant several personal characteristics. For example, if an average earnings profile for electrical engineers is too crude (i.e., the group of electrical engineers in the U.S. is too heterogeneous), the earnings profile of white, male electrical engineers, employed in the automobile industry, can be determined, thereby making the group for which an earnings profile is determined more homogeneous.[3]

Of special importance for practical use is a condensed version of the 1960 census available on magnetic tape. This is a 0.1 percent random sample of the total U.S.

---

[1] In cases where price level changes are significant, an adjustment for these changes can be made. Specifically, $I^*(t)$ will equal $I^\circ(t)$ adjusted for expected price level changes.
[2] $P_r(t)$ is the conditional probability of a person of age $\pi$ dying in year $t$.
[3] For the practical construction of such refined profiles, see [9].

population included in the census. Since a complete census is taken every 10 years, current data will soon be available.

Mortality tables, needed for formula (5), are available for every country and region. Such tables are extensively used by life insurance companies in determining their premium scale and reserves.

## HUMAN CAPITAL VALUE ASSOCIATED WITH THE FIRM

We have discussed thus far the conceptual and practical problems involved in measuring the capital value of a person or a homogeneous group of persons. The determination of the total value of a firm's labor force is a straightforward extension. The firm's labor force will be divided into homogeneous groups of employees such as unskilled employees, semi-skilled, skilled, engineers of different kinds, salesmen, managerial staff, etc. Average earnings profiles, based on census data, will be constructed for each group and the present value of human capital calculated. The sum of present values over the various employee groups will provide the total human capital value associated with the firm. A simple hypothetical example of such a computation is provided in the Appendix.

The firm's value of human capital thus measured is based on average earnings data of homogeneous groups of employees in the U.S. A given firm, however, may employ persons of higher or lower quality than the average and accordingly pay different wages and salaries than those indicated by the census-based data. If the firm employs a large number of employees of different kinds it will be possible to determine earnings profiles based on the firm's own wage scale. Specifically, cross-sectional data on wages currently paid to groups of employees will be substituted for the census data to determine the earnings profiles. We can thus compute for a firm's labor force a *general* value of human capital and a *specific* value, the former based on overall census data and the latter on the specific wage scale of the firm. It should be emphasized again that the specific value of human capital can be computed only if the firm's labor force is large, i.e., when there is an ample amount of cross-sectional data to form the earnings profiles. The appropriate discount rate for determining the firm's human capital value seems to be the cost of capital. This is the rate used in capital budgeting decisions and also the opportunity cost of the firm's resources.

## IMPLICATIONS OF HUMAN CAPITAL REPORTING

Disclosure of human capital values by business enterprises will provide financial statement users with valuable information. The relevance of this information lies in the fact that it concerns organizational changes in the firm's labor force hitherto not reported by accountants. Following are some inferences for decision makers (investors as well as management) that could be drawn from reported values of human capital.

(a) The determination of human capital values suggests a new set of financial ratios. For example:

The ratio of human to nonhuman capital indicates the degree of labor intensiveness in the firm. The extent of labor intensity is believed to have widespread implications for the firm's operations. For example, economists, especially in the area of industrial organization, investigate the effect of labor (or capital) intensity of inter- and intra-industry variations in rates of return. The relative degrees of labor and capital intensity within countries are believed to affect world trade.[4] Lacking direct measures for labor intensity, economists use indirect ones such as value added per employee, or sales per employee. Such measures are crude since they treat all employees as equal; a highly skilled engineer and a janitor are given the same weight in the measure. The suggested ratio of human to nonhuman capital assigns different weights to different employees according to their earning power. Labor intensity thus measured reflects the quality as well as the quantity of the labor force.

The firm's total value of human capital can be disaggregated according to sub-groups of the labor force (see example in the Appendix). Several ratios are suggested by such a disaggregation; for example, the ratio of the value of scientific staff to the total value of human capital. This ratio indicates the extent of "skill (scientific) intensity" in the firm. Skill intensive industries are those with a relatively large scientific and research staff, e.g., chemical products, electronics, pharmaceuticals, etc. The effect of skill intensity on rate of return and growth is a currently debated issue. Here again researchers use extremely crude measures to detect the effect of skill intensity such as R & D expenses, number of college graduates as a percentage of the total number of employees, etc. Such measures are not sensitive to variations within the scientific employee group, whereas the suggested measure reflects such variations.

(b) Reported human capital values will provide information about changes in the structure of the labor force. For example, differences over time in the values of a firm's human capital may result from changes in the age distribution (i.e., "vintage") of employees. Recall that human capital values are determined by capitalizing earnings over the expected useful life (to the enterprise) of employees. Therefore, a change in the age distribution of the labor force would obviously affect the firm's human capital values. Suppose, for example, that no change has taken place in the structure of the labor force during 1969 (i.e., no employees were hired or laid off). In this case, the value of the firm's human capital at the end of 1969 would be smaller than that of the previous year (assuming, of course, no changes in the earnings profiles). The firm's time series of human capital value thus contains information about changes in the structure of the labor force. The phenomenon of an "aging firm" often discussed in organization theory, will be indicated by such a time series when other factors (e.g., number of employees) are held constant. It has been suggested that the aging of the firm's labor force affects its rate of growth and relative share in the industry vis-à-vis the "younger" and more aggressive firms. Such hypotheses can be tested by using the reported values of human capital.

(c) The difference between the general and specific values of human capital (discussed in the preceding section) is another source of valuable information for management and the analyst. The specific value of human capital is based on the firm's actual wage scale while the general value is based on industry-wide wage averages. The difference between the two therefore indicates the level of the firm's wage scale relative to the industry average. Specifically, if the industry-wide wage averages are taken as a standard, this difference indicates to what extent the firm's wage scale is above, on a par with, or below the standard. Such information, which is not currently communicated to users, may explain the observed phenomenon of firms which consistently pay higher wages than the industry averages. It is sometimes

---

[4] This is the well-known Heckscher-Ohlin factor proportions theory which asserts that each country exports that commodity which is most intensive in the country's abundant factor.

argued that such firms employ the professional elite and hence experience a higher rate of return or growth than their competitors. Others are skeptical about such a hiring policy claiming that when wages are equal to employees' marginal productivity[5] then no extra returns can result from employing superior employees. Reporting the general and specific values of human capital will thus enable users to investigate the effects of specific wage and hiring policies.

Management might try to increase profits in the short run by hiring low quality employees. Such a policy can produce damaging effects which will be realized only in the long run. However, if human capital values are reported they will *currently* reflect the change in hiring policy and thereby deter management.

## CONCEPTUAL ISSUES IN REPORTING HUMAN CAPITAL VALUES

The problem of reporting human capital values in financial statements has two distinct aspects: (a) the measurement of the value of the firm's work force which is the subject of this article, and (b) measurement and amortization of the firm's *investment* in human resources. The few articles concerning human capital reporting in financial statements [4, 5, 6, 13] deal exclusively with the second aspect.[6]

> It is often assumed that the objective of human resource accounting is to determine the net worth, or dollar value of an individual employee to a firm. This is not the case. Rather, we are trying to develop concepts and techniques for measuring a firm's investment in its human organization, the rate at which those investments are being consumed, and which investments are more productive than others. This is not the same as measuring the value of individuals, and surely raises *fewer objections*. [13, p. 46, emphasis supplied]

What are the objections that can be raised against the incorporation of human capital values in accounting reports?

(a) It can be argued that human capital (excluding a slave society) cannot be purchased or owned by the firm and therefore would not be recognized as an asset in accounting. This is obviously true with respect to individual employees who can usually resign at will;[7] however, it is not so obvious with respect to the firm's *labor force* as a whole. As long as employees can be replaced it does not matter for our purpose whether the labor force always contains the same persons or is a rapidly changing group. The labor force as a whole is constantly associated with the firm and it can be constructively regarded as being "owned" by it.

Moreover, in modern economies where firms are usually purchased as going concerns (e.g., merger), payment is often made for intangible assets such as a stable and high quality labor force.[8] For example, it is customary in the insurance industry

---

[5] This will be the case when the firm's production function is homogeneous to the first degree.

[6] Most of the research on the subject has been conducted by R. Lee Brummet, Willard Graham Professor of Business Administration at the University of North Carolina, and William J. Pyle of the Institute for Social Research at the University of Michigan. Preliminary results of this research are reflected in the 1969 financial reports of R. G. Barry Corporation which was the first to report investment in human resources. For a description of this case, see [13].

[7] This statement ignores long-term employment contracts whose importance in the U.S. is declining.

[8] All payments for intangible assets are aggregated by accountants in the goodwill resulting from acquisition.

to determine the value of the sales force at the time of acquisition or sale. This is usually done by forecasting the firm's future earnings, determining its present value, and then allocating a portion of the present value to the human resources. A firm's human capital can thus be purchased and in a sense "owned" by it.

(b) It can be argued that the labor force is not an asset since it does not have a "service potential" extending beyond the current period. Specifically, employees are paid for rendering *current* services, and no asset is formed by these payments. If this were true then no firm would invest in (as opposed to maintain) human capital. However, the prevalence of programs such as orientation courses for new employees, executive programs, employees' training programs, facilities for improving employees' morale, etc., is evidence to the contrary. Such expenditures are made with the expectation of future returns, i.e., they increase the service potential embodied in human capital and this creates an asset.

The problem of reporting human capital values is closely related to the issue of long-term leases and other executory contracts. In both cases the firm rents the services of capital (human in the former, physical in the latter) owned by others. Those who favor the presentation of leased assets on the balance sheet would similarly endorse the reporting of human capital.

> Accounting at present recognizes most market transactions involving goods, services or money as one of the elements of the transaction. Present accounting also generally ignores, except in special circumstances, transactions involving an exchange of a promise for a promise. Leases, purchase commitments, executive and other labor contracts are generally denied recognition until the services or goods specified in the contract are either used, delivered, or paid for. Many of these contracts meet the standards of verifiability, freedom from bias, and quantifiability at least as well as other reported events. [1, p. 32]

In accordance with the suggested presentation of long-term leases, human capital values may be presented on the assets side of the balance sheet and the present value of the firm's liability to pay wages and salaries on the liabilities side. The two values are equal by definition: Changes in the values of human capital from period to period would not be recognized as income but would merely be matched by changes in the liability.

(c) Some accountants might accept the notion of human capital being an asset yet object to reporting it on the grounds that it cannot be "objectively" measured. We feel, however, that the preceding sections demonstrated that the degree of objectivity in human capital measurements, which are usually based on census data, is not lower than that of many conventional valuations in accounting. For example, depreciation charges are often estimated from industry-wide equipment mortality data,[9] the determination of reserves by life insurance companies is based on general mortality tables, pension liabilities and product guarantees are also statistically estimated.

The above arguments suggest that human capital values may be an integral part of financial statements. This conclusion is consistent with the recommendations of

---

[9] See in this context a recent suggestion for using the life expectancy of physical assets for estimating depreciation [10].

the AAA committee in *A Statement of Basic Accounting Theory*:

> External users may wish to know degrees of employee morale, customer satisfaction, product quality, and reputation of a given entity. If quantification of these were possible, a substantial amount of additional relevant information could be provided the external users. The accountant must constantly be alert to the possible applications of new measurement methods to develop additional quantifiable information for external users. [1, p. 29]

## CONCLUDING REMARKS

The value of the human capital associated with a business enterprise is not reflected in its financial reports. While some initial strides have been made toward measuring and amortizing the investment in human resources, the determination of human capital values is still an unsolved (and untouched) problem. The economic theory of human capital provides the basis for a practical solution to this problem.

The major limitation in the concept and measurement procedures advanced above is that the firm's value of human capital is not necessarily equal to the portion of the firm's income contributed by the labor force. Specifically, labor is one of several inputs in the production process; its value, therefore, should be determined on the basis of that portion of total income contributed by it. Such a determination of value accords with the well-known accounting concept of "service potential." However, in real life, input factors are interdependent and there is probably no practical way of dividing the total contribution among them. Consequently, accounting values of physical assets are determined by their market prices and not by their relative contribution to the firm. Therefore it seems reasonable that values of human capital may also be similarly determined. In the absence of market prices for human capital, the best approximation to its value is the measurement procedure based on census or firm earnings data.

## APPENDIX

The computation of the firm's value of human capital is demonstrated in the following hypothetical example. Table 1 shows the decomposition of employees in the firm by age groups and degrees of skill. Table 2 shows average annual earnings for each age and skill group. These data can be obtained from the census or from the firm's own current wages. The data in Tables 1 and 2 are sufficient for calculating the present values of future earnings for each group of employees, i.e., the values of human capital. These values (assuming a capitalization rate of 10 per cent) are presented in

---

[10] This value is obtained by the following calculation. Assume, for simplicity, that all the 700 employees are 25 years old. The future earnings stream (based on Table 2) for each employee is:
$5,000 a year for the next 10 years,
$5,500 a year for years 11 to 20,
$6,000 a year for years 21 to 30, and
$5,500 a year for years 31 to 40.
The present value of this series of 40 numbers multiplied by 700 (the number of employees in the group) is equal to $35,822,500. This discount rate is 10 percent. All other values in Table 3 were similarly calculated.

Table 3. For example, the total human capital value of the 700 unskilled employees in the age group 25–34 is \$35,822,500.[10] The total human capital associated with the firm is \$69,184,080. The degree of skill intensity in the firm is measured by the ratio of professionals to total human capital value:

$$\frac{11,058,790}{69,184,080} = 0.16.$$

### TABLE 1

### Distribution of Employees by Age and Skill

| Age | Unskilled | Semi-skilled | Skilled | Professionals | Total |
|-----|-----------|--------------|---------|---------------|-------|
| 25–34 | 700 | — | 10 | 40 | 750 |
| 35–44 | 300 | 40 | 10 | 30 | 380 |
| 45–54 | — | 10 | 20 | 20 | 50 |
| 55–64 | — | — | — | 10 | 10 |
| Total | 1,000 | 50 | 40 | 100 | 1,190 |

### TABLE 2

### Average Annual Earnings (Dollars) Classified by Age and Skill

| Age | Unskilled | Semi-skilled | Skilled | Professionals |
|-----|-----------|--------------|---------|---------------|
| 25–34 | 5,000 | 6,000 | 7,500 | 10,000 |
| 35–44 | 5,500 | 7,000 | 8,000 | 12,000 |
| 45–54 | 6,000 | 7,500 | 9,000 | 13,000 |
| 55–64 | 5,500 | 7,000 | 9,000 | 15,000 |

### TABLE 3

### Total Values of Human Capital (Dollars) By Age and Skill (Capitalization Rate = 10 Percent)

| Age | Unskilled | Semi-skilled | Skilled | Professionals | Total |
|-----|-----------|--------------|---------|---------------|-------|
| 25–34 | 35,822,500 | — | 764,310 | 4,281,760 | 40,868,570 |
| 35–44 | 15,908,400 | 2,686,880 | 786,990 | 3,546,990 | 22,929,260 |
| 45–54 | — | 626,670 | 1,529,540 | 2,308,440 | 4,464,650 |
| 55–64 | — | — | — | 921,600 | 921,600 |
| Total | 51,730,900 | 3,313,550 | 3,080,840 | 11,058,790 | 69,184,080 |

# REFERENCES

[1] AAA, *A Statement of Basic Accounting Theory* (American Accounting Association, 1966).

[2] G. S. Becker, *Human Capital* (Columbia University Press, National Bureau of Economic Research No. 80, 1964).

[3] M. J. Bowman, and R. G. Meyers, "Schooling, Experience, and Gains and Losses in Human Capital Through Migration," *Journal of the American Statistical Association*, LXII (September 1967) pp. 875–98.

[4] R. L. Brummet, E. G. Flamholtz, and W. C. Pyle, "Human Resource Measurement—A Challenge for Accountants," *The Accounting Review*, XLIII (April 1968), pp. 217–30.

[5] ———, ———, and ———, (Editors), *Human Resource Accounting: Development and Implementation in Industry* (Ann Arbor, Michigan: Foundation for Research on Human Behavior, 1969).

[6] J. Douthat, "Accounting for Personnel Training and Development Costs," *Training and Development Journal*, XXIV (June 1970), pp. 2–6.

[7] I. Fisher, *The Theory of Interest* (A. M. Kelley, Reprint of Economic Classics, 1961).

[8] M. Friedman, "The Quantity Theory of Money—A Restatement," in *Studies in the Quantity Theory of Money* (The University of Chicago Press, 1956).

[9] G. Hanoch, "Personal Earning and Investment in Schooling," unpublished Ph.D. dissertation, University of Chicago, 1965.

[10] Y. Ijiri, and R. S. Kaplan, "Probabilistic Depreciation and Its Implications for Group Depreciation," *The Accounting Review*, XLIV (October 1969), pp. 743–56.

[11] J. Mincer, "Investment in Human Capital and Personal Income Distributions," *The Journal of Political Economy*, LXVI (August 1958), pp. 281–302.

[12] ———, "On-the-Job Training: Costs, Returns, and Some Implications," *The Journal of Political Economy*, LXX (October 1962), pp. 50–79.

[13] W. Pyle, "Accounting for Your People," *Innovation*, X (1970), pp. 46–55.

[14] A. Schwartz, "Migration and Earnings in the U.S.," unpublished Ph.D. dissertation, University of Chicago, 1968.

[15] T. W. Schultz, "Investment in Human Capital," *American Economic Review*, LI (March 1961), pp. 1–17.

[16] ———, "Reflections on Investment in Men," *The Journal of Political Economy*, Supplement, LXX (October 1962), pp. 1–8.

[17] ———, *The Economic Value of Education* (Columbia University Press, 1963).

[18] L. Sjaasted, "The Costs and Returns of Human Migration," *The Journal of Political Economy*, LXX (October 1962), pp. 80–93.

[19] U.S. Bureau of the Census, *U.S. Census of the Population: 1960.* Vol. I. Characteristics of the Population, Parts 1–50. (Washington, D.C.: U.S. Government Printing Office, 1963). See especially, Subject Reports: Education Attainment, Final Report PC(2)5B. (U.S. Government Printing Office, 1963).

# V-D 4 *Toward a Theory of Corporate Social Accounting*

KAVASSERI V. RAMANATHAN

A contemporary problem of concern to all technology-rich industrialized societies is that of continuing to provide a high level of motivation for private enterprise while ensuring that its aggregate impact upon society is consistent with social goals and aspirations. This is an exceedingly complex problem for several reasons. Traditional performance criteria for private enterprise have emphasized results which may be in conflict with societal priorities. There are many divergent views as to the most desired social goals and aspirations. The qualitative dimensions of social goal formulation and evaluation add further to the complexity. Yet, the problem is of such significance that there is a pressing need to explore its many dimensions and find ways of formulating solutions.

The nature of the problem can be related further to performance as it is typically viewed from a management perspective. A corporate management's attention, decisions and actions are focused more on those components of the firm's performance which are included in the firm's formal measurement system. To the extent that a firm's social impacts are not subjected to formal measurement process, these aspects are not likely to enter into the firm's planning decisions or performance evaluation.

The traditional view of corporate performance is idealized in the quest to maximize profits. It also is widely acclaimed that a firm's only social responsibility in a free market system is to maximize its profits, for in so doing, it is presumed to maximize its contribution to society. Under this notion, the profits of a firm which operates within the society's legal framework would provide the all-inclusive criterion for evaluating its social performance. However, the economic depression phenomenon of arriving at full equilibrium with substantial unemployment; the relentless disparities in income and employment opportunities among different social groups; and the serious erosion in the quality of environment caused by productive activities have led to sharp criticisms of the use of profits as an all-inclusive criterion of corporate social performance.[1]

Kavasseri V. Ramanathan, "Toward A Theory of Corporate Social Accounting," *The Accounting Review*, July 1976, pp. 516–528. Reprinted with the permission of *The Accounting Review*.

[1] The literature on this debate is voluminous. Sethi [1974] contains discussions on most of the pertinent issues.

A comprehensive analysis of the social impact of private enterprise suffers, at the present time, from a general absence of reliable data on aggregate social costs and benefits of business and on how these are shared among various social groups. However, some progress has been reached in recent years toward gathering and reporting data on corporate social performance, both as a result of internal initiatives of progressive corporations and in response to external influences. Thus, Beresford's [1973] annual survey reports that 298 of the Fortune 500 industrial firms disclosed some type of social performance data in their 1973 annual reports. The majority of these disclosures were in the environmental control category. Other broad categories used in the Beresford survey were minority employment, responsibility to employees, community activities and product improvement. Disclosure practices varied considerably as regard to scope, format, use of quantitative and financial measures and the significance of items disclosed. The trend appears to be toward greater disclosure. Apparently, this follows from firms' increasing concern with their social responsibility and their attempts to institute some form of social audit [Ackerman, 1973; Dierkes and Bauer, 1973].

There have been several other attempts to gather data on corporate social performance from firms on an ad hoc or routine basis by private research groups such as the Council of Economic Priorities [American Accounting Association, 1975; pp. 57–63]. Further, several statutory agencies, such as the Federal Trade Commission, Environmental Protection Agency, Occupational Safety and Hazards Agency and the Office of Equal Employment Opportunity, are requiring data from firms in specific aspects of social concern. Recently, the Securities and Exchange Commission has proposed increased disclosure of corporate environmental policy, plans and performance.

The challenges involved in accounting for corporate social performance has engaged the particular attention of the major accounting institutions in the United States. The Study Group on Objectives of Financial Statements [1973, pp. 53–55 and 66] proposed as an objective of financial statements the reporting on those activities of the firm which have major social impacts. An American Institute of Public Accountants' committee is studying the problems of developing measurement systems for corporate social accounting. The National Association of Accountants' Committee on Accounting for Corporate Social Performance published its report in the February 1974 issue of *Management Accounting*. Several American Accounting Association Committees have been concerned with the broad area of social accounting [1971, 1972, 1973, 1974, 1975, 1976]. The Association also has sponsored a major research study on social cost measurement problems.

Despite such widespread and growing concern and support for accounting for corporate social performance, progress has been slow and sporadic. "Apparently, no corporation has yet designed or implemented anything approaching a systematic information system for its socially relevant actions" [American Accounting Association, 1975, p. 64]. Historically, the theory and practice of accounting has evolved in four interrelated areas—a framework of objectives, valuation concepts, measurement methodology and reporting standards. There is no reason to believe that evolution in social accounting will not follow the same course. This paper will concentrate on developing a theoretical framework consisting of a proposed set of social accounting objectives and concepts in the belief that an acceptable framework of objectives is fundamental to the development of social accounting theory in the areas of valuation, measurement methods and reporting standards.

## BASIC PREMISES

Although there is considerable debate about which corporate actions constitute socially responsible corporate behavior, there appears to be a general acceptance of two assumptions.

1.  The solutions to many of the current social problems require the active and willing involvement of private business organizations; and
2.  To the extent that measured corporate profits are an inadequate guide to policy, a broader scheme of corporate performance measurement is necessary.

The absence of a broader scheme of corporate social performance measurement is partly due to the recency of the public's concern over corporate social impact. But in a large measure it also is due to the failure to arrive at an operational definition of the role of a corporation in its broader social context [Preston, 1975; Bell, 1971, Ch. 6]. The elements of such a definition and the philosophical justification for a broader scheme of corporate social performance measurement is to be found in the notion of a social contract whereby a firm agrees to perform certain socially desirable functions in return for certain rewards. This notion of a social contract, which is of fundamental importance to this paper, is explained well by Shocker and Sethi [1974, p. 67]:

> Any social institution—and business is no exception—operates in society via a social contract, expressed or implied, whereby its survival and growth are based on:
> (1) the delivery of some socially desirable ends to society in general, and
> (2) the distribution of economic, social, or political benefits to groups from which it derives its power.
> In a dynamic society, neither the sources of institutional power nor the needs for its services are permanent. Therefore, an institution must constantly meet the twin tests of legitimacy and relevance by demonstrating that society requires its services and that the groups benefiting from its rewards have society's approval.

### Social Performance Criteria—the Macro Context

The development of a set of social performance criteria is essential for bringing the notion of social contract from the level of ideas to the realm of operationality and to provide answers to the following types of questions:

1.  What are the performance dimensions implied by the social contract?
2.  What is socially responsible performance?
3.  How is it to be measured and evaluated in the aggregate social context?

The task of developing social performance criteria, particularly at the macro-level, is unlikely to be the exclusive province of any one group of specialists or of any one discipline. There is ample evidence to suggest that such criteria will result from the combined efforts of philosophers, historians, sociologists, psychologists, political scientists, measurement theorists and others [See footnote 4].

### Social Performance Criteria—the Micro Context

Once such macro-level dimensions and criteria for social performance measurement become generally available and accepted, the unique tasks of the accountant are (1) to develop corresponding micro-level criteria applicable to specific firms and (2) to design and operate internal accounting systems which will make the resulting corporate social performance measures routinely available. Several difficult issues must be resolved before these tasks can be completed. Chief among these are the choice of performance dimensions to be included in the corporate measurement system, the selection of measures and measurement procedures and development of methods for independent verification of reported data. The firm-level measurement system developed ultimately must be such that reported social performance data would be useful not only for internal decision making, but also for external evaluation of the firm's performance within the framework of macro-level social performance criteria.

### Definition of Social Accounting

The purpose of social accounting is to help evaluate how well a firm is fulfilling its social contract. It would accomplish this purpose by providing visibility to the impact of a firm's activity upon society. While the micro-level measurement system provides the information regarding the corporation's social performance, the macro-level performance criteria provide the evaluative framework. In light of this background, social accounting is:

> the process of selecting firm-level social performance variables, measures, and measurement procedures; systematically developing information useful for evaluating the firm's social performance; and communicating such information to concerned social groups, both within and outside the firm.

## PROPOSED OBJECTIVES FOR SOCIAL ACCOUNTING

The notion of a social contract offers crucial assistance in objectives formulation by recognizing as two unique roles of a firm (1) the delivery of some socially useful goods and services and (2) the distribution of economic, social or political rewards to social groups from which the firm derives its power. The nature of these two roles warrants further examination.

As a deliverer of socially desirable goods, the firm is cast in the role of an agent of production. In this role, the ultimate test of a firm's success is whether its aggregate contribution to the society is more than its aggregate consumption of the society's resources. Under the traditional classical economics view, a firm's contribution and consumption are presumed to be completely valued in the market place—profits are presumed to be the all-inclusive measure of a firm's net contribution to society.

However, certain types of decisions of an individual firm may affect the actions of other firms or social groups or individuals in ways which are not reflected in the market process. For example, a major bank's decision to close down its branch in the ghetto area may prompt similar actions by other banks operating branches there and, thus, accentuate the economic and social decline of that neighborhood. The adversity caused to this social segment may not be reflected in the bank's net profits. Indeed, the bank's profits presumably will increase as a result of closing down the ghetto area branch. Many such instances are conceivable where the pursuit of private benefits may not result in the optimization of social benefits. Consideration of such external costs and benefits arising from an individual firm's action are necessary for the attainment of a socially optimal allocation of a society's resources. Whether such optimization is arrived through internalization of externalities or through direct government intervention, a common prerequisite to policy making within and outside the firm is information on, and separate consideration of, the externalities which give rise to social costs and benefits [Ronen, 1974].

### Objective 1

*An objective of corporate social accounting is to identify and measure the periodic net social contribution of an individual firm, which includes not only the costs and benefits internalized to the firm but also those raising from externalities affecting different social segments.*

While the first role of a firm under the notion of social contract is that of an agent of production, its second unique role is that of an agent in the resource sharing and benefit distribution processes in society. The resource sharing and benefit policies (e.g., hiring, training, retention and promotion policies; plant location strategies; political philosophies; ethical norms) which a firm adopts have a direct impact upon how the aggregate benefits and sacrifices generated in the society are shared among individuals, communities, social segments and generations. The complexities of making tradeoff decisions among these competing groups are overwhelming, and the absence of theories which deal with interpersonal preferences and aggregate social utility functions are well recognized. Hence, in this second role, the firm's decision process is concerned more with notions of fairness, equity and consistency with social goals than with considerations of optimality.

The social monitoring of individual firm performance in this second role is less direct and more complex than the market-mechanism-based social monitoring of its economic performance. Indeed, the successful attainment of social welfare goals and priorities depends, in a large measure, upon how well embedded they are in the strategies and performance of individual firms—one of the largest organized sectors in modern societies. This relationship between individual firm performance and social welfare is the basis for a second major objective for corporate social accounting.

### Objective 2

*An objective of corporate social accounting is to help determine whether an individual firm's strategies and practices which directly affect the relative resource and power status of individuals, communities, social segments and generations are consistent with widely shared social priorities on the one hand and individuals' legitimate aspirations on the other.*

The foregoing two unique roles—a production agent and a distribution agent—of individual firms in modern society, together with the two corresponding objectives of corporate social accounting, indicate the basic directions, dimensions and challenges involved in measuring corporate social performance. Attainment of these two social accounting objectives is necessary for systematically evaluating how well a firm is fulfilling its social contract.

The two preceding objectives may be viewed as *measurement objectives* of social accounting. Implementing these measurement objectives would ensure that a data base relevant to appraising corporate social performance would be available. However, there remains the task of providing relevant information from this data base to the users of social accounting information. For internal reporting purposes, the firm's management presumably will develop specific reporting objectives consistent with the unique features of the firm's technology, the strategies the firm adopts for fulfilling its social contract and its internal management structure. Obviously, this is not a public policy issue.

However, from the external reporting standpoint, there is need for a public policy on corporate social reporting. The purpose of such a policy is to ensure that social reporting by individual firms would be adequate and relevant for aiding public accountability, evaluation, coordination and monitoring of corporate contributions toward social goals attainment. A further purpose of such a public policy would be to insure that external reporting required of individual firms is cost/benefit-effective from the aggregate social standpoint. In the absence of such a policy, different user groups—the different social constituents of firms—will have different degrees of access to corporate social performance data. Further, an overabundance of data on some aspects of social performance and a paucity of information on other relevant aspects could result. Still further, potentials for biased reporting also exist, e.g., as when a firm reports only favorable aspects of its social performance. Finally, there exists the problem of resolving, without adverse social consequences, conflicts of interest in information needs of the various social constituents. There is thus a compelling need for an explicitly stated *reporting objective* of social accounting:

### Objective 3

*An objective of corporate social accounting is to make available in an optimal manner, to all social constituents, relevant information on a firm's goals, policies, programs, performance and contributions to social goals. Relevant information is that which provides for public accountability and also facilitates public decision making regarding social choices and social resource allocation. Optimality implies a cost/benefit-effective reporting strategy which also optimally balances potential information conflicts among the various social constituents of a firm.*

Of the three proposed social accounting objectives, two relate to the measurement process and the third to the reporting process. All three follow from the notion of a social contract under which the firm has both a productive role and a distributive role in society. While these social accounting objectives provide the basic theoretical framework, implementing these objectives would be facilitated by a set of social accounting concepts discussed in the following section.

## PROPOSED CONCEPTS FOR SOCIAL ACCOUNTING

The central notion in the first measurement objective proposed is that of a firm's periodic net contribution to social goals. Traditional accounting income provides only a partial measure of this contribution because its computation is based only on an analysis of historical transactions in the market place. Many of the "trans-actions" between a firm and the society, e.g., positive and negative externalities, are not handled presently through the market place.

The earlier example of a bank branch withdrawing from a ghetto area provides one example of the nature of such nonmarket transactions between a firm and the society. In this case, the local community is deprived of easily accessible banking services and also perhaps of some employment opportunities. Further, the community would incur additional transportation costs due to more distant commuting for both banking facilities and jobs. Another adverse consequence might be the decline in the value of real estate upon withdrawal of prominent business units from a neighbor-hood. All of these results may be characterized as the consequences of a nonmarket transaction between the bank and the local community.

Nonmarket transactions also could lead to social benefits—e.g., when a bank decides to open a new branch in a ghetto. Furthermore, nonmarket transactions may involve shifting costs or benefits from one social segment to another. This may not affect the firm's contribution to society as a production agent, but could do so in its distributive role. Affirmative action programs by firms represent transactions whose main direct impact upon society is in the redistribution of income and growth opportunities among different social segments. Social accounting requires re-cognition of such nonmarket transactions in addition to the traditional market-based financial transactions. Thus, a fundamental concept in social accounting is that of a *social transaction*.

1.  A *social transaction* represents a firm's utilization or delivery of a socioenvironmental resource which affects the absolute or relative interests of the firm's various social constituents and which is not processed through the market place.

The significance of recognizing social transactions lies in the fact that their net cumulative effect, along with traditionally determined financial net income, provides the proper measure of a firm's aggregate social impact. For the purpose of bridging the measurement gap between a firm's aggregate social impact and its financial net income, two more concepts are necessary:

2.  *Social overheads (returns)* represent the sacrifice (benefit) to society from those resources consumed (added) by a firm as a result of its social transactions. In other words, social overheads is the measured value of a firm's negative externalities, and social returns is the measured value of its positive externalities.

3.  *Social income* represents the periodic net social contribution of a firm. It is computed as the algebraic sum of the firm's traditionally measured net income, its aggregate social overheads and its aggregate social returns.

These two concepts are bound to receive considerable attention from both theoreticians and practitioners in social accounting because of the variety of alternative descriptions and measures applicable for these purposes. A proper evaluation of social overheads/returns would require, in the first instance, an identification of the different externalities and social segments affected by each social transaction. A complete enumeration of these would require an impractically elaborate input-output model. Considerable experimentation will be necessary before practical solutions are found in this area.

Secondly, each consequence needs to be "priced" using rates or prices or opportunity costs derived from an appropriate macro-level framework. The problem of developing rates and pricing social transactions of a firm is roughly analogous to, but incredibly more complex than, the problem of developing overhead rates and transfer prices in multidivision organizations [Ronen, 1974].

The problem of developing social overhead/return rates is a derivative of and is coterminous with, the problem of developing an operational definition of social income. The definition proposed above is admittedly vague. As in financial accounting, one approach would be to accept a definition of social income based on a matching of identifiable social costs and identifiable social benefits. While such an approach might be a necessary first step, a more comprehensive and precise definition of social income should be the subject of further research by social scientists.

The next concept, although not yet formally introduced, was used in stating the reporting objective of social accounting. Also, the central notion in the second objective relates to the impact of a firm's activity upon different social groups, with reference for whom the firm is presumed to be a distributive agent. These are the groups with whom the firm has an expressed or implied social contract.

Traditional accounting does not provide formal recognition to these groups. Only the claims of financial equity-holders and the periodic changes in their equity in the firm are measured in conventional accounting. In order to implement the second objective of social accounting, it is necessary to recognize formally in the accounting system all concerned groups. Thus:

4. *Social constituents* are the different distinct social groups (implied in the second objective and expressed in the third objective of social accounting) with whom a firm is presumed to have a social contract.

Formal recognition of social constituents in the accounting system is facilitated through social equity accounts where:

5. *Social equity* is a measure of the aggregate changes in the claims which each social constituent is presumed to have in the firm.

Obviously, social equity claims may not be enforceable under the existing legal system. But measures of social equity would serve as a useful basis for social decision making and for evaluating corporate social performance.

Finally, as a firm's social transactions enhance social well being or consume social resources, formal recognition of these nonmarket events in the firm's accounting system is facilitated by means of a social assets account. A positive externality of the firm (e.g., a decrease in neighborhood crime) would increase the value of its social assets. A negative externality (e.g., pollution) would deplete the firm's social assets. Thus:

6. *Net social asset* of a firm is a measure of its aggregate nonmarket contribution to the society's well being less its nonmarket depletion of the society's resources during the life of the firm.

The net social asset of a firm obviously is not recognizable under the current legal system and does not represent legal title to any future benefits to the firm. However, measures of net social assets would serve as a useful basis for social decision making and for evaluating corporate social performance.

## METHODOLOGICAL IMPLICATIONS

Considerable experimentation will be necessary before the objectives and concepts proposed can be translated into a methodology of social accounting. The basic approach implied by the proposed concepts is described below, however, and major problems of implementation are discussed in the next section.

A fundamental step in social accounting would be to identify a firm's social transactions. All decisions and activities of a firm, whether or not they involve a market exchange, would be examined to identify the associated externalities. Such externalities then would be formulated as social transactions.

The process of formulating a social transaction involves identifying three elements. The first element is the *social constituent(s)* affected by the externality being considered.[2] Examples of social constituents are consumer groups, employees, minorities, the local community, investors groups, the general public, groups representing environmental aspects, youth groups and senior citizen groups.

The second element in formulating a social transaction is the specific nature of the *impact* of a firm's action upon the social constituent. In general, such impacts might be either technology-derived or management policy-derived. Thus, product safety and improved service efficiency are illustrative of technology-derived impacts upon consumers. Truth in advertising and sensitivity to customer service needs are illustrative of policy-related variables impacting upon consumers. Other examples of social transactions relevant to various social constituents are pollution-caused damage to health and environment, quality of human resource management, degree of commitment to affirmative action and concern for quality of life and welfare of the local community.

The final, and perhaps most difficult, element is the determination of the relevant social overhead/return *rates* to be used for pricing each social transaction. Since social transactions are not subject to market tests, no automatic process reveals the rates relevant for pricing such transactions. Instead, the rates would have to be developed within a macro social framework. In principle, this issue would be similar to the problem of developing cost and credit transfer rates in integrated multiplant operations. However, the practical problems would pose a serious challenge to any group of experts working on the problem. An interim solution might be to develop social overhead/return rates at specific industry levels which could be used by individual firms in that industry.

The proposed methodology would require each firm to undertake an audit of its externalities in order to develop a reasonably complete set of social transactions reflecting the firm's ongoing impact upon society which are not subject to the market

---

[2] It is possible that more than one social constituent might be affected by one externality, thus giving rise to multiple social transactions.

process. The methodology also requires the valuation of each social transaction using social overhead/return rates. The formal accounting for social transactions then would require determination of a social asset effect on the one hand and social income and social equity effects on the other. Certain transactions may involve an exact tradeoff between one type of social benefit (or cost) and another—both affecting the same social constituent. The accounting for such transactions might not involve a social equity effect. On the other hand, certain other social transactions might involve shifting benefits (or costs) from one social constituent to another, e.g., affirmative action. Accounting for this type of transaction might not involve any social income effect.[3]

To illustrate the approach further, consider the case of a bank. Based on the nature of a bank's function and its operating characteristics, the following social constituents and transactions are plausible.

| ILLUSTRATIVE SOCIAL CONSTITUENTS | ILLUSTRATIVE SOCIAL TRANSACTIONS |
|---|---|
| 1. Clients | 1. Quality of services which affect thriftiness, savings habits, etc., of clients<br>2. Client satisfaction with services |
| 2. Employees | 1. Job satisfaction<br>2. Opportunities for personal development and professional growth |
| 3. Local community | 1. Effect on neighborhood economic development<br>2. Effect on education, training, crime prevention, etc., in the neighborhood<br>3. Effect on commuter traffic, congestion, pollution, etc. |
| 4. Minority groups | 1. Minority hiring, training and utilization<br>2. Financial services designed especially to meet minority needs |

*Clients.* The financial earnings of the bank usually are a major indicator of a bank's contribution to its clientele. However, the bank's impact upon them may go beyond that. Through aggressive campaign and management policies, the bank may influence its clientele to achieve greater thrift and more responsible personal fiscal management. Part of the resulting benefits may accrue to the bank in terms of greater client loyalty and business, but the aggregate benefit to the client group may exceed that realized by the bank.

*Employees.* Payroll costs and employee productivity may be reflected by traditional accounting. However, if the job situation leads to personal or professional

---

[3] This may not be true if affirmative action programs lead not only to reduced disparities in income and opportunities among social segments, but also to other secondary benefits like greater political stability, fewer crimes, etc.

enrichment, for instance, this positive benefit should be recognized through a social transaction.

*Local community*. Traditional accounting recognizes only local taxes, utility payments and other such market transaction effects on the community. But the bank's impact upon the community may include greater stability of, and fillip to, the local economy and employment potential. These, in turn, could help lessen crime, enhance educational and training opportunities and, generally, improve the quality of life. On the other hand, the bank's presence might also contribute to traffic problems, congestion and pollution. In all these cases, of course, there is a problem of identifying how much of each effect is attributable to the bank under study.

*Minority groups*. These may be employees, clients or other social segments. Efforts to reduce disparities in income and employment opportunities are examples of an employee-related social transaction. Client-related social transactions are illustrated by special programs to promote minority enterprises and minority capital formation. In all such cases, those evaluating the social transactions would attempt to recognize the social costs and benefits which are not reflected in the bank's market transactions and, hence, are not recognized by traditional accounting.

## PROBLEMS OF IMPLEMENTATION

The objectives, concepts and methodology proposed here hopefully provide a tentative framework for developing pilot empirical applications of corporate social accounting. However several complex problems at the macro and micro levels must be resolved before a comprehensive and generally acceptable approach to social accounting can be developed. These include, at the macro level, the development of generally accepted social goals and social indicators to provide the normative framework within which firm-level performance dimensions and measurement criteria must be developed.[4] It is not the accountant's task to prescribe social goals, programs, or structure, just as it is not his or her task to prescribe a firm's goals, policies or management structure. The accounting theorist would necessarily look to sociologists, political scientists, economists and philosophers, among others, to interpret what is socially desirable and to formulate an operational set of goals—just as he or she relies on economists, behavioral scientists and others to interpret and operationalize a firm's goals and decision/performance system. It is essential that the accountant be familiar with the logic and content of the operationalized social goal set, as he or she is to be guided by it in designing appropriate firm-level social accounting systems. Indeed, he or she might be expected to contribute to the macro-level social goal operationalization process by commenting upon the relative merits and problems of measurement implied by alternative operationalization approaches.

---

[4] Milestones in the "social goals" literature include *Goals for Americans* [The American Assembly, 1960]; *Agenda for the Nation* [Gorden, 1968]; *Toward Balanced Growth: Quantity with Quality* [National Goals Research Staff, 1970); and *Setting National Priorities* [Schultze, et al.]. Milestones in the "social indicators" literature include *Indicators of Social Change* [Sheldon and Moore, 1968]; *Toward a Social Report* [U.S. Dept. of H.E.W., 1969] which is the first attempt to implement the social indicators concepts; and *Social Indicators 1973* [Office of Management and Budget] which provides a substantial volume of relevant social and behavioral information.

The problem of developing relevant social performance measures is particularly challenging at the micro level. On the one hand, they must follow logically from the firm's strategies and technological realities. At the same time, they must be technically congruent with the macro-level social indicators such that firm-level performance scored as positive using these measures also would imply positive contribution toward social goals. One solution might be to develop a social input/output model in which the coefficients capture all the interrelationships between a given set of firm-level social performance criteria and the macro-level social goal dimensions.[5] However, considerable research will be necessary before data for such models become available.

Another major micro-level problem relates to social overhead/return rates. This is a fertile field for research aimed at better understanding the economics of externalities and the behavioral impact of alternative rates upon firm managements and social constituents. Empirical research testing the feasibility and usefulness of alternative approaches to developing rates in selected performance dimensions would be of immediate benefit to the refinement of social accounting methodology.

## CONCLUDING COMMENTS

The proposals in this paper are based on the premise that accounting for a firm's social performance requires a broader definition of a firm's role in society than is reflected in the legal entity notion underlying current accounting practices. Accordingly, the notion of a social contract was introduced which led to the three objectives and five concepts of social accounting proposed earlier. Table 1 summarizes these objectives and concepts. They provide a general framework within which several refinements are possible. More important, they suggest useful directions for further research into the various aspects of social accounting, some of which have been noted earlier. In particular, the concepts of social constituents and social transactions require further debate and empirical testing, and methods appropriate for determining social overheads/returns need to be developed. Alternative versions of the concept of social income are bound to emerge with corresponding implications for measuring social overheads/returns and social equity. In the absence of supporting legal sanctions, the notion of social equity and the determination of its shares attributable to various social constituents will have to be resolved through sociopolitical reasoning. Choices of measures and measurement procedures will have to be resolved based on which alternatives best help meet social accounting objectives. The usefulness and problems of integrating financial accounting and social accounting in one combined system need to be explored. Research into questions of materiality, verifiability and bias will receive fresh impetus as corporate accounting systems are broadened to include social performance data. This paper will have served its purpose if it helps to organize the emerging debate on such issues within a logical framework of objectives and concepts.

---

[5] Knowledge of this type is assumed in the input/output model presented by Charnes, Colantoni, Cooper and Kortanek [1972].

**TABLE 1**

**Proposed Objectives and Concepts for Social Accounting**

Objective 1

An objective of corporate social accounting is to identify and measure the periodic net social contribution of an individual firm, which includes not only the costs and benefits internalized to the firm, but also those arising from externalities affecting different social segments.

Objective 2

An objective of corporate social accounting is to help determine whether an individual firm's strategies and practices which directly affect the relative resource and power status of individuals, communities, social segments and generations are consistent with widely shared social priorities, on the one hand, and individuals' legitimate aspirations, on the other.

Objective 3

An objective of corporate social accounting is to make available in an optimal manner, to all social constituents, relevant information on a firm's goals, policies, programs, performance and contributions to social goals. Relevant information is that which provides for public accountability and also facilitates public decision making regarding social choices and social resource allocation. Optimality implies a cost/benefit-effective reporting strategy which also optimally balances potential information conflicts among the various social constituents of a firm.

Concept 1

A *social transaction* represents a firm's utilization or delivery of a socioenvironmental resource which affects the absolute or relative interests of the firm's various social constituents and which is not processed through the market place.

Concept 2

*Social overheads (returns)* represent the sacrifice (benefit) to society from those resources consumed (added) by a firm as a result of its social transactions. In other words, social overheads is the measured value of a firm's negative externalities, and social returns is the measured value of its positive externalities.

Concept 3

*Social income* represents the periodic net social contribution of a firm. It is computed as the algebraic sum of the firm's traditionally measured net income, its aggregate social overheads and its aggregate social returns.

Concept 4

*Social constituents* are the different distinct social groups (implied in the second objective and expressed in the third objective of social accounting) with whom a firm is presumed to have a social contract.

Concept 5

*Social equity* is a measure of the aggregate changes in the claims which each social constituent is presumed to have in the firm.

Concept 6

*Net social asset* of a firm is a measure of its aggregate nonmarket contribution to the society's well being less its nonmarket depletion of the society's resources during the life of the firm.

# REFERENCES

Ackerman, R., "How Companies Respond to Social Demands," *Harvard Business Review* (July–August 1973), pp. 88–98.

American Accounting Association, Committee on Nonfinancial Measures of Effectiveness, "Report of the Committee on Nonfinancial Measures of Effectiveness," *The Accounting Review*, Supplement to Vol. XLVI (1971), pp. 164–211.

———, Committee on Measures of Effectiveness for Social Programs, "Report of the Committee on Measures of Effectiveness for Social Programs," *The Accounting Review*, Supplement to Vol. XLVII (1972), pp. 336–396.

———, Committee on Environmental Effects of Organizational Behavior, "Report of Committee on Environmental Effects of Organizational Behavior," *The Accounting Review*, Supplement to Vol. XLVIII (1973), pp. 73–119.

———, Committee on Measurement of Social Costs, "Report of the Committee on Measurement of Social Costs," *The Accounting Review*, Supplement to Vol. XLIX (1974), pp. 98–113.

———, Committee on Social Costs, "Report of the Committee on Social Costs," *The Accounting Review*, Supplement to Vol. XLX (1975), pp. 50–89.

———, Committee on Accounting for Social Performance, "Report of the Committee on Accounting for Social Performance," *The Accounting Review*, Supplement to Vol. LI (1976).

Bauer, R. A. and D. H. Fenn, Jr., *The Corporate Social Audit* (Russell Sage Foundation, 1972).

Bell, D., *The Coming of Post-Indistrial Society* (Basic Books, 1971).

Beresford, D., *Compilation of Social Measurement Disclosures in Fortune 500 Annual Reports—1973* (Ernst & Ernst, 1973).

Charnes, A., C. Colantoni, W. W. Cooper, and K. O. Kortanek, "Economic, Social and Enterprise Accounting and Mathematical Models," *The Accounting Review* (January 1972), pp. 85–108.

Dierkes, M. and R. A. Bauer, eds., *Corporate Social Accounting* (Prager Publishers, 1973).

Gordon, K., ed., *Agenda for the Nation* (The Brookings Institution, 1968).

National Goals Research Staff, *Toward Balanced Growth: Quantity with Quality* (U.S. Government Printing Office, 1970).

Office of Management and Budget, Executive Office of the President, *Social Indicators 1973* (U.S. Department of Commerce, Social and Economic Statistics Administration).

Preston, L. E., "Corporation and Society: The Search for a Paradigm," *Journal of Economic Literature* (July 1975), pp. 434–453.

Report of the Study Group on *Objectives of Financial Statements* (American Institute of Certified Public Accountants, October 1973).

Ronen, J., "Accounting for Social Costs and Benefits," in J. J. Cramer, Jr. and G. H. Sorter, eds., *Objectives of Financial Statements* (American Institute of Certified Public Accountants, May 1974), pp. 317–340.

Schultze, C. L., et al., *Setting National Priorities* (The Brookings Institution, annually issued).

Sethi, S. P., ed., *The Unstable Ground: Corporate Social Policy in a Dynamic Society* (Melville Publishing Company, 1974).

Sheldon, E. and W. E. Moore, eds. *Indicators of Social Change: Concepts and Measurements* (Russell Sage Foundation, 1968).

Shocker, A. D., and S. P. Sethi, "An Approach to Incorporating Social Preferences in Developing Corporate Action Strategies," in S. P. Sethi, ed., *The Unstable Ground: Corporate Social Policy in a Dynamic Society* (Melville Publishing Company, 1974), pp. 67–80.

The American Assembly, *Goals for Americans*, The Report of the President's Commission on National Goals (Prentice-Hall, 1960).

U.S. Department of Health, Education and Welfare, *Toward a Social Report* (U.S. Government Printing Office, 1969).

A 6
B 7
C 8
D 9
E 0
F 1
G 2
H 3
I 4
J 5